Lecture Notes in Computer Science 6088

Commenced Publication in 1973
Founding and Former Series Editors:
Gerhard Goos, Juris Hartmanis, and Jan van Leeuwen

T0223392

Lora Aroyo   Grigoris Antoniou
Eero Hyvönen   Annette ten Teije
Heiner Stuckenschmidt   Liliana Cabral
Tania Tudorache (Eds.)

The Semantic Web: Reserach and Applications

7th Extended Semantic Web Conference, ESWC 2010
Heraklion, Crete, Greece, May 30 – June 3, 2010
Proceedings, Part I

Springer

Volume Editors

Lora Aroyo
Free University Amsterdam, The Netherlands
E-mail: l.m.aroyo@cs.vu.nl

Grigoris Antoniou
University of Crete, Heraklion, Greece
E-mail: antoniou@ics.forth.gr

Eero Hyvönen
Aalto University, Finland
E-mail: eero.hyvonen@tkk.fi

Annette ten Teije
Free University Amsterdam, The Netherlands
E-mail: annette@cs.vu.nl

Heiner Stuckenschmidt
Universität Mannheim, Germany
E-mail: heiner@informatik.uni-mannheim.de

Liliana Cabral
The Open University, Milton Keynes,UK
E-mail: l.s.cabral@open.ac.uk

Tania Tudorache
Stanford Biomedical Informatics Research Center, USA
E-mail: tudorache@stanford.edu

Library of Congress Control Number: 2010927493

CR Subject Classification (1998): H.4, H.3.3, H.5, J.4, I.2.4, K.4.2

LNCS Sublibrary: SL 3 – Information Systems and Application, incl. Internet/Web
and HCI

ISSN   0302-9743
ISBN-10   3-642-13485-8 Springer Berlin Heidelberg New York
ISBN-13   978-3-642-13485-2 Springer Berlin Heidelberg New York

springer.com

© Springer-Verlag Berlin Heidelberg 2010
Printed in Germany

Typesetting: Camera-ready by author, data conversion by Scientific Publishing Services, Chennai, India
Printed on acid-free paper   06/3180

Preface

This volume contains papers from the technical program of the 7th Extended Semantic Web Conference (ESWC 2010), held from May 30 to June 3, 2010, in Heraklion, Greece. ESWC 2010 presented the latest results in research and applications of Semantic Web technologies. ESWC 2010 built on the success of the former European Semantic Web Conference series, but sought to extend its focus by engaging with other communities within and outside Information and Communication Technologies, in which semantics can play an important role. At the same time, ESWC has become a truly international conference.

Semantics of Web content, enriched with domain theories (ontologies), data about Web usage, natural language processing, etc., will enable a Web that provides a qualitatively new level of functionality. It will weave together a large network of human knowledge and make this knowledge machine-processable. Various automated services, based on reasoning with metadata and ontologies, will help the users to achieve their goals by accessing and processing information in machine-understandable form. This network of knowledge systems will ultimately lead to truly intelligent systems, which will be employed for various complex decision-making tasks. Research about Web semantics can benefit from ideas and cross-fertilization with many other areas: artificial intelligence, natural language processing, database and information systems, information retrieval, multimedia, distributed systems, social networks, Web engineering, and Web science.

To reflect its expanded focus, the conference call for research papers was organized in targeted tracks:

- Mobility
- Ontologies and Reasoning
- Semantic Web in Use
- Sensor Networks
- Services and Software
- Social Web
- Web of Data
- Web Science

The research papers program received 245 full paper submissions, which were first evaluated by the Program Committees of the respective tracks. The review process included evaluation by Program Committee members, discussions to resolve conflicts, and a metareview for each potentially acceptable borderline submission. After this a physical meeting among Track and Conference Chairs was organized to see that comparable evaluation criteria in different tracks had been used and to discuss remaining borderline papers. As a result, 52 research papers were selected to be presented at the conference and are included in the proceedings. The ESWC 2010 proceedings also include ten PhD symposium papers presented at a separate track preceeding the main conference, and 17 demo papers giving a brief description of the system demos that were accepted for presentation in a dedicated session during the conference.

ESWC 2010 was happy to have had three keynote speakers and a dinner talk by high-profile researchers:

- Noshir Contractor, the Jane S. & William J. White Professor of Behavioral Sciences in the School of Engineering, School of Communication and the Kellogg School of Management at Northwestern University
- Sean Bechhofer, lecturer in the Information Management Group within the School of Computer Science at the University of Manchester
- Wolfgang Wahlster, Director and CEO of the German Research Center for Artificial Intelligence and a professor of Computer Science at Saarland University (Saarbruecken, Germany)
- Aldo Gangemi, senior researcher at the CNR Institute of Cognitive Sciences and Technology in Rome, and head of the Semantic Technology Lab.

Special thanks go to all the Chairs, Program Committee members, and additional reviewers of the different refereed tracks who all contributed to ensuring the scientific quality of ESWC 2010. Many thanks also go to the members of the Organizing Committee for their hard work in selecting outstanding tutorials, workshops, panels, lightning talks, and posters. We would like to also thank the Sponsorship Chair for reaching out to industry and various organizations supporting the 2010 edition of the conference, as well as the local organization, website and conference administration team put together by STI International for their excellent coordination during the conference preparation. Finally, we would like to thank the Proceedings Chair for the hard work in preparing this volume, Springer for the support with the preparation of the proceedings, and the developers of the EasyChair conference management system, which was used to manage the submission and review of papers, and the production of this volume.

May 2010

Lora Aroyo
Grigoris Antoniou
Eero Hyvönen
Annette ten Teije
Heiner Stuckenschmidt
Liliana Cabral
Tania Tudorache

Organization

Organizing Committee

General Chair	Lora Aroyo (VU University Amsterdam, The Netherlands)
Program Chairs	Grigoris Antoniou (University of Crete, Greece)
	Eero Hyvönen (Helsinki University of Technology, Finland)

Events Chairs

Workshop Co-chairs	Kalina Boncheva (University of Sheffield, UK)
	Nicola Henze (University of Hannover, Germany)
Tutorials Co-chairs	Anna Fensel (FTW, Austria)
	Aldo Gangemi (ISTC-CNR, Italy)
Demos/Posters Co-chairs	Liliana Cabral (OU, UK)
	Tania Tudorache (Stanford University, USA)
PhD Symposium Co-chairs	Annette ten Teije (VU University Amsterdam, The Netherlands)
	Heiner Stuckenschmidt (University of Mannheim, Germany)
Semantic Web Technologies Co-ordinators	Harith Alani (OU, UK)
	Martin Szomszor (City eHealth Research Center, UK)
News from the Front Latest Results from EU Projects	Lyndon Nixon (STI International, Austria)
	Alexander Wahler (STI International, Austria)
Panel Chair	Carlos Pedrinaci (OU, UK)
Proceedings Chair	Yiannis Kompatsiaris (ITI, Greece)
Sponsorship Chair	Manolis Koubarakis (University of Athens, Greece)
Publicity Chair	Valentina Prescutti (ISTC-CNR, Italy)

Local Organization Chairs

Treasurer	Alexander Wahler (STI International, Austria)
Local Organizer and Conference Administrator	Lejla Ibralic-Halilovic (STI International, Austria)

Program Committee - Mobility Track

Track Chairs

Matthias Wagner and Hans Gellersen

Members

Sebastian Böhm

Eugen Freiter

Johan Koolwaaij

Christian Kray

Thorsten Liebig

Marko Luther

Jerome Picault

Myriam Ribiere

Thomas Strang

Juan Ignacio Vazquez

Program Committee - Ontologies and Reasoning Track

Track Chairs

Jeff Pan and Adrian Paschke

Members

Franz Baader

Nick Bassiliades

Paolo Bouquet

Diego Calvanese

Huajun Chen

Bernardo CuencaGrau

Mathieu D'Aquin

Martin Dzbor

Thomas Eiter

Giorgos Flouris

Tim Furche

Pascal Hitzler

Laura Hollink

Zhisheng Huang

Elisa Kendall

Francisco Martín-Recuerda

Diana Maynard

Leora Morgenstern

Boris Motik

Leo Obrst

Bijan Parsia

Dimitris Plexousakis

Axel Polleres

Guilin Qi

Yuzhong Qu

Riccardo Rosati

Sebastian Rudolph

Alan Ruttenberg

Harald Sack

Kai-Uwe Sattler

Stefan Schlobach

Michael Schroeder

Pavel Shvaiko

Michael Sintek

Kavitha Srinivas

Giorgos Stamou

Giorgos Stoilos

Umberto Straccia

Heiner Stuckenschmidt

Edward Thomas

Robert Tolksdorf

Holger Wache

Kewen Wang

Benjamin Zapilko

Yuting Zhao

Program Committee - Semantic Web In-Use Track

Track Chairs

Stuart Campbell and Sören Auer

Members

David Aumueller
Domenico Beneventano
Andreas Blumauer
John Breslin
Vadim Chepegin
Richard Cyganiak
Andreas Doms
Muriel Foulonneau
Tim Furche
Martin Gaedke
John Goodwin
Mark Greaves
Gunnar Aastrand Grimnes
Tudor Groza
Olaf Hartig
Bernhard Haslhofer
Sebastian Hellmann
Martin Hepp
Robert Hoehndorf
Martin Kaltenböck
Birgitta König-Ries

Jens Lehmann
Steffen Lohmann
Markus Luczak-Rösch
Michele Missikoff
Claudia Müller
Axel-Cyrille Ngonga Ngomo
Massimo Paolucci
Tassilo Pellegrini
Barbara Pirillo
Yves Raimond
Harald Sack
Leo Sauermann
Sebastian Schaffert
Bernhard Schandl
Stefan Schulte
Jo Walsh
Michael Witbrock
Jun Zhao
Sven Abels
Georgi Pavlov

Program Committee – Sensor Networks Track

Track Chairs

Alan Smeaton and Oscar Corcho

Members

Luis Bermudez
Boyan Brodaric
Michael Compton
Ixent Galpin
Raúl García-Castro
Alasdair Gray
Cory Henson
Jonas Jacobi
Krzysztof Janowicz
Laurent Lefort

Kirk Martinez
Holger Neuhaus
Noel O'Connor
Gregory O'Hare
Kevin Page
Vinny Reynolds
Ingo Simonis
Heiner Stuckenschmidt
Kerry Taylor
Andreas Wombacher

Program Committee - Services and Software Track

Track Chairs

Andreas Metzger and Elena Simperl

Members

Stephan Bloehdorn
Matthias Book
Antonio Bucchiarone
Cyril Carrez
Dragan Gasevic
Dragan Ivanovic
Dimka Karastoyanova
Mick Kerrigan
Reto Krummenacher
Stephen Lane
Kim Lauenroth
Tiziana Margaria

Barry Norton
Michael Parkin
Carlos Pedrinaci
Srinath Perera
Pierluigi Plebani
Noël Plouzeau
Dumitru Roman
Fabrizio Silvestri
Michael Stollberg
Martin Treiber
Sanjiva Weerawarana

Program Committee - Social Web Track

Track Chairs

Julita Vassileva and Jie Bao

Members

Sören Auer
Scott Bateman
Dave Beckett
Edward Benson
Shlomo Berkovsky
Dave Braines
John Breslin
Chris Brooks
Francesca Carmagnola
Federica Cena
Richard Cyganiak
Antonina Dattolo
Mike Dean
Darina Dicheva
Yihong Ding
Ying Ding
Jon Dron
Anna Fensel

Steve Harris
Tom Heath
Aidan Hogan
Akshay Java
Robert Jäschke
Lalana Kagal
Dae-Ki Kang
Pranam Kolari
Georgia Koutrika
Milos Kravcik
Markus Krötzsch
Tsvi Kuflik
Juanzi Li
Enrico Motta
Meenakshi Nagarajan
Daniel Olmedilla
Alexandre Passant
Jyotishman Pathak

Guilin Qi
Yuzhong Qu
Juan F. Sequeda
Paul Smart
Sergey Sosnovsky
Steffen Staab
Christopher Thomas

Haofen Wang
Mary-Anne Williams
Jie Zhang
Haizheng Zhang
Lina Zhou
Cristina Gena

Program Committee – Web of Data Track

Track Chairs

Paul Groth and Denny Vrandecic

Members

Harith Alani
Anupriya Ankolekar
Christian Bizer
Uldis Bojars
Paolo Bouquet
Simone Braun
Vinay Chaudhri
Anne Cregan
Philippe Cudré-Mauroux
Richard Cyganiak
Peter Haase
Harry Halpin
Andreas Harth
Tom Heath
Martin Hepp
Rinke Hoekstra
Dietmar Jannach
Craig Knoblock
Georgi Kobilarov
Peter Mika

Malgorzata Mochol
Wolfgang Nejdl
Alexandre Passant
Yuzhong Qu
Yves Raimond
Leo Sauermann
Ansgar Schrep
Juan F. Sequeda
Patrick Sinclair
Katharina Siorpaes
Harold Solbrig
York Sure
Martin Szomszor
Hideaki Takeda
Jamie Taylor
Mischa Tuffield
Valentin Zacharias
Jun Zhao
Thanh Tran

Program Committee - Web Science Track

Track Chairs

Noshir Contractor and Leslie Carr

Members

Ian Brown
Harry Halpin

Nick Gibbins
Kieron O'Hara

Program Committee - Demo and Poster Track

Track Chairs

Liliana Cabral and Tania Tudorache

Members

Harith Alani
Sören Auer
Neil Benn
John Breslin
Christopher Brewster
Emilia Cimpian
Gianluca Correndo
Philippe Cudré-Mauroux
Mathieu d'Aquin
Danica Damljanovic
Klaas Dellschaft
Ying Ding
Leigh Dodds
Sean Falconer
Anna Fensel
Miriam Fernandez
Raúl García-Castro
Hugh Glaser
Tudor Groza
Olaf Görlitz
Peter Haase
Connor Hayes
Tom Heath
Masahiro Hori
Matthew Horridge
Luigi Iannone
Holger Lewen
Vanessa Lopez

Alexander Löser
Francisco Martin-Recuerda
Diana Maynard
Adrian Mocan
Knud Möller
Lyndon Nixon
Natasha Noy
Martin O'Connor
Alexandre Passant
Carlos Pedrinaci
Chantal Reynaud
Marco Rospocher
Marta Sabou
Elena Simperl
Patrick Sinclair
Katharina Siorpaes
Nenad Stojanovic
Heiner Stuckenschmidt
Mari Carmen Suárez-Figueroa
Martin Szomszor
Vlad Tanasescu
Thanh Tran
Mischa Tuffield
Giovanni Tummarello
Johanna Voelker
Holger Wache
Stuart Wrigley
Milena Yankova

Program Committee - PhD Symposium

Track Chairs

Heiner Stuckensmidt and Annette ten Teije

Members

Karl Aberer
Barry Bishop
Paolo Bouquet
Paul Buitelaar
Philipp Cimiano
Isabel Cruz
Jérôme Euzenat
Fabien Gandon
Chiara Ghidini
Paul Groth
Siggi Handschuh
Patrick Lambrix
Thomas Lukasiewicz
Gergely Lukácsy
Diana Maynard
Peter Mika
Dunja Mladenic

Mathias Niepert
Natasha Noy
Jeff Pan
Terry Payne
Valentina Presutti
Sebastian Rudolph
Marta Sabou
Stefan Schlobach
Pavel Shvaiko
Elena Simperl
Sergej Sizov
Umberto Straccia
Valentina Tamma
Johanna Voelker
Holger Wache
Mathieu d'Aquin
Jacco van Ossenbruggen

Referees

Alessandro Adamou
Dimitra Alexopoulou
Sofia Angeletou
Zelalem Bachore
Samantha Bail
Peter Barna
Sebastian Bochm
Stefano Bortoli
Daniele Broccolo
Stuart Campbell
Leyla Jael García Castro
Matteo Casu
Gong Cheng
Vadim Chepegin
Smitashree Choudhury
Jianfeng Du
Kai Eckert
Giorgos Flouris
Angela Fogarolli
Flavius Frasincar
Eugen Freiter
Fatih Gedikli
George Giannakopoulos

Gunnar Aastrand
  Grimnes
Ralf Heese
Daniel Herzig
Geerd-Dietger Hoffmann
Matthew Horridge
Wei Hu
Giovambattista Ianni
Ekaterini Ioannou
Antoine Isaac
Prateek Jain
Malte Kiesel
Sheila Kinsella
Pavel Klinov
Haris Kondylakis
Efstratios Kontopoulos
Johan Koolwaaij
Jacek Kopecky
Jakub Kotowski
Kalliopi Kravari
Christian Kray
Thomas Krennwallner
Vikash Kumar

Günter Ladwig
Georg Lausen
Thorsten Liebig
Dong Liu
Xin Liu
Nuno Lopes
Vanessa Lopez
Marko Luther
Theofilos Mailis
Maria Maleshkova
Michael Martin
Carlos Nana Mbinkeu
Georgios Meditskos
Christian Meilicke
Benedikt Meuthrath
Franco Maria Nardini
Nadejda Nikitina
Olaf Noppens
Vit Novacek
Andrea Giovanni
  Nuzzolese
Jasmin Optiz
Magdalena Ortiz

Ignazio Palmisano
Rahul Parundekar
Rafael Penaloza
Srinath Perera
Jerôme Picault
Valentina Presutti
Maryam Ramezani
Nataliya Rassadko
Michael Reiter
Yuan Ren
Myriam Ribiere
Myriam Ribire
Frank Sawitzki
Anne Schlicht
Stefan Schulz
Kostyantyn

Shchekotykhin
Wei Shen
Nikolaos Simou
Sergey Sosnovsky
Natalia Stash
Heiko Stoermer
Thomas Strang
Olga Streibel
Thanassis Tiropanis
George Tsatsaronis
Joerg Unbehauen
Johanna Völker
Inaki Vazquez
Thomas Waechter
Andreas Wagner
William Waites

Shenghui Wang
Zhe Wang
Jesse Wang
Klara Weiand
Branimir Wetzstein
Gang Wu
Honghan Wu
Markus Zanker
Benjamin Zapilko
Viesturs Zarins
Yuqing Zhai
Xiaowang Zhang
Xiao Zhang
Antoine Zimmermann

Sponsoring Institutions

Table of Contents – Part I

Semantic Web in Use Track

Sensor Networks Track

Table of Contents – Part II

Services and Software Track

Social Web Track

Web of Data Track

Demo and Poster Track

PhD Symposium

Incremental Reasoning on Streams and Rich Background Knowledge

Davide Francesco Barbieri, Daniele Braga, Stefano Ceri,
Emanuele Della Valle, and Michael Grossniklaus

Politecnico di Milano – Dipartimento di Elettronica e Informazione
Piazza L. da Vinci, 32 - 20133 Milano – Italy
{dbarbieri,braga,ceri,dellavalle,grossniklaus}@elet.polimi.it

Abstract. This article presents a technique for Stream Reasoning, consisting in incremental maintenance of materializations of ontological entailments in the presence of streaming information. Previous work, delivered in the context of deductive databases, describes the use of logic programming for the incremental maintenance of such entailments. Our contribution is a new technique that exploits the nature of streaming data in order to efficiently maintain materialized views of RDF triples, which can be used by a reasoner.

By adding expiration time information to each RDF triple, we show that it is possible to compute a new complete and correct materialization whenever a new window of streaming data arrives, by dropping explicit statements and entailments that are no longer valid, and then computing when the RDF triples inserted within the window will expire. We provide experimental evidence that our approach significantly reduces the time required to compute a new materialization at each window change, and opens up for several further optimizations.

1 Introduction

Streaming data is an important class of information sources. Examples of data streams are Web logs, feeds, click streams, sensor data, stock quotations, locations of mobile users, and so on. Streaming data is received continuously and in real-time, either implicitly ordered by arrival time, or explicitly associated with timestamps. A new class of database systems, called data stream management systems (DSMS), is capable of performing queries over streams [1], but such systems cannot perform complex reasoning tasks. Reasoners, on the other hand, can perform complex reasoning tasks, but they do not provide support to manage *rapidly* changing worlds.

Recently, we have made the first steps into a new research direction: Stream Reasoning [2] is a new multi-disciplinary approach that can provide the abstractions, foundations, methods, and tools required to integrate data streams, the Semantic Web, and reasoning systems. Central to the notion of stream reasoning is a paradigmatic change from persistent knowledge bases and user-invoked reasoning tasks to transient streams and continuous reasoning tasks.

L. Aroyo et al. (Eds.): ESWC 2010, Part I, LNCS 6088, pp. 1–15, 2010.

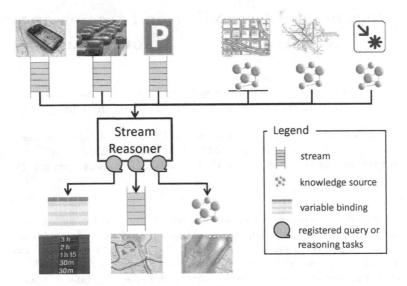

Fig. 1. Mobile Scenario

The first step for enabling Stream Reasoning is the development of languages and systems for querying RDF data also in the form of data streams. Streaming SPARQL [3], Continuous SPARQL (C-SPARQL) [4,5], and Time-Annotated SPARQL [6] are three recent independent proposals for extending SPARQL to handle both static RDF graphs and transient streams of RDF triples. This paper builds on our previous works on C-SPARQL.

In Fig. 1, we show a Stream Reasoner. It takes several streams of rapidly changing information and several static sources of background knowledge as input. In the context of a mobile scenario, examples of sources of streaming data can be the positions of users, the traffic in the streets, and the availability of parking lots, whereas examples of background knowledge can be the city layout, the public transportation schedules, and the descriptions of points of interest and of events in a given area. Several reasoning tasks, expressed in the form of C-SPARQL queries, are registered into the stream reasoner, and the system continuously generates new answers. These answers can be in the standard SPARQL output form (i.e., variable bindings and graphs) or in the form of streams. In our mobile scenario, for instance, we can register two C-SPARQL queries: one continuously monitors the status of the public transportation system and returns the delays as variable bindings, the other one monitors the sensors for traffic detection and generates a stream of aggregate information for each major road. Current implementations of the proposed SPARQL extensions, however, assume only a simple entailment (see Section 2 of [7]). They do not try to handle reasoning on streaming information, e.g., providing strategical suggestions about how to perform goals.

In existing work on logical reasoning, the knowledge base is always assumed to be static (or slowly evolving). There is work on changing beliefs on the basis of new observations [8], but the solutions proposed in this area are far too complex to be applicable to gigantic data streams of the kind we image in a mobile context. However, the nature of data streams is different from arbitrary changes, because change occurs in a "regular" way at the points where the streaming data is observed.

In this article, we present a technique for stream reasoning that incrementally maintains a materialization of ontological entailments in the presence of streaming information. We elaborate on previous papers [9,10] that extend to logic programming results from incremental maintenance of materialized views in deductive databases [11]. Our contribution is a new technique that takes the order in which streaming information arrives at the Stream Reasoner into explicit consideration. By adding expiration time information to each RDF statement, we show that it is possible to compute a new complete and correct materialization by (a) dropping explicit statements and entailments that are no longer valid, and (b) evaluating a maintenance program that propagates insertions of explicit RDF statements as changes to the stored implicit entailments.

The rest of the paper is organized as follows. Section 2 presents a wrap up of the background information needed to understand this paper. In particular, it presents the state of the art in incremental maintenance of materializations of ontologies represented as logic programs. Section 3 presents our major contribution in the form of Datalog rules computing the incremental materialization of ontologies for window-based changes of ontological entailments. In Section 4 we present our implementation experience. Section 5 provides experimental evidence that our approach significantly reduces the time required to compute the new materialization. Finally, we close the paper by sketching future works in Section 6.

2 Background

2.1 Stream Reasoning

A first step toward stream reasoning has been to combine the power of existing data-stream management systems and the Semantic Web [12]. The key idea is to keep streaming data in relational format as long as possible and to bring it to the semantic level as aggregated events [5]. Existing data models, access protocols, and query languages for data-stream management systems and the Semantic Web are not sufficient to do so and, thus, they must be combined.

C-SPARQL [4,5] introduces the notion of RDF streams as the natural extension of the RDF data model to this scenario, and then extend SPARQL to query RDF streams. An RDF stream is defined as an ordered sequence of pairs, where each pair is constituted by an RDF triple and its timestamp τ.

$$\ldots$$
$$(\langle subj_i, pred_i, obj_i \rangle \, , \tau_i)$$
$$(\langle subj_{i+1}, pred_{i+1}, obj_{i+1} \rangle \, , \tau_{i+1})$$
$$\ldots$$

Fig. 2 shows an example of a C-SPARQL query that continuously queries a RDF stream as well as a static RDF graph. The RDF stream describes the users sitting in trains and trains moving from a station to another one. The RDF graph describes where the stations are located, e.g., a station is in a city, which is in a region.

```
1.  REGISTER QUERY TotalAmountPerBroker COMPUTE EVERY 1sec AS
2.  PREFIX ex: <http://example/>
3.  SELECT DISTINCT ?user ?type ?x
4.  FROM <http://mobileservice.org/meansOfTransportation.rdf>
5.  FROM STREAM <http://mobileservice.org/positions.trdf>
5.  [RANGE 10sec STEP 1sec]
6.  WHERE {
7.      ?user ex:isIn ?x .
8.      ?user a ex:Commuter .
9.      ?x a ?type .
10.     ?user ex:remainingTravelTime ?t .
11.     FILTER (?t >= "PT30M"xsd:duration )
12. }
```

Fig. 2. An example of C-SPARQL query that continuously queries a RDF stream as well as a static RDF graph

At line 1, the REGISTER clause instructs the C-SPARQL engine to register a continuous query. The COMPUTE EVERY clause states the frequency of every new computation. In line 5, the FROM STREAM clause defines the RDF stream of positions used in the query. Next, line 6 defines the window of observation of the RDF stream. Streams, by their very nature, are volatile and consumed on the fly. The C-SPARQL engine, therefore, observes them through a window that contains the stream's most recent elements and that changes over time. In the example, the window comprises RDF triples produced in the last 10 seconds and the window slides every second. The WHERE clause is standard SPARQL as it includes a set of matching patterns, which restricts users to be commuters and a FILTER clause, which restricts the answers to users whose remaining traveling time is at least 30 minutes. This example shows that, at the time of the presentation in the window, it is possible to compute the time when triples both of the window and of ontological entailments will cease to be valid.

2.2   Expressing Ontology Languages as Rules

Using rules is a best practice (see Section 2.1 of [9]) in implementing the logical entailment supported by ontology languages such as RDF-S [13] and OWL2-RL [14]. For example, Fig. 3 presents the set of rule used by the Jena Generic Rule Engine [15] to compute RDF-S closure. The first rule (rdfs2) states that if there is a triple <?x ?p ?y> and the domain of the property ?p is the class

```
[rdfs2:   (?x ?p ?y), (?p rdfs:domain ?c) -> (?x rdf:type ?c)]
[rdfs3:   (?x ?p ?y), (?p rdfs:range ?c) -> (?y rdf:type ?c)]
[rdfs5a:  (?a rdfs:subPropertyOf ?b), (?b rdfs:subPropertyOf ?c)
             -> (?a rdfs:subPropertyOf ?c)]
[rdfs5b:  (?a rdf:type rdf:Property) -> (?a rdfs:subPropertyOf ?a)]
[rdfs6:   (?a ?p ?b), (?p rdfs:subPropertyOf ?q) -> (?a ?q ?b)]
[rdfs7:   (?a rdf:type rdfs:Class) -> (?a rdfs:subClassOf ?a)]
[rdfs8:   (?a rdfs:subClassOf ?b), (?b rdfs:subClassOf ?c)
             -> (?a rdfs:subClassOf ?c)]
[rdfs9:   (?x rdfs:subClassOf ?y), (?a rdf:type ?x) -> (?a rdf:type ?y)]
[rdfs10:  (?x rdf:type rdfs:ContainerMembershipProperty)
             -> (?x rdfs:subPropertyOf rdfs:member)]
[rdf1and4: (?x ?p ?y) -> (?p rdf:type rdf:Property),
                        (?x rdf:type rdfs:Resource),
                        (?y rdf:type rdfs:Resource)]
[rdfs7b:  (?a rdf:type rdfs:Class) -> (?a rdfs:subClassOf rdfs:Resource)]
```

Fig. 3. Rules Implementing RDF-S in Jena Generic Rule Engine

?c (represented by the triple `<?p rdfs:domain ?c>`) then the resource ?x is of
type ?c (represented by the triple `<?x rdf:type ?c>`).

In the rest of the paper, we adopt logic programming terminology. We refer
to a set of rules as a *logic program* (or simply program) and we assume that any
RDF graph can be stored in the extension of a single ternary predicate P. Under
this assumption, the rule rdfs2 can be represented in Datalog as follows.

$$P(x, rdf : type, c) :- P(p, rdfs : domain, C), P(s, p, y)$$

2.3   Incremental Maintenance of Materializations

Maintenance of a materialization when facts change, i.e., facts are added or
removed from the knowledge base, is a well studied problem. The state of the art
approach implemented in systems such as KAON[1] is a declarative variant [9] of
the delete and re-derive (DRed) algorithm proposed in [16]. DRed incrementally
maintains a materialization in three steps.

1. Overestimate the deletions by computing all the direct consequences of a
   deletion.
2. Prune the overestimated deletions for which the deleted fact can be re-
   derived from other facts.
3. Insert all derivation which are consequences of added facts.

More formally, a logic program is composed by a set of rules **R** that we can
represent as $H :- B_1, \ldots, B_n$, where H is the predicate that forms the head of
the rule and $B_1, \ldots, B_n$ are the predicates that form the body of the rule. If we

---

[1] The Datalog engine is part of the KAON suite, see http://kaon.semanticweb.org

call the set of predicates in a logic program $\mathbf{P}$, then we can formally assert that $H, B_i \in \mathbf{P}$. A *maintenance program*, which implements the declarative version of the DRed algorithm, can be automatically derived from the original program with a fixed set of rewriting functions (see Table 2) that uses seven maintenance predicates (see Table 1) [9].

Table 1. The maintenance predicates (derived from [9])

Name	Content of the extension
P	the current materialization
P^{Del}	the deletions
P^{Ins}	the explicit insertion
P^{Red}	the triples marked for deletion which have alternative derivations
P^{New}	the materialization after the execution of the maintenance program
P^+	the net insertions required to maintain the materialization
P^-	the net deletions required to maintain the materialization

Given a materialized predicate P and the set of extensional insertions P^{Ins} to and deletions P^{Dels} from P, the goal of the rewriting functions is the definition of two maintenance predicates P^+ and P^-, such that the extensions of P^+ and P^- contain the net insertions and deletions, respectively, that are needed to incrementally maintain the materialization of P.

Table 2. Rewriting functions (derived from [9])

Predicate		
Name	Generator Parameter	Rewriting Result
δ_1^{New}	$P \in \mathbf{P}$	$P^{New} \text{ :- } P, not\, P^{Del}$
δ_2^{New}	$P \in \mathbf{P}$	$P^{New} \text{ :- } P^{Red}$
δ_3^{New}	$P \in \mathbf{P}$	$P^{New} \text{ :- } P^{Ins}$
δ^+	$P \in \mathbf{P}$	$P^+ \text{ :- } P^{Ins}, not P$
δ^-	$P \in \mathbf{P}$	$P^- \text{ :- } P^{Del}, not P^{Ins}, not\, P^{Red}$
Rule		
Name	Generator Parameter	Rewriting Result
δ^{Red}	$H \text{ :- } B_1, \ldots, B_n$	$H^{Red} \text{ :- } H^{Del}, B_1^{New}, \ldots, B_n^{New}$
δ^{Del}	$H \text{ :- } B_1, \ldots, B_n$	$\{H^{Del} \text{ :- } B_1, \ldots, B_{i-1}, B_i^{Del}, B_{i+1}, \ldots, B_n\}$
δ^{Ins}	$H \text{ :- } B_1, \ldots, B_n$	$\{H^{Ins} \text{ :- } B_1^{New}, \ldots, B_{i-1}^{New}, B_i^{Ins}, B_{i+1}^{New}, \ldots, B_n^{New}\}$

We can divide the rewriting functions shown in Table 2 in two groups. One group of functions apply to predicates, while the other group of functions apply to rules. The former functions use the predicates defined in Table 1 to introduce the rules that will store the materialization after the execution of the maintenance program in the extension of the predicate P^{New}. The latter functions introduce the rules that populate the extensions of the predicates P^{Del}, P^{Red}, and P^{Ins}.

These three rewriting functions are executed for each rule that has the predicate P as head. While the function δ^{Red} rewrites each rule in exactly one maintenance rule, the two functions δ^{Del} and δ^{Ins} rewrite each rule with n bodies B_i into n maintenance rules.

To exemplify how these rewriting functions work in practice, let us return to the scenario exemplified in Sect. 2.1. To describe that scenario, we introduced the predicate $isIn$ that captures the respective position of moving objects (e.g., somebody is in a train, the train is in station, somebody else is in a car, the car is in a parking lot, etc.). A simple ontology for a mobility scenario could express transitivity and be represented using the following Datalog rule.

$$(R)\ isIn(x, z) :\text{-}\ isIn(x, y), isIn(y, z)$$

By applying the rewriting functions presented in Table 2 to the rule (R) and the predicate $isIn$, we obtain the maintenance program shown in Table 3. Each row of the table contains the applied rewriting function and the rewritten maintenance rule.

Table 3. The maintenance program automatically derived from a program containing only the rule R by applying the rewriting functions show in Table 2

Rule	Rewriting Function
$isIn^{New}(x,y) :\text{-} isIn(x,y), not\, isIn^{Del}(x,y)$	$\delta_1^{New}(isIn)$
$isIn^{New}(x,y) :\text{-} isIn^{Red}(x,y)$	$\delta_2^{New}(isIn)$
$isIn^{New}(x,y) :\text{-} isIn^{Ins}(x,y)$	$\delta_3^{New}(isIn)$
$isIn^{+}(x,y) :\text{-} isIn^{Ins}(x,y), not\, isIn(x,y)$	$\delta^{+}(isIn)$
$isIn^{-}(x,y) :\text{-} isIn^{Del}(x,y), not\, isIn^{Ins}(x,y), not\, isIn^{Red}(x,y)$	$\delta^{-}(isIn)$
$isIn^{Red}(x,z) :\text{-} isIn^{Del}(x,z), isIn^{New}(x,y), isIn^{New}(y,z)$	$\delta^{Red}(R)$
$isIn^{Del}(x,z) :\text{-} isIn^{Del}(x,y), isIn(y,z)$	$\delta^{Del}(R)$
$isIn^{Del}(x,z) :\text{-} isIn(x,y), isIn^{Del}(y,z)$	$\delta^{Del}(R)$
$isIn^{Ins}(x,z) :\text{-} isIn^{Ins}(x,y), isIn^{new}(y,z)$	$\delta^{Ins}(R)$
$isIn^{Ins}(x,z) :\text{-} isIn^{new}(x,y), isIn^{Ins}(y,z)$	$\delta^{Ins}(R)$

3   Maintaining Materialization of RDF Streams

As we explained earlier in this paper, incremental maintenance of materializations of ontological entailments after knowledge changes is a well studied problem. However, additions or removals of facts from the knowledge base induced by data streams are governed by windows, which have a known expiration time. The intuition behind our approach is straightforward. If we tag each RDF triple (both explicitly inserted and entailed) with a *expiration time* that represents the last moment in which it will be in the window, we can compute a new complete and correct materialization by dropping RDF triples that are no longer in the window and then evaluate a maintenance program that

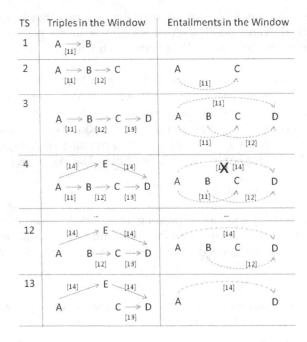

Fig. 4. Our approach to incrementally maintain the materialization at work

1. computes the entailments derived by the inserts,
2. annotates each entailed triple with a expiration time, and
3. eliminates from the current state all copies of derived triples except the one with the highest timestamp.

Note that this approach supports the immediate deletions of both window facts and entailed triples which are dropped by inspection to their expiration times. Instead it requires some extra work for managing insertions as new timestamps need to be computed. This approach is more effective than overestimating the deletions and then computing re-derivations, as we will demonstrate in Section 5.

Figure 4 illustrates our approach. Let us assume that we have a stream of triples in which all the triples use the same predicate *isIn* introduced in Section 2.3. Let us also assume that we register a simple C-SPARQL query that observes an RDF stream through a sliding window of 10 seconds and computes the transitive closure of the *isIn* property.

In the 1st second of execution, the triple <A isIn B> enters the window. We tag the triple with the expiration time 11 (i.e., it will be valid until the 11th second) and no derivation occurs. The transitive closure only contains that triple. In the 2nd second the triple <B isIn C> enters the window. We can tag it with the expiration time 12 and we can materialize the entailed triple <A isIn C>. As the triple <A isIn B> expires in the 11th second, the entailed triple <A isIn C> also expires then and, thus, we tag it with the expiration time 11 (i.e., Step 2 of our approach). As the 11th second passes, we will have to just drop the

Table 4. The maintenance predicates of our approach

Name	Content of the extension
P	the current materialization
P^{Ins}	the triples that enter the window
P^{New}	the triples which are progressively added to the materialization
P^{Old}	the triples for which re-derivations with a longer expiration time were materialized
P^{+}	the net insertions required to maintain the materialization
P^{-}	the net deletions required to maintain the materialization

triples tagged with 11 and the materialization will be up to date (i.e., Step 1 of our approach).

Let us then assume that in the 3rd second, the triple <C isIn D> enters the window. We tag it with the expiration time 13 and compute two entailments: the triple <B isIn D> with expiration time 12 and the triple <A isIn D> with expiration time 11. In the 4th second, the two triples <A isIn E> and <E isIn D> enter the window. Both triples are tagged with the expiration time 14. We also derive the entailed triple <A isIn D> with time expiration 14. The triple <A isIn D> was previously derived, but its expiration time was 11 and, therefore, that triple is dropped. The rest of Fig. 4 shows how triples are deleted when they expire.

More formally, our logic program is composed of a set of rules **R** that we can represent as $H[T]$:- $B_1[T_1], \ldots, B_n[T_n]$, where H is the predicate that forms the head of the rule and it is valid until T. $B_1[T_1], \ldots, B_n[T_n]$ are the n predicates that form the body of the rule with their respective n expiration times $T_1 \ldots T_n$. As in the case illustrated in Section 2.3, we can formally assert that $H, B_i \in \mathbf{P}$ where **P** denotes the set of predicates in a logic program.

Table 5. The rewriting functions of our approach

Predicate		
Name	Generator Parameter	Rewriting Result
Δ_1^{New}	$P \in \mathbf{P}$	$P^{New}[T]$:- $P[T], not P[T_1], T_1 = (now - 1)$
Δ_2^{New}	$P \in \mathbf{P}$	$P^{New}[T]$:- $P^{Ins}[T], not\, P^{Old}[T]$
Δ_1^{Old}	$P \in \mathbf{P}$	$P^{Old}[T]$:- $P^{Ins}[T_1], P[T], T1 > T$
Δ_2^{Old}	$P \in \mathbf{P}$	$P^{Old}[T]$:- $P^{Ins}[T_1], P^{Ins}[T], T1 > T$
Δ_1^{-}	$P \in \mathbf{P}$	$P^{-}[T]$:- $P[T_1], T_1 = (now - 1), not\, P^{Ins}[T_1]$
Δ_2^{-}	$P \in \mathbf{P}$	$P^{-}[T]$:- $P^{Old}[T]$
Δ^{++}	$P \in \mathbf{P}$	$P^{++}[T]$:- $P^{New}[T], not\, P[T_1]$
Δ^{+}	$P \in \mathbf{P}$	$P^{+}[T]$:- $P^{++}[T], not\, P^{Old}[T_1]$

Rule		
Name	Generator Parameter	Rewriting Result
Δ^{Ins}	H :- $B_1, \ldots, B_n$	$\{H^{Ins}[T]$:- $B_1^{New}[T_1], \ldots, B_{i-1}^{New}[T_{i-1}],$ $B_i^{Ins}[T_i], B_{i+1}^{New}[T_{i+1}], \ldots, B_n^{New}[T_n],$ $T = min(T_1, \ldots, T_n)\}$

A maintenance program, which implements our approach in a declarative way, can be automatically be derived from the original program with a fixed set of rewriting functions (see Table 5) that uses five maintenance predicates (see Table 4) inspired by the approach of Volz et al. [9].

Given a materialized predicate P and set of extensional insertions P^{Ins} determined by the new triple entering the window, the goal of the rewriting functions is the definition of the maintenance predicates P^+ and P^- whose extension contains the net insertions and the net deletions needed to incrementally maintain the materialization of P. The extension of the maintenance predicate P^- contains the extensions of predicate P that expires as well as the extension of predicate P^{Old}. In Table 5 we formally defines our rewriting functions. Note that P^{++} is only an auxiliary predicate with not special meaning.

By applying the rewriting functions presented in Table 5 to the rule (R) and the predicate $isIn$ defined in Section 2.3, we obtain the maintenance program shown in Table 6.

Table 6. The maintenance program automatically derived from a program containing only the rule R by applying the rewriting functions show in Table 5

Rule	Function
$isIn^{New}(x,y)[T] :\text{-} isIn(x,y)[T], not\, isIn(x,y)[T_1], T_1 = (now - 1)$	$\Delta_1^{New}(isIn)$
$isIn^{New}(x,y)[T] :\text{-} isIn^{Ins}(x,y)[T], not isIn^{Old}(x,y)[T]$	$\Delta_2^{New}(isIn)$
$isIn^{Old}(x,y)[T] :\text{-} isIn^{Ins}(x,y)[T_1], isIn(x,y)[T], T1 > T$	$\Delta_1^{Old}(isIn)$
$isIn^{Old}(x,y)[T] :\text{-} isIn^{Ins}(x,y)[T_1], isIn^{Ins}(x,y)[T], T1 > T$	$\Delta_2^{Old}(isIn)$
$isIn^-(x,y)[T] :\text{-} isIn(x,y)[T_1], T_1 = (now - 1), not\, isIn^{Ins}(x,y)[T_1]$	$\Delta_1^-(isIn)$
$isIn^-(x,y)[T] :\text{-} isIn^{Old}(x,y)[T]$	$\Delta_2^-(isIn)$
$isIn^{++}(x,y)[T] :\text{-} isIn^{New}(x,y)[T], not\, isIn(x,y)[T_1]$	$\Delta^{++}(isIn)$
$isIn^+(x,y)[T] :\text{-} isIn^{++}(x,y)[T], not\, isIn^{Old}(x,y)[T_1]$	$\Delta^+(isIn)$
$isIn^{Ins}(x,z)[T] :\text{-} isIn^{Ins}(x,y)[T_1], isIn^{New}(y,z)[T_2], T = min(T_1,T_2)$	$\Delta^{Ins}(R)$
$isIn^{Ins}(x,z)[T] :\text{-} isIn^{New}(x,y)[T_1], isIn^{Ins}(y,z)[T_2], T = min(T_1,T_2)$	$\Delta^{Ins}(R)$

4   Implementation Experience

Figure 5 illustrates the architecture of our current prototype, implemented by using the Jena Generic Rule Engine. The *Incremental Maintainer* component orchestrates the maintenance process. It keeps the current materialization in the *Permanent Space* and uses the *Working Space* to compute the net inserts and deletes. Both spaces consist of an RDF store for the triples and a hashtable which caters for efficient management of the expiration time associated with each triple.

The maintenance program (see Fig. 6) is loaded into the rule engine that operates over the RDF store in the working space. The management of expiration times is performed by using four custom built-ins, *GetVT*, *GetDiffVT*, *SetVT* and *DelVT*, that are triggered by the maintenance program[2]. GetVT retrieves

---

[2] For more information on how to write built-ins for Jena Generic Rule Engine see [15].

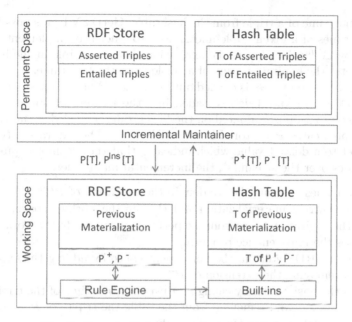

Fig. 5. Overview of the prototype implementation

```
[New1: (?A isIn ?B), GetVT(?A isIn ?B, ?T), noValue(?A isInExp ?B)
    -> (?A isInNew ?B), SetVT(?A isInNew ?B, ?T)]
[New2: (?A isInIns ?B), GetVT(?A isInIns ?B, ?T), noValue(?A isInOld ?B)
    -> (?A isInNew ?B), SetVT(?A isInNew ?B, ?T)]
[Old1: (?A isInIns ?B), GetVT(?A isInIns ?B, ?T1),
    (?A isIn ?B), GetVT(?A isIn ?B, ?T), lessThan(?T, ?T1)
    -> (?A isInOld ?B), DelVT(?A isInIns ?B, ?T)]
[Old2: (?A isInIns ?B), GetVT(?A isInIns ?B, ?T1),
    (?A isInIns ?B), GetDiffVT(?A isIn ?B, ?T1, ?T), lessThan(?T, ?T1)
    -> (?A isInOld ?B), DelVT(?A isInIns ?B, ?T)]
[Rem1: (?A isInExp ?B), GetVT(?A isInExp ?B, ?T), noValue(?A isInIns ?B)
    -> (?A isInRem ?B), DelVT(?A isInExp ?B, ?T) ]
[Rem2: (?A isInOld ?B) -> (?A isInRem ?B) ]
[Add2: (?A isInNew ?B), GetVT(?A isInNew ?B, ?T), noValue(?A isIn ?B)
    -> (?A isInAdd2 ?B), SetVT(?A isInAdd2 ?B, ?T) ]
[Add1: (?A isInAdd2 ?B), GetVT(?A isInAdd2 ?B, ?T), noValue(?A isInOld ?B)
    -> (?A isInAdd ?B), SetVT(?A isInAdd ?B, ?T) ]
[Ins1: (?A isInIns ?B), GetVT(?A isInIns ?B, ?T1),
    (?B isInNew ?C), GetVT(?B isInNew ?C, ?T2), min(?T1, ?T2, ?T)
    -> (?A isInIns ?C), SetVT(?A isInIns ?C, ?T)]
[Ins2: (?A isInNew ?B), GetVT(?A isInNew ?B, ?T1),
    (?B isInIns ?C), GetVT(?B isInIns ?C, ?T2), min(?T1, ?T2, ?T)
    -> (?A isInIns ?C), SetVT(?A isInIns ?C, ?T)]
```

Fig. 6. The maintenance program shown in Table 6 implemented in Jena Generic Rule Engine

the expiration time of a triple from the hashtable; GetDiffVT gets possible other expiration times of a given triple and is used to efficiently implement the rules generated by Δ_2^{Old}; SetVT sets the expiration time of a triple in the hashtable; DelVT deletes the expiration time of a triple from the hashtable.

The maintenance process is carried out as follows. When the system is started up, the background knowledge is loaded into the permanent space. Then, the maintenance program is evaluated on the background knowledge and the extension of all predicates P is stored in the RDF store. The expiration time of all triples is set to a default value which indicates that they cannot expire. As the window slides over the stream(s), the incremental maintainer:

(a) puts all triples entering the window in the extension of P^{Ins},
(b) loads the current materialization and P^{Ins} in the working space,
(c) copies the expiration times from the permanent space into the working space,
(d) evaluates the maintenance program,
(e) updates the RDF store in the permanent space by adding the extension of P^+ and removing the extension of P^-,
(f) updates the hash tables by changing the expiration time of the triples in the extension of P^+ and removing from the table the triples of P^-, and
(g) clears the working space for a new evaluation.

5   Evaluation

This section reports on the evaluation we carried out using various synthetically generated data sets that use the transitive property $isIn$. Although we limit our experiments to the transitive property, the test is significant because widely used vocabularies in Web ontological languages are transitive (e.g., rdfs:subClassOf, rdfs:subPropertyOf, owl:sameAs, owl:equivalentProperty, owl:equivalentClass and all properties of type owl:TransitiveProperty). Moreover, transitive properties are quite generative in terms of entailments and, thus, stress the system.

Our synthetic data generator generates trees of triples all using $isIn$ as property. We can control the depth of the tree and the number of trees generates. All generated triples are stored in a pool. An experiment consists of measuring the time needed to compute a new materialization based on the given the background knowledge, the triples in the window as well as the triples that enter and exit the window at each step. When we start an experiment, we first extract a subset of triples from the pool to form the background knowledge. Then, we stream the rest of the triples from the pool. We control both the dimension of the window over the stream of triples and the number of triples entering and exiting the window at each step.

In our experiments we compare three approaches: (a) the *naive* approach of re-computing the entire materialization at each step, (b) the maintenance program shown in Table 3 implementing [9], denoted as *incremental-volz*), and (c) our maintenance program shown in Tables 6 and in Fig. 6, denoted as *incremental-stream*. Intuitively, the naive approach is dominated with a small number of

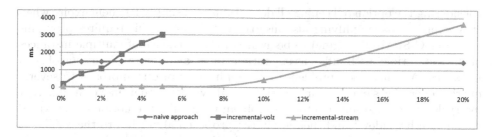

Fig. 7. Evaluation results: the time (ms) required to maintain the materialization as a function of the percentage of the background knowledge subject to change

streaming triples, and dominates when streaming triples are a large fraction of the materialization.

We run multiple experiments[3] using different settings of the experimental environment, by changing the size of the background knowledge, the size of the window, and the number of triples entering and exiting the window at each step. In Fig. 7, we plot the results of one of these experiments (which qualitatively are very similar). We compare the materialization maintenance time as a function of the percentage of the background knowledge subject to change. As one can read from the graph, the incremental-volz [9] approach is faster that the naive approach only if the changes induced by the streaming triples encompass less that 2.5% of the background knowledge. Our incremental-stream approach is an order of magnitude faster than incremental-volz for up to 0.1% of changes and continues to be two orders of magnitude faster up to 2.5% of changes. It no longer pays off with respect to the naive approach when the percentage of change is above 13%.

6   Conclusion and Future Work

In this paper, we have shown how previous work from the field of deductive databases can be applied to the maintenance of ontological entailments with data streams. Our approach is an extension of the algorithm developed by Volz et al. [9], that uses logic programming to maintain materializations incrementally. Data streams use the notion of windows to extract snapshots from streams, that are then processed by the query evaluator; we leverage this fact to define the triples that are inserted into and deleted from the materialization. We have also presented an implementation as an extension of the Jena Generic Rule Engine; our implementation uses hash tables to manage triple expiration time. We have shown that our approach outperforms existing approaches when the window size is a fraction (below 10%) of the knowledge base: this assumption holds for all known data stream applications.

We foresee several extensions to this work. With our approach, at insertion time we explicitly remove old triples which have multiple derivations, but we are

---

[3] We run all experiment on a Intel® Core™ Duo 2.20 GHz with 2 GB of RAM.

considering the option of keeping all derivations and simply let them expire when they expire, thus simplifying also insertions. Of course, this requires programs (e.g., our C-SPARQL engine) to be aware of the existence of multiple instances of the same triple, with different expiration times, and ignore all but one of such instances. Another open problem is the application of our approach to several queries over the same streams, with several windows that move at different intervals. A possible solution to this problem is to build the notion of "maximal common sub-window" and then apply the proposed algorithm to them. This is an original instance of multi-query optimization, that is indeed possible when queries are preregistered (as with stream databases and C-SPARQL). Finally, we intend to explore a "lazy" approach to materialization, in which only entailments that are needed to answer registered queries are computed. In our future work, we plan to address these issues.

Acknowledgements

The work described in this paper has been partially supported by the European project LarKC (FP7-215535). Michael Grossniklaus's work is carried out under SNF grant number PBEZ2-121230.

References

1. Garofalakis, M., Gehrke, J., Rastogi, R.: Data Stream Management: Processing High-Speed Data Streams (Data-Centric Systems and Applications). Springer, Heidelberg (2007)
2. Della Valle, E., Ceri, S., van Harmelen, F., Fensel, D.: It's a Streaming World! Reasoning upon Rapidly Changing Information. IEEE Intelligent Systems 24(6), 83–89 (2009)
3. Bolles, A., Grawunder, M., Jacobi, J.: Streaming SPARQL - extending SPARQL to process data streams. In: Bechhofer, S., Hauswirth, M., Hoffmann, J., Koubarakis, M. (eds.) ESWC 2008. LNCS, vol. 5021, pp. 448–462. Springer, Heidelberg (2008)
4. Barbieri, D.F., Braga, D., Ceri, S., Della Valle, E., Grossniklaus, M.: C-SPARQL: SPARQL for Continuous Querying. In: Proc. Intl. Conf. on World Wide Web (WWW), pp. 1061–1062 (2009)
5. Barbieri, D.F., Braga, D., Ceri, S., Grossniklaus, M.: An Execution Environment for C-SPARQL Queries. In: Proc. Intl. Conf. on Extending Database Technology, EDBT (2010)
6. Rodriguez, A., McGrath, R., Liu, Y., Myers, J.: Semantic Management of Streaming Data. In: Proc. Intl. Workshop on Semantic Sensor Networks, SSN (2009)
7. McBride, B., Hayes, P.: RDF Semantics. W3C Recommendation (2004), http://www.w3.org/TR/rdf-mt/
8. Gaerdenfors, P. (ed.): Belief Revision. Cambridge University Press, Cambridge (2003)
9. Volz, R., Staab, S., Motik, B.: Incrementally maintaining materializations of ontologies stored in logic databases. J. Data Semantics 2, 1–34 (2005)
10. Staudt, M., Jarke, M.: Incremental maintenance of externally materialized views. In: Vijayaraman, T.M., Buchmann, A.P., Mohan, C., Sarda, N.L. (eds.) VLDB, pp. 75–86. Morgan Kaufmann, San Francisco (1996)

11. Ceri, S., Widom, J.: Deriving production rules for incremental view maintenance. In: Lohman, G.M., Sernadas, A., Camps, R. (eds.) VLDB, pp. 577–589. Morgan Kaufmann, San Francisco (1991)
12. Della Valle, E., Ceri, S., Barbieri, D.F., Braga, D., Campi, A.: A First Step Towards Stream Reasoning. In: Proc. Future Internet Symposium (FIS), pp. 72–81 (2008)
13. Brickley, D., Guha, R.: RDF Vocabulary Description Language 1.0: RDF Schema. W3C Recommendation (2004), http://www.w3.org/TR/rdf-schema/
14. Motik, B., Grau, B.C., Horrocks, I., Wu, Z., Fokoue, A., Lutz, C.: Owl 2 web ontology language: Profiles. W3C Recommendation (2009), http://www.w3.org/TR/owl2-profiles/
15. Reynolds, D.: Jena 2 inference support (2009), http://jena.sourceforge.net/inference/
16. Gupta, A., Mumick, I.S., Subrahmanian, V.S.: Maintaining views incrementally. In: Buneman, P., Jajodia, S. (eds.) SIGMOD Conference, pp. 157–166. ACM Press, New York (1993)

Mobile Semantic-Based Matchmaking: A Fuzzy DL Approach

Michele Ruta, Floriano Scioscia, and Eugenio Di Sciascio

Politecnico di Bari
via Re David 200, I-70125
Bari, Italy
{m.ruta,f.scioscia,disciascio}@poliba.it

Abstract. Novel wireless handheld devices allow the adoption of revised and adapted discovery approaches originally devised for the Semantic Web in mobile ad-hoc networks. Nevertheless, capabilities of such devices require an accurate re-design of frameworks and algorithms to efficiently support mobile users. The paper focuses on an implementation of concept abduction and contraction algorithms in (fuzzy) $\mathcal{ALN}(D)$ DL settings to perform semantic matchmaking and provide logical explanation services. OWL-DL Knowledge Bases have been properly exploited to enable standard and non-standard inference services. The proposed framework has been implemented and tested in a *fire hazards* prevention case study: early experimental results are reported.

1 Introduction

Current mobile devices are increasingly effective and powerful but anyway they maintain some limitations which have to be taken into account when designing systems and applications. The paper proposes a novel matchmaking framework suitable for resource-constrained devices and contexts where canonical discovery is unfeasible or even impractical. Particularly, we propose a revision of abduction and contraction algorithms presented in [1] in order to allow an exploitation of them in mobility. Note that, even if they have rising performances, battery powered handheld devices are networked by means of wireless low-throughput links and are basically unable to run heavy reasoning algorithms explicitly devised for PCs and servers over the Internet. Knowledge Representation techniques and approaches –which originally enhanced code-based discovery [2]– have been revised to be effectively suitable in volatile ubiquitous computing contexts by-passing the presence of fixed workstations.

The proposed framework and approach has been applied and tested in a mobile *fire risk prevention* case study even if it is cross-applicable to several scenarios. New approaches to disaster prevention focus on providing assistance to discover possible risks in given areas and activities before disasters happen. Thanks to a continuous surveillance of context parameters and taking into account a knowledge-based domain and risk modeling, possible hazards can be detected in order to quickly perform recovery procedures to take danger under

L. Aroyo et al. (Eds.): ESWC 2010, Part I, LNCS 6088, pp. 16–30, 2010.

control. In what follows an illustrative example is presented to better explain potentialities our approach provides and to let emerge its novelty. A performance examination referred to the case study has been also carried out allowing to evaluate system behavior.

We selected Description Logics (DLs) as reference logic formalism family [3] and particularly we referred to a sublanguage deriving from OWL DL[1], $\mathcal{ALN}(D)$, to model ontologies and environmental annotations whereas the proposed system adopts DIG 2.0[2] as reference syntax. Noteworthy is the exploitation of fuzzy DL operators to better model vague real-world requirements in matchmaking issues.

The remaining of the paper is structured as follows: in the next Section we survey most relevant related work, Section 3 is devoted to present a background of the proposed approach; afterward, in Section 4 we move on to description of theoretical framework. Relevant features of proposed algorithms and architecture are better clarified in Section 5 with the aid of a simple illustrative case study whereas Section 6 reports on experimental evidences related to the implemented prototype. Finally conclusions close the paper.

2   Related Work

Most mobile reasoning engines currently provide only simple rule processing through forward/backward chaining. Interesting instances include mobile Prolog engines [4] –which are reduced version of PC engines– and the mobile composable reasoner in [5]. Their expressiveness, however, is too limited to support advanced applications such as semantic-based matchmaking and resource discovery.

Adapting tableaux algorithms –used in most "wired" DL reasoners– to mobile computing platforms may allow more expressive languages to be used, but efficient implementation of useful non-standard reasoning services is still an open problem due to resource limitations. Most optimization techniques [6] cannot be adopted in mobile systems, since they decrease running time but increase main memory usage.

Pocket KRHyper [7] was the first reasoning engine for mobile devices. It supports the Description Logic $\mathcal{ALCHIR}+$ and was built as a Java ME (Micro Edition) library. Pocket KRHyper was exploited by the authors in a DL-based matchmaking framework between user profiles and descriptions of mobile resources/services [8]. However, its limitations in size and complexity of managed logical expressions are very tight because "out of memory" errors are frequent. To overcome those limitations, Steller and Krishnaswamy [9] introduced a set of tableaux optimizations to reduce memory consumption. Proposed techniques were implemented in *mTableau*, a modified version of Pellet, a popular open-source reasoning engine for Java Standard Edition (SE). Comparative performance tests were performed on a PC, showing faster turnaround times than

[1] OWL Web Ontology Language, W3C Recommendation 10 February 2004,
http://www.w3.org/TR/owl-features/
[2] DIG 2.0: The DIG Description Logic Interface,
http://dig.cs.manchester.ac.uk/overview.html

both unmodified Pellet and Racer, another widely used reasoner in the Semantic Web. Nevertheless, Java SE as a technology is not tailored to the current generation of mobile computing devices, even though some experimental projects are trying to port Java SE to mobile and embedded devices. Both the above systems only support standard satisfiability and subsumption inference services. Consequently, they can only distinguish among full, potential and partial match types (adopting the terminology of [10]). This is due to the fact that satisfiability and subsumption provide only binary "yes/no" answers. Abductive matchmaking is needed to determine what part of a request is not fully satisfied by a supplied resource, thus enabling a more fine-grained semantic ranking as well as explanation of outcomes.

In [11], a different approach to adapt logic-based reasoning services to pervasive computing contexts was proposed. It was based on simplifying the underlying logical languages and admitted axioms in a KB, so that standard and non-standard reasoning services could be reduced to set-based operations. KB management and reasoning services were then executed through a data storage layer, based on a mobile RDBMS (Relational DBMS). A specialized database schema template allowed KB classification and inference algorithms to be performed through a small set of SQL queries. The proposed discovery model was suitable for pervasive contexts characterized by a large amount of "lightweight" resources with a low level of semantic sophistication. This approach was further investigated in [12], by increasing the expressiveness of the language and allowing larger ontologies and more complex descriptions, through the adoption of a mobile OODBMS (Object-Oriented DBMS). Though the approach has relevant benefits, a native language implementation can certainly grant greater flexibility in extending algorithms of the core reasoning engine to more expressive logical languages and in implementing additional inference services.

3   Background

In what follows most relevant basics for the proposed approach will be provided with specific reference to (fuzzy) Description Logics and matchmaking.

3.1   Description Logics

Description Logics (DLs) are a family of logic formalisms for Knowledge Representation [3]. Basic syntax elements are: *concept* names, *role* names, and *individuals*. They can be combined using *constructors* to build complex concept and role *expressions*. Each DL is featured by a different set of constructors. A constructor used in every DL is the one allowing the *conjunction* of concepts, usually denoted as ⊓; some DL include also disjunction ⊔ and complement ¬ to close concept expressions under boolean operations. Roles can be combined with concepts using *existential role quantification* and *universal role quantification*. Other constructs may involve counting, as *number restrictions*. Many other constructs can be defined, so increasing the expressiveness of the related DL but also the computational complexity of related inference services [13]. *OWL-DL* is a language based on DLs theoretical studies which allows a great expressiveness keeping computational completeness and decidability.

In a DL framework, an ontology $\mathcal{T}$ (a.k.a. Terminological Box or TBox) is composed by a set of axioms in the form: $A \sqsubseteq D$ or $A \equiv D$ where A is an atomic concept and D is generic $\mathcal{ALN}$ concept. In particular, we call simple-TBox all those set of axioms such that if A appears in the left hand side (lhs) of a concept equivalence axioms then it cannot appear also in the lhs of any concept inclusion axiom. In this paper we refer to the $\mathcal{ALN}$(D) (Attributive Language with Unqualified Number Restrictions with Concrete Domains) subset of OWL-DL, which has polynomial computational complexity for standard and non-standard inferences in "bushy but not deep" TBoxes [14].

With respect to $\mathcal{ALN}$, $\mathcal{ALN}$(D) allows to model a set of *features* f having D as domain, and a set of unary predicates p in D. Each feature can be seen as: $p(f)$ where $f : \Delta \rightarrow R$. So the following relation ensues:

$$p(f)^{\mathcal{I}} = \{c \in \Delta \mid f(c) \in p^{D}\} \tag{1}$$

For instance, if we consider the integers concrete domain D, p can be represented by one of $\geq_k (\cdot)$, $\leq_k (\cdot)$ or $=_k (\cdot)$ operators, where k is a given value in the domain associated to f.

Hereafter, for compactness we will formalize examples by adopting DL syntax (instead of OWL-DL or its syntactic variant DIG [15]), whereas in our prototypes DIG is exploited because it is less verbose w.r.t. OWL.

3.2   Fuzzy DL

OWL DL becomes less suitable when facts to be represented do not have a precise definition. For instance, let us suppose we have to model the description of a "large fuel depot containing a lot of liquefied petroleum gas with various expert workers operating in the warehouse, and also accessible to non-authorized staff members" in a *fire hazard* domain. A plain translation into OWL DL is difficult, as it involves so called fuzzy or vague concepts, like "large", "a lot", "various", whose unambiguous definition is practically unfeasible. Hence we have to consider a fuzzy extension of $\mathcal{ALN}$(D) DL, and exploit its syntax and semantics.

Basically, a fuzzy set A w.r.t. a universe X is characterized by a membership function $\mu_A : X \rightarrow [0,1]$ assigning an A-*membership degree*, $\mu_A(x)$, to each element x in X. $\mu_A(x)$ gives us an estimation of "how much" x belongs to A. Typically, if $\mu_A(x) = 1$, then x definitely belongs to A, while $\mu_A(x) = 0.5$ means that x is could be an element of A [16]. The notion of degree of membership $\mu_A(x)$ of an element $x \in X$ w.r.t. the fuzzy set A over X can also be seen as the degree of truth in $[0,1]$ of the statement "x is A". Hence a *fuzzy set* A can be defined as set of ordered pairs composed by each X element along with the corresponding value for the membership function:

$$A = \{(x, \mu_A(x)) \mid x \in X\} \tag{2}$$

According to the specific applications, different membership functions can be exploited. The most frequent and widespread are *Trapezoidal*, *Triangular*, *Left shoulder* and *Right shoulder* functions (see [16] for details). They will be also used in the approach proposed here.

3.3 Matchmaking

Given an ontology T and two generic concepts C and D, DL matchmakers expose at least two basic standard reasoning services: concept **subsumption** and concept **satisfiability**. In a nutshell they can be defined as in the following:

Concept subsumption. Check if C is more specific than (implies) D with respect to the information modeled in T. In formulae we write $T \models C \sqsubseteq D$.

Concept satisifiability. Check if the information in C is not consistent with respect to the information modeled in T. In formulae we write $T \models C \sqsubseteq \bot$.

Subsumption and satisfiability may be powerful tools in case a Boolean answer is needed. However, in more advanced scenarios where the so called *Open World Assumption* (OWA) is made, *yes/no* answers do not provide satisfactory results. Often an outcome explanation is required. In [14] Concept Abduction Problem (CAP) $\langle \mathcal{L}, C, D, T \rangle$ was introduced and defined as non standard inference problem for DLs, to provide an explanation when subsumption does not hold. In a few words, given an ontology T and two concepts C and D in a DL $\mathcal{L}$, if $T \models C \sqsubseteq D$ is `false` then we compute a concept H (for hypothesis) such that $T \models C \sqcap H \sqsubseteq D$. That is, H is a possible explanation why resource features do not imply requested ones or, in other words, H represents missing capabilities in the resource C in order to completely satisfy a request D w.r.t. T. Actually, given a CAP there is more than one valid solution. Some minimality criteria have to be defined. We refer the interested reader to [14] for further details.

If the conjunction $C \sqcap D$ is unsatisfiable in the TBox T representing the ontology, *i.e.*, C, D are not compatible with each other, the requester can retract some requirements G (for Give up) in D, to obtain a concept K (for Keep) such that $K \sqcap C$ is satisfiable in T (Concept Contraction Problem, CCP). CCP is formally defined as follows. Let $\mathcal{L}$ be a DL, C, D be two concepts in $\mathcal{L}$ and T be a set of axioms in $\mathcal{L}$, where both C and D are satisfiable in T. A Concept Contraction Problem, identified by $\langle \mathcal{L}, C, D, T \rangle$ is finding a pair of concepts $\langle G, K \rangle \in \mathcal{L} \times \mathcal{L}$ such that $T \models D \equiv G \sqcap K$, and $K \sqcap C$ is satisfiable in T. Then K is a contraction of D according to C and T. Like for the abduction problem, some minimality criteria in the contraction must be defined [14], since usually one wants to give up as few things as possible.

4   Framework and Approach

Here implementation of algorithms featuring the matchmaking described above is analyzed. Each request and supply (from now on D and S) as well as the given TBox T will be expressed in $\mathcal{ALN}$(D) Description Logic[3].

---

[3] We refer the reader to [14,10] for exhaustive examples and wider argumentation.

4.1 Algorithms

Algorithm 4.1. Concept Contraction	Algorithm 4.2. Concept Abduction

Require: $\langle \mathcal{L}, D, S, \mathcal{T} \rangle$ with $\mathcal{L} = \mathcal{ALN}(D)$, acyclic $\mathcal{T}$
Ensure: $\langle G, K \rangle$ with concept G, K in $\mathcal{L}$
  if $D == \perp$ **then**
    return $\langle \perp, \top \rangle$
  else
    $G := \top$
    $K := \top \sqcap D$
    for all concept name A in K **do**
      $U := unfolding(\langle \mathcal{L}, A, \mathcal{T} \rangle)$
      for all concept name A in U **do**
        if there exists B in S such that $B = \neg A$
        then
          $G := G \sqcap A$
          remove A from K
        end if
      end for
    end for
    for all concept $C := (\geq xR)$ in K **do**
      if there exists $(\leq yR)$ in S and $y < x$ **then**
        replace C with $(\geq yR)$
        $G := G \sqcap C$
      end if
    for all concept $\forall R.E$ in K **do**
      if there exists $\forall R.F$ in S **then**
        $\langle G', K' \rangle := Contract(\langle \mathcal{L}, E, F, \mathcal{T} \rangle)$
        $G := G \sqcap \forall R.G'$
        replace $\forall R.E$ in K with $\forall R.K'$
      end if
    end for
    for all concept $C := (\leq xR)$ in K **do**
      if there exists $(\geq yR)$ in S and $y > x$ **then**
        replace C with $(\leq yR)$
        $G := G \sqcap C$
      end if
    end for
    for all predicate $\geq_x g$ in K **do**
      if there exists $\leq_y g$ in S and $y < x$ **then**
        replace $\geq_x g$ with $\geq_y g$
        $G := G \sqcap C$
      end if
    end for
    for all predicate $\leq_x g$ in $K <$ **do**
      if there exists $\geq_y g$ in S and $y > x$ **then**
        replace $\leq_x g$ with $\leq_y g$
        $G := G \sqcap C$
      end if
    end for
  end if
 	
  return $\langle G, K \rangle$
	Require: $\langle \mathcal{L}, D, S, \mathcal{T} \rangle$ with $\mathcal{L} = \mathcal{ALN}(D)$, acyclic $\mathcal{T}$
	Ensure: H in $\mathcal{L}$
	  $H := \top$
	  for all concept name A in D **do**
	    if does not exist B in S such that $B \sqsubseteq A$ **then**
	      $H := H \sqcap A$
	    end if
	  end for
	  for all concept $(\geq xR)$ in D **do**
	    if does not exist $(\geq_y R)$ in S with $y \geq x$ **then**
	      $H := H \sqcap (\geq xR)$
	    end if
	  end for
	  for all concept $(\leq xR)$ in D **do**
	    if does not exist $(\leq yR)$ in S with $x \geq y$ **then**
	      $H := H \sqcap (\leq xR)$
	    end if
	  end for
	  for all concept $\geq_x g$ in D **do**
	    if does not exist $\geq_y g$ in S with $y \geq x$ **then**
	      $H := H \sqcap \geq_x g$
	    end if
	  end for
	  for all concept $\leq_x g$ in D **do**
	    if does not exist $\leq_y g$ in S with $x \leq y$ **then**
	      $H := H \sqcap \leq_x g$
	    end if
	  end for
	  for all concept $\forall R.E$ in D **do**
	    if there exists $\forall R.F$ in S **then**
	      $H' := Abduce(\langle \mathcal{L}, E, F, \mathcal{T} \rangle)$
	      $H := H \sqcap \forall R.H'$
	    else
	      $H := H \sqcap \forall R.E$
	    end if
	  end for
	  return H

The matchmaking starts when are available the unfolded versions of D and S, expressed in Conjunctive Normal Form (CNF) [14]. The *Unfolding* and *Normalization* procedures aiming to pre-process D and S are outlined later on. Given the $\mathcal{ALN}(D)$ DL, an acyclic TBox $\mathcal{T}$ and a concept C in $\mathcal{ALN}(D)$, the *unfolding* procedure reported hereafter produces a new concept equivalent to C w.r.t. $\mathcal{T}$.

$A \rightarrow A \sqcap C$ if $A \sqsubseteq C \in \mathcal{T}$
$A \rightarrow C$ if $A \equiv C \in \mathcal{T}$
$A \rightarrow A \sqcap \neg B_1 \sqcap ... \sqcap \neg B_k$ if $disj(A, B_1, ..., B_k) \in \mathcal{T}$

Furthermore, the *Conjunctive Normal Form* of a concept can be obtained by applying the following substitutions (after the unfolding procedure) until no more substitutions are possible:

$$C \sqcap \bot \rightarrow \bot$$
$$(\geq n\,R) \sqcap (\leq m\,R) \rightarrow \bot \text{ if } n > m$$
$$A \sqcap \neg A \rightarrow \bot$$
$$(\geq n\,R) \sqcap (\geq m\,R) \rightarrow (\geq n\,R) \text{ if } n > m$$
$$(\leq n\,R) \sqcap (\leq m\,R) \rightarrow (\leq n\,R) \text{ if } n < m$$
$$\forall R.D_1 \sqcap \forall R.D_2 \rightarrow \forall R.(D_1 \sqcap D_2)$$
$$\forall R.\bot \rightarrow \forall R.\bot \sqcap (\leq 0\,R)$$

For an unfoldable TBox $\mathcal{T}$ in $\mathcal{ALN}(\text{D})$ DL, any concept expression after normalization and unfolding can be expressed as the conjunction of five concept sets [11]: (i) all atomic concepts and negations; (ii) all universal quantifiers; (iii) all $\geq$ number restrictions; (iv) all $\leq$ number restrictions; (v) all predicates over concrete domains.

Concept Contraction. Let $\mathcal{T}$ be an unfoldable TBox in $\mathcal{ALN}(\text{D})$ DL, and D and S a demand and supply in $\mathcal{T}$. Then a Concept Contraction Problem between D and S can be solved by Algorithm 4.1. The basic principle is to match separately each of the five concepts sets in the normalized and unfolded expression for D with the corresponding one in S. When $S \sqcap D$ is satisfiable in $\mathcal{T}$, the "best" possible solution is $\langle \top, D \rangle$, that is, give up nothing –if possible. Hence, a Concept Contraction problem is an extension of a satisfiability one. Since usually one wants to give up as few things as possible, some minimality criteria in the contraction must be defined [17]. In most cases a pure logic-based approach could be not sufficient to decide between which beliefs to give up and which to keep. There is the need of modeling and defining some extra-logical information to be taken into account. For example, we can think to relax some constraints in the original D introducing a *penalty* given by the following function $\prod_C = f(p_D, p_S)$ where p_D e p_S are the conflicting predicates respectively within the demand and the supply.

Concept Abduction. A similar structural approach can be pursued to solve a Concept Abduction Problem. Algorithm 4.2 reports the procedure details, where D and S are compared piecewise. Also in this case, one can think to a *penalty function* which increases when the number of missing concepts in S w.r.t. to D grows. The penalty function for the abduction problem can be expressed as $\prod_A = f(p_D, p_S)$ where p_D e p_S are missing predicates or restrictions respectively in D and S.

4.2   System Architecture

The mobile reasoning engine was designed to be as modular as possible. Core components provide a framework that supports the two basic system tasks: (1) parsing and manipulation of Knowledge Bases in DIG format and (2) execution of the previously described algorithms for standard and non-standard inference services. Each additional module provides support for a set of logic constructors in both the parsing and reasoning steps. They extend abstract classes and interfaces provided in the core components in order to fit within the software

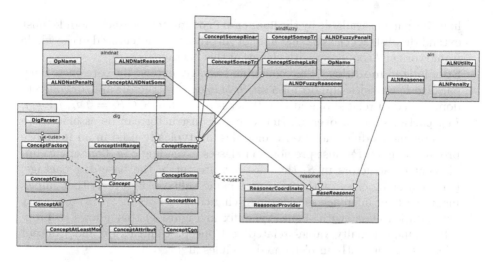

Fig. 1. UML component diagram of the mobile reasoning engine

framework and seamlessly augment the base reasoner capabilities. System architecture is depicted in Figure 1 where solid arrows with full arrowhead indicate inheritance relationship and dashed arrows denote a generic dependency relationship, when not specified further through UML stereotypes (such as the <<use>> one). Classes inside each package and their relationships are shown. Hereafter components are individually described in detail.

- **Package dig** - Provides the core DIG parsing capabilities, supporting basic $\mathcal{ALN}$(D) constructors. It allows to read a DIG Knowledge Base and build an in-memory model of the TBox. *Factory method* design pattern is used to create Java objects representing concepts during DIG parsing. The abstract class Concept provides base fields and methods to represent and process DL concepts. A subclass is defined for each concept type in $\mathcal{ALN}$(D) (atomic concepts, atomic negations, conjunctions, existential and universal quantifications, number restrictions and concrete features).
- **Package reasoner** - Implements the backbone of the inference algorithms described in Section 4.1, while allowing them to be extended by additional modules. As explained above, structural inference algorithms –as well as CNF normalization and unfolding– have a strong regularity, where each type of constructors is examined at a time. Therefore, it is possible to extend the support to new constructors by adding blocks within the general algorithmic structure. The same considerations apply to concrete features, which depend on the evaluation of operators over a concrete domain. This scenario is precisely a case for the adoption of the *template method* design pattern. ReasonerCoordinator implements the general algorithms for CNF normalization, Unfolding, Satisfiability, Concept Contraction and Concept Abduction. Then, depending on logic constructors and concrete domains used in the KB, it delegates processing of different types of constructs to specialized reasoning modules, which

have been made available by the ReasonerProvider class. Each module must extend the abstract class BaseReasoner, in order to be integrated in the whole framework and cooperate with classes of this package.

- **Specialized modules** - The remaining packages extend the core ones. Each package P_i provides support for a set S_i of logic constructors and/or concrete domains (with related operators). It is assumed that $S_i \cap S_j = \emptyset \; \forall i, j, i \neq j$, *i.e.*, packages do not overlap. Hence, each constructor can be associated to at most one module and several modules are typically used in an inference procedure. Each P_i must provide: (1) classes extending dig.Concept to implement constructors in S_i that are not present in the base dig package; (2) a reasoning class (with -Reasoner name suffix in Figure 1) that implements parts of inference services involving constructors in S_i; (3) a penalty computation class (with -Penalty suffix in Figure 1) that allows to properly compute penalty values related to Concept Contraction and Concept Abduction. Currently implemented modules are:

  - aln - Supports $\mathcal{ALN}$ DL. No concrete domains are supported.
  - alndnat - Extends $\mathcal{ALN}$ support to $\mathcal{ALN}(D)$ DL with the concrete domain of natural numbers and the <=, >= and = operators.
  - alndfuzzy - Extends $\mathcal{ALN}$ support to $\mathcal{ALN}(D)$ DL with the concrete domain of real numbers; accepted operators are the fuzzy membership functions $trz_{(a,b,c,d)}(\cdot)$ (trapezoidal), $tri_{(a,b,c)}(\cdot)$ (triangular), $ls_{(a,b)}(\cdot)$ (left shoulder) and $rs_{(a,b)}(\cdot)$ (right shoulder) where a, b, c and d are related parameters. Standard DIG syntax was extended in order to express this kind of operators.

Penalty computation requires a deeper examination. The penalty contribution of each conflicting (resp. missing) element e in a Concept Contraction (resp. Abduction) Problem is computed as $p(e) = 1/n$, with n the total number of concepts in the conjunctive expression in which e appears. For example, let us consider the the CNF-normalized formula $A \sqcap B \sqcap \forall R.(C \sqcap D)$. If $e = B$ then $p(e) = 1/3$ because B appears in the conjunction of three elements; however, if $e = \forall R.C$ then $p(e) = 1/2$ because C appears within the conjunction of two concepts. Therefore, total penalty computation is not only additive, but also multiplicative. In order to implement it correctly, during the whole execution of the inference algorithm the ReasonerCoordinator manages an in-memory tree containing the elementary penalty values computed by each invocation of a reasoning module. At the end the total penalty can be safely obtained by computing products and sums in the order induced by a visit of the tree.

The devised modular architecture has two main benefits:

1. Efficiency. Only the modules that are needed by constructors used in the current KB are actually invoked.
2. Maintainability. The system can be easily extended to support new logic constructors and concrete domains. Only new modules adhering to the base software framework must be added in order to expand reasoning capabilities to more expressive logic languages or new types of concrete domains with

- $Activity \sqsubseteq Thing$
- $Container \sqsubseteq Thing$
- $Bin \sqsubseteq Container$
- $Cylinder \sqsubseteq Container$
- $FixedTank \sqsubseteq Container$
- $HumanPresence \sqsubseteq Thing$
- $ExternalPresence \sqsubseteq HumanPresence$
- $InternalPresence \sqsubseteq HumanPresence$
- $ExperiencedStaff \sqsubseteq InternalPresence$
- $InexperiencedStaff \sqsubseteq InternalPresence$
- $Substance \sqsubseteq Thing$
- $Fuel \sqsubseteq Substance$
- $CompressedGasFuel \sqsubseteq Fuel$
- $DissolvedGasFuel \sqsubseteq Fuel$
- $LiquefiedGasFuel \sqsubseteq Fuel$
- $LiquefiedPetroleumGas \sqsubseteq LiquefiedGasFuel \sqcap \exists hasFlashPoint \sqcap$
  $\forall hasFlashPoint(=_{233.15} temperature\_K)$
- $LiquidFuel \sqsubseteq Fuel$
- $Petrol \sqsubseteq LiquidFuel \sqcap \exists hasFlashPoint \sqcap \forall hasFlashPoint(=_{253.15} temperature\_K)$
- $DieselFuel \sqsubseteq LiquidFuel \sqcap \exists hasFlashPoint \sqcap \forall hasFlashPoint(=_{338.15} temperature\_K)$
- $Combustive \sqsubseteq Substance$
- $CompressedGasCombustive \sqsubseteq Combustive$
- $LiquefiedGasCombustive \sqsubseteq Combustive$
- $RequiredStaffSize \equiv rs_{(4,10)} unit$
- $RequiredLiquefiedGasFlashPoint \equiv \exists hasFlashPoint \sqcap$
  $\forall hasFlashPoint(trz_{(230,273.15,298.15,315)} temperature\_K)$
- $RequiredLiquefiedGasContainerMass \equiv \exists hasMass \sqcap \forall hasMass(ls_{(75,500)} mass\_kg)$

Fig. 2. Relevant axioms in the fire prevention ontology used in the case study

specific operators (*e.g.*, the time domain with Allen's time interval relations or plane geometry with RCC8 relations [18]).

5 Case Study

The proposed framework and the implemented tool have been tested in a fire risk detection case study. The goal was to investigate whether fuzzy $\mathcal{ALN}(\mathrm{D})$ was expressive enough to capture the semantics of current Italian regulations[4] about fire prevention certifications.

Basically, fire risk assessment can be modeled as a matchmaking problem. Regulatory requirements play the role of "request" and the description of a location is a "supply". Annotations related to a given context can be conveyed via the semantic-enhanced versions of most common pervasive computing protocols such as Bluetooth, RFID or even ZigBee [2,19]. Semantic descriptions related to a given environment will be automatically extracted from subjects and/or objects dipped into it and put at disposal for reasoning. The more requirements in the request are contradicted or not met by the supply, the highest the penalty will be [14] and the lowest the overall "fire safety score". Concept Contraction and Abduction were used to detect conflicting characteristics and not explicitly fulfilled requirements, respectively.

Both requests and supplies are represented by conjunctive concept expressions referring to the same ontology. A relevant fragment of it is reported in Figure 2, which is necessary to fully understand the following example.

Let us consider a small example extracted from our case study. The example focuses on warehouses of flammable liquefied gas fuel. The concept expressions for the fire safety regulatory requirements and three warehouse instances are reported hereafter.

---

[4] Italian D.M. 16/02/1982 and later amendments.

D – Requirements for warehouses of flammable liquefied gas fuel in order to receive the safety certification for fire risk prevention in Italy. Only experienced staff must be allowed. Furthermore regulations dictate the required staff size, the maximum quantity of fuel per container and the allowed temperature limits for fuel flash point (the lowest temperature at which it can vaporize to form an ignitable mixture in air). Using concepts appropriately defined in the domain ontology, the fire safety "request" can be expressed as follows:

$Activity \sqcap \exists hasHumanPresence \sqcap \forall hasHumanPresence.(ExperiencedStaff \sqcap$
$RequiredStaffSize \qquad \sqcap \neg ExternalPresence) \qquad \sqcap \exists containsFuel \qquad \sqcap$
$\forall containsFuel.(LiquefiedGasFuel \qquad \sqcap RequiredLiquefiedGasFlashPoint \qquad \sqcap$
$\exists storedIn \sqcap \forall storedIn.(Cylinder \sqcap RequiredLiquefiedGasContainerMass))$

S₁ – This fuel warehouse contains liquefied petroleum gas in 400 kg cylinders. Five expert workers operate in the warehouse, which is also accessible to non-authorized staff members. The description can be expressed in DL w.r.t. the domain ontology as:

$Activity \sqcap \exists hasHumanPresence \sqcap \forall hasHumanPresence.(ExperiencedStaff \sqcap =_5$
$unit \qquad \sqcap \quad ExternalPresence) \qquad \sqcap \quad \exists containsFuel \qquad \sqcap$
$\forall containsFuel.(LiquefiedPetroleumGas \sqcap \exists storedIn \sqcap \forall storedIn.(Cylinder \sqcap$
$\exists hasMass \sqcap \forall hasMass.(=_{400} mass\_kg))$

S₂ – This fuel warehouse contains liquefied petroleum gas in 200 kg cylinders. Eleven expert workers operate in the warehouse, which is not accessible to other people. The description can be expressed in formula as:

$Activity \sqcap \exists hasHumanPresence \sqcap \forall hasHumanPresence.(ExperiencedStaff \sqcap =_{11}$
$unit \qquad \sqcap \quad \neg ExternalPresence) \qquad \sqcap \quad \exists containsFuel \qquad \sqcap$
$\forall containsFuel.(LiquefiedPetroleumGas \sqcap \exists storedIn \sqcap \forall storedIn.(Cylinder \sqcap$
$\exists hasMass \sqcap \forall hasMass.(=_{200} mass\_kg))$

S₃ – This fuel warehouse contains liquefied petroleum gas in 600 kg cylinders. Three expert workers operate in the warehouse, which is also accessible to non-authorized staff members. The description can be expressed in DL w.r.t. the domain ontology as:

$Activity \sqcap \exists hasHumanPresence \sqcap \forall hasHumanPresence.(ExperiencedStaff \sqcap =_3$
$unit \qquad \sqcap \quad ExternalPresence) \qquad \sqcap \quad \exists containsFuel \qquad \sqcap$
$\forall containsFuel.(LiquefiedPetroleumGas \sqcap \exists storedIn \sqcap \forall storedIn.(Cylinder \sqcap$
$\exists hasMass \sqcap \forall hasMass.(=_{600} mass\_kg))$

Results are reported in Table 1. The second and third column show the Give Up and Keep part of the result of the Concept Contraction procedure executed by the mobile matchmaker. The last column reports the overall safety score, computed as the percentage of the number of elements in the (unfolded and normalized expression of the) request that are in conflict or missing from the supply, as determined by Concept Contraction and Abduction. Warehouse S_2 is the best matching instance, basically infringing no safety requirement, as can be seen from the Give Up outcome that contains only the top concept. On the contrary, both S_1 and S_3 contradict some requirements, so their score is significantly lower.

At a deeper analysis, it should be noted that S_2 has not a 100% score, even though it has to Give Up no elements. This is due to modeling concrete features –such as number of staff members and substance mass limits– with fuzzy

Table 1. Matchmaking results

Instance	Give Up	Keep	Score
S_1	$G = \forall\ hasHumanPresence.$ $(\neg ExternalPresence)$	$K = Activity \sqcap \exists hasHumanPresence$ $\forall\ hasHumanPresence.(ExperiencedStaff \sqcap$ $RequiredStaffSize) \sqcap \exists containsFuel \sqcap$ $\forall\ containsFuel.(LiquefiedGasFuel \sqcap$ $RequiredLiquefiedGasFlashPoint \sqcap$ $\exists storedIn \sqcap \forall\ storedIn(Cylinder \sqcap$ $RequiredLiquefiedGasContainerMass))$	45.6%
S_2	$G = \top$	$K = S_2$	87.2%
S_3	$G = \forall\ hasHumanPresence.$ $(RequiredStaffSize \sqcap$ $\neg ExternalPresence) \sqcap$ $\forall\ containsFuel.(\forall\ storedIn.$ $(RequiredLiquefied$ $GasContainerMass))$	$K = Activity \sqcap \exists hasHumanPresence$ $\forall\ hasHumanPresence.ExperiencedStaff \sqcap$ $\exists containsFuel \sqcap$ $\forall\ containsFuel.(LiquefiedGasFuel \sqcap$ $RequiredLiquefiedGasFlashPoint \sqcap$ $\exists storedIn \sqcap \forall\ storedIn.Cylinder)$	33.8%

membership functions, whose truth value is a continuous function in the $[0, 1]$ range. Consequently, a concrete feature in a supply will match semantically the corresponding one in the request *to a certain extent*. Let us consider liquefied gas fuel mass in our example: request prescribes mass to be between 75 kg and 500 kg, with a left-shoulder membership function. This means that containers of 75 kg or less will be "completely safe", those of 500 kg or more will be "completely unsafe" (like in S_3), those in between will have a proportional safety degree. So the match between the requirement in the request and the 200 kg cylinders in S_2 gets a semantic truth degree of $\frac{500-200}{500-75} = 0.706$. Similarly, S_1 has only one element to Give Up entirely but it receives a poor score: this is due to the fact that the number of staff members and fuel cylinder mass are close to the limits specified in the request.

6   Experimental Results

In order to evaluate performance of the proposed system, tests were carried out using the Java ME virtual machine and profiler of Sun Java Wireless Toolkit 2.5.2 for CLDC[5] on a notebook PC with Intel Core Duo T2300 CPU, 1 GB RAM memory and Ubuntu 9.04 operating system[6]. Using a synthetic TBox, 100 request/supply pairs were generated randomly. Generated expressions contain 17.64 ± 4.73 concepts on average (minimum 1, maximum 26) after CNF normalization and unfolding of TBox axioms.

Matchmaking was executed using Concept Contraction and Abduction inference services. Each matchmaking test was executed at two different speed settings for the Java virtual machine, 100 and 1000 bytecode instructions/ms. Based on our experience, these settings are roughly comparable to performance in CPU-bound processes for current mid-range (100 $) Java-equipped mobile phones and high-end (400 $) Java-enabled smartphones, respectively. Execution

---

[5] Sun Java Wireless Toolkit for CLDC: http://java.sun.com/products/sjwtoolkit/
[6] The usage of a simulation environment allowed us to repeat tests with different settings in order to produce more objective results not depending on hardware/software features of a given mobile device so facilitating reproducibility.

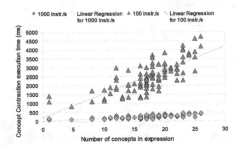
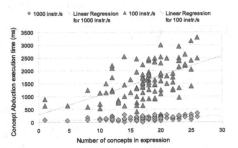

Fig. 3. Concept Contraction performance in 100 tests

Fig. 4. Concept Abduction performance in 100 tests

time for Contraction and Abduction procedures were evaluated, as well as the peak of main memory allocation above the baseline memory usage, which was measured at idle system state before matchmaking request submission.

Figure 3 and Figure 4 report execution times for Concept Contraction and Abduction, respectively. At 1000 bytecode instructions/ms, computation times are rather low (on average, 248.15 ± 89.71 for Contraction and 161.8 ± 68.74 for Abduction), surely acceptable for mobile scenarios requiring on-the-fly matchmaking. At 100 bytecodes/ms there is a corresponding tenfold increase in turnaround time (2551.59 ± 834.96 for Contraction and 1630.65 ± 648.72 for Abduction on average). From a practical standpoint, using devices with low computational capabilities such as standard mobile phones, latencies would be somewhat high w.r.t. user expectations. It should be noted, however, that time is linear in the size of the input with a good approximation, $e.g.$, at 1000 bytecodes/ms correlation coefficients are $R_c^2 = 0.58$ and $R_a^2 = 0.32$ for Contraction and Abduction respectively. This means that acceptable performance could be often achieved by appropriately limiting query complexity in accordance with the computational capabilities of the particular mobile device.

As a further remark, it can be noticed that Contraction is generally slower than Abduction, but it exhibits a more regular behavior w.r.t. the size of the input. Both observations can be justified by the fact that Abduction process stops as soon as a clash is found between concepts in the request and those in the supply.

Finally, Figure 5 reports the main memory consumption peak during the matchmaking process. Results are obviously independent of virtual machine speed. Obtained values are very low (30.95 ± 9.1 kB on average), evidencing that our modular reasoner architecture does not impair memory efficiency. Memory consumption exhibits a positive correlation with the size of concept expressions (correlation coefficient $R^2 = 0.53$). Consequently, it can be deemed that the matchmaker is capable of dealing with complex $\mathcal{ALN}(D)$ concept expressions even on mid-range Java mobile phones with few hundred kilobytes of memory.

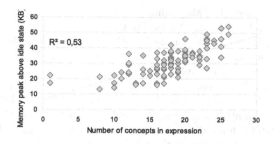

Fig. 5. Main memory usage peak during matchmaking w.r.t. idle state. Linear regression line is plotted.

7 Conclusion and Future Work

We have proposed a novel matchmaking framework useful in contexts where stable networks and powerful workstations are lacking. Original abduction and contraction algorithms presented in [14] have been enriched to support fuzzy DL operators and adapted to handheld devices. The obtained framework has been validated in a fire hazard case study to support in advance emergency detection and recovery. Resulting approach is general purpose as it is fully reusable in several scenarios enabling multiple applications. Early evaluations of system working proved its feasibility and usefulness.

Future work includes: wider tests on the proposed system in order to carry out further optimizations for improving system performances; extension of the prototype to both support more expressive logic formalisms and add resource composition service; finally novel non-standard inferences useful in several application scenarios (such as Least Common Subsumer (LCS) search) will be integrated and tested.

Acknowledgments

The authors acknowledge partial support of Apulia Region Strategic Project PS_121 - Telecommunication Facilities and Wireless Sensor Networks in Emergency Management.

References

1. Di Noia, T., Di Sciascio, E., Donini, F., Mongiello, M.: Semantic matchmaking in a p-2-p electronic marketplace. In: Proceedings of the ACM Symposium on Applied Computing, pp. 582–586 (2003)
2. Di Noia, T., Di Sciascio, E., Donini, F.M., Ruta, M., Scioscia, F., Tinelli, E.: Semantic-based bluetooth-rfid interaction for advanced resource discovery in pervasive contexts. International Journal on Semantic Web and Information Systems 4(1), 50–74 (2008)

3. Baader, F., Calvanese, D., Mc Guinness, D., Nardi, D., Patel-Schneider, P.: The Description Logic Handbook. Cambridge University Press, Cambridge (2002)
4. Koch, F.: 3APL-M platform for deliberative agents in mobile devices. In: Proceedings of the fourth international joint conference on Autonomous agents and multiagent systems, p. 154. ACM, New York (2005)
5. Tai, W., Brennan, R., Keeney, J., O'Sullivan, D.: An Automatically Composable OWL Reasoner for Resource Constrained Devices. In: 2009 IEEE International Conference on Semantic Computing, pp. 495–502. IEEE, Los Alamitos (2009)
6. Horrocks, I., Patel-Schneider, P.: Optimizing description logic subsumption. Journal of Logic and Computation 9(3), 267–293 (1999)
7. Sinner, A., Kleemann, T.: KRHyper - In Your Pocket. In: Nieuwenhuis, R. (ed.) CADE 2005. LNCS (LNAI), vol. 3632, pp. 452–457. Springer, Heidelberg (2005)
8. Kleemann, T., Sinner, A.: User Profiles and Matchmaking on Mobile Phones. In: Umeda, M., Wolf, A., Bartenstein, O., Geske, U., Seipel, D., Takata, O. (eds.) INAP 2005. LNCS (LNAI), vol. 4369, pp. 135–147. Springer, Heidelberg (2006)
9. Steller, L., Krishnaswamy, S.: Pervasive Service Discovery: mTableaux Mobile Reasoning. In: International Conference on Semantic Systems (I-Semantics), Graz, Austria (2008)
10. Colucci, S., Di Noia, T., Pinto, A., Ragone, A., Ruta, M., Tinelli, E.: A nonmonotonic approach to semantic matchmaking and request refinement in e-marketplaces. International Journal of Electronic Commerce 12(2), 127–154 (2007)
11. Ruta, M., Di Noia, T., Di Sciascio, E., Piscitelli, G., Scioscia, F.: Semantic-based mobile registry for dynamic RFID-based logistics support. In: 10th International Conference on Electronic Commerce. ACM Press, New York (2008) doi: 10.1145/1409540.1409576
12. Ruta, M., Scioscia, F., Di Noia, T., Di Sciascio, E.: Reasoning in Pervasive Environments: an Implementation of Concept Abduction with Mobile OODBMS. In: Proceedings of IEEE/WIC/ACM International Joint Conference on Web Intelligence and Intelligent Agent Technology, pp. 145–148. IEEE, Los Alamitos (2009)
13. Brachman, R., Levesque, H.: The Tractability of Subsumption in Frame-based Description Languages. In: 4th National Conference on Artificial Intelligence (AAAI-84), pp. 34–37. Morgan Kaufmann, San Francisco (1984)
14. Di Noia, T., Di Sciascio, E., Donini, F.: Semantic matchmaking as non-monotonic reasoning: A description logic approach. Journal of Artificial Intelligence Research 29, 269–307 (2007)
15. Bechhofer, S., Möller, R., Crowther, P.: The DIG Description Logic Interface. In: Proceedings of the 16th International Workshop on Description Logics (DL'03), CEUR Workshop Proceedings, Rome, Italy, September 2003, vol. 81 (2003)
16. Straccia, U.: A fuzzy description logic for the semantic web. In: Fuzzy Logic and the Semantic Web, Capturing Intelligence, pp. 167–181. Elsevier, Amsterdam (2005)
17. Gärdenfors, P.: Knowledge in Flux: Modeling the Dynamics of Epistemic States. Bradford Books, MIT Press, Cambridge (1988)
18. Lutz, C., Miličić, M.: A tableau algorithm for description logics with concrete domains and general tboxes. Journal of Automated Reasoning 38(1), 227–259 (2007)
19. Ruta, M., Scioscia, F., Di Noia, T., Di Sciascio, E.: A hybrid ZigBee/Bluetooth approach to mobile semantic grids. International Journal of Computer Systems Science and Engineering (2010)

Replication and Versioning
of Partial RDF Graphs

Bernhard Schandl

University of Vienna
Department of Distributed and Multimedia Systems
bernhard.schandl@univie.ac.at

Abstract. The sizes of datasets available as RDF (e.g., as part of the
Linked Data cloud) are increasing continuously. For instance, the recent
DBpedia version consists of nearly 500 millions triples. A common strategy to avoid problems that arise e.g., from limited network connectivity
or lack of bandwidth is to replicate data locally, therefore making them
accessible for applications without depending on a network connection.
For mobile devices with limited capabilities, however, the replication
and synchronization of billions of triples is not feasible. To overcome this
problem, we propose an approach to replicate parts of an RDF graph
to a client. Applications may then apply changes to this partial replica
while being offline; these changes are written back to the original data
source upon reconnection. Our approach does not require any kind of additional logic (e.g., change logging) or data structures on the client side,
and hence is suitable to be applied on devices with limited computing
power and storage capacity.

1 Introduction

The RDF data model has been designed to facilitate the publication of semantically meaningful data about resources on the Web. It is innately intended to be
used in a decentralized, distributed, and uncontrolled manner. Because of these
requirements, RDF has been designed so that data from different sources can
be easily merged and integrated, its vocabulary is extensible, and it employs
an open world semantics, which essentially means that data consumers (applications or end users) can never be assured that they are aware of all relevant
information.

According to current estimates[1], the Linked Data cloud consists of more than
13 billions RDF triples, which are distributed across hundreds of sources. They
can be accessed using a variety of means, ranging from directly de-referencing
HTTP URIs, over issuing selective queries via SPARQL, to downloading data
dumps and deploying them in local triple stores. It is a matter of the concrete

---

[1] Linked Data Set Statistics:
http://esw.w3.org/topic/TaskForces/CommunityProjects/LinkingOpenData/
DataSets/Statistics

L. Aroyo et al. (Eds.): ESWC 2010, Part I, LNCS 6088, pp. 31–45, 2010.
© Springer-Verlag Berlin Heidelberg 2010

application which method is the appropriate one, since they expose different characteristics w.r.t. efficiency and performance.

Especially in the mobile domain it is very unlikely that an application will access all of them online, since mobile network connectivity is not always available for reasonable prices. To overcome this problem, and to decrease response times, data from remote sources can be replicated locally, and applications can operate on these local copies. However, it is not practical to duplicate several billions RDF triples to a mobile device with limited computing power and memory capacity, and often this is not required at all for a specific application; e.g., because the application is only able to operate on resources of certain types.

The replication of data from external sources, which can be selected based on the specific application context, is relatively straightforward for read-only data. However, we expect the Semantic Web to evolve into a read-and-write system; this claim is supported by the currently ongoing efforts towards a standardization of update functionality for the SPARQL query language [1], or the specification of write-back mechanisms for non-RDF data sources[2].

When applications modify partially replicated data, the problem of synchronization upon reconnection becomes apparent. The computation of a *diff* (i.e., sets of added and removed triples) involving partial RDF graphs is not straightforward, even if we leave aside the problems that blank nodes impose on comparing RDF graphs [2,3]. RDF is set-based and does not provide opaque identifiers for single triples, therefore they can only be identified by explicitly and fully naming their subject, predicate, and object. Hence it is difficult to compare incomplete RDF graphs (which is required for merging changes from different sources) without additional information.

One can overcome this problem by instantiating services that monitor and track changes to RDF graphs and therefore make added and removed triples explicit; e.g., by marking triples as deleted instead of physically removing them. However this approach requires hooking into existing software infrastructure used by applications (in particular, triple stores) and is therefore not applicable in many scenarios. In this paper, we present an approach how parts of RDF graphs can be replicated to clients for local modification, whereas the replicas are enriched with triples that describe which parts of the (full) base graph are missing. For this, binary strings are added to the partial replica; these strings are mapped to an ordering of the triples in the base graph. Upon reconnection, this additional information can be used to identify which triples have been added and removed without the need for additional tracking infrastructure on the client side.

In the following, we outline the requirements and the general design of our approach (Section 2). We introduce the concept of triple bitmaps, with which partial graphs are enriched in order to allow the computation of diffs (Section 3), and we explain how changes to partial graphs can be merged with the original data (Section 4). We present some implementation details (Section 5) and address several known limitations of our approach, as well as general problems in

---

[2] Pushback: `http://esw.w3.org/topic/PushBackDataToLegacySources`

the context of replicating and merging RDF graphs (Section 6). We conclude with a discussion of related work (Section 7).

2 Approach and Model

2.1 Requirements

In this section, we introduce the requirements that have led to the specification of our partial graph replication algorithm. As stated before, our general objective is to allow Semantic Web-based applications (which we denote as *clients* in the following) to replicate parts of base RDF graphs (which are stored in a remote *repository*), to make changes to these local replicas, and to synchronize changes back to the base graphs upon reconnection. In particular, the framework aims to fulfill the following requirements:

- *No additional client-side processing.* Our approach should be applicable to environments with limited processing and storage capacity, like mobile devices and handhelds. Moreover, the approach should be compatible with any RDF storage system on the client's side and should therefore not require modifications or hooks. It should also not rely on mechanisms that track changes on the client side, e.g., by marking deleted triples.
- *No additional data structures on the client side.* For the same reasons (namely, avoiding to interfere with client-side RDF storage and processing infrastructure), and to reduce client-side workload, it is desirable that the approach does not require additional data structures beyond the RDF model on the client side. For the server side, we do not impose this requirement since here usually more resources are available, and server environments are more easy to control and maintain than distributed client systems.
- *Support for light-weight clients.* Subsuming the previous two requirements, our approach should be designed in a manner that allows it to be applied in mobile environments.
- *Stateless graph repositories.* The repository (which holds the base graphs to be replicated to clients) should not require to maintain status information (e.g., information about partial graphs) about clients in order to keep a separation of concerns between the repository and the clients.
- *Flexibility w.r.t. subgraph selection.* The approach should not assume a certain graph structure, or a specific ratio of the sizes of the base graph and the partially replicated graph; it should be able to handle any such ratio with acceptable performance and scalability.

2.2 Workflow

In the design of our approach we follow the naming convention of the popular *Subversion* system[3] (SVN) for file versioning. In SVN, a server (called *repository*)

---

[3] Subversion: http://subversion.tigris.org

hosts a set of versioned files, which are arranged in a hierarchical directory structure. A client can transfer these files, or a subset thereof, to a local *working copy*; this step is called *checkout*. This working copy is enriched with metadata containing information about its base revision, which are stored in additional hidden files. Then, modifications are applied to the working copy. The client can *update* its working copy with recent changes from the repository at any time. During this step, modifications from other clients (which have been applied to the repository) are *merged* with the client's working copy. When concurrent changes are merged, *conflicts* can occur, which have to be resolved on the client side. The client's modifications are then transferred to the repository in the course of the *commit* action.

For the specification of our partial graph versioning system, we follow the naming convention of SVN. While SVN treats files as atomic units of versioning, we apply versioning to *(named) RDF graphs*. However, as described before our approach additionally enables clients to checkout *partial RDF graphs*, which has significant impact on the workflow of versioning:

- First of all, our approach should be applicable to devices with limited computing power and memory, hence we operate with partial graphs on the client side. However, the same restriction applies to updates that are transmitted from the repository to the client: as these updates can as well become very large we must ensure that clients are not overburdened with calculation of diffs and merging operations.
- As we will see later, the lack of client-side infrastructure (as defined in the requirements) leads to the problem that the client is not aware of its partial RDF graph's characteristics: for instance, after a partial checkout the client cannot decide which fraction of the original graph was retrieved. Therefore, partial graphs cannot be merged on the client.
- The detection of conflicting modifications (which can occur on the syntactical or the semantic layer) requires domain knowledge and often involves relatively expensive reasoning. The need for partial reasoning has already been recognized [4], and there exist proposals how this can be accomplished on mobile devices (e.g., [5]). However, complete underlying data is required for this task, which in our scenario is the case only on the repository.

Because of these reasons we have specified a modified replication and versioning workflow for partial RDF graphs, as depicted in Figure 1. The most significant change is the shift of merge operations from the client to the repository; this is due to the fact that only the repository has complete information about graphs and modifications, while clients have only partial information.

A second significant change is that clients cannot receive updates from the repository, because this would again require capabilities for merging and conflict detection on the client side. Instead, clients must always commit their changes to the repository and can then checkout a new partial graph. Consequently, the lifetime of a working copy is limited to one checkout-commit cycle.

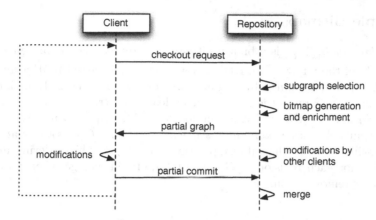

Fig. 1. Partial Graph Versioning Workflow

2.3   Partial Graphs

The key concept in our approach is the enrichment of *partial graphs* with *triple bitmaps*. A partial graph contains a subset of the triples of a given RDF graph (the *base graph*). Triple bitmaps encode which triples from the base graph are missing in the partial graph. Partial graphs are enriched with the necessary triple bitmaps and are transferred to the client, which applies changes to it. When the modified partial graph is committed, the repository is able to analyze the submitted triple bitmaps and infer which triples from the base graph were missing in the original partial graph, and consequently can infer which modifications were applied to the partial graph. In the following we formally describe our approach.

We define an RDF graph $G \in \mathbb{G}$ as a set of tuples $(s, p, o) \in \mathbb{UB} \times \mathbb{U} \times \mathbb{UBL}$, called *triples* [6]. We denote with S_G the set of *subjects* in G, i.e., all elements that appear at the subject (s) position of any triple in G (according to the RDF specification, this can only be URIs and blank nodes); therefore $S_G \subset \mathcal{P}(\mathbb{UB})$.

For *graph equivalence* between two graphs G and G' we reuse the definition from [7], which requires a bijection $\mathcal{M}$ that maps all elements (URIs, literals, and blank nodes) from G to corresponding elements in G', and vice versa [3]. While this mapping is straightforward for URIs and literals, it may be problematic for blank nodes, which must be *grounded* in order to ensure that two graphs can be compared (cf. Section 6). With "grounding" we denote the process of assigning unique identity to blank nodes.

A *partial RDF graph* $\overline{G}$ derived from its *base graph* G is an RDF graph that consists of two groups of triples: (*1*) the set of *base triples* $\overline{G}_b$, i.e., triples that are also contained in G; and (*2*) the set of *bitmap triples* $\overline{G}_t$ of the form $< s', p, o >$, where each s' is derived from an element $s \in S_G$, $p = \mathtt{tbt:bitmap}$[4], and o is a *triple bitmap literal*, related to s, G and $\overline{G}$, which we denote with $B_{(s,G,\overline{G})}$. Therefore, $\overline{G} = \overline{G}_b \cup \overline{G}_t$, where $\overline{G}_b \subseteq G$ and $\overline{G}_t = \bigcup_{s \in S_{\overline{G}_b}} B_{(s,G,\overline{G}_b)}$.

---

[4] $\mathtt{tbt:bitmap}$ is the abbreviated notation of a specific property that represents a resource's triple bitmap.

3   Triple Bitmaps

A *triple bitmap* $B_{(s,G,\overline{G})}$ is a binary bitmap that represents the presence (0) or absence (1) of the triples of an RDF graph G within a partial RDF graph $\overline{G}$. A triple bitmap is determined by a tuple $(s, G, \overline{G})$, where s is an RDF language element that appears as the subject of at least one triple in both G and $\overline{G}$; i.e., $s \in S_G$ and $s \in S_{\overline{G}}$. The construction of such a triple bitmap is described in Algorithm 1. It uses a *monotonic sequential ordering* $O(G, s)$ over all triples in G for which s is on the subject position (i.e., S_G)[5]. This ordering must be recoverable for each revision of G, since $O(G, s)$ will change when triples are added to, or removed from G.

Input: RDF element s, graph G, partial graph $\overline{G}$
Output: Triple bitmap $B_{(s,G,\overline{G})}$

bitmap $\leftarrow$ empty bitmap with size $|O(G, s)|$;
forall *triples* t_i *in* $O(G, s), 0 \leq i \leq |O(G, s)|$ **do**
    if $t_i \in \overline{G}$ **then** bitmap $[i] \leftarrow 0$;
    else bitmap $[i] \leftarrow 1$;
    i $\leftarrow$ i + 1 ;
end

Algorithm 1. Construction of a Triple Bitmap

We have chosen to build bitmaps based on distinct subjects, instead of distinct predicates or objects. This design decision is based on an analysis of typical RDF data found on the Web, which exhibit a certain ratio between the number of distinct resources and the number of triples in which each resource participates. For instance, in the 2009 Billion Triple Challenge dataset[6] only 1.3 millions out of more than 128 millions distinct subjects participate in more than 100 triples, and only ≈25,000 subjects appear in more than 1,000 triples (cf. Table 1). The vast majority of subjects occur in 2 to 10 statements. The distribution of distinct objects is entirely different: two thirds of all distinct objects appear in only one statement. Constructing bitmaps based on triple objects would therefore lead to a large number of bitmaps consisting of only one bit. The number of distinct predicates is far below the number of subjects or objects, which leads to a high number of statements per distinct predicate; in this case triple bitmaps would become very long.

A similar distribution can be found in a highly important Linked Data source, the DBpedia 3.3 dataset[7]. Of 25,455 randomly selected subjects, none appears

---

[5] Such an ordering can be defined for all RDF graphs: either, the underlying storage mechanism already provides a *natural ordering*; if this it not the case a generic lexical sorting as proposed e.g., in [8] can be employed.

[6] 2009 Billion Triple Challenge: `http://vmlion25.deri.ie`

[7] DBpedia: `http://dbpedia.org`

Table 1. Billion Triple Challenge 2009 data det statistics: distribution of participating triples per distinct subject, predicate, and object

# of Partici- pating Triples	Distinct Subjects		Distinct Predicates		Distinct Objects	
Total	128,079,322	(100.00%)	136,188	(100.00%)	279,710,101	(100.00%)
1	9,873,704	(7.71%)	23,222	(17.05%)	189,702,670	(67.82%)
2–10	99,168,416	(77.43%)	50,029	(36.74%)	82,011,684	(29.32%)
11–100	17,734,849	(13.85%)	38,812	(28.50%)	7,247,533	(2.59%)
100–1,000	1,276,612	(1.00%)	15,947	(11.71%)	704,735	(0.25%)
≥1,001	25,741	(0.02%)	8,178	(6.00%)	43,479	(0.02%)

in only a single triple, while the vast majority (89.85%) appeared in 11 to 100 triples; 10.12% occur in 100 to 1,000 triples. Contrary, of 639,321 randomly selected objects, 634,198 appear in 10 or less triples, therefore the number of bitmap triples would be very high, which causes additional storage overhead.

3.1 Serialization of Triple Bitmaps

As we will see later, triple bitmaps are encoded as RDF literals in order to enrich a partial graph. For this purpose, we can encode a triple bitmap $b_{(s,G,\overline{G})}$ as a plain string consisting of a sequence of zero and one digits. Since this is quite verbose, and to facilitate interoperability with RDF-related standards, we apply *base64*-encoding [9] to the bitmap. This encoding is supported by a designated XML data type (`xsd:base64Binary`) and is recommended for representing arbitrary binary content in RDF [10]. To determine the precise length of the bitmap, it is padded with a 1 before the most significant bit; then the bitmap is padded with zeroes to fit the 6 bit pattern for base64-encoding. Figure 2 depicts the subsequent steps in the encoding process. In this example, four out of 21 statements from the original graph are not present in the partial graph; therefore the triple bitmap contains four 1s (positions 4, 8, 11, and 12).

Bit #	21 20 19 18 17	16 15 14 13 12 11 10 9	8 7 6 5 4 3 2 1
Original Bitmap	0 0 0 0 0	0 0 0 0 1 1 0 0	1 0 0 0 1 0 0 0
1-padded Bitmap	1 0 0 0 0 0	0 0 0 0 1 1 0 0	1 0 0 0 1 0 0 0
base64–padded Bitmap	0 0 1 0 0 0 0 0	0 0 0 0 1 1 0 0	1 0 0 0 1 0 0 0
base64-encoded Bitmap	E	A	y	I

Fig. 2. Base64-Encoding of Triple Bitmaps

3.2   Enriching Partial Graphs with Triple Bitmaps

We can now enrich the partial graph $\overline{G}$ with the set of bitmap triples $\overline{G}_t$, which contains one triple bitmap triple per distinct subject in $\overline{G}_b$. For the subject we do not directly use s but add a unique prefix[8], forming a new URI s'[9]:

$$\overline{G}_t = \{< s', \texttt{tbt:bitmap}, "B_{(s,G,\overline{G})} \ "\char`^\char`^\texttt{xsd:base64Binary} > \mid s \in S_{\overline{G}}\} \quad (1)$$

Such an enrichment technique is in line with the RDF formal semantics [11] and has been used in previous works, e.g., for non-deterministic labeling of RDF nodes in order to facilitate signing of RDF graphs [8] (the author calls this technique to *"make meaningless changes to an RDF graph"*). An example of the construction of a triple bitmap and the enrichment of a partial graph is depicted in Figure 3. Here, the base graph consists of four triples of which only two (#1 and #3) are included in the partial graph (non-replicated triples are depicted in grey). The resulting triple bitmap consisting of two zeroes and two ones ("1010"), which yields the string "a" after padding and base64-encoding.

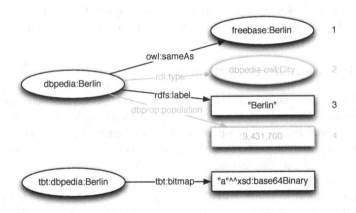

Fig. 3. Graph, partial graph, and bitmap triple

Our approach requires the transmission and storage of one triple bitmap per subject in $\overline{G}$. Bitmaps are encoded as triples, which consist of the subject, a (fixed) predicate, and the serialization of the triple bitmap, whereas each object requires one bit. According to the data presented in Table 1, more than 80% of all triple bitmaps are shorter than 16 bits and can thus be represented using two

---

[8] Without loss of generality this prefix can be freely chosen, as long as it is guaranteed that it does not conflict with other subject URIs used in $\overline{G}$; this condition can however be ensured by various means, e.g., by introducing a special URI schema (as in our example), or by using HTTP URIs within a domain registered solely for this purpose.

[9] Blank nodes must be grounded beforehand so that they are uniquely identifiable and hence a prefixed URI s' can be determined.

bytes. In the Virtuoso triple store, for instance, each triple requires a storage capacity of around 35 bytes [12], which means that the cost of transmitting and storing additional bits in a triple bitmap is much lower than storing additional triples. Therefore we decided to attach triple bitmaps to subjects rather than to objects.

During a partial checkout the repository sends the partial graph $\overline{G}$ (i.e., a subset of the triples of the base graph G plus one bitmap triple for each distinct subject in $\overline{G}$) to the client, where it is buffered in a local triple store. The revision number of the graph is maintained on the client side as part of the graph URI. Applications can now access and modify these data independent from the network connection.

4   Merging Partial Graphs

The triple bitmap for each subject s in the partial graph $\overline{G}$ allows us to determine whether triples have been added or, more importantly, removed from the partial graph without requiring to explicitly track these change operations. The only condition to be fulfilled by the client is that the triple bitmaps may not be modified or deleted; in this case it would become impossible to retrace which triples from the base graph were missing in the unmodified partial graph. However, since the set of bitmap triples $\overline{G}_t$ does not interfere with the rest of the contents of the partial graph $\overline{G}_b$, and an RDF graph entails all of its subgraphs [11] (in our case, $\overline{G} \models \overline{G}_b$), this condition can usually be maintained.

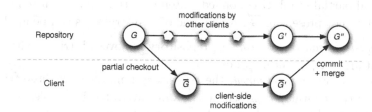

Fig. 4. Evolvement of modified partial graphs

It is unlikely that applications (which are not aware of the special semantics of the bitmap triples) modify or delete these triples "by accident". The typical update operations on RDF graphs as defined e.g., in [1] (i.e., insertion and deletion of triples) have no effects on other triples in the graph. The only exception are *resource deletions*: since in RDF resources can occur only within triples, to "remove a resource" means effectively to remove all triples in which the resource appears. To avoid this, our proposed method to enrich graphs with triple bitmaps is to add a prefix to the actual resource's URI (cf. Figure 3). Thus we create a separate resource for the bitmap triple and therefore reduce the probability of its accidental removal, while this separate resource is still implicitly connected to its base resource through their URI. For the merge operation this implies that if a committed partial graph $\overline{G}'$ contains a bitmap triple with subject s' but no triples with the corresponding subject s, the repository can apply one of two strategies:

1. *Partial resource removal*: the repository removes only triples that were present in the partial graph, according to the triple bitmap for s; or
2. *Complete resource removal*: the repository removes all triples where s occurs in the subject position, regardless of the contents of the triple bitmap.

These strategies represent two different assumptions on the client's intention that the repository can take: in the first case, it assumes that the client intended to remove a set of triples with subject s that is exactly the set of triples that have been checked out in the partial graph $\overline{G}$; in the second case the repository assumes that the client's intention was to remove all triples with subject s.

The decision which strategy to take can be supported by checking whether s is the object of other triples in $\overline{G}'$. If such triples exist, it is unlikely that the client's intention was to remove the resource s entirely since in this case the triples where s stands in the object position would have been removed, too. Therefore, in this case a partial resource removal should be chosen.

Another situation in which bitmap triples may be accidentally removed are bulk deletions that affect multiple subject resources. Let us assume that a committed partial graph $\overline{G}'$ contains triples with a subject resource s without a corresponding triple bitmap statement. Let us further assume that s was already present in the base graph G, but $\overline{G}'$ contains statements with subject s that were not present in G. In this case, the repository cannot decide whether the original partial graph $\overline{G}$ contained statements that have been removed and are therefore not present in $\overline{G}'$. Again, one of two strategies can be applied:

1. *Optimistic resource removal*: the repository removes all triples with subject s that are not present in $\overline{G}'$; or
2. *Pessimistic resource removal*: the repository removes only those triples for which a triple bitmap is present in $\overline{G}'$, and leaves all other triples untouched, including triples with subject s that are not present in $\overline{G}$.

An extreme case of this class of operations is the removal of all triples in the graph; i.e., $\overline{G}'$ is empty. Such a situation cannot be handled using any kind of the heuristics mentioned before; in this case the repository has to decide whether to ignore the commit and leave G in its previous state, or to interpret the commit as total delete and remove all triples from G.

As an alternative to the a-priori selection of a certain removal strategy, the repository can reject the modification and return it to the client. This is a similar behavior as in SVN, where certain types of conflicting concurrent modifications must be resolved manually by the user.

The merge procedure (cf. Figure 4) considers three graphs as input: the modified partial graph $\overline{G}'$ as received from the client, the base graph G from which the original partial graph $\overline{G}$ was extracted, and the current revision of G, denoted as G'. Since the contents of the original partial graph (i.e., $\overline{G}$) can be computed using the triple bitmaps contained in $\overline{G}'$, we can apply a standard RDF diff algorithm [2] to detect and compare changes. Its result is a merged graph G'' which reflects all changes applied to G. In case of unresolved conflicts, the algorithm terminates without returning a merged graph, and the commit must be revised by the client (e.g., through an appropriate user interface). Conflicts can be detected by comparing either the two changesets $C_{G,\overline{G}'}$ and $C_{G,G'}$ (whereas a changeset C consists of one set of added triples C^a and one set of removed triples C^r [7,13,14]), or by comparing G' with the full graph that can be reconstructed from $\overline{G}'$. Algorithms for conflict detection on various levels of semantics have already been presented (e.g., [15]) and are out of the scope of this paper.

5 Implementation

We have implemented the presented approach as part of the MobiSem Replication Framework[10]. The prototype is based on the Jena Semantic Web library and provides the necessary methods to extract parts of an RDF graph, to compute and serialize triple bitmaps, and to reconstruct graphs based on partial commits. Modules for blank node grounding and conflict detection can be plugged into the framework since these tasks are highly depending on the schema that is used in the data; our implementation does not impose restrictions on these aspects.

6 Limitations and Discussion

Our proposed algorithm is able to cope with changes to partial RDF graphs, as long as the triple bitmaps that are attached to the partial graph remain intact. Even in situations where subjects without corresponding triple bitmap exist (or vice versa) the algorithm is able to terminate; however in this case assumptions on the client's intentions must be made. If this is not desirable, the repository can revoke changes which are not clearly resolvable.

As shown in Section 3, the computation, transmission, and storage of triple bitmaps is feasible under consideration of the structure of real RDF data sets. In extreme cases, however, this approach may become inefficient. First, if the base graph contains a large number of subject resources but only very few triples per subject, a large number of short triple bitmaps is added to the partial graph. On the other hand, if the base graph contains only few subjects while each subject is described by a large number of statements, triple bitmaps become very large and may become unmanageable. In these cases a modified variant of our approach can be applied where triple bitmaps are not attached to subjects, but to predicates or objects, depending on the structure of the data. This can be done without loss of functionality as long as the repository's interpretation of bitmap triples for each graph remains consistent over time.

---

[10] MobiSem Project: http://www.mobisem.org

A general problem in the context of RDF versioning and replication is the treatment of blank nodes. The comparison of two graphs requires blank nodes in the graphs to be matched, so that changes in the triples where these nodes occur can be detected. A number of solutions for blank node grounding have been discussed in the literature (including node renaming [7], usage of existing or artificial inverse-functional properties [16], explicit identity assertions like `owl:sameAs` and `owl:equivalentClass`, or feature vector comparison [17]). Our approach does not consider blank nodes differently from named nodes, therefore it requires an additional strategy to ground blank nodes as part of the calculation of diffs between the base graph and a committed partial graph.

A second problem in this context is the detection of conflicts that occur due to concurrent modifications to the same graph. Various approaches to tackle conflicts on the structural or semantic layer have been presented in the literature (e.g., [7,15,18]). However, this issue is out of the scope of our algorithm; instead we provide a hook for a conflict detection function as part of our merge algorithm.

7   Related Work

The problems of versioning RDF graphs and tracking changes in the context of Semantic Web-based information systems have been acknowledged early. Kiryakov and Ognyanov [13] have introduced the basic foundations of versioning w.r.t. the semantics of the RDF model; based on their work models and ontologies for *RDF deltas* have been specified [2]. The characteristics of such deltas under the conditions of RDF Schema semantics have been analyzed [14]. Efficient storage structures [19] and aggregation algorithms [7] for versioned triple data were designed, and the semantics of graph merge operations have been studied in detail [20]. This research has lead to a number of concrete systems and frameworks, including SemVersion [16], the discontinued Graph Versioning System (GVS)[11], and the Talis Platform[12].

On a higher level, versioning can also be applied to knowledge bases under consideration of the semantics imposed by the underlying ontology language; an example of a complete framework for such high-level changes is presented by Plessers et al. [21]. Papavassiliou et al. [18] introduce the notion of higher-level changes to RDF graphs that are validated against preconditions. Similar to [7] they propose to aggregate atomic changes to higher-level composite changes and provide a reasoning-based algorithm to detect them.

The need for replication of RDF data has likewise been addressed in previous works: for instance, the Boca Semantic Web framework [22] provides support for graph replication and synchronization, both in real-time and in batch mode. This is accomplished on the named graph level, therefore it does not allow for the replication of arbitrary sub-graphs. Moreover, it requires that modifications are tracked on the client side, which requires special client-side software. In the relational database world, algorithms for replication and synchronization are

---

[11] Graph Versioning System: http://gvs.hpl.hp.com
[12] Talis Platform: http://www.talis.com/platform/

already well-established; through the usage of hybrid databases such mechanisms can also be applied to RDF data (as implemented, e.g., within the Virtuoso integration middleware [23]). Replication of RDF data has also been proposed on a peer-to-peer basis [24]. Our approach differs from these works in that it does not require any kind of special infrastructure on the client side; instead, partial graphs are (re)constructed by the repository only.

None of these approaches have explicitly considered the special conditions of management of subsets of RDF graphs in a distributed situation. There exist various approaches for the specification of graph subsets; e.g., Concise Bounded Descriptions [25], RDF Molecules [26], and Minimum Self-contained Graphs [27]; mostly they have been specified to overcome problems in conjunction with blank nodes. Some of these approaches have been applied in the context of versioning (e.g., GVS uses RDF Molecules as versioning subject), but none of them allows for unrestricted selective replication and synchronization of graph subsets. Therefore we consider previous works on modification tracking and versioning of RDF graphs as complementary to our work.

8   Summary and Conclusions

It is reasonable to replicate data sets from remote sources (e.g., the Linked Data Cloud) to mobile devices. This allows users to operate in offline mode, which is helpful in situations with limited connectivity or in situations where data transmission over a network is too expensive or too slow. However, under consideration of the limited resources available on mobile devices it is impractical to replicate large data sets. In this paper we have presented an approach that provides the possibility to replicate subsets of RDF graphs to clients, which can be processed and modified locally, and later written back to the base graph. Subsets of RDF graphs are enriched with triple bitmaps, which indicate the missing triples in the partial replica. Upon reconnection, these triple bitmaps can be utilized to determine which modifications have been made by the client. Hence, our algorithm does not require to set up special infrastructure on the client side, which increases its applicability for a wide range of situations.

The presented algorithm is based on the characteristic of RDF that triples can be added to a graph without interfering with the graph's original semantics. For the algorithm to work correctly it is important to ensure that the injected triple bitmaps are not accidentally modified or deleted. To decrease the probability of this case, triple bitmaps use a dedicated vocabulary and are not explicitly connected to the resources they describe. The algorithm is able to intercept certain error situations; however, in several cases a definite decision cannot be made. In such situations, the repository can either assume certain client intentions and perform corresponding actions, or refuse the modification; in this case the client must solve the ambiguity.

Our algorithm has been designed especially for mobile applications, where one cannot rely on a stable network connection, and because of limited resources the full replication of large data sets is not feasible. In the future we plan to extend the possible application fields, e.g., to collaborative ontology and data authoring, and to integrate the proposed method with further algorithms for conflict detection.

Acknowledgements. This work has been funded by FIT-IT grant 815133 from the Austrian Federal Ministry of Transport, Innovation, and Technology. The author thanks Gunnar Aastrand Grimnes for providing statistics of the 2009 Billion Triples Challenge dataset.

References

1. Schenk, S., Gearon, P.: SPARQL 1.1 Update (W3C Working Draft October 22, 2009), World Wide Web Consortium (2009), http://www.w3.org/TR/sparql11-update/
2. Berners-Lee, T., Connolly, D.: Delta: An Ontology for the Distribution of Differences Between RDF Graphs. World Wide Web Consortium (2006), http://www.w3.org/DesignIssues/Diff (retrieved December 15, 2008)
3. Klyne, G., Carroll, J.J.: Resource Description Framework (RDF): Concepts and Abstract Syntax (W3C Recommendation February 10, 2004). World Wide Web Consortium (2004)
4. Fensel, D., van Harmelen, F.: Unifying Reasoning and Search to Web Scale. IEEE Internet Computing 11(2), 96, 94–95 (2007)
5. Steller, L.A., Krishnaswamy, S., Gaber, M.M.: A Weighted Approach to Partial Matching for Mobile Reasoning. In: Bernstein, A., Karger, D.R., Heath, T., Feigenbaum, L., Maynard, D., Motta, E., Thirunarayan, K. (eds.) ISWC 2009. LNCS, vol. 5823, pp. 618–633. Springer, Heidelberg (2009)
6. Muñoz, S., Pérez, J., Gutiérrez, C.: Minimal Deductive Systems for RDF. In: Franconi, E., Kifer, M., May, W. (eds.) ESWC 2007. LNCS, vol. 4519, pp. 53–67. Springer, Heidelberg (2007)
7. Auer, S., Herre, H.: A Versioning and Evolution Framework for RDF Knowledge Bases. In: Virbitskaite, I., Voronkov, A. (eds.) PSI 2006. LNCS, vol. 4378, pp. 55–69. Springer, Heidelberg (2007)
8. Carroll, J.J.: Signing RDF Graphs. In: Fensel, D., Sycara, K., Mylopoulos, J. (eds.) ISWC 2003. LNCS, vol. 2870, pp. 369–384. Springer, Heidelberg (2003)
9. Josefsson, S.: The Base16, Base32, and Base64 Data Encodings (RFC 4648). Network Working Group (October 2006)
10. Koch, J., Velasco, C.A.: Representing Content in RDF 1.0 (W3C Working Draft October 29, 2009). World Wide Web Consortium (2009), http://www.w3.org/TR/Content-in-RDF10/
11. Hayes, P.: RDF Semantics (W3C Recommendation February 10, 2004). World Wide Web Consortium (2004)
12. Erling, O., Mikhailov, I.: RDF Support in the Virtuoso DBMS. In: Auer, S., Bizer, C., Müller, C., Zhdanova, A.V. (eds.) Stochastic Automata: Stability, Nondeterminism and Prediction. LNI, vol. 113, pp. 59–68. GI (2007)
13. Kiryakov, A., Ognyanov, D.: Tracking Changes in RDF(S) Repositories. Transformation for the Semantic Web KTSW 2002 (2002)

14. Zeginis, D., Tzitzikas, Y., Christophides, V.: On the Foundations of Computing Deltas between RDF Models. In: Aberer, K., Choi, K.-S., Noy, N., Allemang, D., Lee, K.-I., Nixon, L.J.B., Golbeck, J., Mika, P., Maynard, D., Mizoguchi, R., Schreiber, G., Cudré-Mauroux, P. (eds.) ASWC 2007 and ISWC 2007. LNCS, vol. 4825, pp. 631–644. Springer, Heidelberg (2007)
15. Ma, Y., Jin, B.: An Combination Approach to Tackling Semantic Conflicts Based on RDF Model. In: Third International Conference on Semantics, Knowledge and Grid. IEEE, Los Alamitos (2007)
16. Völkel, M., Groza, T.: SemVersion: An RDF-based Ontology Versioning System. In: Proceedings of the IADIS International Conference on WWW/Internet (ICWI 2006), vol. 1, pp. 195–202. IADIS (October 2006)
17. Grimnes, G.A., Edwards, P., Preece, A.D.: Instance Based Clustering of Semantic Web Resources. In: Bechhofer, S., Hauswirth, M., Hoffmann, J., Koubarakis, M. (eds.) ESWC 2008. LNCS, vol. 5021, pp. 303–317. Springer, Heidelberg (2008)
18. Papavassiliou, V., Flouris, G., Fundulaki, I., Kotzinos, D., Christophides, V.: On Detecting High-Level Changes in RDF/S KBs. In: Bernstein, A., Karger, D.R., Heath, T., Feigenbaum, L., Maynard, D., Motta, E., Thirunarayan, K. (eds.) ISWC 2009. LNCS, vol. 5823, pp. 473–488. Springer, Heidelberg (2009)
19. Tzitzikas, Y., Theoharis, Y., Andreou, D.: On Storage Policies for Semantic Web Repositories that Support Versioning. In: Bechhofer, S., Hauswirth, M., Hoffmann, J., Koubarakis, M. (eds.) ESWC 2008. LNCS, vol. 5021, pp. 705–719. Springer, Heidelberg (2008)
20. Carroll, J.J.: Matching RDF graphs. In: Horrocks, I., Hendler, J. (eds.) ISWC 2002. LNCS, vol. 2342, pp. 5–15. Springer, Heidelberg (2002)
21. Plessers, P., De Troyer, O.: Ontology change detection using a version log. In: Gil, Y., Motta, E., Benjamins, V.R., Musen, M.A. (eds.) ISWC 2005. LNCS, vol. 3729, pp. 578–592. Springer, Heidelberg (2005)
22. Feigenbaum, L., Martin, S., Roy, M.N., Szekely, B., Yung, W.C.: Boca: An Open-Source RDF Store for Building Semantic Web Applications. Briefings in Bioinformatics 8(3), 195–200 (2007)
23. OpenLink Software Inc. Virtuoso Replication and Synchronization Services (2006), http://virtuoso.openlinksw.com/Whitepapers/html/DMI_Replication_Services.htm
24. Nejdl, W., Wolf, B., Qu, C., Decker, S., Sintek, M., Naeve, A., Nilsson, M., Palmér, M., Risch, T.: EDUTELLA: A P2P Networking Infrastructure Based on RDF. In: Proceedings of the 11th International Conference on World Wide Web, pp. 604–615 (2002)
25. Stickler, P.: CBD – Concise Bounded Description (W3C Member Submission June 3, 2005). World Wide Web Consortium (2005), http://www.w3.org/Submission/CBD
26. Ding, L., Finin, T., Peng, Y., da Silva, P.P., McGuinness, D.L.: Tracking RDF Graph Provenance Using RDF Molecules. In: Gil, Y., Motta, E., Benjamins, V.R., Musen, M.A. (eds.) ISWC 2005. LNCS, vol. 3729, Springer, Heidelberg (2005)
27. Morbidoni, C., Tummarello, G., Erling, O., Bachmann-Gmür, R.: RDFSync: Efficient remote synchronization of RDF models. In: Aberer, K., Choi, K.-S., Noy, N., Allemang, D., Lee, K.-I., Nixon, L.J.B., Golbeck, J., Mika, P., Maynard, D., Mizoguchi, R., Schreiber, G., Cudré-Mauroux, P. (eds.) ASWC 2007 and ISWC 2007. LNCS, vol. 4825, pp. 533–546. Springer, Heidelberg (2007)

Finding Your Way through the Rijksmuseum with an Adaptive Mobile Museum Guide

Willem Robert van Hage[1], Natalia Stash[2], Yiwen Wang[2], and Lora Aroyo[1]

[1] VU University Amsterdam
wrvhage@few.vu.nl, l.m.aroyo@cs.vu.nl
[2] Eindhoven University of Technology
n.v.stash@tue.nl, y.wang@tue.nl

Abstract. This paper describes a real-time routing system that implements a mobile museum tour guide for providing personalized tours tailored to the user position inside the museum and interests. The core of this tour guide originates from the CHIP (Cultural Heritage Information Personalization) Web-based tools set for personalized access to the Rijksmuseum Amsterdam collection. In a number of previous papers we presented these tools for interactive discovery of user's interests, semantic recommendations of artworks and art-related topics, and the (semi-)automatic generation of personalized museum tours. Typically, a museum visitor could wander around the museum and get attracted by artworks outside of the current tour he is following. To support a dynamic adaptation of the tour to the current user position and changing interests, we have extended the existing CHIP mobile tour guide with a routing mechanism based on the SWI-Prolog Space package. The package uses (1) the CHIP user profile containing user's preferences and current location; (2) the semantically enriched Rijksmuseum collection and (3) the coordinates of the artworks and rooms in the museum. This is a joint work between the Dutch nationally funded CHIP[1] and Poseidon[2] projects and the prototype demonstrator can be found at http://www.chip-project.org/spacechip.

Keywords: Interactive museum tours, mobile museum guide, semantic web, recommender systems, user modeling.

1 Introduction

Cultural heritage and museum collections provide a wide variety of objects, which could be of interest to different visitors. To meet the diversity of preferences and backgrounds of visitors museum curators offer tours on different topics. However, these topics usually are selected based on the highlights of the collection and the resulting tours include a fixed and predefined sequence of artworks to

---

[1] http://www.chip-project.org
[2] http://www.esi.nl/poseidon

L. Aroyo et al. (Eds.): ESWC 2010, Part I, LNCS 6088, pp. 46–59, 2010.
© Springer-Verlag Berlin Heidelberg 2010

view. An audio tour provides more freedom in determining your own sequence of artworks while visiting a museum. However, the set of artworks to choose from is still a predefined one and is the same for all visitors. Currently, museums turn to multimedia guides in order to bridge the gap between the visitor's interests and the static museum tours. Personalization is one way to provide dynamics related to visitor's interests, which subsequently could enhance visitor's experiences [5]. An adaptive mobile museum guide acts as a museum expert and provides the user with information adapted to the current situation [2]. For example, the *MIT Media Lab*[3] audio and visual narration adapts to the user's interest acquired from the physical path in the museum and length of the user stops. The mobile museum guides developed within *Hippie* [3] and *PEACH* [4] projects provide content adaptation based on technical restrictions of specific presentation devices as well as visitor's preferences and knowledge. The difference between two projects is that Hippie museum guide uses stationary and mobile devices in a sequential way (e.g., a user prepares his museum visit on the personal computer at home and then uses the mobile device while actually visiting the museum), the PEACH museum guide combines both mobile and stationary devices in parallel. The mobile museum guide built within *Sotto Voce* [1] project takes into account the special needs of groups visiting a museum and facilitates social interaction between group members. *AgentSalon* [6] system users are provided with mobile devices and are monitored while exploring the museum. The system can infer an overlap between users' interests and experiences and fosters communication between the users with stationary devices. *ARCHIE* [10] provides a socially-aware handheld guide that stimulates interaction between group members. They can communicate with each other either directly (by voice) or indirectly (by collaborative games) by means of their mobile guides. By using a personal profile it allows to adapt the interface and tailor the information to the needs and interests of each individual user. The user profile evolves slowly by observing how the user interacts with the digital content, e.g. asking for more, or bookmarking it, may indicate interest while stopping an explanation prematurely may indicate a lack of it. The *Kubadji* mobile tour guide[4] aims at deriving visitor's interests from implicit behavior (e.g. artworks viewing times), recommendation of items of interest and personalization of the content delivered for these items via the handheld device. Besides it uses collaborative filtering approach for predicting visitor's viewing times of unseen exhibits from his viewing times at visited exhibits. The context-aware museum tour guide presented in [11] is used to give directions to the visitor and is adjusted as the tour progresses dropping one or more exhibits if the visitor falls behind the tour or suggesting additional exhibits or taking a break at a nearby restaurant if the visitor has extra time. The environment also supports peer-to-peer interactions between visitors, allowing them to find each other, share ratings and comments about exhibits. A number of museums, e.g. Tate Modern, Science Museum Boston, are already exploring the potential of personalized museum guides, currently available on their websites.

---

[3] http://www.media.mit.edu/

[4] http://www.kubadji.org/

A major bottleneck in realization of this personalization is how to collect the necessary information about the user's (constantly evolving) interests [5] without intruding on the visitor too much. Typically, for large scale online access personalization can be achieved through usage of stereotypes (e.g. students, novices, art experts, children) or through deducing a user profile from observation of their online browsing and searching (or in museum) viewing behavior. In this way, personalized virtual tours are ways for visitors to construct their own narratives[5]. In addition, the indoor localization of people and objects plays a critical role in order to implement and deploy successfully such a system. Two tasks are considered in this context [2]:

- **Detecting user's location** inside the museum requires a positioning system that considers the boundaries and constraints (i.e. the walls, doors, stairs) of the physical indoor space. Methods using different hardware solutions have been proposed to increase the accuracy of the indoor user position.
- **Assessing user's context** in terms of artworks in her neighborhood, which artworks have been already seen by the users, how much time has the user already spent in the museum and additional temporal constraints (e.g. how much time is available), what are visitor's general interests in art, and potentially also their physiological and the emotional state [2].

Having the limited resources of mobile guides in mind, most of representation and processing of relevant knowledge needs to be carried out remotely in the infrastructure. To reduce complexity and to ensure reusability of the knowledge representations and inference mechanisms a flexible web-based approach is required that allows different types of systems to exchange and augment information on users and particular situations [2]. In the following sections we discuss briefly the CHIP project, the routing mechanism of SWI-Prolog Space package and pay a special attention to the **SPACE-CHIP** demonstrator.

2   CHIP Demonstrator

The CHIP (Cultural Heritage Information Presentation) project is a cross-disciplinary research project, combining aspects from cultural heritage and information technologies. The team has been working at the Rijksmuseum Amsterdam since early 2005, as part of the Dutch CATCH (Continuous Access to Cultural Heritage) program on techniques to provide a personalized access to the museum collection both online and inside the museum, therefore also allowing to link visitor's experience in both environments. We have used explicit semantics in order to enrich the museum collection and in this way to be able to discover relationships between the objects in the collection, and use those to generate personalized recommendations and tours for each user. The main goal of the project so far, was to explore how explicit semantics can improve the users' satisfaction with respect to the recommendation of artworks and related art concepts. All

---

[5] Virtual Museum (of Canada), http://www.museevirtuel-virtualmuseum.ca/

the CHIP Web-based tools[6] for browsing the online collections, planning personalized museum tours, getting recommendations about interesting artworks to see, and quickly finding their ways in the museum use a common distributed user model, which collects user interaction data and interprets it in terms of user's interests used further for generating recommendations and personalized tours. The **Art Recommender** helps the user to discover his art interests in the Rijksmuseum collection and store them in a user profile (also visible to the user). The **Tour Wizard** helps the user to generate personalized tours through the museum based on his user model and visualizes them on the museum map and on a historical timeline. By default, two tours are generated automatically for each user based on his ratings–*Tour of Favorites* containing artworks positively rated by the user and *Tour of Recommended Artworks* containing 20 top recommended artworks. The user can also create tours by searching for concrete artworks. The e-Culture Semantic Search[7] open API helps him find semantically related topics and artworks to include in the personalized tours. For example, if the user searches for "Rembrandt" he gets not only artworks created by Rembrandt himself but also artworks created by Rembrandt's teachers and students, as well as artworks by artists in the same style as Rembrandt. Finally, the **Mobile Museum Guide** allows users to access their tours created with the Tour Wizard on their mobile devices in the museum. Technical details about the design and implementation of the CHIP Art Recommender, Tour Wizard and Mobile Museum Guide (ver 0.1 and ver 1.0) can be found in [9]. However, so far all those tools considered only user preferences are constraints for the adaptation. In order to realize this in the real physical space we need to also consider spatial constraints in generating both recommendations and museum tours. In this paper we propose a method for on-the-fly adaptation of museum tours based on a spatial model of the museum.

The first two versions of the **CHIP Mobile Guide**[8] used two different hardware settings to allow users to use on their handhelds the museum tours created with the online CHIP Tour Wizard. The Mobile Guide is implemented as a Web-based application and is therefore viewable in any browser. For demonstration purposes we have created also an iPhone simulation of the graphical user interface. The simulation can be used if a user wants to get familiar with the mobile environment before going to the museum. The Mobile Guide automatically detects the screen resolution of the user and based on this information chooses to display the Mobile Guide for a mobile device or the simulation. As the other CHIP tools the Mobile Museum Guide provides an extensive description of each artwork and a set of artworks related to it. Visitors can also search for specific artworks exhibited in the museum and can also give a rating to objects they find interesting or like.

When the user selects a tour to follow the Mobile Guide checks the availability and the positioning of all the artworks in the tour in the museum. It is

---

[6] See http://www.chip-project.org/demo
[7] http://e-culture.multimedian.nl/
[8] http://www.chip-project.org/demo/mobileguide

possible that the user has created the tour in advance but by the time that he actually managed to visit the museum some artworks could have been removed or replaced. Next the user adds artworks to the tour that qualify according to contextual and user criteria. Similarly the user can remove artworks from the tour. The user can also specify tour constraints, such as the length of the tour in terms of the maximum number of artworks included in a tour or in terms of the maximum time to spend in the museum. Based on these constraints, the tour can adapt dynamically while the user is in the museum. The user can change those adaptation parameters at any point during the usage of the Mobile Guide (e.g. before starting a tour, while following a tour). The user can also choose an option of adapting the tour based on his ratings given to artworks while using a Mobile Guide.

Suppose the user follows a tour of recommended artworks and he has chosen an option of adapting the tour. If he provides a rating to an artwork that he sees CHIP demonstrator updates the user model and as consequence the list of recommended artworks. However, this version of the Mobile Guide does not take spatial constraints as well as information about already seen artworks into account. In section 3 we show how SWI-Prolog Space package allows to solve this problem and in section 4 we present details about the implementation of the third version of the CHIP Mobile guide including those spatial constrains, http://www.chip-project.org/spacechip.

3   Finding Routes through the Rijksmuseum

The Art Recommender supplies a list of recommended artworks that are ordered by the estimated likelihood that the user will find them appealing based on manual ratings. Even though the rooms in the Rijksmuseum have themes, such as works about the Dutch republic or works by Rembrandt and his pupils, these themes do not necessarily coincide with the preferences of the user. This means that even a small set of recommended artworks can be distributed over the entire museum. In order to improve the user experience of the museum visit, we reorder the results of the Art Recommender so that there is an efficient way to walk from one to the other. This route minimizes the walking effort, while maximizing the number of top recommendations. Also, it takes into account a optional caps to the walking distance and the number of artworks. This helps the user to decide where to go given limited time. (The feeling of missing something important can cause people to linger too long in the "wrong" rooms and therefore to miss their favorite works.)

An Easy Traveling Salesman Problem. Computing an efficient route through a museum is very similar to the traveling salesman problem. However, for a few reasons, theoretically at least, a significantly easier problem than the general traveling salesman problem, for which the greedy nearest-neighbor search algorithm is considered a sub-optimal solution. First, if you consider the artwork displays, rooms, doors, hallways, and stairs to be nodes in a connectivity graph, then this graph is not fully connected, because there are walls and floors in the way. This is illustrated in Fig. 1. Second, the rooms are considered units when the exhibits are created, which means it makes sense to view all works from a single room together. This means it is nearly always a good idea to delay transitions across doors until all displays in a room have been visited. And third, floor transitions take a lot of effort, especially up by stairs, or either way by elevator, because you have to wait for the elevator. For these reasons there are only a few sensible paths through the museum. Locations are grouped per room and then per floor. If you set the transition weight of the edges in the connectivity graph to the experienced distance instead of the actual distance then nearest neighbor search will always send the visitor to works within the same room first before making the transition to another room (or even floor), which is good in the case of the Rijksmuseum, but which is bad in the case the general traveling salesman problem, because it causes local optima.

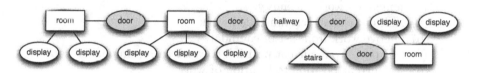

Fig. 1. Example connectivity graph

Implementation of the Nearest Neighbor Router. The SWI-Prolog space package [8] provides nearest neighbor search. However, this nearest neighbor search is unaware of the restrictions posed by the walls and floors. Therefore, we base our routing on a connectivity graph search algorithm that uses intersection queries as opposed to nearest neighbor queries. First we compute a connectivity graph between all the artwork displays, rooms, stairwells, etc. that takes into account where the doors are. Then we compute the weighted shortest path between all the displays. The weight is based on graph distance, the type of the transition (*e.g.* moving to another floor is more expensive), and on the distance between locations inside a room (*e.g.* how far displays are from each other or from a door). This shortest distance matrix is used to compute an efficient path along all the recommended artworks. The exact method we use to calculate the routes is as follows:

- Pre-compute artwork distance matrix once
  1. define that stairs, hallways, toilets, are rooms
  2. define works are at a display in the museum
     (a) give the display a $\langle x, y, z \rangle$ coordinate
  3. define what it means to be connected
     (a) places (displays, doors) space_intersect with same room
     (b) places are stated to be connected (stairs to stairs on other floor) by
         A chip:connectsTo *B*

4. assert A chip:connectsTo B for each connected pair $\langle A, B \rangle$
5. make connectivity graph of chip:connectsTo
6. compute weights for each transition
   (a) graph distance plus distance within room
   (b) door transitions get a higher graph distance than display-display transitions
   (c) stairs transitions get an even higher graph distance
7. compute and cache upper triangle matrix of weighted graph shortest path distances between all places
- Apply routing algorithm for each request
   1. fetch set of recommended works (given by Art Recommender)
   2. fetch current position (given by user interface)
   3. fetch remaining time in museum (given by user interface)
   4. fetch maximum number of artworks to route (given by user interface)
   5. greedy nearest neighbor search in weighted distance graph until list of recommended works is empty:
      (a) look up nearest recommended work
      (b) remove work from list of candidates
      (c) add path from current position to work to recommended route
      (d) set current position to location of work
      (e) add length of path to total length of recommended route
   6. while total path length of recommended route takes longer than remaining time in museum
      (a) remove furthest artwork from current position
      (b) apply greedy nearest neighbor search again (step 5)

4 SPACE-CHIP Demonstrator

4.1 Usage Scenario

Imagine the following usage scenario: Our user prepares a visit to the Rijksmuseum. He provides his opinion about a number of Rijksmuseum artworks and topics through the Art Recommender e.g. rates the painting "Woman Reading a Letter" and the artist that made the painting Johannes Vermeer with 4 stars meaning he likes them. These ratings result in the list of recommended artworks that form a Tour of Recommended Artworks that the user can view in the Tour Wizard [9]. The user is going to follow this tour inside the museum with the help of the CHIP Mobile Guide. The routed tour is shown in Fig. 3. We use icons

---

[9] For the demonstration purposes we simulate the user's experience with the mobile device by showing the tour map in the Tour Wizard tool. In difference with the original version of the tool in this Tour Wizard we indicate with icons the (imaginary) artworks locations. Semantically enriched data about Rijksmuseum collection only provides information about the room number where a particular artwork is located but does not provide information about the exact artwork location.

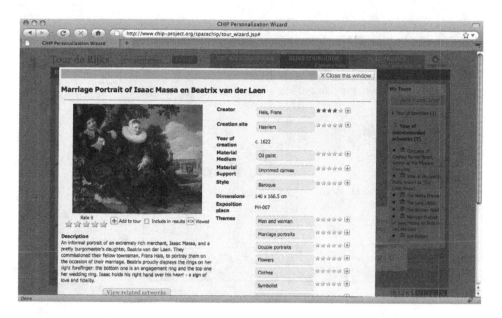

Fig. 2. Artwork description page

in a different color to indicate artworks that are in the tour and connect them with the tour line. The user location is indicated with an icon at the entrance door on the ground floor. During the visit the user views artworks that are in the tour but is also attracted by other artworks outside his tour. In order to give a notification to the system that the user has viewed an artwork he has to click on a corresponding icon on the museum map and in the popup window showing artwork description (see Fig. 2) he has to click on "Viewed" icon. If the user clicks on a "Viewed" icon for an artwork that is in his tour then the tour route remains the same. Otherwise the tour may be re-routed taking into account the user's interest in that artwork. He can also give ratings to any artwork he sees. These actions result in the tour being dynamically adapted taking into account the history of his visit (seen artworks), changing interests and current location. (However if the user wants to follow the initial sequence of recommended artworks and does not want the tour to be adapted he can select a corresponding option in the tour configuration). If the user, for example, likes the works by Frans Hals and Ferdinand Bol he comes across on his way to the recommended Johannes Vermeer works, he can add a rating by selecting the work on the map and submitting a new rating (see Fig. 2). This automatically updates the tour. The updated tour is shown in Fig. 4. For the sake of clarity we have highlighted the works from the original tour with red, the new Frans Hals recommendations with yellow and the new Ferdinand Bol work with blue.

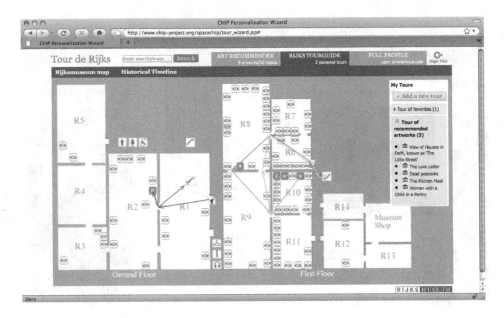

Fig. 3. Initial route of the tour of recommended recommended artworks

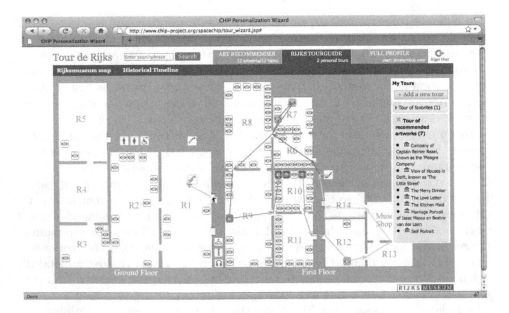

Fig. 4. Re-routed tour of recommended artworks

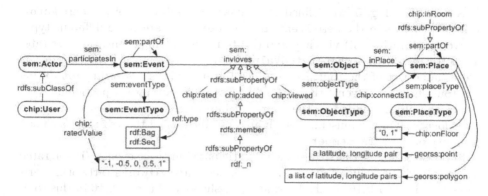

Fig. 5. Mapping CHIP user model (UM) to the simple event model (SEM)

4.2 Mapping the CHIP User Model to SEM

In order to provide data exchange between CHIP and SWI-Prolog Space package we mapped the original CHIP user model (UM) [9] specified using RDF/XML to the Simple Event Model (SEM)[10] which is proposed by van Hage et al. [7] and is just a formalization in RDF using SEM.

```
:Saskia a sem:Actor ;
      sem:participatesIn :event_1, :event_2, :event_3 .

:event_1 a sem:Event ;
      sem:eventType :rating ;
      chip:rated :artwork_9 ;
      chip:ratedValue "0.5" .

:event_2 a sem:Event ;
      sem:eventType :viewing ;
      sem:partOf :event_3 ;
      chip:viewed :artwork_16 .

:event_3 a sem:Event, rdf:Seq ;
      sem:eventType :tour ;
      rdf:_1 :artwork_16 ;
      rdf:_2 :artwork_5 ;
      rdf:_3 :artwork_9 .
```

Fig. 6. Code example of the CHIP User Model based on SEM

[10] For this work we use this version: http://semanticweb.cs.vu.nl/2009/04/event/.
A newer version is available at http://semanticweb.cs.vu.nl/2009/11/sem/

As shown in Fig. 5, we defined `chip:User` as a sub class of the `sem:Actor`, who participates in the `sem:Event`. In our case, there are three different types of events: (i) rating, (ii) viewing, and (iii) tour. In a rating event, the user rates a `sem:Object` with a `chip:ratedValue` from "-1" to "1". The viewing events are usually part of the tour events, since the user views a `sem:Object` during the tour. In a tour event, the user adds a `sem:Object` into a particular tour. All of the objects added in the tour will be ordered in a sequence based on their locations in the museum, which are described using the `rdf:_n`[11] as a sub property of the `rdfs:member`.

Suppose Saskia is a CHIP user who participated in three events: (i) she rated artwork_9 with a value of "0.5"; (ii) she added three artworks (artwork_5, artwork_9 and artwork_16) in the tour; and (iii) she viewed artwork_16 in this tour. Using the routing algorithm, artworks are ordered in a sequence: artwork_16, artwork_5 and then artwork_9. In Fig. 6 we give the corresponding code that describes these information in the user profile and tour profile.

To indicate the locations of objects in the museum, we use various properties: `chip:inRoom`, `chip:onFloor`, `georss:point`[12] and `georss:polygon`. There are also many different types of places in our case, such as display (the place type for artworks), room, door, hallway, stair, elevator, restroom, etc. Two places are connected by using the `chip:connectsTo` property.

5   Evaluation

We consider two issues for evaluation: (1) that recommendations are useful for the users and (2) that sequence of recommendations follows an efficient route through the museum in a reasonable time that allows real-time interaction with the system.

With respect to the first issue we performed a study *Effectiveness of recommendations, novices versus experts*. Our conclusion was that the **Art Recommender** helps novices to elicit or clarify their art preferences from their implicit or unclear knowledge about the museum collection[9]. Compared to the novices, the experts (mainly museum domian experts) do not seem to benefit from it a lot, although there is a slight increase of 0.23 (the increase for the novices is 1.18) which indicates that the system also helps the experts to elicit their art preferences.

With respect to the second issue, we measured the speed of the router. To determine the speed of the router we measured the CPU time taken on a 2.66 GHz Intel processor, given enough memory to store the cached distance matrix between the artworks. The result is shown in Fig. 7. Even though the performance curve shows exponential growth in terms of the number of artworks that needs to be routed, the total time needed for the routing stays within reasonable bounds for the number of artworks in a realistic tour through the Rijksmuseum. This performance could be significantly improved by further optimizing the data

---

[11] http://www.w3.org/TR/rdf-schema/
[12] http://georss.org/simple

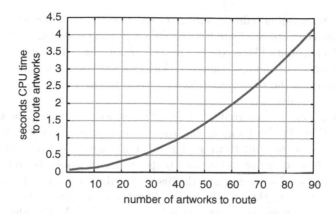

Fig. 7. Time performance of the router for n artworks. The router needs exponential time to derive an efficient route, but stays within a reasonable time for real-time response for the number of artworks that a realistic tour comprises.

structure that stores the distance matrix. At the moment this is a binary tree. An array matrix would provide faster access. Furthermore, we guarantee that the router always favors within-room transitions over between-room transitions, which in turn are always favored over floor transitions. Given the limited connectivity between the rooms and floors this guarantees an efficient path.

6   Discussion and Future Work

Existing adaptive mobile museum guides differ in the ways they construct the user model, the ways they provide personalized experience inside the museums, devices that they use. Many projects focus on social communication between the visitors (e.g. friends, group members) while following a tour. Currently, CHIP does not take social aspect into account–neither for generating recommendations, nor for communication inside the museum. This could be one of the improvements to the CHIP demonstrator. The strong points of CHIP however are the distributed user model and the ability to view the CHIP Mobile Guide in any browser. No additional software installation is required while typically museums would provide the visitors with the PDA's running pre-installed software and ask them to provide some personal information to start creating their user models. In the presence of Wifi inside the Rijksmuseum the visitor could use his own device (iPod touch or iPhone) to follow the CHIP Mobile Guide that uses the user model and the tours information stored on the CHIP server.

We consider several directions for future work.

First, implementing the demonstrator for the use in the realistic situation (inside the museum) with the real time data. In the current prototype we simulated the user's experience with the mobile device by showing the tour map in the Tour Wizard tool. To indicate the fact that the user has seen an artwork he has to first click on a corresponding icon on the map and then on a "Viewed" icon in the popup window that opens. Time issues while following the tour in this way are not taken into account. The next step in developing the demonstrator would be the implementation of the real-time user localization and re-routing the user by taking into account the time that he spends viewing artworks, moving between artworks, taking stairs, etc.

Second, designing and evaluating the user interface for guiding the user in the realistic situation. At the moment the user is only provided with the museum map that indicates the tour route and the current user location. Based on the map the user has to figure out where to go next. It would be interesting to consider the possibility of guiding the user "locally" by an indication about where to go next from the current point, like turn left/right, etc. It would be also interesting to consider using technologies like Google Goggles[13] to show information about an artwork when the user points with his device on it.

And third, experimenting with various re-routing algorithms. Current algorithm can provide re-routing of a tour or sequencing of a given set of artworks from the tour (generated by CHIP Art Recommender and Tour Wizard tools) based on user's position or closeness to a certain artwork from the tour. In addition to this artworks set, the routing mechanism uses the museum coordinates. It does not take into account the information from the user model. It would be interesting however to consider more complex algorithms that would also take user preferences into account and possibly decide to add more artworks to the tour that might be interesting for the user based on the user closeness to them.

Acknowledgments. The work on the CHIP project is funded by the Dutch Science Foundation CATCH program and is in collaboration with the Rijksmuseum Amsterdam. Part of this work has been carried out as a part of the Poseidon project in collaboration with Thales Nederland, under the responsibilities of the Embedded Systems Institute (ESI). This project is partially supported by the Dutch Ministry of Economic Affairs under the BSIK program.

References

1. Aoki, P.M., Grinter, R.E., Hurst, A., Szymanski, M.H., Thornton, J.D., Woodruff, A.: Sottovoce: exploring the interplay of conversation and mobile audio spaces. In: SIGCHI Conference on Human factors in computing systems (2002)
2. Kruger, A., Jorg, B., Heckmann, D., Kruppa, M., Wasinger, R.: Adaptive Mobile Guides. In: Brusilovsky, P., Kobsa, A., Nejdl, W. (eds.) Adaptive Web 2007. LNCS, vol. 4321, pp. 521–549. Springer, Heidelberg (2007)
3. Oppermann, R., Specht, M.: A nomadic information system for adaptive exhibition guidance. In: ICHIM99 Conference (1999)
4. Rocchi, C., Stock, O., Zancanaro, M., Kruppa, M., Kruger, A.: The museum visit: generating seamless personalized presentations on multiple devices. In: 9th International Conference on Intelligent User Interfaces (2004)

---

[13] http://www.google.com/mobile/goggles/

5. Roes, I., Stash, N., Wang, Y., Aroyo, L.: A personalized walk through the museum: The CHIP interactive tour guide. In: ACM CHI-Student Research Competition (2009)
6. Sumi, Y., Mase, K.: Interface Agents that facilitate knowledge interactions between community members. In: Cognitive Technologies Series, pp. 405–427. Springer, Heidelberg (2004)
7. van Hage, W.R., Malaisé, V., de Vries, G., Schreiber, G., van Someren, M.: Combining ship trajectories and semantics with the simple event model (sem). In: 1st ACM International Workshop on Events in Multimedia. Sheridan Publishers (2009)
8. van Hage, W.R., Wielemaker, J., Schreiber, G.: The space package: Tight integration of space and semantics. In: 8th International Semantic Web Conference Workshop: TerraCognita (2009)
9. Wang, Y., Stash, N., Aroyo, L., Gorgels, P., Rutledge, L., Schreiber, G.: Recommendations based on semantically enriched museum collections. Journal of Web Semantics 6(4), 43–58 (2008)
10. Luyten, K., Van Loon, H., Teunkens, D., Gabriëls, K., Coninx, K., Manshoven, E.: ARCHIE: Disclosing a Museum by a Socially-aware Mobile Guide. In: 7th International Symposium on Virtual Reality, Archaeology and Cultural Heritage VAST (2006)
11. Chou, S.-C., Hsieh, W.-T., Gandon, F.L., Sadeh, N.M.: Semantic Web Technologies for Context-Aware Museum Tour Guide Applications. In: 19th International Conference on Advanced Information Networking and Applications, pp. 709–714. IEEE Computer Society, Washington (2005)

A Hybrid Model and Computing Platform for Spatio-semantic Trajectories*

Zhixian Yan[1], Christine Parent[1],
Stefano Spaccapietra[1], and Dipanjan Chakraborty[2],**

[1] EPFL, Switzerland
{firstname.surname}@epfl.ch
[2] IBM Research, India Lab
cdipanjan@in.ibm.com

Abstract. Spatio-temporal data management has progressed significantly towards efficient storage and indexing of mobility data. Typically such mobility data analytics is assumed to follow the model of a stream of (x,y,t) points, usually coming from GPS-enabled mobile devices. With large-scale adoption of GPS-driven systems in several application sectors (shipment tracking to geo-social networks), there is a growing demand from applications to understand the *spatio-semantic* behavior of mobile entities. Spatio-semantic behavior essentially means a semantic (and preferably contextual) abstraction of raw spatio-temporal location feeds. The core contribution of this paper lies in presenting a *Hybrid Model* and a *Computing Platform* for developing a semantic overlay - analyzing and transforming raw mobility data (GPS) to meaningful semantic abstractions, starting from raw feeds to semantic trajectories. Secondly, we analyze large-scale GPS data using our computing platform and present results of extracted spatio-semantic trajectories. This impacts a large class of mobile applications requiring such semantic abstractions over streaming location feeds in real systems today.

1 Introduction

Over the last few years, there has been a tremendous surge in applications and services that exploit real-time location of mobile end points. This is possible in turn due to the large-scale embedding of GPS-driven location sensors in several mobile end points that range from smart phones (e.g. iPhone, Nokia N-series) to specialized GPS chips on shipments, parcels etc. Popular trends suggest large-scale adoption of such mobile end points in future. E.g. Berg Insight (www.berginsight.com) forecasts increase in shipments of GPS-enabled GSM/WCDMA handsets to 770 million units in 2014, representing an coverage rate of 55%. Of course, apart from GPS, other tracking techniques like satellites, radar and RFID also promote location monitoring. Applications and services

---

* This work is supported by the Swiss FNRS grant 200021-116647/1.
** While the author was in EPFL as Academic Guest.

L. Aroyo et al. (Eds.): ESWC 2010, Part I, LNCS 6088, pp. 60–75, 2010.

consuming this spatio-temporal data range from real-time applications to statistical analytics applications. While real-time applications (e.g. location-based advertising) have typically drawn on raw feeds, statistical applications usually require abstracted analytical views on the data for analysis (e.g. geo-marketing, workforce management, study of tele-density by telcos, traffic management etc).

As such, study on raw mobility tracking data has mostly centered around moving object databases and corresponding statistical analytics. Moving object database community has primarily focusing on: (1) Definitions/extensions of trajectory related datatypes such as *moving point* and *moving region* [7][18]; (2) Efficient storage of mobility data, building indexing and querying techniques [3]. Statistical data mining community has on the other hand progressed significantly on approximation functions (e.g. regression or compression) for spatio-temporal mobility data, mining and learning algorithms for pattern discovery [8], primarily considering the raw geometrical perspective on movement.

In this paper, we explore the complimentary challenge that lies in developing appropriate spatio-semantic abstractions of raw spatio-temporal location feeds, catering to a large number of real-time applications. This is because, in recent years, there has been an increase in applications requiring such *abstracted semantic* view on the real-time movement of mobile entities. E.g. Geo-fencing based applications essentially focus on generating high-level events when mobile end points cross domain boundaries or deviate from pre-defined trajectories. Social Networking applications start to exploit real-time location for enriched geo-social collaborations [2] and communications. There is a strong emphasis on developing techniques for higher level, *semantic* events (e.g. Harry just *reached office*, Sally is *shopping in the Owings Mills mall*, Dave is *stuck in traffic* - inferred at varying semantic abstractions from raw GPS-driven location feeds. Solutions used today mostly require human intervention (e.g. applications integrated with twitter) for such semantic (and contextual) abstractions of spatio-temporal data. Our paper is towards providing a model and computing platform for such abstracted spatio-semantic feeds at different levels.

Research relevant to our goal has primarily explored approaches for developing new conceptual models where semantics of movement can be explicitly expressed through application-aware trajectory modeling [16][19][1]. This has resulted in development of high-level semantically meaningful trajectory concepts [5]. However, the primary challenge not yet addressed is to have a generic model to develop these abstracted spatio-semantic trajectories from low-level real-life GPS and other mobility feeds. Apart from handling several issues related to noisy data, a key novelty in our method is to be able to provide a generic set of computing methodologies to represent a spatio-temporal raw data feed at different semantically abstracted levels, starting with basic abstractions (e.g. *stop*, *moves*) to enriched higher-level abstractions (e.g. *office*, *shop*).

To summarize, the core contributions of our paper are: (1) *A hybrid spatio-semantic trajectory model that progressively abstracts high-level semantic concepts from low-level location feeds.* (2) *A computing platform that encapsulates several mobile data abstraction algorithms to enable such semantic enrichment of mobility data.* (3) *Evaluation of the model and computing platform against large-scale real GPS location feeds and presentation of experimental analysis.*

2   Related Work

The GeoPKDD (*Geographic Privacy-aware Knowledge Discovery and Delivery*) [5] and MODAP (*Mobility, Data Mining, and Privacy*) projects emphasize the need to develop high-level semantic concepts related to mobility data. However, they focus on data warehousing and mining for trajectories of moving objects, with an aim to preserve privacy of the owner. A systematic approach towards incremental semantic abstraction of raw trajectory data is not addressed.

A body of work exists in defining semantic abstractions over trajectory data [16][1][6][13][19][17]. Spaccapietra et al. [16] provide a trajectory structure as a sequence of *moves* and *stops* in between, with *begin* and *end* events to represent a trajectory. Work also exists on analysis of tourist movements [1] and semantic interpretation of stops [6] and moves [13]. In addition, reasoning has been applied to mobility data: Yan et al. design ontologies for conjunctive query processing over trajectory-related knowledge [19]; Wessel et al. [17] propose a situational reasoning engine to recognize events from trajectories with description logic.

While these papers focus on definitions and interpretation/analysis of semantic trajectory models relevant for different application domains, the ability to infer several such basic semantic concepts at different abstracted levels from real GPS feeds has remained a challenge. Our model and computing platform enables this. We carefully adopt key concepts from related literature in semantic trajectory modeling for our spatio-semantic representation of trajectories. Further, we take a computational perspective on the spatio-temporal data for extraction of such key concepts and define a conceptual model (called *episodes*) that encapsulates several such semantic trajectory concepts (e.g. *stop, move, begin, end*). This enables us to process raw GPS events in our computing platform.

Complementary to semantic trajectory representation literature, another body of related work on trajectory data analysis is in applying conventional data mining and machine learning methods for clustering [12], classification [11], outlier detection [10], finding convoys [9] and sequential rule-driven pattern mining [4], over real GPS data feeds. The common goal of such statistical analytics is to extract knowledge about trajectories in terms of patterns. Interestingly, the patterns extracted from this body are represented on raw mobility data and are disconnected from the associated *semantic* interpretation of such data.

To the best of our knowledge, our work is the first to bridge the gap between these two bodies of research and presents a model and computing platform for spatio-semantic knowledge discovery from GPS feeds.

3   Spatio-semantic Trajectory Model

As discussed, related work has focused either on high-level semantic representation models of user's mobility or low-level analytics on spatio-temporal GPS data. Our proposal is a hybrid *Spatio-Semantic* trajectory model that: (1) encapsulates raw GPS spatio-temporal trajectory data; (2) allows for progressive abstraction of the raw data to higher-level semantic representation of such data; (3) encapsulates well-known concepts used in literature for trajectories, e.g. stop-move in [16]. The model is usable by several applications requiring varying degrees of such comprehensive trajectory representations from data as well as semantic perspectives (and hence hybrid). Our key design considerations are:

- *Raw Data characteristics:* Model should consider characteristics of raw mobility tracking data (e.g. spatial and temporal gaps, uncertainties) to create simple *low-level* representations (e.g. hourly, daily, monthly and geo-fenced trajectories)
- *Progressive computation possible:* Model should be designed so that a layered computing platform can systematically generate higher-level semantic abstractions from underlying lower-level trajectory representations

Therefore, our hybrid model consists of (1) *Data Model:* to encapsulate the trajectory definitions available from raw data perspective; (2) *Conceptual Model:* a key mid-level abstraction of a trajectory that allows for progressive abstraction of the raw mobility data; (3) *Semantic Model:* to encapsulate spatio-semantic behavior of the trajectory. Fig. 1 provides a high-level view of such models.

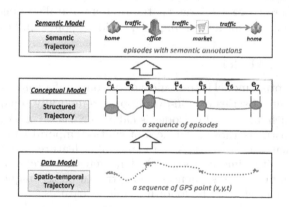

Fig. 1. The Hybrid Spatio-Semantic Trajectory Model

3.1   Data Model

Data model is the first abstraction level over the raw mobility (GPS) data. The raw mobility data is traditionally captured by mobile location sensors, and continuously records the evolving position where a moving object temporally resides. So, raw mobility data is essentially as a long sequence of spatio-temporal tuples (*position, timestamp*) collected over varying time lengths. Most real-life location traces today are essentially GPS-like tuples (*longitude, latitude, timestamp*), (x, y, t) in short. From now on, we use the term *GPS feed* to represent the *raw* sequence of (x, y, t) spatio-temporal mobility data.

In our Data Model, we decompose each GPS feed into *subsequences* so that each such subsequence represents one meaningful unit of movement. We call these meaningful units *"spatio-temporal trajectories"*. Consequently, a spatio-temporal trajectory has a starting point (x, y, t) and an ending point (temporally ordered) that delimits the subsequence, along with a time interval $[t_{begin}, t_{end}]$.

Definition 1 (Spatio-temporal Trajectory $\mathcal{T}_{spa}$). *A spatio-temporal trajectory $\mathcal{T}_{spa}$ is a cleansed subsequence of raw GPS feed for a given moving object in a given time interval $[t_{begin}, t_{end}]$. It is a list of triples (x, y, t) which is ordered by increasing t, i.e. $\mathcal{T}_{spa} = \{p_1, p_2, \ldots, p_n\}$ where $p_i = (x_i, y_i, t_i)$ represents a spatio-temporal point.*

Several issues are relevant for systematic computation of a sequence of $\mathcal{T}_{spa}$ from a computational perspective. E.g. the raw GPS feed need to be cleansed, missing points interpolated and errors in data acquisition corrected. We provide such *Data Preprocessing* methods in our computing platform in Section 4.1. A key concept in computing this model is to identify the meaningful *dividing points* in a raw GPS feed that separates two temporally ordered $\mathcal{T}_{spa}$. A dividing point identifies the *end* of one trajectory $\mathcal{T}_{spa}$ and the *begin* of the next one. Note that the exact begin and end coordinates may not be co-located (e.g. due to data collection gaps). Typical examples of such dividing points could be temporal (daily, hourly trajectories) or spatial (trajectory of a car in a city) or places in the raw feed where there are large spatial or temporal disconnections. Section 4.2 describes the policy for identifying such dividing points and computing $\mathcal{T}_{spa}$.

3.2   Conceptual Model

Intuitively, conceptual model is the logical partitioning of a *single* spatio-temporal trajectory $\mathcal{T}_{spa}$ into a series of non-overlapping temporally separated *episodes*. A $\mathcal{T}_{spa}$ having such annotated episodes is called a *Structured Trajectory* ($\mathcal{T}_{str}$).

An *episode* abstracts those sequences of spatio-temporal tuples that show a high degree of correlation w.r.t. some identifiable feature (e.g. velocity, angle of movement, density, time interval etc). This generic *structural* representation enables us to compute such sequences using structured techniques (described in Section 4.3). An *episode* has the following salient features:

- *Encapsulates semantic trajectory concepts:* High-level trajectory concepts such as *begin, end, stops, moves* [16] become *sub-classes* of *episode*. Moreover, it also encapsulates additional meaningful trajectory concepts such as *jumps, pattern-driven movement* sequences (not necessarily *stop* or *move*), which is defined in literature for domains such as trajectory of wild life [14].
- *Computed automatically:* Episodes can be computed with relevant *Trajectory Structure* algorithms. This is because the correlations are essentially geometric characteristics of GPS feed like *velocity, acceleration, orientation, density,* or other *spatio-temporal* correlations.
- *Enables Data Compression:* Instead of semantic annotation of each GPS records directly (which is possible), episodes essentially enable single semantic tagging of correlated GPS tuples having similar features. This reduces the data size to represent trajectories at the conceptual level. E.g. Fig. 1 shows semantic annotation of seven episodes in the conceptual model which is more efficient than annotation of each GPS tuple in the data model.

Definition 2 (Structured Trajectory $\mathcal{T}_{str}$). *A structured trajectory $\mathcal{T}_{str}$ consists of a sequence of trajectory units, called "episode", i.e. $\mathcal{T}_{str} = \{e_1, e_2, \ldots, e_m\}$*

- *A episode (e) groups a subsequence of $\mathcal{T}_{spa}$ with k consecutive GPS points having some similar characteristics $\{p_1^{(e_i)}, \ldots, p_k^{(e_i)}\}$ derived from $\mathcal{T}_{spa}$.*
- *For data compression, episode is a tuple that stores only the subsequence's temporal duration and spatial extent. $e_i = (time_{from}, time_{to}, bounding_{rectangle}, center)$.*

3.3   Semantic Model

In *Semantic Model*, a trajectory $\mathcal{T}_{sem}$ is an annotated enhancement of a *structured trajectory* $\mathcal{T}_{str}$ enriched with semantic knowledge. Such annotations can be made on episodes in the $\mathcal{T}_{str}$ as well as on the whole $\mathcal{T}_{str}$.

A typical example of a *Semantic Model* is in Fig. 1 (upper layer), where GPS feed are enriched with an employee's spatio-semantic movement pattern: he goes to work from *home* (morning); after *work* (later afternoon), he leaves for shopping in *market*, and finally reaches *home* (evening).

Our model is designed so that it can integrate data from third party sources (e.g. landuse data, road network, points of interest), or social network data related to locations. The model instances can even be inferred through learning patterns from underlying GPS feeds. Our computing platform describes semantic enrichment methodologies that can be applied on such third party data towards computing instances of the semantic model (Section 4.4).

Definition 3 (Semantic Trajectory $\mathcal{T}_{sem}$). *A semantic trajectory $\mathcal{T}_{sem}$ is a structured trajectory with added semantic annotation: episodes are enriched in terms of semantic episodes (se) with geographic or application knowledge. i.e.*
$\mathcal{T}_{sem} = \{se_1, se_2, \ldots, se_m\}$*, where semantic episode $se_i = (sp_i, t_{in}^{(sp_i)}, t_{out}^{(sp_i)})$*

- *sp_i (semantic position) is a meaningful location object, which can be real-world objects from geographic knowledge (e.g. building, roadSegment, administrativeRegion, landuse), or more application domain knowledge (e.g. home, office that belong to specific people in a given application).*
- *$t_{in}^{(sp_i)}$ is the incoming timestamp for trajectory entering this semantic position (sp_i), and $t_{out}^{(sp_i)}$ is the outcoming timestamp for trajectory leaving sp_i. They can be approximated by $time_{from}$ and $time_{to}$ in episode.*
- *From data compression point of view, many episodes in one or more structured trajectories $\mathcal{T}_{str}$ can be located in the same sp_i in $\mathcal{T}_{sem}$.*

Our hybrid model is generic and different ontological frameworks for trajectory modeling [19] [17] can be represented with such model. We do not describe additional examples, but focus on the second contribution - a computing platform that enables population of our hybrid model instances from live GPS feeds.

4   Trajectory Computing Platform

The *Trajectory Computing Platform* exploits the Spatio-Semantic Trajectory model and build trajectory instances of the models at every level (*spatio-temporal, structural, semantic*), from large-scale real-life GPS feed. Fig. 2 shows the four layers in our platform, each containing several techniques for progressive computation of the trajectory instances.

1) **Data Preprocessing Layer:** This layer cleanses the raw GPS feed, in terms of preliminary tasks such as outliers removal and regression-based smoothing. The outcome of this step is a cleansed sequence of (x, y, t).

2) **Trajectory Identification Layer:** This layer divides the cleansed (x, y, t) GPS spatio-temporal points into several meaningful subsequences (spatio-temporal trajectories $\mathcal{T}_{spa}$). This step exploits gaps present in the underlying data and in addition, exploits well-defined polices for temporal and spatial demarcations (e.g. time interval for a day, week, city area etc).

3) **Trajectory Structure Layer:** This layer is responsible for computing *episodes* present in each spatio-temporal trajectory and generates structured trajectories $\mathcal{T}_{str}$. It contains several algorithms for computing correlations between temporally occurring sequence of GPS points.

4) **Semantic Enrichment Layer:** This layer semantically annotates $\mathcal{T}_{str}$ and computes semantic trajectories $\mathcal{T}_{sem}$. It integrates episodes with relevant semantic data from 3rd party sources, and includes algorithms for such integration. E.g. we use spatial join for inferring semantic regions (e.g. landuses), map-matching for inferring road networks, and hidden Markov model for inferring semantic points (e.g. points of interests).

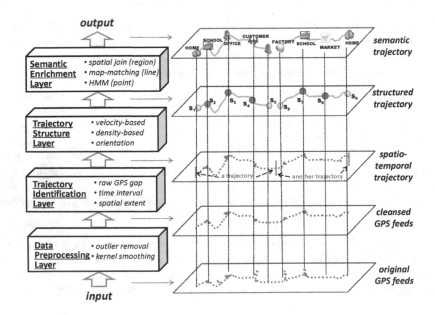

Fig. 2. Spatio-Semantic Trajectory Computing Platform

4.1 Data Preprocessing Layer

Due to GPS measurements and sampling errors from mobile devices, the recorded position of a moving object is not always precise or correct [20]. There is work on determining possible causes for such uncertainty [3]. Data of spatio-temporal tracks from mobile sensors in real world is usually unreliable, imprecise, incorrect and contain noisy records. The *Data Preprocessing Layer* has techniques to clean this data before fitting our *hybrid* model on the data.

Adopting GPS preprocessing techniques for data cleaning [15], we have built techniques to detect (1) *outliers*: observations that deviate significantly from the desired correct position; (2) *random noise*: GPS signals can have noise from several sources. E.g. ionospheric effects and clocks of satellites can contribute towards white noise of ±15 meters (www.kowoma.de/en/gps/errors.htm).

For *outliers*, we adopt threshold-driven techniques on velocity and remove points that do not give us a reasonable correlation with expected velocity. Each GPS feed has domain knowledge of the moving object (e.g. car, human, cycle etc). This lets us compute such speed thresholds from the data. For *random noises*, we design a Gaussian kernel based local regression model to smooth out the GPS feed. The smoothed position $(\widehat{x}, \widehat{y})$ is the weighted local regression based on the past points and future points within a sliding time window, where the weight is a Gaussian kernel function $k(t_i)$ with the kernel bandwidth σ (Formula 1). To control the smoothing related information loss, we adopt a reasonably small value for σ (e.g. 5 × GPS sampling frequency) so that only nearby points can affect the smoothed position. This is necessary as we wanted to calibrate the technique to handle only the noise while avoiding under-fitting.

$$(\widehat{x}, \widehat{y}) = \frac{\sum_i k(t_i)(x_{t_i}, y_{t_i})}{\sum_i k(t_i)}, where \ k(t_i) = e^{-\frac{(t_i - t)^2}{2\sigma^2}} \tag{1}$$

Fig. 3, 4, 5 show an example of our smoothing algorithm on a real data set taken from wild-life tracking data on 15.03.2008. It contains 52 GPS (x,y,t) records. Fig. 3 shows the smoothed longitude (X in cartesian coordinate). Fig. 4 shows the smoothed latitude (Y in cartesian coordinate) and Fig. 5 plots the original GPS feed before smoothing and the smoothed one.

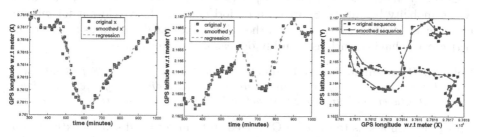

Fig. 3. Smooth GPS (x)   **Fig. 4.** Smooth GPS (y)   **Fig. 5.** Original/smoothed

4.2   Trajectory Identification Layer

This layer uses the processed data and extracts relevant non-overlapping spatio-temporal trajectories $\mathcal{T}_{spa}$ (*data model*). The central issue here is to determine reasonable identification policies, to identify *dividing points* (x_i, y_i, t_i) (introduced earlier) and divide the continuous GPS sequence into consecutive trajectories at appropriate positions. We present three types of trajectory identification policies we have implemented for various trajectory scenarios: *Raw GPS Gap*, *Predefined Time Interval* and *Predefined Spatial Extent*.

Policy 1 (Raw GPS Gap). *Divide the (x,y,t) sequence into several spatio-temporal trajectories according to the raw GPS gaps.*

(1) Given a large time interval $\Delta_{duration-large}$, for any two consecutive GPS records $p_i(x_i, y_i, t_i)$ and $p_{i+1}(x_{i+1}, y_{i+1}, t_{i+1})$, if the temporal gap $t_{i+1}-t_i > \Delta_{duration-large}$, then p_i is the ending point of current trajectory whilst p_{i+1} is the staring point of the forthcoming trajectory.

(2) Given both time interval $\Delta_{duration}$ and spatial distance $\Delta_{distance}$, for any two consecutive GPS records p_i and p_{i+1}, if the temporal gap $t_{i+1}-t_i > \Delta_{duration}$ and the spatial gap $\sqrt{(x_{i+1}-x_i)^2 + (y_{i+1}-y_i)^2} > \Delta_{distance}$, then p_i is the ending point of current trajectory whilst p_{i+1} is the staring point of the forthcoming trajectory.

This policy used significant temporal (and spatial) gaps in GPS feed to logically separate two consecutive spatio-temporal trajectories. This is because GPS-alike tracking devices are usually turned off (automatically or manually) when the object does not move for a long while (e.g. to save power). The first sub-policy exploits large temporal gaps $\Delta_{duration-large}$ to extract spatio-temporal trajectories. This is typically relevant for vehicle movement scenarios. E.g. our dataset of 17,241 car GPS traces (2,075,213 GPS records) resulted in 83,134 spatio-temporal trajectories. The second sub-policy uses both temporal and spatial gaps, where the two parameters are determined by statistical analysis of GPS feeds (e.g. gap distribution, type of movement - vehicular, pedestrian etc).

Policy 2 (Predefined Time Interval). *Divide the stream of GPS feed into several subsequences contained in given time intervals, e.g. hourly trajectory, daily trajectory, weekly trajectory, monthly trajectory.*

This policy allows us to meaningfully divide a GPS feed into periods for analyzing mobility behaviors. Short-term period is particularly relevant for human movements. Wild-life monitoring on the other hand usually requires longer-term trajectory behaviors such as monthly or seasonal patterns.

Policy 3 (Predefined Space Extent). *Divide the stream of GPS feed into several subsequences according to a spatial criteria, e.g. fixed distance, geo-fenced regions, movement between predefined points in network constrained trajectories.*

This policy allows us to divide a GPS feed in terms of fixed spatial extent; in a specific domain zone (e.g. Lausanne downtown), where trajectories ought to be created according to their entering and leaving the zone; or between two given positions of crossings.

4.3   Trajectory Structure Layer

After identifying spatio-temporal trajectories, the next task is to compute their internal structures, and to construct structured trajectories T_{str} consisting of meaningful episodes. The core issue in *trajectory structure* is to group continuous GPS points into an episode. We have implemented *velocity, density, orientation* and *time series* based algorithms for identifying episodes. In this paper, the focus is on the whole trajectory data computing platform. Thus we only address a representative one, i.e. *velocity-based* approach, which we have found quite useful in analyzing our current data sets.

In this approach, we focus on two kinds of episodes (i.e. *stops* and *moves*). The idea is to determine whether a GPS point $p(x, y, t)$ belongs to a stop episode or a move episode by using a speed threshold (Δ_{speed}). Hence, *if the instant speed of p is lower than Δ_{speed}, it is a part of a stop, otherwise it belongs to a move.* Fig. 6 traces the speed evolution of a vehicle, showing how stops can be determined by a given Δ_{speed}. Besides Δ_{speed}, we also use a second parameter - *minimal stop time* τ in order to avoid false positives (e.g. short-term *congestions* with low velocity should not be a stop episode).

Determining the value for Δ_{speed} is a challenge: *if Δ_{speed} is too high, many stops appear; on the contrary, if Δ_{speed} is too low, probably no stops are computed.* Fig. 6 simply shows a constant Δ_{speed} applied all across the trajectory. This is not practical in real-world scenarios, where Δ_{speed} should rather be dynamic according to the context of the moving object. For example, vehicles with different levels of performance (bicycles or motor cars), different road networks (a highway or a secondary road), different weather conditions (sunny or snowy days) call for diverse speed thresholds. However, it is not easy to get these contexts. To avoid this, we design a generic method for determining Δ_{speed}, based on class of moving objects being monitored (which is available) and the real-time underlying movement area. This can be applied to most real-life GPS feeds.

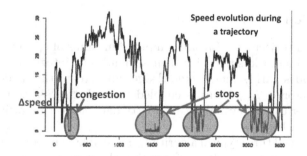

Fig. 6. Velocity-based Stop Identification

Definition 4 (Dynamic Velocity Threshold - Δ_{speed}). *For each GPS point $p(x, y, t)$ of a given moving object (obj$_{id}$), the Δ_{speed} is dynamically related to the moving object (by objectAvgSpeed - the avg. speed of this moving object) and the positionAvgSpeed - the* *avg. speed of moving objects in this position* $\langle x, y \rangle$; *i.e.* $\Delta_{speed} = min\{\delta_1 \times \overline{objectAvgSpeed},$ $\delta_2 \times \overline{positionAvgSpeed}\}$

$\overline{objectAvgSpeed}$ is easy to calculate. We approximate $\overline{positionAvgSpeed}$ through space division. We divide the mobility space into regular cells (or directly using the available landuse data) and calculate the average speed in each cell $\overline{cellAvgSpeed}$. Algorithm 1 provides the pseudocode to determine Δ_{speed}. We analyze sensitivity of the coefficients δ (e.g. 30%) through experiments.

Algorithm 1. getDynamicΔ_{speed} (gpsPoint, obj_{id}, δ)

---

    input : gpsPoint $p = (x, y, t)$, moving object obj_{id}
    output: dynamic speed threshold Δ_{speed}
1 get the average speed of this moving object obj_{id}: $\overline{objectAvgSpeed}$;
2 get the average speed of the cell that (x,y) belongs to: $\overline{cellAvgSpeed}$;
3 compute the dynamic speed threshold by Definition 4;
4 **return** Δ_{speed}

In some scenarios, GPS tracking data have instant speeds (s) values captured by the devices. We use them for calculating Δ_{speed} and identifying stops; otherwise, s is approximated by the average speed between the previous spatio-temporal point $(x_{i-1}, y_{i-1}, t_{i-1})$ and the next one $(x_{i+1}, y_{i+1}, t_{i+1})$, i.e. $s_i = \frac{\|\langle x_{i+1}, y_{i+1}\rangle - \langle x_{i-1}, y_{i-1}\rangle\|_2^2}{t_{i+1} - t_{i-1}}$. This is possible as GPS data is usually sampled frequently (e.g. a few minutes or even every second).

Algorithm 2 provides the pseudocode for determining *velocity-based trajectory structure*: firstly, we compute the instant speed if not available from GPS devices; secondly, we compute the dynamic Δ_{speed} (using Algorithm 1) and annotate the GPS point with 'M' or 'S' tag; finally, stops and moves are computed with the consecutive same tags, using preconditions on minimal stop time τ.

4.4 Semantic Enrichment Layer

Once structured trajectories $\mathcal{T}_{str}$ are computed in terms of episodes such as *stop* and *move*, the final task is to enrich their semantics by integrating these spatio-temporal episodes with semantic knowledge, and create the model for spatio-semantic trajectories $\mathcal{T}_{sem}$. This is enabled through the Semantic Enrichment Layer. This layer utilizes available third party data sources to gather additional context about each episode.

We have designed three typical algorithms to be able to integrate landuse data, road networks and maps as well as information about points of interest with each episode in the structured trajectory. Landuse data is integrated using *spatial join* with semantic regions for computing $\mathcal{T}_{sem}^{(region)}$; *Map-matching* algorithm is used with semantic lines (road networks) for computing $\mathcal{T}_{sem}^{(line)}$ and *hidden Markov model (HMM)* is used with semantic points (e.g. points of interets) for computing $\mathcal{T}_{sem}^{(point)}$. In this paper, we only illustrate the first case: $\mathcal{T}_{sem}^{(region)}$.

Algorithm 2. *Velocity-based trajectory structure*

Input: a raw trajectory $\mathcal{T}_{raw} = \{p_1, p_2, \cdots, p_n\}$
Output: a structured trajectory $\mathcal{T}_{str} = \{e_1, e_2, \ldots, e_m\}$ where e_i is a tagged trajectory
episode (stop $\mathcal{S}$ or move $\mathcal{M}$)

```
1  begin
2      /* initialize: calculate GPS instant speed if needed */
3      ArrayList⟨x, y, t, tag⟩ gpsList ← getGPSList(𝒯_spa);
4      if no instant speed from GPS device then
5          compute GPS instant speed s_i for all p_i = (x, y, t) ∈ gpsList;

6      /* episode annotation: tag each GPS point with 'S' or 'M' */
7      forall p_i = (x, y, t) ∈ gpsList do
8          // get dynamic Δ^(i)_speed by Algorithm 1
9          Δ^(i)_speed ← getDynamicΔ_speed (p, obj_id, δ);
10         // tag GPS point as a stop point 'S' or a move point 'M'
11         if instant speed s_i < Δ^(i)_speed then
12             tag current point p_i(x, y, t) as a stop point 'S';
13         else
14             tag current point p_i(x, y, t) as a move point 'M';

15     /* compute episodes: grouping consecutive same tags*/
16     forall consecutive points with the same tag 'S' do
17         // compute stop episode
18         get the total time duration t_interval of these points;
19         if t_interval > τ the minimal possible stop time then
20             stop ← (time_from, time_to, center, boundingRectangle);
21             𝒯_str.(stop, 'S'); // add the stop episode
22         else
23             change the 'S' tag to 'M' for all these points; // as "congestion"

24     forall consecutive points with the same tag 'M' do
25         // compute move episode
26         move ← (stop_from, stop_to, duration) // create a move episode
27         𝒯_str.(move, 'M'); // add the move episode
28     return the structured trajectory 𝒯_str;
29  end
```

We use *spatial join* to compute $\mathcal{T}_{sem}^{(region)}$. *Spatial join* is used to calculate the topological correlations between episodes and semantic regions. For each episode (e.g. stop), we use either the spatial *bounding rectangle* of the episode or the *center* to do spatial join. Further, we apply landuse data that describes the use of natural environment to tag each episode. To do this, we divide the landuse space into cells (depending on density) and correlate each episode to available landuse

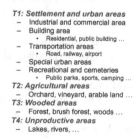

T1: *Settlement and urban areas*
  – Industrial and commercial area
  – Building area
      • Residential, public building ...
  – Transportation areas
      • Road, railway, airport
  – Special urban areas
  – Recreational and cemeteries
      • Public parks, sports, camping ...
T2: *Agricultural areas*
  – Orchard, vineyard, arable land ...
T3: *Wooded areas*
  – Forest, brush forest, woods ...
T4: *Unproductive areas*
  – Lakes, rivers, ...

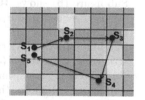

Fig. 7. Landuse Ontology   **Fig. 8.** Real Landuse   **Fig. 9.** Synthetic Landuse

cells. As an example, Fig. 8 shows the landuse about Lausanne downtown, where we divided the space into 100×100 m^2 cells. Each cell has semantic annotations from the landuse ontology in Fig. 7 from Swisstopo (www.swisstopo.admin.ch).

For some trajectory scenarios, when real landuse cells are not available, we generate Gaussian distributed synthetic cells. Fig. 9 shows a sample trajectory with five stop episodes. S_1 and S_5 share the same landuse; S_3 and S_4 belong to the same landuse category (shown in same color). In this case, semantic trajectory $\mathcal{T}_{sem}$ is a sequence of four landuse cells with a temporal duration ($cell_{id}, time_{in}, time_{out}$).

5   Experiment Analysis

We have validated our model and computing platform against different kinds of real-life GPS feed. Table 1 provides a short summary of the data used in our experimental analysis. Milan car and Laussane taxi are two big datasets from the GeoPKDD project and Swisscom (www.swisscom.ch) respectively. In addition, we use two public Athens datasets from R-tree portal (www.rtreeportal.org).

Table 1. Trajectory datasets - real life GPS feed

	Dataset	# objects	# GPS records	Traking time	Sampling frequency
(1)	car (Milan)	17,241	2,075,213	1 week	avg. 40 seconds
(2)	bus (Athens)	2	66,095	108 days	30 seconds
(3)	truck (Athens)	50	112,203	33 days	30 seconds
(4)	taxi (Lausanne)	2	3,347,036	5 months	1 second

In order to present trajectory computing results, we have implemented a hybrid trajectory visualization tool using Java 2D API. Fig. 10 provides a snapshot of the tool presenting four sub-figures corresponding to original *GPS feeds*, *spatio-temporal trajectory*, *structured trajectory*, and *semantic trajectory* computed from the truck dataset. The order of sub-figures (from left to right) follows the progressive computation of trajectories from the raw feed.

- Sub-figure (a) visualizes the spatial locations of 112,203 raw GPS records, in terms of their 2D geometric coordinates (x, y), without any further meanings (output of *Data Preprocessing* Layer).
- Sub-figure (b) shows 310 spatio-temporal trajectories obtained from the (x, y, t) cleansed sequence (output of *Trajectory Identification* Layer). To distinguish, the neighboring trajectories are shown in different colors.
- Sub-figure (c) displays the trajectory episodes (i.e. stops and moves) and visualizes structured trajectories (output of *Trajectory Structure* Layer). There are 1826 stops (visualized as *points*) and 1849 moves (as *lines between points*).
- Sub-figure (d) shows the output of *Semantic Enrichment* Layer. It displays enriched stop episodes, where 1826 stops are mapped to 160 landuse cells (visualized as *squares*) in 5 types. Cells from different types are drawn with distinct colors.

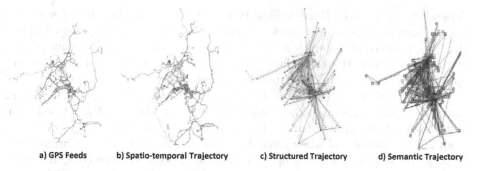

a) GPS Feeds   b) Spatio-temporal Trajectory   c) Structured Trajectory   d) Semantic Trajectory

Fig. 10. Visualization - from GPS feed to semantic trajectories

An interesting aspect to observe is the decrease in the data size as trajectories are abstracted to the higher level model. To demonstrate this, we compute the *semantic abstraction rate* as $log_2(\frac{\#GPS}{\#dataComputed})$, where $\#GPS$ is the number of the initial GPS records and $\#dataComputed$ is the number of computed model instances, i.e. the number of trajectories, episodes (stops and moves), and semantic episodes (e.g. landuse cells). For example we observe that for taxi dataset, 3,347,036 GPS records are abstracted to 1,145 trajectories with 1,874 stops and 2,925 moves in structured trajectories, and even lesser 816 semantic stops in semantic trajectories. This is because the higher layer trajectory encapsulates multiple concepts from the underlying lower layer trajectory. Fig. 11 shows the abstraction results for the four datasets.

Another interesting (and reasonable) observation is that the abstraction rate is proportional to the GPS sampling frequency. From left to right in Fig. 11, the GPS recording frequency is respectively one record per 40 seconds (on average), 30 seconds, 30 seconds, and one second. We see the higher recording frequency (like taxi data), the more is the compression (i.e. the higher abstraction rate).

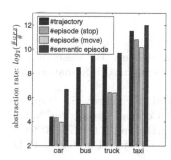

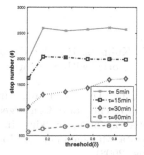

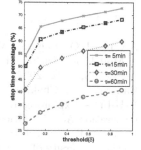

Fig. 11. Different levels of data abstraction

Fig. 12. Δ_{speed} w.r.t. total stop number

Fig. 13. Δ_{speed} w.r.t. total stop time

As mentioned before, the coefficients for speed thresholds play a role in determining the number of stop and move episodes and as pointed out before, is dependent on several factors (vehicle type, road type etc). Results presented in Fig. 11 have used the same coefficient of speed thresholds ($\delta_1 = \delta_2 = \delta = 0.3$) and the same minimal stop duration ($\tau = 15\ mins$) to provide a comparative picture of the abstraction. However, these parameters effect the number of trajectory episodes and needs to be calibrated accordingly.

We analyzed the sensitivity of δ and τ in identifying stop episodes. Fig. 12 shows the number of stops we get with different δ and τ for the Athens truck data. With higher τ (from five minutes to one hour), the number of stops decreases from 2601 to about 633 when given $\delta = 0.15$; whilst with higher δ (from 0.015 to 0.9), the stop number goes up then saturates, because stops computed with higher coefficient δ (i.e. higher Δ_{speed}) usually have longer duration. Therefore stop number decrease as some stops join together. Nevertheless, we observe that the total percentage of time duration for stops always increases when the minimal stop time τ becomes smaller or the speed threshold δ increases (see Fig. 13). We are investigating means to dynamically calibrate these parameters.

6   Conclusion

In this paper, we propose a hybrid spatio-semantic model and a computing platform for trajectories of moving objects. Our hybrid model can represent trajectories in terms of both spatio and semantic mobility characteristics, supporting different levels of data abstraction. Through experimental analysis of real-life GPS feeds, we demonstrate how our model and platform achieve the purpose of progressive abstraction of the raw mobility data. We present spatio-semantic trajectory computing results in various live mobility feeds, and present insights on parameters that guide the sensitivity of such computing platform. This approach can be applied to other location feeds like cellular location data. Our future work focuses on inferring spatio-semantic trajectories from diverse location (and sensory) sources.

References

1. Alvares, L.O., Bogorny, V., Kuijpers, B., Macedo, J., Moelans, B., Vaisman, A.: A Model for Enriching Trajectories with Semantic Geographical Information. In: ACM-GIS, p. 22 (2007)
2. Banerjee, N., Chakraborty, D., Dasgupta, K., Mittal, S., Nagar, S., Saguna: R-U-In? - Exploiting Rich Presence and Converged Communications for Next-Generation Activity-Oriented Social Networking. In: MDM, pp. 222–231 (2009)
3. Frentzos, E.: Trajectory Data Management in Moving Object Databases. PhD thesis, University of Piraeus (2008)
4. Giannotti, F., Nanni, M., Pinelli, F., Pedreschi, D.: Trajectory Pattern Mining. In: KDD, pp. 330–339 (2007)
5. Giannotti, F., Pedreschi, D.: Mobility, Data Mining and Privacy - Geographic Knowledge Discovery. Springer, Heidelberg (2008)
6. Gómez, L., Vaisman, A.: Efficient Constraint Evaluation in Categorical Sequential Pattern Mining for Trajectory Databases. In: EDBT, pp. 541–552 (2009)

7. Güting, R., Schneider, M.: Moving Objects Databases. Morgan Kaufmann, San Francisco (2005)
8. Han, J., Lee, J.-G., Gonzalez, H., Li, X.: Mining Massive RFID, Trajectory, and Traffic Data Sets. In: KDD Tutorial (2008)
9. Jeung, H., Yiu, M.L., Zhou, X., Jensen, C.S., Shen, H.T.: Discovery of Convoys in Trajectory Databases. In: VLDB, pp. 1068–1080 (2008)
10. Lee, J.-G., Han, J., Li, X.: Trajectory Outlier Detection: A Partition-and-Detect Framework. In: ICDE, pp. 140–149 (2008)
11. Lee, J.-G., Han, J., Li, X., Gonzalez, H.: TraClass: Trajectory Classification Using Hierarchical Region-Based and Trajectory-Based Clustering. In: VLDB, pp. 1081–1094 (2008)
12. Lee, J.-G., Han, J., Whang, K.-Y.: Trajectory Clustering: a Partition-and-Group Framework. In: SIGMOD, pp. 593–604 (2007)
13. Mouza, C., Rigaux, P.: Mobility Patterns. GeoInformatica 9(4), 297–319 (2005)
14. Santer, R.D., Yamawaki, Y., Rind, F.C., Simmons, P.J.: Motor Activity and Trajectory Control During Escape Jumping in the Locust Locusta Migratoria. Journal of Comparative Physiology A 191(10), 965–975 (2005)
15. Schüssler, N., Axhausen, K.: Processing GPS Raw Data Without Additional Information. Transportation Research 8 (2009)
16. Spaccapietra, S., Parent, C., Damiani, M.L., de Macedo, J.A., Porto, F., Vangenot, C.: A Conceptual View on Trajectories. Data and Knowledge Engineering 65, 126–146 (2008)
17. Wessel, M., Luther, M., Möller, R.: What Happened to Bob? Semantic Data Mining of Context Histories. In: Description Logics (2009)
18. Wolfson, O., Xu, B., Chamberlain, S., Jiang, L.: Moving Objects Databases: Issues and Solutions. In: SSDBM, pp. 111–122 (1998)
19. Yan, Z., Macedo, J., Parent, C., Spaccapietra, S.: Trajectory Ontologies and Queries. Transactions in GIS 12(1), 75–91 (2008)
20. Zhang, J., Goodchild, M.F.: Uncertainty in Geographical Information, 1st edn. CRC, Boca Raton (2002)

Reactive Policies for the Semantic Web*

Piero A. Bonatti[1], Philipp Kärger[2], and Daniel Olmedilla[3]

[1] Università di Napoli Federico II, Italy
[2] L3S Research Center & Leibniz University of Hannover, Germany
[3] Telefónica Research & Development, Madrid, Spain

Abstract. Semantic Web policies are general statements defining the behavior of a system that acts on behalf of real users. These policies have various applications ranging from dynamic agent control to advanced access control policies. Although policies attracted a lot of research efforts in recent years, suitable representation and reasoning facilities allowing for *reactive* policies are not likewise developed. In this paper, we describe the concept of reactive Semantic Web policies. Reactive policies allow for the definition of events and actions, that is, they allow to define reactive behavior of a system acting on the Semantic Web. A reactive policy makes use of the tremendous amount of knowledge available on the Semantic Web in order to guide system behaviour while at the same time ensuring trusted and policy-compliant communication. We present a formal framework for expressing and enforcing such reactive policies in combination with advanced trust establishing techniques featuring an interplay between reactivity and agent negotiation. Finally, we explain how our approach was applied in a prototype which allows to define and enforce reactive Semantic Web policies on the Social Network and communication tool Skype.

1 Introduction

Semantic Web policies [11,30] attracted a lot of research effort in the last years. Typically, policies are declarative behaviour descriptions used in the upper-most levels in the Semantic Web layer cake, thus establishing trust and enforcing privacy settings among Semantic Web systems. Current Semantic Web policy languages allow to define conditions that must be fulfilled by a peer in order to be allowed to perform a certain action on a system. These languages are based on the assumption, that certain actions (e.g., access to an RDF store [1] or to copy Web content [28]) are only allowed if certain conditions are fulfilled. In this paper, we extend this model to so-called *reactive policies*, which—in contrast to the current Semantic Web policies—allow to define (1) events triggering the evaluation of conditions and (2) actions which are taken as reactions for such an evaluation. Reactive policies make it possible to declaratively define what are the reactions to a specific situation or event within one single language. This way, reactive policies reflect the dynamics of the Semantic Web: updates

---

* The authors' efforts were partly funded by the European COST Action IC0801 "Agreement Technologies".

L. Aroyo et al. (Eds.): ESWC 2010, Part I, LNCS 6088, pp. 76–90, 2010.

in the knowledge stored on some Semantic Web peer are turned into reactions in the real world, thus closing the gap between knowledge and behaviour on the Semantic Web while at the same time ensuring trusted and policy-compliant communication.

Making privacy decisions and establishing trust among systems or agents that do not know each other beforehand is a difficult task. One of the most prominent ways to address this challenge is policy-based trust negotiation [33], a protocol to exchange evidences (typically digitally signed credentials) and policies to mutually establish trust among strangers.

In this paper, we present a policy language to define declarative, exact, and detailed behaviour description of Semantic Web systems with Event-Condition-Action rules (ECA rules [32]). Our framework combines ideas from reactive languages on the Semantic Web [5] with advanced policy reasoning and trust negotiations such that reactivity is based on secure evidences. To achieve this, we formally define a policy language that features an extension to the formal trust negotiation process [13,12] based on an interplay between negotiations and reactive rule evaluation.

In our language, policies have the form **ON** *Event* **IF** *Condition* **DO** *Action* and are interpreted according to the standard ECA semantics: in case *Event* occurs and, at the same time, *Condition* is evaluated to true, the action *Action* is performed. *Events* are any kind of change in the environment that is propagated by exploiting the infrastructure of the internet; examples are "a flight is rescheduled", "an auction will end in 10 minutes", or "a money transaction is completed". *Conditions*, on the one hand, make use of the mass of information exposed on the Semantic Web such as "is the requester listed in my FOAF[1] profile?" and, on the other hand, they allow for security checks that may, for example, only be carried out by a trust negotiation, such as "is the flight change notification coming from an authorized peer belonging to the airline?" or "is the requester a citizen of the city Hannover?" (to prove those attributes, the exchange of signed credentials is required). Finally, the *actions* will turn the Semantic Web knowledge into real world changes such as "rebook the flight according to my preferences", "redirect the call to my mobile phone", or "dispatch the goods".[2] It is worth noting that the requirement for *reactive* Semantic Web Policies, based on reactive rules, has already been sketched in several publications [12,11,3,21], however, a unified language that combines reactive behaviour control with advanced trust establishing techniques was not given until now.

In summary, the framework for reactive Semantic Web policies presented in this paper has the following features:

- a declarative policy language for reactive policies with well-defined semantics
- seamless integration of Semantic Web sources into the reasoning process
- support for trust negotiations
- support for strong and lightweight evidences

---

[1] FOAF=Friend of a Friend, www.foaf-project.org
[2] We refer the reader to [4] where more examples are given for the use of reactive policies on the Semantic Web.

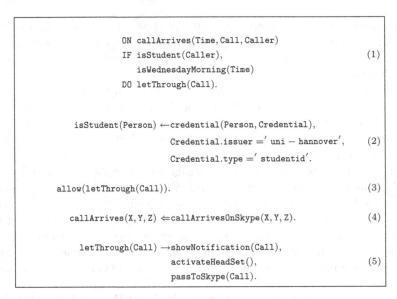

Fig. 1. An example policy accepting student's calls on Wednesday morning

We further illustrate how the presented framework can be used in social systems and describe its use in our application SPoX [22] where reactive policies are enforced for the Social Network and communication tool Skype.

The remainder of this paper is structured as follows. In the next section we will first provide an overview of our policy framework and the principle of trust negotiation. Then, the syntax and the semantics of our policy language is provided. In Section 3 we describe how we used our approach to implement reactive policy control for Skype. In Section 4 we compare our approach to related work and we conclude the paper in Section 5.

2   A Framework for Reactive Policies

Before we formally define the language and the negotiation protocol, we present an informal description of the procedure illustrating the basic principles of our approach.

An example policy is given in Figure 1 where it is stated that phone calls from students are automatically accepted on Wednesday morning. If a call comes in, in order to let Rule (1) apply, the predicate $isStudent(\_)$ has to be proven which requires the predicate $credential(\_,\_)$ to be true. The intuition behind this predicate is, that it is true if the peer given in the first argument provided a credential (which will then be bound to the second argument). In such a case, the fact $credential(peer, cred)$ would be added to the state of the system. Typically, in an initial state, when a call comes in, $credential(\_,\_)$ is not true. Thus, the policy owner will initiate a request back for a credential. The goal of the procedure is to make $credential(\_,\_)$ true, i.e., adding it as a fact to the state. The reply to the initiator of the call comprises two parts: the request for proving *isStudent*(_) and the policy itself that tells the other peer how to prove *isStudent*(_). The idea behind this reply is that the policy owner asks the caller about evidences which help to prove *isStudent*(_). From the policy that is sent along with the response, the caller learns that a student credential is required. If possible, the caller sends back the credential and the negotiation is successful. Of course, the credential itself can be again protected by a policy (e.g., the calling peer may disclose a student credential only to university employees) which would lead to a request back forming a multi-step negotiation. Finally, if the negotiation is successful and it is Wednesday morning, the action part of Rule (1) can be executed. The execution of actions has to undergo a policy check again (automated re-actions have to be checked to ensure execution safety, as discussed later in the paper) so for each action a that is going to be executed, the predicate *allow*(a) has to be proven. In our example, accepting the call is always allowed (see empty body in Rule (3)).

2.1 Evidences and Filtered Policies

Due to space limitations, we do not detail the negotiation model here and remain with the example given above. We only recall two important principles presented in [13,12] which we adopt for our framework.

Strong and lightweight evidences. Evidences for properties provided by a peer in order allow another peer's decision may be strongly certified by cryptographic techniques, or may be reliable to some intermediate degree with lightweight evidence gathering and validation [11]. Our framework supports both, strong evidences and lightweight evidences. Examples for strong evidences are digitally signed credentials (such as the student ID in Figure 1). Lightweight evidences include so-called declarations, such as the signing of a license agreement or provision of a user name and password.

Policy filtering. As described in the example above, a request for evidences from another peer comprises the policies whose evaluation requires those evidences. This is needed in order to provide the peer receiving the request with reasons why the request is sent (otherwise a calling student would not be able to understand the benefit of providing her student credential). Another reason is that the policies implicitly contain all possible options (e.g., sets of credentials to disclose) to fulfill them. However, policies are sensitive resources and it may be necessary to hide parts of them [12] (see for example Policy (6) in Section 3: since the password itself is part of the policy, sending a non-filtered policy would unintentionally disclose the password). Moreover, not all parts of the policies are important for the receiver of a request which is another motivation for filtering. The policy filtering mechanism and how the filtered policy is used to select a "promising" set of credentials from a portfolio are not included in this paper: we refer to reader to [12] where this principle is described in detail.

2.2   Using External Semantic Data

Policy decisions may not only depend on credentials that are provided or not, but also on other sources such as if someone is a friend in a FOAF profile (see [23] for more examples) or if it is Wednesday morning (see Figure 1). For this, we support a specific predicate called in-predicate that allows calls to external methods to be integrated into the policy evaluation process. With this predicate, ground facts do not have to be present explicitly but can be retrieved on demand from external sources during the reasoning process. In the present work we use this feature to incorporate social data from the (Semantic) Web into the reasoning process as it was presented in [23]. For the in-predicate we adopt the syntax introduced in [29].

2.3   Syntax

In the following, we define the Syntax of our policy language. It is composed of three different types of rules: the reactive rules in ECA form (Rule (1) in Figure 1), definition rules to define complex events (Rule (4)) and complex actions (Rule (5)), and implication rules (Rules (2) and (3)) which form the declarative part of the policy and are processed like normal logic programming rules.

A policy P is a set of definition rules, reactive rules and inference rules. A definition rule is either an event definition or an action definition. Let E_a, E_c (atomic and complex events, resp.), A_a, A_c (atomic and complex actions, resp.) be sets of atoms and let e_a,e_c,a_a,a_c be respective elements of those sets.

The set of events E over E_a and E_c is the set of atoms e of the form $e ::= e_a \mid e_1 \bigtriangledown e_2 \mid e_c$ where e_1, e_2 are arbitrary elements of E. Given $e \in E$, an event definition is any expression of the form "$e_c \Leftarrow e$.".

A set of actions A over A_a and A_c is the set of atoms of the form $a ::= a_a \mid a_1, a_2 \mid a_c$ where a_1, a_2 are arbitrary elements of A. Given $a \in A$, an action definition is any expression of the form "$a_c \to a$.". [3]

Let $Cond$ be a set of atoms. A reactive rule r is any rule of the form "ON e IF $c_1, \ldots, c_m, not\ c_{m+1}, \ldots, not\ c_n$ DO a." with $c_1, \ldots, c_n \in Cond$.

An implication rule is of the form "$head \leftarrow c_1, \ldots, c_m, not\ c_{m+1}, \ldots, not\ c_n$." with $head ::= c_0 \mid allow(a)$ and $c_i(0 \le i \le n) \in Cond$, $a \in A_a \cup A_c$.

State predicates. A distinguished subset of predicates, called *state predicates*, may change their extension dynamically (as a consequence of message exchanges, updates, etc.). State predicates comprise credential, declaration, the in predicate (see Section 2.2), as well as predicates that define the attributes of compound objects like credentials and declarations (like the attribute issuer of a credential in Rule (2)). Conceptually, in the logical model, state predicates are defined by sets of ground facts, while their actual implementation may be ad hoc or cast into the system on evaluation time. For simplicity, we assume that

---

[3] It is worth mentioning that our approach can easily be extended to allow more complex action constructs, e.g., following the ideas presented in [8]. We leave such directions for future work.

policy rules do not change during negotiations. On the contrary, the dynamics of the system is reflected in the state predicates whose validity may change.

In contrast to traditional non-reactive trust negotiation approaches, in the presented framework, peer interactions are triggered by a variety of events instead of requests only. For example, in the model in [13,12] the value of the meta-term *peer* is in general clearly identified by the requester in the negotiation's context. Since in our approach, sources for policy evaluations may not only be requests with a single requester peer, we use binary state predicates for representing credentials and declarations, where the first argument explicitly mentions the peer in charge of providing missing evidence and the second argument denotes the evidence itself. For example a peer may try to make a condition $credential(p, c)$ true by asking peer p for the credential c. Accordingly, we will call *peer variable* of a rule r any variable occurring as the first argument of `credential` or `declaration` in r's body.

Although our language implements negation as failure in general, negation of provisional predicates is prohibited. Provisional predicates are state predicates that are proven by another peer—typically declarations or credentials. As it has been stated in [12], this restriction ensures that policies are monotonic, that is, as more credentials are released the set of permissions does not decrease. Moreover, the restriction on negation makes the implication rules build a stratified program; therefore negation as failure has a clear, PTIME computable semantics that can be equivalently formulated as the perfect model semantics, the well-founded semantics or the stable model semantics [6].

2.4   Semantics

We will first give a procedural description of the policy evaluation process. Subsequently, we will detail this description by a formal definition of the semantics. Procedurally, the evaluation of a reactive policy happens as follows:

1. If an event occurs, the event expressions of all reactive rules are evaluated to determine if the event expression matches the event happened. All reactive rules whose event part applies are called *pending*.
2. For all pending reactive rules r all evidences from the condition part are collected that are not known from the current state but can be proven by other peers (for example, the evidence stating that the origin of a signal is a student and thus can provide a student ID credential).
3. Those requests together with the corresponding filtered policy are sent to the parties defined in the evidence's peer variable and thus initiate a negotiation.
4. If the condition of r is not true but there are remaining evidences which can be proven by other peers, the negotiation goes on.
5. If the condition of r evaluates to true, its variable results are bound to the action part, it is checked if the action execution is authorized (i.e., $allow(action)$ is true) and the actions in question are executed.

Events. An event triggers the evaluation of a rule if it matches the rule's event part as follows:

Definition 1. An event expression e is true for a given atomic event e_A and a reactive policy P, denoted $e \vdash_P e_A$, if one of the following conditions is true

1. e is an atomic event and there is a substitution σ such that $e\sigma = e_A$
2. e is an event expression of the form $e_1 \triangledown e_2$ and there is a substitution σ such that $e_1\sigma \vdash_P e_A \vee e_2\sigma \vdash_P e_A$ (disjunctive connection of events)
3. there is a substitution σ, an event definition $e_c \Leftarrow e_{def}. \in P$, and $e_c\sigma = e$ as well as $e \vdash_P e_{def}$ holds.

We want to note here that this rather simple event algebra can be easily extended by more complex algebras (for example [18]). We leave further extensions in that direction for future work.

Condition evaluation. In the following we define what satisfies a condition part of a reactive rule and which message exchanges and negotiations are needed. We assume the reader to be familiar with the basics of Logic Programming, including SLD-derivations and *mgu* (most general unifier) [6].

Definition 2. [State atom, context, support] A *state atom* (resp. *state literal*) is an atom (resp. literal) whose predicate is a state predicate. A *context* is a set of ground state atoms. (Note that a context is a Herbrand model containing only state atoms.) A *support* of a goal G from a set of implication rules P is a goal G_n containing state literals only and occurring as the last step in a complete, finite SLD-derivation $G, G_1, G_2, \ldots, G_n$. With a slight abuse of notation, goals will be identified with the *set* of literals constituting the goal (instead of a sequence of literals).

We will use contexts to express the set of facts that are true for the current state of the negotiation. Supports will be used to denote the set of predicates that are collected from the policy and that are not true (yet). Those predicates are candidates for requests to other peers in order to collect evidences to prove the initial goal. For example, if a student Alice calls the peer from our running example on a Wednesday 11AM, the peer's context contains the fact $isWednesdayMorning('11AM')$, the support for the goal $isStudent(alice)$ contains $credential(alice, Credential)$. As soon as Alice provides a credential c, the fact $credential(alice, c)$ will be added to the context.

Note that a support is not necessarily a context because, in general, a support is not ground but may still contain unbound variables. Roughly speaking, the support of a goal is the set of literals that are to be verified in order to prove the goal. A goal can only be verified, if the literals in its support hold in the context. Hence, starting from the support of G, the problem of deriving G from the context is reduced to pattern matching against the current context. This is formalized by the following lemma describing the validity of a goal G given a policy and a context.

Lemma 1. *Let P be a set of implication rules of a policy and let C be a context. Then $P \cup C \models G$ iff there exists a support S of G from P and a substitution σ such that $S\sigma \subseteq C$.*

Resulting Actions. Now, since we expressed what satifies the event part and the condition part of a reactive rule, we define our language's semantics by stating which actions are executed and which messages are exchanged given a certain policy, a local state, and a history of events and exchanged messages. The formal framework consists of the following components:

- a (global) *history* (of message/signal exchanges) $\mathcal{H}$;
- a mapping *Pol* associating each peer p to a policy $Pol(p)$;
- a mapping *Ctx* that for each peer p and time t returns a context $Ctx(p,t)$ (called the *negotiation state*);
- a *multiset* of *pending rules* $Pending(p,t)$ for each peer p and time point t;
- a set of *executed actions* $Exe(p,t)$ for each peer p and time point t.

The history $\mathcal{H}$ is a finite set of *messages* $\langle p_1, p_2, M, t \rangle$, where p_1 is the sender, p_2 is the recipient, M is the message content, and $t \in \mathbb{N}$ represents a time point.

Beyond the agents potentially participating in negotiations, the set of peers also comprises some special peers called *environmental peers* that represent the system and the environment in which the system is situated. Environmental peers account for *signals*: events that are not requests or disclosures generated by an agent in the system. Examples for signals are notifications about environmental changes, updates in an RDF document, an arriving call, or the change of the on line status of a peer. The set of possible messages comprises:

- *signals* where M is a ground event and p_1 is an environmental peer;
- *requests* where $M = \langle G, FilteredPol \rangle$; intuitively, p_1 asks p_2 for evidence that can help in proving G from the filtered Policy *FilteredPol*;
- *disclosures* where M is a context consisting of a logical description of a set of credentials and declarations.

The system behavior is constrained as follows:

Pending and executing rules. At any time, a *signal* may activate a reactive rule thus making the rule pending; i.e., its condition part needs to be evaluated as a goal against the set of implication rules (see Lemma 1). This has several effects, including the start of a negotiation. Formally, for all signals $\langle p_1, p_2, e, t \rangle \in \mathcal{H}$ (where e is an event) and for all pending rules $R = (\text{ON } e' \text{ IF } G \text{ DO } a)$ in $Pol(p_2)$ such that $e \vdash_{Pol(p_2)} e_A$ and $mgu(e_A, e') = \sigma$, if $G\sigma$ has at least one support from $Pol(p_2)$ then it holds that:

- p_2 has to request for evidences that are to be provided by other peers. Or, more formally, there have to be requests for all peers p_3 occurring in some support of $G\sigma$ from $Pol(p_2)$. Further, $\mathcal{H}$ must contain a request $\langle p_2, p_3, \langle G\sigma, FilteredPol \rangle, t' \rangle$ (with $t' < t$), where *FilteredPol* is a filtering of $Pol(p_2)$ satisfying the faithfulness condition below. To identify correctly the recipients p_3, the first argument of all **credential** and **declaration** atoms must be ground in all supports (guaranteed by the call-safeness conditions discussed later in the paper)

– the set of pending rules is cumulative, that is $Pending(p_2, t) := Pending(p_2, t-1) \uplus \{R\sigma\}$ for all R that are pending at time t.[4]

If $G\sigma$ does not have any support, that is, if the condition part of R is not fulfilled, then the event e does not cause the execution of the pending rule R.

Faithfulness. Filtered policies always correctly approximate the real policy in the following sense: for all requests $\langle p_1, p_2, \langle G, FilteredPol \rangle, t \rangle \in \mathcal{H}$, and for all contexts C, it holds that

$$FilteredPol \cup C \models G \text{ implies } Pol(p_1) \cup C \models G.$$

Note that the converse is not required to hold: not all conclusions that are valid in $Pol(p_1) \cup C$ also hold in the filtered version $FilteredPol \cup C$. This is due to the fact that policy filtering may remove relevant information from $Pol(p_1)$ during filtering either for confidentiality or efficiency (see Section 2.1).

Disclosure Safety. Each disclosure during a negotiation process must be authorized by the local policy. Formally, for all $\langle p_1, p_2, C, t \rangle \in \mathcal{H}$ (where C is a context), and for all atoms $P(p_1, e) \in C$ where $P \in \{\texttt{credential}, \texttt{declaration}\}$,

$$Pol(p_1) \cup Ctx(p_1, t) \models allow(release(e)).$$

Relevance. No evidence should be disclosed without need, that is, all disclosed evidence should be relevant to some previous request. Our notion of relevance is justified by Lemma 1: since all the proofs of a goal G depend on some support, we require all disclosed evidence to occur in some of those supports. Formally, for all disclosures $\langle p_1, p_2, C, t \rangle \in \mathcal{H}$ (where C is a context), and for all atoms $P(p_1, e) \in C$ where $P \in \{\texttt{credential}, \texttt{declaration}\}$, there exists a time point $t' < t$ and a request $\langle p_2, p_1, \langle G, FilteredPol \rangle, t' \rangle \in \mathcal{H}$ such that $P(p_1, e)$ belongs to a support of G from $FilteredPol$.

Evidence acquisition. The context is cumulative as well, that is, facts are never removed from the context.[5] Formally, $Ctx(p, t) := Ctx(p, t-1) \cup \bigcup \{C \mid \langle p_1, p, C, t \rangle \in \mathcal{H}\}$.

Execution Safety. $Exe(p, t)$ is the set of all actions that are executed as a result of a pending rule's successful evaluation. Formally, $Exe(p, t)$ is the set of all actions a such that for some $R = (\texttt{ON } e \texttt{ IF } G \texttt{ DO } a_1, \ldots, a_n)$ in $Pending(p, t)$, the following two conditions hold

---

[4] In a real system, pending rules may not always be simply accumulated: they may be eliminated when the corresponding negotiations terminate or a timeout occurs. For the sake of simplicity we make this conceptual simplification.

[5] This is again a conceptual simplification: in real systems the elements of a context are first cryptographically verified, and—as a consequence—some may be discarded and thus removed from the set of facts in the context; moreover, context elements may be eliminated when the corresponding credential expires.

1. $Pol(p) \cup Ctx(p,t) \models G$
2. $Pol(p) \cup Ctx(p,t) \models allow(execute(a))$.

All other reactive rules remain pending. Accordingly, $Pending(p, t+1)$ is the multiset of all rules of $Pending(p,t)$ such that either G or $allow(execute(a))$ is not a logical consequence of $Pol(p) \cup Ctx(p,t)$.

Call Safeness. As it has been stated before, the peer responsible for providing a state predicate has to be instantiated (grounded) in some argument of the atom. For defining this formally, we introduce call safeness as follows.

A *call typing* is a mapping τ : Pred $\rightarrow \wp(\mathbb{N})$ that associates each predicate symbol p to a set of argument indexes. Intuitively, if $\tau(p) = \{1,3\}$ then the first and third argument are going to be ground in each call to p. We require that $\tau(\texttt{credential}) = \tau(\texttt{declaration}) = \{1\}$.

We extend τ to atoms in the natural way: If $\tau(p) = \{i_1, \ldots, i_k\}$ then for all atoms $A = p(t_1, \ldots, t_n)$ let $\tau(A) = \{t_{i_1}, \ldots, t_{i_k}\}$.

An implication rule R with head A is *call safe* iff for all atoms B occurring in the body of R and for all variables X occurring in B, $X \in \tau(B)$ implies $X \in \tau(A)$.

Moreover, a goal G is *call safe* iff for all atoms A occurring in G, $\tau(A)$ is ground.

Proposition 1. *If a goal G is call safe, then all of its supports from a call safe program are call safe, too. In particular, the first arguments of all* credential *and* declaration *predicates in the support are ground.*

A *reactive* rule ON e IF G DO a is *call safe* iff for all atoms B occurring in G and for all variables $X \in \tau(B)$, X occurs in e.

This guarantees that the most general unifier of e and the occurred event makes G call safe and, consequently, all credential and declaration predicates in G are associated to specific agents. This condition ensures that at any stage during a negotiation, the receivers of request messages are determined.

3 Implementation

In this section we describe how the approach of reactive policies has been successfully used to provide advanced privacy control for the Social Network and communication tool Skype. Our policy framework allows to enforce policies on Skype such as the one given in Figure 1: calls, notifications, and chat messages are either accepted or initiated only if certain conditions are fulfilled.

Example policies and features exploited. The following example policies show how the features presented in the previous sections are exploited for our scenario. **(A)** Notifications about on line status changes are only shown for specific persons, who may be tagged as family members on some Social Platform. **(B)** Or such notifications are shown if people change the status who can prove that they belong to a certain company by disclosing a company member credential. **(C)** Chat messages may only be accepted if the local computer is not in presentation mode. **(D)** Another way of controlling incoming messages is to require the sender to provide a password before the message shows up.

The use of external Social Semantic Web data is exploited in Example A (retrieve person tags from Social Platforms). Example B requires credential exchange and trust negotiation to ensure a policy aware disclosure of company credentials. Example C integrates external information from the local client into the policy decision process and Example D exploits the declaration predicate for automatically retrieving a password. The policy rule from example D looks as follows:

$$
\begin{aligned}
&\texttt{ON chatArrives(Time, Chat, Sender)} \\
&\texttt{IF declaration(Sender, password} = \texttt{A)}, \\
&\quad \texttt{not (A} =' \texttt{let\_me\_in')} \\
&\texttt{DO reject(Chat)}.
\end{aligned}
\tag{6}
$$

Those examples fit the scenario of Skype, however, our framework plugged into other systems offers other potentials as mentioned in Section 1, such as the automated rebooking of flights according to user preferences and time schedule (e.g., retrieved from a PIM[6]) [4].

Architecture. We implemented our framework on top of the policy engine Protune[7]. We further developed a Skype plugin that (1) observes events from Skype and passes them to the policy engine, (2) uses the Skype-inherent application channel[8] for transferring negotiation messages and (3) performs actions in Skype, such as cancelling a call, changing the mood message, or sending a chat message. The result was a tool called SPoX (Skype Policy Extension) [22], a reactive policy engine that is influencing the behaviour of a Skype client. For more details about this tool we refer the reader to [22] and to www.L3S.de/ $\sim$kaerger/SPoX, due to space restrictions we will focus in this section on some particular features of this tool directly related to the interplay of reactivity and negotiation handling.

Credentials and declarations. In SPoX, the concept of declarations is used to link users across different Social Web platforms. One can state, for example, that only Flickr friends are allowed to call. In order to find out if a caller is a Flickr friend, a state predicate $flickrName(Peer, Name)$ is used that, according to the semantics definition (see Lemma 1), leads to a request to the call initiator. The SPoX client on the caller's peer will receive the request for the declaration and, if provided by the caller, will send back the instantiated fact thus disclosing her Flickr name. Of course, disclosing the Flickr name can again be protected

---

[6] Personal Information Manager (e.g., Outlook)
[7] www.L3S.de/protune
[8] This channel is typically used for game information,
   see http://skype.easybits.com/

by a policy and would lead to a multistep negotiation. It has to be noted that for such a declaration there is no easy way to verify if a requester's Flickr name is actually the one provided. However, there are technologies such as OpenID that provide solutions in this case. Digitally signed credentials can be used used as well in SPoX as strong authentication in a similar way. Those credentials are as well transferred using the Skype application channel, e.g., for proving that someone is a student (see the example in Figure 1).

The Social Web as negotiation context. As described in Section 2.2, external sources can be easily integrated in the reasoning process and the gathered facts become part of the context as soon as they are required to make a goal true. In SPoX we exploited this concept for integrating arbitrary external Social Web sources into the negotiation process, such as DBLP (in order to prove co-authorship relations), FOAF, Twitter (to prove if someone is following me), Flickr, and Skype (e.g., prove if somebody is a contact or blocked). Also an extension for gathering social data from any OpenSocial[9] platform has been recently added (cf. [24]).

In conclusion, a combination of reactive behaviour description, Semantic Web data and trust negotiation, as it is needed for an advanced policy control in Skype, is provided by our interplay of triggering events and negotiation message exchange. Our formal model ensures that any action taken in Skype fulfills the given policies, either by adding facts gathered from the Semantic Web to the negotiation state or by exchanging evidences thus mutually and automatically establishing trust among Skype peers.

4   Related Work

The concept of reactive Semantic Web policies touches two research areas: advanced policy reasoning and trust management on the one side and reactive rules on the Web on the other. In the following, we will detail related approaches from both areas separately. As a third category, we compare our approach to general policy languages that support a certain notion of reactivity.

Reactivity on the Web. Adding declarative, reactive rules to enrich systems with reactivity features has been extensively studied in the 90s in the area of database systems, with the introduction of Active Databases [32]. Later, in order to specify the reactive behavior of Semantic Web agents, the concept of Reactivity on the (Semantic) Web has been introduced in several publications [19,27,26,5]. Several frameworks have been developed for reactive rules on the Semantic Web, e.g., r^3 [2] and MARS [9]. Although these approaches share our strategy to provide reasoners for reactive rules, a general difference is that the present work adds a level of trust on top of reactive rule reasoning by an explicit handling of credentials, interactions among agents, contextual disclosure of information and the exchange of policies and evidences.

---

[9] See **www.opensocial.org**

Semantic Web policies. Among the most prominent Semantic Web policy languages there are KAoS [16], Rei [20], and Protune [12]. These policy languages allow for automated reasoning in order to enforce a policy and, with most of them, policies can also be exchanged between entities [7,10,12,17] which is essential for automated agent interaction and negotiations on the Semantic Web. Therefore, they are typically based on languages with well-defined semantics and interoperable formats; that is in most of the cases description logics (e.g., KAoS and Rei) or rule-based semantics (e.g., Cassandra [7], Peertrust, and Protune).[10] However, the semantics of current Semantic Web policy languages is restricted to definitions of the conditions to be fulfilled in order to make a decision. In contrast, the present approach combines handling of general events and triggering of reactions with trust negotiation and credential exchange.

Policies and reactivity. There are other policy languages that do not appear in the realm of the Semantic Web and some of them support a certain level of reactivity. Ponder [15] (and its successor Ponder2 [31]) is a policy language for pervasive systems that supports—beyond classical authorization policies— reactive obligation policies. Those obligation policies are specifically used to trigger internal auditing if a security violation happens and are not meant to react to external events. Ponder does also not feature agent interaction and misses a well-defined semantics. Contrarily, PDL (Policy Description Language) [25] is a policy language based on ECA rules that provides a well-defined semantics. PDL, similar to Ponder, does not feature agent interaction or other trust establishing techniques. It further restricts actions to contain only constants and thus does not allow for variable bindings crossing events, condition, and action expressions.

5   Conclusions

Reactive Semantic Web policies combine the features of reactive behaviour control on the Web with the trust and security features of advanced policies. Automatically guiding a system's behaviour on the Semantic Web does not only need an advanced reactive rules reasoner incorporating arbitrary, heterogeneous data sources, it also needs to consider the upper most layers in the Semantic Web stack: obeying as well as enforcing Semantic Web policies, automated agreement with other systems and trusted interactions with Semantic Web agents. In this paper, we describe a policy language that allows to define reactive behaviour control in a declarative way and that features advanced trust negotiation based on exchanges of evidences and policies. We gave a formal definition of our language's semantics and defined how the exchange of information may lead to an establishing of trust. We successfully exploited our approach to enforce reactive Semantic Web policies in the Social Network and communication tool Skype.

---

[10] For a more comprehensive overview and comparison of policy languages we refer the reader to [14].

References

1. Abel, F., De Coi, J.L., Henze, N., Koesling, A.W., Krause, D., Olmedilla, D.: Enabling advanced and context-dependent access control in rdf stores. In: Aberer, K., Choi, K.-S., Noy, N., Allemang, D., Lee, K.-I., Nixon, L.J.B., Golbeck, J., Mika, P., Maynard, D., Mizoguchi, R., Schreiber, G., Cudré-Mauroux, P. (eds.) ASWC 2007 and ISWC 2007. LNCS, vol. 4825, pp. 1–14. Springer, Heidelberg (2007)
2. Alferes, J.J., Amador, R.: r^3- A foundational ontology for reactive rules. In: Meersman, R., Tari, Z. (eds.) ODBASE'07. LNCS, vol. 4803, pp. 933–952. Springer, Heidelberg (2007)
3. Alferes, J.J., Amador, R., Kärger, P., Olmedilla, D.: Towards reactive semantic web policies: Advanced agent control for the semantic web. In: Sheth, A.P., Staab, S., Dean, M., Paolucci, M., Maynard, D., Finin, T., Thirunarayan, K. (eds.) ISWC 2008. LNCS, vol. 5318. Springer, Heidelberg (2008)
4. Alferes, J.J., Amador, R., Kärger, P., Olmedilla, D.: Towards reactive semantic web policies—motivation scenario and implementation details. Technical report, L3S Research Center (October 2008),
   http://www.L3S.de/~kaerger/reports/reactive_policies.pdf
5. Alferes, J.J., May, W.: Evolution and reactivity for the web. In: Reasoning Web, pp. 134–172 (2005)
6. Baral, C.: Knowledge representation, reasoning and declarative problem solving. Cambridge University Press, Cambridge (2003)
7. Becker, M.Y., Sewell, P.: Cassandra: Distributed access control policies with tunable expressiveness. In: POLICY 2004 (2004)
8. Behrends, E., Fritzen, O., May, W., Schenk, F.: Combining eca rules with process algebras for the semantic web. In: RuleML, pp. 29–38 (2006)
9. Behrends, E., Fritzen, O., May, W., Schubert, D.: An eca engine for deploying heterogeneous component languages in the semantic web. In: Grust, T., Höpfner, H., Illarramendi, A., Jablonski, S., Mesiti, M., Müller, S., Patranjan, P.-L., Sattler, K.-U., Spiliopoulou, M., Wijsen, J. (eds.) EDBT 2006. LNCS, vol. 4254, pp. 887–898. Springer, Heidelberg (2006)
10. Bonatti, P.A., Samarati, P.: Regulating service access and information release on the web. In: CCS 2000, pp. 134–143. ACM Press, New York (2000)
11. Bonatti, P.A., Duma, C., Fuchs, N., Nejdl, W., Olmedilla, D., Peer, J., Shahmehri, N.: Semantic web policies - a discussion of requirements and research issues. In: Sure, Y., Domingue, J. (eds.) ESWC 2006. LNCS, vol. 4011, pp. 712–724. Springer, Heidelberg (2006)
12. Bonatti, P.A., Olmedilla, D.: Driving and monitoring provisional trust negotiation with metapolicies. In: 6th IEEE Policies for Distributed Systems and Networks (POLICY 2005), Stockholm, Sweden, June 2005, pp. 14–23. IEEE Computer Society, Los Alamitos (2005)
13. De Coi, J.L., Olmedilla, D.: A flexible policy-driven trust negotiation model. In: IEEE/WIC/ACM International Conference on Intelligent Agent Technology, Silicon Valley, CA, USA (November 2007)
14. De Coi, J.L., Olmedilla, D.: A review of trust management, security and privacy policy languages. In: International Conference on Security and Cryptography (SECRYPT 2008). INSTICC Press (July 2008)
15. Damianou, N., Dulay, N., Lupu, E., Sloman, M.: The ponder policy specification language. In: Sloman, M., Lobo, J., Lupu, E.C. (eds.) POLICY 2001. LNCS, vol. 1995, pp. 18–38. Springer, Heidelberg (2001)

16. Uszok, A., et al.: Kaos policy and domain services: Toward a description-logic approach to policy representation, deconfliction, and enforcement. In: POLICY 2003 (2003)
17. Gavriloaie, R., Nejdl, W., Olmedilla, D., Seamons, K.E., Winslett, M.: No registration needed: How to use declarative policies and negotiation to access sensitive resources on the semantic web. In: Bussler, C.J., Davies, J., Fensel, D., Studer, R. (eds.) ESWS 2004. LNCS, vol. 3053, pp. 342–356. Springer, Heidelberg (2004)
18. Gehani, N.H., Jagadish, H.V., Shmueli, O.: Composite event specification in active databases: Model and implementation. In: 18th VLDB Conference (1992)
19. Grust, T., Höpfner, H., Illarramendi, A., Jablonski, S., Mesiti, M., Müller, S., Patranjan, P.-L., Sattler, K.-U., Spiliopoulou, M., Wijsen, J. (eds.): EDBT 2006. LNCS, vol. 4254. Springer, Heidelberg (2006)
20. Kagal, L., Finin, T.W., Joshi, A.: A policy based approach to security for the semantic web. In: Fensel, D., Sycara, K., Mylopoulos, J. (eds.) ISWC 2003. LNCS, vol. 2870, pp. 402–418. Springer, Heidelberg (2003)
21. Kärger, P.: Advanced semantic web policies: Evolution reactivities, and priorities. In: Sheth, A.P., Staab, S., Dean, M., Paolucci, M., Maynard, D., Finin, T., Thirunarayan, K. (eds.) ISWC 2008. LNCS, vol. 5318. Springer, Heidelberg (2008)
22. Kärger, P., Kigel, E., Jaltar, V.Y.: Spox: combining reactive semantic web policies and social semantic data to control the behaviour of skype. In: Bernstein, A., Karger, D.R., Heath, T., Feigenbaum, L., Maynard, D., Motta, E., Thirunarayan, K. (eds.) ISWC 2009. LNCS, vol. 5823. Springer, Heidelberg (2009)
23. Kärger, P., Kigel, E., Olmedilla, D.: Reactivity and social data: Keys to drive decisions in social network applications (2009)
24. Kärger, P., Siberski, W.: Guarding a walled garden - semantic privacy preferences for the social web. In: Proceedings of the 7th Extended Semantic Web Conference. Springer, Heidelberg (2010)
25. Lobo, J., Bhatia, R., Naqvi, S.: A policy description language. In: Proc. of AAAI, pp. 291–298 (1999)
26. May, W., Alferes, J.J., Bry, F.: Towards generic query, update, and event languages for the semantic web. In: Ohlbach, H.J., Schaffert, S. (eds.) PPSWR 2004. LNCS, vol. 3208, pp. 19–33. Springer, Heidelberg (2004)
27. Papamarkos, G., Poulovassilis, A., Wood, P.T.: Event-condition-action rule languages for the semantic web. In: Cruz, I.F., Kashyap, V., Decker, S., Eckstein, R. (eds.) SWDB, pp. 309–327 (2003)
28. Seneviratne, O., Kagal, L., Berners-Lee, T.: Policy-aware content reuse on the web. In: Bernstein, A., Karger, D.R., Heath, T., Feigenbaum, L., Maynard, D., Motta, E., Thirunarayan, K. (eds.) ISWC 2009. LNCS, vol. 5823, pp. 553–568. Springer, Heidelberg (2009)
29. Subrahmanian, V.S., Bonatti, P.A., Dix, J., Eiter, T., Kraus, S., Ozcan, F., Ross, R.B.: Heterogenous Active Agents. MIT Press, Cambridge (2000)
30. Tonti, G., Bradshaw, J.M., Jeffers, R., Montanari, R., Suri, N., Uszok, A.: Semantic web languages for policy representation and reasoning: A comparison of KAoS, Rei, and Ponder. In: Fensel, D., Sycara, K., Mylopoulos, J. (eds.) ISWC 2003. LNCS, vol. 2870, pp. 419–437. Springer, Heidelberg (2003)
31. Twidle, K.P., Lupu, E., Dulay, N., Sloman, M.: Ponder2 - a policy environment for autonomous pervasive systems. In: POLICY (2008)
32. Widom, J., Ceri, S. (eds.): Active Database Systems: Triggers and Rules For Advanced Database Processing. Morgan Kaufmann, San Francisco (1996)
33. Winslett, M.: An introduction to trust negotiation. In: Nixon, P., Terzis, S. (eds.) iTrust 2003. LNCS, vol. 2692, pp. 275–283. Springer, Heidelberg (2003)

Categorize by: Deductive Aggregation of Semantic Web Query Results

Claudia d'Amato[1], Nicola Fanizzi[1], and Agnieszka Ławrynowicz[2]

[1] Dipartimento di Informatica, Universita degli Studi di Bari, Italy
{claudia.damato,fanizzi}@di.uniba.it
[2] Institute of Computing Science, Poznan University of Technology, Poland
alawrynowicz@cs.put.poznan.pl

Abstract. Query answering on a wide and heterogeneous environment such as the Web can return a large number of results that can be hardly manageable by users/agents. The adoption of grouping criteria of the results could be of great help. Up to date, most of the proposed methods for aggregating results on the (Semantic) Web are mainly grounded on syntactic approaches. However, they could not be of significant help, when the values instantiating a grouping criterion are all equal (thus creating a unique group) or are almost all different (thus creating one group for each answer). We propose a novel approach that is able to overcome such drawbacks: given a query in the form of a conjunctive query, grouping is grounded on the exploitation of the semantics of background ontologies during the aggregation of query results. Specifically, we propose a solution where answers are deductively grouped taking into account the subsumption hierarchy of the underlying knowledge base. In this way, the results can be shown and navigated similarly to a faceted search. An experimental evaluation of the proposed method is also reported.

1 Introduction

The users of the (Semantic) Web often perform interactive, and exploratory data retrieval, where queries often result in an overwhelming number of the returned answers. However typically, only a small part of the result set is relevant to the user thus making necessary the analysis of the retrieved results to identify those relevant ones. This phenomenon, known as *information overload*, constitutes a ceaseless challenge for researchers. It may occur in situations when the user, at the beginning of a search, submits a broad query to avoid exclusion of possibly interesting results, only further possibly reformulating it into a more precise narrower query. It is also inherent to the task of browsing through a collection of resources instead of searching among them. Manually separating the interesting items from the uninteresting ones is a tedious and time consuming job. For this reason, various services have been set up to manage the information overload. They may be categorized as variations of two complementary approaches: (a) predefined category structures; (b) fully automatic search engines.

Predefined category structures are maintained by humans, who organize resources into a hierarchy, grouping appropriate ones together under a meaningful

L. Aroyo et al. (Eds.): ESWC 2010, Part I, LNCS 6088, pp. 91–105, 2010.

category description. This is meant to support user browsing activity. The main drawback of such an approach is that the categories are frequently obsolete, since they are not updated so quickly as new documents and new topics appear. In turn, the mechanisms used by automatic search engines, enable them to stay relatively up-to-date, what makes the search engines the premier choice for most Web users. However, when the number of the results is huge, even despite their ranked order, manually investigating them is a big effort without any additional navigation tools. In order to facilitate browsing and managing results of a Web search/query, methods for grouping answers on the ground of user defined criteria would be exploited.

In this paper, we propose to marry the benefits of two complementary approaches for handling information overload by offering a method that, given a query in the form of a conjunctive query [1,2,3,4,5], produces a dynamic categorization over ranked query results. The key feature of the method is in the exploitation of the *semantics* of knowledge bases of reference (in the form of ontologies) for grouping results with respect to a user defined criteria. Specifically, given a certain grouping criterion, expressed as a (complex) concept from a knowledge base of reference, results are grouped in agreement with (part of) the subsumption hierarchy deductively obtained by considering the specified concept and the given ontology.

Currently, besides of the usual syntactic based approach (grounded on the use of keywords) adopted by the main Web search engines such as Google or Yahoo, the other approaches that are generally exploited for grouping structured query answers are based on the semantics drawn from SQL, the standard language for querying relational databases. An example is given by the implementation of the aggregation operators (COUNT, MIN, MAX, AVG, SUM, GROUP BY) for SPARQL in Virtuoso[1]. However, besides of the fact that these implementations are not part of the SPARQL standard, these latter approaches (differently from the method that we propose) do not assume to perform any reasoning involving background knowledge during the query results aggregation, and as such they are purely syntactic as well. The same happens for grouping/aggregating features that are to be included in the ongoing SPARQL 2 standard.

The main contributions of the paper are summarized as follows: (a) we introduce a novel way for grouping query answers (*semantic grouping*) where grouping is done on the ground of a knowledge base of reference; (b) we propose a technique for aggregating query results consisting on a dynamic generation of a navigable hierarchy on top of the retrieved results, that is based on their semantics. Such a hierarchy constitutes a multi-valued classification of the results that may be seen as a novel approach for generating a *dynamic faceted classification* over retrieved results, enabling further faceted search/browsing over them; (c) we present the experimental results of the application of our proposed method to ontologies expressed in *Web Ontology Language (OWL)*[2], whose semantics is based on *description logic (DL)* [6].

---

[1] http://virtuoso.openlinksw.com/
[2] http://www.w3.org/TR/owl-features/

The rest of the paper is organized as follows. In Sect. 2, a motivating example for our work is presented. In Sect. 3, we introduce the basics of the knowledge representation formalism of choice: description logics and the notion of conjunctive queries over DL knowledge bases. In Sect. 4, we present our proposed approach. Sect. 5 reports on the experimental evaluation of our method while Sect. 6 discusses the work related to ours. In Sect. 7, conclusions are drawn.

2   Motivating Example

Let us discuss the need for and advantage of semantic query answer aggregation on the ground of a motivating example.

Example 1 (Motivating scenario). Maria and Sebastian are searching for a weekend break offer. In order to get faster insight into the results retrieved by their query, they would like to have the answers grouped by a destination criterion. After getting first insight into the results, they perform further exploration, submitting another, most specific query for destinations located in mountains, and for budget accommodations offered in these destinations with a request to group the results w.r.t. destinations, and additionally w.r.t. accommodations offered.

Let us suppose that there is a Web service that exploits a SPARQL endpoint that retrieves the results from Semantic Web datasets. Furthermore the Web service uses an ontology as background knowledge on the given domain (an instance is presented in Example 3). In the following, instances of SPARQL queries for the user needs illustrated in Example 1 are shown.

Example 2 (Example queries in SPARQL syntax).
$Q_{1\_group\_by}$ = SELECT ?x ?y WHERE { ?x rdf:type :WeekendBreakOffer .
?x :hasDestination ?y } GROUP BY ?y
$Q_{2\_group\_by}$ = SELECT ?x ?y ?z WHERE { ?x rdf:type :WeekendBreakOffer.
?x :hasDestination ?y . ?y :locatedIn ?v . ?v rdf:type :Mountains .
?x :hasAccomodation ?z . ?z rdf:type :BudgetAccomodation } GROUP BY ?y ?z

Let us assume an application of the classical semantics of the GROUP BY clause known from SQL in the evaluation of the query Q_1. Let us assume further that instances that bind to variable y are town names. In such a case, the results will be partitioned so that one row for each town name is created. Considering that there may be possibly many towns satisfying the query conditions, there will be also too many groups to provide significant added value.

Note also that classical semantics of GROUP BY clause, which is to partition the results by identical values, disregards the presence of any background knowledge, even if there is available some. Consider for example that the towns are annotated by terms from the ontology such as City, EuropeanDestination, ItalianDestination, PolishDestination. Considering such annotations as a grouping condition, it would be possible to aggregate the results into a smaller number of 'semantic' groups. The classical semantics of GROUP BY disregards also semantic relationships between groups like subclass-superclass relation (e.g. ItalianDestination, and EuropeanDestination). Exploiting the background ontology would enable making such relations explicit.

Another problem with the syntactic approach may happen when all the results in the grouping condition, e.g. all destinations in our case, refer to the same town. This gives as grouping result a unique row which synthesizes all instances, thus giving almost null information.

Summarizing, a merely syntactic approach, as the one used by the GROUP BY clause in the database context, could not be of great help when many destinations are found, or when the results refer to the same destination. To manage situations like these, a *semantic group by* could be adopted, namely a method that is able to group query results on the ground of a knowledge base of reference.

3   Preliminaries

3.1   Representation and Inference

Description logics (DLs) [6] are a family of knowledge representation languages (endowed with a model-theoretic semantics and reasoning services) that have been adopted as theoretical foundation for OWL language.Basic elements in DLs are: *atomic concepts* (denoted by A), and *atomic roles* (denoted by R, S). *Complex descriptions* (denoted by C and D) are inductively built by using concept and role *constructors*.

Semantics is defined by *interpretations* $\mathcal{I}=(\Delta^{\mathcal{I}}, \cdot^{\mathcal{I}})$, where non-empty set $\Delta^{\mathcal{I}}$ is the domain of the interpretation and $\cdot^{\mathcal{I}}$ is an interpretation function which assigns to every atomic concept A a set $A^{\mathcal{I}} \subseteq \Delta^{\mathcal{I}}$, and to every atomic role R a binary relation $R^{\mathcal{I}} \subseteq \Delta^{\mathcal{I}} \times \Delta^{\mathcal{I}}$. The interpretation function is extended to complex concept descriptions by the inductive definition as presented in Tab. 1. A DL *knowledge base*, KB, is formally defined as: $\mathcal{KB} = (\mathcal{T}, \mathcal{A})$, where $\mathcal{T}$ is called a TBox, and it contains axioms dealing with how concepts and roles are related to each other, such as those, used further in the paper, defining role domain, and role range, written $\mathsf{Domain}(R, C)$ (where $(a, b) \in R^{\mathcal{I}}$ implies $a \in C^{\mathcal{I}}$), $\mathsf{Range}(R, C)$ (where $(a, b) \in R^{\mathcal{I}}$ implies $b \in C^{\mathcal{I}}$), and where $\mathcal{A}$ is called an ABox, and it contains assertions about individuals such as $C(a)$ (that means the invidual a is an instance of the concept C) and $R(a, b)$ (a is R-related to b).

As regards the inference services, we recall the definition of *instance-checking* and *subsumption* that are further used in the paper. *Instance-checking* amounts

Table 1. Syntax and semantics of example DL constructors

Constructor	Syntax	Semantics
Universal concept	$\top$	$\Delta^{\mathcal{I}}$
Bottom concept	$\bot$	$\emptyset$
Negation of arbitrary concepts	$(\neg C)$	$\Delta^{\mathcal{I}} \backslash C^{\mathcal{I}}$
Intersection	$(C \sqcap D)$	$C^{\mathcal{I}} \cap D^{\mathcal{I}}$
Union	$(C \sqcup D)$	$C^{\mathcal{I}} \cup D^{\mathcal{I}}$
Value restriction	$(\forall R.C)$	$\{a \in \Delta^{\mathcal{I}} \mid \forall b.(a, b) \in R^{\mathcal{I}} \rightarrow b \in C^{\mathcal{I}}\}$
Full existential quantification	$(\exists R.C)$	$\{a \in \Delta^{\mathcal{I}} \mid \exists b.(a, b) \in R^{\mathcal{I}} \wedge b \in C^{\mathcal{I}}\}$

to determine whether an individual, say a, belongs to a concept extension, i.e. whether $C(a)$ holds for a certain concept C. As regards *subsumption*, given two concept descriptions C and D in a TBox $\mathcal{T}$, C subsumes D (denoted by $D \sqsubseteq C$) if and only if, for every interpretation $\mathcal{I}$ of $\mathcal{T}$ it holds that $D^{\mathcal{I}} \subseteq C^{\mathcal{I}}$. C equivalent to D (denoted by $C \equiv D$) amounts to $C \sqsubseteq D$ and $D \sqsubseteq C$.

3.2   Conjunctive Queries

Queries admitted in this work are expressed in the form of *conjunctive queries* [1,2,3,4,5]. Let N_C, N_R, N_I be the sets of *concept names, role names* and *individual names* respectively and let N_V be a countably infinite set of variables disjoint from N_C, N_R, and N_I. Let by $\mathbf{x}$ and $\mathbf{y}$ denote the sets of distinguished and nondistinguished variables, respectively, where $\mathbf{x}, \mathbf{y} \subseteq N_V$. A conjunctive query, denoted with $Q(\mathbf{x}, \mathbf{y})$, is the finite conjunction of a non-empty set of *atoms*. An *atom* is an expression of kind $A(t_1)$ (concept atom) or $R(t_1, t_2)$ (role atom), where A is a concept name, R is a role name, and t_1 and t_2 are individuals from N_I or variables from $\mathbf{x}$ or $\mathbf{y}$.

An answer to a query $Q(\mathbf{x}, \mathbf{y})$ w.r.t. KB is an assignment θ of individuals to distinguished variables such that $KB \models \exists \mathbf{y} : Q(\mathbf{x}\theta, \mathbf{y})$.

Example 3 (Conj. Query). Given the following knowledge base:

$\mathcal{T} = \{$ City $\sqsubseteq$ Destination, EuropeanDestination $\sqsubseteq$ Destination, ItalianDestination $\sqsubseteq$ EuropeanDestination, PolishDestination $\sqsubseteq$ EuropeanDestination, Hotel $\sqsubseteq$ Accomodation, BudgetAccomodation $\sqsubseteq$ Accomodation, B&B $\sqsubseteq$ BudgetAccomodation, Hostel $\sqsubseteq$ BudgetAccomodation, SkiingSite $\sqsubseteq$ Site, SightSeeingSite $\sqsubseteq$ Site, $\top \sqsubseteq \forall$ hasSite.Site, $\top \sqsubseteq \forall$ hasDestination.Destination, $\top \sqsubseteq \forall$ hasAccomodation.Accomodation$\}$.

$\mathcal{A} = \{$ locatedIn(ZAKOPANE, TATRA),hasSite(ZAKOPANE, SKI_LIFTS_NOSAL), SkiingSite(SKI_LIFTS_NOSAL), locatedIn(CHOCHOLOW, TATRA), hasSite(CHOCHOLOW, HIGHLANDERS_WOODEN_HOUSES), SightSeeingSite(HIGHLANDERS_WOODEN_HOUSES), Mountains(TATRA), locatedIn(TRENTO, ALPS), Mountains(ALPS), WeekendBreakOffer(O1), hasAccomodation(O1,A1), B&B(A1), hasDestination(O1, ZAKOPANE),PolishDestination(ZAKOPANE), WeekendBreakOffer(O2),hasAccomodation(O2,A2),B&B(A2), hasDestination(O2, CHOCHOLOW), PolishDestination(CHOCHOLOW), WeekendBreakOffer(O3),hasAccomodation(O3,A3),Hostel(A3), hasDestination(O3, TRENTO), ItalianDestination(TRENTO),City(TRENTO) $\}$.

we formalize conjunctive queries corresponding to the ones from Example 2 as:
$$Q_1(x,y) = \text{WeekendBreakOffer}(x) \wedge \text{hasDestination}(x,y)$$

$Q_2(x,y,z) = \text{WeekendBreakOffer}(x) \wedge \text{hasDestination}(x,y) \wedge \text{locatedIn}(y,v) \wedge \text{Mountains}(v) \wedge \text{hasAccomodation}(x,z) \wedge \text{BudgetAccomodation}(z)$

4   Deductive Aggregation: Semantic Grouping

Let us consider the knowledge base and the example queries from Example 3. Supposing the case in which many offers are available, the user would be interested in grouping the results with respect to the different destinations. However, as already discussed in the previous section, a merely syntactic approach, as the one used by the *group by* clause in the database context, could not be of great help in cases in which several destinations are found or all results refer to the same destination. In order to manage cases like this, a *semantic group by* could be adopted, namely a method that is able to group query results on the ground of a knowledge base of reference. Specifically, looking at the knowledge base in the example above, results could be grouped on the ground of the pertaining country of a destination (ItalianDestination, PolishDestination).

In this section we present a method that is able to perform the *semantic group by* on the ground of concepts that are more specific (in the knowledge base of reference) than the concept adopted by the user for grouping the results.

4.1   Basics of the Semantic Aggregation

The general idea behind *semantic group by* is to categorize the results with regard to concept hierarchies inferred for each variable appearing in a grouping condition. Thus, in order to formalize our proposition of a *semantic group by*, we introduce a special second order predicate categorize_by.

Definition 1 (categorize_by). *A conjunctive query with a* semantic aggregate subgoal *is of the form*

$$categorize\_by([X_1, X_2, ..., X_m]) : Q(\mathbf{x}, \mathbf{y})$$

where $[X_1, X_2, ..., X_m]$ *is a grouping list of variables appearing in* $\mathbf{x}$.

In Example 4 we present the conjunctive queries with the categorize_by clause for the scenario discussed throughout this paper.

Example 4 (Example queries with the categorize_by clause).

$Q_{1\_categorize\_by}(x, y) = categorize\_by(y)$: WeekendBreakOffer(x) ∧ hasDestination(x, y)

$Q_{2\_categorize\_by}(x, y, z) = categorize\_by(y, z)$: WeekendBreakOffer(x) ∧ hasDestination(x, y) ∧ locatedIn(y, v) ∧ Mountains(v) ∧ hasAccomodation(y, z) ∧ BudgetAccomodation(z)

Further, we formally define the notion of *semantic category*.

Definition 2 (Semantic category). *Given is query*

$$Q = categorize\_by([X_1, X_2, ..., X_m]) : Q(\mathbf{x}, \mathbf{y})$$

A semantic category *is a tuple of concepts* $\langle C_1, C_2, \ldots, C_m \rangle$, *where each* C_i *corresponds to* X_i *in the grouping variables list of* Q.

Semantic categories form a multi-valued classification $\mathcal{H}$, induced by a subsumption relation between concepts appearing in the same place in tuples. Then, the operational semantics for **categorize_by** clause is to first create $\mathcal{H}$, a partially ordered set of semantic categories, based on the inferred semantic types of grouping variables, and then to assign the tuples to the most specific semantic categories.

4.2   Inferring the Type of the Variables

Let v_i be a query variable used in the grouping clause of a query. For each such variable a (complex) concept C^i is derived as follows. Let B_C be a set of the concepts explicitly mentioned in the query atoms of the form $C(v_i)$, $C \in B_C$. Let B_D, and B_{Rn} be sets of the concepts inferred by the role atoms $R(v_i, \cdot)$ or $R(\cdot, v_i)$, by taking into account the domain and range of role R, respectively, $\mathsf{Domain}(R, C_D)$, $C_D \in B_D$, $\mathsf{Range}(R, C_R)$, $C_R \in B_{Rn}$. Now, let $\mathcal{B}_i := B_C \cup B_D \cup B_{Rn}$. The concept C^i is an intersection:

$$C^i := \bigcap_{C_p^i \in \mathcal{B}_i} C_p^i$$

A concept C^i corresponding to query variable v_i, included in the CATEGORIZE BY clause, is derived. Then it is classified in the subsumption hierarchy of the concepts in the knowledge base. A sub-hierarchy of concepts rooted at these concepts will be used in the next step, which determines the final multivalued classification of semantic categories used for grouping the query answers.

Example 5 (Determining the type of variable). Consider query $Q_{2\_categorize\_by}$ (x, y, z) from Example 4, and variable z appearing in the grouping variables list. Then the concept inferred for the variable z is:

$$C^z := \mathsf{Accomodation} \sqcap \mathsf{BudgetAccomodation}$$

4.3   Constructing a Tree of Semantic Categories

The primary motivation for this work is to enable better results exploration for the user by reducing information overload by means of presenting him/her the groupings of the results. From this perspective we are rather interested in some compromise between generating the complete multi-valued classification of semantic categories versus meeting the demands of a real time computation of the results, and improving the user experience, not overloading him/her with too many groupings (the initial problem). Therefore, in this work, we restrict our analysis to the case of DL concept subsumption hierarchies, and semantic category hierarchies in the form of trees. The extension of the proposed ideas to graphs is possible, although not yet considered in this paper.

Concept Hierarchy for a Single Variable. A basic approach for generating a sub-hierarchy of concepts to be rooted at the concept C^i, corresponding to a grouping variable v_i, is to reproduce a part of a classified subsumption hierarchy produced by a DL reasoner.

In some cases, however, this may not be enough to obtain a meaningful hierarchy of groups. Consider for example the situation, where the concept C^i is a leaf in the classified subsumption hierarchy, e.g. PolishDestination in the knowledge base from Example 3. Another case where this basic approach would not be of help is when all the retrieved results for variable v_i, e.g. all destinations from the discussed example, fall under the same type, e.g. again PolishDestination.

In such cases more advanced approach could be adopted, that is based on an iterative application of a concept refinement operator, for example adapted from such concept specialization operators like the ones proposed in [7,8] to the case of a purely deductive approach. The application of the refinement operator would introduce further, unnamed, complex concepts into the sub-hierarchy rooted at C^i. For example, the concept PolishDestination could be then specialized into concepts: PolishDestination ⊓ ∃hasSite.SkiingSite and PolishDestination ⊓ ∃hasSite.SightSeeingSite to differentiate two Polish destinations from the knowledge base, ZAKOPANE, and CHOCHOLOW, based on the sites they offer.

Multiple Variables: Tree Product. Let us define the subtrees trees by the quadruple (N, E, r, ℓ), where N is the set of nodes, E is the set of edges between nodes (n_a, n_b), $r \in N$ stands for the root node and ℓ is the labeling function assigning each node with the corresponding concept.

Now, let us consider the case of two variables, say v_i and v_j in the CATEGORIZE BY clause and their related subtrees, $T_i = (N_i, E_i, r_i, \ell_i)$ and $T_j = (N_j, E_j, r_j, \ell_j)$, in the subsumption hierarchy. Multiple variables will be processed by iterating the binary product operation presented in the following. A formal sketch of the algorithm is shown in Figure 1. The product $T_i \times T_j := (N_{ij}, E_{ij}, r_{ij}, \ell_{ij})$ of the two subtrees is computed recursively. The root of the product tree is made up by the node $r_{ij} = \langle r_i, r_j \rangle \in N_{ij}$ labeled with $\ell_{ij}(r_{ij}) = \langle \ell(r_i), \ell(r_j) \rangle$. For each couple of children nodes c_i of r_i and c_j of r_j, a new child $r' = \langle c_i, c_j \rangle$ of r_{ij} is obtained. Hence r' is the root of the subtree that constitutes the product T' of the subtrees T'_i and T'_j, rooted respectively, at c_i and c_j. The product subtree T' is finally connected to the product tree under construction T_{ij}.

An important feature of the product is that its complexity is polynomial (note that if the trees are represented with matrices then the proposed product corresponds to a matrix product).

Figure 2 illustrates the general idea of generation of the tree product, and Figure 3 presents the tree product for our motivating scenario.

Alternative Tree Products. In some cases the level-wise computation of product trees would yield poorly structured trees, when one of them is rooted with a primitive concept, for example. In such cases it may be advisable to use alternative definition of the tree product operator (derived from graph product operators), which is able to retain all of the structural information contained in the subsumption hierarchies.

$\times(T_i, T_j) : (N_{ij}, E_{ij}, r_{ij}, \ell_{ij})$
begin
$E_{ij} \leftarrow \emptyset$
$r_{ij} \leftarrow \langle r_i, r_j \rangle$
$N_{ij} \leftarrow \{r_{ij}\}$
$\ell_{ij}(r_{ij}) \leftarrow \langle \ell(r_i), \ell(r_j) \rangle$
for each (c_i, c_j) **where** $(r_i, c_i) \in E_i$ **and** $(r_j, c_j) \in E_j$ **do**
$\quad T_i' \leftarrow \text{SUBTREE}(T_i, c_i)$
$\quad T_j' \leftarrow \text{SUBTREE}(T_j, c_j)$
$\quad (N', E', r', \ell') \leftarrow \times(T_i', T_j')$
$\quad N_{ij} \leftarrow N_{ij} \cup N'$
$\quad$**for each** $node \in N'$ **do**
$\quad\quad\quad \ell(node) \leftarrow \ell'(node)$
$\quad E_{ij} \leftarrow E_{ij} \cup E' \cup \{\langle r_{ij}, r' \rangle\}$
return $(N_{ij}, E_{ij}, r_{ij}, \ell_{ij})$
end

Fig. 1. Tree product operator

Definition 3 (alternative tree products). *Given two trees* $T_1 = (V_1, E_1, r_1, \ell_1)$ *and* $T_2 = (V_2, E_2, r_2, \ell_2)$, *their* product, *denoted* $T_1 \times T_2$, *is a tree* $T_p = (V_p, E_p, r_p, \ell_p)$ *defined as follows:*

- *the vertex set is a subset of the Cartesian product* $V_p \subseteq V_1 \times V_2$;
- $r_p = (r_1, r_2) \in V_p$;
- $\ell_p(u, v) = (\ell_1(u), \ell_2(v))$;
- *two product vertices* $(u_1, u_2) \in V_p$ *and* $(v_1, v_2) \in V_p$ *are connected in* T_p, *i.e.* $((u_1, u_2), (v_1, v_2)) \in E_p$, *iff* u_1, u_2, v_1, v_2 *satisfy the conditions specified in the following table:*

Rooted product	$\bigcup_{u \in V_1} \{((u,v),(u,v')) \mid (v,v') \in E_2\}$
Co-normal product	$(u_1, v_1) \in E_1 \vee (u_2, v_2) \in E_2$
Tensor product	$(u_1, v_1) \in E_1 \wedge (u_2, v_2) \in E_2$

Note, that for the last two operators it is not guaranteed that a tree is obtained.

4.4 From Trees to Groups

Having produced a tree of semantic categories, the next step is to assign results (tuples) to the semantic categories. We propose to perform it incrementally in line with the ranking of the results provided by the query answering engine. For each tuple the projection of the bindings of variables appearing in the CATEGORIZE BY clause is taken into account. Then starting from the root of a tree and following paths to its leaves the membership check of instances to concepts in the tree nodes are performed in order to find the most specific nodes under which to place the result tuple. Such technique allows to obtain more populated hierarchy in a longer time frame, where completeness increases over time. A sketch of the algorithm is shown in Figure 4.

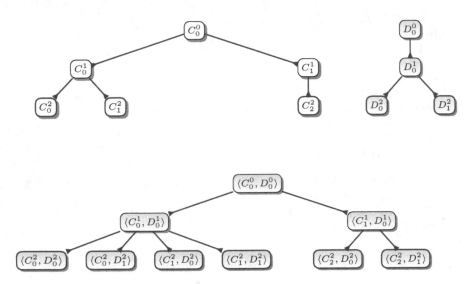

Fig. 2. Tree product example: the lower tree is the product of the two upper trees

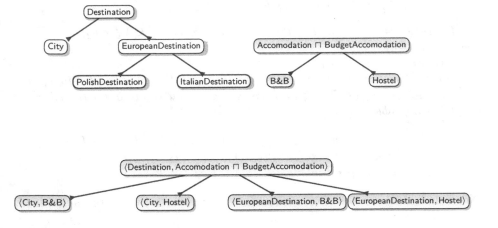

Fig. 3. Tree product illustration for query $Q_{2\_categorize\_by}$ from Example 4

The time complexity of the proposed population algorithm depends on a complexity of instance membership checks. The population algorithm itself has the complexity $O(nkb^m)$, where n is the number of answers, k the number of grouping variables, b the branching factor, and m is the maximum depth of the tree. Besides this simple algorithm, also other solutions could be adopted, e.g. such in which a non-standard inference of computing *most specific concept* [9] would

POPULATE(T, KB, $\mathcal{H}$)
input:
$T = (a_{ij})_{i=1,r}^{j=1,n}$: query answer table
KB: knowledge base
$\mathcal{H}$: semantic category hierarchy
Q: query
output:
$\mathcal{H}$: populated semantic category hierarchy

begin
   $i \leftarrow 0$
   while !RESOURCES_UP() **and** $i < r$
      $a_i \leftarrow$ T.GETANSWER(I);
      ASSIGNTOMOSTSPECIFICSEMANTICCATEGORIES(a_i, $\mathcal{H}$, $\mathcal{H}$.ROOT(), KB, Q);
return $\mathcal{H}$
end

ASSIGNTOMOSTSPECIFICSEMANTICCATEGORIES(a_i, $\mathcal{H}$, $\mathcal{H}$.NODE(), KB, Q)
begin
   $\langle (C_0), ..., (C_n) \rangle \leftarrow \mathcal{H}$.NODE().GETSEMANTICCATEGORY();
   assigned $\leftarrow$ **false**;
   followsUnderNode $\leftarrow$ **true**;
   $j \leftarrow 0$;
   while followsUnderNode **and** $j < n$
      $a_{ij} \leftarrow a_i$.GETBINDING(j);
      if $\neg(KB \models C_j(a_{ij}))$ **then**
         followsUnderNode $\leftarrow$ **false**;
      $j \leftarrow j + 1$;
   if followsUnderNode **then**
      for each $\mathcal{H}$.NODE().CHILD()
         if ASSIGNTOMOSTSPECIFICSEMANTICCATEGORIES(a_i, $\mathcal{H}$, $\mathcal{H}$.NODE().CHILD(), KB, Q)**then**
            assigned $\leftarrow$ **true**;
      if assigned=false **then**
         $\mathcal{H}$.NODE().ASSIGN(a_i);
         assigned $\leftarrow$ **true**;
return assigned;
end

Fig. 4. Population of a semantic category hierarchy

be employed. It should be noted, hovever, that for some description logics the most specific concept may not exist.

Example 6 (Assignment of the results to semantic categories). The results of query $Q_{2\_categorize\_by}$ from Example 4 are assigned to the semantic categories shown in Figure 3 as follows: (O1, ZAKOPANE, A1): $\langle$EuropeanDestination, B&B$\rangle$, (O2, CHOCHOLOW, A2): $\langle$EuropeanDestination, B&B$\rangle$, (O3, TRENTO, A3): $\langle$City, Hostel$\rangle$, (O3, TRENTO, A3) : $\langle$EuropeanDestination, Hostel$\rangle$.

5   Experimental Evaluation

We have developed a proof-of-concept implementation of our approach in Java, on top of Pellet reasoner[3]. Please note, that state-of-the-art reasoners (including Pellet) do not support conjunctive queries with truly undistinguished variables. Therefore, our prototype implementation supports only *DL-safe queries* [10], i.e. queries, where all variables are assumend to be bound to named individuals.

---
[3] http://clarkparsia.com/pellet/

Table 2. Characteristics of test datasets

dataset	DL	#concepts	#obj. roles	#individuals
FINANCIAL	$\mathcal{ALCIF}$	60	16	17941
NTN	$\mathcal{SHIF}$	49	29	728
VICODI	$\mathcal{ALHI}$	194	10	16942
LUBM	$\mathcal{SHI}(\mathbf{D})$	43	25	17174

Table 3. Tested queries

dataset	query
FINANCIAL	$Q_1(x, y) = categorize\_by(x, y)$: Client(x) ∧ hasCreditCard(x, y) ∧ CreditCard(y)
FINANCIAL	$Q_2(x, y, z) = categorize\_by(x, y, z)$: Client(x) ∧ livesIn(x, y) ∧ hasAgeValue(x, z)
NTN	$Q_3(x, y) = categorize\_by(x, y)$: Agent(x) ∧ relativeOf(x, y)
NTN	$Q_4(x, y, z) = categorize\_by(x, y, z)$: CognitiveAgent(x) ∧ collaboratesWith(x, y) ∧ knows(x, z)
VICODI	$Q_5(x, y) = categorize\_by(x, y)$: Scientist(x) ∧ hasRole(y, x)
VICODI	$Q_6(x, y, z) = categorize\_by(x, y, z)$: Leader(x) ∧ hasRole(y, x) ∧ related(x, z) ∧ Individual(y) ∧ Location(z)
LUBM	$Q_7(x, y) = categorize\_by(x, y)$: Faculty(x) ∧ teacherOf(x, y)
LUBM	$Q_8(x, y, z) = categorize\_by(x, y, z)$: Person(x) ∧ memberOf(x, y) ∧ subOrganizationOf(x, z)

We have empirically tested our approach using four benchmark datasets: FINANCIAL[4], NEW TESTAMENT-NAMES (NTN)[5], VICODI[6], and LUBM[7] (see: Table 2). The experiments were conducted on a laptop computer with a 1.67 GHz Intel processor, 1014 MB of RAM, running Windows Vista.

For each of the datasets we tested 2 queries (see: Table 3). Let us take query Q_1 as an example. Variable x in Q_1 bounds to the names of clients, and variable y to the IDs of credit cards, so the classical, *syntactic group by* would create 892 groups. In turn, our proposed *semantic grouping*, creates the six following semantic categories: ⟨Client, CreditCard⟩ ⟨Man, Classic⟩, ⟨Man, Gold⟩, ⟨Man, Junior⟩, ⟨Woman, Classic⟩, ⟨Woman, Gold⟩, ⟨Woman, Junior⟩.

For each of the queries we tested how our method scales with the growing number of results for each query. Figure 5 presents the total times of computing, and populating a semantic category hierarchy.

Note that the Web users usually browse not more than a few dozens of the retrieved results. For this number of the results, the basic implementation of our proposed approach performes well, in real-time, on the tested cases, and scales linearly with the number of the processed results.

Note further, that not all the nodes of the generated semantic category hierarchy would become ultimately populated. This observation may lead to an optimization of the proposed algorithm for the cases where some precomputation would be possible to identify concepts without an extension. These concepts could be then stored on an index, and the nodes containing them removed from the semantic category hierarchy in a preprocessing step, thus reducing the further complexity of the hierarchy population. We tested this technique experimentaly reaching a significant decrease in execution time (for the hardest query, Q_8, and

---

[4] FINANCIAL, http://www.cs.put.poznan.pl/alawrynowicz/financial.owl
[5] NTN, http://protegewiki.stanford.edu/index.php/Protege_Ontology Library
[6] VICODI, http://kaon2.semanticweb.org/download/test_ontologies.zip
[7] LUBM, http://swat.cse.lehigh.edu/projects/lubm/

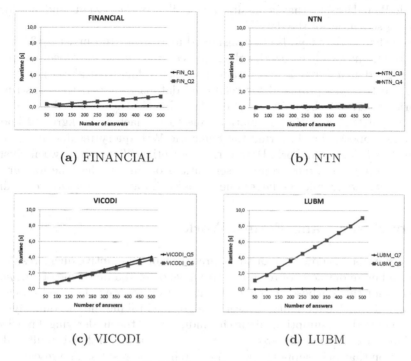

Fig. 5. Results of the experiments

for 500 results, the execution time was shorter more than 5 times than this reported in the figure for the basic approach).

6   Related Work

To the best of our knowledge, ours is the first proposal for grouping conjunctive query results on the ground of semantics of the underlying knowledge base.

While aggregate queries were extensively studied for relational databases, there are very few results for aggregate queries over ontologies, especially those that target to meet the peculiarities of the KR formalisms of the Semantic Web. In [11] the syntax and semantics for epistemic aggregate queries over ontologies were proposed, and query answering for typical aggregate functions studied for an ontology language $DL\text{-}Lite_\mathcal{A}$. That work was motivated by the non-adequacy of certain answer semantics for conditional aggregate queries over ontologies due to the open world assumption. In [12] the meaning and implementation of grouping and aggregate queries over RDF graphs were studied, motivated by the drawback of the previous works where the grouping and aggregate operations had not take the graph structure of the base data into account.

However, none of the above approaches exploited the peculiar feature of the Semantic Web datasets, that is possible availability of the background ontologies expressing semantics of the data.

Some other works may also be considered as relevant to ours. In [13] an approach to automatically categorize the results of SQL queries has been proposed that consisted on a dynamic generation of a labeled, hierarchical category structure. Since this was proposed for relational database model, the constructed categories could only be built based on the values in the retrieved tuples, and not on any extra semantic information, due to the lack of background knowledge. The proposal for clustering the Semantic Web query results [14,15] may be considered as related work. However, an essential difference between clustering query results, and our proposed semantic grouping, is that the former one involves *induction*, while the latter one is based simply on *deductive* reasoning.

7   Conclusions and Future Work

The paper proposes a method for the aggregation of concjuntive query results on the ground of an ontology of reference. We have defined a new type of *categorize by* queries for this purpose. To enable such queries, we have designed a method where in a deductive modality, answers are grouped taking into account dynamically generated subsumption hierarchy induced by the underlying knowledge base. This subsumption hierarchy has the form of a hierarchical, multi-valued classification that may support a faceted search of the results. The research presented in the paper may constitute a proposal for the next generation query languages oriented to knowledge bases annotated with ontology languages.

To the best of our knowledge, this work is the first to propose grouping of conjunctive query results on the ground of semantics of the underlying knowledge base. As such it may be an important first step towards the proposed direction of semantic grouping, and inspiration to conduct future work on the proposed idea. In particular, in the future, alternative versions of the components of the proposed method may be investigated such as different tree/graph product operators, or different techniques of assigning answers to semantic groups. An interesting future research may concern an investigation on a possible integration of semantic grouping into query processing, and query execution plans.

References

1. Calvanese, D., De Giacomo, G., Lenzerini, M.: On the decidability of query containment under constraints. In: Proc. of the 17th ACM SIGACT SIGMOD SIGART Symposium on Principles of Database Systems (PODS'98), pp. 149–158 (1998)
2. Horrocks, I., Tessaris, S.: Querying the semantic web: A formal approach. In: Horrocks, I., Hendler, J. (eds.) ISWC 2002. LNCS, vol. 2342, pp. 177–191. Springer, Heidelberg (2002)

3. Calvanese, D., De Giacomo, G., Lembo, D., Lenzerini, M., Rosati, R.: Data complexity of query answering in description logics. In: Doherty, P., Mylopoulos, J., Welty, C. (eds.) Proceedings of the Tenth International Conference on Principles of Knowledge Representation and Reasoning (KR'06). AAAI Press, Menlo Park (2006)

4. Ortiz, M., Calvanese, D., Eiter, T.: Data complexity of answering unions of conjunctive queries in $\mathcal{SHIQ}$. In: Parsia, B., Sattler, U., Toman, D. (eds.) Proceedings of the International Workshop on Description Logics (DL'06). CEUR-WS, vol. 189. CEUR (2006)

5. Glimm, B., Horrocks, I., Lutz, C., Sattler, U.: Conjunctive query answering for the description logic $\mathcal{SHIQ}$. J. Artif. Int. Res. 31(1), 157–204 (2008)

6. Baader, F., Calvanese, D., McGuinness, D., Nardi, D., Patel-Schneider, P. (eds.): The Description Logic Handbook. Cambridge University Press, Cambridge (2003)

7. Iannone, L., Palmisano, I., Fanizzi, N.: An algorithm based on counterfactuals for concept learning in the Semantic Web. Appl. Intell. 26(2), 139–159 (2007)

8. Lehmann, J., Hitzler, P.: A refinement operator based learning algorithm for the $\mathcal{ALC}$ description logic. In: Blockeel, H., Ramon, J., Shavlik, J., Tadepalli, P., et al. (eds.) ILP 2007. LNCS (LNAI), vol. 4894, pp. 147–160. Springer, Heidelberg (2008)

9. Baader, F., Küsters, R.: Computing the least common subsumer and the most specific concept in the presence of cyclic $\mathcal{ALN}$-concept descriptions. In: Herzog, O., Günter, A. (eds.) KI 1998. LNCS, vol. 1504, pp. 129–140. Springer, Heidelberg (1998)

10. Motik, B., Sattler, U., Studer, R.: Query answering for OWL-DL with rules. Journal of Web Semantics: Science, Services and Agents on the World Wide Web 3(1), 41–60 (2005)

11. Calvanese, D., Kharlamov, E., Nutt, W., Thorne, C.: Aggregate queries over ontologies. In: ONISW '08: Proc. of the 2nd international workshop on Ontologies and Information systems for the Semantic Web, pp. 97–104. ACM, New York (2008)

12. Seid, D., Mehrotra, S.: Grouping and aggregate queries over Semantic Web databases. In: International Conference on Semantic Computing, pp. 775–782. IEEE Computer Society, Los Alamitos (2007)

13. Chakrabarti, K., Chaudhuri, S., Hwang, S.w.: Automatic categorization of query results. In: SIGMOD '04: Proc. of the 2004 ACM SIGMOD international conference on Management of data, pp. 755–766. ACM, New York (2004)

14. Ławrynowicz, A.: Grouping results of queries to ontological knowledge bases by conceptual clustering. In: Nguyen, N.T., Kowalczyk, R., Chen, S.-M. (eds.) ICCCI 2009. LNCS, vol. 5796, pp. 504–515. Springer, Heidelberg (2009)

15. Ławrynowicz, A.: Query results clustering by extending SPARQL with CLUSTER BY. In: Meersman, R., Herrero, P., Dillon, T.S. (eds.) OTM 2009 Workshops. LNCS, vol. 5872, pp. 826–835. Springer, Heidelberg (2009)

Natural Language Interfaces to Ontologies: Combining Syntactic Analysis and Ontology-Based Lookup through the User Interaction

Danica Damljanovic, Milan Agatonovic, and Hamish Cunningham

Department of Computer Science, University of Sheffield
Regent Court, 211 Portobello Street, Sheffield, UK
{d.damljanovic,m.agatonovic,h.cunningham}@dcs.shef.ac.uk

Abstract. With large datasets such as Linked Open Data available, there is a need for more user-friendly interfaces which will bring the advantages of these data closer to the casual users. Several recent studies have shown user preference to Natural Language Interfaces (NLIs) in comparison to others. Although many NLIs to ontologies have been developed, those that have reasonable performance are domain-specific and tend to require customisation for each new domain which, from a developer's perspective, makes them expensive to maintain. We present our system FREyA, which combines syntactic parsing with the knowledge encoded in ontologies in order to reduce the customisation effort. If the system fails to automatically derive an answer, it will generate clarification dialogs for the user. The user's selections are saved and used for training the system in order to improve its performance over time. FREyA is evaluated using Mooney Geoquery dataset with very high precision and recall.

Keywords: Natural language interfaces, ontologies, question-answering, learning, clarification dialogs.

1 Introduction

With billions of triples being published in recent years, such as those from Linked Open Data[1], there is a need for more user-friendly interfaces which will bring the advantages of these data closer to the casual users. Research has been very active in developing various interfaces for accessing structured knowledge, from faceted search, where knowledge is grouped and represented through taxonomies, to menu-guided and form-based interfaces such as those offered by KIM [16]. While hiding the complexity of underlying query languages such as SPARQL[2], these interfaces still require that the user is familiarised with the queried knowledge

---

[1] http://esw.w3.org/topic/SweoIG/TaskForces/CommunityProjects/
LinkingOpenData
[2] http://www.w3.org/TR/rdf-sparql-query/

L. Aroyo et al. (Eds.): ESWC 2010, Part I, LNCS 6088, pp. 106–120, 2010.

structure. However, casual users should be able to access the data despite their queries not matching exactly the queried data structures [8]. Natural Language Interfaces (NLIs), which are often referred as closed-domain Question Answering (QA) systems, have a very important role as they are intuitive for the end users and preferred to keyword-based, menu-based or graphical interfaces [9].

Most QA systems contain the classifier module which is used to detect the question category or the type of the question. The successful parsing is based on this identification. However, the syntactic patterns for this classification are usually derived from the dataset which must be large in order to work efficiently [7]. Moreover, as Ferret et al. point out: "answers to [some] questions can hardly be reduced to a pattern." [7, p.7]. In addition, it is not trivial to translate successfully parsed question into the relevant logical representation or a formal query which will lead to the correct answer [14].

We present an approach where instead of encoding the specific rules into our NLI system (which would increase the chance of being domain-specific), we use the knowledge encoded in ontologies as the primary source for understanding the user's question, and only then try to use the output of the syntactic parsing in order to provide the more precise answer. This allows more freedom and flexibility to the user, as questions do not need to fall within the predefined categories. If the system is not able to automatically derive an answer, it will generate clarification dialogs. The user's choice is then saved and used for *training* the system in order to improve its performance over time. While engaging the user in this kind of interaction might be an overload at the beginning, our intention is to see whether our learning mechanism can reduce this by the time. On the route to achieving this, we have developed FREyA a system which combines several usability methods and is named after **F**eedback, **R**efinement and **E**xtended Vocabulary **A**ggregation. We evaluate our approach using Mooney Geoquery dataset[3].

This paper is structured as follows. In the next section we present related work. In Section 3, we describe FREyA and demonstrate through examples how it works. In Section 4 we present evaluation results with Mooney dataset. Finally, we conclude and draw future directions in Section 5.

2   Related Work

While NLI systems which have a good performance require a customisation (such as in the case of ORAKEL [1]), several systems have been developed for which the customisation is not mandatory (e.g., PANTO [19], Querix [10], AquaLog [13]), QuestIO [5], NLP-Reduce [10]). However, as is reported in [13] the customisation usually improves the recall. On the other hand, some of these systems rely on grammatically correct questions which fall within the boundaries of system capabilities.

In case of ORAKEL, customisation is performed through the user interaction, using a software called FrameMapper, where the linguistic argument structures,

---

[3] http://www.cs.utexas.edu/users/ml/nldata.html

such as verbs or nouns with their arguments, are mapped to the relations in the ontology. While their intention is to involve application developers in this customisation, our system is intended to be used by end-users from the start. We are aware that initial system given to the end-users can be seen as overload as the users will be heavily engaged into the dialogs, until the system *learns* enough to be able to automatically suggests the correct answer.

AquaLog [13] is capable of learning the user's jargon in order to improve his experience by the time. Their learning mechanism is good in a way that it uses ontology reasoning to learn more generic patterns, which could then be reused for the questions with similar context. Our approach is different in that it shares the input from all users and reuses it for the others, not favorising jargon of the particular user.

Querix [11] is another ontology-based question answering system which relies on clarification dialogs in case of ambiguities. Our system is similar to Querix in many aspects, with the main difference that the primary goal of the dialog in our system is not only to resolve ambiguities, but also to map question terms to the relevant ontology concepts. Therefore, our system does not rely on the vocabulary of the ontology, but tries to align it with that of the user.

Our intention with FREyA is to balance between heavy customisation which is usually required by application developers, in order to port the system to a different domain, and the end users who need to explore the available knowledge without being constrained with the query language.

3   FREyA

In the previous work ([5], [18]), we have developed QuestIO (Question-based Interface to Ontologies), which translates a Natural Language (NL) or a keyword-based question into SPARQL, and returns the answer to the user after executing the formal query against an ontology. Although this approach uses very shallow NLP, it is quite efficient for very small and domain-specific ontologies. Also, it performs quite well for the set of ill-formed and grammatically incorrect questions [5]. However, the trade-off is that many grammatically correct questions which do require more deep analysis would remain unanswered, or partially answered. For example, if the question is *What is the largest city in Nevada?*, QuestIO would be able to list cities in Nevada, but it would ignore the word *largest* which is in this case crucial to deliver semantic meaning. In addition, when ontologies are spanning diverse domains, automatically deriving an answer becomes an issue due to ambiguities. Finally, QuestIO displays the result of executing SPARQL queries as a table in which the user finds the answer. Therefore, we have started to work on methods which would, in comparison to our previous work:

- improve understanding of the question's semantic meaning
- provide the concise answer to the user's question
- communicate the system's interpretation of the query to the user
- assist the user formulate the query which falls within the boundaries of the system capabilities

These methods have been thoroughly discussed in [3]. Their combination is the base of FREyA which is named after **F**eedback, **R**efinement and **E**xtended Vo-cabular**y** **A**ggregation. The implementation of FREyA can be broken down into several steps:

- Identification and verification of *ontology concepts*
- Generating SPARQL
- Identification of the *answer type* and presenting the results to the user

3.1 Identification and Verification of Ontology Concepts

Our algorithm for translating a NL question into the set of Ontology Concepts (OCs)[4] combines the syntactic parsing with ontology reasoning in order to iden-tify the user's information need correctly. In cases when the algorithm does not derive conclusions automatically, it generates suggestions for the user. By engag-ing the user into the dialog, we have a better chance of identifying his information need when it is expressed ambiguously through the question.

Figure 1 shows step-by-step process which starts with finding ontology-based annotations in the query and ends with a set of ontology concepts, which are then used in subsequent steps to generate a SPARQL query. Further we describe each step in more details.

Identification of Ontology Concepts. We use the knowledge available in the ontology to identify the ontology-based annotations in the question, which we call Ontology Concepts. Generated annotations contain links to ontology resources (e.g. URIs). If there are ambiguous annotations in the query, we engage the user into the dialog. For example, if someone is enquiring about *Mississippi*, we might not be able to automatically derive whether OC refers to *geo:River*[5], or *geo:State*. To resolve this ambiguity, we generate a clarification dialog where the user selects one of the two. Note that we apply disambiguation rules which are based on the ontology reasoning before we model the clarification dialog. For example, for the question *which rivers flow through Mississippi?*, modeling a clarification dialog is not necessary, as due to the context of the question we automatically derive that *Mississippi* refers to *geo:State*.

We use GATE [2] application, and an ontology-based gazetteer called On-toRoot Gazetteer [5] to perform this step. OntoRoot Gazetteer relies on the human understandable lexicalisations of ontology resources and therefore, the quality of produced annotations depends directly on them (see [5]). However, it is not often the case that ontology resources are followed by human understand-able lexicalisations (e.g., labels). This is especially the case for properties. In addition, Natural Language is so complex that words like *total, smallest, higher*

---

[4] Note that we use the term *Ontology Concept* to refer to all types of ontology resources such as classes, instances, properties and literals.

[5] For clarity of presentation, we use prefix *geo:* instead of http://www.mooney.net/ geo#in all examples.

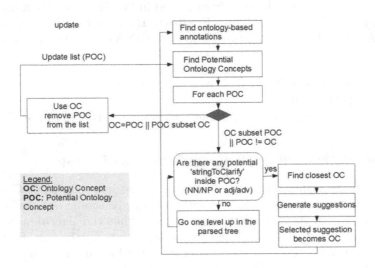

Fig. 1. Validation of potential ontology concepts through the user interaction

than or *how many* cannot be automatically understood/encoded into the relevant structure without additional processing. Some formal languages such as SPARQL even do not support some of these structures (e.g., it is not possible to do count queries in SPARQL). Therefore, NLIs to ontologies would have to translate any additional semantic meanings into the relevant operations with the ontology concepts (e.g. superlative means applying maximum or minimum function to the datatype property value).

Identification of Potential Ontology Concepts. *Potential Ontology Concepts* (POCs) are derived from the syntactic parse tree, and refer to question terms which could be linked to an ontology concept. Syntactic parse tree is generated by Stanford Parser [12]. We use several heuristic rules in order to identify POCs. For example, each NP (noun phrase) or NN (noun) is identified as a POC. Also, if a noun phrase contains adjectives, these are considered POCs as well. Next, the algorithm iterates through the list of POCs, attempting to map them to OCs.

Mapping POCs to OCs. A Potential Ontology Concept is mapped to Ontology Concept in two ways:

1. *Automatically*: if it overlaps with an Ontology Concept in a way that OC spans over POC:
   - both POC and OC refer to exactly the same text span in the question ($OC == POC$); for example, in *which rivers flow through Texas?*, *rivers* can be identified as OC, as referring to the class *geo:River*, while it can also be identified as POC. In this case, POC is automatically mapped to OC, as $OC == POC$ (the starting and ending offsets are identical)

- POC refers to the text span which is contained within the span to which OC refers ($POC \subset OC$);
2. *By engaging the user*: when the user verifies it by choosing it from the list of the available suggestions

Generating Suggestions. Suggestions are generated for each POC which does not overlap with OC, or in cases when POC spans over OC ($OC \subset POC\|POC! = OC$). First, our algorithm identifies the *closest OC* to this POC by walking through the syntax tree, and then uses ontology reasoning to generate suggestions. Based on the type of the closest OC, rules for generating suggestions vary (see Table 1).

Table 1. Generating suggestions based on the type of the closest OC

Type of the closest OC	Generating suggestions
class or instance	*get all classes connected to OC by exactly one property, and all properties defined for this OC*
datatype property of type number	*maximum, minimum and sum function of OC*
object property	*get all domain and range classes for OC*

Option *none* is always added to the list of suggestions (see Table 2). This allows the user to ignore suggestions, if they are irrelevant. That is, the system would assume that the POC in the dialog should not be mapped to any suggested OCs, and therefore the system would learn by the time that this POC is either: 1) incorrectly identified, or 2) cannot be mapped to any OC as the ontology does not contain relevant knowledge. While this option will not be of a huge benefit to the end-users, it is intended to identify flaws in the system and encourage improvements.

The task of creating and ranking the suggestions before showing them to the user is quite complex, and this complexity arises as the queried knowledge source grows.

Ranking Suggestions. Initial ranking is based on the string similarity between POC and suggestions, and also based on synonym detection as identified by Wordnet [6] and Cyc[6]. For string similarity we combine Monge Elkan[7] metrics with Soundex[8] algorithm. When comparing the two strings the former gives a very high score to those which are exact parts of the other. For example, if we compare *population* with *city population*, the similarity would be maximised as the former is contained in the latter. The intuition behind this is the way ontology concepts are usually named. Soundex algorithm compensates for any spelling mistakes that the user makes - this algorithm gives a very high similarity to the two words which are spelled differently but would be pronounced similarly.

---

[6] http://sw.opencyc.org/

[7] See http://www.dcs.shef.ac.uk/~sam/stringmetrics.html#monge

[8] http://en.wikipedia/wiki/Soundex

Table 2. Sample queries and generated suggestions for relevant POCs

Query	POC	Closest OC	Suggestions
population of cities in california	population	geo:City	1. city population 2. state 3. has city 4. is city of 5. none
population of california	population	geo:california	1. state population 2. state pop density 3. has low point ... n. none
which city has the largest population in california	largest population	geo:City	1. max(city population) 2. min(city population) 3. sum(city population) 4. none

3.2 Generating SPARQL

After all POCs are resolved, the query is interpreted as a set of OCs. Firstly, we insert any potential *joker* elements in between OCs, if necessary. For example, if the first two OCs derived from a question are referring to *a property* and *a class* respectively, one *joker* class would be added before them. For instance, the query *what is the highest point of the state bordering Mississippi?* would be translated into the list of the following OCs:

```
geo:isHighestPointOf  geo:State  geo:border  geo:mississippi
PROPERTY               CLASS      PROPERTY    INSTANCE
```

These elements are transformed into the following:

```
?        geo:isHighestPointOf geo:State geo:border geo:mississippi
JOKER    PROPERTY1            CLASS1    PROPERTY2  INSTANCE
```

Next step is *generating set of triples from OCs*, taking into account the domain and range of the properties. For example, from the previous list, two triples would be generated[9]:

```
? - geo:isHighestPointOf - geo:State;
geo:State - geo:borders - geo:mississippi (geo:State);
```

Last step is *generating SPARQL query*. Set of triples are combined and based on the OC type, relevant parts are added to *SELECT* and *WHERE* clauses. Following the previous example, the SPARQL query would look like:

---

[9] Note that if *geo:isHighestPointOf* would have *geo:State* as a domain, the triple would look like:*geo:State - geo:isHighestPointOf - ?;*.

```
prefix rdf: <http://www.w3.org/1999/02/22-rdf-syntax-ns#>
prefix geo: <http://www.mooney.net/geo#>
select ?firstJoker  ?p0  ?c1  ?p2  ?i3
where { { ?firstJoker ?p0 ?c1 .
filter (?p0=geo:isHighestPointOf) . }
?c1 rdf:type geo:State .
?c1  ?p2 ?i3 .
filter (?p2=geo:borders) .
?i3 rdf:type geo:State .
filter (?i3=geo:mississippi) . }
```

3.3 Answer Type Identification

The result of the SPARQL query is a graph, and an important decision to make is how to display results to the user. In order to show the concise answer, we must identify the *answer type* of the question. To achieve this, we combine the output of the syntactic parsing with the ontology-based lookup coupled with several heuristic rules (see [4] for detailed algorithm). Figure 2 shows how we display the answer for the query *Show lakes in Minnesota*.

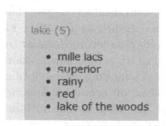

Fig. 2. List showing the answer of the query *Show lakes in Minnesota*

In addition, as feedback can help the user familiarise himself with the queried knowledge structure, we also render *the system's interpretation of the query*: this is visualised as a graph, where we place the answer type in the center, and the answer on the nearest circle, see Figure 3. We use JIT library[10] for graph visualisation.

3.4 Learning

We use an approach inspired by Reinforcement Learning (RL) [17] to improve ranking of suggestions shown to the user. While many question-answering systems apply supervised learning, we decide to use semi-supervised approach due to several reasons. Firstly, supervised learning goes in-line with automatic classification of the question, where each question is identified as belonging to the

---

[10] www.thejit.org

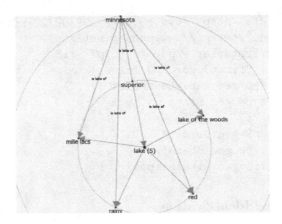

Fig. 3. Graph showing the system interpretation of the query *Show lakes in Minnesota*

one predefined category. Our intention with FREyA is to avoid automatic classification and allow the user to enter queries of any form. Secondly, we want to minimise customisation of the NLI system which would be required when using supervised learning, as to map some question terms to the underlying structure. For example, we want the system itself to suggest that *where* should be mapped to the specific ontology concept such as *Location*, rather than the application developer browsing the ontology structure in order to place this mapping.

The first important aspect of RL is the identification of the goal to be achieved, which is in our case the correct ranking of suggestions. Each suggestion has its *initial ranking* calculated based on synonym detection and string similarity as explained previously. These are used in the untrained system. Each time the suggestion is selected by the user, it receives a reward of +1 while all alternative ones receive -1. The system then learns to place the correct suggestion at the top for any *similar* questions. *Similar* is identified by a combination of a POC and the closest OC. This increases robustness of our learning mechanism as our learning model is not updated per question, but per each combination of POC and the closest OC. In addition, we apply some generalisation rules derived from the ontology. For example, if the closest OC is *geo:Capital*, we would save its superclass *geo:City* in our learning model in order to reuse the same rule for all *cities*, not only *capitals*.

An example which demonstrate how the learning algorithm works, is shown in Figure 4. For query *What is the highest point of the state with the largest area?* there is only one token (*state*) annotated as referring to OC, whereas there are three POCs. We start with the last POC *largest area*. Suggestions are generated based on the closest OC which is *geo:State*. As *geo:stateArea* is a datatype property of type number, generated suggestions would, among others, contain the following: *max(geo:stateArea, min(geo:stateArea), sum(geo:stateArea)*. If the user selects the first one, the system will *learn* that the *largest area* refers to the maximum value of *geo:stateArea*.

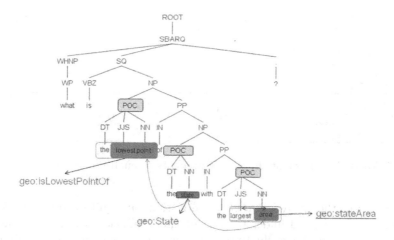

Fig. 4. Mapping POCs to OCs

We then skip the next POC as it overlaps with the ontology concept *state*. The last POC *the lowest point* is then used to generate suggestions. The closest OC is again, *geo:State*. There will be several suggestions and the user is very likely so select *geo:isLowestPointOf*, although this one will be ranked third[11]. However, for the next user, the system will learn to rank *geo:isLowestPointOf* first.

Figure 5 shows the syntax tree for the query *what is the population of New York*. As *New York* is identified as it could be referring to both *geo:State* and *geo:City*, we first ask the user to disambiguate (see Figure 5 a.)). If he selects for example *geo:City*, we start iterating through the list of POCs. The first POC (*New York* as *geo:City*) overlaps with already identified OC, which causes its immediate verification so we skip it. The next one (*population*) is used, together with the closest OC *geo:City*, to generate suggestions. Among them there will be *geo:cityPopulation* and after the user select this from the list of available options, *population* is mapped to the datatype property *geo:cityPopulation* (see Figure 5 b.)). Note that if the user selected that *New York* refers to *geo:State*, suggestions would be different, and following his selection, *population* would probably be mapped to refer to *geo:statePopulation* as the closest OC would be *geo:State*.

4   Evaluation

We have evaluated our approach on the 250 questions from the Mooney Geoquery dataset. Although the ontology contains rather small portion of knowledge about

---

[11] Note that although *lowest* is a superlative it will not be further used to generate suggestions as *geo:isLowestPointOf* is an object property, while in case of *largest area*, one of the options was *max(geo:stateArea)*, as *geo:stateArea* is datatype property of type number.

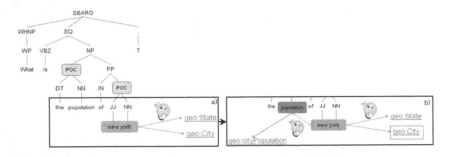

Fig. 5. Validation of potential ontology concepts through the user interaction

the geography of the United States, the questions are quite complex and the system must have a good understanding of the semantic meaning in order to correctly answer them. We evaluate *correctness, ranked suggestions,* and *learning mechanism.*

4.1   Correctness

We report correctness of FREyA in terms of precision and recall, which are measures adapted from information retrieval (see [15],[14]). *Recall* is defined as the number of questions correctly answered by an NLI system, divided by the total number of questions in the dataset. *Precision* measures the number of questions correctly answered divided by the number of questions for which the answer is returned at all [1].

Table 3 shows the number of questions correctly answered automatically, as opposed to those which have been answered correctly only after engaging the user into at most 2 clarification dialogs. Finally, there is a system failure to answer questions correctly in 7.6% of the time (e.g., questions with negation). Recall and precision values are equal, reaching 92.4%. This is due to FREyA always returning an answer, although partial or incorrect.

Table 3. Results of running FREyA with 250 questions from Mooney Geoquery dataset

	Correct		Incorrect
no dialogs	1 dialog	2 dialogs	
72	127	32	19
28.8%	50.8%	12.8%	7.6%

If we neglect the fact that it required quite an engagement of the user in order to correctly answer questions, FREyA's performance favorably compares to other similar systems. PANTO [19] is a similar system which was evaluated with the Mooney geography dataset of 877 questions (they removed duplicates from the original set of 879). They reported precision and recall of 88.05% and

85.86% respectively. NLP-Reduce [10] was evaluated with the original dataset, reporting 70.7% precision and 76.4% recall. Kaufmann et al.[11] selected 215 questions which syntactically represent the original set of 879 queries. They reported the evaluation results over this subset for their system Querix with 86.08% precision and 87.11% recall. Our 250 questions are a superset of these 215. It should be noted that FREyA had quite poor performance in comparison to others if we consider automatically answered questions only. However, the intention with FREyA is to allow users full control over the querying process.

4.2 Ranked Suggestions

We use *Mean Reciprocal Rank (MRR)* to report the performance of our ranking algorithm. MRR is a statistic for evaluating any process that produces a list of possible responses (suggestions in our case) to a query, ordered by probability of correctness. The *reciprocal rank* of a suggestion is the multiplicative inverse of the correct rank. The *mean reciprocal rank* is the average of the reciprocal ranks of results for a sample of queries (see Equation 1).

$$MRR = \frac{1}{|Q|} \sum_{i=1}^{Q} \frac{1}{rank_i} \tag{1}$$

We have manually labeled the correct ranking for suggestions which have be generated when running FREyA with 250 questions. This was the gold standard against which our ranking mechanism achieved MRR of 0.81. However, for some cases it is very hard to judge automatically which suggestion to place as number one. It is very likely that different users would select different suggestions for the questions phrased the same way. This emphasises the importance of the dialogs when modeling NLI systems.

4.3 Learning

From the above set of 250 questions, we have randomly selected 103 which required one clarification dialog with the user in order to get the correct answer. Then, we have ran our initial ranking algorithm and compared results with manually labeled gold standard. MRR was 0.72. Table 4 shows the distribution of the rankings.

Table 4. Evaluation with 103 questions from Mooney geography dataset

Correct rank	Number of questions
1	64 (62.13%)
2 or 3	22 (21.36%)
4 or more	17 (16.5%)

We then grouped 103 questions by OC, and then randomly chose training and evaluation sets from each group. We repeated this two times. Table 5 shows the structure of the dataset grouped by OC for both iterations. Note that these two iterations are independent - they have both been performed starting with an untrained system.

Table 5. Distribution of the training and evaluation datasets for 103 questions

OC	Iteration 1		Iteration 2	
	Training	Evaluation	Training	Evaluation
geo:State	26	19	19	26
geo:City/Capital	20	19	19	20
geo:River	12	6	9	9
geo:Mountain	1	0	0	1
total	59	44	47	56

After learning the model with 59 questions from the iteration 1, MRR for the evaluation questions (44 of them) has reached 0.98. Overall MRR (for all 103 questions) increased from 0.72 to 0.77. After training the model with 47 questions during the iteration 2, overall MRR increased to 0.79. Average MRR after running these two experiments was 0.78, which shows the increase of 0.06 in comparison to MRR of the initial rankings. Therefore, we conclude that for the selection of 103 questions from the Mooney Geoquery dataset, our learning algorithm improved our initial ranking by 6%.

5   Conclusion and Future Work

We presented FREyA, a NLI to ontologies which balances between heavy customisation (which is usually required by application developers, in order to port the NLI system to a different domain), and the end users who need to explore the available knowledge without being constrained with the query language. FREyA combines the output of the syntactic parser with the ontology-based lookup in order to approve the user's information need and, if necessary, engage the user into the dialog. Our evaluation with Mooney Geoquery dataset, shows that FREyA compares favorably to other similar systems. Moreover, this system is *learning* from the user's clicks in order to improve its performance over time. Our evaluation with 103 questions from the Mooney dataset revealed that the learning algorithm improved the initial rankings of suggestions by 6%.

At present, we are experimenting with large datasets such as LDSR[12], which have been developed as a part of LarKC project[13]. LDSR includes several subgraphs of Linked Open Data. We are preparing a user-centric evaluation in order to measure the user's experience with FREyA.

---

[12] http://ldsr.ontotext.com
[13] http://www.larkc.eu

Acknowledgments

We would like to thank Abraham Bernstein and Esther Kaufmann from the University of Zurich, for sharing with us Mooney dataset in OWL format, and J. Mooney from University of Texas for making this dataset publicly available.

This research has been partially supported by the EU-funded MUSING (FP6-027097) and LarKC (FP7-215535) projects.

References

1. Cimiano, P., Haase, P., Heizmann, J.: Porting natural language interfaces between domains: an experimental user study with the orakel system. In: IUI '07: Proceedings of the 12th international conference on Intelligent user interfaces, pp. 180–189. ACM, New York (2007)
2. Cunningham, H.: Information Extraction, Automatic. Encyclopedia of Language and Linguistics, 2nd edn., pp. 665–677 (2005)
3. Damljanovic, D., Bontcheva, K.: Towards enhanced usability of natural language interfaces to knowledge bases. In: Devedzic, V., Gasevic, D. (eds.) Special issue on Semantic Web and Web 2.0, vol. 6, pp. 105–133. Springer, Berlin (2009)
4. Damljanovic, D., Agatonovic, M., Cunningham, H.: Identification of the Question Focus: Combining Syntactic Analysis and Ontology-based Lookup through the User Interaction. In: 7th Language Resources and Evaluation Conference (LREC). ELRA, La Valletta (May 2010)
5. Damljanovic, D., Tablan, V., Bontcheva, K.: A text-based query interface to owl ontologies. In: 6th Language Resources and Evaluation Conference (LREC). ELRA, Marrakech (May 2008)
6. Fellbaum, C. (ed.): WordNet - An Electronic Lexical Database. MIT Press, Cambridge (1998)
7. Ferret, O., Grau, B., Hurault-plantet, M., Illouz, G., Monceaux, L., Robba, I., Vilnat, A.: Finding an answer based on the recognition of the question focus (2001)
8. Hurtado, C.A., Poulovassilis, A., Wood, P.T.: Ranking approximate answers to semantic web queries. In: Aroyo, L., Traverso, P., Ciravegna, F., Cimiano, P., Heath, T., Hyvönen, E., Mizoguchi, R., Oren, E., Sabou, M., Simperl, E.P.B. (eds.) ESWC 2009. LNCS, vol. 5554, pp. 263–277. Springer, Heidelberg (2009)
9. Kaufmann, E., Bernstein, A.: How useful are natural language interfaces to the semantic web for casual end-users? In: Franconi, E., Kifer, M., May, W. (eds.) ESWC 2007. LNCS, vol. 4519. Springer, Heidelberg (2007)
10. Kaufmann, E., Bernstein, A., Fischer, L.: NLP-Reduce: A naive but domain-independent natural language interface for querying ontologies. In: Franconi, E., Kifer, M., May, W. (eds.) ESWC 2007. LNCS, vol. 4519, Springer, Heidelberg (2007)
11. Kaufmann, E., Bernstein, A., Zumstein, R.: Querix: A natural language interface to query ontologies based on clarification dialogs. In: Cruz, I., Decker, S., Allemang, D., Preist, C., Schwabe, D., Mika, P., Uschold, M., Aroyo, L.M. (eds.) ISWC 2006. LNCS, vol. 4273, pp. 980–981. Springer, Heidelberg (2006)
12. Klein, D., Manning, C.D.: Fast exact inference with a factored model for natural language parsing. In: Becker, S., Thrun, S., Obermayer, K. (eds.) Advances in Neural Information Processing Systems 15 - Neural Information Processing Systems, NIPS 2002, pp. 3–10. MIT Press, Cambridge (2002),
http://books.nips.cc/papers/files/nips15/CS01.pdf

13. Lopez, V., Uren, V., Motta, E., Pasin, M.: Aqualog: An ontology-driven question answering system for organizational semantic intranets. Web Semantics: Science, Services and Agents on the World Wide Web 5(2), 72–105 (2007)
14. Mooney, R.J.: Using multiple clause constructors in inductive logic programming for semantic parsing. In: Proceedings of the 12th European Conference on Machine Learning, pp. 466–477 (2001)
15. Popescu, A.M., Etzioni, O., Kautz, H.: Towards a theory of natural language interfaces to databases. In: IUI '03: Proceedings of the 8th international conference on Intelligent user interfaces, pp. 149–157. ACM, New York (2003)
16. Popov, B., Kiryakov, A., Kirilov, A., Manov, D., Ognyanoff, D., Goranov, M.: KIM – Semantic Annotation Platform. In: Fensel, D., Sycara, K., Mylopoulos, J. (eds.) ISWC 2003. LNCS, vol. 2870, pp. 834–849. Springer, Heidelberg (2003)
17. Sutton, R.S., Barto, A.G.: Reinforcement Learning: an Introduction. MIT Press, Cambridge (1998)
18. Tablan, V., Damljanovic, D., Bontcheva, K.: A natural language query interface to structured information. In: Bechhofer, S., Hauswirth, M., Hoffmann, J., Koubarakis, M. (eds.) ESWC 2008. LNCS, vol. 5021, pp. 361–375. Springer, Heidelberg (2008)
19. Wang, C., Xiong, M., Zhou, Q., Yu, Y.: Panto: A portable natural language interface to ontologies. In: Franconi, E., Kifer, M., May, W. (eds.) ESWC 2007. LNCS, vol. 4519, pp. 473–487. Springer, Heidelberg (2007)

GeoWordNet: A Resource for Geo-spatial Applications

Fausto Giunchiglia, Vincenzo Maltese, Feroz Farazi,
and Biswanath Dutta

DISI - Università di Trento, Trento, Italy

Abstract. Geo-spatial ontologies provide knowledge about places in the world and spatial relations between them. They are fundamental in order to build semantic information retrieval systems and to achieve semantic interoperability in geo-spatial applications. In this paper we present GeoWordNet, a semantic resource we created from the full integration of GeoNames, other high quality resources and WordNet. The methodology we followed was largely automatic, with manual checks when needed. This allowed us accomplishing at the same time a never reached before accuracy level and a very satisfactory quantitative result, both in terms of concepts and geographical entities.

Keywords: Geo-spatial ontologies, WordNet.

1 Introduction

As part of the effort to achieve semantic interoperability in the Web, there is a pressing need and growing interest in geo-spatial ontologies, aiming at the so called geo-spatial semantic Web [2, 3]. For geo-spatial ontology we mean an ontology including geo-spatial entities (optionally associated with some properties/metadata), geographic classes (also called features) and topological relations [17] (such as *part-of, overlaps, near*) between them. For instance, a geo-spatial ontology can provide the information that *Florence* (the entity) is a *city* (its class) in *Italy* (its ancestor) and, among other information, the corresponding latitude and longitude coordinates. In some contexts, tools which maintain this kind of information are also called semantic gazetteers (for instance in [12]) or semantic geo-catalogs [4].

Geo-spatial ontologies are of fundamental importance in many applications, such as (among others) semantic Geographic Information Systems [4, 5], semantic annotation (but also matching and discovery) of geo-spatial Web services [6, 7], geographic semantics-aware web mining [15] and Geographical Information Retrieval (GIR) [10, 13]. In particular, restricted to GIR, there are various competitions, for instance GeoCLEF[1], specifically for the evaluation of geographic search engines. In all such applications, ontologies are mainly used for word sense disambiguation [9], semantic (faceted) navigation [14], document indexing and query expansion [10, 13], but in general they can be used in all the contexts where semantic interoperability is an issue.

---

[1] http://ir.shef.ac.uk/geoclef/

L. Aroyo et al. (Eds.): ESWC 2010, Part I, LNCS 6088, pp. 121–136, 2010.
© Springer-Verlag Berlin Heidelberg 2010

Unfortunately, the current geographical standards, for instance the specifications provided by the Open Geospatial Consortium (OGC)[2], do not represent an effective solution to the interoperability problem. In fact, they specifically aim at syntactic agreement [11]. For example, if it is decided that the standard term to denote a harbour (defined in WordNet as "*a sheltered port where ships can take on or discharge cargo*") is *harbour*, they will fail in applications where the same concept is denoted with *seaport*. Similarly, current gazetteers do not represent a satisfactory solution. In fact, they are no more than just yellow pages for place names and, consisting of ambiguous plain descriptions, they do not support logical inference [12]. As a response to this problem, some frameworks have been recently proposed to build and maintain geo-spatial ontologies [5, 14, 15], but to the best of our knowledge no comprehensive, sufficiently accurate and large enough ontologies are currently available.

WordNet[3], even if not specifically designed for this, is de facto used as knowledge base in many semantic applications (for instance in [18, 19, 20, 25]). Unfortunately, its coverage of geographic information is very limited [10], especially if compared to geographic gazetteers that usually contain millions of place names. In addition, WordNet does not provide latitude and longitude coordinates as well as other relevant information which is of fundamental importance in geo-spatial applications.

To overcome these limitations, there have been some recent attempts to integrate WordNet with geographical resources. Angioni et al. [8] propose a semi-automatic technique to integrate terms (classes and instances) from GEMET. Volz et al. [9] created a new ontology from the integration of WordNet with a limited set of classes and corresponding instances from GNS and GNIS[4]. The same resources are used by Buscardi et al. [10] to enrich 2,012 WordNet synsets with latitude and longitude coordinates. Unfortunately, all the above mentioned approaches are very limited in the number of terms (classes and instances) covered and accuracy. In particular, the problem in accuracy is mainly due to the semi-automatic approaches used.

Our main contribution to this problem is the creation of the GeoWordNet semantic and linguistic resource obtained from the integration of GeoNames[5] with WordNet plus the Italian section of MultiWordNet[6]. The methodology we followed is largely automatic, with manual intervention for the critical parts, thus accomplishing at the same time a never reached before accuracy and a very satisfactory quantitative result. We first created a multilingual knowledge base in which we imported WordNet and MultiWordNet. Then, for each place in GeoNames we automatically extracted metadata such as latitude and longitude coordinates, altitude, alternative names (available in multiple languages) and the spatial relations between them and integrated them in the knowledge base. This was achieved by first identifying those classes in Geo-Names for which there existed already a corresponding synset in WordNet and then by enriching WordNet (i.e. the knowledge base) with new synsets for the uncovered classes. The new synsets were then connected to the most appropriate synset through *hypernym* (is-a) or *part meronym* (pat-of) relations. Synsets for individual places were

---

[2] http://www.opengeospatial.org/

[3] http://wordnet.princeton.edu/wordnet

[4] http://earth-info.nga.mil/gns/html/index.html and
http://geonames.usgs.gov respectively

[5] http://www.geonames.org

[6] http://multiwordnet.fbk.eu

then automatically created as instances of the previously identified or created synsets. The last step consisted in the importing of corresponding metadata.

The rest of the paper is organized as follows. In Section 2 we briefly describe the overall process followed for the construction of GeoWordNet. Individual phases are extensively described in Sections 3-6. Some interesting critical issues faced during the process are presented in Section 7. Section 8 presents some final statistics. Section 9 concludes the paper and outlines future work.

2   Creating GeoWordNet

Being our main goal to improve the geo-spatial search experience of end users and to support semantic interoperability in geo-spatial applications, we enriched WordNet with a huge number of geo-spatial concepts, entities and relations between them. We posed particular attention not only to the quantity, but also to the quality of the information being integrated. Towards this goal we organized the process in four phases (see Fig. 1), described in the next four sections:

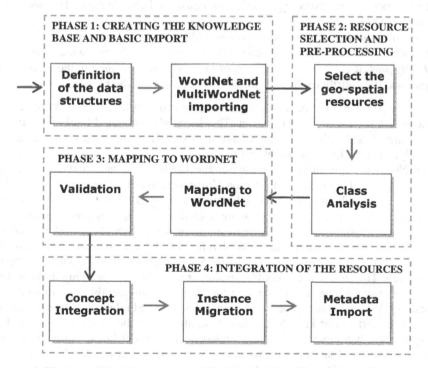

Fig. 1. A global view of the phases of the GeoWordNet creation process

- **PHASE 1: Creating the knowledge base and basic import.** It consisted of the definition of some suitable data structures to store knowledge in multiple languages coming from different sources such as WordNet and MultiWordNet.

- **PHASE 2: Resource selection and pre-processing.** It consisted of the selection of the most appropriate resources of geo-spatial terms, analysis of the classes and entities contained, and creation of the corresponding concepts.
- **PHASE 3: Mapping to WordNet.** Concepts created with the previous step were mapped with those in WordNet. The mapping produced was manually validated.
- **PHASE 4: Integration of the resources.** It consisted of the full integration of the geo-spatial concepts with WordNet (including spatial relations between them), migration of the instances of such concepts (the places) and of the creation of the corresponding metadata (properties).

3 Creating the Knowledge Base and Basic Import

Our knowledge base is organized into four distinct parts:

- **Linguistic part:** it contains terms, synsets and lexical relations between them. This part is instantiated in multiple languages (e.g., English and Italian);
- **Ontological part:** it stores concepts and semantic hierarchical (e.g., *is-a*, *part-of*) and associative relations (e.g., *similar-to*, *cause-of*) between them. This section is language independent;
- **Domain knowledge:** concepts are organized into facet hierarchies [24] codifying knowledge about a specific domain. This section is also language independent;
- **Entity part**: it contains the instances of the concepts contained in the ontological part and their attributes (possibly different according to their kind);

We initially populated the data structures with information taken from WordNet 2.1 and the Italian section of MultiWordNet. This is mainly motivated by the importance that the English and Italian languages have respectively in the context of the Living Knowledge[7] and the Live Memories[8] projects.

WordNet is a large lexical database for the English language, developed at the Cognitive Science Laboratory at Princeton University. WordNet groups words of different part of speech (nouns, verbs, adjectives and adverbs) into sets of cognitive synonyms, called synsets, each expressing a distinct concept. In other words, each synset groups all the words with same meaning or sense. Synsets are interlinked by means of conceptual-semantic and lexical relations. Typical semantic relations are *hypernym* (is-a) and *part meronym* (part-of). An example of lexical relation is *Participle of verb*. The structure of WordNet makes it a useful tool for computational linguistics and natural language processing and it is also frequently used in semantic applications. We imported all the words, synsets and lexical relations between them in the linguistic part of our knowledge base, instantiated for the English language. For each synset we then created a language independent concept in the ontological part. Semantic hierarchical and associative relations are codified at this level. We decided to do not import WordNet instances for two main reasons. First, they are not a significant number and no attributes are provided for them. Second, we plan to import huge quantities of entities and corresponding metadata from other resources, starting from

---

[7] http://livingknowledge-project.eu
[8] http://www.livememories.org

GeoNames. Note that the official number of entities in WordNet is 7671 [16], while we found out that they are 6988 instead. Synsets representing entities are connected to other synsets with at least one *instance hypernym* relation. We identified and manually verified the wrong ones by selecting those with no uppercased lemma.

MultiWordNet is a multilingual lexical database including many languages such as Italian, Spanish, Romanian and Latin. The Italian part is strictly aligned with WordNet 1.6. Therefore, in order to align such information with those already imported by WordNet 2.1, we first had to design an ad hoc procedure to map the two versions. This has been done by first using an already existing mapping[9] between WordNet 1.6 and 2.0 and then – using some heuristics - creating our own mapping between WordNet 2.0 and 2.1. Notice that for adjectives and adverbs we had to directly compute the mapping between WordNet 1.6 and 2.1 since not available elsewhere. We then instantiated the linguistic part of our knowledge base for the Italian language by importing words and synsets and - using the mapping – we connected each synset to the corresponding concept in the ontological part. Notice that due to the partial coverage of the language in MultiWordNet and the well known problem of gaps in languages (i.e. given a lexical unit in a language, it is not always possible to identify an equivalent lexical unit in another language) not all concepts have a corresponding synset in Italian. Detailed statistics are provided in Section 8.

4 Resource Selection and Pre-processing

Unfortunately, WordNet has quite limited coverage in geo-spatial information and lacks of latitude and longitude coordinates [10]. Therefore, it is essential to look elsewhere if we want an adequate amount of geographical information.

4.1 Selecting the Geo-spatial Resources

In order to enrich WordNet with the desired information, the first step in the process was the selection of one or more suitable sources of geo-spatial terms. In principle, there are various ways to collect such terms. For example, this can be done by extracting them from texts on the geo-spatial literature, by analysing the millions or billions of user queries stored in the query logs of existing search engines, by analyzing geo-spatial glossaries, or by selecting them from existing geo-spatial gazetteers. We chose the latter approach. In fact, geo-spatial gazetteers already contain high quality and huge quantities of readymade and usable names of geo-spatial classes (features or feature types) as well as corresponding instances (places), sometimes organized in hierarchies, thus providing also (spatial) relations between them. Last but not least, we especially looked to those providing latitude and longitude coordinates. On the basis of quantity and quality criteria, we evaluated several candidates including Wikipedia[10], YAGO [1], DBPedia[11], GEMET[12] and the ADL gazetteer[13], but they are limited

---

[9] http://www.cse.unt.edu/~rada/downloads.html#wordnet
[10] http://www.wikipedia.org/
[11] http://dbpedia.org/About
[12] http://www.eionet.europa.eu/gemet/about
[13] http://www.alexandria.ucsb.edu/gazetteer/

either in locations, classes, relations or metadata. GeoNames and TGN, instead, both met our requirements:

- **Thesaurus of Geographical Names (TGN).**[14]. TGN is a poly-hierarchical (i.e. multiple parents are allowed) structured vocabulary for place names. It also provides alternative names, feature types and geographic (approximate) coordinates. It includes administrative political (e.g., cities, nations) and physical (e.g., mountains, rivers) entities. The temporal coverage of TGN ranges from prehistory to the present (some historical nations and empires are also included). It currently contains around 1.1 million names and 646 feature types, focusing on places particularly important for the study of art and architecture.

- *GeoNames.* GeoNames is perhaps the most famous geo-spatial database. It includes geographical data such as place names in various languages, latitude, longitude, altitude and population collected from several data sources. Latitude and longitude coordinates are stored according to the WGS84 (World Geodetic System 1984) standard. It currently contains over 8 millions geographical names for around 7 millions unique places. At top level, the places are categorised into 9 broader categories (called feature classes), further divided into 663 sub-classes or features, most of them with a natural language description. A special *null* class contains unclassified entities. In Table 1 they are given in detail. GeoNames provides an interface which allows users to manually edit and add new names. The data is available free of charge through a number of web services. The database is also available for free download under a creative commons attribution license.

Table 1. Feature classes and sub-classes in GeoNames

Feature Class	Description	Number of classes
A	Administrative divisions of a country. It also represents states, regions, political entities and zones	16
H	Water bodies, e.g., ocean, sea, river, lake, stream, etc.	137
L	Parks, areas, etc.	49
P	Populated places, e.g., capitals, cities, towns, small towns, villages, etc.	11
R	Roads and railroads	23
S	Spots, buildings and farms	242
T	Mountains, hills, rocks, valleys, deserts, etc.	97
U	Undersea areas	71
V	Forests, heaths, vineyards, groves, etc.	17

We used GeoNames as the main source. Being a thesaurus, TGN is instead used for consultation in order to better disambiguate GeoNames classes and relations.

---

[14] http://www.getty.edu/research/conducting_research/
vocabularies/tgn

4.2 Class Analysis

This step is motivated by the following two objectives: (i) to make explicit the semantic of each class name, thus disambiguating each of them to a single concept, and (ii) to categorise and organise the semantically related concepts in a subsumption hierarchy. Notice in particular that relations in GeoNames are only implicitly provided (i.e. the kind is not explicitly mentioned). Relations between instances can be mainly mapped to a generic *part meronym* (part-of) relation, including administrative and physical containment. Relations between classes and instances can be mapped to *instance hyponym* (instance-of) relation; no relations between classes are explicitly provided (i.e., the classes are provided in a flat list).

(i) We found that out of the 663 classes in GeoNames, for 57 of them no definition is provided at all. For these names we tried to understand the exact intended meaning, most of the time by considering the context of the term used, i.e. the corresponding feature class, and the instances (the places) associated to it. It was also observed that, even though the definitions are provided for the remaining terms, in some cases they are either ambiguous or not clear enough. Consider for instance the class *astronomical station*. GeoNames defines it as "*a point on the earth whose position has been determined by observations of celestial bodies*". Conversely, we decided that a more appropriate definition is "*a station from which celestial bodies and events can be observed*" and therefore we substituted it.

(ii) Once each of the 663 class names were refined and disambiguated to a single concept, following basic principles from Library Science we started categorising those semantically related concepts based upon their similar and dissimilar characteristics [22] and organised them in a hierarchical order. The result was a set of unconnected hierarchies. In choosing the characteristics, geo-spatial aspects were considered. Consider for instance the class *intermittent pond*. One may treat it as "a type of pond" and one may prefer to treat it as "a kind of intermittent thing". The former one is motivated by "geographical" feature. While, the latter one is motivated by its "temporal" aspect. Both views are correct from the classification point of view, but their correctness in a context is highly dependable on the purpose of the classification. In our case we chose the former one.

5 Mapping to WordNet

Concepts identified with the first phase were mapped - mainly manually with the help of some automatic discovery facilities - to WordNet synsets. We first tried to identify those concepts having an exact match with a synset in WordNet. For this purpose, it is clear that a syntactic match is not enough to judge about its existence. We rather worked at the conceptual level. For exact match at conceptual level we mean that a corresponding word for the class name exists in WordNet, and exactly one synset denotes the same meaning. For an easier identification of such synsets, we started from those concepts first which were more generic in nature according to the categorisation we did in the previous step. Consider for instance the following hierarchy:

valley ("*a long depression in the surface of the land that usually contains a river*")
   ravine ("*a deep narrow steep-sided valley (especially one formed by running water)*")
      canyon ("*a ravine formed by a river in an area with little rainfall*")
      gorge ("*a deep ravine (usually with a river running through it)*")
   hanging valley ("*a valley the floor of which is notably higher than the valley or shore to which it leads; most common in areas that have been glaciated*")

We first looked in WordNet for a suitable synset for the concept *valley* and then we proceeded with the concept *ravine*, visiting the whole tree top-down. This order allowed restricting the search in WordNet to those synsets that are more specific than the previous one. In this way we found 306 exact correspondences with the Geo-Names classes. In case of mismatch, we created a new synset in WordNet and identified the most appropriate synset denoting a more generic meaning for the class name. In other words we identified a suitable parent (according to the *hypernym* relation) for it. We faced several different situations and solved them accordingly. Due to space limitation, we present here only some notable examples:

- *A more generic synset exists and no synset is available for the term.* Consider the class *palm grove*, defined in GeoNames as "*a planting of palm trees*". This concept is not available in WordNet, but the more generic synset for *grove* ("*garden consisting of a small cultivated wood without undergrowth*") is available. In this case we created a new synset for *palm grove* in WordNet and linked it with *grove* using a *hypernym* relation.

- *A more generic synset exists but a synset is available for the term.* Consider the class *water tank*. GeoNames defines the term as "*a contained pool or tank of water at, below, or above ground level*", while WordNet defines it as "*a tank that holds the water used to flush a toilet*". WordNet does not provide any other sense for this term. It is clear that these two definitions are not equivalent. However, both definitions are more specific than *tank*, defined in WordNet as "*a large (usually metallic) vessel for holding gases or liquids*". In this situation we created a new sense for the term *water tank*. We positioned it as a sibling of the already existing one, by connecting it to *tank* using the *hypernym* relation.

- *Linking synsets using the part meronym.* We occasionally considered appropriate to introduce some *part meronym* relations instead of the *hypernym* relation. For instance, an *icecap depression* (defined in GeoNames as "*a comparatively depressed area on an icecap*") is a part of an *icecap* (defined in GeoNames as "*a dome-shaped mass of glacial ice covering an area of mountain summits or other high lands; smaller than an ice street*") and not something more specific. A similar discourse can be done for *canal bend* and *section of canal* which are both parts of *canal*.

- *Missing words in an existing synset.* It is interesting to note that in few cases we found that, even though the candidate term is not available, there is a synset denoting the same meaning in WordNet. In other words, the synset contains synonyms for the candidate term. It is clear that such cases are very difficult to detect just using automatic tools. One such example is the term *leprosarium*. This term is not available in WordNet, but there is a synset for the equivalent term *lazaret*. In these cases we added the GeoNames term to the corresponding

WordNet synset. Another example is *metro station*, added in the synset for *subway station*.

- **Multiple synset candidates.** The most subtle case is perhaps when the candidate concept has close match with multiple synsets in WordNet. This is due to the well known polysemy problem (see for instance [23]), namely very fine grained distinctions are provided. The solutions we adopted are described in Section 7.

To assess the quality of the mapping produced, a validation work was carried out by some experts in Library Science, particularly skilled in knowledge organization. The experts were different to those who were involved in the first phase of our work. This in order to assure that the validation work was not influenced by any unexpected external factor or bias. In order to carry out the validation work, the validators had to look at factors like the soundness of the description for the concepts (determined during the first phase), suitability of the selected synsets in WordNet, suitability of assigned names for the plural forms of concepts, and so on (see Section 7 for a list and corresponding description of the most interesting issues). In case of disagreement we iterated on the previous steps till all the conflicting cases were solved.

6 Integration of the Resources

Once the mapping has been produced and validated, the next phase consisted in the integration of the two resources. This phase is fully automatic and consisted of the following three steps:

- **Concept Integration.** We integrated GeoNames classes with WordNet (previously imported into the knowledge base). Here, by integration we mean the integration of the concepts built during the first phase (along with their description) which were not found in WordNet during the second phase, together with the *hypernym* and *part meronym* relations necessary to connect them to the existing concept network. For each new concept we created a corresponding English synset[15] by specifying the word, which is the name of the class, the gloss, which is the description of the class, and the part of speech, which is always noun. For the cases in which a synset already existed, but it did not contain the name of the class, we just added it to the list of words of the synset. For the classes having an exact match with WordNet, we just saved a reference to the existing concept/synset for future use (see next steps).
- **Instance migration.** This step is about importing the locations contained in GeoNames into the knowledge base. Notice that in WordNet, the specific *instance hypernym* relation is used to link a synset denoting an entity to the synset denoting the corresponding class (or classes). We rather created a new object in the entity part of our knowledge base, clearly distinguishing between concepts and instances. We created a new object for each of the about 7 millions entities in GeoNames and related each of them to the concept of the corresponding class previously identified or created. We also created *part meronym* relations between such entities, according to the information provided in GeoNames. For instance,

---

[15] We will also create corresponding Italian synsets in the near future.

we codify the information that *Florence* is part of the *Tuscany* region in *Italy*. As final note, the locations of the special *null* class were treated as instances of the generic class *location*.

- **Metadata Importing.** Locations in GeoNames are equipped with some metadata including the place name, alternative names in multiple languages (the specific languages can be identified), latitude, longitude, altitude and population. For instance, for the Italian city *Florence* the alternative names which are provided are *Firence, Firenze, Florencia, Florencija, Florens, Florenz, Florència, Flórens*; latitude is 43.7666667; longitude is 11.25; average altitude is 87 meters; population is 371,517 habitants. We attached all such information to the corresponding object (focusing on English and Italian names for the moment) created for the geographical entity in the entity part of the knowledge base.

7   Critical Issues

This section describes the main issues we faced during the present work and the solutions we adopted for them. Due to the space limitation, only few of the issues, those considered particularly important and interesting, are described.

7.1   Facility: The Service vs. Function Approach

The term *facility* is a key term in GeoNames. Being generic, a quite considerable amount of more specific classes are present in GeoNames. A mistake in the analysis of this term would have major consequences. In WordNet there are 5 different noun senses for the term, most of them focusing more on the notion of "service", rather than on the notion of "function":

- **facility,** installation (a building or place that provides a particular service or is used for a particular industry) *"the assembly plant is an enormous facility"*
- **adeptness,** adroitness, deftness, **facility**, quickness (skillful performance or ability without difficulty) *"his quick adeptness was a product of good design"; "he was famous for his facility as an archer"*
- **facility**, readiness (a natural effortlessness) *"they conversed with great facility"; "a happy readiness of conversation"--Jane Austen*
- **facility** (something designed and created to serve a particular function and to afford a particular convenience or service) *"catering facilities"; "toilet facilities"; "educational facilities"*
- **facility** (a service that an organization or a piece of equipment offers you) *"a cell phone with internet facility"*

On the other hand, the description of the term provided in GeoNames (*"a building or buildings housing a center, institute, foundation, hospital, prison, mission, courthouse, etc."*) is rather generic and incomplete as includes only building or group of buildings. There are classes which are not buildings but still they can be treated as facilities, e.g., farms and parks. This is in line with the first sense in WordNet, where a facility can be a building or even a place. On one side many buildings provide services. Building housing banks usually provide transaction services; building housing hospitals usually provide health care services; building housing libraries usually provide access to the catalogue and book consultation. However, there are also buildings (or generic constructions) which do not provide any service, but are rather intended to have a function. For instance, houses are used for living purposes, while roads, streets and bridges have a transportation function (but no specific service is provided).

We decided to adhere to the WordNet vision and clearly distinguish between buildings and places providing a service (placed under the first sense) and those having just a (specific or generic) function (placed under the forth sense).

7.2 Plurals and Parenthesis

92 classes in GeoNames are present both in singular form, e.g., *populated place* and *vineyard*, and in plural form, e.g., *populated places* and *vineyards*. Furthermore, 99 classes are represented as a mixed singular-plural form, e.g., *arbour(s)*, *marsh(es)* and *distributary(-ies)*, sometimes in conjunction with the singular or plural form also.

From our analysis, singular forms represent single entities; plural forms indicate groups of entities; mixed forms are used when it is not easy to distinguish between the two previous cases. The approach we followed is to avoid plurals, identifying for each plural or mixed form a corresponding, more appropriate, name. For instance, we substituted *lakes* with *lake chain* and *mountains* with *mountain range*.

7.3 Dealing with Polysemy

242 class names in GeoNames are polysemous, namely they have two or more similar, or related, meanings. It is not always easy to understand the correct meaning meant, especially in the cases in which no description is provided.

To find out the right concept, we compared the description, if available, of a class to each of the meanings of that class in WordNet. In some cases (15), we found out that a part of the description matches with one sense and another part of the description matches with another sense. Examples of such classes are *university*, *library* and *market*. During disambiguation such situations were overcome by comparing related terms in WordNet, for instance the ancestors, with the GeoNames feature class.

To be more concrete consider the following example for the term *university*. University is defined in GeoNames as: *"an institution for higher learning with teaching and research facilities constituting a graduate school and professional schools that award master's degrees and doctorates and an undergraduate division that awards bachelor's degrees"*. It can be then summarized to be an institution for higher learning including teaching and research facilities that awards degrees. The term university has three meanings in WordNet:

- **university** (the body of faculty and students at a university)
- **university** (establishment where a seat of higher learning is housed, including administrative and living quarters as well as facilities for research and teaching)
- **university** (a large and diverse institution of higher learning created to educate for life and for a profession and to grant degrees)

The first meaning has little connection with GeoNames description and is excluded. The second meaning is relevant as it describes a university as an establishment for higher learning which also facilitates research and teaching. The third meaning is also relevant as it describes that it is a large institution of higher learning to educate for life and to grant degrees. To better disambiguate between the two remaining candidate meanings we then compared the hypernym hierarchy of the two synsets with the feature class provided for the term in GeoNames. The third meaning is a descendant of *social group*. The second meaning is a descendant of *construction*, which is closer to the feature class S (spots, building and farms). As a consequence, we finally selected the second meaning.

When such kind of analysis was not enough to disambiguate, we selected the instances from all close matched senses of WordNet and looked for their co-occurrence with the instances in GeoNames. In case of a match at instance level, we chose the corresponding sense. For example, consider the candidate term *palace*. GeoNames defines it as "*a large stately house, often a royal or presidential residence*". The first and forth senses for the term in WordNet look like possible candidates. They define it as "*a large and stately mansion*" and "*official residence of an exalted person (as a sovereign) correspond to it*" respectively. Following the proposed approach, we found that *Buckingham Palace* is the only instance in common with the first sense whereas no instances in common at all were found with the fourth sense. Therefore, we chose the first sense.

7.4 Unique Name Provision

In GeoNames, the same name is occasionally used to denote different concepts in different feature classes. This is particularly frequent for the classes under the feature class T - which denotes mountains, hills, rocks - and U - which denotes undersea entities. Some examples are *hill*, *mountain*, *levee* and *bench*. However, when feasible, it is always preferable to provide unique names to each semantically individual concept. And this is what we did, namely we identified a unique name to each concept. For the above examples, we distinguished between *hill* and *submarine hill*, between *mountain* and *seamount*, between *levee* and *submarine levee*, and between *bench* and *oceanic bench*. Such terms are not just arbitrarily assigned. They are rather collected from authentic literature available on Geography, Oceanography and Geology (e.g., Encyclopaedia Britannica[16]).

7.5 Physical vs. Abstract Entities

It is important to note that, since GeoNames always provides latitude and longitude coordinates for the entities, all of them must be seen as physical entities, that is having physical existence. However, when mapping the concepts from GeoNames to WordNet, we observed that for 27 of such concepts, WordNet only provides abstract senses, namely they are categorized as descendant of *abstract entity*. For example, for the concept *political entity* ("*a unit with political responsibilities*") WordNet provides a single synset at distance 6 from *abstract entity*. It is clear that, it would be incorrect to associate a geo-political entity, say *India*, under the abstract concept provided by WordNet. In these cases we rather preferred to create a new synset in WordNet

---

[16] http://www.britannica.com/

somewhere under *physical entity*. In the specific case, we created the new synset with the term *geo-political entity* defined as *"the geographical area controlled or managed by a political entity"* and connected it, through *hypernym* relation, to *physical object*.

8 Statistics

In this section we provide some interesting statistics regarding the imported resources as well as the constructed resource, GeoWordNet. In Table 2 we report statistical data about what we imported from WordNet 2.1 and the Italian MultiWordNet. Excluding the 6988 entities and related relations, WordNet was completely imported into the knowledge base. MultiWordNet, mainly due to the heuristics used to reconstruct the mapping with WordNet 2.1, was only partially imported. In particular, we imported all words, 88.4% of the senses and 86.3% of the synsets. We did not import the 318 (Italian) lexical and semantic relations provided.

Table 2. Statistical data for WordNet 2.1 and MultiWordNet

WordNet 2.1		MultiWordNet	
Object	**Instances**	**Object**	**Instances**
Synset	110,609	Synset	33,356
Relation	204,481	Relation	-
Word	147,252	Word	45,156
Sense	192,620	Sense	59,656
Word exceptional form	4,728	Word exceptional form	-

Statistics about GeoNames (as from the version downloaded on 15th March 2009) are reported in Table 3. In particular, it shows the number of alternative names in multiple languages, names explicitly marked as preferred, and number of natural languages covered (those having an ISO 639 code).

Table 3. Statistical data for GeoNames

GeoNames	
Object	**Instances**
Location	6,907,417
Alternative name	855,341
Preferred name	92,289
Natural language	230

We analyzed the 663 GeoNames classes and their descriptions and compared them with those in WordNet. The result of our analysis is summarized in Table 4.

Table 5 shows the amount and kind of relations we created. Notice that for each relation we also created the corresponding inverse relations. Therefore, the provided numbers must be doubled (726 relations between classes, 13,814,834 relations between instances and classes, and 4,530,566 relations between instances).

Table 4. Main results of the GeoNames class analysis

GeoNames Classes	Instances	%
Which have a description in GeoNames	606	91.40
Which have no description in GeoNames	57	8.60
For which we provided or changed the description	92	13.88
For which we found a corresponding synset in WordNet	306	46.15
For which only one noun synset is available in WordNet	160	24.13
For which multiple noun synsets are available in WordNet	242	36.50
For which one part of the description matches with one synset and another part of the description matches with another synset	15	2.26
For which the description does not match with any of the synsets	38	5.73
For which we had to create a new synset in WordNet	357	53.84

Table 5. Statistics about the number of relations created

Objects involved	Kind of relation	Quantity
Relations between classes	Hypernym	327
	Part meronym	36
Relations between instances and classes	Instance hypernym	6,907,417
Relations between instances	Part meronym	2,265,283

9   Conclusions and Future Work

In this paper we presented GeoWordNet, a semantic and linguistic resource we created from the full integration of GeoNames with WordNet and the Italian portion of MultiWordNet. The methodology we followed is largely automatic, with manual intervention for the critical parts. This allowed obtaining a very satisfactory quantitative and qualitative result. By providing information about places in the world and proprieties like latitude and longitude coordinates, GeoWordNet supports interoperability in geo-spatial applications.

GeoWordNet is only the first step towards the creation of a huge and high quality knowledge base that we call the Universal Knowledge. The future work will mainly include the integration of other geo-spatial resources (like TGN) as well as concepts and instances from other domains (including people, organizations, events) and thus the instantiation of the domain part following the faceted approach (e.g., see [24, 22]).

Acknowledgments. This work has been partially funded by the FP7 Living Knowledge FET IP European Project. Thanks to Gaia Trecarichi and Veronica Rizzi for the pleasant and fruitful discussions about geo-spatial issues. We also want to thank Ilya Zaihrayeu and Marco Marasca for their contribution to the definition of the data structures and Abdelhakim Freihat for the importing of the Italian MultiWordNet.

References

1. Suchanek, F.M., Kasneci, G., Weikum, G.: YAGO: a core of semantic knowledge unifying WordNet and Wikipedia. In: Proc. of the 16th WWW, pp. 697–706 (2007)
2. Egenhofer, M.J.: Toward the Semantic GeoSpatial Web. In: The 10th ACM Int. Symposium on Advances in Geographic Information Systems (ACM-GIS), pp. 1-4 (2002)
3. Kolas, D., Dean, M., Hebeler, J.: Geospatial semantic web: Architecture of ontologies. In: Rodríguez, M.A., Cruz, I., Levashkin, S., Egenhofer, M.J. (eds.) GeoS 2005. LNCS, vol. 3799, pp. 183–194. Springer, Heidelberg (2005)
4. Shvaiko, P., Vaccari, L., Trecarichi, G.: Semantic geo-catalog: a scenario and requirements. Poster at the 4th Ontology Matching Workshop (OM) at the ISWC (2009)
5. Abdelmoty, A.I., Smart, P., Jones, C.B.: Building Place Ontologies for the Semantic Web: issues and approaches. In: Proc. of the 4th ACM workshop on GIR (2007)
6. Janowicz, K., Schade, S., Bröring, A., Keßler, C., Stasch, C., Maue', P., Diekhof, T.: A transparent Semantic Enablement Layer for the Geospatial Web. In: The Terra Cognita Workshop at ISWC (2009)
7. Roman, D., Klien, E., Skogan, D.: SWING – A Semantic Web Service Framework for the Geospatial Domain. In: The Terra Cognita Workshop (2006)
8. Angioni, M., Demontis, R., Tuveri, F.: Enriching WordNet to Index and Retrieve Semantic Information. In: Proc. of 2nd Int. Conf. on Metadata and Semantics Research (2006)
9. Vorz, R., Kleb, J., Mueller, W.: Towards ontology-based disambiguation of geographical identifiers. In: Proc. of the 16th WWW Conference (2007)
10. Buscardi, D., Rosso, P.: Geo-wordnet: Automatic Georeferencing of wordnet. In: Proc. of the 5th Int. Conference on Language Resources and Evaluation, LREC (2008)
11. Kuhl, W.: Geospatial semantics: Why, of What, and How? Journal of Data Semantics (JoDS) III, 1–24 (2005)
12. Keßler, C., Janowicz, K., Bishr, M.: An agenda for the Next Generation Gazetteer: Geographic Information Contribution and Retrieval. In: The Int. Conference on Advances in Geographic Information Systems (ACM SIGSPATIAL GIS) (2009)
13. Jones, C.B., Adbelmoty, A.I., Fu, G.: Maintaining Ontologies for Geographical Information Retrieval on the Web. In: Meersman, R., Tari, Z., Schmidt, D.C. (eds.) CoopIS 2003, DOA 2003, and ODBASE 2003. LNCS, vol. 2888, pp. 934–951. Springer, Heidelberg (2003)
14. Auer, S., Lehmann, J., Hellman, S.: LinkedGeoData - Adding a Spatial Dimension to the Web of Data. In: Bernstein, A., Karger, D.R., Heath, T., Feigenbaum, L., Maynard, D., Motta, E., Thirunarayan, K. (eds.) ISWC 2009. LNCS, vol. 5823, pp. 731–746. Springer, Heidelberg (2009)
15. Chaves, M.S., Silva, M.J., Martins, B.: A Geographic Knowledge Base for Semantic Web Applications. In: Proc. of 20th Brazilian Symposium on Databases, SBBD (2005)
16. Miller, G.A., Hristea, F.: WordNet Nouns: classes and instances. Computational Linguistics 32(1), 1–3 (2006)
17. Egenhofer, M.J., Dube, M.P.: Topological Relations from Metric Refinements. In: Proc. of the 17th ACM SIGSPATIAL Int. Conference on Advances in GIS (2009)
18. Giunchiglia, F., Zaihrayeu, I.: Lightweight Ontologies. The Encyclopedia of Database Systems (2007)
19. Giunchiglia, F., Yatskevich, M., Shvaiko, P.: Semantic Matching: algorithms and implementation. Journal on Data Semantics IX (2007)
20. Giunchiglia, F., Maltese, V., Autayeu, A.: Computing minimal mappings. In: Proc. of the 4th Ontology Matching Workshop at the ISWC (2009)

21. Hill, L.L., Frew, J., Zheng, Q.: Geographic names: the implementation of a gazetteer in a georeferenced digital library. D-Lib Magazine 5(1) (1999)
22. Ranganathan, S.R.: Prolegomena to library classification. Asia Publishing House (1967)
23. Mihalcea, R., Moldovan, D.I.: EZ Wordnet: principles for automatic generation of a coarse grained WordNet. In: Proc. of FLAIRS (2001)
24. Giunchiglia, F., Dutta, B., Maltese, V.: Faceted Lightweight Ontologies. In: Borgida, A.T., Chaudhri, V.K., Giorgini, P., Yu, E.S. (eds.) Conceptual Modeling: Foundations and Applications. LNCS, vol. 5600, pp. 36–51. Springer, Heidelberg (2009)
25. Giunchiglia, F., Zaihrayeu, I., Farazi, F.: Converting classifications into owl ontologies. In: Proceedings of Artificial Intelligence and Simulation of Behaviour Convention Workshop on Matching and Meaning, Edinburgh, UK (2009)

Assessing the Safety of Knowledge Patterns in OWL Ontologies

Luigi Iannone, Ignazio Palmisano, Alan L. Rector, and Robert Stevens

University of Manchester
Kilburn Building
Oxford Road M13 9PL
Manchester, UK
`lastname@cs.manchester.ac.uk`

Abstract. The availability of a concrete language for embedding knowledge patterns inside OWL ontologies makes it possible to analyze their impact on the semantics when applied to the ontologies themselves. Starting from recent results available in the literature, this work proposes a sufficient condition for identifying *safe* patterns encoded in OPPL. The resulting framework can be used to implement OWL ontology engineering tools that help knowledge engineers to understand the level of extensibility of their models as well as pattern users to determine what are the safe ways of utilizing a pattern in their ontologies.

1 Introduction

OWL ontologies may be built for the most disparate purposes. Yet, as soon as they are made public, the problem of their extension arises. The presence of the `owl:import` primitive in the language testifies to the inclination of OWL to encourage ontology re-use. The addition of any axiom to an ontology does, however, modify its semantics. The extent of the impact of these alterations can be evaluated, but , at the moment, not anticipated or formally analyzed when an ontology is either being developed or recently released. The knowledge engineers, at the current state of the art, have only annotations for documenting what are the possible extensions of their ontology, and there is no formal language for their encoding.

The effect of this limitation is better explained using an analogy. Let us suppose for a moment that the Java programming language did not provide the `final` primitive to specify that a certain Java class/method cannot be sub-classed/overridden. API developers could not prevent their users from extending portions of the API object model that are meant to be fixed and non extensible. The consequence would be that all the assumptions about some pieces of code behaving in a fixed and pre-determined way would no longer hold, thus making the re-use of third party code more unpredictable and unreliable. One could argue that knowledge re-use is meant to be more flexible than the code counterpart, that is why we observe that nothing as strict as the `final` primitive is needed. What we claim, though, is that it would be useful if the knowledge engineer, whilst developing their ontologies, could specify what and how to extend it in order to remain compliant with its original meta-model. The users could then decide whether to follow such guidelines or not, but natural language annotations are too

L. Aroyo et al. (Eds.): ESWC 2010, Part I, LNCS 6088, pp. 137–151, 2010.

ambiguous for their specification. Secondly, but equally importantly, a formal language could also help the original ontology creators in understanding which ones, amongst many envisaged extensions are actually harmless with respect to the original semantics of the ontology itself.

We recently [1] proposed the adoption of OPPL 2, a declarative manipulation language for ontologies, as a language for embedding knowledge patterns into OWL ontologies. In this paper, we now propose a formal framework for evaluating the impact that the usage of such patterns (written in OPPL) could have on the semantics of an ontology. We aim to provide a methodology for deciding which patterns are actually safe to use in combination with an ontology i.e.: they do not disrupt its original semantics.

The remainder of this paper is structured as follows: Sect. 2 recaps the main features of our concrete language for embedding patterns into an OWL Ontology; Sect. 3 illustrates our proposal for the evaluation of a pattern's impact on an ontology; Sect. 4 briefly surveys the state of the art on the subject; Sect. 5 Discusses the implications of our approach and outlines possible future directions for the investigation in this area.

2   OPPL Patterns

One of the main criticisms of the current way of re-using ontologies is that OWL artefacts are often *opaque* because of their size and their complexity [2]. The rationales, especially those behind the major ontologies, designed to be re-used, are often difficult to grasp. Consider, for instance, the following axiom taken from the Dolce Ultra-Light ontology[1] (in Manchester OWL Syntax):

```
InformationRealization equivalentTo
            PhysicalObject and realizes some InformationObject
            or (Event and hasParticipant some PhysicalObject)
```

It is an implementation of the *Information Realization* pattern that "[...] represents the relations between information objects like poems, songs, formulas, etc., and their physical realizations like printed books, registered tracks, physical files, etc. [2]". There is no distinction between entities or constructs that are fixed parts of the pattern and those which are variable and can be modified in order to re-use the same pattern in different situations. As an example, if we restrict ourselves to the first disjunct:

```
InformationRealization equivalentTo
            PhysicalObject and realizes some InformationObject
```

the pattern describes a relationship between three entities: a sub-class of *Information-Realization*, a sub-property of *realizes*, and a sub-class of *InformationObject*. The fixed aspects of the pattern is the conjunction between being a *PhysicalObject* with, as a filler for a sub-property of *realizes*, a sub-class of *InformationObject*.

Although this appears in the natural language description of the pattern, an automatic tool cannot adequately derive this kind of information when dealing with the OWL exemplar usage of this pattern. This is why in [1] the adoption of OPPL as a concrete language for embedding knowledge patterns into OWL ontologies was proposed. In [3], OPPL was initially motivated by the need of ontology developers to transform one

---

[1] http://www.loa-cnr.it/ontologies/DUL.owl

ontology to an axiomatically richer form. The aim of its pattern sub-language is, instead, to encapsulate recurring knowledge structures (set of parameterized operations on OWL axioms) expressed in OWL. For a example-based description of the OPPL pattern sub-language we refer the reader to [1]; the complete OPPL grammar is available online[2].

Here we limit ourselves to report the basic structure of an OPPL pattern: *Variables* and *Actions*. Variables, just as in full OPPL, have one of the following types: CLASS, OBJECTPROPERTY, DATAPROPERTY, INDIVIDUAL, CONSTANT. They can be *input* variables, whose values should be provided by the user, or *generated* variables, whose value depends on other variables.

All variables, except for those of the CONSTANT kind, can be scoped; this means that the set of allowed values for a variable can be restricted:

(a) `superClassOf` and `subClassOf` for CLASS variables; the values must be super-classes (sub-classes) of a class expression: `?x:CLASS[subClassOf A]`.
(b) `superPropertyOf` and `subPropertyOf` for DATAPROPERTY and OBJECT-PROPERTY variables; the values must be super-properties (sub-properties) of a property expression.
(c) `instanceOf` for INDIVIDUAL variables; the values must be instances of a class expression: `?x:INDIVIDUAL[instanceOf A and hasP some B]`.

Let us consider the *partWhole* pattern, which describes a whole as having some parts and constrains all the possible parts to be among those in the values of the `?part` variable; this pattern will be referenced in the remainder of the paper.

```
?whole:CLASS, ?part:CLASS, ?allParts:CLASS = createUnion(?part.VALUES)
BEGIN
    ADD ?whole subClassOf has_direct_part some ?part,
    ADD ?whole subClassOf has_direct_part only ?allParts
END;
```

It is the simplest OPPL version of the recurring knowledge pattern that binds an object to all its parts and imposes that such an object cannot have other parts than those specified in the values of the `?part` variable. The pattern presents two input variables (`?whole` and `?part`) and a generated one (`?allParts`) that is the union of all the values assigned to `?part`. It can be instantiated to populate one's ontology, with the only assumption that such an ontology contains the `has_direct_part` object property. One can, for example, invoke the pattern as follows:

```
partWhole(Molecule,Atom)
partWhole(Atom, {Proton, Neutron, Electron})
```

The results of the instantiation are[3]:

```
Molecule subClassOf has_direct_part some Atom
Molecule subClassOf has_direct_part only Atom
Atom subClassOf has_direct_part some Proton
Atom subClassOf has_direct_part some Neutron
Atom subClassOf has_direct_part some Electron
Atom subClassOf has_direct_part only (Proton or Electron or Neutron)
```

To the best of our knowledge, there is no alternative concrete language to express knowledge patterns and use them inside tools. An attempt to build a framework for

---

[2] http://www.cs.man.ac.uk/~iannonel/oppl/documentation.html
[3] This is only an illustrative example, not a correct ontology for Physics (i.e., Hydrogen atoms need not have neutrons).

automatically extracting patterns from an ontology and apply them to another one is described in [2]. It does not, however, attempt to store the extracted pattern in any form, hence it cannot be re-used. Moreover, it relies on SPARQL [4] for implementing the extraction mechanism, which, in the authors' own words, allows only for partial extractions that often require manual refinements (see Sect. 3.1 in [2]).

Besides the ability to store and re-use knowledge patterns using the same vocabulary of the embedding ontology, having a concrete language (such as OPPL) opens other directions of investigation concerning the repercussions of the use of a particular pattern in an ontology. In particular, as we shall see in the next section, one can determine whether the instantiations of such patterns in an ontology have consequences on its semantics. This makes it possible both for the pattern authors and their users to anticipate the circumstances under which the usage of a pattern in combination with an ontology will cause changes in the model, and prevent undesirable alterations.

3   Evaluating the Impact of Using a Pattern

A concrete language for encoding patterns inside ontologies provides a means for ontology engineers to specify how their ontologies could be extended; e.g., the *partWhole* pattern, when instantiated, will produce sets of axioms; this set can then be either added to the ontology itself or to an extension. Sometimes, however, adding an axiom to an ontology can affect its semantics in ways that are not in line with the principle of re-using and extending an ontology. Let us illustrate this by means of an example, by using *partWhole* in combination with two ontologies $\mathcal{O}_1$ and $\mathcal{O}_2$:

$\mathcal{O}_1$	$\mathcal{O}_2$
	owl:import $\mathcal{O}_1$
Molecule $\sqsubseteq$ $\top$, *Atom* $\sqsubseteq$ $\top$	*Proton* $\sqsubseteq$ $\top$, *Electron* $\sqsubseteq$ $\top$, *Neutron* $\sqsubseteq$ $\top$
*has_part** $\sqsubseteq$ *has_part*	*Atom* $\sqcap$ *Proton* $\sqsubseteq$ $\bot$, *Atom* $\sqcap$ *Neutron* $\sqsubseteq$ $\bot$, *Atom* $\sqcap$ *Electron* $\sqsubseteq$ $\bot$
	Proton $\sqcap$ *Electron* $\sqsubseteq$ $\bot$, *Proton* $\sqcap$ *Neutron* $\sqsubseteq$ $\bot$, *Neutron* $\sqcap$ *Electron* $\sqsubseteq$ $\bot$

Now let us instantiate `partWhole`, and add the resulting axioms, listed in the previous section, to $\mathcal{O}_2$. One non obvious outcome of the whole process is that now a reasoner can derive that *Molecule* and *Atom* are disjoint[5]. Irrespective of whether this may or may not make sense in the particular domain, we have just proved that the instantiation of a pattern, which was aimed at extending the initial ontology, has some side-effects that act on the semantics of entities defined in our imported ontology ($\mathcal{O}_1$). This means that there are axioms, using only symbols from $\mathcal{O}_1$, which do not hold in $\mathcal{O}_1$ but hold in $\mathcal{O}_2$, after the above pattern instantiations; e.g., $\models$ *Atom* $\sqcap$ *Molecule* $\sqsubseteq$ $\bot$. This means that $\mathcal{O}_1$ is being extended without preserving its original semantics.

The main shortcoming of *disruptively* extending ontologies in this way can be better illustrated by the following scenario. Let us suppose that we have a software application that uses $\mathcal{O}_1$ for its functionalities. Now imagine we have to add one functionality that requires that we extend $\mathcal{O}_1$. If our extension does not preserve the semantics of $\mathcal{O}_1$, there

---

[4] http://www.w3.org/TR/rdf-sparql-query/

[5] From: *Molecule* $\sqsubseteq$ $\forall has\_direct\_part.Atom$, *Molecule* $\sqsubseteq$ $\exists has\_direct\_part.Atom$, *Atom* $\sqcap$ *Proton* $\sqsubseteq$ $\bot$,

Atom $\sqcap$ *Neutron* $\sqsubseteq$ $\bot$, *Atom* $\sqcap$ *Electron* $\sqsubseteq$ $\bot$ *Atom* $\sqsubseteq$ $\forall has\_direct\_part.(Proton \sqcup Electron \sqcup Neutron)$

is no guarantee that all the functionalities in our pre-existing version of the application will keep working after replacing $\mathcal{O}_1$ with it. This means we will have to, at least, re-test, and, in the worst case, re-write, the portion of the application which is now incompatible with the changes produced by our extension. This is one of the reasons why, in the recent literature the notion of *conservative extensions* of an ontology [4] received a lot of attention. Intuitively, a conservative extension of an ontology is another ontology that has the same interpretation for the symbols it shares with the original one. A consequence of this definition is that queries on the shared vocabulary have the same results irrespective of whether they are carried out on the original ontology or on one of its conservative extensions. Producing conservative extensions when re-using ontologies is, therefore, very important to avoid the drawbacks described in the little scenario above. Since in [1] we proposed OPPL patterns as means to produce re-usable ontology, the question becomes whether it is possible to decide if a pattern will produce a conservative extension of the ontology it is applied to. We already know from [5] that determining whether an ontology *safely extends* (is a conservative extension of) another ontology is not decidable for expressive Description Logics such as OWL-DL. Deciding whether a pattern will produce a safe extension presents the further complication of taking variables into account.

To the best of our knowledge, the only workaround for the undecidability mentioned above is the identification of classes of axioms that produce a conservative extension when added to an ontology. Belonging to one of such classes is only a sufficient condition for safety, and, so far, only one class has been fully characterised and depends on the notion of the *locality* of an axiom (see Def. 25 in [5]). Intuitively, an axiom is local w.r.t. a signature when, once reduced to the symbols in the signature, it results in either a tautology or in an axiom that already holds in the ontology under consideration. The idea is that the axiom does not modify the set of valid interpretations for the symbols in the signature w.r.t. the one they have in the original ontology. This means that whenever an axiom which is local w.r.t. a signature is added to an ontology, the resulting ontology is a safe (conservative[6]) extension of the original one. In the remainder of this section we extend the notion of locality to patterns, in order to provide a solution for determining whether a pattern produces safe extensions for an ontology. Let us start by defining a pattern in an abstract way[7].

Definition 3.1 (Variable Names). *Called V_{Class} the set of class variable names, V_{Op} the set of object property variable names, V_{Dp} the set of data property variable names, V_{Ind} the set of individual variable names, and V_{Const} the set of constant variable names, we call $V = \{V_{Class} \cup V_{Op} \cup V_{Dp} \cup V_{Ind} \cup V_{Const}\}$ the set of disjunct sets of variable names.*

Definition 3.2 (Variable Expression). *We can define a variable expression inductively as follows:*

---

[6] There are different kinds of conservative extensions in literature. Analysing the difference between them is beyond the scope of this paper. Here we use the term conservative extension in its *deductive* meaning, i.e.: those preserving the results of every query when restricted to the symbols in the signature. We refer the reader to [4] and [5] for further particulars.

[7] Without using OPPL proprietary syntax, i.e.: Manchester OWL Syntax.

Called VE_{Class} the set of class *variable expressions, VE_{Op} the set of object properties variable expressions, VE_{Dp} the set of data properties variable expressions, VE_{Ind} the set of individual variable expressions, VE_{Const} the set of constants, $VE_{Assertion}$ the set of* assertion *variable expressions, $VE = \{VE_{Class} \sqcup VE_{Assertion} \sqcup VE_{Ind} \sqcup VE_{Dp} \sqcup VE_{Op}\}$ the set of variable expressions,*

- *if $v \in V$, then $v \in VE$;*
- *if $v \in V_{Class}$, then $\neg v \in VE_{Class}$;*
- *if $v \in V_{Op}$ and e is a (variable) class expression, then $\exists v.e, \forall v.e \in VE_{Class}$;*
- *if $v \in V_{Dp}$ and e is a data type expression, then $\exists v.e, \forall v.e \in VE_{Class}$;*
- *if $v \in VE_{Class}$ and i is an individual, then $v(i) \in VE_{Assertion}$;*
- *if $v \in VE_{Ind}$ and e is a (variable) class expression, then $e(v) \in VE_{Assertion}$;*
- *if $v, f \in V_{Ind}$ and p is a (variable) property expression (data or object) then $p(v, f) \in VE_{Assertion}$;*
- *if $v \in V_{Ind}$, then $\{v\} \in VE_{Class}$;*
- *if $v \in VE_{Class}$ and C is a (variable) class expression, then $v \sqcap C, v \sqcup C \in VE_{Class}$;*

*Moreover, if $v \in V_{Class}$, $v_f \in VE$ is a **generated** variable obtained applying a function $f(v)$ to v, where f returns variable expressions; e.g., $p \in V_{Op}, f : V_{Class} \times V_{Op} \rightarrow VE = \exists p.v$; this will be represented as $v_f = \exists p.v$.*

Variable expressions can only be assigned to generated variables, while input variables are restricted to named entities and data type constants[8]. All the variable names in this paper will start with a question mark $(?x, ?y, \ldots)$. In order to specify the kind of a variable, we will borrow the notation from OPPL— as it is more compact—and write: *?x:CLASS* in place of $?x \in V_{Class}$, or *?p:DATAPROPERTY* in place of $?p \in V_{Dp}$.

Furthermore, the function *VALUES*, used it in the *partWhole*, always appears in combination with other aggregating functions, such as, for example, $\sqcup$ and $\sqcap$. Hence the expression: *?x:CLASS, ?z:CLASS*$= \sqcap ?x.VALUES$ means that $?z \in VE_{Class}$ is a generated variable containing all the values of $?x$.

Definition 3.3 (Variable axiom)
A variable axiom α over V is an OWL-DL axiom containing at least a variable expression $ve \in VE$.

Therefore, if $v \in VE_{Class}$ and C a (variable or not) class expression according to Def. 3.2, then $v \sqsubseteq C$ and $C \sqsubseteq v$ are variable axioms.

We can now define a pattern as follows:

Definition 3.4 (Pattern). *Called α_i an OWL-DL axiom or a variable axiom over V_p, $1 \le i \le n, n \ge 1$, a pattern over V is: $p = (V, \{\alpha_1, \ldots, \alpha_n\})$*

Patterns without variable axioms will not be considered in this paper, since their locality can be decided straightforwardly by applying the results in [5] to each plain OWL-DL axiom in the pattern. We focus, instead, on patterns containing at least one variable axiom, in order to find a procedure to determine whether their instantiations produce safe extensions of the ontologies in which they are used in combination.

---

[8] This limitation keeps the OPPL query sub-language, not used here for patterns, decidable.

In order to define instantiations we need to introduce the notion of binding as follows:

Definition 3.5 (**Binding**). *A binding b over V is a set of assignments from variable names to variable expressions, where the type of variable expression is determined by the type of variable:*
$$b = \{v \to \text{value}, (v, value) \in \{V_{Class} \times VE_{Class}\} \sqcup \{V_{Op} \times VE_{Op}\} \sqcup \{V_{Dp} \times VE_{Dp}\} \sqcup \{V_{Ind} \times VE_{Ind}\} \sqcup \{V_{Const} \times VE_{Const}\}\}.$$
*A binding is **complete** over V if it contains an assignment for all the non generated variables in V. b(v) will denote the value assigned to the variable v inside b.*

We can now define instantiations:

Definition 3.6 (**Instantiation**). *Let $p = (V, \{\alpha_1, \ldots, \alpha_n\})$ a pattern over V according to Def. 3.4, and B a set of complete bindings over V, with vinV and $b \in B$. Then:*

- *An axiom instantiation $\sigma_b(\alpha_i)$ consists of replacing every occurrence of each variable v in α_i with b(v), therefore obtaining an OWL DL axiom;*
- *A pattern instantiation over a single binding is defined as:*
  $$\sigma_b(p) = \bigcup_{1 \le i \le n} \sigma_b(\alpha_i);$$
- *A pattern instantiation over the whole B corresponds to:*
  $$\sigma_B(p) = \bigcup_{b \in B} \sigma_b(p).$$

Given a signature[9] **S** over a generic Description Logic $\mathcal{L}$, a pattern is said to be *local* w.r.t. **S** if all the axioms resulting from all its possible instantiations are local with respect to **S**. More formally:

Definition 3.7 (**Local patterns**). *Let $p = (V, \{\alpha_1, \ldots, \alpha_n\})$ a pattern over V according to Def. 3.4, and S a signature of a Description Logic $\mathcal{L}$.*
*Then p is **local** w.r.t. S iff:*
$\forall b$, *where b is a complete binding over V,*

$$\alpha \in \sigma_b(p) \Rightarrow \alpha \text{ is local with respect to } S.$$

The problem now becomes to define an algorithm that decides whether a pattern can produce non local axioms in one of its instantiation. The one we propose in this paper uses the semantic locality test τ function detailed in [5] (see Proposition 30)[10], and is reported in Alg. 1. The idea behind it is to produce a set of bindings that are generic enough to encompass all the possible combinations of values assigned to the variables used by the pattern. Then, the algorithm proceeds to apply the classic locality test τ on each of these bindings. It stops when it either finds a binding which produces an instantiation containing an axiom that fails the locality test or when all the bindings have been examined. Such bindings are built considering only the non generated variables since

---

[9] A *signature* (or *vocabulary*) **S** of a DL is defined in [6] as:" the (disjoint) union of a set C of atomic concepts $(A, B, \ldots)$ representing sets of elements, a set R of atomic roles $(r, s, \ldots)$ representing binary relations between elements, and a set I of individuals $(a, b, c, \ldots)$ representing elements".

[10] Please notice that this reference pre-dates OWL 2 specification and is restricted to class axioms. It can be extended to encompass both property and individual axioms.

the locality of $\mathcal{L}$-constructs containing generated variables only depends on whether the **generating** variables are or not in the signature. Therefore, a generated variable can be seen as a function of one or more non generated one, and does not contribute directly to the locality of an axiom.

Proposition 3.1 (Completeness). *Let $p(V, \{\alpha_1, \ldots, \alpha_n\})$ be a pattern defined over a set of variables as in Def. 3.4. If the pattern is not local, our algorithm terminates returning* `false` *(i.e.: Alg. 1 is complete w.r.t. locality test failures).*

Proof. Let us suppose there is some binding b_{out} and some i such that $\sigma_{b_{out}}(\alpha_i)$ fails the locality test τ. If we consider how τ has been recursively defined in Proposition 30 of [5] cited above, the locality depends, ultimately, on whether (some of) the symbols used in the axioms appear or not in the signature S. That is to say that, given an axiom α in a Description Logic $\mathcal{L}$ and a signature S, the only way to change the locality of α is, to remove (add) symbols used in α from (to) S. Now the first part of our algorithm (from line 1 to 10 in Alg. 1), creates a set of bindings B whose elements cover all the possible permutations of variable assignments to values within or outside the signature S. This means that, whatever the assignments contained in b_{out}, a binding $b \in B$ exists whose assignments are in the same situation[11] w.r.t. S as those in b_{out}. Therefore, the locality test τ will fail on b too when applied to α_i, hence, given the generality of b_{out} we can conclude that our algorithm is complete w.r.t. locality test failures.

The soundness of our algorithm comes from the fact that it is built upon the locality test τ itself.

Proposition 3.2 (Soundness). *Let $p(V, \{\alpha_1, \ldots, \alpha_n\})$ be a pattern defined over a set of variables as in Def. 3.4. If our algorithm terminates returning* `false`, *the pattern is not local.*

Proof. Let us suppose our algorithm terminates returning `false`. *This can only happen if there is a b inside the set of bindings built in the first part of the algorithm (from line 1 to 10 in Alg. 1) which causes an instantiation of some axiom α_i to fail the locality test. Therefore, according to Def. 3.7, p is not local.*

3.1 Algorithm Trace

Now consider again the *partWhole* pattern. Suppose we want to test its locality before applying it to the ontology $\mathcal{O}_2$, and we choose as our signature the whole set of symbols appearing either in $\mathcal{O}_1$ or in $\mathcal{O}_2$ (variable types are as defined in *partWhole*):

$$S = \{Atom, Molecule, Electron, Proton, Neutron, has\_part, has\_direct\_part\}$$

$$\alpha_1 = ?whole \sqsubseteq \exists has\_direct\_part.?part$$

$$\alpha_2 = ?whole \sqsubseteq \forall has\_direct\_part.?allParts$$

---

[11] Please notice that we are **not** asserting they are the **same** assignments, as it is irrelevant for the locality test. What really matters is whether the values are or not in **S**.

Algorithm 1. Locality check for patterns

Require: A pattern $p(V, \{\alpha_1, \ldots, \alpha_n\})$.
  A signature $\mathbf{S}$ over a Description Logic $\mathcal{L}$.
Ensure: The locality of p w.r.t. $\mathbf{S}$.

1: $V_{input} \leftarrow \{v \in V, v \text{ is not generated}\} = \{v_1, v_2 \ldots v_n\}, n = |V_{input}|$
2: **for** $1 \leq j \leq n$ **do**
3:     **for** $b \in B$ **do**
4:         $\mathbf{S} \leftarrow \mathbf{S} \cup \{v_j^{\mathbf{S}}\}, v_j^{\mathbf{S}}$ a symbol name
5:         $v_j^{\neg \mathbf{S}}$ a symbol name, $v_j^{\neg \mathbf{S}} \notin \mathbf{S}$
6:         $b' \leftarrow b \cup \{v_j \rightarrow v_j^{\mathbf{S}}\}, b'' \leftarrow b \cup \{v_j \rightarrow v_j^{\neg \mathbf{S}}\}$
7:         $B \leftarrow (B \setminus b) \cup \{b', b''\}$
8:     **end for**
9: **end for**
10: *found* $\leftarrow$ false
11: **for** $\neg found \wedge B \neq \emptyset$ **do**
12:     Select $b \in B$
13:     *found* $\leftarrow \neg \tau(\sigma_b(p), \mathbf{S})$
14:     $B \leftarrow B \setminus \{b\}$
15: **end for**
16: **return** $\neg found$

Our *partWhole* pattern is:

$$partWhole(\{ ?part, ?whole, ?allParts\}, \{\alpha_1, \alpha_2\})$$

If we run our algorithm, the following results will be generated:

Updated signature	$\mathbf{S} \leftarrow \mathbf{S} \cup \{whole^{\mathbf{S}}, part^{\mathbf{S}}\}$
Set of complete bindings $B = \{b_1, b_2, b_3, b_4\}$	$b_1 = \{ ?part \rightarrow part^{\mathbf{S}}, ?whole \rightarrow whole^{\mathbf{S}}\}$
	$b_2 = \{ ?part \rightarrow part^{\mathbf{S}}, ?whole \rightarrow whole^{\neg \mathbf{S}}\}$
	$b_3 = \{ ?part \rightarrow part^{\neg \mathbf{S}}, ?whole \rightarrow whole^{\mathbf{S}}\}$
	$b_4 = \{ ?part \rightarrow part^{\neg \mathbf{S}}, ?whole \rightarrow whole^{\neg \mathbf{S}}\}$
Instantiated axiom	$\sigma_{b_1}(\alpha_1) = whole^{\mathbf{S}} \sqsubseteq \exists has\_direct\_part.part^{\mathbf{S}}$

$\tau(\sigma_{b_1}(\alpha_1)) = \texttt{false}$ because it is neither a tautology nor did it hold previously in $\mathcal{O}_2$; therefore, *partWhole* is not local w.r.t. $\mathbf{S}$ when applied to $\mathcal{O}_2$.

3.2 Algorithm Complexity

The computational complexity of the proposed algorithm is non polynomial in n, where n is the number of non generated variables. The algorithm, indeed, builds as many bindings as necessary to represent the possible combinations of value assignment to variables with respect to their belonging or not to a signature; therefore, two possible values for each non generated variable, which brings 2^n combinations. The aim of this work is not to propose and efficient version of it, nevertheless we observe that:

- If one changes the strategy for creating the bindings, from the current breadth-first exploration of a tree whose nodes are variable assignments, to a depth-first one, the locality check can be moved and performed as soon as a new complete

binding b is created. This means that if it returns `false` for some b, there is no
need to proceed in creating any other bindings. We preferred to write our algorithm
without this optimisation for the sake of clarity, but its introduction would make the
non polynomial exploration only the worst case.

- Patterns represent abstractions over recurring knowledge structures. Although an
  upper limit on the number of variables in a pattern does not exist, we observe that
  the introduction of a variable in a pattern often requires more than one axiom to go
  with it for representing the piece of recurring knowledge it is abstracting over. In
  other words, a variable axiom such as $?x{:}CLASS \sqsubseteq ?y{:}CLASS$ has little meaning
  if there are no other axioms further characterising both $?x$ and $?y$. However, such
  axioms, in their turn, decrease the level of generality of the pattern and its applicability to other ontologies. This means that there is a physiological balance between
  the number of variables in patterns, its meaningfulness, and its generality; this leads
  to think that real world patterns will have a limited number of input variables, and
  therefore acceptable performance for locality checks even in the worst case.

3.3   Determination of Safe Combinations

The example in Sec. 3.1, however, also raises the question of whether it is possible
to invoke our *partWhole* pattern in a safe way. If we observe the instantiations our
algorithm creates, we notice that, all the $\sigma_b(\alpha_i)$ for each b containing the assignment
$?whole \rightarrow whole^{\neg S}$, as they become of the form $\bot \sqsubseteq \exists \ldots$ or $\bot \sqsubseteq \forall \ldots$. This means
that our *partWhole* pattern is local, whenever it is instantiated assigning to $?whole$ a
value outside the signature $\mathbf{S}$.

We could then think of modifying the second part of our algorithm (from line 11 on-
wards in Alg. 1), so that combinations of assignments that produce local instantiations
are returned, if they exists. These modifications are reported in Alg. 2.

Algorithm 2. Extended Locality check for patterns

Require: A pattern $p(V, \{\alpha_1, \ldots, \alpha_n\})$.
  A signature $\mathbf{S}$ over a Description Logic $\mathcal{L}$.
Ensure: The binding configurations that result in local instantiations for p.

```
 1: identical to line 1–9 in Alg. 1
 2: LocalBindings ← ∅
 3: for B ≠ ∅ do
 4:     Select b ∈ B
 5:     if τ(σ_b(p), S) then
 6:         LocalBindings ← LocalBindings ∪ {b}
 7:     end if
 8:     B ← B \ {b}
 9: end for
10: return LocalBindings
```

This algorithm does not stop when it detects the first binding that produces a non
local instantiation $(\tau(\sigma_b(p), \mathbf{S}) = \text{false})$, but it examines all the bindings. This makes
it impossible to use the depth first optimization mentioned above, nevertheless, finer
grained ones could be introduced.

We observe that, for example, not every axiom, in a pattern, depends on all the variables. Therefore, we could determine the axioms that use the smallest number of variables, let us call them $\{\alpha_{min_1}, \ldots \alpha_{min_k}\}$, compute the bindings restricted to those variables and check the locality instantiating such axioms. The only bindings we will expand to the other variables are those amongst the restricted ones that produced local instantiations on $\{\alpha_{min_1}, \ldots \alpha_{min_k}\}$. In this way we can significantly prune the number of bindings to examine with respect to the non polynomial worst case.

3.4 Maximization of Safe Instantiations

Consider now a very small ontology $\mathcal{O}_{Food}$ and a pattern *foodWithout*:

$\mathcal{O}_{Food}$	*Ingredient* $\sqsubseteq$ $\top$, *Meat* $\sqsubseteq$ *Ingredient*, *Eggs* $\sqsubseteq$ *Ingredient*, *Salad* $\sqsubseteq$ *Ingredient*, *Food* $\sqsubseteq$ $\top$, *Food* $\sqsubseteq$ $\forall contains.Ingredient$
foodWithout	$(\{\,?x{:}CLASS, ?y{:}CLASS, ?forbidden{:}CLASS = \bigsqcup ?y.VALUES\}, \{\alpha\})$ $\alpha = ?x \sqsubseteq Food \sqcap \forall contains. (\neg ?forbidden)$
Possible bindings	$b_1 = \{\,?x{:}CLASS \rightarrow x^{\mathbf{S}}, ?y{:}CLASS \rightarrow y^{\mathbf{S}}\}$ $b_2 = \{\,?x{:}CLASS \rightarrow x^{\mathbf{S}}, ?y{:}CLASS \rightarrow y^{\neg\mathbf{S}}\}$ $b_3 = \{\,?x{:}CLASS \rightarrow x^{\neg\mathbf{S}}, ?y{:}CLASS \rightarrow y^{\mathbf{S}}\}$ $b_4 = \{\,?x{:}CLASS \rightarrow x^{\neg\mathbf{S}}, ?y{:}CLASS \rightarrow y^{\neg\mathbf{S}}\}$

If we ran Alg. 2 it would return b_3 and b_4 as the only binding configurations that produce local instantiations. In particular[12]:

$$\sigma_{b_3}(p) \; x^{\neg\mathbf{S}} \sqsubseteq Food \sqcap \forall contains.(y^{\mathbf{S}}) \quad \rightarrow \quad \bot \sqsubseteq Food \sqcap \forall contains. (\neg y^{\mathbf{S}}) \text{ (tautology)}$$
$$\sigma_{b_4}(p) \; x^{\neg\mathbf{S}} \sqsubseteq Food \sqcap \forall contains.(\neg y^{\mathbf{S}}) \quad \rightarrow \quad \bot \sqsubseteq Food \qquad\qquad \text{ (tautology)}$$

This means that, given a signature **S**, if we instantiate our *foodWithout* pattern using, as values for *?x:CLASS*, entities that do not belong to **S** we will produce instantiations that will not modify the semantics of the entities in **S**. However, if we edited our pattern *foodWithout* by scoping *?x:CLASS* as *?x:CLASS*[subClassOf *Food*], we would constrain[13] *?x:CLASS* to have as values only sub-classes of *Food*. This implies $\sigma_{b_2}(p) \rightarrow x^{\mathbf{S}} \sqsubseteq Food$, which holds if we consider that of $x^{\mathbf{S}}$ is a value for *?x:CLASS*, constrained inside the scope declared above to be $\sqsubseteq Food$.

Therefore, by changing the scope of one of the variables, one extra safe binding configuration would be determined, thus limiting the unsafe ones to be those configurations in which a user assigns to both *?x:CLASS* and *?y:CLASS* values that appear in **S**. Unfortunately, there is no simple way, for the time being, to modify any of the algorithms above in order to provide indications on how to scope variables so as to include previously non local binding configurations into the local ones. We limit ourselves to observe that, in order to solve this problem, it is necessary to compute, given an axiom

---

[12] In applying the τ locality test all the entities outside **S** are transformed into $\bot$.
[13] Please see Sect. 2 for details on how to scope variables.

α and an ontology $\mathcal{O}$, with $\not\models_{\mathcal{O}} \alpha$, what are, if any, the possible combinations of axioms $AxiomSet_1, \ldots, AxiomSet_n$ such that, if $\mathcal{O}_i = \mathcal{O} \cup AxiomSet_i$ then $\forall i, \models_{\mathcal{O}_i} \alpha$. In particular, in our settings, our α would be the result of the instantiations that fail the locality test, and the sets of axioms we would be interested in are those that can translated into variable scope restrictions like the one on $?x{:}CLASS$ in the *foodWithout* example above. Unfortunately, to the best of our knowledge this problem has not been solved yet in the literature, but it represents an interesting future direction of investigation.

The results discussed in this section, however, make it possible, give a pattern encoded in OPPL, to decide what values assigned to its variables will provide conservative extensions of the ontology it is used in combination with. Given a signature, indeed, our algorithms return the binding configurations leading to local instantiations. The purpose of such binding configurations is only to distinguish between variable values that belong or not to the input signature, which, as we showed above, is all is needed in order to determine the locality of the pattern instantiations. Thus, users know in advance, for example, that the *partWhole* pattern can be used safely w.r.t. $\mathbf{S}=\{Molecule, Atom\}$ only when $?whole{:}CLASS$ has values outside $\mathbf{S}$, whichever those values are.

3.5 Implementation

Both algorithms described above have been implemented in the PATTERNS plugin[14] for Protégé 4. Some screenshots presenting the *partWhole* pattern and its safety analysis results are reported, in Fig. 1. The *parthWhole* pattern has two input variables, which can therefore be bound to any named class entity in the ontology; the signature $\mathbf{S}$ used in the depicted safety check is $\mathbf{S} = \{Molecule, Atom\}$.

When both variables are not bound, the possible situations are 2^2, i.e.,

- ?whole, ?part $\in \mathbf{S}$
- ?whole, ?part $\notin \mathbf{S}$
- only one of ?whole or ?part $\in \mathbf{S}$;

These four cases are depicted on the lower left part of Fig. 1; green circles mark the cases in which instantiation is safe, i.e., no changes occur to the semantics of the entities contained in $\mathbf{S}$, while red circles mark the unsafe cases.

If one of the variables is bound, the number of cases decreases to 2^1; the lower right part of Fig. 1 represents the case in which *?part* is bound to *Atom*, which belongs to the signature. In this case, it is clear that the safety of the pattern is determined by *?whole*: whenever it is included in the signature, the resulting action could change the semantics of the symbols in $\mathbf{S}$.

4 Related Work

Knowledge patterns have been gaining considerable attention as a means of promoting good ontology engineering practice. Our contribution to this aim builds upon previous work on the nature and cataloguing of such patterns. Clark *et al.* were the first, to the

---

[14] http://www.cs.man.ac.uk/~iannonel/oppl/patterns/

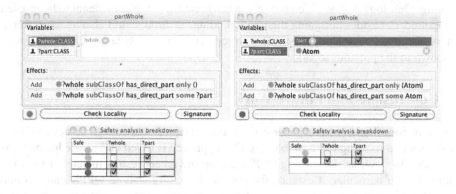

Fig. 1. The *partWhole* pattern instantiation and safety analysis breakdown, without any user assigned variable (left) and with one assigned variable (right). The signature for the safety check is $S = \{Molecule, Atom\}$.

best of our knowledge, to use the label *knowledge patterns*, defining them as: 'first order theories whose axioms are not part of the target knowledge-base, but can be incorporated via renaming of their non logical symbols' (see Section 2 in [7]). In the subsequent years, researchers seemed to focus on pattern categorisation (see, for instance, [8] and its references) aiming to create organised catalogues that engineers could browse and adopt in their knowledge bases. Staab *et al.*, in [9], propose a framework based on RDF for creating catalogues of patterns that are (partially - according to the authors themselves) *executable/portable* in any implementation language. Vrandecic, in [10], proposes the creation of scripts (called *macros* in the paper) that, without changing the semantics of the underlying knowledge representation language – OWL-DL in this case – capture sets of axioms that can be reused.

Locality has been often used in literature to support re-use through modularization. In [11], for instance, a methodology for extracting the right portion of axioms from an ontology and safely import it inside another one is proposed. This approach has a point of view that is orthogonal to the one in this paper, as it deals with the problem of some-one building an ontology trying to re-use as much as possible from third party sources, and to remain coherent with the semantics of what they are re-using. In [11] as well as in other variations based on safe extensions [12], users individuate ontologies they wish to re-use, select the vocabulary to which they wish to restrict and extract, where possible, a proper sub-set of such ontologies to incorporate them in their own. This, despite guaranteeing that users embed (approximately) the minimal required knowledge from the re-used ontologies into the one they are creating, does not help in determining how to extend the ontology and does not prevent the user to subsequently alter, in a non conservative way, the re-used knowledge. Our work, therefore, can be seen as complementary to the re-use by modularization. If knowledge engineers were able to embed patterns in their ontology, encoded in a concrete language such as OPPL, users could then extract from such ontology the modules that are relevant to their purposes (using the methodologies just cited), but, also, decide, perhaps using the methods illustrated here, how safe it is to use the exposed patterns in the ontology extension they are creating. Ontology engineers, conversely, when creating ontologies meant to be re-used and extended, besides designing them in a modular fashion, could also attach patterns whose usage can be *certified* to be safe with respect to the vocabulary each module uses, as shown in the previous section.

5 Conclusions and Future Work

The main contribution of this paper is the proposal of a framework to achieve safe extensions when re-using OWL ontologies. Our approach is based on knowledge patterns embedded in OWL artefacts using OPPL, and on the recent results in safely extending ontologies. In particular, it extends the notion of locality tests to OPPL patterns and provides an algorithm for determining whether a pattern is local or not with respect to a signature. In addition we provided an extension of this algorithm to compute, in case of patterns that turn out not to be local in general, the combinations of values, w.r.t. an input signature, that result in local instantiations. When implemented inside a tool, these algorithms can help the knowledge engineers in creating and using patterns anticipating the effects on the semantics of the ontologies in which they use the patterns. Thus, when a user decides to use an OPPL pattern wishing to extend an ontology, the tool can point out, given a signature, what are the allowed combinations of value assignments that will produce conservative extensions of the original ontology. Conversely, ontology engineers can evaluate in advance what are the safe uses of the patterns they are designing for extending their own ontologies and even get an idea on how extensible are such ontologies are while still preserving the semantics of the original vocabulary. An implementation of the algorithm is currently available in the PATTERNS plugin for Protégé.

Future work in this field includes the optimisation of this technique together with the exploitation of OPPL features, such as the scoping of variables, in order to achieve safer versions of non local patterns. Another interesting observation is that this work relies on ontologies exposing the patterns for their re-use and evaluates the impact of instantiating them in new ontologies. This leaves out all the ontologies that have already been created without any patterns. The detection and the induction of patterns from existing ontologies becomes, then, a promising research direction. Discovering the presence of regularities in a model and characterising them in the form of a pattern could support ontology design and re-use in many ways:

- The model, or a portion of it, is expressed in the form of patterns and so becomes clearer to understand thanks to their greater level of abstraction
- Portions of a model which are non compliant to the discovered patterns can be individuated more easily and corrected if the pattern is recognized as valid and normative for the model. that is, a 'house-style' can be more consistently applied.
- If the induction process reveals that a pattern, which is unsafe according to the criteria provided in this work, has been used inside an ontology, this can lead to the discovery and hopefully to the correction of modeling errors that will enhance the quality of the model itself.

References

[1] Iannone, L., Rector, A.L., Stevens, R.: Embedding knowledge patterns into owl. In: Aroyo, L., Traverso, P., Ciravegna, F., Cimiano, P., Heath, T., Hyvönen, E., Mizoguchi, R., Oren, E., Sabou, M., Simperl, E. (eds.) ESWC 2009. LNCS, vol. 5554, pp. 218–232. Springer, Heidelberg (2009)

[2] Presutti, V., Gangemi, A.: Content ontology design patterns as practical building blocks for web ontologies. In: Li, Q., Spaccapietra, S., Yu, E., Olivé, A. (eds.) ER 2008. LNCS, vol. 5231, pp. 128–141. Springer, Heidelberg (2008)

[3] Egaña, M., Rector, A.L., Stevens, R., Antezana, E.: Applying ontology design patterns in bio-ontologies. In: Gangemi, A., Euzenat, J. (eds.) EKAW 2008. LNCS (LNAI), vol. 5268, pp. 7–16. Springer, Heidelberg (2008)

[4] Ghilardi, S., Lutz, C., Wolter, F.: Did i damage my ontology? a case for conservative extensions in description logics. In: Doherty, P., Mylopoulos, J., Welty, C.A. (eds.) KR, pp. 187–197. AAAI Press, Menlo Park (2006)

[5] Cuenca Grau, B., Horrocks, I., Kazakov, Y., Sattler, U.: Modular reuse of ontologies: Theory and practice. J. of Artificial Intelligence Research (JAIR) 31, 273–318 (2008)

[6] Grau, B.C., Horrocks, I., Kazakov, Y., Sattler, U.: Just the right amount: extracting modules from ontologies. In: WWW '07: Proceedings of the 16th international conference on World Wide Web, pp. 717–726. ACM, New York (2007)

[7] Clark, P., Thompson, J., Porter, B.W.: Knowledge patterns. In: KR, pp. 591–600 (2000)

[8] Blomqvist, E., Sandkuhl, K.: Patterns in ontology engineering: Classification of ontology patterns. In: ICEIS, vol. (3), pp. 413–416 (2005)

[9] Staab, S., Erdmann, M., Maedche, A.: Engineering ontologies using semantic patterns. In: IJCAI Workshop on E-business & The Intelligent Web (2001)

[10] Vrandecic, D.: Explicit knowledge engineering patterns with macros. In: Proceedings of the Ontology Patterns for the Semantic Web Workshop at the ISWC 2005, Galway, Ireland (November 2005)

[11] Jiménez-Ruiz, E., Cuenca Grau, B., Sattler, U., Schneider, T., Llavori, R.B.: Safe and economic re-use of ontologies: A logic-based methodology and tool support. In: Bechhofer, S., Hauswirth, M., Hoffmann, J., Koubarakis, M. (eds.) ESWC 2008. LNCS, vol. 5021, pp. 185–199. Springer, Heidelberg (2008)

[12] Grau, B.C., Horrocks, I., Kazakov, Y., Sattler, U.: Extracting modules from ontologies: A logic-based approach. In: Stuckenschmidt, H., Parent, C., Spaccapietra, S. (eds.) Modular Ontologies. LNCS, vol. 5445, pp. 159–186. Springer, Heidelberg (2009)

Entity Reference Resolution via Spreading Activation on RDF-Graphs

Joachim Kleb and Andreas Abecker

FZI Research Center for Information Technology Karlsruhe
Haid-und-Neu-Str. 10-14
76131 Karlsruhe, Germany
surname@fzi.de

Abstract. The use of natural language identifiers as reference for ontology elements—in addition to the URIs required by the Semantic Web standards—is of utmost importance because of their predominance in the human everyday life, *i.e.* speech or print media. Depending on the context, different names can be chosen for one and the same element, and the same element can be referenced by different names. Here homonymy and synonymy are the main cause of ambiguity in perceiving which concrete unique ontology element ought to be referenced by a specific natural language identifier describing an entity. We propose a novel method to resolve entity references under the aspect of ambiguity which explores only formal background knowledge represented in RDF graph structures. The key idea of our domain independent approach is to build an entity network with the most likely referenced ontology elements by constructing steiner graphs based on spreading activation. In addition to exploiting complex graph structures, we devise a new ranking technique that characterises the likelihood of entities in this network, *i.e.* interpretation contexts. Experiments in a highly polysemic domain show the ability of the algorithm to retrieve the correct ontology elements in almost all cases.

1 Introduction

The World Wide Web provides access to content produced by people all over the world including people of very different cultural and local backgrounds. Hence a large variety of content providers create articles using different writing styles—based on their different background—that contain the same or similar information. Thus the comparison of information becomes harder as different terms for equal or similar information are common involving the problem of ambiguity. For example, the same person can be called "John Doe" in one and "John D." or "Johnny" in another source.

In ontology-based applications, one has to associate additional literal relations to concepts and instances, in order to cover their different identifiers used in input media. This raises the problem of ontology-element identification concerning the retrieval of information in knowledge bases (KBs). Here a specific ontology element cannot necessarily be determined uniquely in a KB, solely based on its natural language identifier (NLI, identifiers using natural language names), due to their ambiguity. As opposed to URIs, NLIs do not guarantee uniqueness. For example, the DBPedia ontology[1]

---

[1] http://dbpedia.org

L. Aroyo et al. (Eds.): ESWC 2010, Part I, LNCS 6088, pp. 152–166, 2010.

includes six different ontology elements sharing the same NLI "George Bush". But exact reference resolution in case of ambiguity can benefit from exploiting co-occurrence information. In particular, the relational network between entities in an ontology graph includes information that can enable the unique identification of entities. For instance, only one of the above mentioned "George Bush"s has *a farm in Texas*.

Current approaches typically use this co-occurrence information as importance measures for nodes [7] or use heuristics on the graph structure [11]. Also, many try to transfer NLP approaches to this domain [26,14,9], mostly focusing on a specific domain, using domain-specific measures. So far, in the field of ontology-based entity disambiguation, domain-independent complex structures in semantic graphs have not been exploited. Only certain aspects of entity-networks have been used, *e.g.* relations of a certain type. Also no ranking measures for entity networks have been proposed.

We present a novel approach for entity disambiguation, applied to RDF(S)-ontologies, which determines the most likely references for a given NLI. By exploiting the structure of graphs with spreading activation (SA), we identify a steiner graph covering only the most likely ontology elements which denote reasonable references for the given NLIs, from the set of all elements referable by an NLI (surrogates). Our approach does not need pre-learned knowledge and is also applicable to huge entity-networks. Its weighting and prominence scheme allow for a valued consideration of ontology elements and includes a new ranking model. It uses the activation value of a connector node, characterising the semantic coherence of a steiner graph which includes the result of the disambiguation process in form of the most likely surrogates.

This paper is structured as follows: After a short background section 2, Sect. 3 defines the problem of entity-reference resolution and devises our algorithm. Section 4 contains the used measures and the ranking procedure, whereas related work is surveyed in Sect. 5. Section 6 describes the evaluation of our approach in detail, based on a polysemic domain. The paper concludes with a summary and outlook in Sect. 7.

2 Background

Representation of Names in the Semantic Web. For representing knowledge in a KB, we refer to the Semantic Web standard ontology languages RDF(S) and OWL. Those specify the identification of an ontology element by its $rdf{:}ID$ tag. This must be a URI guaranteeing a nearly unique identification of an element[2]. According to the standard, $rdfs{:}label$ specifies a literal in form of a natural language name which identifies an ontology element, *i.e.* a natural language identifier (NLI). Here, without loss of generality, we disregard the language tagging facility of RDF(S) literals. A label does not guarantee for a unique identification, as multiple elements can share the same label but are not equal. It has been designed in order to enable access to an element based on human language expressions[3]. Hence, the search for ontology elements via their NLIs implies

---

[2] Two RDF URI references are equal if they compare as equal.

[3] NLIs can be associated via other property relations as well. For example, SKOS (http://www.w3.org/2004/02/skos/) defines the relations hasPrefLabel and hasAlterLabel for this purpose.

the problem of ambiguity, *e.g.* "Karlsruhe" in the geo-ontology is associated to a city, an administrative region in Germany and a spring in Africa.

Ambiguity. According to the Encyclopedia Britannica, ambiguity is a *"factual, explanatory prose, [...]"* and *"[...] considered an error in reasoning or diction"*. It leads to a non-exclusive connection between ontology elements. In an ontology, the following types of ambiguity can be found: *(a) Multi-reference ambiguity within instances of one concept* and *(b) Multi-reference ambiguity across concepts* (cf. [26]). Both include the problem of synonymy, *i.e.* several NLIs are associated to one element and can be used interchangeably. As identifiers are not unique, it is also possible that an NLI refers to an element outside of the examined ontology domain, and thus there is no corresponding element included in the ontology at all.

Co-occurrence. In order to overcome this problem, we make use of the co-occurrence of entities in input data, *e.g.* a text document, and try to reproduce this co-occurrence on an RDF(S)-graph. Focusing on text, co-occurrence means the joined appearance of entities in a document. Regarding RDF(S)-graphs, co-occurrence means the possibility to retrieve paths between the ontology elements.

Spreading Activation. Like Quillian's original spreading-activation idea [20], almost all later extensions (cf. [5,1]) transfer an initial activation to a selection of nodes in a network. Source nodes fire and transfer (spread) their activation to their adjacent nodes. This is done iteratively until no node is left which is allowed to fire. Whenever a node gets activations via multiple paths, this results in a high overall activation of this node. Often such nodes are important for the result sets of the algorithms. The activation values are often decreased in each iteration with a decay factor.

3   Entity Reference Resolution Based on Entity Identifiers

In order to retrieve **the** ontology element that stands for an ambiguous identifier found in the context of a document, we first collect all ontology elements that can be referred by this identifier (NLI) in the ontology, *e.g.* "John Doe" leads to the elements A, B and C (cf. Fig. 1). This set of elements is called a surrogate set for this identifier. In order to obtain the **reference** for an ontology element (equivalent to the meant element for this identifier in the text), we use the connections between elements of different surrogate sets, *e.g.* between a surrogate for identifier *John Doe, Karl Foo* and identifier *Fritz Hall*, means between A, D and E for example. Our **hypothesis** is, that identifiers co-occurring in a text must be also related in an ontology and thus can represented by connected elements. These connections are included in a spanning graph. A spanning graph between a subset of elements of the overall graph is called **steiner graph** We search for a steiner graph connecting at least one surrogate of each surrogate set to each other and thus each identifier to the others[4]. As this is a combinatorial problem, multiple of such steiner graphs can be found in the same ontology graph (cf. Fig. 1, here two possible graphs are shown). Thus there must be a ranking method evaluating these steiner graphs in order to obtain the graph representing the references and thus the ontology elements that stand for each identifier originally found in the text.

---

[4] There may occur several members of a surrogate set, if they have been equally weighted.

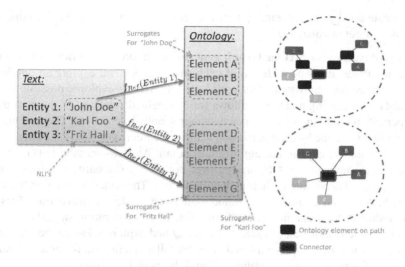

Fig. 1. Left: NLI based surrogate retrieval; Right: Examples for steiner graphs

More formally: An RDF(S)-ontology can be represented as triple list $G \subseteq V \times E \times V$, where the nodes $v \in V$ represent classes, instances and literals while the edges $e \in E$ denote to object-properties. Any ordered triple $\langle u, e, v \rangle$ states that node u is related to node v via edge e. We assume that edges are undirected, following the design principle that edges in a semantic graph imply a semantic meaning to both adjacent nodes and thus are navigable in both directions[5], e.g. $u \xrightarrow{lives\ in} v$ implies $u \xleftarrow{accommodate} v$.

Let I be the set of all **given** initial entity NLIs. $L_v := \{l_1^v, l_2^v, \dots, l_p^v\}$ denotes the set of possible identifiers for a node v, whereas an entity n, e.g. a named entity in a text document, is identified by its textual identifier $i \in I$. The set of ontology surrogates S_i for a given entity identifier i corresponds to the nodes with an associated label equal to the entity identifier, formally given as follows

$$v \in S_i \text{ iff } \exists\, l^v \in L_v, \; l^v = i \tag{1}$$

The references of an entity n—with an associated identifier i—are initially indicated by its surrogates in the graph given by

$$f_{Ref}(n) = S_i \tag{2}$$

We **search** for (multiple) steiner graphs Z, formally defined by

$$Z := \{\langle v, e, u \rangle \in (V^Z, E^Z, V^Z) \mid V^Z \subseteq V \text{ s.t. } V^Z \cap S_i \neq \emptyset \text{ for each } S_i \in S\} \tag{3}$$

Each of them includes for each entity n in the set of entities N and their corresponding identifiers $i \in I$ at least one surrogate node $v \in S_i$, for each $S_i \in S$. S states the union

---

[5] OWL includes the *owl:inverse* property to allow the definition of inverse relations and *owl:symmetricProperty* to express symmetry.

of all surrogate sets $\bigcup_{i \in I} S_i$. Steiner points are represented by $V^Z \notin S$. The edge set E^Z of Z is a subset or equal to E.

Spreading Activation for Steiner Graph generation. In order to retrieve a graph including at least one surrogate node out of each surrogate set, we explore an ontology graph using *spreading activation*. Our approach (cf. Alg. 1) explores possible paths among entity-representing nodes and allows for a weighted selection of the next path steps. It permits the ranking of constructed steiner graphs (see above). The ranking of the steiner graphs is done by their activation values (see Sect. 4).

In the following we explain our algorithm in detail: At first—method INITIALISATION —all surrogate nodes $v \in S_i$ are retrieved for each given entity identifier i and inserted in queue Q according to their activation values. The nodes included in the surrogate sets $S_i \in S$ build the processing foundation as we aim for a construction of result graphs including at least one node out of each set. In every iteration step, the node v with the highest activation value is selected from Q and explored. Hence the most important node per iteration step is explored. The overall activation a_v for node v results from the sum of activations per identifier $a_{v,i}$ and the $nodePrestige(v)$.

After selecting the most activated node, we explore its vicinity. Nodes adjacent to v are retrieved by the method GETPATHSTEPSOFINTEREST(v). We consider only edges with a $degree(e) \leq deg_{max}$. This allows us a restriction to edges of a certain degree that implies that these edges represent rather important connections than connections to multiple nodes by the same edge type. We denote the first as semantically more expressive (see Sect. 4). We also consider the presence of adjacent nodes in Q or X (X includes the already analysed nodes). The queues contain important nodes, since all of them hold connections to at least one surrogate.

Each returned $u, e \in pathSteps$ is analysed in combination with node v in the method ANALYSECONNECTION(u, e, v). Each node v has associated sets $P_{v,i}$[6], each indicating the best path(s) to a surrogate for an identifier i. For each path only the first node p per path is included. If a node is a surrogate node itself, a reflexive auxiliary relation is used. In this method all available best path connections of node v are considered if they denote better surrogate connections for node u via e. The decision concerning a best path is based on the path distances, $dist_{v,i}$ resp. $dist_{u,i}$. In case u has no connection to a member of surrogate set S_i or its distance to a member of this surrogate set is longer than the distance via v, v is used as best parent. If the distances are equal, the node with a greater overall activation is used. If the analysis denotes equal paths, the one via v is also used since they are equally important. In case of a retrieved connection to a new surrogate set, u may denote a full-Connector. The method (IS-FULLCONNECTOR(u)) examines if a node u holds connections to all surrogate sets, whereas the parents are not allowed to be equal for all paths. In this case it would be the "root" of a sub-graph Z and thus inserted into the result set R.

For all identifier connections of v the activations to spread from v to u are calculated. If the value of an identifier i is higher than the stored activation for this identifier $a_{u,i}$, the activation value is updated. If the parent association $P_{u,i}$ or the activation value $a_{u,i}$ of a node u changes, this change is back-propagated to all already

---

[6] If there are multiple equally valued paths then $|P_{v,i}| > 1$.

Algorithm 1.

---

1 **Initialisation** $Q \leftarrow S; X = \emptyset; R = \emptyset; \forall u \in S : depth_u = 0;$;
2 $\forall i, \forall u \in S : if\ u \in S_i\ then\ dist_{u,i} \leftarrow 0, P_{u,i} \leftarrow u\ else\ dist_{u,i} \leftarrow \infty, P_{u,i} \leftarrow \emptyset;$
3 **while** Q *is non-empty* **do**
4   Retrieve node v, with highest overall activation, from Q and insert in X;
5   **if** IS-FULLCONNECTOR(v) **then** insert v in R;
6   **foreach** $(u, e) \in$ GETPATHSTEPSOFINTEREST(v) **do**
7   ANALYSECONNECTION(u, e, v);
8   **if** $((u \notin X)\ and\ (a_u > a_{min})\ and\ (depth_u < depth_{max}))$ **then** insert it into Q with $depth_v + 1$
9   **end**
10 **end**
11 **Func** GETPATHSTEPSOFINTEREST(v)
12     $pathSteps \leftarrow \emptyset$;
13   **foreach** $(u, e) \in incoming(v) \bigcup outgoing(v)$ **do**
14   **if** $((degree(e) \le deg_{max}) || (u \in (Q \cup X)))$ **then**
15         $insert(e, u)$ into $pathSteps$;
16   **end**
17   **return** $pathSteps$;
18 **end**
19 **Func** ANALYSECONNECTION(u, e, v)
20   **foreach** *identifier* $i \in I$ **do**
21   **if** $dist_{v,i} + 1 \le dist_{u,i}$ **then**
22   **if** $dist_{v,i} + 1 < dist_{u,i}$ **then**
23                 $P_{u,i} \leftarrow \emptyset$;
24                 $dist_{u,i} = dist_{v,i} + 1$;
25   **end**
26   **else**
27   **foreach** $p \in P_{u,i}$ **do**
28   **if** $a_v > a_p$ **then** $p \leftarrow \emptyset$;
29   **end**
30   add v to $P_{u,i}$;
31   **end**
32   **if** IS-FULLCONNECTOR(u) **then** insert u in R;
33   COSTUPDATE(u, i);
34   **end**
35   **if** v *spreads more activation to* u *from* t_i **then**
36   update $a_{u,i}$ with this new activation;
37   ACTIVATIONUPDATE(u, i);
38   **end**
39   **end**
40 **end**

---

analysed adjacent nodes of u (COSTUPDATE(u, i) for parent and distance update, ACTIVATIONUPDATE(u, i) for activation update), since their activation value or parent relation for the identifier in question may also need to be changed. Each node affected by the back-propagation is analysed according to a possible optimisation of its parent associations or activation values.

After the connection analysis the node u is considered for further exploration of its vicinity. If its activation exceeds the minimum activation threshold and its depth $depth_u$ is lower than the maximum depth, it is inserted in Q on condition that the node is not already a member of Q or X. The parameter $depth_{max}$ specifies the maximum depth allowed for a node in the graph—which is used as a performance optimiser.

The output of our algorithm is a set of full-connectors in R, sorted according to their activation value. A graph can be reconstructed by an iterative exploration of the parent nodes associated to each node. The surrogates per identifier within this graph represent the final result of our algorithm.

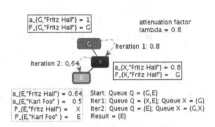

Fig. 2 illustrates our algorithm[7]. The nodes E, G are connected through node X. E is a surrogate node for identifier "Karl Foo" while G is a surrogate node for "Fritz Hall". The figure represents the status of the algorithm

Fig. 2. Example

after two iterations without back-propagation and shows the retrieval of the connector node E. The example includes two iterations; the status of the queues is shown in the lower right corner.

4   Measures and Ranking

The activation of a node represents its prestige and its connectivity to keyword surrogates. The higher the activation, the more keyword surrogates of different identifiers are connected and the closer they are.

Initial Activation. The initial activation of keyword surrogates is calculated by

$$a_{u,i} = \frac{nodePrestige(u)}{|S_i|}) \times proximity(u,i) \tag{4}$$

As suggested in [3,13], we use the function $nodePrestige(u)$ in order to express the importance of u in an ontology graph. Common measures are *indegree* or *outdegree* of u (for an overview of $nodePrestige$-Measures, see [22]). We introduce the multiplication with $proximity(u,i)$ that denotes to the reliability of the identifier i in context of node u, *e.g.* due to non-exact recognition of the identifier in the pre-analysis-phase. A typical example for pre-analysis is the Levensthein-distance in text recognition.

Activation Spreading. The calculation of the spreading activation from a node u to v via $e_{u,v}$ is calculated per identifier i

$$a_{v,i} = a_{u,i} \times \lambda \times degree(e_{u,v})$$
$$degree(e_{u,v}) := \frac{|e_{u,v}|}{|e_u|} \tag{5}$$

---

[7] Note: This is an excerpt from the example in Fig. 1. For the sake of brevity, here only two initial keywords "Karl Foo" and "Fritz Hall" are considered.

The variable λ is an attenuation factor for decreasing activation over the path length and thus per iteration. The $degree(e_{u,v})$ represents the structural coherence between two adjacent nodes. The higher the value, the tighter the connection between two nodes depending on the edge type. This is illustrated in Fig. 3.

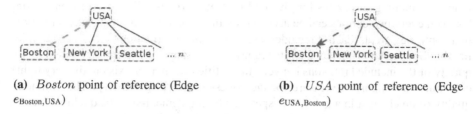

(a) *Boston* point of reference (Edge $e_{\text{Boston,USA}}$)

(b) *USA* point of reference (Edge $e_{\text{USA,Boston}}$)

Fig. 3. Example of Edge Degree

Figure 3 shows a relation of type $rdf.inCountry$ between two sets of instances. From the perspective of *Boston*, the degree of the edge to USA, $e_{\text{Boston,USA}}$ is 1, since there is one edge in total (Fig. 3a). From the perspective of USA, there are n edges in total and all of the same type, but only one of them is associated to *Boston*. Hence the edge degree for $e_{\text{USA,Boston}}$ is $\frac{1}{n}$ (Fig. 3b). The point of view is important, since the degree represents the semantic expressivity during exploration. In consequence, it characterises the importance for *Boston* to be of type USA, and for USA having an associated city *Boston* based on the degree of relations that are of the same type.

Overall Activation. The overall activation of a node v is calculated as the sum of the identifier-dependent activations and the prestige of v.

$$a_v = \sum_{i \in I} a_{v,i} + nodePrestige(v) \tag{6}$$

The overall activation is used to estimate the processing order in queue Q. The node with the highest activation value is considered as node for exploration. A $nodePrestige$ is not included in the spreading phase (only if surrogate), but considered to be of importance to the ranking measure.

Ranking. Based on the activation functions above, the calculation of importance is done during the execution of the algorithm. Apart from the ranking position in queue Q the activation value is also considered as ranking value for the generated result graphs. As stated in Sect. 3, a connecting node is the root r of a generated result graph Z and thus holds connections to at least one surrogate of each identifier. The quality of the connections is expressed by the identifier activation $a_{r,i}$. The prestige of a node as well as the proximity of each identifier is included in each identifier-dependent activation value. We consider the overall activation value of a_r, also including $nodePrestige$ of $r \in R$, as a valid measure for the quality of a result graph. In our algorithm the constructed result graphs are ordered according to their overall activation value. In consequence the top k results in R, defined by the parameter Top_k, are consistent with the best k results for the entity resolution process.

Steiner Graphs and Semantic Coherence. A steiner graph Z denotes an excerpt of the ontology graph including at least one surrogate node for each given NLI (cf. Eq. 3). The significance of Z is given through the quality of its semantic coherence. We adapt the notion of *semantic coherence* (SC) from [7] to the problem of entity resolution and to the used algorithm, by defining it as the *cohesiveness* and *expressivity* of a steiner graph Z including surrogates for given NLIs. **Cohesiveness:** The information existing between every two entities can be accessed by the exploration of their mutual relations in an ontology graph. Each Z includes a subset of this information that can be qualified first by the amount of included entities. Further, the shape of a graph Z, defined by the quality of the included relations between the entities (from non-existent till very tight), constitutes an important measure for the cohesiveness. **Expressivity:** The individual quality of an element in a graph Z is specified by an element-specific quality measure, *i.e.* the *overall activation*. This value is derived by the quality and amount of connected keyword surrogates as well as their individual *initial activations*. Further, the overall activation is computed by the *activation spreading* influenced by the shape of the paths between the nodes. The quality of each individual node is recursively calculated by the quality of its surrounding nodes. This peaks out in the quality of the connector node, the first node with associated paths to all entities and the representative of a graph Z. The overall activation of the connector node constitutes the significance of a steiner graph Z and its *ranking* value.

5   Related Work

Related research fields are word-sense disambiguation on graphs, ontology-element spotting and disambiguation, as well as keyword and entity search on graphs.

In the context of **graph based algorithms**, Veronis and Ide [25] used SA to disambiguate the senses of given words in a thesaurus. A gloss text associated to each word is used for disambiguation. During the spreading phase each word entailed in the gloss activates its associated sense while the sense itself has an associated gloss again. Recently, Tsatsaroni *et al.* [24] applied this approach to WordNet [6], including a modification that allows to use direct associations between senses. Rada *et al.* [21,22] build graphs from textual context information and use them for disambiguation based on co-occurring context words. Bhattacharya *et al.* [4] also represent textual co-references using hypergraphs. They merge different graphs based on their similarities in order to identify the exact entities. Mailaise *et al.* [15] used an SA-based approach for disambiguation between annotations used for TV programme description, including human feedback to increase the precision. This class of approaches builds upon the linguistic domain. They focus either on lexicons or on measures given through natural-language analysis. The use of graphs does not include the specifics of ontologies. Mostly background knowledge is not explored independently from the domain.

In the context of **ontology-element disambiguation** Banek *et al.* [2] recently associated a WordNet Synset to each ontology element. The disambiguation utilises the synonyms for identifying similar elements. A similar approach by Nguyen *et al.* [17] *et al.* uses an associated bag-of-words vector to each entity including certain nouns, co-occurring entities and further Wikipedia knowledge. Nguyen *et al.* also used the

KIM-ontology for disambiguation [16]. They used the textual distance between two entities in a learning corpus and preferred entities of the same concept affiliation. Garcia *et al.* [7] used a modified PageRank-Algorithm [18]; here, the textual co-occurrence of entities is used to calculate the relevance of a possible surrogate without including other ontological knowledge. Garcia *et al.* presented a modification of the algorithm including Wikipedia information [8]. Hassel *et al.* [11] presented an approach based on the DBLP-ontology which disambiguates authors occurring in mails published in the DBLP-mailing list. They used ontology relations of length one or two, in particular the co-authorship and the areas of interest. The approach by Volz *et al.* [26] used contextual information for detecting the concept affiliation of entities. Kleb *et al.* [14] used concept-dependant text patterns for the disambiguation of text information. Gruhl *et al.* [9] trained an SVM classifier in order to spot ontology entities. Here, many common ideas from information retrieval (IR) have been transferred to this domain. However, we neither require training data to learn classifiers for recognition, nor focus on the analysis of textual knowledge. Our approach could use this information later, in order to improve its weighting scheme (cf. 7). But currently, we focus on exploring complex structural background knowledge. Apart from disambiguation, Hasan [10] used spreading activation with user feedback for enabling user-driven search for information items, *i.e.* the user is allowed in an interactive approach to increase/decrease the activation of a node in order to influence the retrieval of connected graphs between entity references.

Keyword search on graphs also retrieves connected graphs including the searched keywords, but does not focus primarily on disambiguation. Bhalotia *et al.* [3] presented the BANKS system which performs an iterated search starting from all surrogates, with a best-first expansion based on the exploration of backward edges. This approach has been optimised by Kacholia *et al.* [13] regarding a spreading-activation based forward-backward exploration search using two iterators. We took up the idea of spreading activation; however, we use other measures for calculating the activation and we discard the distinction between edge directions. We also consider multiple best surrogate connections and disregard nodes with the same parent for all identifiers. Further, Kacholia's algorithm terminates with the first result found, while our algorithm finds all possible results. The recent approach BLINKS [12], based on [13], selects clusters according to the smallest cardinality. Thanh *et al.* [23] presented a search algorithm for RDF-Graphs based on one iterator per surrogate set. Recently, Kasneci *et al.* [12] proposed an approximation algorithm for Steiner trees that allows for a fast retrieval of relationship graphs based on minimal weights. In contrast to keyword search, our input information often covers more than 2-3 keywords (average for keyword search) by regarding all entity identifiers in a text. Also synonymy of input strings is not given in this field. Keyword search focuses for the retrieval of short paths following the assumption of a tight relation between the input words. This is a-priori not given for entity disambiguation.

We focus on the relational structure and specific properties of an ontology and propose a generic algorithm for disambiguation using the semantic relations between entities. We allow for an adaption of our weighting scheme by the use of preanalysis tasks.

6 Evaluation

6.1 Ontology and Input Data

Nearly all ontologies contain NLIs for ontology elements. This often implies ambiguity—but for the evaluation of our algorithm we need a *highly* polysemic domain. Regarding existing benchmarks, entity- disambiguation approaches either do not use ontologies (cf. Trec-conferences[8] or [27,4]) or do not provide their data-set publicly [7,8,16,17]. As classical entity disambiguation approaches do not include an ontology they can not be used for comparison. For the data-set [11], the NLP process for retrieving surrogates is unclear. Thus we had to construct our own evaluation scenario. In order to reflect the ambiguity of ontology elements we used a highly ambiguous **geography ontology** which is a refinement from [26,14]. It currently contains 132,087,082 RDF(S) triples, including 18 classes, 50 relations, and instance data collected from Geonames.org (information from NGA, GNIS and 36 additional sources[9]). Each instance and concept of the ontology has an associated hasName and hasAlterName relation, equivalent to the SKOS relations hasPrefLabel and hasAlterLabel. An excerpt of the ontology is shown in Fig. 4. The property hasGeographicFeature has eight associated subproperties defining the specific relations between the subclasses of GeographicFeature.

The ontology includes 6,085,125 different ontology-element identifiers. 5,109,884 of them are associated to exactly one element and thus unique. 975,241 are associated to multiple elements (in average to 4.44 elements). This results in an overall average ambiguity of 1.55 elements per identifier. The most ambiguous identifier is "First Baptist Church" with 2,085 associated elements.

As **input data** we use news articles (cf. [26,14]) crawled from the European Media Monitor (EMM [19]) which collects news of European newspapers and clusters them topic-wise. We chose the topic *natural disasters* in order to guarantee for documents including geographic entities. The included entities have been manually annotated with their exact ontology surrogate. For our evaluation, we used 46 documents. Within the corpus there are 353 mentions of identifiers pointing to 237 entities. 74 of them are unique; the most ambiguous identifier with 1,739 surrogates is "San Antonio". In average a document includes 7.67 entities. Of those 2 refer to exactly one surrogate node ($|S_i| = 1$) leaving 37.06 surrogates for each of the remainder entities. The maximum of included entities in a document was 35, and the highest overall ambiguity, the accumulated sum of entity ambiguities in a document, was 1,914.

6.2 Evaluation Process

The process describes an ontology based reference resolution for given entity identifiers. At first all entity identifiers occurring in a document are collected and used as input data. Based on the identifiers we calculate possible steiner graphs including ontology surrogates. As stated in Sect. 4 we use as result the selection of surrogates entailed in the graph with the highest activated connector node. The quality of our algorithm is

---

[8] http://trec.nist.gov/
[9] http://www.geonames.org/about.html

evaluated by comparing the entity-associated annotation in the text (including the best ontology reference based on human choice) and the reference retrieved by our algorithm. We construct steiner graphs including the searched entity-representing surrogates based on the annotations in the reference corpus. The top_1 ranked graph includes the surrogates used as result references for evaluation. We calculate the standard IR measures. The *recall* ($R_Z := \frac{|relevant\ entities \cap retrieved\ entities|}{|relevant\ entities|}$) is the ratio between the amount of correctly identified entities in the result list and all relevant entities that should be included in the result list. *Precision* ($P_Z := \frac{|relevant\ entities \cap retrieved\ entities|}{|retrieved\ entities|}$) is the ratio of the number of correctly identified entities in the result list and all retrieved entities. The *F-measure* ($f_{measure} := \frac{2*R_Z*P_Z}{R_Z+P_Z}$) is the harmonic mean between recall and precision.

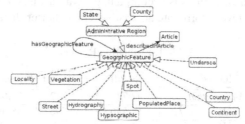

Fig. 4. Geoname Ontology Excerpt

(a) Connector: Israel   (b) Connector: Gaza

Fig. 5. Example of Steiner Graphs

We used the following algorithm thresholds: The maximum depth ($depth_{max}$) was set to 4 as this resulted in an acceptable processing time. Every possible activation value was considered using 0 as minimum activation (a_{min}). From another set of experiments we could conclude that a minimum value for activation is advantageous in combination with a high maximum depth. We restricted the edge degree (deg_{max}) to 1 and thus only considered the strongest relations in the graph. Only the highest ranked result graph, Top_1, has been used for evaluation. An example is given in Fig. 5. Here, two result graphs for the NLIs *Gaza*, *Sederot*, *Zaitoun* and *Israel* are given. Graph 5a is higher ranked than graph 5b indicated by a higher activated connecting node (see Sect. 4). In consequence only graph 5a would be considered for the result analysis.

6.3   Evaluation Results

Table 1 shows the evaluation results. In addition to the two included identifiers, each referring to exactly one ontology element, our algorithm retrieves 1.9268 additional exact surrogate association in average. Thus, in nearly four out of 7.67 identifiers, the algorithm returns exactly one surrogate as reference for each of them. In each case these surrogates were the correct references by comparison to the annotations. The algorithm achieved a recall of 97.73%[10]. Two different causes for the loss of recall can be identified here. The first kind of documents includes entities which references are widespread in the ontology graph. Visually these geographic places are distributed over several continents. This turns out as problematic by the use of the current metric. A perfect result graph in this case would include long path distances between the surrogates. However, there is often one element in a surrogate set that could be accessed via a shorter distance. This is due to the fact that spreading is influenced by an attenuation factor and thus decreased over path length. In the latter case not all entities are distributed. Here often one local cluster of entities is accompanied by a far distant entity. Here we also have been able to retrieve a surrogate accessible via a shorter distance. Result sets R,

Table 1. Evaluation Results

Method	Recall	Precision	F-measure
SA algorithm	97.731	48.342	64.687
Random $(\|R_i\| = 1 \| \forall R_i)$	38.596	38.596	38.596
Random $(\|R_i\| = \eta \| \forall R_i)$	64.286	5.028	9.322

containing η surrogates randomly selected from the set of possible surrogates S_i for each identifier, have been used for comparison with the result of our algorithm. Tab. 1, row 3, shows the results based on $S_i = 1$ whereas Tab. 1, row 4, contains the result for a random subset size η. The average of 10 evaluations is shown for both. Our approach performed much better than these baselines. 97.7% recall indicates that almost all entity references have been retrieved. 48% precision states that for almost every second entity the correct reference has been retrieved as first result. This was done in a domain with 37.40 possible references per identifier. The information regarded for disambiguation was restricted to the entity names. Except for edge degree, there was no use of further information or heuristics, like conceptual closeness. During the evaluation, the algorithm discovered at least 10 annotation mistakes in the test corpus, resulting from the geographic domain and the fact that it is not easy for a human annotator to manually annotate places, he has never been to, with the correct identifier.

The evaluation confirms our hypothesis to resolve the correct entity-representing ontology elements by the use of co-occurrence information, *i.e.* a steiner graph. Here 97% of all searched ontology elements have been retrieved. Based on this foundation a further improvement of precision is possible, as the selection within the retrieved surrogates must be improved and not so much the retrieval itself.

7   Conclusion and Outlook

We presented a novel and general applicable reference resolution algorithm under the aspect of ambiguity that allows the determination of corresponding surrogates of

---

[10] The represented precision and recall values are based on *all* identifiers found in a document.

entity identifiers based on their co-occurrence in RDF(S)-graphs. Starting from natural language identifiers, we exploit the graph representation of an ontology in order to construct spanning graphs between ontology-element surrogates. The graph itself is generated by exploration, starting from the most activated node until a connector between the elements of the different surrogate sets is retrieved. We search for all possible connectors and rank them according to their activation values. The resulting set includes the URIs of the most probable ontology elements per identifier.

We examined the quality of our approach by retrieving referencing ontology elements based on NLIs in a highly polysemic domain. We achieved 97.73% recall and 48.34% precision. As a next step, we will extend our evaluation by the annotation of further data. We will include other domains in order to verify our first promising results on other data-sets and in other domains.

Our current approach does not regard concept identifiers. The consideration of schema information would allow for the retrieval of surrogates with a certain nearness according to their instance-to-concept relation. Here the concept identifiers in the input data as well as the conceptual relations in the graph could be considered, *e.g.* surrogates with the same concept affiliation are considered to be more likely. Also relational identifiers can be used. The design of our algorithm allows this already by now.

We did not to focus on linguistic preprocessing here, as our focus was on structural processing and measures. However, parameters like the distance between identifiers in text that could be an indicator for path length between surrogates, can be included. Also phrases like "lies in" can be used to indicate certain concept affiliation or patterns between identifiers that could be mapped to an ontology graph.

Currently our approach is restricted to the identification of full-connectors, *i.e.* connectors related to one surrogate per given identifier at least. Using partial connectors in order to retrieve local clusters and thus tighter connected graphs is a next step. We will also modify the spreading between nodes and the consideration of best parents in order to allow for a more fine-grained distinction between best-parents. This will decrease the amount of possible surrogates per set and thus improve the precision of our algorithm.

References

1. Anderson, J.R.: A spreading activation theory of memory. Journal of Verbal Learning and Verbal Behavior (1983)
2. Banek, M., Vrdoljak, B., Tjoa, A.M.: Word sense disambiguation as the primary step of ontology integration. In: Bhowmick, S.S., Küng, J., Wagner, R. (eds.) DEXA 2008. LNCS, vol. 5181, pp. 65–72. Springer, Heidelberg (2008)
3. Bhalotia, G., Hulgeri, A., Nakhe, C., Chakrabarti, S., Sudarshan, S.: Keyword searching and browsing in databases using banks. In: Proc. ICDE. IEEE Computer Society, Los Alamitos (2002)
4. Bhattacharya, I., Getoor, L.: Collective entity resolution in relational data. IEEE Data Eng. Bull. 29(2) (2006)
5. Collins, A.M., Loftus, E.F.: A spreading-activation theory of semantic processing. Psychological Review 82(6) (1975)
6. Fellbaum, C. (ed.): WordNet An Electronic Lexical Database. The MIT Press, Cambridge (1998)

7. García, N.F., del Toro, J.M.B., Sánchez, L., Bernardi, A.: Identityrank: Named entity disambiguation in the context of the news project. In: Franconi, E., Kifer, M., May, W. (eds.) ESWC 2007. LNCS, vol. 4519, pp. 640–654. Springer, Heidelberg (2007)
8. García, N.F., del Toro, J.M.B., Sánchez, L., Centeno, V.L.: Semantic annotation of web resources using identityrank and wikipedia. In: Proc. AWIC (2007)
9. Gruhl, D., Nagarajan, M., Pieper, J., Robson, C., Sheth, A.P.: Context and domain knowledge enhanced entity spotting in informal text. In: Bernstein, A., Karger, D.R., Heath, T., Feigenbaum, L., Maynard, D., Motta, E., Thirunarayan, K. (eds.) ISWC 2009. LNCS, vol. 5823, pp. 260–276. Springer, Heidelberg (2009)
10. Hasan, M.M.: A spreading activation framework for ontology-enhanced adaptive information access within organisations. In: van Elst, L., Dignum, V., Abecker, A. (eds.) AMKM 2003. LNCS (LNAI), vol. 2926, pp. 288–296. Springer, Heidelberg (2004)
11. Hassell, J., Aleman-Meza, B., Arpinar, I.B.: Ontology-driven automatic entity disambiguation in unstructured text. In: Cruz, I., Decker, S., Allemang, D., Preist, C., Schwabe, D., Mika, P., Uschold, M., Aroyo, L.M. (eds.) ISWC 2006. LNCS, vol. 4273, pp. 44–57. Springer, Heidelberg (2006)
12. He, H., Wang, H., Yang, J., Yu, P.S.: Blinks: ranked keyword searches on graphs. In: Proc. SIGMOD. ACM Press, New York (2007)
13. Kacholia, V., Pandit, S., Chakrabarti, S., Sudarshan, S., Desai, R., Karambelkar, H.: Bidirectional expansion for keyword search on graph databases. In: Proc. VLDB (2005)
14. Kleb, J., Volz, R.: Ontology based entity disambiguation with natural language patterns. In: Proc. ICDIM (2009)
15. Malais, V., Gazendam, L., Brugman, H.: Disambiguating automatic semantic annotation based on a thesaurus structure. In: Proc. TALN (2007)
16. Nguyen, H.T., Cao, T.H.: A knowledge-based approach to named entity disambiguation in news articles. In: Orgun, M.A., Thornton, J. (eds.) AI 2007. LNCS (LNAI), vol. 4830, pp. 619–624. Springer, Heidelberg (2007)
17. Nguyen, H.T., Cao, T.H.: Named entity disambiguation on an ontology enriched by wikipedia. In: Proc RIVF 2008 (2008)
18. Page, L., Brin, S., Motwani, R., Winograd, T.: The pagerank citation ranking: Bringing order to the web. Technical report, Stanford Digital Library Technologies Project (1998)
19. Pouliquen, B., Steinberger, R., Ignat, C., Käsper, E., Temnikova, I.: Multilingual and cross-lingual news topic tracking. In: Proc. COLING. ACL (2004)
20. Quillian, M.R.: A revised design for an understanding machine. Machine Translation (1975)
21. Rada, M.: Unsupervised large-vocabulary word sense disambiguation with graph-based algorithms for sequence data labeling. In: Proc. HLT. ACL (2005)
22. Sinha, R., Rada, M.: Unsupervised graph-based word sense disambiguation using measures of word semantic similarity. In: Proc. ICSC. IEEE Computer Society, Los Alamitos (2007)
23. Tran, T., Wang, H., Rudolph, S., Cimiano, P.: Top-k exploration of query candidates for efficient keyword search on graph-shaped RDF data. In: Proc. ICDE. IEEE, Los Alamitos (2009)
24. Tsatsaronis, G., Vazirgiannis, M., Androutsopoulos, I.: Word sense disambiguation with spreading activation networks generated from thesauri. In: Proc. IJCAI (2007)
25. Veronis, J., Ide, N.M.: Word sense disambiguation with very large neural networks extracted from machine readable dictionaries. In: Proc. COLING. ACL (1990)
26. Volz, R., Kleb, J., Mueller, W.: Towards ontology-based disambiguation of geographical identifiers. In: Proc. WWW Workshop I^3 (2007)
27. Wick, M.L., Culotta, A., Rohanimanesh, K., McCallum, A.: An entity based model for coreference resolution. In: Proc. SIAM (2009)

A Generic Approach for Correcting Access Restrictions to a Consequence

Martin Knechtel[1] and Rafael Peñaloza[2]

[1] SAP Research Center Dresden
martin.knechtel@sap.com
[2] Theoretical Computer Science TU Dresden, Germany
penaloza@tcs.inf.tu-dresden.de

Abstract. Recent research has shown that annotations are useful for representing access restrictions to the axioms of an ontology and their implicit consequences. Previous work focused on assigning a label, representing its access level, to each consequence from a given ontology. However, a security administrator might not be satisfied with the access level obtained through these methods. In this case, one is interested in finding which axioms would need to get their access restrictions modified in order to get the desired label for the consequence. In this paper we look at this problem and present algorithms for solving it with a variety of optimizations. We also present first experimental results on large scale ontologies, which show that our methods perform well in practice.

1 Introduction

In several applications it is desirable to have one, usually large, ontology, but offer different users access to different views of this ontology. In other words, each user has access to only a subset of the ontology, selected in accordance to an appropriate criterion. Different criteria can be used: access rights is only one of them, others are granularity, certainty, relevancy, trust etc., without loss of generality we focus on access rights in this paper while the results remain applicable to all the other lattice-based applications. Axioms have a privacy level and users get assigned a security clearance. A user can then only see those axioms whose privacy level is dominated by the security clearance of the user. In order to maintain only one ontology, we want to be able to store and retrieve the access information of users and axioms in an easy way. The approach proposed in [2] is to use a labeling lattice $(L, \leq)$; i.e. a set L of labels together with a partial order $\leq$ such that every finite set of labels has a join (least upper bound) and a meet (greatest lower bound) w.r.t. $\leq$. Every axiom a in the ontology $\mathcal{O}$ is assumed to have a label $\mathsf{lab}(a) \in L$, and each user receives also a label $\ell \in L$. The sub-ontology to which a user with label ℓ has access is defined as

$$\mathcal{O}_{\geq \ell} := \{a \in \mathcal{O} \mid \mathsf{lab}(a) \geq \ell\}.$$

A desirable property in ontologies is that they express as least explicit information as possible, while all the implicitly encoded knowledge is accessible through

L. Aroyo et al. (Eds.): ESWC 2010, Part I, LNCS 6088, pp. 167–182, 2010.

reasoning. Whenever we obtain a consequence c from an ontology, we need to be able to detect which users are allowed to see this consequence; in other words, if the user has a label ℓ, we need to decide whether c also follows from the sub-ontology $\mathcal{O}_{\geq \ell}$. The solution presented in [2] is to compute a so-called *boundary* for the consequence c; that is, an element ν_c of L such that c is a consequence of $\mathcal{O}_{\geq \ell}$ iff $\ell \leq \nu_c$.

The general problem can be seen similar to reducing inference control to access control in databases [8,7]. Inference control assumes a set of defined secrets and checks at runtime on every response to a user's query whether this response together with the user's a priori knowledge and already delivered answers implies any secret. In contrast to that, access control is enforced by following a policy which regulates access on explicit data. For knowledge bases, we extended access control to implied knowledge by computing a boundary for a consequence as described above. A security administrator can change the boundary only by changing the implying axioms' labels. For this purpose, he might be interested in support to find the minimal set of those axioms.

Just as ontology development and maintenance is an error prone activity, so is the adequate labeling of axioms according to their access requirements. A wrong access labeling may allow a user to deduce consequences for which he should have no security clearance. One may also encounter the dual problem, where a consequence is restricted to a user having the adequate security clearance. Both of these errors can be detected by looking at the boundary computed for the consequence. The first case occurs when the boundary is set too high up in the lattice, while the second case arises when the boundary is lower than expected.

The problem we want to solve then is that of repairing the labeling: we want to find a relabeling of the ontology such that the boundary computed under this new labeling yields the desired privacy level. This problem differs from that of ontology repair in that we do not aim to modify the axioms in the ontology, but only the labeling they receive. Our approach focuses on finding a minimal sub-ontology $\mathcal{S}$ such that, if we relabel all axioms in $\mathcal{S}$ to the goal label ℓ_g, and leave all other labels unchanged, then the boundary is changed to ℓ_g. Such a set will be called a *change set*. In order to commit as least changes as possible, we will prefer change sets of smaller cardinality.

We show that the ideas of axiom pinpointing [13,12,11,4,3] can be adapted to the search of a change set with minimum cardinality. We present black-box methods, improving upon the Hitting Set Tree approach to axiom pinpointing [10,14] that yield the desired change set. The methods take advantage of our search of a set with minimum cardinality, as well as the axiom labeling to reduce the search space and hence also the execution time. The experimental results at the end of the paper show that these enhancements improve the execution time.

2   Basic Notions and Results

To keep our presentation and results as general as possible, we impose only minimal restrictions to our ontology language. We just assume that an *ontology* is a finite set, whose elements are called *axioms*, such that every subset of an ontology is itself an ontology. If $\mathcal{O}' \subseteq \mathcal{O}$ and $\mathcal{O}$ is an ontology, then $\mathcal{O}'$ is called a *sub-ontology* of $\mathcal{O}$. An ontology language specifies which sets of axioms are admitted as ontologies. Given an ontology language, a *monotone consequence relation* $\models$ is a binary relation between ontologies $\mathcal{O}$ and *consequences* c such that if $\mathcal{O} \models c$, then for every ontology $\mathcal{O}' \supseteq \mathcal{O}$ it holds that $\mathcal{O}' \models c$. If $\mathcal{O} \models c$, we say that c *follows from* $\mathcal{O}$ or that $\mathcal{O}$ *entails* c.

If $\mathcal{O} \models c$, we may be interested in finding the axioms responsible for this fact. A sub-ontology $\mathcal{S} \subseteq \mathcal{O}$ is called a *MinA* for $\mathcal{O}, c$ if $\mathcal{S} \models c$ and for every $\mathcal{S}' \subset \mathcal{S}, \mathcal{S}' \not\models c$. The dual notion of a MinA is that of a diagnosis. A *diagnosis* for $\mathcal{O}, c$ is a sub-ontology $\mathcal{S} \subseteq \mathcal{O}$ such that $\mathcal{O} \setminus \mathcal{S} \not\models c$ and $\mathcal{O} \setminus \mathcal{S}' \models c$ for all $\mathcal{S}' \subset \mathcal{S}$.

For a lattice $(L, \leq)$ and a set $K \subseteq L$, we denote as $\bigoplus_{\ell \in K} \ell$ and $\bigotimes_{\ell \in K} \ell$ the *join* (least upper bound) and *meet* (greatest lower bound) of K, respectively. We consider that ontologies are *labeled* with elements of the lattice. More formally, for an ontology $\mathcal{O}$ there is a labeling function lab that assigns a *label* $\mathsf{lab}(a) \in L$ to every element a of $\mathcal{O}$. We will often use the notation $L_{\mathsf{lab}} := \{\mathsf{lab}(a) \mid a \in \mathcal{O}\}$. For an element $\ell \in L$, we denote as $\mathcal{O}_{\geq \ell}$ the sub-ontology $\mathcal{O}_{\geq \ell} := \{a \in \mathcal{O} \mid \mathsf{lab}(a) \geq \ell\}$. The sub-ontologies $\mathcal{O}_{\leq \ell}, \mathcal{O}_{=\ell}, \mathcal{O}_{\neq \ell}, \mathcal{O}_{\not\geq \ell}$, and $\mathcal{O}_{\not\leq \ell}$ are defined analogously. This notion is also extended to sets of labels in the natural way, e.g. $\mathcal{O}_{=K} := \{a \in \mathcal{O} \mid \mathsf{lab}(a) = \ell$ for some $\ell \in K\}$. Conversely, for a sub-ontology $\mathcal{S} \subseteq \mathcal{O}$, we define $\lambda_{\mathcal{S}} := \bigotimes_{a \in \mathcal{S}} \mathsf{lab}(a)$ and $\mu_{\mathcal{S}} := \bigoplus_{a \in \mathcal{S}} \mathsf{lab}(a)$. An element $\ell \in L$ is called *join prime relative to* L_{lab} if for every $K_1, \ldots, K_n \subseteq L_{\mathsf{lab}}, \ell \leq \bigoplus_{i=1}^n \lambda_{K_i}$ implies that there is $i, 1 \leq i \leq n$ such that $\ell \leq \lambda_{K_i}$. Join prime elements relative to L_{lab} are called *user labels*. The set of all user labels is denoted as U. When dealing with labeled ontologies, the reasoning problem of interest consists on the computation of a *boundary* for a consequence c. Intuitively, the boundary divides the user labels ℓ of U according to whether $\mathcal{O}_{\geq \ell}$ entails c or not.

Definition 1 (Boundary). *Let $\mathcal{O}$ be an ontology and c a consequence. An element $\nu \in L$ is called a* boundary *for $\mathcal{O}, c$ if for every join prime element relative to L_{lab} ℓ it holds that $\ell \leq \nu$ iff $\mathcal{O}_{\geq \ell} \models c$.*

Given a user label ℓ_u, we will say that the user *sees* a consequence c if $\ell_u \leq \nu$ for some boundary ν. The following lemma relating MinAs and boundaries was shown in [2].

Lemma 1. *If $\mathcal{S}_1, \ldots, \mathcal{S}_n$ are all MinAs for $\mathcal{O}, c$, then $\bigoplus_{i=1}^n \lambda_{\mathcal{S}_i}$ is a boundary for $\mathcal{O}, c$.*

A dual result, which relates the boundary with the set of diagnoses, also exists. The proof follows easily from the definitions given in this section.

Lemma 2. *If $\mathcal{S}_1, \ldots, \mathcal{S}_n$ are all diagnoses for $\mathcal{O}, c$, then $\bigotimes_{i=1}^n \mu_{\mathcal{S}_i}$ is a boundary for $\mathcal{O}, c$.*

Example 1. Let $(L_d, \leq_d)$ be the lattice shown in Figure 1, and $\mathcal{O}$ a labeled ontology from a marketplace in the Semantic Web with the following axioms

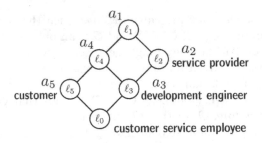

Fig. 1. Lattice $(L_d, \leq_d)$ with 4 user labels and an assignment of 5 axioms to labels

$a_1 : EUecoService \sqcap HighperformanceService(ecoCalculatorV1)$
$a_2 : HighperformanceService$
$\quad \sqsubseteq ServiceWithLowCustomerNr \sqcap LowProfitService$
$a_3 : EUecoService \sqsubseteq ServiceWithLowCustomerNr \sqcap LowProfitService$
$a_4 : ServiceWithLowCustomerNr \sqsubseteq ServiceWithComingPriceIncrease$
$a_5 : LowProfitService \sqsubseteq ServiceWithComingPriceIncrease$

where the function lab assigns to each axiom the labels as shown in Figure 1. This ontology entails $c : ServiceWithComingPriceIncrease(ecoCalculatorV1)$. The MinAs for $\mathcal{O},c$ are $\{a_1, a_2, a_4\}, \{a_1, a_2, a_5\}, \{a_1, a_3, a_4\}, \{a_1, a_3, a_5\}$, and its diagnoses are $\{a_1\}, \{a_2, a_3\}, \{a_4, a_5\}$. Using Lemma 2, we can compute the boundary as $\mu_{\{a_1\}} \otimes \mu_{\{a_2,a_3\}} \otimes \mu_{\{a_4,a_5\}} = \ell_1 \otimes \ell_2 \otimes \ell_4 = \ell_3$. Valid user labels are $\ell_0, \ell_2, \ell_3, \ell_5$ which represent user roles as illustrated. For ℓ_0 and ℓ_3, c is visible.

3   Modifying the Boundary

Once the boundary for a consequence c has been computed, it is possible that the knowledge engineer or the security administrator considers this solution erroneous. For instance, the boundary may express that a given user u is able to deduce c, although this was not intended. Alternatively, the boundary may imply that c is a confidential consequence, only visible to a few, high-clearance users, while in reality c should be publicly available. The problem we face is how to change the labeling function so that the computed boundary corresponds to the desired label in the lattice. This problem can be formalized and approached in several different ways. In our approach, we fix a goal label ℓ_g and try to modify the labeling of as least axioms as possible so that the boundary equals ℓ_g.

Definition 2. *Let $\mathcal{O}$ be an ontology, c a consequence, lab a labeling function, $\mathcal{S} \subseteq \mathcal{O}$ and $\ell_g \in L$ the goal label. The modified assignment $\mathsf{lab}_{\mathcal{S},\ell_g}$ is given by*

$$\mathsf{lab}_{\mathcal{S},\ell_g}(t) = \begin{cases} \ell_g, & \text{if } t \in \mathcal{S}, \\ \mathsf{lab}(t), & \text{otherwise.} \end{cases}$$

A sub-ontology $\mathcal{S} \subseteq \mathcal{O}$ is called a change set *for ℓ_g if the boundary for $\mathcal{O},c$ under the labeling function $\mathsf{lab}_{\mathcal{S},\ell_g}$ equals ℓ_g.*

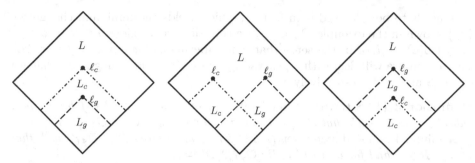

Fig. 2. Hide consequence from some user roles (left), allow additional user roles to see consequence (right) and both at the same time (middle)

Obviously, the original ontology $\mathcal{O}$ is always a change set for any goal label if $\mathcal{O} \models c$. However, we are interested in performing minimal changes to the labeling function. Hence, we search for a change set of minimum cardinality. It follows from [5] that this problem is NP-complete.

Let ℓ_g denote the goal label and ℓ_c the computed boundary for c. There are three possible cases for ℓ_g and ℓ_c to differ, which are illustrated in Figure 2: either (i) $\ell_g < \ell_c$ (left), (ii) $\ell_c < \ell_g$ (right), or (iii) ℓ_g and ℓ_c are incomparable (middle). The sets L_c and L_g contain the user labels before and after the label changes respectively. Consider the first case, where $\ell_g < \ell_c$. Then, from Lemma 2 it follows that any diagnosis S is a change set for ℓ_g: since $\ell_g < \ell_c$, then for every diagnosis S', $\ell_g < \mu_{S'}$. But then, under the new labeling lab_{S,ℓ_g} we get that $\mu_S = \ell_g$. And hence, when the greatest lower bound of all $\mu_{S'}$ is computed, we obtain ℓ_g as a boundary. Using an analogous argument and Lemma 1, it is possible to show that if $\ell_c < \ell_g$, then every MinA is a change set for ℓ_g. The third case can be solved using a combination of the previous two: if ℓ_g and ℓ_c are incomparable, we can first set as a partial goal $\ell'_g := \ell_g \otimes \ell_c$. Thus, we can first solve the first case, to set the boundary to ℓ'_g, and then, using the second approach, modify this new boundary once more to ℓ_g. Unfortunately, this approach does not yield a change set of minimum cardinality, even if the smallest diagnosis or MinA is computed, as shown in the following example.

Example 2. Let $\mathcal{O},c$ and lab be as in Example 1. We then know that $\ell_c := \ell_3$ is a boundary for $\mathcal{O},c$. Suppose now that the goal label is $\ell_g := \ell_4$. Since $\ell_c < \ell_g$, we know that any MinA is a change set. Since all MinAs for $\mathcal{O},c$ have exactly three elements, any change set produced this way will have cardinality three. However, $\{a_2\}$ is also a change set, whose cardinality is obviously smaller.

To understand why the minimality of MinAs is not sufficient for obtaining a minimum change set, we can look back to Lemma 1. This lemma says that in order to find a boundary, we need to compute the join of all λ_S, with S a MinA, and λ_S the meet of the labels of all axioms in S. But then, for any axiom $a \in S$ such that $\ell_g \leq \text{lab}(a)$, modifying this label to ℓ_g will have no influence in the result of λ_S. In Example 2, there is a MinA $\{a_1, a_2, a_4\}$, where two axioms, namely a_1 and a_4 have a label greater or equal to $\ell_g = \ell_4$. Thus, the only axiom that needs to be relabeled is in fact a_2, which yields the minimum change set $\{a_2\}$ shown in the example. Basically, we consider every axiom $a \in \mathcal{O}$ such that $\ell_g \leq \mathsf{lab}(a)$ as *fixed* in the sense that it is superfluous for any change set. For this reason, we will deal with a generalization of MinAs and diagnoses, that we call IAS and RAS, respectively.

Definition 3 (IAS,RAS). *A minimal inserted axiom set (IAS) for ℓ_g is a subset $I \subseteq \mathcal{O}_{\ngeq \ell_g}$ such that $\mathcal{O}_{\geq \ell_g} \cup I \models c$ and for every $I' \subset I : \mathcal{O}_{\geq \ell_g} \cup I' \not\models c$.*

A minimal removed axiom set (RAS) for ℓ_g is a subset $R \subseteq \mathcal{O}_{\nleq \ell_g}$ such that $\mathcal{O}_{\nleq \ell_g} \setminus R \not\models c$ and for every $R' \subset R : \mathcal{O}_{\nleq \ell_g} \setminus R' \models c$.

The following theorem justifies the use of IAS and RAS when searching for change sets of minimum cardinality.

Theorem 1. *Let ℓ_c be a boundary for $\mathcal{O},c$, ℓ_g the goal label, I an IAS for ℓ_g of minimum cardinality and R an RAS for ℓ_g of minimum cardinality. Then, the following holds:*

  - *if $\ell_g < \ell_c$, then R is a change set of minimum cardinality,*
  - *if $\ell_c < \ell_g$, then I is a change set of minimum cardinality.*

4   Computing the Smallest IAS and RAS

In this section, we show how the smallest IAS and RAS can be computed. We first present the most obvious approach that is based in the computation of all MinAs and diagnoses. Afterwards, we show how this idea can be improved by considering fixed portions of the ontology, as described before. We further improve this approach by showing that it usually suffices to compute only partial IAS and RAS, thus reducing the search space and execution time of our method.

4.1   Using Full Axiom Pinpointing

Although we have shown in Example 2 that MinAs and diagnoses do not yield change sets of minimum cardinality directly, these change sets can still be deduced from the set of all MinAs and diagnoses, as shown by the following lemma.

Lemma 3. *Let I (R) be an IAS (RAS) for ℓ_g, then there is a MinA (diagnosis) $\mathcal{S}$ such that $I = \mathcal{S} \setminus \mathcal{O}_{\geq \ell_g}$ ($R = \mathcal{S} \setminus \mathcal{O}_{\leq \ell_g}$).*

Lemma 3 shows that we can compute the set of all IAS by first computing all MinAs and then removing the set of fixed elements $\mathcal{O}_{\geq \ell_g}$ from it[1]. Thus, the most naïve approach for computing a change set of minimum cardinality is to first find all MinAs, then compute the set of all IAS by removing all elements in $\mathcal{O}_{\geq \ell_g}$, and finally search for the IAS having the least elements.

---

[1] To avoid unnecessary repetitions, we henceforth focus our discussion on the computation of the smallest IAS except for very specific cases. It should be noted, however, that the case of RAS can be treated in a similar fashion.

The task of computing all MinAs, also called axiom pinpointing, has been widely studied in recent years, and there exist black-box implementations based on the hitting set tree (HST) algorithm [10,14]. The HST algorithm makes repeated calls to an auxiliary procedure that computes a single MinA. Further MinAs are found by building a tree, where nodes are labeled with MinAs. If the MinA labeling a node has n axioms ($\mathcal{S} := \{a_1, \ldots, a_n\}$), then this node will have n children: the i-th child is labeled with a MinA obtained after removing a_i from the ontology. This ensures that each node is labeled with a MinA distinct from those of its predecessors. Although not stated explicitly in the axiom pinpointing literature, it is clear that the same HST algorithm can be used for computing all diagnoses. The only variant necessary is to have a subroutine capable of computing one such diagnosis, which can be obtained by dualizing the algorithm computing one MinA (see Algorithm 2 for an example on how this dualization works). In our experiments, we used this approach as a basis to measure the improvement achieved by the optimizations that will be introduced next.

4.2   Using Fixed Sub-ontologies and Cardinality Limit

Rather than computing the set of IAS indirectly by first computing MinAs and then removing the fixed axioms, we would like to use a procedure that finds them directly. Moreover, since our goal is to find the *smallest* IAS, we want this procedure to stop once the IAS being computed is ensured to have cardinality larger than or equal to that of the best IAS found so far. In Algorithm 1 we present a variation of the logarithmic MinA extraction procedure presented in [6] that is able to compute an IAS or stop once this has reached a size n.

We also show the RAS variant in Algorithm 2 to illustrate how the duality between IAS and RAS transfers to the algorithms that compute them.

Given a goal label ℓ_g, if we want to compute an IAS of size at most n for a consequence c, then we would make a call to extract-partial-IAS($\mathcal{O}_{\geq \ell_g}, \mathcal{O} \setminus \mathcal{O}_{\geq \ell_g}, c, n$). Similarly, a call to extract-partial-RAS($\mathcal{O} \setminus \mathcal{O}_{\leq \ell_g}, \mathcal{O} \setminus \mathcal{O}_{\leq \ell_g}, c, n$) yields an RAS of size at most n. The second parameter defines the axioms which are allowed to be contained in the RAS. One of the advantages of the HST algorithm is that the labels of any node are always ensured not to contain the label of any of its predecessor nodes. In particular this means that even if we do not always compute a full IAS (like in Algorithm 1, where the output may be only a subset of size n of an IAS), the algorithm will still correctly find all IAS that do not contain any of the partial IAS found during the execution. Since we are interested in finding the IAS of minimum cardinality, we can set the limit n to the size of the smallest IAS found so far. If extract-partial-IAS outputs a set with fewer elements, we are sure that this is indeed a full IAS, and hence we can update our best result to this newly found set. The HST algorithm will not find all IAS in this way, but we can be sure that one IAS with the minimum cardinality will be found.

The idea of using only partial information for finding the smallest IAS can be taken a step further. We can in fact modify the HST algorithm itself, so that it looks only at a reduced search space, while still finding a smallest IAS. Algorithm 3 shows the modified HST method.

Algorithm 1. Compute (partial) IAS

Procedure extract-partial-IAS($\mathcal{O}_{fix}, \mathcal{O}_{test}, c, n$)
Input: $\mathcal{O}_{fix}$: fixed axioms; $\mathcal{O}_{test}$: axioms; c: consequence; n: limit
Output: first n elements of a minimal $\mathcal{S} \subseteq \mathcal{O}_{test}$ such that $\mathcal{O}_{fix} \cup \mathcal{S} \models c$
1: **Global** $l := 0, n$
2: **return** extract-partial-IAS-r($\mathcal{O}_{fix}, \mathcal{O}_{test}, c$)
Subprocedure extract-partial-IAS-r($\mathcal{O}_{fix}, \mathcal{O}_{test}, c$)
1: **if** $n = l$ **then**
2:      **return** $\emptyset$
3: **if** $|\mathcal{O}_{test}| = 1$ **then**
4:      $l := l + 1$
5:      **return** $\mathcal{O}_{test}$
6: $\mathcal{S}_1, \mathcal{S}_2 := $ halve($\mathcal{O}_{test}$)   (partition $\mathcal{O}_{test}$ so that $||\mathcal{S}_1| - |\mathcal{S}_2|| \leq 1$)
7: **if** $\mathcal{O}_{fix} \cup \mathcal{S}_1 \models c$ **then**
8:      **return** extract-partial-IAS-r($\mathcal{O}_{fix}, \mathcal{S}_1, c$)
9: **if** $\mathcal{O}_{fix} \cup \mathcal{S}_2 \models c$ **then**
10:     **return** extract-partial-IAS-r($\mathcal{O}_{fix}, \mathcal{S}_2, c$)
11: $\mathcal{S}_1' := $ extract-partial-IAS-r($\mathcal{O}_{fix} \cup \mathcal{S}_2, \mathcal{S}_1, c$)
12: $\mathcal{S}_2' := $ extract-partial-IAS-r($\mathcal{O}_{fix} \cup \mathcal{S}_1', \mathcal{S}_2, c$)
13: **return** $\mathcal{S}_1' \cup \mathcal{S}_2'$

There are two main differences between the original HST method as described in [10,14] and the procedure hst-extract-smallest-IAS. The first one, as already explained before, is that the nodes of the generated tree are not necessarily labeled with an IAS, but may contain only a partial IAS. The reduction in the search space here is clear: since nodes have less axioms, the search tree has a lower branching factor. Moreover, the set of (possibly partial) IAS still to be found is also reduced, since no superset of any label set found so far is allowed. The second difference is that the tree is not expanded at each node for all the axioms in it, but rather only on the first $m - 1$, where m is the size of the smallest IAS found so far. This further reduces the search space by decreasing the branching factor of the search tree. Notice that the highest advantage of this second optimization appears when the HST is constructed in a depth-first fashion. In that case, a smaller IAS found further below in the tree will reduce the branching factor of all its predecessors. The following theorem shows that Algorithm 3 is correct.

Theorem 2. *Let $\mathcal{O}$ be an ontology, c a consequence with $\mathcal{O} \models c$, and ℓ_g a goal label. If n is the minimum cardinality of an IAS for ℓ_g, then Algorithm 3 outputs an IAS I such that $|I| = n$.*

Proof. Algorithm 3 always outputs an IAS since I is only modified when the output of extract-partial-IAS has size strictly smaller than the limit m, and hence only when this is an IAS itself. Suppose now that the output I is such that $n < |I|$, and let I_0 be an IAS such that $|I_0| = n$, which exists by assumption. Then, every set obtained by calls to extract-partial-IAS has size strictly greater

---

Algorithm 2. Compute (partial) RAS

Procedure extract-partial-RAS($\mathcal{O}_{\text{nonfix}}, \mathcal{O}_{\text{test}}, c, n$)
Input: $\mathcal{O}_{\text{nonfix}}$: axioms; $\mathcal{O}_{\text{test}}$: axioms; c: consequence; n: limit
Output: first n elements of a minimal $\mathcal{S} \subseteq \mathcal{O}_{\text{test}}$ such that $\mathcal{O}_{\text{nonfix}} \setminus \mathcal{S} \not\models c$
 1: **Global** $l := 0, \mathcal{O} := \mathcal{O}_{\text{nonfix}}, n$
 2: **return** extract-partial-RAS-r($\emptyset, \mathcal{O}_{\text{test}}, c$)

Subprocedure extract-partial-RAS-r($\mathcal{O}_{\text{fix}}, \mathcal{O}_{\text{test}}, c$)
 1: **if** $n = l$ **then**
 2:    **return** $\emptyset$
 3: **if** $|\mathcal{O}_{\text{test}}| = 1$ **then**
 4:    $l := l + 1$
 5:    **return** $\mathcal{O}_{\text{test}}$
 6: $\mathcal{S}_1, \mathcal{S}_2 := \text{halve}(\mathcal{O}_{\text{test}})$
 7: **if** $\mathcal{O} \setminus (\mathcal{O}_{\text{fix}} \cup \mathcal{S}_1) \not\models c$ **then**
 8:    **return** extract-partial-RAS-r($\mathcal{O}_{\text{fix}}, \mathcal{S}_1, c$)
 9: **if** $\mathcal{O} \setminus (\mathcal{O}_{\text{fix}} \cup \mathcal{S}_2) \not\models c$ **then**
10:    **return** extract-partial-RAS-r($\mathcal{O}_{\text{fix}}, \mathcal{S}_2, c$)
11: $\mathcal{S}_1' := \text{extract-partial-RAS-r}(\mathcal{O}_{\text{fix}} \cup \mathcal{S}_2, \mathcal{S}_1, c)$
12: $\mathcal{S}_2' := \text{extract-partial-RAS-r}(\mathcal{O}_{\text{fix}} \cup \mathcal{S}_1', \mathcal{S}_2, c)$
13: **return** $\mathcal{S}_1' \cup \mathcal{S}_2'$

---

than n, since otherwise, I and m would be updated. Consider now an arbitrary set $\mathcal{S}$ found during the execution through a call to extract-partial-IAS, and let $\mathcal{S}_n := \{a_1, \ldots, a_n\}$ the first n elements of $\mathcal{S}$. Since $\mathcal{S}$ is a (partial) IAS, it must follow that $I_0 \not\subseteq \mathcal{S}_n$. Then, there must be an $i, 1 \leq i \leq n$ such that $a_i \notin I_0$. But then, I_0 will still be an IAS after axiom $\{a_i\}$ has been removed. Since this argument is true for all nodes, it in particular holds at all leaf nodes, but then they cannot be leaf nodes, since a new IAS, namely I_0 can still be found by expanding the HST. This contradicts that I is the output of the algorithm. $\square$

Efficient implementations of the original version of the HST algorithm rely on several optimizations. Two standard optimizations described in the literature are node-reuse and early path termination (see, e.g. [10,14,2]). Node-reuse keeps a history of all nodes computed so far in order to avoid useless (and usually expensive) calls to the auxiliary procedure that computes a new node. Early path termination, on the other hand, prunes the hitting set tree by avoiding expanding nodes when no new information can be derived from further expansion. In order to avoid unnecessary confusion, we have described the modified HST algorithm without including these optimizations. However, it should be clear that both, node-reuse and early path termination, can be included in the algorithm without destroying its correctness. All the implementations used in the experimental results contain these two optimizations.

4.3 Label-Based Optimization

Up to now, our approach has only looked at the axioms individually in an attempt to compute the IAS, but the labels of these axioms have been ignored,

---

Algorithm 3. Modified HST algorithm to find smallest IAS for ℓ_g

---

Procedure hst-extract-smallest-IAS($\mathcal{O}, (L, \leq), c, \ell_g$)
Input: $\mathcal{O}$: labeled ontology; $(L, \leq)$: lattice; c: consequence of $\mathcal{O}$; ℓ_g: goal label
Output: IAS I of minimum cardinality
1: **Global** $I := \mathcal{O}, m := |\mathcal{O}|, \mathcal{O}_{\text{fix}} := \mathcal{O}_{\geq \ell_g}, \mathcal{O}_{\text{nonfix}} := \mathcal{O} \setminus \mathcal{O}_{\text{fix}}$
2: expand-hst-IAS($\mathcal{O} \setminus \mathcal{O}_{\text{fix}}, c$)
3: **return** I

Procedure expand-hst-IAS($\mathcal{O}, c$)
Input: $\mathcal{O}$: ontology; c: consequence
Side effects: modifications to I and m
1: **if** $\mathcal{O}_{\text{fix}} \cup \mathcal{O} \not\models c$ **then**
2:    **return**
3: **else**
4:    $\mathcal{S} :=$ extract-partial-IAS($\mathcal{O}_{\text{fix}}, \mathcal{O}, c, m$)
5:    **if** $|\mathcal{S}| < |I|$ **then**
6:       $I := \mathcal{S}$
7:       $m := |I|$
8:    **for** the first $(m - 1)$ axioms t in $\mathcal{S}$ **do**
9:       expand-hst-IAS($\mathcal{O} \setminus \{t\}, c$)

---

except for the fixed axioms, whose label is greater than or equal to ℓ_g. The experiments in [2] show that it is usually faster to compute the set of labels that contain a MinA than a MinA itself. This is not surprising since usually a single lattice element ℓ labels more than one axiom, and hence when testing whether there is an axiom labeled with ℓ that belongs to a MinA we are simultaneously performing this test for several axioms. Intuitively, the same should be true for the computation of IAS. Hence, our search for the smallest IAS can be further improved if IAS are computed through a two-step procedure: (1) without computing the IAS we compute the set of labels K of axioms in the IAS, (2) we then find the IAS from only the axioms that have labels in K. Notice that for a given set of labels K, there can in fact be several IAS having labels in K. We can use a HST algorithm to find all of them before trying to compute a new label set.

Interestingly, this approach can also be improved when searching for the smallest IAS by using (partial) label sets of length at most that of the smallest IAS found so far. Algorithm 4 shows a simple procedure for computing such partial label sets, up to a given length n. Let L_{IAS} be the set obtained by an application of partial-lab-IAS($\mathcal{O}, (L, \leq), L_{\geq \ell_g}, c, n$), where $L_{\geq \ell_g} := \{\ell \in L \mid \ell \geq \ell_g\}$. Then, every IAS contained in $\mathcal{O}_{L_{\text{IAS}}}$ has at least one axiom labeled with each element ℓ of L_{IAS}; otherwise, ℓ would not have been added to the set during the application of the algorithm. That in particular means that for every IAS I contained in $\mathcal{O}_{L_{\text{IAS}}}$ it holds that $|L_{\text{IAS}}| \leq |I|$. Thus, there is no risk on stopping the computation of the label set when it is large enough, if we are only searching for the smallest IAS. Moreover, any IAS that can be deduced from this set of labels will not give any new information, so we can further avoid the second step that extracts specific IAS from the set of labels. Algorithm 5 shows how the two

---

Algorithm 4. Compute labels of (partial) IAS

Procedure partial-lab-IAS($\mathcal{O}, (L, \leq), L_{\text{fix}}, c, n$)
Input: $\mathcal{O}$ ontology; $(L, \leq)$ lattice; L_{fix}: fixed labels; c: consequence; n: limit
Output: $L_{\text{IAS}} \subseteq L$: set of labels of at least one (partial) IAS of size at most n

1: $\mathcal{S} := \mathcal{O}$; $L_{\text{IAS}} := \emptyset$
2: **for** every $k \in (L \setminus L_{\text{fix}})$ **do**
3:    **if** $\mathcal{S} \setminus \mathcal{O}_{=k} \models c$ **then**
4:       $\mathcal{S} := \mathcal{S} \setminus \mathcal{O}_{=k}$
5:    **else**
6:       $L_{\text{IAS}} := L_{\text{IAS}} \cup \{k\}$
7:       **if** $|L_{\text{IAS}}| = n$ **then**
8:          **return** L_{IAS}
9: **return** L_{IAS}

---

step computation of IAS can be combined with the modified HST approach of Algorithm 3 to efficiently obtain the smallest IAS.

The algorithm works as follows. It fist computes a set of labels of an IAS L_{IAS}. Using the restricted ontology having only axioms labeled with elements of L_{IAS}, it starts then the modified hitting set tree algorithm trying to find an IAS of smaller size. However, when the hitting set tree cannot be expanded further due to the fact that no other IAS appear in the ontology in use, the algorithm does not stop, but rather goes back to compute a new label set. Intuitively, is a nesting of two HST methods. The outer one only computes label sets in the style of [2], and the inner one uses restricted sub-ontologies based on the results of the outer one to compute the actual IAS. As said before, the method also uses the optimization in which the sets used in each of the hitting set trees are restricted in size, according to the smallest IAS found so far. Additionally, the inner HST is not called whenever the label set found by the outer procedure is already larger than the smallest IAS known, since no IAS found from that sub-ontology will be smaller, and hence is irrelevant in our search for the IAS with least axioms. The following theorem, stating the correctness of Algorithm 5, can be shown following an argument similar to the proof of Theorem 2.

Theorem 3. *Let $\mathcal{O}$ be an ontology, c a consequence with $\mathcal{O} \models c$, and ℓ_g a goal label. If n is the minimum cardinality of an IAS for ℓ_g, then Algorithm 5 outputs an IAS I such that $|I| = n$.*

5 Empirical Evaluation

We implemented and evaluated our algorithms empirically with large practical ontologies. The following sections describe our test setting and the results.

5.1 Test Data and Test Environment

We test on a PC with 2GB RAM and Intel Core Duo CPU 3.16GHz. We implemented all approaches with Java 1.6, CEL 1.0, Pellet 2.0 and OWL API trunk

---

Algorithm 5. Label optimized HST algorithm to find smallest IAS

Procedure lab-hst-extract-smallest-IAS$(\mathcal{O}, (L, \leq), c, \ell_g)$
Input: $\mathcal{O}$: labeled ontology; $(L, \leq)$: lattice; c: consequence; ℓ_g: goal boundary
Output: IAS I of minimum cardinality
1: **Global** $I := \mathcal{O}, m := |\mathcal{O}|, L_{\text{fix}} := \{\ell \in L \mid \ell \geq \ell_g\}, \mathcal{O}_{\text{fix}} := \mathcal{O}_{\geq \ell_g}, (L, \leq),$
   $\mathcal{O}_{\text{nonfix}} := \mathcal{O} \setminus \mathcal{O}_{\text{fix}}$
2: expand-lab-hst-IAS$(\mathcal{O} \setminus \mathcal{O}_{\text{fix}}, c)$
3: **return** I

Procedure expand-lab-hst-IAS$(\mathcal{O}, c)$
Input: $\mathcal{O}$: ontology; c: consequence
Side effects: modifications to I and m
1: **if** $\mathcal{O}_{\text{fix}} \cup \mathcal{O} \not\models c$ **then**
2:     **return**
3: $M :=$ partial-lab-IAS$(\mathcal{O}, (L, \leq), L_{\text{fix}}, c, m)$
4: **if** $|M| < m$ **then**
5:     expand-hst-IAS-aux$(\mathcal{O}, \mathcal{O}_{=M}, c)$
6: **else**
7:     **for** the first $m - 1$ labels $\ell \in M$ **do**
8:         expand-lab-hst-IAS$(\mathcal{O}_{\neq \ell}, c)$

Procedure expand-hst-IAS-aux$(\mathcal{O}, \mathcal{O}_{\text{test}}, c)$
Input: $\mathcal{O}$: ontology; $\mathcal{O}_{\text{test}}$: axioms; c: consequence
Side effects: modifications to I and m
1: **if** $\mathcal{O}_{\text{fix}} \cup \mathcal{O}_{\text{test}} \not\models c$ **then**
2:     expand-lab-hst-IAS$(\mathcal{O}, c)$
3: **else**
4:     $\mathcal{S} :=$ extract-partial-IAS$(\mathcal{O}_{\text{fix}}, \mathcal{O}_{\text{test}}, c, m)$
5:     **if** $|\mathcal{S}| < m$ **then**
6:         $I := \mathcal{S}$
7:         $m := |I|$
8:     **for** the first $(m - 1)$ axioms t in $\mathcal{S}$ **do**
9:         expand-hst-IAS-aux$(\mathcal{O} \setminus \{t\}, \mathcal{O}_{\text{test}} \setminus \{t\}, c)$

---

revision 1150. Since we need lattices, labeled ontologies and computed boundaries of their consequences, the test data used in [2] was feasible also in this context and we will describe the test data here only briefly. The two labeling lattices are similar to ones encountered in real-world applications: the nonlinear lattice $(L_d, \leq_d)$ was already introduced in Figure 1, the linear order $(L_l, \leq_l)$ has 6 elements $L_l = L_d = \{\ell_0, \ldots, \ell_5\}$ with $\leq_l := \{(\ell_n, \ell_{n+1}) \mid \ell_n, \ell_{n+1} \in L_l \wedge 0 \leq n \leq 5\}$.

We used the two ontologies O^{SNOMED} and O^{FUNCT} with different expressivity and types of consequences for our experiments. The Systematized Nomenclature of Medicine, Clinical Terms (SNOMED CT) is a comprehensive medical and clinical ontology built using the Description Logic (DL) $\mathcal{EL}^+$. From the January/2005 release of the DL version, which contains 379,691 concept names, 62 object property names, and 379,704 axioms, and entails more than five million subsumptions, we used a sampled set of 27,477 positive subsumptions. Following [6], for each subsumee A of any subsumption $A \sqsubseteq B$ we precomputed the reachability-based module with CEL and stored these modules. This module is guaranteed to contain all axioms of any MinA for $A \sqsubseteq B$, so it can be used as the start ontology when searching for MinA, thus also for diagnoses, IAS and RAS rather than searching the complete ontology. O^{FUNCT} is an OWL-DL ontology for functional description of mechanical engineering solutions [9]. It has 115 concept names, 47 object property names, 16 data property names, 545 individual names, 3,176 axioms, and the DL expressivity is $\mathcal{SHOIN}(\mathbf{D})$. Its 716 consequences are 12 subsumption and 704 instance relationships (class assertions).

To obtain labeled ontologies, axioms in both labeled ontologies received a random label assignment of elements from $L_l = L_d$. As black-box subsumption and instance reasoner we used the reasoner Pellet since it can deal with the expressivity of both ontologies. For the expressive DL $\mathcal{SHOIN}(\mathbf{D})$ it uses a tableau-based algorithm and for $\mathcal{EL}+$ it uses an optimized classifier for the OWL 2 EL profile, which is based on the algorithm described in [1].

We computed the boundary ℓ_c of each consequence c of the ontologies with the algorithms described in [2] and then computed the change set described in this paper to reach goal boundary ℓ_g which is constantly ℓ_3 in all experiments. Consequences where $\ell_c = \ell_g$ were not considered. Thus, from the 716 consequences in O^{FUNCT}, we have 415 remaining with labeling lattice $(L_d, \leq_d)$ and 474 remaining with $(L_l, \leq_l)$. From the 27,477 consequences in O^{SNOMED} we have 23,695 remaining with labeling lattice $(L_d, \leq_d)$ and 25,897 with $(L_l, \leq_l)$.

5.2   Results

Table 1 contains results for the 4 combinations of the 2 ontologies and the 2 labeling lattices. For each of them we tested 4 variants, leading to 16 measurement series overall. We tested the variants *full axiom pinpointing* limited to 10 MinA, *fixed axioms*, *fixed axioms and cardinality limit* and *fixed axioms and cardinality limit and label-based optimization* all of the last three limited to 10 IAS and 10 RAS. Running with fixed axioms without cardinality limit can be done easily by skipping Line 7 in Algorithm 3.

Since we limit the number of MinAs, IAS and RAS, our algorithms might not find the smallest change set before reaching the limit. We measure the quality of the presented variants given those limitations at execution time. Table 1 lists the ratio of correct solutions where at least 1 correct change set was computed, and the ratio of optimal solutions where the limit was not reached during the computation and thus yielded the shortest change set possible. Notice however that the ratio of cases with the minimal change set successfully computed might be higher, including those where the limitation was reached but the minimal change set was already found.

Full axiom pinpointing is clearly outperformed by the other variants. Remarkably, label-based optimization seems not to pay off in our setting. A reason might be the small subset of the ontology, on which the Hitting Set Tree algorithms is working on already by fixing axioms. Furthermore in O^{SNOMED} we work on the

Table 1. Results of the optimizations in 4 test settings

Ont.	Lat.	Variant and Runtime Limit	Time (minutes)	Ratio of correct solutions	Ratio of optimal solutions
O^{Funct}	nonlinear	full PP, ≤ 10 MinA	44.05	96%	47%
		fixed axioms, ≤ 10 IAS/RAS	20.36	100%	91%
		fixed axioms, partial, ≤ 10 IAS/RAS	7.11	100%	99%
		fixed axioms, partial, lab-opt., ≤ 10 IAS/RAS	7.85	100%	99%
	linear	full PP, ≤ 10 MinA	54.46	98%	49%
		fixed axioms, ≤ 10 IAS/RAS	16.65	100%	96%
		fixed axioms, partial, ≤ 10 IAS/RAS	8.00	100%	99%
		fixed axioms, partial, lab-opt.	7.56	100%	100%
O^{Snomed}	nonlinear	full PP, ≤ 10 MinA	184.76	100%	75%
		fixed axioms, ≤ 10 IAS/RAS	16.00	100%	99%
		fixed axioms, partial, ≤ 10 IAS/RAS	9.81	100%	100%
		fixed axioms, partial, lab-opt., ≤ 10 IAS/RAS	11.70	100%	100%
	linear	full PP, ≤ 10 MinAs	185.35	100%	75%
		fixed axioms, ≤ 10 IAS/RAS	41.66	100%	95%
		fixed axioms, partial, ≤ 10 IAS/RAS	27.50	100%	98%
		fixed axioms, partial, lab-opt., ≤ 10 IAS/RAS	32.80	100%	98%

extracted reachability-modules so that the search space is further reduced already. To conclude, fixed sub-ontologies and cardinality limit are optimizations with reasonable impact.

6   Conclusions

Previous work has studied labeled ontologies and methods to compute boundaries for their consequences. In the present paper we have looked at the problem of finding an adequate relabeling of the ontology in case that the boundary obtained differs from the desired one. Our approach focuses on the search of a change set of minimum cardinality. We identified simple cases, namely where the boundary ℓ_c and the goal label ℓ_g are comparable w.r.t. to the lattice ordering, in which known methods from ontology repair can be adapted. In particular, we showed that if $\ell_c < \ell_g$, then any MinA yields a change set, while if $\ell_g < \ell_c$, then diagnoses correspond to change sets. The remaining case, where ℓ_c and ℓ_g are incomparable is reduced to the previous one by using $\ell_c \otimes \ell_g$ as an intermediate goal label.

In order to find a change set with minimum cardinality, we presented a variation of the HST algorithm used in axiom-pinpointing. Our variations are based on three insights: (i) some axioms are irrelevant for the computation of a change set; thus, they can be removed from the search space from the beginning; (ii) since we are interested only in a change set of minimum cardinality, we can improve the search by avoiding unnecessarily large solutions; and (iii) axioms can be grouped by their labels to first reduce the ontology from which the change set will be computed. We implemented algorithms to test the benefit of using the optimizations obtained by these three insights, and tested them on large-scale ontologies. Our first results show that the first two ideas yield tangible improvements in both the execution time and the quality of the solution. However, trying to optimize the search through the labels does not seem to pay off. All our algorithms are black-box based, which means that they can be used with any off-the-shelf reasoner, without the need of modifications.

As future work we intend to study the problem of finding change sets for several consequences (each with its own goal label) simultaneously. An availability policy could further restrict the set of axioms and their allowed label changes. We will also look more closely at the case where the boundary and the goal label are incomparable, and try to develop methods that improve both, the quality of the change set and its computation time. Moreover, we will look at other criteria for the minimality of change sets and more flexible restrictions on the goal label.

References

1. Baader, F., Brandt, S., Lutz, C.: Pushing the $\mathcal{EL}$ envelope. In: Proc. of IJCAI'05, Edinburgh, UK (2005)
2. Baader, F., Knechtel, M., Peñaloza, R.: A generic approach for large-scale ontological reasoning in the presence of access restrictions to the ontology's axioms. In: Bernstein, A., Karger, D.R., Heath, T., Feigenbaum, L., Maynard, D., Motta, E., Thirunarayan, K. (eds.) ISWC 2009. LNCS, vol. 5823, pp. 49–64. Springer, Heidelberg (2009)
3. Baader, F., Peñaloza, R.: Automata-based axiom pinpointing. Journal of Automated Reasoning (to appear, 2010); Special Issue: IJCAR 2008 (2008)
4. Baader, F., Peñaloza, R.: Axiom pinpointing in general tableaux. Journal of Logic and Computation 20(1), 5–34 (2010); Special Issue: Tableaux'07
5. Baader, F., Peñaloza, R., Suntisrivaraporn, B.: Pinpointing in the Description Logic $\mathcal{EL}^+$. In: Hertzberg, J., Beetz, M., Englert, R. (eds.) KI 2007. LNCS (LNAI), vol. 4667, pp. 52–67. Springer, Heidelberg (2007)
6. Baader, F., Suntisrivaraporn, B.: Debugging SNOMED CT using axiom pinpointing in the description logic $\mathcal{EL}^+$. In: Proc. of KR-MED'08 (2008)
7. Biskup, J., Embley, D.W., Lochner, J.-H.: Reducing inference control to access control for normalized database schemas. Inf. Process. Lett. 106(1), 8–12 (2008)
8. Farkas, C., Jajodia, S.: The inference problem: a survey. SIGKDD Explor. Newsl. 4(2), 6–11 (2002)
9. Gaag, A., Kohn, A., Lindemann, U.: Function-based solution retrieval and semantic search in mechanical engineering. Proc. of ICED'09 (2009)
10. Kalyanpur, A., Parsia, B., Horridge, M., Sirin, E.: Finding all justifications of OWL DL entailments. In: Aberer, K., Choi, K.-S., Noy, N., Allemang, D., Lee, K.-I., Nixon, L.J.B., Golbeck, J., Mika, P., Maynard, D., Mizoguchi, R., Schreiber, G., Cudré-Mauroux, P. (eds.) ASWC 2007 and ISWC 2007. LNCS, vol. 4825, pp. 267–280. Springer, Heidelberg (2007)

11. Kalyanpur, A., Parsia, B., Sirin, E., Hendler, J.A.: Debugging unsatisfiable classes in OWL ontologies. J. Web Sem. 3(4), 268–293 (2005)
12. Meyer, T., Lee, K., Booth, R., Pan, J.Z.: Finding maximally satisfiable terminologies for the description logic $\mathcal{ALC}$. In: Proc. of AAAI'06 (2006)
13. Schlobach, S., Cornet, R.: Non-standard reasoning services for the debugging of description logic terminologies. In: Proc. of IJCAI'03, pp. 355–362 (2003)
14. Suntisrivaraporn, B.: Polynomial-Time Reasoning Support for Design and Maintenance of Large-Scale Biomedical Ontologies. PhD thesis, TU Dresden (2008)

Dealing with Inconsistency When Combining Ontologies and Rules Using DL-Programs*

Jörg Pührer, Stijn Heymans, and Thomas Eiter

Institute of Information Systems 184/3
Vienna University of Technology
Favoritenstraße 9–11, A–1040 Vienna, Austria
{puehrer,heymans,eiter}@kr.tuwien.ac.at

Abstract. Description Logic Programs (DL-programs) have been introduced to combine ontological and rule-based reasoning in the context of the Semantic Web. A DL-program loosely combines a Description Logic (DL) ontology with a non-monotonic logic program (LP) such that dedicated atoms in the LP, called DL-atoms, allow for a bidirectional flow of knowledge between the two components. Unfortunately, the information sent from the LP-part to the DL-part might cause an inconsistency in the latter, leading to the trivial satisfaction of every query. As a consequence, in such a case, the answer sets that define the semantics of the DL-program may contain spoiled information influencing the overall deduction. For avoiding unintuitive answer sets, we introduce a refined semantics for DL-programs that is sensitive for inconsistency caused by the combination of DL and LP, and dynamically deactivates rules whenever such an inconsistency would arise. We analyze the complexity of the new semantics, discuss implementational issues and introduce a notion of stratification that guarantees uniqueness of answer sets.

1 Introduction

Recently, combinations of rule formalisms and ontologies (in particular *Description Logic (DL) theories* [1]) have gained increasing interest in the Semantic Web community. This is reflected in the Semantic Web Layer Architecture that envisions a Rules Layer complementing the Ontology Layer as a means for sophisticated representation and reasoning. A major issue in systems integrating rules and ontologies is how to realize the semantics of their combination.

A popular approach in this respect is *loose coupling*, i.e., the two components, ontology and rules, act separately but communicate via a well-defined interface. A realization of this approach is given by *Description Logic Programs (DL-programs)* [2], which combine a DL ontology with a logic program (LP). The semantics of the formalism is given by an extension of the *stable-model semantics* [3] that allows for using default negation for *non-monotonic reasoning*. DL-programs follow the answer set programming paradigm [4], where the program can be seen as a problem and the resulting stable models, called *answer*

---

* This work is partially supported by the Austrian Science Fund (FWF) projects P20840 and P21698, and by the EC FP7 project OntoRule (IST-2009-231875).

L. Aroyo et al. (Eds.): ESWC 2010, Part I, LNCS 6088, pp. 183–197, 2010.

sets correspond to different solutions of this problem. The interface between the logic programming part and the Description Logic ontology, which is seen as a black box, is realized by dedicated atoms in the premises of the rules, called *DL-atoms*, which allow for a bidirectional exchange of information. The flow of information from the rules to the ontology provides a powerful tool, as results from the program can be used as assertions in the DL for further deduction.

However, it is possible that the assertions by which the ontology is extended cause an inconsistency. We say that in such a case the respective DL-atom is DL-inconsistent. As then the respective query is trivially true, we may end up with counterintuitive results, even though both the DL and the LP are perfectly consistent in separation.

In this work, we introduce a semantics, called the *DL-inconsistency tolerant semantics*, that aims at avoiding this effect by dynamically switching rules off whenever DL-inconsistency occurs. Thus, information derived from an inconsistency only cannot influence the reasoning in the LP-part.

The main contributions of this paper can be summarized as follows:

– We introduce a refined semantics for DL-programs that avoids unintuitive answer sets caused by DL-inconsistency and properly extends the answer set semantics for normal logic programs.
– We analyze the complexity of deciding whether a DL-program has an answer set under the new semantics. The problem turns out to be NEXP-TIME-complete for many popular Description Logics. Moreover, we show that reasoning in our formalism can be reduced to reasoning in HEX-programs [5]. An implementation of our approach is targeted within the OntoRule project.
– We define a stratification property that guarantees the uniqueness of answer sets under the new semantics and EXPTIME-completeness of deciding answer set existence. Based on these results, we present an algorithm for computing the answer set of a stratified program whenever one exists.

The remainder of the paper is organized as follows. In the next section, we give preliminaries on normal logic programs under the answer set semantics, Description Logics, and DL-programs. Section 3 explains the problem to be tackled in the paper, using an illustrative running example, and introduces the concept of DL-inconsistency. After introducing our new semantics in Section 4, we deal with various computational aspects in Section 5, discussing complexity and implementation issues, and introducing an adequate notion of stratification for the refined semantics. For brevity, we include here only selected proofs.

2   Preliminaries

2.1   Normal Programs under the Answer Set Semantics

An LP-signature $\Sigma = \langle \mathcal{F}, \mathcal{P} \rangle$ is a first-order signature such that $\mathcal{F}$ is a nonempty finite set of 0-ary function symbols (constants) and $\mathcal{P}$ is a nonempty finite set of predicate symbols. A *term* is any variable from a set of variables $\mathcal{V}$ or constant symbol from $\mathcal{F}$. An *atom* is of form $p(t_1, \ldots, t_n)$, where $p \in \mathcal{P}$ is a predicate symbol of arity $n \geq 0$ and $t_1, \ldots, t_n$ are terms. A *(classical) literal* l is an atom a or a negated atom $\neg a$. A *negation as failure literal* (or *NAF-literal*) is a literal l or a default-negated literal *not* l. A *normal rule* (simply, *rule*) r is of the form

$$a \leftarrow b_1, \ldots, b_k, not\ b_{k+1}, \ldots, not\ b_m, \qquad m \geq k \geq 0, \qquad (1)$$

where $a, b_1, \ldots, b_m$ are classical literals. The literal a is the *head* of r, denoted by $H(r)$, and the conjunction $b_1, \ldots, b_k, not\ b_{k+1}, \ldots, not\ b_m$ is the *body* of r; its *positive* (resp., *negative*) part is $b_1, \ldots, b_k$ (resp., $not\ b_{k+1}, \ldots, not\ b_m$). We denote by $B(r)$ the set of body literals $B(r)^+ \cup B(r)^-$, where $B(r)^+ = \{b_1, \ldots, b_k\}$ and $B(r)^- = \{b_{k+1}, \ldots, b_m\}$. A *(normal) program* Π (over Σ) is a finite set of rules; Π is *positive* iff it is "*not* "-free.

The *Herbrand universe* of a program Π is the set $\mathrm{HU}(\Pi) \subseteq \mathcal{F}$ of all constant symbols in Π (if no such symbol exists, $\mathrm{HU}(\Pi) = \{c\}$ for an arbitrary constant symbol c from $\mathcal{F}$). Moreover, the *Herbrand base* of a program Π, denoted $\mathrm{HB}(\Pi)$, is the set of all ground (classical) literals with predicate symbols appearing in Π and constant symbols from $\mathrm{HU}(\Pi)$. The notions of *ground terms, atoms, literals* etc. are as usual. We denote by $gr_S(\Pi)$ the grounding of Π w.r.t. a set $S \subseteq \mathcal{F}$ of constants, i.e., the ground rules originating from rules in Π by replacing, per rule, each variable by each possible combination of constants in S.

A set of literals $X \subseteq \mathrm{HB}(\Pi)$ is *consistent* iff $\{p, \neg p\} \not\subseteq X$ for every atom $p \in \mathrm{HB}(\Pi)$. An *interpretation* I relative to Π is a consistent subset of $\mathrm{HB}(\Pi)$. I *satisfies* the positive (resp., negative) body of a rule r, symbolically $I \models B(r)^+$ (resp., $I \models B(r)^-$), if $B(r)^+ \subseteq I$ (resp., $I \cap B(r)^- = \emptyset$). I *satisfies* the body of r, denoted $I \models B(r)$, if $I \models B(r)^+$ and $I \models B(r)^-$. I *satisfies* a rule r, symbolically $I \models r$, if $H(r) \in I$ whenever $I \models B(r)$. An interpretation $I \subseteq \mathrm{HB}(\Pi)$ is a *model* of a program Π, denoted by $I \models \Pi$, if every $r \in gr_{\mathrm{HU}(\Pi)}(\Pi)$ is satisfied by I. An *answer set* of a positive program Π is the least model of Π w.r.t. $\subseteq$.

Answer sets were traditionally defined in terms of the *Gelfond-Lifschitz reduct* [3]. We here use the equivalent definition of answer sets by means of the *FLP-reduct* of Π relative to an interpretation $I \subseteq \mathrm{HB}(\Pi)$, denoted Π^I_{FLP}, following Faber, Leone, and Pfeifer [6]. It has been introduced for an intuitive handling of aggregates in answer set programming and is a special case of the *t-reduct* that we use for defining the semantics introduced in this paper. The FLP-reduct of Π relative to an interpretation $I \subseteq \mathrm{HB}(\Pi)$, denoted Π^I_{FLP}, is the set of rules $r \in gr_{\mathrm{HU}(\Pi)}(\Pi)$ such that $I \models B(r)$. Then, I is an answer set of Π iff I is a minimal model of Π^I_{FLP}.

Example 1. As a simple example, consider the program P that consists of the three rules $c(t)$, $a(t) \leftarrow not\ b(t)$, and $b(t) \leftarrow c(t), not\ a(t)$. It has two answer sets, viz. $I_1 = \{c(t), a(t)\}$ and $I_2 = \{c(t), b(t)\}$.

2.2   Description Logics

The approach to resolving inconsistencies caused by DL-atoms is to a large extent independent of a specific Description Logic (DL) [1]. For a particular DL knowledge base Φ, we will assume that

- it is defined over a signature $\Sigma_o = \langle \mathcal{F}, \mathcal{P}_o \rangle$ with individuals from $\mathcal{F}$ and concept and role names from $\mathcal{P}_o$,
- it is able to deal with ground unary or binary literals, i.e., an expression $\Phi \cup \{C(a), \neg C(a), R(a, b), \neg R(a, b)\}$ is well-defined for unary (binary) predicates C (R) from $\mathcal{P}_o$ and individuals a from $\mathcal{F}$, and
- it defines an entailment relation $\models$ such that $\Phi \models Q(t)$ is defined for DL-queries $Q(t)$ and indicates that all models of Φ satisfy $Q(t)$.

A *DL-query* $Q(t)$ is either

(a) a concept inclusion axiom F or its negation $\neg F$; or
(b) of the forms $C(t)$ or $\neg C(t)$, where C is a concept and t is a term; or
(c) of the forms $R(t_1, t_2)$ or $\neg R(t_1, t_2)$, where R is a role and t_1, t_2 are terms.

Exemplary DLs that satisfy these minimum requirements are $\mathcal{SHOIN}(\mathbf{D})$ and $\mathcal{SROIQ}(\mathbf{D})$ which provide the logical underpinnings of the Web ontology languages OWL DL and OWL 2 (see [7; 8; 9] for further background). In what follows we assume that the reader is familiar with standard DL syntax.

Example 2 (Product Database). As our running example, we will adapt an example that has been used previously in the context of DL-programs [10].

A small computer store obtains its hardware from several vendors. It uses the following DL knowledge base Φ_{ex}, which contains information about the product range that is provided by each vendor. For some parts, a shop may already be contracted as supplier and shops which are known to be disapproved for some reason can never become an actual supplier.

$$\geq 1 \ supplier \sqsubseteq Shop; \quad \top \sqsubseteq \forall supplier.Part;$$
$$\exists supplier.\top \sqcap disapproved \sqsubseteq \bot;$$
$$Shop(s_1); \quad Shop(s_2); \quad Shop(s_3); \quad disapproved(s_2);$$
$$Part(harddisk); \quad Part(cpu); \quad Part(case);$$
$$provides(s_1, cpu); \quad provides(s_1, case); \quad provides(s_2, cpu);$$
$$provides(s_3, harddisk); \quad provides(s_3, case);$$
$$supplier(s_3, case);$$

Here, the first two axioms determine *Shop* and *Part* as domain and range of the property *supplier*, respectively, while the third axiom constitutes the incongruity between shops that are contracted as supplier but are explicitly disapproved.

2.3 DL-Programs

Syntax. A signature $\Sigma = \langle \mathcal{F}, \mathcal{P}_o, \mathcal{P}_p \rangle$ for DL-programs consists of a set $\mathcal{F}$ of 0-ary function symbols and sets $\mathcal{P}_o$, $\mathcal{P}_p$ of predicate symbols such that $\Sigma_o = \langle \mathcal{F}, \mathcal{P}_o \rangle$ is a DL-signature and $\Sigma_p = \langle \mathcal{F}, \mathcal{P}_p \rangle$ is an LP-signature.

Informally, a DL-program consists of a Description Logic ontology Φ over Σ_o and a normal program Π over Σ_p, which may contain queries to Φ. Roughly, in such a query, it is asked whether a certain Description Logic formula or its negation logically follows from Φ or not.

A *DL-atom* $a(\mathbf{t})$ has the form

$$\mathrm{DL}[S_1 \ op_1 \ p_1, \ldots, S_m \ op_m \ p_m; \ Q](\mathbf{t}), \qquad m \geq 0, \tag{2}$$

where each S_i is either a concept or a role predicate from $\mathcal{P}_o$, $op_i \in \{\uplus, \uplus, \cap\}$, p_i is a unary, resp. binary, predicate symbol from $\mathcal{P}_p$, and $Q(\mathbf{t})$ is a DL-query. We call $\gamma = S_1 \ op_1 \ p_1, \ldots, S_m \ op_m \ p_m$ the *input signature* and $p_1, \ldots, p_m$ the *input predicate symbols* of $a(\mathbf{t})$. Moreover, literals over input predicate symbols are *input literals*. Intuitively, $op_i = \uplus$ (resp., $op_i = \uplus$) increases S_i (resp., $\neg S_i$) by the extension of p_i, while $op_i = \cap$ constrains S_i to p_i. A *DL-rule* r has the form (1), where any literal $b_1, \ldots, b_m \in B(r)$ may be a DL-atom. A *DL-program* $\mathcal{KB} = (\varPhi, \varPi)$ consists of a DL ontology $\varPhi$ and a finite set of DL-rules $\varPi$.

Example 3. Consider the DL-program $\mathcal{KB}_{ex} = (\varPhi_{ex}, \varPi_{ex})$, with $\varPhi_{ex}$ as in Example 2 and $\varPi_{ex}$ given as follows, choosing not-deterministically a vendor for each needed part:

(1) *needed(cpu)*;   *needed(harddisk)*;   *needed(case)*;
(2) *alreadyContracted*$(P) \leftarrow$ DL[; *supplier*](S, P), *needed*(P);
(3) *offer*$(S, P) \leftarrow$ DL[; *provides*](S, P), *needed*(P), not *alreadyContracted*(P);
(4) *chosen*$(S, P) \leftarrow$ *offer*(S, P), not *notChosen*(S, P);
(5) *notChosen*$(S, P) \leftarrow$ *offer*(S, P), not *chosen*(S, P);
(6) *supplied*$(S, P) \leftarrow$ DL[*supplier* $\uplus$ *chosen*; *supplier*](S, P), *needed*(P);
(7) *anySupplied*$(P) \leftarrow$ *supplied*(S, P), *needed*(P);
(8) *fail* $\leftarrow$ not *fail*, *needed*(P), not *anySupplied*(P).

Rule (2) extracts information on which parts already have a fixed vendor assigned from the DL, whereas Rule (3) imports the available offers for the needed parts not yet assigned. Rules (4)-(5) nondeterministically decide whether an offer should be chosen. Rule (6) summarizes the purchasing results by first sending the chosen assignments of vendors and parts from the LP-part to the ontology, and then querying for the overall *supplier* relation. Finally, Rules (7)-(8) ensure that for every needed part there is a vendor chosen who supplies it. Note that Rule (8) acts as a constraint where the occurrences of the auxiliary atom *fail* in both, head and positive body, prevents all interpretations containing *needed*(t) but not *anySupplied*(t) for any term t from being an answer set. As we will see in Section 3, $\varPhi_{ex}$ has one intended and one counterintuitive answer set.

Semantics. In the sequel, let $\mathcal{KB} = (\varPhi, \varPi)$ be a DL-program over $\varSigma = \langle \mathcal{F}, \mathcal{P}_o, \mathcal{P}_p \rangle$. By $gr(\varPi)$ we denote the grounding of $\varPi$ w.r.t $\mathcal{F}$, i.e., the set of ground rules originating from DL-rules in $\varPi$ by replacing, per DL-rule, each variable by each possible combination of constants in $\mathcal{F}$.

An *interpretation* I (over $\varSigma_p$) is a consistent subset of literals over $\varSigma_p$. We say that I satisfies a classical literal l under $\varPhi$, denoted $I \models^{\varPhi} l$, iff $l \in I$, and a ground DL-atom $a = DL[S_1 op_1 \ p_1, \ldots, S_m op_m p_m; Q](\mathbf{c})$ under $\varPhi$, denoted $I \models^{\varPhi} a$, if $\varPhi \cup \tau^I(a) \models Q(\mathbf{c})$, where the extension $\tau^I(a)$ of a under I is defined as $\tau^I(a) = \bigcup_{i=1}^m A_i(I)$ such that

- $A_i(I) = \{S_i(\mathbf{e}) \mid p_i(\mathbf{e}) \in I\}$, for $op_i = \uplus$;
- $A_i(I) = \{\neg S_i(\mathbf{e}) \mid p_i(\mathbf{e}) \in I\}$, for $op_i = \cup$;
- $A_i(I) = \{\neg S_i(\mathbf{e}) \mid p_i(\mathbf{e}) \notin I\}$, for $op_i = \cap$.

We say that I *satisfies* the positive (resp., negative) body of a ground DL-rule r under Φ, symbolically $I \models^\Phi B(r)^+$ (resp., $I \models^\Phi B(r)^-$), if $I \models^\Phi l$ (resp., $I \not\models^\Phi l$) for all $l \in B(r)^+$ (resp., $l \in B(r)^-$). I *satisfies* the body of r under Φ, denoted $I \models^\Phi B(r)$, whenever $I \models^\Phi B(r)^+$ and $I \models^\Phi B(r)^-$. I satisfies a ground DL-rule r under Φ, symbolically $I \models^\Phi r$, if $I \models^\Phi H(r)$ whenever $I \models^\Phi B(r)$. I is a model of a DL-program $\mathcal{KB} = (\Phi, \Pi)$, denoted $I \models \mathcal{KB}$, iff $I \models^\Phi r$ for all $r \in gr(\Pi)$. We say $\mathcal{KB}$ is *satisfiable* (resp., *unsatisfiable*) iff it has some (resp., no) model.

In this paper, we base the answer set semantics of DL-programs on the Faber-Leone-Pfeifer reduct, rather than on the Gelfond-Lifschitz reduct.

Definition 1. *Let $\Sigma = \langle \mathcal{F}, \mathcal{P}_o, \mathcal{P}_p \rangle$ be a signature for DL-programs, Φ a DL knowledge base over $\langle \mathcal{F}, \mathcal{P}_o \rangle$, Π a set of ground DL-rules over $\Sigma_p = \langle \mathcal{F}, \mathcal{P}_p \rangle$, and I an interpretation over Σ_p. The FLP-reduct $\Pi_{FLP}^{I,\Phi}$ of Π under Φ relative to I is the set of rules $r \in \Pi$ such that $I \models^\Phi B(r)$. Moreover, the FLP-reduct $\mathcal{KB}_{FLP}^I$ of a (possibly non-ground) DL-program $\mathcal{KB} = (\Phi, \Pi)$ relative to I is given by $gr(\Pi)_{FLP}^{I,\Phi}$.*

Definition 2. *Let $\mathcal{KB}$ be a DL-program over $\Sigma = \langle \mathcal{F}, \mathcal{P}_o, \mathcal{P}_p \rangle$. An interpretation I over Σ_p is an* answer set *of $\mathcal{KB}$ if it is a minimal model of $\mathcal{KB}_{FLP}^I$. The set of all answer sets of $\mathcal{KB}$ is denoted by $AS(\mathcal{KB})$.*

We use this answer set semantics (we will sometimes refer to it as *FLP-semantics*), as it naturally handles DL-atoms which are not *monotonic*.

Definition 3. *For a DL-program $\mathcal{KB} = (\Phi, \Pi)$, a ground DL-atom l is* monotonic *relative to $\mathcal{KB}$, if for all interpretations I, J with $I \subseteq J$, $I \models^\Phi l$ implies $J \models^\Phi l$. $\mathcal{KB}$ is* monotonic *if $gr(\Pi)$ contains only DL-atoms that are monotonic relative to $\mathcal{KB}$.*

It was shown in [5] that for DL-programs that do not employ the $\cap$ operator, the FLP-semantics coincides with strong answer set semantics, as originally introduced for DL-programs [2] using the Gelfond-Lifschitz reduct. Note that this operator is rarely used in practice and can in many cases (e.g., for *t-stratified* DL-programs, cf. Section 5) be removed by simple translations.

We will later refer to the class of *positive DL-programs*, defined in [2] as follows.

Definition 4. *A DL-program $\mathcal{KB}$ is* positive, *if it is monotonic and $B(r)^- = \emptyset$ for each rule $r \in \Pi$.*

Note that a DL-atom a that does not employ the operator $\cap$ is always monotonic as $I \subseteq J$ implies $\tau^I(a) \subseteq \tau^J(a)$.

3   Inconsistency When Combining Ontologies and Rules

We will now look at the semantics of our example DL-program in order to illustrate the core problem we want to tackle in our approach.

Example 4. $\mathcal{KB}_{ex}$ has two answer sets, I_1 and I_2, both containing the same atoms of predicates *needed*, *offer*, *alreadyContracted*, and *anySupplied*:

$$I' = \{\ needed(cpu), needed(harddisk), needed(case), alreadyContracted(case),$$
$$offer(s_1, cpu), offer(s_2, cpu), offer(s_3, harddisk),$$
$$anySupplied(cpu), anySupplied(harddisk), anySupplied(case)\}$$

The remaining atoms of I_1 are given by

$$I_1 \setminus I' = \{chosen(s_1, cpu), chosen(s_3, harddisk), notChosen(s_2, cpu),$$
$$supplied(s_1, cpu), supplied(s_3, harddisk), supplied(s_3, case)\}\ ,$$

expressing a solution where the cpu is provided by shop s_1, whereas harddisk and case are delivered by vendor s_3.

The second answer set might seem surprising at first sight:

$$I_2 \setminus I' = \{chosen(s_2, cpu), chosen(s_3, harddisk), notChosen(s_2, cpu),$$
$$supplied(s_1, cpu), supplied(s_1, harddisk), supplied(s_1, case),$$
$$supplied(s_2, cpu), supplied(s_2, harddisk), supplied(s_2, case),$$
$$supplied(s_3, cpu), supplied(s_3, harddisk), supplied(s_3, case),$$
$$supplied(cpu, cpu), supplied(cpu, harddisk), supplied(cpu, case),$$
$$supplied(harddisk, cpu), supplied(harddisk, harddisk),$$
$$supplied(harddisk, case), supplied(case, cpu), supplied(case, harddisk),$$
$$supplied(case, case)\}$$

Apparently a situation is described in which each of the shops s_1, s_2, and s_3 supplies each of the needed hardware parts *cpu*, *case*, and *harddisk*, although the intention was that only a single shop supplies one part. Moreover, we also have atoms like *supplied(cpu, harddisk)* in I_2, completely lacking intuition, as the first argument of predicate *supplied* is supposed to refer to vendors only. The reason for the unintuitive results lies in an inconsistency emerging in the combination of the ontology and the logic programming part of $\mathcal{KB}_{ex}$. Note that atom $chosen(s_2, cpu) \in I_2$ suggests that shop s_2 has been chosen to deliver the cpu, although this shop is identified as disapproved in the DL-part (cf. Example 2). Consider any ground instance a' of DL-atom $a = \mathrm{DL}[supplier \uplus chosen;\ supplier](S, P)$ in Rule (6) of extended logic program $\varPi_{ex}$. We then have $\tau^I(a') = \{supplier(\mathbf{e}) \mid chosen(\mathbf{e}) \in I\}$ and therefore $supplier(s_2, cpu) \in \tau^I(a')$. As a consequence, $\varPhi \cup \tau^I(a')$ is inconsistent since $\neg supplier(s_2, cpu)$ follows from the axioms $\exists supplier.\top \sqcap disapproved \sqsubseteq \bot$ and $disapproved(s_2)$ in $\varPhi_{ex}$. Due to this inconsistency every ground instance of a is true under I_2.

Whenever information, passed from the logic programming part $\varPi$ to the ontology $\varPhi$ of a DL-Program, is inconsistent with $\varPhi$, unintuitive answer sets may arise as a consequence of trivial satisfaction of DL-atoms. In such cases we call the respective DL-atom *DL-inconsistent*.

Definition 5. *Let* $\mathcal{KB} = (\Phi, \Pi)$ *be a DL-program and* I *an interpretation relative to* Π. *A ground DL-atom* $a = \mathrm{DL}[\gamma; Q](\mathbf{c})$ *is DL-consistent under* I *w.r.t.* Φ, *if (1)* $\Phi \models Q(\mathbf{c})$ *or (2)* $\Phi \cup \tau^I(a)$ *is consistent, otherwise* a *is DL-inconsistent under* I *w.r.t.* Φ.

Intuitively, we are interested in avoiding using rules that have DL-inconsistent atoms in their bodies. Note that we use a notion of "inconsistence" that pertains to updates of the ontology: if some atom $Q(\mathbf{c})$ is entailed by the original ontology, we assume it is DL-consistent, even if updates via γ make the ontology inconsistent. Indeed, if $\Phi \models Q(\mathbf{c})$, we also have $\Phi \cup \tau^I(a) \models Q(\mathbf{c})$ for any update $\tau^I(a)$ due to monotonicity of usual Description Logics. If we would not take this case into account, we would disregard the whole rule (as seen in Definition 6).

4 DL-Inconsistency Tolerant Semantics

In what follows we introduce and discuss a refined semantics for DL-programs that limits the negative side effects of DL-inconsistency. The central idea is to deactivate a rule whenever a DL-atom contained in its body becomes DL-inconsistent, in order to behave *tolerant* in the sense that flawed information does not influence the derived results. This way literals with unexpected argument types such as *supplied(cpu, harddisk)* in Example 4, can be avoided in the information flow from the ontology to the logic program.

Definition 6. *Let* $\mathcal{KB} = (\Phi, \Pi)$ *be a DL-program and* I *an interpretation.* I *t-satisfies the body of a ground DL-rule* r *under* Φ, *denoted* $I \models_t^{\Phi} B(r)$ *if* $I \models^{\Phi} B(r)$ *and all DL-atoms in* $B(r)$ *are DL-consistent under* I *w.r.t.* Φ. *Moreover,* I *t-satisfies* r *under* Φ, *symbolically* $I \models_t^{\Phi} r$, *if* $I \models_t^{\Phi} B(r)$ *implies that* $I \models^{\Phi} H(r)$. I *is a* t-model *of a set* Q *of ground DL-rules under* Φ *denoted* $I \models_t^{\Phi} Q$ *if* $I \models_t^{\Phi} r$ *for all* $r \in Q$. *Finally,* I *is a* t-model *of* $\mathcal{KB}$, *denoted* $I \models_t \mathcal{KB}$, *if* $I \models_t^{\Phi} gr(\Pi)$.

Note that every model of $\mathcal{KB}$ is also a t-model of $\mathcal{KB}$. Moreover, if DL-atoms occur only in the negative bodies of rules in Π, also the converse holds. The reason for the latter is that a rule that is not applicable under DL-inconsistency tolerant semantics only because of a DL-inconsistent DL-atom $a \in B(r)^-$ for some rule $r \in \Pi$ would also not be applicable under standard semantics as a would be satisfied as a consequence of DL-inconsistency.

Example 5. Consider the ground instantiation

$$r = supplied(cpu, harddisk) \leftarrow \mathrm{DL}[supplier \uplus chosen; supplier](cpu, harddisk),$$
$$needed(harddisk)$$

of Rule (6) of our running example. For interpretation I_2, as defined in Example 4, we have that $I_2 \models^{\Phi} B(r)$ but, as the DL-atom in $B(r)$ is DL-inconsistent under I_2 w.r.t. Φ_{ex}, it holds that $I_2 \not\models_t^{\Phi} B(r)$. As $H(r) \in I_2$, both $I_2 \models^{\Phi} r$ and $I_2 \models_t^{\Phi} r$. More general, since I_2 is a model of $\mathcal{KB}_{ex}$ it is also a t-model of $\mathcal{KB}_{ex}$. However, as we will see next, I_2 is not a *t-answer set* of $\mathcal{KB}_{ex}$.

For defining the notion of a t-answer set, we first give a modified version of the FLP-reduct, called *t-reduct*.

Definition 7. *Let $\Sigma = \langle \mathcal{F}, \mathcal{P}_o, \mathcal{P}_p \rangle$ be a signature for DL-programs, Φ a DL knowledge base over $\langle \mathcal{F}, \mathcal{P}_o \rangle$, Π a set of ground DL-rules over $\Sigma_p = \langle \mathcal{F}, \mathcal{P}_p \rangle$, and I an interpretation over Σ_p. The t-reduct $\Pi_t^{I,\Phi}$ of Π under Φ relative to I is the set of rules $r \in \Pi$ such that $I \models_t^\Phi B(r)$. Moreover, the t-reduct $\mathcal{KB}_t^I$ of a (possibly non-ground) DL-program $\mathcal{KB} = (\Phi, \Pi)$ relative to I is given by $gr(\Pi)_t^{I,\Phi}$.*

Definition 8. *Let $\mathcal{KB}$ be a DL-program. An interpretation I is a t-answer set of $\mathcal{KB}$, if I is a subset-minimal t-model of $\mathcal{KB}_t^I$. The set of all t-answer sets of $\mathcal{KB}$ is denoted by $\mathrm{AS}^t(\mathcal{KB})$.*

Example 6. For the program $\mathcal{KB}_{ex}$ of the product database example, the only t-answer set is given by interpretation I_1, as defined in Example 4. As stated in Example 5, I_2 is a t-model of $\mathcal{KB}_{ex}$; however, I_2 is not a minimal t-model of $(\mathcal{KB}_{ex})_t^{I_2}$, as required in Definition 8 for being a t-answer set. In fact, the ground instance of Rule (6) in Example 5 is not contained in $(\mathcal{KB}_{ex})_t^{I_2}$. Therefore, we can remove the head of the rule, atom $supplied(cpu, harddisk)$, from I_2 such that the resulting interpretation I_2' is still a t-model of $\mathcal{KB}_{ex}$.

Whenever no DL-atoms are present in a DL-program $\mathcal{KB} = (\Phi, \Pi)$, DL-inconsistency tolerant semantics reduces to answer set semantics of the ordinary logic program Π. Therefore, the next result is a proper extension to a similar one that is folklore for standard logic programs.

Theorem 1. *For every t-answer set I of a DL-program $\mathcal{KB}$, I is a minimal t-model of $\mathcal{KB}$.*

Note that the converse does not generally hold. E.g., consider the set

$$I_3 = I' \cup \{chosen(s_2, cpu), chosen(s_3, harddisk), notChosen(s_2, cpu),$$
$$notChosen(s_2, harddisk)\} \,,$$

where I' is given as in Example 4. I_3 is a minimal t-model of $\mathcal{KB}_{ex}$ but, since the ground instantiation

$$fail \leftarrow not\ fail, needed(cpu), not\ anySupplied(cpu)$$

of Rule (8) from our example is not contained in $(\mathcal{KB}_{ex})_t^{I_3}$, we can remove atom $anySupplied(cpu)$ from I_3 such that the resulting interpretation I_3' is still a t-model of $(\mathcal{KB}_{ex})_t^{I_3}$. Consequently, by Definition 8, I_3 is no t-answer set of $\mathcal{KB}_{ex}$.
    The next result relates the refined semantics to the FLP-semantics.

Proposition 1. *Let $\mathcal{KB} = (\Phi, \Pi)$ be a monotonic DL-program and let I be an answer set of $\mathcal{KB}$. If all DL-atoms in $gr(\Pi)$ are DL-consistent under I w.r.t. Φ, then I is a t-answer set of $\mathcal{KB}$.*

Note that DL-programs with no occurrences of the ⩑ operator are monotonic and, as remarked in Section 2, this operator can typically be avoided in applications.

While counterintuitive literals a là *supplied*(*cpu*, *harddisk*) cannot occur in a t-answer set, Proposition 1 suggests that results that are intuitive are preserved under the refined semantics, as answer sets of a DL-program where inconsistency is immaterial are selected. On the other hand, a DL-program may have t-answer sets that do not correspond to any answer set (due to inconsistency avoidance).

Example 7. Consider the DL-program $\mathcal{KB} = (\Phi, \Pi)$ where $\Phi = \{\neg C(a)\}$ and $\Pi = \{p(a); \quad fail \leftarrow not\ fail, \mathrm{DL}[C \uplus p; C](a)\}$. Clearly, $\mathcal{KB}$ has no answer set, as the DL-atom in Π is DL-inconsistent; its single t-answer set is $I = \{p(a)\}$.

5   Computational Aspects

Translation to FLP Semantics. The DL-inconsistency tolerant semantics of DL-programs can be simulated by the FLP semantics as in Definition 2 using a linear rule-by-rule transformation $\rho(\cdot)$ on generalized normal programs, defined as

$$\rho(\Pi) = \{\rho(r) \mid r \in \Pi\} \cup$$
$$\{a' \leftarrow \mathrm{DL}[\gamma; \top \sqsubseteq \bot], not\ \mathrm{DL}[; Q](\mathbf{t}) \mid r \in \Pi, not\ a \in A(r)\}, \quad \text{where}$$
$$\rho(r) = H(r) \leftarrow B(r) \cup A(r), \quad \text{and}$$
$$A(r) = \{not\ a' \mid a = \mathrm{DL}[\gamma; Q](\mathbf{t}) \in B(r)\}.$$

In the translation for each DL-atom $a = \mathrm{DL}[\gamma; Q](\mathbf{t})$ occurring in the body of a rule r, we add a new atom a' to the negative body of r and a rule that deduces a' exactly when $I \models^{\Phi} \mathrm{DL}[\gamma; \top \sqsubseteq \bot]$ and $I \not\models^{\Phi} \mathrm{DL}[; Q](\mathbf{t})$ for some interpretation I, i.e., when $\Phi \cup \tau^{I}(a)$ is inconsistent and $\Phi \not\models Q(\mathbf{c})$, and thus a is DL-consistent. Deduction of a' thus causes the body of the transformed rule to be false under FLP-semantics corresponding exactly the case where the atom a is DL-inconsistent. Thus for a rule r in Π under a DL-inconsistency tolerant semantics and its corresponding rule $\rho(r)$ in the transformed program $\rho(\Pi)$ under FLP-semantics, we have that r and $\rho(r)$ have bodies whose truth values correspond under the respective semantics, thus effectively mimicking the DL-inconsistency tolerant semantics with the FLP-semantics.

Theorem 2. *For every DL-program* $\mathcal{KB} = (\Phi, \Pi)$, $\mathrm{AS}^{t}(\mathcal{KB}) = \{I \cap \mathrm{HB}(\Pi) \mid I \in \mathrm{AS}((\Phi, \rho(\Pi)))\}$.

By means of this translation, the t-answer sets of $\mathcal{KB}$ can be computed utilizing DLVHEX, a solver for *non-monotonic logic programs* admitting *higher-order atoms* and *external atoms*, or *HEX-programs* for short [5], that have a semantics based on the FLP-reduct. A plug-in for evaluating DL-programs, without the ⩑ operator, is available for DLVHEX that gives access to the DL-knowledge base by means of a third-party DL-reasoner [11; 12].

Due to the close relationship to HEX-programs, results on their computational complexity carry over to DL-inconsistency tolerant semantics of DL-programs. In particular, as corollaries of Theorem 7 and 8 in [5], due to the existence of transformation $\rho(\cdot)$, we obtain the following two results.

Theorem 3. *Given a DL-program $\mathcal{KB} = (\Phi, \Pi)$, where query answering in Φ is in complexity class C, deciding whether $\mathcal{KB}$ has a t-answer set is in* NEXPTIME^C.

Theorem 4. *Given a DL-program $\mathcal{KB} = (\Phi, \Pi)$, where query answering in Φ is in* EXPTIME, *deciding whether $\mathcal{KB}$ has a t-answer set is* NEXPTIME-*complete.*

Hardness in Theorem 4 follows from the special case of DL-programs without any DL-atoms, for which the DL-inconsistency tolerant semantics reduces to the standard answer set semantics of normal logic programs. It is known that answer set existence for this class of programs is NEXPTIME-complete. On the other side, membership follows again from the translation to HEX-programs, as it is known that checking the answer sets of HEX-programs is NEXPTIME-complete under the restriction that the external atoms can be evaluated in exponential time [5].

The result is especially interesting as query answering is in EXPTIME for many important DLs such as the basic DL $\mathcal{ALC}$, the DL underlying OWL-Lite ($\mathcal{SHIF}$), and the DLs corresponding to the fragments OWL 2 EL, OWL 2 RL, OWL 2 QL of the upcoming standard for a Web Ontology Language [9].

Another important aspect of the complexity results is that for DL-programs, reasoning under DL-inconsistency tolerant semantics is not harder than under the FLP-semantics.

Stratification. Eiter et al. [2] defined an iterative least model semantics for DL-programs that have a certain stratification property (which we will here refer to as *standard stratification*). The idea of stratification is to layer a program into a number of ordered strata that can be efficiently evaluated one-by-one where lower strata do not depend on higher strata.

A DL-program $\mathcal{KB}$ which is standard stratified has at most one answer set that coincides with its iterative least model and conversely, if $\mathcal{KB}$ has an iterative least model it coincides with the unique answer set of $\mathcal{KB}$. However, a DL-program that is standard stratified may have multiple t-answer sets. Too see this, note that a positive DL-program always has a standard stratification with a single stratum. Consider, e.g., the DL-program $\mathcal{KB} = (\Phi, \Pi)$, with

$$\Pi = \{\ h(c),$$
$$a(c) \leftarrow \mathrm{DL}[B \uplus b, H \uplus h; H](c),$$
$$b(c) \leftarrow \mathrm{DL}[A \uplus a, H \uplus h; H](c)\}\ ,$$

where $\Phi \models A(c)$ and $\Phi \models B(c)$. This program has two t-answer sets, viz. $I_1 = \{a(c), h(c)\}$ and $I_2 = \{b(c), h(c)\}$.

In the following, we define a different kind of stratification (which we call *t-stratification*) that guarantees a unique t-answer set iff the respective t-stratified program has a t-answer set. The major difference to standard stratification is to enforce that the information necessary for evaluating DL-atoms must be already available on a strictly lower stratum then the current one during a computation.

Definition 9. *A t-stratification of a DL-program $\mathcal{KB} = (\Phi, \Pi)$ is a mapping $\mu : \mathrm{HB}(\Pi) \cup \mathrm{D}(\Pi) \rightarrow \{0, 1, \ldots, k\}$, where $\mathrm{D}(\Pi)$ is the set of DL-atoms occurring in $gr(\Pi)$, such that*

(i) for each $r \in gr(\Pi)$, $\mu(H(r)) \geq \mu(l')$ for all $l' \in B(r)^+$, $\mu(H(r)) > \mu(l')$ for all $l' \in B(r)^-$, and $\mu(H(r)) > \mu(l')$ for each DL-atom $l' \in B(r)$, and

(ii) $\mu(a) \geq \mu(l)$ for each input literal l of each DL-atom $a \in D(\Pi)$.

We call $k \geq 0$ the length of μ. For every $i \in \{0, \ldots, k\}$, we then define the DL-programs $\mathcal{KB}_{\mu,i}$ as (Φ, Π_i), where $\Pi_i = \{r \in gr(\Pi) \mid \mu(H(r)) = i\}$ and $\mathcal{KB}^*_{\mu,i}$ as $(\Phi, \Pi^*_{\mu,i})$ where $\Pi^*_{\mu,i} = \{r \in gr(\Pi) \mid \mu(H(r)) \leq i\}$. Likewise, we define $HB_{\mu,i}(\Pi)$ (resp., $HB^*_{\mu,i}(\Pi)$) as the set of all $l \in HB(\Pi)$ such that $\mu(l) = i$ (resp., $\mu(l) \leq i$). We say that a DL-program $\mathcal{KB}$ is t-stratified, if it has a t-stratification μ of length $k \geq 0$. It is easy to see that for DL-programs without DL-atoms, t-stratification reduces to standard stratification of logic programs. Moreover, checking whether a DL-program is t-stratified and computing a t-stratification can be done by modified algorithms for standard stratification in linear time.

Note that by Definition 9, $\mathcal{KB}^*_{\mu,0}$ is always a positive DL-program without DL-atoms. Consequently, Π_0 coincides with a positive logic program, for which DL-inconsistency tolerant semantics coincides with the answer set semantics of logic programs. Therefore, the following proposition holds.

Proposition 2. Let $\mathcal{KB}$ be a DL-program $\mathcal{KB} = (\Phi, \Pi)$ with t-stratification μ. Then, $\mathcal{KB}^*_{\mu,0}$ has a unique minimal t-model that is also the unique t-answer set of $\mathcal{KB}^*_{\mu,0}$.

Next we want to establish uniqueness of t-answer sets for arbitrary strata.

Lemma 1. Let $\mathcal{KB}$ be a DL-program $\mathcal{KB} = (\Phi, \Pi)$ with t-stratification μ. If I_1 and I_2 are t-answer sets of $\mathcal{KB}^*_{\mu,i}$ for $i \geq 0$, then $I_1 = I_2$.

As a consequence of this lemma and Proposition 2, we get the next result.

Theorem 5. Let $\mathcal{KB}$ be a t-stratified DL-program $\mathcal{KB} = (\Phi, \Pi)$. If $\mathcal{KB}$ has a t-answer set, then this t-answer set is unique.

As can be seen in the next result, the t-answer set of a t-stratified DL-program is *compositional* in the sense that, roughly speaking, we get t-answer sets for the part of the DL-program that is below a certain stratum, if we remove all atoms of higher strata from I.

Theorem 6. Let $\mathcal{KB}$ be a DL-program $\mathcal{KB} = (\Phi, \Pi)$ with t-stratification μ. If I is a t-answer set of $\mathcal{KB}^*_{\mu,i}$ for $i > 0$, then $I \cap HB^*_{\mu,i-1}(\Pi)$ is a t-answer set of $\mathcal{KB}^*_{\mu,i-1}$.

Approaching from this result, we aim at computing the t-answer set I of $\mathcal{KB}$ step-by-step, starting with $I \cap HB^*_{\mu,0}(\Pi)$ and extending the interpretation one stratum a time until we reach $I = I \cap HB^*_{\mu,k}(\Pi)$. Hence, we define a series of sets $\Delta_{i,h}$ for each stratum i, that can be seen as the results of repeatedly applying a consequence operator.

Definition 10. Let $\mathcal{KB}$ be a DL-program $\mathcal{KB} = (\Phi, \Pi)$ with t-stratification μ and I_{i-1} a t-answer set of $\mathcal{KB}^*_{\mu,i-1}$ for some $i > 0$. We define sets of literals $\Delta_{i,h}$ for $h \geq 0$ as follows:

(i) $\Delta_{i,0} = \emptyset$ and

(ii) $\Delta_{i,m} = \bigcup_{o<m} \Delta_{i,o} \cup \{H(r) \mid \mu(H(r)) = i, I_{i-1} \cup \Delta_{i,m-1} \models_t^\Phi B(r)\}$ for $m > 0$.

As $gr(\Pi)$ contains only a finite number of rules, and $\Delta_{i,h} \subseteq \Delta_{i,h+1}$ for all h, we must always reach some fixpoint Δ_i. That is, $\Delta_i = \Delta_{i,f}$ when $\Delta_{i,f} = \Delta_{i,f+1}$.

In order to establish our main result on computing the unique t-answer set (whenever one exists), we make use of the following lemma.

Lemma 2. *Let $\mathcal{KB}$ be a DL-program $\mathcal{KB} = (\Phi, \Pi)$ with t-stratification μ. If I_1 and I_2 are t-models of $\mathcal{KB}_{\mu,i}^*$ for $i \geq 0$ such that $I_1 \cap \mathrm{HB}_{\mu,i-1}^*(\Pi) = I_2 \cap \mathrm{HB}_{\mu,i-1}^*(\Pi)$ then $I_1 \cap I_2$ is a t-model of $\mathcal{KB}_{\mu,i}^*$.*

Intuitively, when we can extend a t-model of lower strata of the DL-program to a further stratum, there is always a subset minimal extension of this t-model.

By computing the t-answer set of $\mathcal{KB}_{\mu,0}^*$ and subsequently Δ_i for each stratum i, we can compute the t-answer set of $\mathcal{KB}$, whenever it exists:

Theorem 7. *Let $\mathcal{KB}$ be a DL-program $\mathcal{KB} = (\Phi, \Pi)$ with t-stratification μ and let I be a t-answer set of $\mathcal{KB}_{\mu,i}^*$ for some $i > 0$. Then, $I = I'$ where $I' = (I \cap \mathrm{HB}_{\mu,i-1}^*(\Pi)) \cup \Delta_i$.*

Proof. Towards a contradiction assume $I \neq I'$. From Theorem 5 follows that $I' \notin \mathrm{AS}^t(\mathcal{KB}_{\mu,i}^*)$. As I is a minimal t-model of $\mathcal{KB}_{\mu,i}^*$, we get $I \cap I' \not\models_t^\Phi \Pi_{\mu,i}^*$. From this and Lemma 2 follows by modus tollens that $I' \not\models_t^\Phi \Pi_{\mu,i}^*$. Hence, there is a rule $r \in \Pi_{\mu,i}^*$ with $I' \models_t^\Phi B(r)$ and $I' \not\models_t^\Phi H(r)$. Consider the case that $\mu(H(r)) < i$. Then, $I' \not\models_t^\Phi r$ is a contradiction to $I \models_t^\Phi r$, since $I \cap \mathrm{HB}_{\mu,i-1}^*(\Pi) = I' \cap \mathrm{HB}_{\mu,i-1}^*(\Pi)$. Now consider case $\mu(H(r)) = i$ and number $m \leq 0$ such that $\Delta_{i,m} = \Delta_i$. As $\Delta_{i,m} \subseteq I'$ and $I' \not\models_t^\Phi H(r)$, we have $H(r) \notin \Delta_{i,m}$. Moreover, since $I' \models_t^\Phi B(r)$ and $I' = (I \cap \mathrm{HB}_{\mu,i-1}^*(\Pi)) \cup \Delta_{i,m}$, by Definition 10 we have that $H(r) \in \Delta_{i,m+1}$. As then $\Delta_{i,m} \neq \Delta_{i,m+1}$, we have a contradiction to $\Delta_{i,m}$ being the fixpoint Δ_i. $\qquad \square$

So far we established that in case there is a t-answer set we can compute it stratum by stratum. In the following, we provide means for deciding the existence of a t-answer set during this computation.

Theorem 8. *Let $\mathcal{KB}$ be a DL-program $\mathcal{KB} = (\Phi, \Pi)$ with t-stratification μ and I_{i-1} a t-answer set of $\mathcal{KB}_{\mu,i-1}^*$ for some $i > 0$. If $I_i = I_{i-1} \cup \Delta_i$ is a t-model of $\mathcal{KB}_{\mu,i}^*$ then I_i is a t-answer set of $\mathcal{KB}_{\mu,i}^*$.*

This enables us to pursue the following approach. After computing $I_i = I_{i-1} \cup \Delta_i$ for a stratum i, we check whether $I \models_t^\Phi \Pi_{\mu,i}^*$. If yes, we know by Theorem 8 that I_i is a t-answer set of $\mathcal{KB}_{\mu,i}^*$ and we are either done or continue our computation for stratum $i + 1$. If $I \not\models_t^\Phi \Pi_{\mu,i}^*$, we know by Theorem 7 that $\mathcal{KB}_{\mu,i}^*$ has no t-answer set and stop the computation.

Algorithm 1 for computing the t-answer set of a given DL-program $\mathcal{KB}$ with a t-stratification follows precisely this strategy after having computed the unique t-answer set of $\mathcal{KB}_{\mu,0}^*$. This can be done by a standard answer set solver as $\mathcal{KB}_{\mu,0}^*$ does not involve DL-atoms. Overall, the algorithm runs in exponential

---

Algorithm 1. Computing the t-answer set of a t-stratified DL-program $\mathcal{KB}$

Require: $\mathcal{KB} = (\Phi, \Pi)$, μ is a t-stratification of $\mathcal{KB}$ of length $k \geq 0$
1: $I_0 :=$ the unique t-answer set of $\mathcal{KB}^*_{\mu,0}$ // computable in exponential time
2: **for** $i := 1$ **to** k **do**
3:     // compute Δ_i
4:     $\Delta' := \emptyset$
5:     **repeat**
6:       $\Delta_i := \Delta'$
7:       **for all** $r \in gr(\Pi_i)$ **do**
8:         // loop may have exponentially many iterations
9:         // the following check requires two queries to Φ per DL-atom in $B(r)$:
10:       **if** $\Delta_i \cup I_{i-1} \models^{\Phi}_t B(r)$ **then**
11:         $\Delta' := \Delta' \cup \{H(r)\}$
12:       **end if**
13:       **end for**
14:     **until** $\Delta_i = \Delta'$ // number of iterations limited by number of rules in $gr(\Pi_i)$

15:     $I_i := I_{i-1} \cup \Delta_i$
16:     **if** $I_i \not\models^{\Phi}_t gr(\Pi^*_{\mu,i})$ **then**
17:       **print** "$\mathcal{KB}$ has no t-answer set."
18:       **return**
19:     **end if**
20: **end for**
21: **return** I_k // I_k is the unique t-answer set of $\mathcal{KB}$

---

time with an additional effort of external calls to a DL-reasoner for evaluating the DL-queries of DL-atoms in lines 10 and 16. The time necessary for this evaluations depends on the complexity of query answering in the respective DL. Altogether, there may be an exponential number of such calls.

Theorem 9. *Given a DL-program $\mathcal{KB} = (\Phi, \Pi)$ with t-stratification μ, where query answering in Φ is in complexity class C, deciding whether $\mathcal{KB}$ has a t-answer set is in* $\mathrm{ExpTime}^{C}$.

When query answering in Φ is possible in exponential time, in the worst case the algorithm has to perform an exponential number of exponential time calls which can in turn be done in exponential time.

Theorem 10. *Given a DL-program $\mathcal{KB} = (\Phi, \Pi)$ with t-stratification μ, where query answering in Φ is in* $\mathrm{ExpTime}$, *deciding whether $\mathcal{KB}$ has a t-answer set is* $\mathrm{ExpTime}$-*complete.*

Hardness follows from $\mathrm{ExpTime}$-completeness of ordinary stratified logic programs. For lightweight DLs such as those underlying OWL 2 EL, OWL 2 RL, and OWL 2 QL, where query answering has polynomial data complexity, reasoning for DL-programs is feasible in polynomial time under data complexity (where all of $\mathcal{KB}$ except facts in Φ and Π is fixed).

6   Conclusion and Outlook

We have introduced a refined semantics for DL-programs to overcome counter-intuitive results that are caused by inconsistency that emerges when combining rules and ontologies. For programs without DL-atoms our semantics coincides with the standard answer set semantics of logic programs. Moreover, we defined the property of t-stratification which guarantees that a DL-program has at most one answer set and gave an algorithm for computing it. Furthermore, we analyzed the computational complexity of the new semantics. The core of our approach is the definition of a new satisfaction relation for DL-rules such that for the body to be satisfied, additionally all its DL-atoms need to be DL-consistent.

An implementation of DL-inconsistency tolerant semantics is targeted in the context of the EU FP7 project OntoRule, with a focus on stratified programs and integration of F-Logic Programming [13].

References

1. Baader, F., Calvanese, D., McGuinness, D., Nardi, D., Patel-Schneider, P.: The Description Logic Handbook: Theory, Implementation and Applications. Cambridge University Press, Cambridge (2003)
2. Eiter, T., Ianni, G., Lukasiewicz, T., Schindlauer, R., Tompits, H.: Combining answer set programming with description logics for the semantic web. Artificial Intelligence 172(12-13), 1495–1539 (2008)
3. Gelfond, M., Lifschitz, V.: The stable model semantics for logic programming. In: ICLP'88, pp. 1070–1080. The MIT Press, Cambridge (1988)
4. Baral, C.: Knowledge Representation, Reasoning and Declarative Problem Solving. Cambridge University Press, Cambridge (2003)
5. Eiter, T., Ianni, G., Schindlauer, R., Tompits, H.: A uniform integration of higher-order reasoning and external evaluations in answer-set programming. In: IJCAI'05, pp. 90–96. Professional Book Center (2005)
6. Faber, W., Leone, N., Pfeifer, G.: Recursive aggregates in disjunctive logic programs: Semantics and complexity. In: Alferes, J.J., Leite, J. (eds.) JELIA 2004. LNCS (LNAI), vol. 3229, pp. 200–212. Springer, Heidelberg (2004)
7. Horrocks, I., Patel-Schneider, P.F.: Reducing OWL entailment to description logic satisfiability. In: Fensel, D., Sycara, K., Mylopoulos, J. (eds.) ISWC 2003. LNCS, vol. 2870, pp. 17–29. Springer, Heidelberg (2003)
8. Horrocks, I., Patel-Schneider, P.F., van Harmelen, F.: From $\mathcal{SHIQ}$ and RDF to OWL: The making of a Web ontology language. J. Web Sem. 1(1), 7–26 (2003)
9. Motik, B., Patel-Schneider, P.F., Parsia, B. (eds.): OWL 2 Web Ontology Language: Structural Specification and Functional-Style Syntax (2008), W3C Working Draft 02 December 2008
10. Eiter, T., Lukasiewicz, T., Schindlauer, R., Tompits, H.: Well-founded semantics for description logic programs in the semantic web. In: Antoniou, G., Boley, H. (eds.) RuleML 2004. LNCS, vol. 3323, pp. 81–97. Springer, Heidelberg (2004)
11. Eiter, T., Ianni, G., Krennwallner, T., Schindlauer, R.: Exploiting Conjunctive Queries in Description Logic Programs. AMAI (1-4), 115–152 (2008)
12. Krennwallner, T.: Integration of Conjunctive Queries over Description Logics into HEX-Programs. Master's thesis, Vienna University of Technology (2007)
13. Kifer, M., Lausen, G., Wu, J.: Logical foundations of object-oriented and frame-based languages. J. ACM 42(4), 741–843 (1995)

Aligning Large SKOS-Like Vocabularies: Two Case Studies

Anna Tordai, Jacco van Ossenbruggen, Guus Schreiber, and Bob Wielinga

VU University Amsterdam, Amsterdam The Netherlands

Abstract. In this paper we build on our methodology for combining and selecting alignment techniques for vocabularies, with two alignment case studies of large vocabularies in two languages. Firstly, we analyze the vocabularies and based on that analysis choose our alignment techniques. Secondly, we test our hypothesis based on earlier work that first generating alignments using simple lexical alignment techniques, followed by a separate disambiguation of alignments performs best in terms of precision and recall. The experimental results show, for example, that this combination of techniques provides an estimated precision of 0.7 for a sample of the 12,725 concepts for which alignments were generated (of the total 27,992 concepts). Thirdly, we explain our results in light of the characteristics of the vocabularies and discuss their impact on the alignments techniques.

Keywords: Vocabulary alignment, case study, cultural heritage, methodology.

1 Introduction

As Semantic Web technology gains prevalence the field of ontology alignment is becoming more and more important. Within the MultimediaN E-Culture project [11] we use a large number of vocabularies for the annotation of artwork metadata. Despite the large amount of work done on developing ontology alignment techniques [7], in a practical setting it is still hard to predict, for two given vocabularies, which combination of techniques can best be used to create an alignment between them.

In previous work [12] we took a first step towards a methodology for selecting such a combination. We applied three alignment techniques to two vocabularies from the E-Culture repository, and looked which combination of techniques gave the best results. In this study, we take a second step by questioning to what extent we can use an analysis of the characteristics of the vocabularies to predict the performance of the different techniques, and to predict which combination will generate the best results. To answer this question, we perform two case studies, in each we align a large domain-specific vocabulary to a lexical resource. We analyze the vocabularies being aligned and predict the performance of four selected alignment techniques. We then apply all four techniques to generate alignments, followed by manual evaluation of representative samples to assess

L. Aroyo et al. (Eds.): ESWC 2010, Part I, LNCS 6088, pp. 198–212, 2010.

the performance of each technique. Finally, we discuss our findings and compare them to our initial predictions.

2 Related Work

Work on procedures and guidelines for ontology and vocabulary alignment is still limited. The Ontology Alignment Evaluation Initiative(OAEI[1]) campaigns provide a standardized way of comparing alignment tools, with tools such as Falcon [10] having the best performance in the 2007 [6] and RiMOM [13] among the top performers in 2008 [2] and 2009 [5] campaigns. Unfortunately, there are no clear selection criteria for these tools and many of the off-the-shelf tools are either unavailable or do not work on data other than that of the OAEI campaigns. Euzenat et al. [4] identify applications requirements and propose a case-based method for recommending alignment techniques but the work remains at a high level of abstraction. In a survey of alignment techniques, Aleksovski et al. [1] list techniques for alignment problems based on real world applications. They recommend using those techniques for similar application. In both cases there is a lack of a systematic method of comparison and evaluation of techniques with respect to domains and vocabulary characteristics. Eckert et al. [3] used machine learning techniques for alignment generation but found that combining the results of multiple alignment tools by a system of voting works just as well as machine learning. This result suggests that machine learning techniques, while useful in other areas such as natural language processing, have little added value in the field of ontology alignment. Ghazvinian et al. [8] compare the performance of off-the-shelf alignment tool and a simple lexical algorithm for creating alignments between medical ontologies using the OAEI gold standard. They concluded that the simple lexical algorithm performs better than the alignment tool.

Our conclusion is that we need to develop our own methods for aligning vocabularies with clear selection criteria.

3 Alignment Techniques

In previous work we learned that for vocabularies containing many synonyms or alternative labels, simple string matching techniques can already yield relatively good results at low computational costs. In contrast, off-the-shelf structural tools such as Falcon tend to find few or no extra alignments, but are computationally so expensive that they cannot be run on large vocabularies. For this study, we tested Falcon on our data set but it ran out of memory. A test run on a relatively small subset of a source vocabulary required 15 Gb of memory and 46 hours of runtime to generate alignments. Ghazivinian et al. [8] reported similar problems with Falcon, and other off-the-shelf tools. In this paper we focus on relatively simple alignment techniques based on string matching. Variations within these techniques, however, still have a significant influence on the quality

---

[1] http://oaei.ontologymatching.org/

of the alignments generated. Our goal is to be able to predict which variation will perform best, based on an analysis of the characteristics of the vocabularies being aligned.

3.1 Vocabulary Characteristics

We focus on vocabularies that are either represented directly in SKOS or can be easily mapped to the SKOS model. Since relatively few organisations publish their vocabularies in this format, this typically means the SKOS version is the result of a conversion from some other format. Both the conventions during the development of the original format and the decisions made during the conversion influence the characteristics of the resulting SKOS vocabularies, especially when the source and target vocabulary follow different conventions. This is typically a source of potential alignment problems.

Consider the use of plural versus singular nouns forms in labels. Lexical resources tend to prefer singular, while the ISO standard for thesauri[2] prescribes the use of the plural form, and yet other vocabularies contain both forms.

Another example is the use of preferred and alternative labels versus the use of synonyms of equivalent status. The first is common practice in many domain-specific thesauri, the latter is commonly found in dictionaries and other lexical resources.

Another potential source of matching problems are the spelling conventions of words with upper case characters, diacritics and hyphens. For example, "Fin-de-siècle" may be spelled in this way in one vocabulary but as "fin de siecle" in another.

Finally, vocabularies tend to differ in the treatment of homonyms, that is, terms with the same label that have different meanings. Some vocabularies prevent homonyms by explicitly adding qualifiers to labels so that each label is unique. Others allow multiple concepts to have the same label, and rely on the concept's place in the hierarchy or its scope note to clarify its meaning.

For all the examples given above, it is *a priori* not clear how the different conventions should be handled during the alignment and how this might influence the results.

3.2 Alignment Generation Techniques

In this paper we thus focus on three morphological techniques based on simple string matching, using either exact string matching, string matching after normalization of hyphens and diacritics, and string matching after conversion of plurals to singular form. We also look at the effect of using only preferred labels versus the use of both preferred and alternative labels. Application of these techniques yields a single alignment candidate for some concepts, but due to the many homonyms, many concepts have multiple ambiguous alignment candidates which need to be disambiguated in a separate step.

---

[2] http://www.niso.org/workrooms/iso25964

3.3 Disambiguation Techniques

In previous work we described two types of disambiguation techniques for ambiguous candidate alignments. Both techniques use the broader/narrower relationships of the source and target vocabularies (hyper/hyponym in lexical sources).

In the Child Match technique we follow, for each source concept with multiple alignments in the target vocabulary, the hierarchy "downwards" and count the number of alignments between "child" concepts of aligned concepts. We assume that concepts with similar meaning will have similar hierarchies below them. This means there should be more alignments between their children, than for homonym concepts which may be lexically similar but differ in meaning. We then count the number of alignments that have at least one or more child alignments and consider them to be correct close matches. If multiple concepts have more than one child alignment we choose the alignment with the highest number of child alignments. In some cases both alignments have the same (highest) number of child alignments, and then both alignments are chosen. The Parent Match technique is a mirroring of the Child Match technique. We find correct alignments by following the hierarchies "upward", and count the number of aligned "parent" concepts to distinguish the correct target concept from its homonyms.

4 Case Study Setup

To answer our research questions we performed the following study. We first analyse the characteristics of the our vocabularies in our dataset. Based on this analysis we make a number of predictions about the performance on the different alignment techniques described. We then apply four different techniques and discuss the alignments sets they produce, and how these sets overlap. Lastly, we manually evaluate representative samples, and discuss the quality of the results.

4.1 Characteristics of the Vocabularies

For the two case studies we use Getty's Art and Architecture Thesaurus (AAT)[3] and its Dutch version, AATNed[4]. The two vocabularies are closely linked, in fact the AATNed was based on the AAT and extended with additional terms. We chose Princeton WordNet version 2.0 as the target vocabulary for the English language AAT and Cornetto[5], a WordNet-like lexical resource for Dutch, as the target for AATNed.

For WordNet we used the RDF version published by W3C, the other vocabularies were originally in XML but were converted to SKOS[6] by the MultimediaN E-Culture project. We describe them in a little more detail below:

---

[3] http://www.getty.edu/research/conducting_research/vocabularies/aat/
[4] http://www.aat-ned.nl/
[5] http://www2.let.vu.nl/oz/cornetto/index.html
[6] http://www.w3.org/2004/02/skos/

AAT is a structured vocabulary in English containing terms related to fine art, architecture and archival materials. It is organized in 7 facets with 36 hierarchies and contains $2,949$ guide terms and $27,992$ concepts. There are broader/narrower and related relations between the concepts and each has exactly one preferred label and possibly multiple alternative labels with a total of $92,089$ alternative labels for concepts. Ambiguous preferred labels are distinguished from each other with the use of qualifiers. An important feature in terms of alignment is that the preferred labels are in plural form if a plural form is linguistically possible.

AATNed is a structured vocabulary in Dutch, closely related to the English AAT. It is organized in 34 hierarchies with $2,873$ guideterms and $30,817$ concepts. There are broader/narrower and related relations between concepts, each one having exactly one preferred label. As in the AAT, qualifiers are used to distinguish homonymous preferred labels. Concepts can also have alternative labels with a total number of $24,817$ for concepts, a number significantly lower than for the AAT. As in the AAT, preferred labels tend to be in plural form. We found $20,457$ singular labels for the same number of concepts meaning that $10,360$ preferred labels have no singular form. These concepts tend to describe processes, states or certain materials such as "marble" or "cement" that are already in singular form or have no plural form.

WordNet is a large lexical database for the English language. It contains $115,424$ synsets with $203,147$ labels. A synset may contain over thirty labels and one label may appear in multiple synsets (homonyms). There are 17 relations between synsets such as the hyponym and meronym relations. Important differences with the AAT are that all labels are equivalent in the sense that there is no distinction between a preferred label and alternative label, labels tend to be in singular form and contain no diacritics.

Cornetto is a large lexical database in Dutch containing $70,370$ synsets and $103,762$ labels. There are 57 relations between the synsets than in WordNet, such as the "has hypernym" and "causes" relations. An important distinction between Cornetto and WordNet is that Cornetto has fewer synsets and significantly fewer labels than WordNet.

Finally, an important difference between the source vocabularies (AAT and AATNed) and the target vocabularies (WordNet and Cornetto) is that the first describe the cultural heritage domain while the latter describe more general perceptions of the world, which is often visible in the different way the hierarchies are organized. The difference in ontological commitments means that even lexical matches do not necessarily have the same meaning. One example is the concept "artist" in AAT referring exclusively to artists in the fine arts, while in WordNet the meaning also includes musical and other types of artist. As a result, finding true exact matches between the concepts is difficult, therefore our aim is to generate close matches instead. Each of the four vocabularies can be navigated through using the Europeana Thesaurus Navigator[7].

---

[7] http://eculture.cs.vu.nl/europeana/session/thesaurus

4.2 Predictions/Hypotheses

Based on the analysis of the characteristics of the vocabularies in our dataset, we make the following predictions.

First, AAT, AATNed and Cornetto contain diacritics in their labels, while WordNet does not. The vocabularies also differ in their use of capital letters and finally they also differ in the use of hyphens. We predict that these differences will have a significant negative effect on all alignment techniques that use simple string matching without normalization of the labels, and that this effect will outweigh the possibly negative effects of normalisation.

Second, both the AAT and AATNed contain lexical variations of their preferred label as alternative labels of the same concept. We predict that an alignment tool not restricted to preferred labels would therefore generate significantly more alignments using the lexical variations, but at the cost of lower precision.

Third, the large number of synonym labels in the target vocabularies increases the likelihood of finding alignments and therefore increasing recall. However, we also expect the precision to be low as both WordNet and Cornetto contain a large number of homonyms.

Finally, WordNet and Cornetto labels are mostly in singular form, while in AAT and AATNed there is a preference for plurals. We predict that this mismatch will have a significant negative effect on the alignment, and that this will outweigh any negative effects of errors introduced by automatically converting all terms to singular form.

4.3 Alignment Generation

We selected four alignment techniques based on the possibilities described in Section 3; three morphological techniques and a lexical technique.

Our baseline technique uses simple string-matching. It was also used in [12] in order to compare performances. It generates alignments between unique preferred labels of the source vocabularies (AAT and AATNed) and unique labels of the target vocabularies (WordNet and Cornetto). Concepts with homonymous labels are simply ignored.

The second technique matches unique singular labels. For AATNed, we use the 20, 457 singular labels present in the original vocabulary. Since AAT is missing explicit singular labels, we generated them by first applying the built-in Porter stemmer of SWI Prolog[8] to the preferred label of each concept. We then matched the resulting stem to the alternative labels of the same concept. If we found a match, we added the label as a singular preferred label to the concept. This yielded 9, 129 singular labels. This is just a third of the total number of concepts, significantly less than in AATNed. The main reason for this is that the stem of a plural does not always yield the singular form, stemming for example the word "houses" to "hous", which would subsequently not match the alternative label "house". In addition, the Porter stemmer removes more affixes than just the plural affixes, therefore applying it to the alternative labels could yield multiple

---

[8] http://www.swi-prolog.org/

matches to the stemmed preferred labelnot all of which being the singular form of the preferred label. A better approach would be the use of an algorithm that only removes plural affixes. Concepts with homonymous labels are simply ignored. We refer to this technique as the Singular Non-ambiguous technique or SN for short.

The third technique matches unique normalized singular preferred labels or normalized preferred labels if no singular label is available. These are matched to normalized labels from WordNet or Cornetto. Normalization includes replacing diacritics with a non-diacritic character ("ó" to "o"), replacing hyphens and underscores by spaces, and turning each label into lower case. Note that normalization may infrequently introduce ambiguity. For example, after normalization the Indian style "Amber" and the material "amber" have the same preferred label. Concepts with homonymous labels are simply ignored. We call this technique the Normalized Non-ambiguous technique or NN for short.

With the fourth technique, called Lexical, we match all normalized labels of the source thesauri to normalized labels of the target thesauri, regardless of whether they are unique, in order to generate as many as possible candidate alignments.

We applied all four techniques to generate mappings from AAT to WordNet, and from AATNed to Cornetto. Before applying the techniques, we removed qualifiers from the preferred labels of the AAT and AATNed as neither WordNet nor Cornetto have qualifiers. This means that we introduce ambiguity in the AAT labels, and we need to rely on the disambiguation techniques to repair this in a later phase. We then apply the Child Match and Parent Match disambiguation techniques described in Section 3 on the set of ambiguous alignments.

4.4   Manual Evaluation

Unlike in previous work where the entire set of generated alignments $(4, 375)$ were evaluated manually, we expected in these case studies to generate significantly more alignments. Evaluating a large number of alignments manually is not feasible. We sampled alignments from various subsets we expected to have different properties. These samples were evaluated manually. We also performed inter-rater agreement evaluations to check the quality of the manual evaluation. Subsequently, we extrapolate from the results of the evaluated samples to estimate the precision of the subsets using the method described in Van Hage et al. [9].

4.5   Summary of Case Study Setup

In **Step 1** we preprocess the data-sets by removing qualifiers from the preferred labels In **Step 2** we apply the four alignment techiques to the vocabularies to generate close-match alignments. In **Step 3** we apply two disambiguation techniques that use the structure of the vocabularies. In **Step 4** we perform manual evaluation of samples of data classifying each alignment into one of seven categories: exact-match, close-match, broader, narrower, related, unsure

Table 1. Number of alignments generated between AAT and WordNet

Method	Alignments	Aligned AAT Concepts	% of AAT Concepts
Baseline	2,296	2,296	8%
SN	4,299	4,299	15%
NN	4,365	4,365	15.5%
Lexical	42,039	12,725	45%
Total	42,039	12,725	45%

Table 2. Disambiguated alignments of the Lexical tool for AAT-WordNet

Segment	Kept Alignments	Disambiguated Concepts	Removed Alignments
Child Match only	590	554	3,205
Parent Match only	2,485	2,011	7,035
Overlap	236	234	1,580
Distinct Total	3,311	2,665	11,820

and not related. We also record the amount of time the evaluation takes. In **Step 5** independent raters evaluate random samples of evaluated alignments in order to calculate inter-rater agreement statistics (Cohen's Kappa). In **Step 6** we estimate based on the results of the evaluated alignments the performance of the alignment and disambiguation techniques. The focus here is on alignments evaluated as exact-match and close-match.

5   Alignment Results

5.1   AAT-WordNet

Alignment Generation. We generated four sets of alignments using the four alignment techniques. Table 1 displays the number of alignments per technique with the number of AAT concepts aligned and the percentage of the total AAT concepts. The baseline generates the fewest alignments which was expected, this is caused by the large number of preferred labels in plural form. The SN technique is more successful aligning almost twice as many concepts. The NN tool only generates 66 alignments more than the SN tool. Combined, the three morphological tools generate 4,592 distinct alignments which is 16.4% of the AAT concepts. The Lexical tool generates almost ten times more alignments for three times the amount of concepts the morphological tools generate. This is caused by the large number of alternative labels of the AAT and allowing for ambiguous alignments.

Combining Alignments. Examining the overlap between the alignments generated by the four tools revealed that all alignments generated by the morphological tools were also generated by the Lexical tool. Fig. 1 shows the overlaps between the three morphological tools. There is a large overlap between all three tools along with a large overlap between the SN and NN tools. The figure also shows that 191 NN alignments were *not* found by the Baseline and SN tools. Most of these alignments are upper case labels matched to lower case labels or

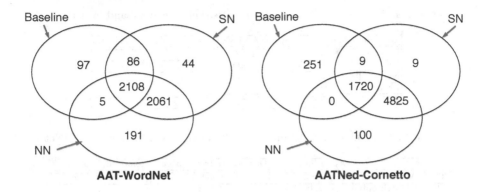

Fig. 1. Overlap in alignments generated by the morphological tools

normalized diacritics e.g.: "venetian blind" matching "Venetian blind". An example of an alignment only found by SN is "Maltese cross". When normalized the term matches two synsets in WordNet and becomes ambiguous. The Lexical tool generated an 37,447 alignments for 8,990 concepts excluding alignments displayed in Table 2. Further analysis showed that 2,116 of these alignments were not ambiguous. These non-ambiguous alignments are between unique AAT alternative labels and unique WordNet labels.

Disambiguation. Of the 12,725 concepts that were aligned, 6,887 concepts have more than one alignment with a total of 36,201 alignments. We applied Child Match and Parent Match disambiguation techniques where we rely on the structure of the thesauri. Analysis of the results of the disambiguations showed that 908 alignments were also generated by the morphological tools. We removed these alignments as our goal is to improve the performance of the Lexical tool.

Table 2 displays the results of the disambiguation process showing the alignments that were kept, the number of disambiguated concepts and the alignments that were rejected. The Parent Match technique disambiguated three and a half times more concepts than the Child Match technique. There is a small overlap between the two. Examples of correctly disambiguated alignments are the concept "vehicle" as in motorized vehicle which is disambiguated from "vehicle" meaning expression or medium because of alignments between its children such as "aircraft" and "tricycle". Of the 6,887 concepts, 2,665 concepts (39%) were disambiguated.

By combining the non-ambiguous alignments found by the four techniques with the results of the disambiguation techniques we have 10,0019 alignments for 9,208 AAT concepts.

5.2   AATNed-Cornetto

Alignment Generation. The result of the alignment process is shown in Table 3. Similarly to AAT-WordNet case, Baseline generated the fewest number

Table 3. Alignments generated between AATNed and Cornetto

Method	Alignments	Aligned AATNed Concepts	% of AAT Concepts
Baseline	1,980	1,980	6.5%
SN	6,563	6,563	21%
NN	6,644	6,644	22%
Lexical	20,331	10,773	35%
Total	20,331	10,773	35%

Table 4. Disambiguated alignments for AATNed-Cornetto

Segment	Kept Alignments	Disambiguated Concepts	Removed Alignments
Child Match only	342	327	1,140
Parent Match only	1,281	920	1,667
Overlap	106	104	289
Distinct Total	1,729	1,297	3,096

of alignments. The SN tool generated over three times that many alignments as more singular labels were available. In total, the three morphological techniques generated 6, 923 alignments for the same amount of concepts, aligning a little over 22% of AATNed concepts.

The Lexical tool generated 20, 331 alignments for over a third of the total AATNed concepts and there are significantly fewer alignments generated than for AAT-WordNet. This is caused by the lower number of alternative labels in AATNed and fewer sense labels in Cornetto.

Combining Alignments. Again, all alignments generated by the three morphological tools were also generated by the Lexical tool. Fig. 1 shows the overlap between the non-ambiguous tools. There is a large overlap between the three tools. However, the number of alignments found only by Baseline tool is larger than in the English case. There is an even larger overlap between SN and NN tools.

In addition to the alignments shown in Fig. 1, the Lexical tool generated 13, 417 alignments for 4, 414 concepts. An analysis showed that a small subset of these alignments (569) is not ambiguous. This is smaller number than in AAT-WordNet, again caused by the fewer alternative labels.

Disambiguation. Of the 10, 773 concepts that were aligned in total, 3, 899 concepts have more than one alignment with a total of 13, 457 alignments. We applied Child Match and Parent Match and removed 142 alignments also generated by the morphological tools. The results are shown in Table 4. Again, there is a small overlap between the two techniques. Overall 1, 297 concepts were disambiguated, which is a third of the total number of ambiguous concepts. In comparison to the AAT- WordNet case we see that a smaller percentage of the aligned concepts are ambiguous. This is caused by fewer number of alternative labels in AATNed and also fewer labels per concept in Cornetto.

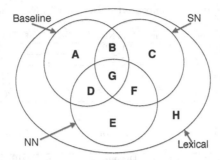

Fig. 2. Venn diagram of segments representing the overlaps of the four tools

6   Evaluation

We manually evaluated samples of generated alignments. The samples were selected from all segments of the Venn diagram shown in Fig. 2. For segment H,
we the samples are from alignments returned by the two disambiguation techniques and their overlap, as well as alignments removed by the two techniques in
order to assess calculate the number of false negatives. We also took a sample of
ambiguous alignments that were not disambiguated to assess the overall performance of the Lexical tool. Finally, we also sampled non-ambiguous alignments
generated using unique alternative labels. In total we selected alignments for one
thousand source concepts from AAT and one thousand concepts from AATNed.
These alignments were scattered along all segments: 400 concepts were sampled
segments A to F, and 600 concepts from segment H.

The alignments were manually evaluated by the first author using the evaluation tool used in [12]. Three extra raters evaluated small samples of the evaluated
set to measure inter-rater agreement. Each rater had a different sample of 50
concepts from with alignments of both cases. Averaged over the three raters
Cohen's kappa was 0.67 (for English) and 0.71 (for Dutch) which is a moderate agreement. This result shows that alignment evaluation is difficult, even for
humans.

6.1   Results for AAT-WordNet

Table 5 displays the result of the manual evaluation. In the columns for the
AAT-WordNet alignments we see that the overlap between the SN and NN tools
marked by segment F has the highest precision (0.9), followed by the segment G
at 0.81. As predicted, the precision of the alignments generated by the Baseline
tool only in segment A, is lower than most other segments at 0.38. This is caused
by plural nouns from AAT incorrectly matching verbs in WordNet.

Table 6 shows the results of the sampling of alignments from the set found
only by the Lexical tool. The disambiguation with the Child Match technique
performs better with a precision of 0.74 while the ParentMatch technique has a
precision of 0.46 and the overlap the highest precision at 0.84. The number of

Table 5. Sampled evaluation from the non-ambiguous segments

Segment	AAT-WordNet				AATNed-Cornetto			
	Segment Size	Sample Size	Correct Alignments	Sample precision	Segment Size	Sample Size	Correct Alignments	Sample precision
A	97	55	21	0.38	251	132	66	0.5
B	86	46	20	0.43	9	9	4	0.44
C	44	44	35	0.79	9	9	5	0.56
D	5	5	5	1.0	0	0	0	0
E	191	50	18	0.36	100	50	24	0.48
F	2061	100	90	0.90	4825	100	92	0.92
G	2108	100	81	0.81	1720	100	87	0.87

Table 6. Sampled evaluation of alignments found only by the Lexical technique

Segment	AAT-WordNet				AATNed-Cornetto			
	Segment Size	Sample Size	Correct Alignments	Sample precision	Segment Size	Sample Size	Correct Alignments	Sample precision
ChildMatch only	590	101	75	0.74	342	88	78	0.89
ParentMatch only	2485	120	55	0.46	1281	135	92	0.68
Child Match Parent Match overlap	236	44	37	0.84	106	47	43	0.91
Discarded ChildMatch only	3205	226	17	0.08	1140	161	19	0.12
Discarded ParentMatch only	7035	178	11	0.06	1667	147	9	0.06
Discarded ChildMatch ParentMatch overlap	1580	119	4	0.03	289	61	5	0.08
Remaining ambiguous alignments	20200	545	62	0.12	8023	306	59	0.19
Lexical only unambiguous al.	2116	100	65	0.65	569	100	74	0.74

false negatives in the discarded segments is low at between 3% and 8%. Looking at the remaining ambiguous alignments that were not disambiguated we have a precision of 0.12. This means from the 20200 ambiguous alignments an estimated 2650 alignments should be close- or exact-matches. The non-ambiguous alignments generated using alternative labels have a precision of 0.65. This is lower than for alignments with preferred labels, supporting the view that alternative labels yield worse alignments than preferred labels. We estimate the precision of all the alignments between AAT and WordNet without disambiguation at 0.17. Thus, only applying lexical alignment without disambiguation yields an unacceptably low precision.

6.2   Results for AATNed-Cornetto

The results of the evaluation displayed in Table 5 and Table 6 show that the overall precision of the techniques is higher for the Dutch than for the English language vocabularies. This is caused by the lower number of labels per concept in both AATNed and Cornetto resulting in fewer alignments per concept.

Similarly to the results of AAT-WordNet, half of the sample alignments generated only by the Baseline tool, (segment A) are incorrect. There were more

Table 7. Precision and coverage of combined alignment techniques

Segment	AAT-WordNet				AATNed-Cornetto			
	Alignm.	Concepts	Prec.	% AAT Concepts	Alignm.	Concepts	Prec.	% AATNed Concepts
1. Union morph. tools	4,592	4,592	0.82	16.4%	6,914	6,914	0.88	22.4%
2. non-amb. Lexical	2,116	2,116	0.65	7.6%	569	559	0.74	1.8%
3. Disambiguated alignments	3,311	2,665	0.53	9.5%	1,729	1,297	0.74	4.2%
1 + 2	6,708	6,695	0.70	23.9%	7,483	7,425	0.86	24.1%
1 + 2 +3	10019	9,208	0.69	32.9%	9,212	8,621	0.84	27.9%

alignments in this segment than in the AAT-WordNet and the evaluation revealed that 60% of these alignments were to Cornetto verbs. Some of the alignments are correct. The labels of processes in AATNED, for example, are often verbs. However, most others matches to verb targets are incorrect. For example, the concept "handwerken" (needle-works) is mapped incorrectly to the verb "handwerken" (needle-working). Again, just as for the AAT-WordNet, the alignments generated by the NN only (segment E) have relatively low precision at 0.48, although this is higher than the 0.36 for AAT-WordNet segment. Most of the erronous alignments are due to to concepts that describe styles and periods aligned to the nationality or language the style gets its name from. These concepts are related but are not the same (e.g. the "Pueblo" style and "pueblo (house)"). The overlap between SN and NN (segment F) has the highest precision, following the trend we have seen in AAT-WordNet.

Table 6 shows that the disambiguation techniques performed slightly better in Dutch than in English. Although difficult to analyze, this is possibly due to more similar hierarchies in the Dutch vocabularies than the English vocabularies. The overlap between the two techniques has the highest precision of 0.91 followed by the alignments found only by the Child Match technique at 0.89 and the Parent Match at 0.68. The number of false negatives ranges from 6% to 12%. The precision of the sample of the subset of 569 non-ambiguous alignments generated by the Lexical tool is 0.74. Finally, we estimated the precision of all alignments between AATNed and Cornetto at 0.46. This is significantly higher than in the AAT-WordNet case, caused by fewer alternative labels in the AATNed and the fewer labels per concept in Cornetto.

6.3   Results of Alignment Technique Combination

We now look at the precision of combined techniques for AAT-WordNet and AATNed-Cornetto. Table 7 displays the number of alignments, concepts, their precision and the percentage of all concepts they represent. The union of morphological tools combined with non-ambiguous Lexical alignments (of alternative labels) align 24% of AAT and AATNed concepts with precision of 0.7 and and 0.86 respectively. By further adding the disambiguated alignments from the

Lexical tool the coverage in terms of aligned concepts increases to 32.9% for the English case and 27.9% for the Dutch case although precision drops slightly to 0.69 and 0.84. However, this seems to be an acceptable trade-off for the boost in coverage.

7 Conclusion

We make the following three conclusions about the performance of the techniques.

1. The simple non-ambiguous morphological matching techniques work well with a high precision but low coverage.
2. The lexical matching technique using alternative labels improves coverage but reduces precision
3. Disambiguation of the lexical matches increases coverage keeping precision at an acceptable level.

Our key findings with respect to the characteristics of the vocabularies are: First, language does not seem to be a factor in the alignment results. All differences can be explained in terms of differences in the vocabulary characteristics such as the difference in the number of alternative labels.

Second, the selection of alignment techniques is mainly influenced by the characteristics of the vocabularies. For example, in this case the use of plural labels in AAT made it necessary to extract singular labels while this was not the case for AATNed nor in the previous case study where all labels where in singular form.

Finally, the number of aligned source concepts is influenced by the difference in domain of the vocabularies, the source vocabularies being specialist cultural heritage vocabularies and the target vocabularies covering a "common sense" domain.

We found that a combination of morphological and lexical alignment techniques with disambiguation works relatively well given the differences in vocabularies. For future work, using additional background knowledge for example about the partitioning of vocabularies with regard to part-of speeches is expected to further increase precision and coverage.

Acknowledgement. The datasets have been kindly provided by RKD and the Cornetto project. We thank Marieke van Erp for her contributions on the alignment evaluation. This research was supported by the MultimediaN project funded through the BSIK programme of the Dutch Government.

References

1. Aleksovski, Z., van Hage, W.R., Isaac, A.: A Survey and Categorization of Ontology-Matching Cases. In: Shvaiko, P., Euzenat, J., Giunchiglia, F., He, B. (eds.) Proceedings of the Workshop on Ontology Matching (OM 2007) at ISWC/ASWC 2007 (2007)

2. Caracciolo, C., Euzenat, J., Hollink, L., Ichise, R., Isaac, A., Malaisé, V., Meil-icke, C., Pane, J., Shvaiko, P., Stuckenschmidt, H., Sváb-Zamazal, O., Svátek, V.: Results of the Ontology Alignment Evaluation Initiative 2008. In: OM 2008 (2008)
3. Eckert, K., Meilicke, C., Stuckenschmidt, H.: Improving Ontology Matching Using Meta-Level Learning. In: Aroyo, L., Traverso, P., Ciravegna, F., Cimiano, P., Heath, T., Hyvönen, E., Mizoguchi, R., Oren, E., Sabou, M., Simperl, E. (eds.) ESWC 2009. LNCS, vol. 5554, pp. 158–172. Springer, Heidelberg (2009)
4. Euzenat, J., Ehrig, M., Jentzsch, A., Mochol, M., Shvaiko, P.: Case-Based Rec-ommendation of Matching Tools and Techniques. deliverable 1.2.2.2.1, Knowledge Web NoE, 2006 (2006)
5. Euzenat, J., Ferrara, A., Hollink, L., Isaac, A., Joslyn, C., Malaisé, V., Meilicke, C., Nikolov, A., Pane, J., Sabou, M., Scharffe, F., Shvaiko, P., Spiliopoulos, V., Stuckenschmidt, H., Sváb-Zamazal, O., Svátek, V., dos Santos, C.T., Vouros, G.A., Wang, S.: Results of the Ontology Alignment Evaluation Initiative. In: OM 2009 (2009)
6. Euzenat, J., Isaac, A., Meilicke, C., Shvaiko, P., Stuckenschmidt, H., Sváb, O., Svátek, V., van Hage, W.R., Yatskevich, M.: Results of the Ontology Alignment Evaluation Initiative 2007. In: OM 2007 (2007)
7. Euzenat, J., Shvaiko, P.: Ontology Matching. Springer, Heidelberg (2007)
8. Ghazvinian, A., Noy, N.F., Musen, M.A.: Creating Mappings for Ontologies in Biomedicine: Simple Methods Work. In: 2009 AMIA Annual Symposium (2009)
9. van Hage, W.R., Isaac, A., Aleksovski, Z.: Sample Evaluation of Ontology-Matching Systems. In: Proceedings of the ISWC workshop on Evaluation of On-tologies and Ontology-based tools, pp. 41–50 (2007)
10. Hu, W., Qu, Y.: Falcon-AO: A Practical Ontology Matching System. J. Web Se-mant. 6(3), 237–239 (2008)
11. Schreiber, G., Amin, A., Aroyo, L., van Assem, M., de Boer, V., Hardman, L., Hildebrand, M., Omelayenko, B., van Ossenbruggen, J., Tordai, A., Wielemaker, J., Wielinga, B.: Semantic Annotation and Search of Cultural-Heritage Collections: The Multimedian E-Culture Demonstrator. J. Web Semant. 6(4), 243–249 (2008)
12. Tordai, A., van Ossenbruggen, J., Schreiber, G.: Combining Vocabulary Alignment Techniques. In: K-CAP '09: Proceedings of the Fifth International Conference on Knowledge Capture, pp. 25–32 (2009)
13. Zhang, X., Zhong, Q., Li, J., Tang, J.: RiMOM Results for OAEI 2008. In: Shvaiko, P., Euzenat, J., Giunchiglia, F., Stuckenschmidt, H. (eds.) OM (2008)

OWL Reasoning with WebPIE:
Calculating the Closure of 100 Billion Triples

Jacopo Urbani, Spyros Kotoulas, Jason Maassen,
Frank van Harmelen, and Henri Bal

Department of Computer Science, Vrije Universiteit Amsterdam
{j.urbani,kot,j.maassen,frank.van.harmelen,he.bal}@few.vu.nl

Abstract. In previous work we have shown that the MapReduce framework for distributed computation can be deployed for highly scalable inference over RDF graphs under the RDF Schema semantics. Unfortunately, several key optimizations that enabled the scalable RDFS inference do not generalize to the richer OWL semantics. In this paper we analyze these problems, and we propose solutions to overcome them. Our solutions allow distributed computation of the closure of an RDF graph under the OWL Horst semantics.

We demonstrate the WebPIE inference engine, built on top of the Hadoop platform and deployed on a compute cluster of 64 machines. We have evaluated our approach using some real-world datasets (UniProt and LDSR, about 0.9-1.5 billion triples) and a synthetic benchmark (LUBM, up to 100 billion triples). Results show that our implementation is scalable and vastly outperforms current systems when comparing supported language expressivity, maximum data size and inference speed.

1 Introduction

In this paper, we address the problem of *massively scalable OWL reasoning* and present WebPIE (Web-scale Parallel Inference Engine). In [15] we already presented a scalable and distributed method for materializing the closure of an RDF graph, using the RDFS semantics. That method encoded RDFS inference using the MapReduce framework, which allowed execution on a compute cluster.

In this paper, we extend our approach to deal with the complexity of the OWL semantics. We chose the OWL Horst fragment [8] of OWL because it provides a complete set of entailment rules represented as *if-then* rules. Because the rules in this fragment are more complex than the RDFS entailment rules, our previous approach is no longer sufficient. For example, previously, we could exploit the fact that all rules require a join between one schema triple and one instance triple. This observation underlies several key papers in this area [6, 15, 16], and allowed replicating schema triples in the main memory of all the nodes and performing the required joins on the fly. In the OWL Horst fragment, however, there are some rules that do not respect this pattern. As a result, this crucial optimization is no longer applicable.

L. Aroyo et al. (Eds.): ESWC 2010, Part I, LNCS 6088, pp. 213–227, 2010.

Hence, the complexity of the OWL entailment rules required us to redesign our approach and to come up with novel optimizations that can deal with this higher complexity. In this paper we first recall the RDFS-specific optimizations (section 2), we then point out what are the major challenges for OWL reasoning and how our approach solves these problems (section 3). To evaluate our technique (section 4), we have implemented the WebPIE engine using Hadoop and performed experiments using both real-world and benchmark data. As real-world data, we have used the UniProt dataset[1], containing about 1.5 billion triples and the LDSR dataset[2] containing about 0.9 billion triples. As a benchmark, we have used the Lehigh University Benchmark (LUBM), for up to 100 billion triples. The obtained results show that our approach can scale to very large size, outperforming all published approaches, both in terms of triple throughput and maximum system size by at least an order of magnitude. To the best of our knowledge it is the only approach that demonstrates Semantic Web reasoning for an input in the order of 10^{11} triples.

2   Previous Work: RDFS Reasoning with MapReduce

To explain the use of MapReduce for reasoning, we first explain the basic idea of the framework, and then briefly recall the optimizations that we used to achieve efficient RDFS reasoning in our previous work, before turning to OWL Horst reasoning in section 3.

MapReduce is a programming model introduced by Google for large data processing [3]. The execution of a MapReduce program applies two user-specified functions, *map* and *reduce*, to the input data. The *map* function processes the input and outputs some intermediate key/value pairs. These pairs are partitioned according to the key and each partition is processed by a *reduce* function.

The closure of an RDF input graph can be computed by applying all rules iteratively on the input until no new data is derived (fixpoint). Single-antecedent rules can be easily implemented by iterating over the input and matching each triple individually. Applying rules is only challenging when there are multiple antecedents, since matching multiple antecedents means performing a join on the input triples, hence placing requirements on how to partition the data across compute nodes.

As an example, let us consider the rule from RDFS [5] which derives `rdf:type` based on the sub-class hierarchy:

$$s \text{ rdf:type } x, x \text{ rdfs:subClassOf } y \Rightarrow s \text{ rdf:type } y \qquad (1)$$

This rule effectively performs a join, which we can implement in MapReduce with a *map* and *reduce* function, as shown in Figure 1. In the *map* operation, we process each triple and output a key/value pair, using as value the original triple, and as key the triples term on which the join should be performed. In the case

---

[1] http://www.uniprot.org
[2] http://www.ontotext.com/ldsr/

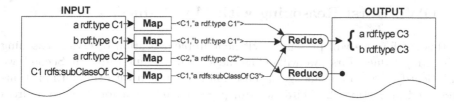

Fig. 1. Encoding the RDFS subclass-type rule in MapReduce

of the above rule, to perform the sub-class join, triples with `rdf:type` should be grouped on their object ("x" in the rule's first antecedent), while triples with `rdfs:subClassOf` should be grouped on their subject (the "x" in the rule's second antecedent). When all emitted tuples are grouped for the reduce phase, these two will group on "x" and the reducer will be able to perform the required join. To calculate the complete closure, the application of all rules should be iterated, until fixpoint.

This example illustrates some important elements of the MapReduce programming model:

- since the *map* operates on single pieces of data without dependencies, input partitions can be created arbitrarily and can be scheduled in parallel across many nodes.
- the *reduce* operates on an iterator of values because the set of values is typically far too large to fit in memory. This means that the reducer can only partially use correlations between these items while processing: it receives them as a stream instead of a set.
- the *reduce* operates on all pieces of data that share a key. By assigning proper keys to data items during the *map* phase, the data is partitioned for the *reduce* phase. A skewed partitioning (i.e. skewed key distribution) will lead to imbalances in the load of the compute nodes. If term x is relatively popular, the node performing the *reduce* for x will be slower than others. To use MapReduce efficiently, we must find balanced partitions of the data.

A naive implementation of such RDFS reasoning is straightforward, but is inefficient because it produces duplicate triples (several rules generate the same conclusions), suffers from poor load-balancing and requires fixpoint iteration. In [15], we introduced three optimizations that vastly improved performance:

Loading schema triples in memory. Typically, schema triples are far less numerous than instance triples. Furthermore, RDFS rules have at most one antecedent that is not a schema triple, so that no joins are required between instance triples. This allowed us to load the schema triples in the memory of each node and stream the instance triples, which improved load balancing.

Data preprocessing to avoid duplicates. We have devised a way to partition triples in a manner that dramatically reduced duplicate derivations.

Ordering the application of the RDFS rules. We have analyzed the RDFS ruleset and devised a rule ordering that removed the need to apply each rule more than once (no fixpoint iteration).

3   OWL Horst Reasoning with MapReduce

In this section, we will present an efficient implementation of OWL reasoning using MapReduce. First, we will define the logic we are interested in. Second, we will identify the main challenges it poses, in comparison with the optimizations presented in Section 2. Third, we will present efficient algorithms to address these challenges.

3.1   OWL Horst Fragment

In this paper, we consider the Horst fragment of OWL [8]. The reasons for this choice are: (a) it is a *de facto* standard for scalable OWL reasoning, implemented by industrial strength triple stores such as OWLIM; (b) it can be expressed by a set of rules; and (c) it strikes a balance between the computationally unfeasible OWL full and the limited expressiveness of RDFS. The OWL Horst ruleset (formally known as pD) consists of the RDFS rules[5] (defined as D) and the rules shown in table 1 (defined as p). Our method performs forward inference. However, we should note:

- Similar to [15], we omit some rules with one antecedent (rules 5a,5b) as these can be parallelized efficiently and are commonly ignored by reasoners as yielding consequences that can also be easily simulated at query-time.
- We do not directly materialize inferences based on owl:sameAs triples. Instead, we construct a table of all sets of resources connected by owl:sameAs relationships (rules 6, 7, 9, 10 and 11 from Table 1). In other words, we represent the equivalence classes under owl:sameAs. Again, this is common practice in industrial strength triple stores. Note that this does not change the computational complexity of the task, since the owl:sameAs relationships are still calculated. The sameAs-table simply provides a more compact representation, reducing the amount of intermediate data that need to be processed and the size of the output.

3.2   Challenges in OWL Reasoning

The OWL Horst rules in Table 1 show that the techniques presented in Section 2 are not always applicable. Here, we present some of the challenges for OWL reasoning.

No rule ordering. For D, there is a rule execution order that allows us to compute the closure by executing each rule only once, in most cases. In the Horst fragment, there is no such ordering. Hence we must repeatedly apply rules until no new triples are derived (fixpoint iteration is required);

Joins between multiple instance triples. In D, at most one antecedent can be matched by instance triples. In p, rules 1, 2, 4, 7, 11, 15 and 16 contain two antecedents that can be matched by instance triples. Thus, loading one side of the join in memory (the schema triples) and processing instance

Table 1. p ruleset

1: p rdf:type owl:FunctionalProperty, $u\ p\ v$, $u\ p\ w$ $\Rightarrow$ v owl:sameAs w

2: p rdf:type owl:InverseFunctionalProperty, $v\ p\ u,\ w\ p\ u$ $\Rightarrow$ v owl:sameAs w

3: p rdf:type owl:SymmetricProperty, $v\ p\ u$ $\Rightarrow$ $u\ p\ v$

4: p rdf:type owl:TransitiveProperty, $u\ p\ w,\ w\ p\ v$ $\Rightarrow$ $u\ p\ v$

5a: $u\ p\ v$ $\Rightarrow$ u owl:sameAs u

5b: $u\ p\ v$ $\Rightarrow$ v owl:sameAs v

6: v owl:sameAs w $\Rightarrow$ w owl:sameAs v

7: v owl:sameAs $w,\ w$ owl:sameAs u $\Rightarrow$ v owl:sameAs u

8a: p owl:inverseOf $q,\ v\ p\ w$ $\Rightarrow$ $w\ q\ v$

8b: p owl:inverseOf $q,\ v\ q\ w$ $\Rightarrow$ $w\ p\ v$

9: v rdf:type owl:Class, v owl:sameAs w $\Rightarrow$ v rdfs:subClassOf w

10: p rdf:type owl:Property, p owl:sameAs q $\Rightarrow$ p rdfs:subPropertyOf q

11: $u\ p\ v,\ u$ owl:sameAs $x,\ v$ owl:sameAs y $\Rightarrow$ $x\ p\ y$

12a: v owl:equivalentClass w $\Rightarrow$ v rdfs:subClassOf w

12b: v owl:equivalentClass w $\Rightarrow$ w rdfs:subClassOf v

12c: v rdfs:subClassOf $w,\ w$ rdfs:subClassOf v $\Rightarrow$ v rdfs:equivalentClass w

13a: v owl:equivalentProperty w $\Rightarrow$ v rdfs:subPropertyOf w

13b: v owl:equivalentProperty w $\Rightarrow$ w rdfs:subPropertyOf v

13c: v rdfs:subPropertyOf $w,\ w$ rdfs:subPropertyOf v $\Rightarrow$ v rdfs:equivalentProperty w

14a: v owl:hasValue $w,\ v$ owl:onProperty $p,\ u\ p\ v$ $\Rightarrow$ u rdf:type v

14b: v owl:hasValue $w,\ v$ owl:onProperty $p,\ u$ rdf:type v $\Rightarrow$ $u\ p\ v$

15: v owl:someValuesFrom $w,\ v$ owl:onProperty $p,$ $\Rightarrow$ u rdf:type v
$\quad u\ p\ x,\ x$ rdf:type w

16: v owl:allValuesFrom $u,\ v$ owl:onProperty $p,$ $\Rightarrow$ x rdf:type u
$\quad w$ rdf:type $v,\ w\ p\ x$

triples in a streaming fashion no longer works because instance triples greatly outnumber instance triples and the main memory of a compute node is not large enough to load the instance triples.

Duplicate derivations. The two challenges above contribute to a third challenge, namely generation of duplicates. First, since there is no rule ordering that can prevent fixpoint iteration, rules will be applied repeatedly and derive the same conclusions.

Multiple joins per rule. In D, all the rules require at most one join between two antecedents. In p, rules 11, 15 and 16 require two joins.

In the next sections, we will describe how we overcome these challenges.

3.3 Overall Structure

Our approach tackles the above challenges interleaving the application of the D rules and the p rules. Algorithm 1 summarizes the control flow of our algorithm. For D, we use the methods from [15], which will not be discussed. In this paper, we will deal with the p rules, for which fixpoint iteration is required.

On a rare occasion (when there are subproperties of *rdfs:subPropertyOf*), the implementation in [15] does not produce the full closure for D without fixpoint iteration. To prevent this, the overall algorithm will stop when the application of the D rules does not produce any new triple so that no derivation is left out.

Algorithm 1. RDFS/OWL reasoner: main control flow

```
calculate_closure(data):
  boolean first_time=true;
  while (true) {
    derived=apply_rules(data, D); // Apply D rules once
    if (derived == null && first_time == false)
      return data; // D derived nothing, return
    data= data + derived;

    do { // Do fixpoint iteration for p rules
      derived=apply_rules(data, p);
      data= data + derived; }
    while (derived != null);

    first_time=false; }
```

If we take a closer look at the rules of the p fragment, we notice that some rules can be implemented exploiting the optimizations introduced for the RDFS reasoning. These are the rules $3,8a,8b,12a,12b,12c,13a,13b,13c,14a,14b$.

Furthermore, rules 1 and 2 require a join on subject and predicate or predicate and object for two instance triples and a join on predicate with a schema triple. We found that these rules were straightforward to implement by partitioning on subject and predicate or predicate and object while the others can be efficiently implemented exploiting the RDFS optimizations. Thus, we will exclude these rules from further discussion.

All other rules from p are indeed challenging and require detailed explanation: Section 3.4 deals with rule 4, Section 3.5 deals with rules 6, 7, 9, 10, 11 and Section 3.6 deals with rules 15 and 16.

3.4   Transitivity Algorithm

Rule 4 of the Horst fragment requires a three-way join between one schema triple and two instance triples. It seems similar to rules 1 and 2, suggesting that it can be implemented by partitioning triples according to (pw) (i.e. partition triples according to subject-predicate and predicate-object) and performing the join in-memory, together with the schema triple. Nevertheless, there is a critical difference with rules 1 and 2: the descendant is likely to be used as an antecedent (i.e. we have chains of resources connected through a transitive relationship). Thus, this rule must be applied iteratively.

Applying rule 4 as above will lead to a large number of duplicates, because every time the rule is applied, the same relationships will be inferred. For a transitive property chain of length n, a naive implementation will generate $O(n^3)$ copies while the maximum output only contains $O(n^2)$ unique pairs.

We can solve this problem if we constrain how triples are allowed to be combined. At the nth iteration of the algorithm we would like not to derive triples which have a graph distance less or equal than 2^{n-2} because these were already derived in the previous execution. We also would like to derive the new triples only once and not by different combinations. The conditions to assure this are:

Algorithm 2. owl:transitivity closure (p rule 4)

```
map(key, triple, n):
 //key: distance of the triple
 //triple: triple in input
 //n: current step

 if (key.step = 2^(n - 2) || key.step = 2^(n -1)) then
  emit({triple.predicate, triple.object}, {flag=L, key.step, triple.subject});
 if (key.step > 2^(n-2) then
  emit({triple.predicate, triple.subject}, {flag=R, key.step, triple.object});

 reduce(key, iterator values):
  for(value in values) do
   if (value.flag = 'L')
     leftSide.add({key.step, value.subject})
   else
     rightSide.add({key.step, value.object})
  for(leftElement in leftSide)
   for(rightElement in rightSide)
    newKey.step = leftElement.step + rightElement.step //distance new triple
    emit(newKey,triple(leftElement.subject, key.predicate, rightElement.object));
```

- on the left side of the join (triples which have the key as object) we allow only triples with distance 2^{n-1} and distance 2^{n-2};
- on the right side of the join (triples which have the key as subject) we allow only triples with the distance greater than 2^{n-2}.

The complete picture is shown in Algorithm 2. The map function filters out all the triples that do not have a transitive predicate by checking the input with the in-memory schema and it selects the triples which suit the possible join by checking their distance value. The reduce function simply loads the two sets in memory and returns new triples with distances corresponding to the sums of the combinations of distances in the input. In the ideal case, this algorithm completely avoids duplicates. Nevertheless, when there are different chains that intersect, it will produce duplicate derivations, but much fewer than without this optimization.

3.5   SameAs Algorithm

Rules 7 and 11 from p are problematic because they involve a two-way and a three-way join between instance triples. Similarly to before, since the join is on the instance data, we cannot load one side in memory but instead we are obliged to perform the join by partitioning the input based on the part of the antecedents involved in the join.

However, in this case, this approach would cause severe load balancing problems. For example, rule 11 involves joins on the subject or the object of an antecedent with no bound variables. As a result, the data will need to be partitioned on subject or object, which follow a very uneven distribution. This will obviously lead to serious load balancing issues, since a single machine will be called to process a large portion of the triples in the system (e.g. consider the number of triples with foaf:person as object).

To avoid these issues, we first apply the logic of rule 7 to find all the groups of synonyms (e.g. resources connected by the owl:sameAs relation) that are present in the datasets and we assign a unique key to each of these groups. In other words, we calculate all non-singleton equivalence classes under owl:sameAs. We store the pairs (resource, group_key) in a table that we call the sameAs-table. Subsequently, we replace in our input all the occurrences of the resources in the sameAs-table with their corresponding group key. In other words, we use a single canonical representation for each equivalence class.

This procedure, which is common practice in existing reasoners, does not explicitly materialize all the derivations by rule 11, but instead produces a more compact representation of these results. This procedure brings as additional advantages that it reduces the complexity of a three-way join of rule 11 to a two-way join applied during the operation of replacement; and it makes the execution of the p rules 6, 9 and 10 trivial and redundant to implement.

We will now describe building the sameAs-table and replacing all items by their canonical representation.

Building the sameAs-table. Our purpose is to calculate all the groups of resources that are connected with the owl:sameAs relation. The graph with owl:sameAs relationships is undirected, since owl:sameAs is symmetric. We turn this into a directed acyclical graph by assigning all nodes id, and having edges point to the node with higher id. The node with the lowest id in a group will be the canonical representation for all nodes that are reachable from it. We now want to efficiently calculate all nodes reachable from the canonical node.

To this end, we have developed a MapReduce algorithm. The intuition behind this algorithm is that edges that create a shorter path to the canonical representation should be created incrementally and in parallel and edges that are no longer needed should be removed. Eventually, all edges will originate from the canonical representation. Algorithm 3 shows this process: the graph is partitioned across nodes and the outgoing edges of a node are replaced by the incoming edge from the node with the lowest id, if such a node exists. This process is repeated until no edges can be replaced.

Replacing resources with their canonical representation. Since our purpose is to replace in the original dataset the resources in the sameAs-table with their canonical representation, we must perform a join between the input data and the information contained in the table. In principle, the join is executed by partitioning the dataset on the single term. Since the term distribution is very uneven, we suffer from a severe load balancing problem. We circumvent this problem by sampling the dataset to discover the most popular terms, and loading their eventual replacements in the memory of all nodes. (In our implementation, we typically sample a random subset of 7% of the dataset). When the nodes read the data in the input, they check whether the resource is already cached in memory. If it is, the nodes replace it on-the-fly and send the outcome to a random reduce task flagging it to be output immediately. For non-popular

---

Algorithm 3. owl:sameas reasoning (*p* rule 7)

```
map(key, edge): //key: irrelevant
  //Partition graph across nodes
  emit(edge.from, {forward, edge.to});
  emit(edge.to, {backward, edge.from});

reduce(key, values):
  //key:
  // value: the nodes of the edge
  toNodes.empty(); // edges to other nodes
  fromNodes.empty(); // edges from other nodes
  fromNodes.add(key);
  for (value in values) // collect all incoming and outgoing edges to node
    if (value.forward) toNodes.add(value);
    else if (value.backward) fromNodes.add(value);
  for (to in toNodes)
    emit(null, {fromNodes.minValue(), to});
```

---

terms, the standard partitioning technique is used to perform the join, but since these terms are not popular, the partitioning will not cause load balancing issues.

Note that this approach is applicable to datasets with any popularity distribution: If we have a large proportion of terms that are significantly more popular than the rest, they will be spread to a large number of nodes, dissipating the load balancing issue. If there is a small proportion of popular terms, there will be enough memory to store the mappings.

3.6   someValuesFrom and allValuesFrom Algorithm

Rules 15 and 16 present the following challenges: (a) they contain two joins, for v and for w. (b) one join is between antecedents that match many triples ((u p x) matches all triples, (x rdf:type w) matches a large subset). In this section, we will focus on rule 15. The algorithm for rule 16 is entirely analogous.

As with all schema triples, triples of the form (v owl:someValuesFrom w) and (v owl:onProperty p) are few and can be loaded into memory. The join between the schema triples can be done in the nodes' memory using the standard techniques. The join between the instance triples (u p x) and (x rdf:type w) is the most challenging part: since these triples are too many to fit in the memory of a single machine, they will need to be partitioned.

To overcome memory limitations, these partitions should be small. Our initial implementation has filtered the instance triples which match against the two schema triples. Then, it partitioned them according to x. Since x is a single resource, one partition may contain many elements. Thus, the available memory of each node was not always sufficient to store the partition and perform the join in-memory. Consequently, this method was abandoned.

To reduce the size of the partitions, we have developed Algorithm 4. It aims at reducing the size of the partitions by performing the joins with the schema triples as soon as possible. We first perform the join between the two schema triples ((v owl:someValuesFrom w) ⋈ (v owl:onProperty p)). Then, *before we partition*, we perform the join between the above and either (u p x) or (x rdf:type

---

Algorithm 4. owl:someValuesFrom reasoning (p rule 15)

```
map(key, triple): //key: irrelevant
   joinSchema = join on the subject between someValuesFrom and onProperties triples
   if (triple.predicate == "rdf:type")
     if (triple.object in joinSchema.someValuesFromObjects)
        entries = joinSchema.getJoinEntries(triple.object)
        for (entry in entries)
          emit({entry.p,triple.subject}, {type=typetriple, resource=entry.
                onPropertySubject});
   else if (triple.predicate in joinSchema.onPropertiesSet)
     emit({triple.predicate,triple.object}, {type=generictriple, resource=triple.subject});

reduce(key, iterator values):
   // key: partition (p,x)
   // values: parts of the instance triples used for the derivation
   types.clear(); generic.clear();
   for (value in values)
     if (value.type = typetriple) types.add(value.resource)
     else generic.add(value.resource)
   for (v in types)
     for (u in generic)
       emit(null, triple(u, "rdf:type", v));
```

---

w), calculating (v owl:someValuesFrom w) ⋈ (v owl:onProperty p) ⋈ (u p x) and (x rdf:type w) ⋈ (v owl:someValuesFrom w) ⋈ (v owl:onProperty p). Now, in both cases, we have all possible bindings for x and p. Thus, we can partition on (xp) and perform the join during the reduce phase. Since partitioning is now done on two variables, each partition is much smaller. The pseudo code is shown in Algorithm 4.

4 Evaluation

We have used the Hadoop framework[3], an open-source Java implementation of MapReduce, to implement and test the algorithms explained in the previous sections[4]. Hadoop uses a distributed file system that uses the local disks of the participating machines, and manages execution details such as data transfer, job scheduling, and error management.

Our implementation was validated against the OWLIM reasoner[5]. It should be noted that our results do not completely coincide with those of OWLIM, since the latter offers limited support of owl:intersectionOf and owl:unionOf, which is not part of the Horst semantics.

We have performed the experiments on the Vrije Universiteit cluster of the DAS-3 distributed supercomputer[6] using up to 64 compute nodes. Nodes were equipped with two dual-core 2.4GHz Opteron processors, 4GB of main memory, 250GB hard disk and a Gigabit Ethernet interconnect.

---

[3] http://hadoop.apache.org
[4] Our open source code is available at https://launchpad.net/reasoning-hadoop
[5] http://www.ontotext.com/owlim/
[6] http://www.cs.vu.nl/das3/

4.1 Datasets

The evaluation was performed using three datasets: *UniProt* is one of the largest (1.51 billion unique triples) curated sets of real-world OWL statements available to date, and has been used before to stress-test the performance of OWL reasoners. *LDSR* includes DBPedia, Freebase, Geonames and other datasets representing general knowledge and consists of 0.9 billion triples. *LUBM* is a widely used benchmark that can generate semi-realistic datasets of arbitrary size. We have chosen to use LUBM because: (a) it is widely used for reasoner evaluation, allowing comparison of our results with existing approaches; (b) there exists no real-world dataset of the size we want to test (up to 100 billion triples); (c) reasoning over arbitrary triples retrieved from the Web would result in useless and unrealistic derivations [7]. All datasets do indeed use the OWL Horst fragment.

4.2 Experimental Results

Performance on real world data: For UniProt, our system derived 2.03 billion triples, as well as a synonyms table for `owl:sameAs` relationships, consisting of equality statements between 35 million entries. The entire process took 6.1 hours on 32 nodes. For LDSR, our system derived 0.94 billion triples in 3.52 hours. Figure 2a shows the sequence of the launched MapReduce jobs for UniProt along with the time spent for each of them. The analysis shows that the computation is dominated by the costs of the equality reasoning, in particular, the costs of replacing all RDF resources by the canonical members of the `sameAs`-equivalence classes. When no `owl:sameAs` statements are present (as in the LUBM case, figure 2b), the costs are more evenly spread across the different phases. A future challenge is to reduce the cost of the equality-reasoning, either by smarter algorithms or by further parallelization of this phase.

Scalability: Table 3a shows how our approach scales with an increasing number of compute nodes, using 10 billion triples generated by LUBM as a fixed input. We define speedup as $\frac{runtime\ for\ baseline}{runtime}$. We use the time on the 8-node configuration as baseline, because in DAS3 a single node does not have enough resources (disk space) to store all the data. Table 3b shows how our approach scales with increasing input size, using a fixed configuration of 64 nodes.

We make the following observations:

- The throughput is significantly (almost 30%) higher for larger datasets. This is attributed to platform startup overhead which is amortized over a larger processing time for large datasets. The platform overhead is also responsible for the superlinear speedup in table 3a. Since the overhead becomes more relevant with fewer nodes, the calculated speedup will be higher than the real one.
- The execution time greatly depends on the complexity of the input: on UniProt and LDSR, we achieve a throughput of 68.3 Ktriples/sec and 74.9 Ktriples/sec respectively, while the throughput on the much simpler LUBM dataset is around 10 times higher (table 3b). If the input is more

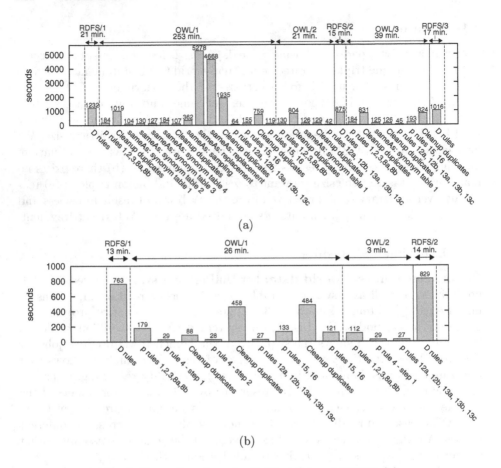

Fig. 2. Execution steps for UniProt (a) and LUBM (b)

Nodes	Runtime (hours)	Speedup		Input (GTriples)	Output (MTriples)	Runtime (hours)	Throughput (Kt/sec)
8	44.4	1.00		1.07	495.5	0.61	455.2
16	22.3	1.99		10.71	4971.7	4.06	684.6
32	10.6	4.17		102.50	47563.1	45.77	606.8
64	5.0	8.78					
	(a)				(b)		

Fig. 3. Scalability over the number of nodes (left) and over input data (right)

complex, the algorithm needs to launch more iterations to reach fixpoint (as shown in Figure 2).
– Considering the effects of the platform overhead, we conclude that the results show linear scalability regarding the size of the input and number of nodes. Currently, the only way to test this is by using the LUBM benchmark data.

We have no evidence on how the algorithm behaves with a real world dataset of 100 billion triples, since such dataset currently does not exist.

5   Related Work

Hogan *et al.* [6] compute the closure of an RDF graph using two passes over the data on a single machine. They implement only a fragment of the OWL Horst semantics to allow efficient materialization and to prevent "ontology hijacking".

Schlicht and Stuckenschmidt [13] show peer-to-peer reasoning for the expressive ALC logic but focusing on distribution rather than performance.

Soma and Prasanna [14] present a technique for parallel OWL inferencing through data partitioning. Experimental results show good speedup but only on very small datasets (1M triples) and runtime is not reported. In contrast, our approach needs no explicit partitioning phase and we show that it is scalable over increasing dataset size.

In [10, 12], we have presented a technique based on data-partitioning in a peer-to-peer network. A load-balanced auto-partitioning approach was used without upfront partitioning cost. Experimental results were however only reported for datasets of up to 200M triples.

In Weaver and Hendler [16], straightforward parallel RDFS reasoning on a cluster is presented. This approach replicates all schema triples to all processing nodes and distributes instance triples randomly. Each node calculates the closure of its partition using a conventional reasoner and the results are merged. To ensure that there are no dependencies between partitions, triples extending the RDFS schema are ignored. This approach is not extensible to richer logics, or complete RDFS reasoning, since, in these cases, splitting the input to independent partitions is impossible.

Newman *et al.* [11] decompose and merge RDF molecules using MapReduce and Hadoop. They perform SPARQL queries on the data but performance is reported over a dataset of limited size (70,000 triples).

Several proposed techniques are based on deterministic rendezvous-peers on top of distributed hashtables [1, 2, 4, 9]. However, because of load-balancing problems due to the data distributions, these approaches do not scale [10].

Some Semantic Web stores support reasoning and scale to tens of billions of triples[7]. We have shown inference on a triple set which is one order of magnitude *larger* then reported anywhere (100 billion triples against 12 billion triples). Furthermore, our inference is 60 times *faster* (10 billion triples in 4 hours against 12 billion triples in 290 hours for LUBM) against the best performing reasoner (BigOWLIM). For UniProt, BigOWLIM 3.1 needs 21 hours to perform forward reasoning on 1.15 billion triples[8] (yielding a throughput of 15.2 Ktriples/sec) while our system needs only 6 hours for 1.5 billion triples (yielding a throughput of 68.3 Ktriples/sec). It should be noted that the comparison of our system with RDF stores is not always meaningful, as our system does not support querying.

---

[7] http://esw.w3.org/topic/LargeTripleStores
[8] D5.5.2 at http://www.larkc.eu/deliverables

6   Conclusion

Summary. In this paper, we have shown a massively scalable technique for parallel OWL Horst forward inference and demonstrated inference over 100 billion triples. Both in terms of processing throughput and maximum data size, our technique outperforms published approaches by a large margin.

Discussion of scope. The computational worst-case complexity of even the OWL Horst fragment precludes a solution that is efficient on all inputs. Any approach to efficient reasoning must make assumptions about the properties of realistic datasets, and optimize for those realistic cases. Some of the key assumptions behind our algorithms are: (a) The schema must be small enough to fit in main memory; (b) for rules with multiple joins, some of the joins must be performed in-memory, which could cause memory problems for some unrealistic datasets or for machines with very limited memory; (c) we assume that there is no ontology hijacking [7]; and (d) all the input is available locally in the distributed filesystem. The difference in performance on UniProt and LUBM shows that the complexity of the input data strongly affects performance Although it is easy to create artificial data which break the performance, we did not observe such cases in realistic data. In fact, the above assumptions (a)-(d) could also serve as guidelines in the design of ontologies and datasets, to ensure that they can be used effectively.

Future challenges. The technique presented is optimized for the OWL-Horst rules. Future work lies in reasoning over user-supplied rulesets, where the system would chose the correct implementation for each rule and the most efficient execution order, depending on the input.

Furthermore, as with all scalable triple stores, our approach cannot efficiently deal with distributed data. Future work should extend our technique to deal with data streamed from remote locations.

In fact, we believe that this paper establishes that computing the closure of a very large centrally available dataset is no longer an important bottleneck, and that research efforts should switch to other modes of reasoning. Query-driven backward-chaining inference over distributed datasets might turn out to be more promising than exhaustive forward inference over centralized stores.

References

[1] Battré, D., Höing, A., Heine, F., Kao, O.: On triple dissemination, forward-chaining, and load balancing in DHT based RDF stores. In: Moro, G., Bergamaschi, S., Joseph, S., Morin, J.-H., Ouksel, A.M. (eds.) DBISP2P 2005 and DBISP2P 2006. LNCS, vol. 4125, pp. 343–354. Springer, Heidelberg (2007)

[2] Cai, M., Frank, M.: RDFPeers: A scalable distributed RDF repository based on a structured peer-to-peer network. In: Proc. of the WWW 2004(2004)

[3] Dean, J., Ghemawat, S.: Mapreduce: Simplified data processing on large clusters. In: Proceedings of USENIX OSDI, pp. 137–147 (2004)

[4] Fang, Q., Zhao, Y., Yang, G., Zheng, W.: Scalable distributed ontology reasoning using DHT-based partitioning. In: Domingue, J., Anutariya, C. (eds.) ASWC 2008. LNCS, vol. 5367, pp. 91–105. Springer, Heidelberg (2008)

[5] Hayes, P. (ed.): RDF Semantics. W3C Recommendation (2004)

[6] Hogan, A., Harth, A., Polleres, A.: Scalable authoritative OWL reasoning for the web. International Journal on Semantic Web and Information Systems 5(2) (2009)

[7] Hogan, A., Polleres, A., Harth, A.: SAOR: Authoritative reasoning for the web. In: Domingue, J., Anutariya, C. (eds.) ASWC 2008. LNCS, vol. 5367, pp. 76–90. Springer, Heidelberg (2008)

[8] ter Horst, H.J.: Completeness, decidability and complexity of entailment for RDF schema and a semantic extension involving the OWL vocabulary. Journal of Web Semantics 3(2-3), 79–115 (2005)

[9] Kaoudi, Z., Miliaraki, I., Koubarakis, M.: RDFS reasoning and query answering on top of DHTs. In: Sheth, A.P., Staab, S., Dean, M., Paolucci, M., Maynard, D., Finin, T., Thirunarayan, K. (eds.) ISWC 2008. LNCS, vol. 5318, pp. 499–516. Springer, Heidelberg (2008)

[10] Kotoulas, S., Oren, E., van Harmelen, F.: Mind the data skew: Distributed inferencing by speeddating in elastic regions. In: Proc. of the WWW 2010 (2010)

[11] Newman, A., Li, Y., Hunter, J.: Scalable semantics the silver lining of cloud computing. In: Proceedings of the 4th IEEE International Conference on eScience (2008)

[12] Oren, E., Kotoulas, S., Anadiotis, G., et al.: MARVIN: distributed reasoning over large-scale Semantic Web data. Journal of Web Semantics (2009)

[13] Schlicht, A., Stuckenschmidt, H.: Peer-to-peer reasoning for interlinked ontologies. To appear in the International Journal of Semantic Computing, Special Issue on Web Scale Reasoning (2010)

[14] Soma, R., Prasanna, V.: Parallel inferencing for OWL knowledge bases. In: International Conference on Parallel Processing, pp. 75–82 (2008)

[15] Urbani, J., Kotoulas, S., Oren, E., van Harmelen, F.: Scalable distributed reasoning using mapReduce. In: Bernstein, A., Karger, D.R., Heath, T., Feigenbaum, L., Maynard, D., Motta, E., Thirunarayan, K. (eds.) ISWC 2009. LNCS, vol. 5823, pp. 634–649. Springer, Heidelberg (2009)

[16] Weaver, J., Hendler, J.: Parallel materialization of the finite RDFS closure for hundreds of millions of triples. In: Bernstein, A., Karger, D.R., Heath, T., Feigenbaum, L., Maynard, D., Motta, E., Thirunarayan, K. (eds.) ISWC 2009. LNCS, vol. 5823, pp. 682–697. Springer, Heidelberg (2009)

Efficiently Joining Group Patterns in SPARQL Queries

María-Esther Vidal[1], Edna Ruckhaus[1], Tomas Lampo[1], Amadís Martínez[1,2],
Javier Sierra[1], and Axel Polleres[3]

[1] Universidad Simón Bolívar, Caracas, Venezuela
{mvidal,ruckhaus,tomas,amadis,javier}@ldc.usb.ve
[2] Universidad de Carabobo, Venezuela
aamartin@uc.edu.ve
[3] Digital Enterprise Research Institute
National University of Ireland, Galway, Ireland
axel.polleres@deri.org

Abstract. In SPARQL, conjunctive queries are expressed by using shared variables across sets of triple patterns, also called basic graph patterns. Based on this characterization, basic graph patterns in a SPARQL query can be partitioned into groups of acyclic patterns that share exactly one variable, or *star-shaped* groups. We observe that the number of triples in a group is proportional to the number of individuals that play the role of the subject or the object; however, depending on the degree of participation of the subject individuals in the properties, a group could be not much larger than a class or type to which the subject or object belongs. Thus, it may be significantly more efficient to independently evaluate each of the groups, and then merge the resulting sets, than linearly joining all triples in a basic graph pattern. Based on this observation, we have developed query optimization and evaluation techniques on *star-shaped* groups. We have conducted an empirical analysis on the benefits of the optimization and evaluation techniques in several SPARQL query engines. We observe that our proposed techniques are able to speed up query evaluation time for join queries with star-shaped patterns by at least one order of magnitude.

1 Introduction

In the context of RDF documents and SPARQL [1] queries, variables in (a combination of) basic graph patterns may be interpreted as either subjects characterized by a property, object values of a property, or properties that relate a subject and an object. These basic graph patterns in a query can be partitioned and reordered into groups of pattern combinations according to exactly one common variable, which we call *star-shaped* groups; the combinations may be over subjects, objects or mixed subjects and objects. For example, subject star-shaped groups of triple patterns around the same variable, commonly occur in complex SPARQL queries, where such groups around the same subject variable, typically describe a "class" of individuals to be queried: that is, a subject *star-shaped* group may be viewed as all the combinations of object values of the properties that characterize the individuals that belong to this "class"[1]. Thus, the

---

[1] We quote "class" to indicate that we are not talking about classes in the sense of OWL or RDFS, but rather groups of individuals characterized by common properties.

L. Aroyo et al. (Eds.): ESWC 2010, Part I, LNCS 6088, pp. 228–242, 2010.
© Springer-Verlag Berlin Heidelberg 2010

number of triples in the group is proportional to the number of individuals in the subject; however, depending on the degree of participation of the subject individuals in the properties, the group may be not much larger than this subject "class". In the common case where *star-shaped* groups denote instances of data such that the combined properties imply quasi functional dependencies, the group may be significantly smaller than any of the participating properties taken on its own. Similar properties hold for object and subject-object *star-shaped* groups. Therefore, it is often beneficial to evaluate such groups jointly.

In this work, we have developed a query optimization technique that provides the basis for an efficient evaluation of common SPARQL queries that can be rewritten as combinations of small *star-shaped* groups. In order to identify an optimal plan for a query, a randomized cost-based optimizer partitions the basic graph patterns that appear in the 'WHERE' clause of a query into small-sized *star-shaped* groups, and also explores different orderings within groups and between groups. We focus in this paper on conjunctive queries, i.e., queries consisting of a single basic graph pattern (BGP) [1, Section 5.1]. However, since BGPs are the basic building block for any other, more complex patterns, such as OPTIONAL, UNION, FILTER, and GRAPH patterns, obviously our method also proves valuable for efficiently evaluating subpatterns within more complex queries. In addition, to efficiently evaluate SPARQL queries, we have developed two different physical join operators for the SPARQL query language that support the evaluation of combinations of such groups: we propose the *njoin* and the *gjoin* operators. The njoin scans the triples of the first pattern, and loops on the second pattern for matching triples. The gjoin evaluates star-shaped groups and matches their results. We have implemented the gjoin operator in the Jena query engine, and have empirically studied the performance of the optimized queries in several RDF query engines: our own system OneQL[2], Jena [3], RDF-3X [4], Sesame [5] and GiaBATA [6]. We have observed that our techniques are able to speed up the query evaluation time – especially for queries where common star-shaped patterns can be found – by several orders of magnitude.

To summarize, the main contributions of this paper are the following:

- We define and have implemented different physical operators for combining patterns: (1) a naive operator njoin, that for each triple that satisfies the first pattern, loops on the second pattern for matching triples, and (2) a gjoin operator which evaluates the *star-shaped* groups jointly, and matches their results.
- We define sampling techniques to estimate the result size and cost of star-shaped group patterns, the size of each property, and the selectivity of their subjects and objects, which help us to identify the most promising star-shaped groups.
- Based on the sampled values, we establish cost metrics that reflect the number of RDF triples that need to be read in order to answer the query. Out cost model extends the model presented in [2], to estimate the evaluation cost and cardinality of the *star-shaped* group physical operator.
- We describe a randomized optimization strategy that identifies a cost-effective plan (wrt. our metrics) and it is based on the Simulated Annealing algorithm. The algorithm explores execution plans of any shape (bushy trees) in contrast with other optimization algorithms that explore a smaller portion, e.g., left-linear plans only.

Bushy trees need to be explored, as query plans of any shape may be generated when combining star-shaped groups.
- In our evaluation we provide an empirical analysis on the predictive capability of our cost model, and the benefits of the proposed evaluation techniques on different RDF query engines.

The remainder of the paper is structured as follows. We start with a motivating example in the following section. Our query evaluation engine along with its underlying cost model and the query optimization strategy are presented in section 3. An extensive experimental study is reported in section 4, and section 5 summarizes the related work. Finally, we conclude in section 6 with an outlook to future work.

2 Motivating Example

As a running example throughout this paper we consider an RDF dataset on US Congress vote results, published as RDF at the *http://www.govtrack.us* website[2]. This dataset registers individuals and property values related to the US bills voting process grouped per year. E.g., for each of the 216 bills voted in 2004, it registers its title, date, voting options and winners; each voter and vote are also registered (there are 100 voters for each election). Table 1 reports the number of triples, and the number of different values for the subject and the object of some of the properties in the 2004 dataset.

Table 1. Cardinality and number of values govtrack.us 2004

property	# triples	# subject values	# object values
voter	21,600	21,600	100
winner	216	216	2
hasBallot	21,600	216	21,600
option	21,600	21,600	3
title	216	216	216

An example query posed against this dataset is *All the bills and their titles where 'Nay' was the winner, and at least one voter voted for the same option (Aye/Nay/NoVote) as voter 'L000174'*. There may be several equivalent (w.r.t. the set of answers) query evaluation strategies or plans where we may apply regrouping or reordering of basic graph patterns. Two equivalent SPARQL queries can be seen in Figures 1(a) and 1(b), and their query plan trees are presented in Figures 2(a) and 2(b), respectively; we denote our njoin and gjoin operators, which we will detail later, by $\bowtie^{njoin}$ and $\bowtie^{gjoin}$, respectively. Intuitively, the gjoin operator always applies when two groups of more than one triple pattern are joined, as opposed to joining a single triple with a group. The tree in Figure 2(a) is left-linear, whereas the tree in Figure 2(b) is a bushy tree where the patterns were partitioned into star-shaped groups.

In an RDF dataset, there is only asserted knowledge, so the evaluation cost is proportional to the number of RDF triples that are read along query evaluation (i.e., the total number of intermediate results).

---

[2] http://www.govtrack.us/data/rdf/

PREFIX vote: <tag:govshare.info,2005:rdf/vote/>
PREFIX dc: <http://purl.org/dc/elements/1.1/>
PREFIX people:<http://www.rdfabout.com/rdf/usgov/>
SELECT ?E ?T
FROM <http://example.org/votes>
WHERE
       {?E vote:winner 'Nay' .
      ?E dc:title ?T .
      ?E vote:hasBallot ?I .
      ?I vote:option ?X .
      ?J vote:option ?X .
      ?E vote:hasBallot ?J .
      ?J vote:voter 'people:L000174'.
      FILTER (?I != ?J) }

(a) SPARQL Query without groupings

PREFIX vote: <tag:govshare.info,2005:rdf/vote/>
PREFIX dc: <http://purl.org/dc/elements/1.1/>
PREFIX people:<http://www.rdfabout.com/rdf/usgov/>
SELECT ?E ?T
FROM <http://example.org/votes>
WHERE
      {{{?E vote:winner Nay .
      ?E dc:title ?T} .
      {?E vote:hasBallot ?I .
      ?I vote:option ?X}} .
      {?J vote:voter people:L000174 .
      ?J vote:option ?X .
      ?E vote:hasBallot ?J}.
      FILTER (?I != ?J)}

(b) SPARQL Query with groupings

Fig. 1. Two Equivalent Queries

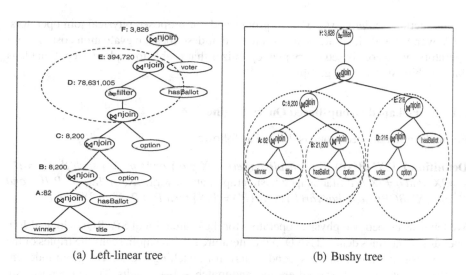

(a) Left-linear tree   (b) Bushy tree

Fig. 2. Query Execution Trees

Let us take a look at the evaluation of the patterns. In plan 2(a), patterns are evaluated in a left linear fashion: for each triple in a pattern, we loop on the next pattern and retrieve the matching triples; this procedure continues until all the patterns are evaluated. Each sub-tree is annotated with its evaluation cost defined in terms of the number of RDF triples that are produced during execution time; the total query evaluation cost is 79,046,033 triples.

In plan 2(b), patterns were partitioned into three star-shaped groups. Similarly, each sub-tree is annotated with its evaluation cost, and some of the sub-trees correspond to the gjoin operator. The estimated cost is dramatically reduced to 34,140 triples; note that the ordering within each group is also relevant, e.g., if the instantiated pattern {?J vote:voter people:L000174} were the right-most pattern in the group instead of the left-most one, the total number of sub-tree **E** intermediate results, would have been larger. This example illustrates how the combination of appropriate partitioning in star-shaped

groups and join reordering may improve the efficiency of query evaluation. It is beneficial to identify small-sized star-shaped groups and to avoid large-sized ones.

For instance, the small-sized group in sub-tree **D**, in Figure 2(b), reduces the number of voter options from 21,600 to 216 due to the voter instantiation {?J vote:voter
people:L000174}. On the other hand, avoiding large-sized star-shaped groups prevents
the explosion of the evaluation cost, e.g., the star-shaped group {?I vote:option ?X. ?J
vote:option ?X} should be not be considered since the join selectivity of the 'option'
object values is low, and a large number of matchings will occur and be accounted as
intermediate answers. Note that in Figure 2(a), the cost of this plan explodes when the
two 'option' property patterns are joined in sequence; this sequential join is marked
with a dashed circle in Figure 2(a).

3   Our Approach

In this section we define *star-shaped* groups and our proposed physical join operators.
Moreover, we will elaborate on a cost model that describes the evaluation cost of these
operators, and a cost-based query plan optimizer that is able to explore execution plans
that combine *star-shaped* groups.

3.1   Star-Shaped Group-Based Query Engine

Formally, a star-shaped group is defined as follows:

Definition 1 ($?X^*$**-BGP**). *Each triple pattern $\{?X\ p\ o\ \}$ or $\{s\ p\ ?X\ \}$ such that $s \neq ?X$,
$p \neq ?X$, and $o \neq ?X$ is a* Star-shaped basic graph pattern w.r.t. $?X$, or $?X^*$-BGP. If P and
P' are $?X^*$-BGPs such that $var(P) \cap var(P') = \{?X\}$ then $P \cup P'$ is an $?X^*$-BGP.

We have developed two physical operators for the evaluation of SPARQL's logical Join
operator, sometimes denoted AND in the literature [7]. The njoin scans the triples of the
first pattern, and loops on the second pattern for matching triples. The gjoin independently evaluates the star-shaped groups, and matches their results. These operators are
described using the terminology presented in [7] for the semantics of SPARQL graph
pattern expressions:

- A *triple pattern* (or a *basic graph pattern*, respectively) is an RDF triple (or a set
  of RDF triples, resp.) where variables may occur in subject, predicate or object
  position.
- Solutions of patterns are described in terms of *mappings* μ which are partial functions from variables to RDF terms.
- The evaluation of a basic graph pattern P, $[[P]]_G$ is the set of all mappings μ where
  $dom(\mu)$ is the set of variables occurring in P, such that $\mu(P) \subseteq G$. Each mapping
  corresponds to a valid pattern instantiation in graph G.
- *Compatible mappings* μ_1, μ_2 are those which coincide in the variables they share,
  and denote matching pattern instantiations.
- If P is a pattern and μ is a mapping, then by $\mu\ |_P$ we denote the mapping obtained
  from restricting μ to the variables in P.

A detailed description of the operators is as follows:

- Nested-Loop Join $\bowtie^{njoin}$: Given two star-shaped group patterns R_1 and R_2, we extend each mapping $\mu_{R_1} \in [[R_1]]_G$ to $\mu'_{R_1} \supseteq \mu_{R_1}$ such that $\mu_{R_2} = \mu'_{R_1} |_{R_2}$ is in $[[R_2]]_G$. I.e., μ_{R_1} and μ_{R_2} are compatible mappings.
- Group Join $\bowtie^{gjoin}$: Given two star-shaped groups R_1 and R_2, each of them is independently evaluated, and the results are combined to match the compatible mappings.

3.2   Star-Shaped Group Cost Model

In this section we define the cost model used for query plan generation. First, we describe the sampling technique used by the star-shaped cost model to estimate costs of intermediate results. Then, we present the application of this sampling technique for gathering RDF statistics, and for estimating the cost and cardinality of star-shaped groups. Finally, we define the formulas used for computing the cardinality, and the cost of a SPARQL query plan.

Adaptive Sampling Techniques. Unlike traditional approaches [8], the use of adaptive sampling techniques for query size and cost estimation does not require to store full summary statistics about the data. An additional advantage of this approach is that no strong assumptions about data characteristics are made upfront, but rather these properties can be estimated dynamically anytime. In [9], an adaptive sampling algorithm for estimating the result size of general queries is presented. It is applicable to any query that can be partitioned into disjoint sets of answers. This technique assumes that there is a population $\mathbb{P}$ of all the different valid instantiations of a predicate P, and that $\mathbb{P}$ is divided into n partitions according to the instantiations of one or more arguments of P. Each element in $\mathbb{P}$ is related to its evaluation cost and cardinality, and the population $\mathbb{P}$ is characterized by the statistics mean and variance of these two parameters.

The objective of the sampling is to identify a sample of the population $\mathbb{P}$, called $\mathbb{EP}$, such that the mean and variance of the cardinality (resp., evaluation cost) of $\mathbb{EP}$ are valid to within a predetermined accuracy and confidence level.

To estimate the mean of the cardinality (resp., cost) of $\mathbb{EP}$, say $\overline{Y}$, within $\frac{Y}{d}$ with probability p, where $0 \leq p < 1$ and $d > 0$, and $\alpha = \frac{d \times (d+1)}{(1 - \sqrt{p})}$, the sampling method assumes an *urn* model.

The urn has n balls from which m samplings are repeatedly taken, until the sum z of the cardinalities (resp., costs) of the samples is greater than $\alpha \times (\frac{S}{Y})$. The estimated mean of the cardinality (resp., cost) is: $\overline{Y} = \frac{z}{m}$.

The values d and $\frac{1}{(1 - \sqrt{p})}$ are associated with the relative error and the confidence level, and S and Y represent the cardinality (resp., cost) variance and mean of $\mathbb{P}$. Since statistics of $\mathbb{P}$ are unknown, the upper bound $\alpha \times \frac{S}{Y}$ is replaced by $\alpha \times b(n)$.

To approximate $b(n)$ for cost and cardinality estimates, k samples are randomly evaluated and the maximum value is taken among them:

$b(n) = max_{i=1}^{k}(card(P_i))$ (resp. $b(n) = max_{i=1}^{k}(cost(P_i))$, where $1 \leq k \leq n$

Cardinality and Cost of Query plans. The cost of query plans and sub-plans is either computed or estimated according to their shape as follows:

– The adaptive sampling method is used to estimate the size and cost of star-shaped groups. The sampling process for groups is simple and gives accurate estimates: the population for the cost and cardinality estimates is comprised of the set of mappings μ in the evaluation of the first pattern in the group. We sample on this population, and for each sampled μ, we evaluate the group and compute its cardinality (number of answers) and the evaluation cost. The samples are averaged in order to compute the final values for cost and cardinality.
– The cost of plans which are not star-shaped is computed according to cost formulas similar to the ones used in relational databases [8,10].

3.3 Star-Shaped Group Query Optimizer

The star-shaped group optimizer is implemented as a Simulated Annealing randomized algorithm which performs random walks over the search space of bushy query execution plans. Random walks are performed in stages, where each stage consists of an initial *plan generation step* followed by one or more *plan transformation steps*. An equilibrium condition or a number of iterations determines the number of transformation steps. At the beginning of each stage, a query execution plan is randomly created in the plan generation step. Then, successive *plan transformations* are applied to the query execution plan in order to obtain new plans. The probability of transforming a current plan p into a new plan p' is specified by an acceptance probability function $P(p, p', T)$ that depends on a global time-varying parameter T called the *temperature*; it reflects the number of stages to be executed. The function P may be nonzero when $cost(p') > cost(p)$, meaning that the optimizer can produce a new plan even when it is worse than the current one, i.e., it has a higher cost. This feature prevents the optimizer from becoming stuck in a local minimum. Temperature T is decreased during each stage and the optimizer concludes when $T = 0$. Transformations applied to the plan during the random walks correspond to the SPARQL axioms of the physical operators implemented by the query and reasoning engine. The transformation rules that implement the axioms that define the $\bowtie^{njoin}$ and $\bowtie^{gjoin}$ operators are as follows:

1. Symmetry:
   - $R_1 \bowtie^{njoin} R_2 \equiv R_2 \bowtie^{njoin} R_1$
   - $R_1 \bowtie^{gjoin} R_2 \equiv R_2 \bowtie^{gjoin} R_1$
2. Associativity:
   - $(R_1 \bowtie^{njoin} R_2) \bowtie^{njoin} R_3 \equiv R_1 \bowtie^{njoin} (R_2 \bowtie^{njoin} R_3)$
   - $(R_1 \bowtie^{gjoin} R_2) \bowtie^{gjoin} R_3 \equiv R_1 \bowtie^{gjoin} (R_2 \bowtie^{gjoin} R_3)$
3. Distributivity (Linear to Bushy)
   - $(R_1 \bowtie^{njoin} R_2) \bowtie^{njoin} R_3 \equiv (R_1 \bowtie^{njoin} R_3) \bowtie^{gjoin} (R_2 \bowtie^{njoin} R_3)$
4. Grouping
   - $(R_1 \bowtie^{njoin} R_2) \bowtie^{njoin} (R_3 \bowtie^{njoin} R_4) \equiv (R_1 \bowtie^{njoin} R_2) \bowtie^{gjoin} (R_3 \bowtie^{njoin} R_4)$

5. Fold into a star-shaped group: P_1 and P_2 are $?X^*$-BGPs such that $var(P_1) \cap var(P_2) = \{?X\}$, then:
   - $P_1 \bowtie^{njoin} P_2 \Rightarrow (P_1 \bowtie^{njoin} P_2)$
6. Unfold a star-shaped group: P_1 and P_2 are $?X^*$-BGPs such that $var(P_1) \cap var(P_2) = \{?X\}$, then:
   - $(P_1 \bowtie^{njoin} P_2) \Rightarrow P_1 \bowtie^{njoin} P_2$

For each iteration in the inner loop of the optimization algorithm, a transformation rule is applied with a random probability. We have assigned a probability value to each transformation rule. To illustrate this, in the running example from Figure 2 the following rules have been applied to transform the left linear plan into the bushy plan:

1. Associativity
   $((P_1 \bowtie^{njoin} P_2) \bowtie^{njoin} P_3) \bowtie^{njoin} P_4 \equiv (P_1 \bowtie^{njoin} P_2) \bowtie^{njoin} (P_3 \bowtie^{njoin} P_4)$
2. Grouping
   $(P_1 \bowtie^{njoin} P_2) \bowtie^{njoin} (P_3 \bowtie^{njoin} P_4) \equiv (P_1 \bowtie^{njoin} P_2) \bowtie^{gjoin} (P_3 \bowtie^{njoin} P_4)$

4 Related Work

In the context of the Semantic Web, several query engines have been developed to access RDF documents efficiently [3,4,6,11,12,13,14]. Jena [3] provides a programmatic environment for SPARQL, and it includes the ARQ query engine and indices which provide an efficient access to large datasets. The ARQ-Optimizer is a system that implements heuristics for selectivity-based Basic Graph Pattern optimization, proposed by Stocker et al. [15]. These heuristics range from simple triple pattern variable counting to more sophisticated selectivity estimation techniques; the optimization process is based on a greedy optimization algorithm which may explore a reduced portion of the space of possible plans, i.e., only left linear plans. Hence, query plans generated by the ARQ-Optimizer can sometimes be far from the optimal plans. The Jena Tuple Database or TDB [13] is a persistent graph storage layer for Jena. TDB works with the Jena SPARQL query engine (ARQ) to support SPARQL together with a number of extensions (e.g., property functions, aggregates, arbitrary length property paths).

Sesame [14] is an open source Java framework for storing and querying RDF data. It supports both SPARQL and SeRQL queries which are translated to Prolog; the join operator is implemented as sideways-passing of variable bindings, which is similar to our Nested Loop Join (njoin) operator.

RDF-3X [4] focuses on an index system, and its optimization techniques were developed to explore the space of plans that benefit from these index structures. The RDF-3X query optimizer implements a dynamic programming-based algorithm for plan enumeration, which imposes restrictions on the size of queries that can be optimized and evaluated. Indeed, in certain cases, these index-based plans could coincide with our optimized plans; however, the RDF-3X optimization strategies are not tailored to identify any type of bushy plans or to scale up to queries with at least one Cartesian product.

GiaBATA [6], a SPARQL engine built on top of the dlvhex reasoning engine for HEX-programs, and the DLVDB [16] ASP solver with persistent storage. DLVDB is an extension of DLV which provides interfaces with external databases, takes advantage of the optimization techniques implemented in the current DBMSs for improving reasoning efficiency. Weiss et al. [17] propose a main memory indexing technique that uses the triple nature of RDF as an asset. Two other approaches [18,19] define two secondary memory index-based representations and evaluation techniques for RDF-based queries. Several different RDF store schemas have been proposed [20,21,22] to efficiently implement an RDF management systems on top of a relational database system. These approaches empirically show that a physical implementation of vertically partitioned RDF tables may outperform the traditional physical schema of RDF tables. Similarly to some of the existing state-of-the-art RDF systems, the optimization techniques are not tailored to identify and evaluate small-sized star-shaped groups.

Finally, we have implemented the star-shaped based optimization and evaluation techniques in our own system, OneQL [10], and we have empirically shown the benefits of these techniques in queries against medium-size datasets. However, because OneQL is implemented in Prolog, it is not able to scale up to very large datasets. To overcome this limitation, we have implemented the star-shaped operators in several of the above-mentioned state-of-the-art RDF engines.

5 Experimental Results

We conducted an experimental study to empirically analyze the effectiveness of the proposed optimization and evaluation techniques in our own and several existing RDF engines. We report on the evaluation time performance of bushy plans comprised of star-shaped groups and identified by our proposed query optimizer. We compare the performance of the RDF query engines OneQL, Sesame, DLVDB, Jena TDB, and the extensions of Jena and RDF-3X that implement the gjoin operator, i.e., the $\bowtie^{gjoin}$.

Dataset and Query Benchmark: we use the real-world dataset on US Congress vote results of the 2004 bills voting process described in Table 1; the total size is 3.613 MB and 67,392 triples. We considered two sets of queries; benchmark one is comprised of 17 queries which are described in Figure 3(a) in terms of the number of patterns in the WHERE clause and the answer size; all the queries have at least one pattern whose object is instantiated with a constant. Benchmark two is a set of 120 queries which are composed of between 1 and 7 gjoin(s) among patterns of very small size. We also use the real-world ontology YAGO [23][3]; the total size of the dataset is 4GB and 44 millions of triples. We consider a benchmark of 10 queries which are comprised of between 17 and 25 basic patterns; for all these queries the answer is empty, except q6 that produces 551 triples. These three benchmarks are published in http:www.ldc.usb.ve/~mvidal/OneQL/datasets.

Evaluation Metrics: we report on runtime performance, which corresponds to the *user time* produced by the *time* command of the Unix operation system. The experiments on dataset one were evaluated on a Solaris machine with a Sparcv9 1281 MHz processor and 16GB RAM; experiments on the dataset Yago and the RDF-3X were executed on a Linux Ubuntu machine with an Intel Pentium Core2 Duo 3.0 GHz and 8GB RAM. Jena extensions were developed in Java (64-bit JDK version 1.5.0_12);

---

[3] Ontology available for download at http://www.mpi-inf.mpg.de/yago-naga/yago/

OneQL is implemented in SWI-Prolog (Multi-threaded, 64 bits, Version 5.6.54); finally, RDF-3X 0.3.3 is implemented in gcc/g++ v4.3.3.

Query Engine Implementations: the *star-shaped* group randomized query optimizer implements a Simulated Annealing algorithm that was run for twenty iterations and an initial temperature of 700; transformation rules were applied according to the probability distribution reported in Table 3(b).

To implement the gjoin operator in Jena 2.3, we modified the method Query Iterator stream in the class com.hp.hpl.jena.sparql.engine.main.OpCompiler. The Jena *GJoin* performs as follows: first, two objects of the QueryIteratorCaching class are created by replicating the input of the method stream; the outer and inner star-shaped groups are independently evaluated by calling the compileOp method with these QueryIteratorCaching objects. Each result set is stored in a different QueryIterator object, and the method QueryIterJoin is called to compute the join matches between the two sets. A new QueryIterator object is created to store the matches and is returned as the output of the method. We call this version of Jena, GJena.

Additionally, we have extended RDF-3X 0.3.3 to respect star-shaped plans produced by our query optimizer; njoin and gjoin are implemented as RDF-3X *Hash Joins*, while njoins in star-shaped groups correspond to RDF-3X *Merge Joins*; we call this version GRDF-3X. Finally, the njoin and gjoin operators were also implemented in DVLDB; for each star-shaped group in a plan, we generate a relational view which only projects the join variables of the star-shaped group.

query	#patterns	answer size
q1	4	3
q2	3	14,033
q3	7	3,908
q4	4	0
q5	4	0
q6	4	47
q7	3	6,600
q8	3	963
q9	7	13,177
q10	9	6,003
q11	9	150
q12	9	0
q13	3	100
q14	3	100
q15	3	1
q16	4	0

(a) Benchmark One

Transformation Rule	Probability
Symmetry	0.9
Associativity	0.9
Linear To Bushy	0.9
Grouping (Folding into a star-shaped group)	0.7
Grouping (Unfold a star-shaped group)	0.3

(b) Transformation Rules Distribution

Fig. 3. Experiment Configuration Set-Up

5.1 Effectiveness of the Star-Shaped Group-Based Optimization Techniques

We study the effectiveness of the star-shaped group-based optimization techniques by empirically analyzing the quality of the optimized plans w.r.t. the rest of the plans of the corresponding queries, and the runtime performance of the optimized plans.

To analyze the quality of the optimized plans, we generated all the plans of q13, q14, q15, and q16 in Figure 3(a), and computed the percentile in which the optimal plan falls. This optimal plan was identified by the star-shaped group randomized optimizer, and all the plans were run on the version of Jena that implements the gjoin operator. Queries q13, q14, q15, and q16 fall in the 83th, 26th, 92th, and 99th percentiles, respectively. These results suggest that the optimizer is able to traverse the space of star-shaped groups and identify those that minimize the evaluation cost.

Table 2 compares the runtime cost of the non-optimized versus optimized versions of the first nine queries of benchmark one in the engines: DLVDB, Sesame, and Jena TDB (all versions).

Table 2. Evaluation Time of Non-Optimized versus Optimized Queries (seconds)

Query	Jena TDB Fixed	Jena TDB Stats	Jena TDB None	Sesame	DLVDB
q1	0m6.952s	0m7.149s	0m6.861s	0m0.34s	0m0.37s
$q1_o$	0m4.072s	0m4.320s	0m4.048s	0m0.03s	0m0.34s
q2	0m29.106s	0m29.443s	0m28.553s	0m1.30s	0m1.23s
$q2_o$	0m28.404s	0m31.121s	0m29.308s	0m1.38s	0m1.16s
q3	129m56.301s	150m7.661s	133m11.581s	Timeout(100s)	14m53.05s
$q3_o$	0m19.945s	0m20.816s	0m20.615s	0m0.56s	0m10.614s
q4	0m32.681s	0m32.364s	0m31.928s	0m2.45s	45m47.620s
$q4_o$	2m43.325s	2m33.943s	2m37.936s	0m52.18s	0m9.189s
q5	0m26.085s	0m26.095s	0m26.187s	0m1.71s	33m1.786s
$q5_o$	0m4.114s	0m4.097s	0m3.902s	0m1.06s	22m14.712s
q6	0m7.958s	0m7.808s	0m7.691s	0m0.26s	0m0.745s
$q6_o$	0m4.939s	0m4.951s	0m4.772s	0m0.02s	0m0.712s
q7	0m20.486s	0m20.736s	0m20.342s	0m1.01s	0m0.761s
$q7_o$	0m20.376s	0m20.381s	0m19.733s	0m0.56s	0m0.699s
q8	0m12.802s	0m12.758s	0m13.033s	0m0.28s	0m0.339s
$q8_o$	0m0.402s	0m11.181s	0m11.677s	0m0.09s	0m0.314s
q9	337m12.276s	333m54.96s	350m14.346s	Timeout (100s)	1191m55.86s
$q9_o$	0m12.238s	0m11.689s	0m11.660s	0m0.58s	415m43.86s

We can observe that in general, the optimization techniques are able to speed up the evaluation time in almost all the SPARQL query engines. Particularly, in query q3, the improvement was produced by the reordering of the patterns, while in query q9, a combination of reordering and star-shaped groups was generated. However, the randomized optimizer was not able to produce the star-shaped groups which would have improved the evaluation time of q4.

Additionally, we study the effectiveness of the star-shaped group-based optimization techniques in different Jena engines. We ran queries q3, q9, q11, q12, q13, q14, q15, and q16 on Jena 2.3 and their respective optimized plans in GJena, and compare their evaluation times (seconds-logarithmic scale) in Figure 4(a). All these plans were composed of small-sized star-shaped groups. We could observe that the evaluation time of the optimized queries was at most 50% of the evaluation time of Jena's native query processing, and in some cases, the time was reduced by up to two orders of magnitude. These results indicate that by identifying groups our optimizer is able to generate significantly better plans for star-shaped queries compared to the "flat" join-reordering techniques in Jena.

Furthermore, we studied the benefits of the star-shaped based optimization and evaluation techniques by empirically analyzing the quality of star-shaped optimized plans w.r.t. the plans optimized by the RDF-3X query optimizer. Nine queries of benchmark one were optimized by OneQL and RDF-3X, and the generated plans were run in OneQL. Each RDF-3X optimized plan was run using the gjoin to evaluate the groups in the bushy plans, and using the njoin to evaluate joins inside the star-shaped groups. Figure 4(b) reports the evaluation time (seconds-logarithmic scale) of these combinations of queries. We can observe that the evaluation time of the star-shaped and RDF-3X optimized plans are competitive, except for queries $q1$ and $q6$ where our optimizer was able to identify plans where all the triples are instantiated, and the most selective ones are evaluated first. These results indicate that the star-shaped based optimization and evaluation techniques may be used in conjunction with the state-of-the-art techniques to provide more efficient query engines; they have encouraged us to develop our physical operators in existing RDF engines like Jena and RDF-3X.

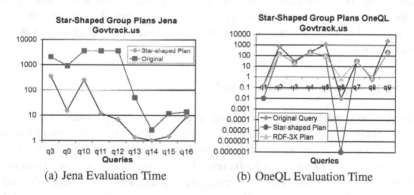

(a) Jena Evaluation Time   (b) OneQL Evaluation Time

Fig. 4. Effectiveness of the Star-shaped Optimizer-Time (seconds-logarithmic scale)

Finally, we studied the behavior of the star-shaped plans in RDF-3X against large datasets. For each query of benchmark three on YAGO, we computed the RDF-3X optimal plan and the star-shaped plan produced by OneQL. We also built the optimal star-shaped group plan of the query *by hand*; each optimal plan was comprised of between two and five star-shaped groups free of Cartesian products. RDF-3X optimized plans were run in RDF-3X, while the other two versions were executed in GRDF-3X. Figure 5(a) reports on the evaluation time (seconds-logarithmic scale) of these queries; optimization time is not considered in any case. We can observe that the star-shaped plans produced by our optimizer can reduce evaluation time by up to three orders of magnitude, and in many cases their evaluation time is close to the optimal cost. We also ran this experiment in Jena; original queries were run in Jena 2.3 and the other two versions were executed in GJena. We observe a similar trend in the evaluation time.

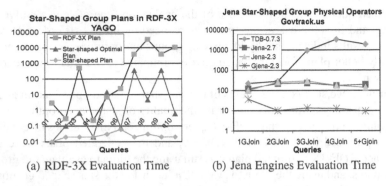

(a) RDF-3X Evaluation Time   (b) Jena Engines Evaluation Time

Fig. 5. Performance of Star-shaped Groups-Time (seconds-logarithmic scale)

5.2 Performance of the Star-Shaped Group Physical Operators

We have conducted an empirical analysis on the benefits of the evaluation techniques implemented on Jena, and we have executed the one hundred and twenty queries of the benchmark two on govtrack.us. We compared the benefits of using our gjoin physical implementation and the njoin implementation provided by Jena versions 2.3, Jena 2.7 and Jena TDB. We could observe that our gjoin implementation was able to speed up the evaluation time by up to three orders of magnitude. Figure 5(b) reports the average time (seconds-logarithmic scale) consumed by the Jena query engine to evaluate the different queries.

6   Conclusions and Future Work

We have defined optimization and evaluation techniques that provide the basics for an efficient evaluation of SPARQL queries. The assumptions of the uniformity of values of subjects and objects in a property, and of independence between properties, may lead to imprecise estimates in real-world problems. Thus, in the future we plan to enhance the star-shaped cost model with Bayesian inference capabilities so as to consider the lack of uniformity of the values in the RDF documents, and correlations between patterns in the SPARQL queries. Furthermore, we plan to conduct an experimental comparison of the performance of our optimizer and the RDF-3X optimizer [24]; also, a detailed experimental study of column-store approaches[22] such as Virtuoso[4] or MonetDB[5] is on our agenda.

Acknowledgements

This research has been partially supported by the DID-USB and the Proyecto ALMA Mater-OPSU. The work of Axel Polleres is supported by Science Foundation Ireland under Grant No. SFI/08/CE/I1380 (Lion-2). We thank Andy Seaborne for his advice on the installation of the different Jena engines.

---

[4] http://virtuoso.openlinksw.com/
[5] http://monetdb.cwi.nl/

References

1. Prud'hommeaux, E., Seaborne, A.: SPARQL query language for RDF. W3C Recommendation (January 2008), http://www.w3.org/TR/rdf-sparql-query/
2. Ruckhaus, E., Ruiz, E., Vidal, M.: OneQL: An Ontology Efficient Query Language Engine for the Semantic Web. In: Proceedings ALPSWS 2007 (2007)
3. Dickinson, I.: The Jena Ontology API.,
   http://jena.sourceforge.net/ontology/index.html
4. Neumann, T., Weikum, G.: RDF-3X: a RISC-style engine for RDF. PVLDB 1(1), 647–659 (2008)
5. Broekstra, J., Kampman, A., Harmelen, F.: Sesame: An Architecture for Storing and Querying RDF Data and Schema Information. In: Spinning the Semantic Web, pp. 197–222 (2003)
6. Ianni, G., Krennwallner, T., Martello, A., Polleres, A.: Dynamic Querying of Mass-Storage RDF Data with Rule-Based Entailment Regimes. In: Bernstein, A., Karger, D.R., Heath, T., Feigenbaum, L., Maynard, D., Motta, E., Thirunarayan, K. (eds.) ISWC 2009. LNCS, vol. 5823, pp. 310–327. Springer, Heidelberg (2009)
7. Perez, J., Arenas, M., Gutierrez, C.: Semantics and Complexity of SPARQL. In: International Semantic Web Conference, pp. 30–43 (2006)
8. Selinger, P., Astrahan, M., Chamberlin, D., Lorie, R., Price, T.: Access Path Selection in a Relational Database Management System. In: Proceedings of ACM Sigmod, pp. 23–34 (1979)
9. Lipton, R., Naughton, J.: Query size estimation by adaptive sampling (extended abstract). In: Proceedings of ACM Sigmod, pp. 40–46 (1990)
10. Lampo, T., Ruckhaus, E., Sierra, J., Vidal, M.E., Martinez, A.: OneQL: An Ontology-based Architecture to Efficiently Query Resources on the Semantic Web. In: The 5th International Workshop on Scalable Semantic Web Knowledge Base Systems at ISWC (2009)
11. Franz Inc.: AllegroGraph, http://www.franz.com/agraph/allegrograph/
12. Harth, A., Umbrich, J., Hogan, A., Decker, S.: YARS2: A Federated Repository for Querying Graph Structured Data from the Web. In: ISWC/ASWC, pp. 211–224 (2007)
13. Seaborne, A.: Jena TDB, http://openjena.org/wiki/TDB
14. Wielemaker, J.: An optimised Semantic Web Query Language Implementation in Prolog. In: Gabbrielli, M., Gupta, G. (eds.) ICLP 2005. LNCS, vol. 3668, pp. 128–142. Springer, Heidelberg (2005)
15. Stoker, M., Seaborne, A., Bernstein, A., Keifer, C., Reynolds, D.: SPARQL Basic Graph Pattern Optimizatin Using Selectivity Estimation. In: Proceedings of the 17th International Conference on World Wide Web (WWW), pp. 595–604 (2008)
16. Terracina, G., Leone, N., Lio, V., Panetta, C.: Experimenting with recursive queries in database and logic programming systems. Theory Pract. Log. Program. 8(2), 129–165 (2008)
17. Weiss, C., Karras, P., Bernstein, A.: Hexastore: sextuple indexing for semantic web data management. PVLDB 1(1), 1008–1019 (2008)
18. Fletcher, G., Beck, P.: Scalable Indexing of RDF Graph for Efficient Join Processing. In: Proceedings of the 18th ACM Conference on Information and Knowledge Management (CIKM), pp. 1513–1516 (2009)
19. McGlothlin, J., Khan, L.: RDFKB: Efficient Support For RDF Inference Queries and Knowledge Management. In: Proceedings of International Database Engineering and Applications Symposium (IDEAS), pp. 259–266 (2009)
20. Abadi, D.J., Marcus, A., Madden, S., Hollenbach, K.: SW-Store: a vertically partitioned DBMS for Semantic Web data management. VLDB J. 18(2), 385–406 (2009)
21. Abadi, D.J., Marcus, A., Madden, S., Hollenbach, K.J.: Scalable Semantic Web Data Management Using Vertical Partitioning. In: Proceedings of the 33th International Conference on Very Large Data Bases (VLDB), pp. 411–422 (2007)

22. Sidirourgos, L., Goncalves, R., Kersten, M.L., Nes, N., Manegold, S.: Column-store support for RDF data management: not all swans are white. PVLDB 1(2), 1553–1563 (2008)
23. Suchanek, F.M., Kasneci, G., Weikum, G.: YAGO: A Large Ontology from Wikipedia and WordNet. Elsevier Journal of Web Semantics 6(3), 203–217 (2008)
24. Neumann, T., Weikum, G.: Scalable join processing on very large RDF graphs. In: Proceedings of the ACM SIGMOD International Conference on Management of Data, Providence, Rhode Island, USA, pp. 627–640. ACM Press, New York (2009)

Reasoning-Based Patient Classification
for Enhanced Medical Image Annotation

Sonja Zillner

Corporate Technology, Siemens AG
Munich, Germany
sonja.zillner@siemens.com

Abstract. Medical imaging plays an important role in today's clinical
daily tasks, such as patient screening, diagnosis, treatment planning and
follow up. But still a generic and flexible image understanding is missing.
Although, there exist several approaches for semantic image annotation,
those approaches do not make use of practical clinical knowledge, such as
best practice solutions or clinical guidelines. We introduce a knowledge
engineering approach aiming for reasoning-based enhancement of medical
images annotation by integrating practical clinical knowledge. We will
exemplify the reasoning steps of the methodology along a use case for
automatic lymphoma patient staging.

1 Introduction

The vision of THESEUS MEDICO[1] is to automatically extract the meaning
from the medical images and to seamlessly integrate the extracted knowledge into
medical processes, such as clinical decision making. In other words, the computer
shall learn to find, catalogue and interpret medical images. This requires the
semantic representation of medical images' content and the preprocessing of
semantic image annotations for seamless integration into clinical applications.

The integration of practical clinical knowledge resources is an essential requirement to achieve the goals of MEDICO. Thus, we are aiming to enhance
medical image annotations by integrating clinical knowledge, such as lymphoma
staging systems. There exist several approaches for semantic image annotation,
such as automatic image parsing [1], manual image annotation [2], [3], the extraction of information from DICOM headers and DICOM structured reports [4],
or the automated extraction from radiology reports. Although those approaches
provide the very important basis for semantic image annotation, they do yet
not make use of practical clinical knowledge, such as best practice solutions or
clinical guidelines for fine-tuning and customizing the established annotations to
reflect the particular requirements of a clinical application or work flow.

Within the MEDICO project, one of the selected use case scenarios aims
for improved image search in the context of patients suffering of lymphoma in

---

[1] http://theseus-programm.de/en-us/theseus-application-scenarios/medico/
default.aspx

L. Aroyo et al. (Eds.): ESWC 2010, Part I, LNCS 6088, pp. 243–257, 2010.
© Springer-Verlag Berlin Heidelberg 2010

the neck area. Lymphoma, a type of cancer originating in lymphocytes, is a systematic disease with manifestations in multiple organs. The selected and discussed use case scenario is focusing on the automatic classification of lymphoma patients.

The contribution of this paper is to introduce a knowledge engineering approach aiming for enhanced medical image annotations by integrating clinical knowledge. The knowledge engineering steps will be exemplified along the selected use case. The Ann-Arbor Staging System of Hodgkin-lymphoma [5] provided us guidance in formally describing the knowledge base enabling the automatic inference of lymphoma patient staging results. Our aim for the knowledge base design was to establish an automatic staging system that maps each patient to uniquely one staging degree. We, thus, can automatically generate additional patient annotation data, that can be used for supporting the clinicians in their daily tasks. By integrating the patient's staging information, into other clinical applications, for instance, the quality of medical care can be optimized or the search and comparison of patients be improved. We have developed an OWL DL ontology that represents the Ann Arbor staging system together with lymphoma patient records and that is suitable for performing automatic lymphoma patient classification.

The remainder of the paper is organized as follows. Section 2 gives an overview of the KEMM Knowledge Engineering Methodology for the medical domain. In Section 3 we will introduce the knowledge resources the use case of ontology-based lymphoma patient staging is based on. Section 4 details the knowledge engineering steps exemplified along the selected use case scenario. Section 5 illustrates the benefits of the reasoning results by introducing a concrete example patient case and Section 6 discusses related approaches. Section 7 concludes this paper with an outlook on future work.

2   Knowledge Engineering in the Medical Domain

Given a formal and explicit representation of practical clinical knowledge, implicit conclusion can be derived. We conceive of reasoning-based enhancement of the ontology and the semantic annotations as an operation that is based on several knowledge resources - such as the information captured in the medical images, text-mining results on the basis of radiology reports, (fragments of) medical ontologies, and formal representations of clinical guidelines - and yields an outcome that can be directly used in clinical applications. A specific knowledge engineering methodology for the medical domain (KEMM) [6] has been designed. The knowledge engineering approach encompasses five steps, i.e. *Knowledge Requirements Analysis, Requirements Decomposition, Knowledge Integration, Complex Query Composition, and Evaluation*, and was derived from the experiences gained during the realization of a clinical use case within the MEDICO project. By specifying the knowledge engineering steps required for the integration of practical clinical knowledge into medical application, the KEMM module "Reasoning-Based Ontology Enhancement" is implemented.

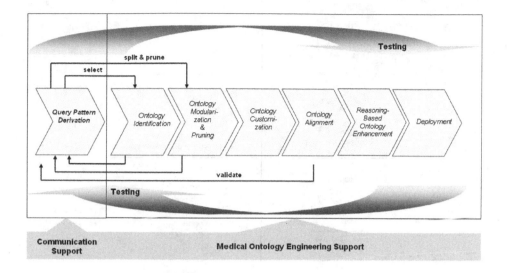

Fig. 1. The KEMM medical knowledge engineering methodology

3   Knowledge Resources

The approach for the automated staging application relies on three different knowledge resources that are described in the following.

Practical Clinical Knowledge. Only practical clinical knowledge that is explicitly and formally described can be integrated into other clinical applications. The Ann-Arbor Staging System for Hodgkin Lymphoma[5] documents precisely the classification of lymphoma patients. The staging depends on two criteria. The first criterion is the place where the malignant tissue is located, its type as well as its frequency of occurrence. The location can be identified with located biopsy as well as with medical imaging methods. The second criterion are systemic symptoms, such as night sweats, weight loss of more than 10 percent or fevers, caused by the lymphoma. Those systemic symptoms are called "B symptoms".

The principal stage is determined by the location of the tumor and reflects the grade of expansion of lymphoma occurrences. Four different stages are recognized:

- Stage I indicates that the cancer is located in a single region, either an affected lymph node or organ within the lymphatic system.
- In Stage II the cancer is located in two separated regions, an affected lymph node or an affected organ within the lymphatic system and a second affected lymph node area. Moreover, the affected areas are confined to one side of the diaphragm - that is, both are above the diaphragm or, both are below the diaphragm.

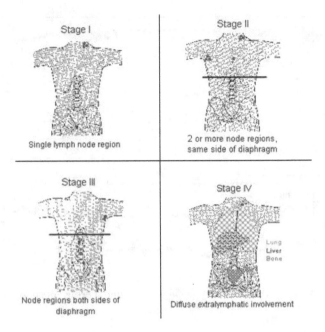

Fig. 2. Ann-Arbor Staging System (Source: http://training.seer.cancer.gov)

- Stage III indicates that the cancer has spread to both sides of the diaphragm, including one extra lymphatic organ or site.
- Stage IV shows diffuse or disseminated involvement of one or more extra lymphatic organs.

Medical Ontologies. For achieving re-usability and interoperability of data, we need an external knowledge model, that covers anatomical information related to lymphatic occurrences. Two ontologies, the Foundational Model of Anatomy (FMA) and the Radiology Lexicon (RadLex), cover anatomical entities and provide the required coverage of anatomical and radiological concepts for the staging scenario. The *FMA* [7] is a very comprehensive specification of anatomy taxonomy, i.e. an inheritance hierarchy of anatomical entities with different kinds of relationships. It covers approximately 70,000 distinct anatomical concepts and more than 1.5 million relations instances from 170 relation types. It provides concepts that describe single lymph nodes, such as 'axilliary_lymph_node', and concepts that describe multiple lymph nodes, such as 'set_of_axilliary_lymph_node'. It contains 425 concepts representing singular lymph nodes and 404 concepts describing sets of lymph nodes.

RadLex[2] is a terminology developed and maintained by the Radiological Society of North America (RSNA) for the purpose of uniform indexing and retrieval of radiology information, including medical images. RadLex contains over 8,000 anatomic and pathologic terms, also those about imaging techniques, difficulties

---

[2] http://www.radlex.org

and diagnostic image qualities. Its purpose is to provide a standardized terminology for radiological practice. RadLex is available in English and German language and covers more than 100 concepts describing lymph node concepts.

The semantic labeling of "B-symptoms" requires an ontology that encompasses cancer-related diseases, symptoms and findings. We identified the *National Cancer Institute Thesaurus (NCI)*[3], a standard vocabulary for cancer research, as appropriate. It contains around 34.000 concepts from which 10521 are related to Disease, Abnormality, Finding, 5901 are related to Neoplasm, 4320 to Anatomy and the rest are related to various other categories such as Gene, Protein, etc.

Semantic Image Annotation and Radiology Reports. The information about number, type and location of lymphatic occurrences can be detected by analyzing medical images. The detected information is formally captured by semantic image annotation. The MEDICO project is based on multiple ways of generating semantic image annotation. For instance methods for automated image parsing, such as [1], allow to hierarchically parse whole body CT images and efficiently segment multiple organs taking contextual information into account. While automated image parsing remains incomplete, manual image annotation remains an important complement. To integrate manual image annotation in the reporting workflow of radiologists is one of the objectives of the Annotation and Image Markup Project ([3],[2]). Currently, users of the MEDICO system can manually add semantic image annotations by selecting or defining anatomical landmarks or arbitrary regions/volumes of interest. Ongoing work within the MEDICO project is focusing on the semi-automatically identification of terms and relations in radiology reports that are generated by clinicians in the process analyzing the patient's disease patterns by investigating medical imaging data.

4   Knowledge-Engineering Steps for Ontology-Based Lymphoma Patient Staging

Our goal is to integrate practical clinical knowledge into medical applications, such as decision support systems, semantic search or quality control applications. This requires the formal and explicit representation of practical clinical knowledge such that implicit conclusion can be derived. The aim of reasoning-based ontology enhancement is to use existing reasoning procedures for discovery of new classification and subsumption results.

We use OWL DL, which is MEDICO's agreed semantic representation language, for representing the knowledge model. Description Logics [8], a family of formal representation languages for ontologies, are designed for classification-based reasoning.

Automatic symbolic reasoning deals with the formal manipulation of explicitly represented sets of symbols (defined within a formal language) using rules

---

[3] http://nciterms.nci.nih.gov/

of inference. One rule of inference used is deduction where from a given set of propositions new ones can be generated and interpreted as logical consequences of these. Sets of propositions constructed in this manner and used to define a particular domain of interest are typically called a knowledge-base. The advantage of this approach is that otherwise implicit knowledge can be explicit and more readily to available to users and applications.

Definition 1 (Entailment). *A knowledge base KB is said to entail a statement α if α follows from the knowledge stored in the KB, which is written KB $\models \alpha$.*

The inference procedures implemented in computational reasoners aim at realizing the entailment relation between logical statements [9], i.e. inference procedures use sets of background axioms that are implicitly used by the reasoning system. The automatic staging of lymphoma patients represented as concepts, relies on the subsumption procedure, i.e. the computing of subsumptions.

Definition 2 (Subsumption Procedure). *Let KB denote a knowledge base and c, d be two concepts in KB, then we call the inference rule π a subsumption procedure, if π can determine for any sentence α of the form ($\forall x \quad x \in c \rightarrow x \in d$) whether or not KB $\models \alpha$.*

We transformed the Ann-Arbor Staging System for Hodgkin Lymphoma [5] into a formal and ontology-based representation suitable for computing subsumptions. For doing so, we follow the following steps:

4.1   First Step: Knowledge Requirements Analysis

For capturing the requirements of the ontology design, we followed the formal approach of [10]. We used competency questions to determine the expressiveness requirements of the knowledge model. The ontology needs to be able

1. to *compute the answers* to the questions using the axioms, definitions, and background axioms of the reasoning system
2. to *represent* the questions *using its terminology*

In the context of automatic classification of lymphoma patients, the Ann-Arbor Staging System specifies the scope as well as the basic constraints for developing competency questions. Each of the staging classes matches to one high-level competency questions and is represented as complex and defined OWL DL class. This provides the basis for *computing the answers*. i.e. the patient classification. By representing patients as OWL DL classes with the corresponding axioms and characteristics, they will be subsumed according to their staging grade.

For determining the *required terminology*, the decision criteria of Ann-Arbor Staging System need to be reflected. The patient classification basically relies on

- the number of lymphatic occurrences
- the relative position of a lymphatic occurrence in relation to the diaphragm

- the type of lymphatic occurrence
- the classification along so-called "B-symptoms".

In the following step, we decomposed the complex competency questions that represent the made ontological commitment into simpler questions which we need to answer in order to answer the given questions. The simpler questions relate to the mentioned decision criteria of the Ann-Arbor Staging System.

4.2 Second Step: Requirements Decomposition

As already mentioned, the goal is to decompose the complex questions conforming to the Ann-Arbor Staging System for Hodgkin Lymphoma into more simple and manageable queries that represent events that can be accessed independently. For accessing the number and location of lymph node occurrences and respectively extra lymphatic organ or site involvement, as well as capture the information about possible systemic symptoms, the following queries, i.e. defined OWL classes, were specified:

- The OWL defined classes N1 and N2 subsume all patients with at least one or at least two involved lymph node regions.
- The OWL defined classes E1 and E2 subsume all patients with at least one or at least two involved extra lymphatic organ or site involvement.
- The OWL defined classes N_AllAboveD and N_AllBelowD subsume all patients with the location of the lymph node regions either only above or only below the diaphragm. For accessing patients with occurrences of lymph nodes on both sides of the diaphragm, one has to make sure that the occurrences are neither located all above nor located all below the diaphragm. This can be formulated by the complex class $\neg$ N_AllAboveD $\sqcup$ $\neg$ N_AllBelowD.
- The location of extra nodal occurrences are identified in an analogous manner, i.e. by establishing the defined classes E_AllAboveD and E_AllBelowD, as well as the corresponding complex axiom for accessing patients with extra nodal occurrences on both sides of the diaphragm.
- The OWL defined class B-Symptom subsumes all patients with at least one systemic symptom, such as fever, night sweats or weight loss, respectively subsumes the OWL defined Class A-Symptom all patients with the absence of systemic symptoms.

Before detailing the staging classification, we will discuss the particular requirements towards the ontology design for realizing the auxiliary queries. For establishing the ontological model basically three different challenges needed to be addressed:

1. The staging of Lymphoma patients relies on many different knowledge resources, such as findings from medical image analysis findings, patient records, medical background knowledge and clinical guidelines. How to select and customize the right (fragment of) relevant knowledge resources for the integration into the staging scenario?

2. How to ensure that the ontological model provides the basis for inferring the number of lymph node occurrences and the number of extra lymphatic involvements?
3. How to identify the relative location – above, below or on both sides of the diaphragm – of the lymphatic occurrences?

The mentioned requirements are addressed in the following steps.

4.3   Third Step: Knowledge Integration

The selection of the right ontologies and knowledge resources covering the domain of interest, the identification of relevant fragments or aspects of knowledge resources as basis for scalable reasoning, and the enhancement and customization of knowledge resources are important aspects for their successful integration into the intended application. The KEMM knowledge engineering methodology [6] specifies the access to the mentioned ingredients for automatic patient classification in its previous modules. We sketch them briefly in the following

Ontology Selection. As human health is a sensitive matter, the quality and the quantity of the medical knowledge to be used in the target application have to be ensured. This implies reusing the work of acknowledged resources when choosing medical ontologies. For capturing the semantics of for the staging of lymphoma patients, ontological concepts describing the organs as well as concepts listing possible regions of lymphatic occurrences are required. As the use case scenario relies only on high-level concepts, both ontologies - FMA and RadLex - are suitable in terms of coverage. For this use case, we decided to use RadLex as primary third party resource to label lymphatic occurrences. As within the MEDICO project, we are confronted with radiology reports in German language, the availability of a German translation was an crucial argument for the above decision. In addition, due to the large size of Radlex, we needed to establish an ontology fragment that is scalable and efficient for reasoning application. For modeling the B-symptoms, we required concepts representing the systemic symptoms that were covered within the NCI vocabulary. As only a very small subset of NCI concepts were used within our scenario, we manually established the NCI fragment accordingly.

Ontology Modularization. Scalable reasoning requires the modularization of large ontologies. These modules need to cover all concepts and relationships for describing the particular scenario, in our case any concept describing a lymph node occurrence or an extra lymphatic involvement. Thus, we semi-automatically generated a RadLex fragment in OWL DL format following three steps:

1. For identifying the concepts representing lymph node occurrences, we selected all 'lymph node' concepts, i.e. concepts that contained the string 'lymph node' in its preferred name label. In addition, all concepts with the string 'node' in its preferred name and a 'lymph node' concept as superconcept were selected. By interviewing our clinical experts, we could derive a list of nine concepts representing extra nodal occurrences.

2. The semantics of the parent-child relationship was translated to OWL DL axioms, such as

RightLowerParaTrachealLymphnode ⊑ (Anatomical_Structure ⊓

⊓ ∃is_child_of.LowerParaTrachealLymphnode)

3. To make sure that the the exact number of lymphatic occurrences can be inferred by the DL reasoner[4], we needed to label the identified concepts for representing lymphatic occurrences as disjoint by adding the correlating axioms.

Ontology Customization. The relative position of lymphatic occurrences is an important decision criteria of the staging system and needs to be reflected by the reasoning procedure. The patient staging results distinguish between patient that have lymphatic occurrences only above, only below or on both sides of the diaphragm. The relative position of lymphatic occurrences to the diaphragm has to be expressed in the knowledge model. For achieving this, we see two options. The information about the relative position of lymphatic occurrences can be either derived by the image segmentation algorithm or derived directly from the underlying ontological model. In other words, this information either comes with the patient record information or with the integrated knowledge model of the human anatomy. The deduction of the relative spatial position of lymphatic occurrences by segmentation algorithms will be addressed within our future work. In the meantime, we need to rely on the selected anatomy knowledge model to capture - as basis for later inference - the relevant spatial information. FMA and RadLex do not explicitly capture the information about the relative position between lymphatic regions or organs and the diaphragm. Thus, we required to enhance the established fragment accordingly. This could be achieved by extending each lymphatic region by an axiom, such as

LowerParaTrachealLymphnode ⊑ (Anatomical_Structure ⊓

⊓∃hasN_Location.aboveDiaphragm)

indicating that the region is above, or respectively, below the diaphragm. The classification of lymphatic regions - and of patients with lymphatic occurrences - above, below or on both sides of the diaphragm was modeled as value partition.

The established RadLex fragment encompasses 123 concepts, whereof 104 represent lymph node occurrences and nine extra nodal occurrences; the remaining concepts are auxiliary concepts required for the classification task.

4.4   Fourth Step: Complex Query Composition

The application queries are the Ann-Arbor Staging classes that are represented as defined OWL DL classes. Each staging class captures the semantics as detailed in Subsection 3. Their formal representation makes use of auxiliary classes introduced in Subsection 4.2. Figure 3 summarizes the transformation of the Ann-Arbor Staging System. Stage-1 is the union of the sets N1 and E1. The class N1 infers all patients with the involvement of at least one lymph node region and E1

---

[4] We use Pellet (http://clarkparsia.com/pellet/) as DL reasoner.

Stages	Description
Stage-I	N1 *or* E1
Stage-II	Stage-II-N *or* Stage-II-mixed
Stage-II-N	N2 *and* (N_AllAboveD *or* N_AllBelowD)
Stage-II-mixed	N1 *and* E1 *and* ((N_AllAboveD and E_AllAboveD) *or* (N_AllBelowD *and* E_AllBelowD))
Stage-III	Stage-III-N *or* StageIII-mixed
StageIII-N	N2 *and not* N_AllAboveD *and not* N_AllBelowD
StageIII-mixed	E1 *and* N1 *and* (*not* (N_AllAboveD and E_AllAboveD) *and not* (N_AllBelowD and E_AllBelowD))
StageIV	E2 *and* (*not* N_AllAboveD *and not* N_AllBelowD)

Fig. 3. Formal Representation of Ann-Arbor Staging System

all patients with the involvement of at least one extra lymphatic organ or site. Stage-II is the union of Stage-II-N or Stage-II-mixed with Stage-II-N gathering all patients with more that two lymph node region that are all on one side of the diaphragm and Stage-II-mixed patients with one involved lymph node region and one involved extra lymphatic organ or site on the same side of the diaphragm. Patients of Stage-III are contained in Stage-III-N or in StageIII-mixed. Stage-III-N identifies all patients that have at least two involved lymph node regions that are spread to both sides of the diaphragm and StageIII-mixed all patients with one involved lymph node region and one involved extra lymphatic organ or site on both sides of the diaphragm. StageIV subsumes all patients that have two or more extra lymphatic organs or site on both sides of the diaphragm. The A-Symptom or B-Symptom classes are not indicated in the table as their semantics was already described in Sect. 4.2.

4.5 Evaluation

Both, complex questions and simple questions, provided us valuable guidance for evaluating the ontological commitment that has been made. This was possible

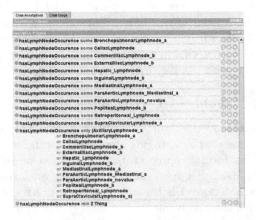

Fig. 4. OWL Representation of an example patient record

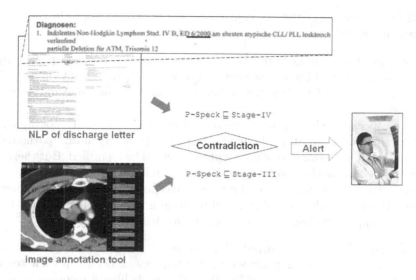

Fig. 5. Contradicting Staging Results can be discovered

by systematically establishing test patients classes according to the simple and the complex questions. Each test patient is equipped with different numbers and kinds of lymphatic occurrences at different locations in the body. The format representing the patient data is determined by the reasoning procedure. Figure 4 represents an example patient with more than 13 lymph node occurrences. By analyzing the reasoning result, we could evaluate whether the created ontology established the expressivity in accordance to the requirements of the use case scenario. In this way, the evaluation (as well as the development) of the classification axioms was straight forward. In addition, we conducted a proof-of-concept study on the basis of real patient records, which we detail in the following section.

5   Clinical Example

The automated patient staging approach is aiming for enhanced medical image annotation providing the basis for improved clinical applications. Thus, we conducted a proof-of-concept study on the basis of real patient records to analyze the practical potential. With the help of our clinical experts, the corresponding medical images were manually annotated and the semantic annotations integrated within our knowledge base. Additional, the information of discharge letters covering diagnose and findings was transformed into the knowledge model.

In the context of one particular patient, we identified a contradiction between the clinicians diagnose in the discharge letter, and the automated staging results based on the image annotation: The so-called Patient Speck[5] is an advanced stage lymphoma patient who was already treated with 3 chemotherapies using

---

[5] The original name was changed.

the CHOP-protocol. As the accomplished treatments did not help to improve the patient's health condition, he was referred to a specialist clinic.

- The patient's discharge letter covers details about the diagnose, past medical diagnose, and findings, assessment and progression and recent therapy. The discharge letter of Patient Speck indicates the diagnose of Ann-Arbor IV-Stage.
- In the specialist clinical, he was screened using Computer Tomography. By analyzing and annotating the medical images, 16 enlarged and pathological lymph nodes on both side of the diaphragm could be identified. But there was no indication for the involvement of extra lymphatic organs. The semantic annotations were transformed into the corresponding OWL DL representation. Relying on the formal Ann-Arbor Staging criteria, the ontology-based staging approach classifies Patient Speck as Ann-Arbor III-Stage.

The clinician's diagnose is contradicting the result of the automated reasoning application. As the staging grade strongly influences clinicians in their sequential treatment decisions, a careful handling thereof is highly recommended. By highlighting such contradicting results medical mistakes can be reduced (see Figure 5). This example case is in line with our argumentation, that the automatic generation of additional patient annotation data helps to improve medical quality control and medical care.

6   Related Work

6.1   Semantic Image Understanding

There exist a wide range of different imaging technologies and modalities, such as 4D 64-slice Computer Tomography (CT), whole-body Magnet Resonance Imaging (MRI), 4D Ultrasound, and the fusion of Positron Emission Tomography and CT (PET/CT) providing detailed insight into human anatomy, function and disease associations. Moreover, advanced techniques for analyzing imaging data generating additional quantitative parameters paving the way for improved clinical practice and diagnosis. However, for advanced applications in Clinical Decision Support and Computer Aided Diagnoses the comparative exploration of similar patient information is required. The missing link here fore is a flexible and generic image understanding. Currently, the large amounts of heterogeneous image data are stored in distributed and autonomous image databases being indexed by keywords without capturing any semantics.

Generic medical image understanding is still a long-term agenda due to the high complexity of the problem. Several challenging research questions need to be addressed for tackling this vision: For determining the scope and level of detail of the semantics of the domain, i.e. the relevant metadata for annotating medical images, one needs to find out what kind of knowledge the clinicians are interested in. The scope of the constraint domain can be determined by the set of derived query patterns [11], [12] that provide guidance in identifying the relevant (fragments of) ontologies [13]. Moreover, the low level features, segmentations and quantitative measures derived from image processing need to be associated with ontologies.

6.2   Knowledge Engineering

There has been a rapid increase in ontology building, especially within the context of the Semantic Web activities initiated by various groups from industry and academia. It has been suggested that these separate activities should be executed in a systematic manner [14],[15], as a result of which several ontology engineering methodologies have been proposed [16],[17], [18].

Some communities concentrated on developing stand-alone ontology engineering methodologies that shall be applicable across domains and tasks. Examples of these are METHONTOLOGY [18], ON-TO-KNOWLEDGE [19] and COMMON-KADS [20]. METHONTOLOGY proposes to align ontology development with software development activities and consequently defines an ontology development life cycle process (similar to software development) that consists of several phases.

Some of these methodologies are the outcome of experiences collected during the ontology development process such as the Enterprise Methodology [16] or the TOVE (Toronto Virtual Enterprise) Methodology[17]. The TOVE methodology is characterized by its definition of the so-called "competency questions" that determine the scope of the ontology to be modeled and for which the future ontology shall be capable of providing answers. In developing of the ontology design for the automatic staging of lymphoma patient, we followed the approach of establishing competency questions.

6.3   Reasoning-Based Patient Classification

There exist several approaches that integrate practical clinical knowledge for improving clinical applications. [21] focuses on the classification of lung tumors and [22] on the classification of glioma tumors. [23] is similar to our exemplified use case, inasmuch as it introduces an application that provides support for the semantic annotation of medical images. [23] relies on the anatomy model and its regional relationships for assisting the labeling of the MRI image content by means of OWL DL reasoning. [24] aims for improved and concise patient data visualization by incorporating clinical knowledge, such as the WHO grading system. The mentioned related approaches do not provide any details about the accomplished knowledge engineering steps and we assume that the use cases could be modeled in accordance to our introduced approach.

7   Conclusion

The usage of OWL DL based reasoning capabilities, provide means to automatically perform lymphoma patient classification. The achieved additional patient annotation again can be used in a multitude of clinical applications, such as the recommendations for treatments, quality control applications, and for improved search and visualization applications for patient information. In our future work, we will focus on the integration of the established OWL DL based classification system into the overall MEDICO system aiming for improve clinical applications. Furthermore, we will analyze the potential of other reasoning approaches, such as rules or theorem proving, in the context of our application scenario.

Acknowledgments. This research has been supported in part by the THESEUS Program in the MEDICO Project, which is funded by the German Federal Ministry of Economics and Technology under the grant number 01MQ07016. The responsibility for this publication lies with the author. We are also thankful to Kamal Najib for his support with implementation tasks.

References

1. Seifert, S., Barbu, A., Zhou, S., Liu, D., Feulner, J., Huber, M., Suehling, M., Cavallaro, A., Comaniciu, D.: Hierarchical parsing and semantic navigation of full body ct data. In: SPIE Medical Imaging (2009)
2. Channin, D., Mongkolwat, P., Kleper, V., Sepukar, K., Rubin, D.: The cabib annotation and image markup project. Journal of Digital Imaging (2009)
3. Rubin, D., Mongkolwat, P., Kleper, V., Supekar, K., Channin, D.: Medical imaging on the semantic web: Annotation and image markup. In: AAAI Spring Symposium Series, Semantic Scientific Knowledge Integration, Stanford, USA (2008)
4. Möller, M., Regel, S., Sintek, M.: Radsem: Semantic annotation and retrieval for medical images. In: Aroyo, L., Traverso, P., Ciravegna, F., Cimiano, P., Heath, T., Hyvönen, E., Mizoguchi, R., Oren, E., Sabou, M., Simperl, E. (eds.) ESWC 2009. LNCS, vol. 5554, pp. 21–35. Springer, Heidelberg (2009)
5. Wittekind, C., Meyer, H., Bootz, F.: TNM Klassifikation maligner Tumoren. Springer, Heidelberg (2005)
6. Wennerberg, P., Zillner, S., Möller, M., Buitelaar, P., Sintek, M.: Kemm: A knowledge engineering methodology in the medical domain. In: Proc. of the 5th International Conference on Formal Ontology in Information Systems, FOIS (2008)
7. Rosse, C., Mejino, J.J.: A reference ontology for biomedical informatics: the foundational model of anatomy. J. of Biomedical Informatics 36 (2003)
8. Baader, F., Calvanese, D., McGuinness, D.L., Nardi, D., Patel-Schneider, P.F. (eds.): The Description Logic Handbook: Theory, Implementation, and Applications. Cambridge University Press, Cambridge (2003)
9. Russel, S., Norvig, P.: Artificial Intelligence: A Modern Approach. Prentice Hall, New Jersey (1995)
10. Uschold, M., Gruninger, M.: Ontologies: Principles, methods and applications. Knowledge Engineering Review 11 (1996)
11. Wennerberg, P., Buitelaar, P., Zillner, S.: Towards a human anatomy data set for query pattern mining based on wikipedia and domain semantic resources. In: Proceedings of a Workshop on Building and Evaluating Resources for Biomedical Text Mining (LREC), Marrakech, Marocco (2008)
12. Buitelaar, P., Wennerberg, P., Zillner, S.: Statistical term profiling for query pattern mining. In: Proceedings of ACL 2008 BioNLP Workshop, Columbus, Ohio, USA (2008)

13. Wennerberg, P., Zillner, S.: Towards context driven modularization of large biomedical ontologies. In: Proceedings of the International Conference of Biomedical Ontology (ICBO), Buffalo, New York, US (2009)
14. Bouaud, J., Bachimont, B., Charlet, J., Zweigenbaum, P.: Methodological principles for structuring an "ontology" (1995)
15. Jones, D., Bench-Capon, T., Visser, P.: Methodologies for ontology development (1998)
16. Uschold, M.: Building ontologies: Towards a unified methodology. In: 16th Annual Conf. of the British Computer Society Specialist Group on Expert Systems (1996)
17. Gruninger, M., Fox, M.S.: The design and evaluation of ontologies for enterprise engineering (1994)
18. López, M.F., Gómez-Pérez, A., Sierra, J.P., Sierra, A.P.: Building a chemical ontology using methontology and the ontology design environment. IEEE Intelligent Systems 14 (1999)
19. Sure, Y., Studer, R.: On-to-knowledge methodology - final version (2002)
20. Schreiber, G., Akkermans, H., Anjewierden, A., Dehoog, R., Shadbolt, N., Vandevelde, W., Wielinga, B.: Knowledge Engineering and Management: The CommonKADS Methodology. The MIT Press, Cambridge (1999)
21. Dameron, O., Roques, E., Rubin, D., Marquet, G., Burgun, A.: Grading lung tumors using owl-dl based reasoning. In: Proceedings of 9th International protégé Conference (2006)
22. Marquet, G., Dameron, O., Saikali, S., Mosser, J., Burgun, A.: Grading glioma tumors using owl-dl and nci-thesaurus. In: Proceedings of the American Medical Informatics Association Conference AMIA (2007)
23. Golbreich, C., Dameron, O., Bierlaire, O., Gibaud, B.: What reasoning support for ontology and rules? the brain anatomy case study. In: Proceedings of the Workshop on OWL Experiences and Directions, Irlande (2005)
24. Zillner, S., Hauer, T., Rogulin, D., Tsymbal, A., Huber, M., Solomonides, T.: Semantic visualization of patient information. In: Proceedings of the 21th IEEE International Symposium on Computer-Based Medical Systems (CBMS), Jyvskyl, Finland (2008)

Facilitating Dialogue - Using Semantic Web Technology for eParticipation

George Anadiotis[1], Panos Alexopoulos[1], Konstantinos Mpaslis[1],
Aristotelis Zosakis[1], Konstantinos Kafentzis[1], and Konstantinos Kotis[2,3]

[1] IMC Technologies, Athens, Greece
{ganadiotis,palexopoulos,kmpaslis,azosakis,kkafentzis}@imc.com.gr
[2] University of the Aegean, AI-Lab, Samos, Greece
kotis@aegean.gr
[3] Prefecture of Samos, IT Department, Samos, Greece
kotis@samos.gr

Abstract. In this paper we describe the application of various Semantic Web technologies and their combination with emerging Web 2.0 use patterns in the eParticipation domain and show how they are used in an operational system for the Regional Government of the Prefecture of Samos, Greece. We present parts of the system that are based on Semantic Web technology and how they are merged with a Web 2.0 philosophy and explain the benefits of this approach, as showcased by applications for annotating, searching, browsing and cross-referencing content in eParticipation communities.

1 Introduction: On eParticipation

There is general agreement among many actors in democratic societies that there is a lack of possibilities for political participation. New media and the internet especially have been heralded as solutions to this problem and while eParticipation, or 'the use of information and communication technologies to broaden and deepen political participation by enabling citizens to connect with one another and with their elected representatives' [12], cannot replace other forms of participation and solve the democratic deficit once and for all, it can help to improve the overall democratic culture in a society.

Even though the uptake of eParticipation solutions depends to a great extent on political commitment and social consensus, a solid technical foundation that provides advanced functionality via a seamless user experience and helps dealing with eParticipation-associated challenges [12] is also of great importance. With that goal in mind, when faced with the challenge to develop and deploy an eParticipation solution for the Regional Government of the Prefecture of Samos, we chose an approach powered by the advanced features of Semantic Web technology, while hiding its complexity behind a user-friendly Web 2.0 facade. The resulting solution has been deployed at http://www.samos-dialogos.gr.

This paper is organised as follows: in this Section, we present the domain and give the necessary background in order to explain the use of ontologies

L. Aroyo et al. (Eds.): ESWC 2010, Part I, LNCS 6088, pp. 258–272, 2010.

in the deliberation process in Section 2, while in Section 3 we elaborate on the mechanisms in place for transparent hybrid-based search and browsing. In Section 4 we describe the reference deliberation ontology developed as part of the project and how it is used to make content available as Linked Data and build distributed applications that use it. Finally, we evaluate our approach in Section 5 and present conclusions and future work in Section 6.

1.1   A Methodology and Platform for eParticipation

In order to facilitate eParticipation, a two-fold approach has been taken, laying the theoretical framework and providing its implementation:

- a *methodology* has been developed, based on extensive study of related literature and deployed projects worldwide
- an *integrated platform* has been implemented, using appropriate tools to support the methodology in every aspect

The methodology is based on three different processes that can run separately, complementing each other and covering online channels of citizen participation. The first is the eConsultation process, initiated in a top-down way by the decision makers, aiming to provide an efficient and easy way to collect intelligent feedback from citizens on different issues. The second process is the ePetition process, initiated in a bottom-up way by citizens, aiming to offer an accessible mechanism through which citizens can raise publicly issues they deem important. Finally, the third process is the eDeliberation process, which requires a closer collaboration between decision makers and citizens in order to formulate policies and achieve consensus on important issues. All three processes have been implemented in the platform, supplemented by offline actions where needed.

In the rest of the paper we focus on eDeliberation, as it is the most engaging and complex process. It essentially constitutes a tight 'serial process' within a specific time-frame, with 7 concrete steps embedded in each deliberative cycle (see Figure 1). Initially we have the agenda setting stage, in which citizens may choose among a list of proposed issues for deliberation. After choice has been made, we move on to the discussion stage, succeeded by a report publishing stage, in which moderators summarize the discussion in a report. Then there is the voting stage, in which citizens have to fill in questionnaires to quantify opinions and finally, after another report has been published to summarize the outcome of the voting stage, an interactive online real-time council takes place. The process concludes with the publishing of an overall report.

The platform supports the implementation of this process via appropriate web-based tools for each step: an e-poll component for agenda setting, a moderated e-forum, e-surveys to quantify opinions, interactive online real-time webcasting of the council, where citizens can offer their feedback directly and a document library component for report publishing. Both the methodology and the platform have evolved through previous experience in the case of the City of Trikala, Greece [9], a finalist in the European eGovernment Awards for 2009.[1]

---

[1] http://www.epractice.eu/en/cases/edialogosawards

Agenda setting   Discussion   Discussion report   Voting   Voting report   Online council   Final report

Fig. 1. Methodology stages for eDeliberation

2   Adding Semantics to eDeliberation

Each deliberation process is focused on a specific domain, determined by the outcome of the agenda setting stage. In order to assist citizens engage in the process, as well as administrators responsible for producing information material for it, domain knowledge can be captured and made available to both user groups by means of a domain ontology. The association of a domain ontology with a deliberation is an optional task, however doing so serves a dual purpose: i) users are given context for the topic under discussion, in a form they can use to annotate content and ii) based on provided annotations and ontological relations, a powerful hybrid search mechanism is implemented.

2.1   Making Domain Knowledge Explicit: Developing Domain Ontologies

So far, four online deliberation processes have been started in the Prefecture of Samos, for which three ontologies have been developed, as two of the deliberations refer to the same domain (Tourism) and are hence associated with the same ontology. The ontologies have been developed by knowledge workers in the Prefecture of Samos, in collaboration with the University of Aegean, AI-Lab. The methodology followed for the development of the domain ontologies was partially based on HCOME [11]. Due to the short time of project implementation, the collaborative part of the methodology was not implemented using a tool such as SharedHCONE or Collaborative Protege, however active involvement of knowledge workers in the ontology engineering process was ensured.

Knowledge was extracted from administration documents provided by the Prefecture (press docs, board decisions docs, legislation, etc), web documents retrieved by knowledge workers and other available domain ontologies. Extraction of conceptualizations from text was performed manually, with all artefacts named in English while providing Greek labels for internationalization purposes. A small number of knowledge workers with less experience in ICT was asked to use a human-centered ontology engineering environment, namely HCONE2 [10], for the engineering of draft versions of the ontologies, while the final versions were developed in Protege.

The domain ontologies developed following the abovementioned methodology were:

- **Recycling Ontology**, aiming to represent knowledge regarding the domain of recycling materials and its impact to the environment. Special focus on the recycling of plastic bags from local companies/organizations has been given due to related administrative board decisions that were taken.
- **Culture Ontology**, aiming to represent knowledge regarding the cultural heritage of the prefecture and the role of the authorities and non-profit organizations to the accentuation of local assets, as well as potential initiatives towards new forms of cultural events/developments.
- **Tourism ontology**, aiming to represent knowledge regarding the touristic development of the prefecture and the role of the authorities and non-profit organizations to the accentuation of local assets as well as potential initiatives towards new forms of touristic developments.

2.2 Making Explicit Knowledge Accessible: Associating Domain Ontologies with the Deliberation Process

Even though knowledge formulation in the form of ontologies can provide substantial benefits to the operation of the platform, its potential will not be fully realized unless it is available to the users in a form that is familiar and easy to use. For this purpose, we chose to pursue a Web 2.0 approach as far as user experience is concerned.

Ontologies that the administrators wish to associate with certain deliberations are acquired (developed from scratch or imported/reused) and stored in an ontological repository. Ontologies are processed before being stored in the repository, in order to ensure that all classes and instances have corresponding labels that are readable and informative.

After a deliberation has been created in the system, administrators may use a GUI to browse the ontological repository and select an ontology they wish to associate with the deliberation. The ontology is then imported in the system in the form of a taxonomy: a stripped-down form of the original ontology, retaining only classes and instances as well as their hierarchical relations, using their labels as taxonomy terms. The ontology will be from that point on available across all the tools encompassed in the deliberation in the form of a taxonomy of domain-related terms that can be used to:

- **Annotate**. A deliberation's domain taxonomy can be used to annotate content associated with the deliberation (web content, forum posts, documents, etc). Users remain agnostic of the underlying complexity of the ontology and are presented with a tree-like structure with auto-complete assistance that they can use to 'tag' resources, as seen in Figure 2.
- **Browse**. In order to enable quick access to popular content within a deliberation, users may browse through a tag cloud used to visualize resource annotation frequency. Clicking on a tag triggers the search mechanism for this tag, limiting its scope to annotations, thus retrieving the resources it has been used to annotate categorized by type and ranked by relevance (see Section 3). Additionally, an overall tag cloud is available, that aggregates terms and their frequencies across deliberations.

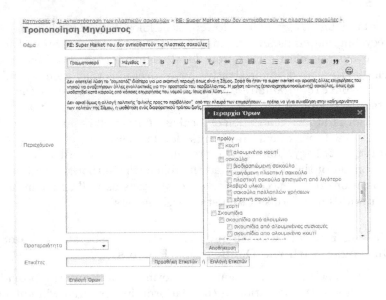

Fig. 2. Content annotation using tags

It must be emphasized however that despite the simplified view of the ontology that users are presented with, a connection of taxonomy terms, or tags, with their counterpart ontological terms is retained. Additionally to the use of a controlled vocabulary to annotate resources, custom tags may also be used in order to allow users to complement the vocabulary with their own terms.

3   Finding Relevant Views

Besides browsing via the tag cloud or navigating via the web front-end menu structure, we wanted to enable users to locate content quickly via an intuitive search mechanism, tailored to our eParticipation context and infrastructure requirements, namely:

- `Usability by general public`. The quintessence of the deliberation process is to involve as broad an audience as possible. Therefore, we had to take a 'least common denominator' approach, focusing on providing an intuitive search mechanism that performs well without presenting users with a complicated set of options.
- `Applicability to heterogeneous content`. In our platform, a variety of tools is used to support the deliberation process, each one generating content with different characteristics. Therefore, according to the 'least common denominator' approach we choose to rely on a combination of full-text search and user-provided annotation, as all the tools generate content that can be annotated, indexed and retrieved.

– **Applicability to user-generated content.** Finally, content is mostly generated by end users, therefore we cannot rely on resources to be properly annotated, even when using the simplest possible form of annotation (tagging). When present though, we want to take this annotation into account.

3.1   A Hybrid Search System

Taking the above points into account, we chose to pursue a hybrid search approach that relies mostly on full-text search and statistical measures to retrieve and rank results, but also uses annotations, where available, to influence ranking as well as domain ontologies to expand results.

Each piece of content generated by the platform tools is treated as a document and indexed using the Lucene engine[2]. The title, tags and actual content of the piece are linguistically analyzed before they are indexed (as discrete fields), using a custom analyzer developed especially for the Greek language that performs tokenization and lemmatization. Additional fields are also used for some specific content types, based on their structure.

The search interface is extremely simple, having only one input field in which keyword search terms are entered (Figure 3). The query string is parsed using the same analyzer used for indexing, ensuring that query terms match index terms, and the resulting terms are looked up in the index. Ranking results is done using standard TF/IDF metrics, however the query performed against the index combines field scores giving different weights to each, promoting the tags field to reflect the fact that we consider explicit annotation as most relevant. Title field is weighted 2nd, content field 3rd and custom content fields follow.

This way we produce results that are ranked based on a mixed model, utilizing annotations, when present, while smoothly blending with an effective full-text search model. This takes place intuitively, by utilizing a different, simpler mechanism than the one utilized in similar existing work [4], as our context differs and hence so do our requirements. Additionally, queries can be further refined or expanded depending on user input.

Query refinement works on the deliberation level, so if users choose to use the search functionality while browsing a specific deliberation space, they can activate an option that restricts the results to content generated only for the deliberation at hand.

Query expansion works by utilizing the same search mechanism, but using a semantically expanded query as input. When the query expansion mechanism is activated, the original user query is first processed by the query expansion engine and then the resulting semantically expanded query is used as input for the search mechanism. Terms retrieved via the semantic expansion mechanism are displayed separately in a special 'expanded query tag cloud' that visualizes which are the extra terms and how frequently they occur. This is used as a means of filtering expanded results, as the user is not only presented with a list

---

[2] http://lucene.apache.org/

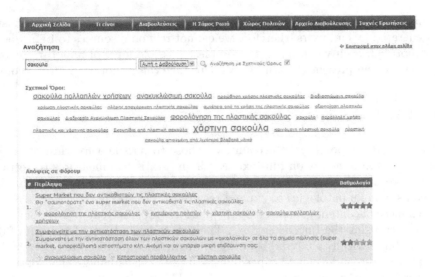

Fig. 3. Search Interface

of related terms, but is also able to preview how many results each of them is associated with. By clicking on a term the user is presented with related results.

3.2   Query Expansion via Contextualization

In order to perform semantic query expansion, we have implemented a component that works by determining for a given query term, terms that are semantically similar in the specific search context. The component works by utilizing domain ontologies and a corresponding semantic query expansion method [1]. Since this mechanism relies on the existence of a domain ontology, it only works for searching within deliberations that have been associated with one, via the process described in Section 2.

The method draws upon ideas and techniques from the areas of ontologies and fuzzy logic and allows for the customization of the semantic similarity assessment mechanism according to the search scenario's particular characteristics. This is made possible through a context model that captures information about which of the domain ontology's relations and to what extent should participate in the similarity assessment process. The parameters of this model are typically determined prior to the deployment of the system and are used by a contextualization algorithm for producing a term semantic similarity index (i.e. pairs of similar terms) that is subsequently used for the expansion [1].

The distinguishing characteristic of this expansion method compared to others is that it may utilize not only the *subclassOf*, *equivalent* and *instanceOf* relations that are typically found within an ontology but virtually any relation between concepts and their instances that has been defined within the domain ontology.

Thus, given a query, the platform's query expansion mechanism works as follows:

- **Query parsing.** Query terms are parsed and compared against taxonomical terms generated via the association process described in Section 2. This is done using the same advanced analyzer used for indexing, thus giving great flexibility in the matching process, and results in a list of taxonomical terms.
- **Query expansion.** As noted in Section 2, taxonomical terms retain their association to their ontological counterparts, by storing their URIs. So at this point, the list of URIs that correspond to the taxonomical terms identified in the query parsing stage are sent to the query expansion component, which then uses the semantic similarity index described above in order to produce a list of ontological terms that are related to the ones given as input.
- **Query execution.** Finally, the list of ontological terms returned by the query expansion component are associated to their taxonomical counterparts (again, via their URIs) and used as input to the hybrid search mechanism. It must be noted that the weight of terms retrieved via the query expansion mechanism is appropriately reduced in order to influence their standing in the overall ranking and reflect the fact that they are deemed less relevant than terms contained in the original query.

4   Sharing Views

As eParticipation matures as a discipline, we expect to see more eParticipation projects being implemented and, consequently, the need to connect these communities and let them share their views to emerge. This is not just a hypothetical projection, as in addition to the City of Trikala, there are already similar projects under way in the City of Arta and the City of Thessaloniki, the 2nd largest in Greece. Although each community has its own characteristics and issues at stake, certain issues will be shared on the local, regional, national and international level, for which the exchange of experience shall be benefitial.

On the other hand, even though a specialized eParticipation framework best serves an integrated approach in a controlled environment, dialogue and argumentation exchange naturally also occur in non-designated environments and in non-prescribed forms. Fora, social networking sites, mailing lists and newsgroups alike, as different as they may be in terms of technical infrastructure, they all provide means to facilitate discussion for the user communities that use them. This is another 'resource', or content provider, that we would like to tap on by enabling exchange and reference to expressed views.

In order to address both of these challenges, we need to adopt an approach that enables us to not only specify the semantics of the exchange (what is the community and its discussions about) but also make it feasible technically, by providing a mechanism to support identification and cross-reference of resources, a transport layer and remote structured querying facilities. In that view, the adoption of Linked Data is a natural choice, as it covers all these requirements in a standardized way via ontologies, URIs and SPARQL [6].

In this section, we describe our approach towards the implementation of this vision, by describing our eDeliberation ontology, its use for making content available as Linked Data as well as an application built on top of this infrastructure that showcases its potential.

4.1 The eDeliberation Ontology

The eDeliberation ontology is a conceptualization of our framework. Its primary goal is to make the structure and semantics of the framework explicit and subsequently to make the content it generates accessible to external applications in the form of Linked Data, rather than constitute a generic knowledge map of the eParticipation domain [14].

Each deliberation process is modelled within the eParticipation platform as an online community whose members make use of certain tools, such as fora, questionnaires and polls, in order to participate in each of the deliberation's stages. All the tools are associated with a community space in the platform. In this process, content such as forum posts, answers to questionnaires or documents is generated and annotated by means of the deliberation's associated domain ontology. This means that the deliberation ontology needs to represent each deliberation stage in connection to the associated tools and the content they generate. Additionally, it should provide a way to make content meaning explicit, by relating its tags to terms derived from the deliberation's domain ontology, as well as provide information about the use of tags in specific annotations.

In order to cover the above requirements, the eDeliberation ontology reuses well established ontologies from the Semantic Web community, namely the SIOC Core Ontology[3], the Tag Ontology[4] and the MOAT Ontology[5], all suited for semantically representing Web 2.0 content. In particular, the SIOC ontology enables the integration of online community information and social web data, the Tag ontology models the relationship between resources, tags and users and the MOAT ontology enables users to define the meaning(s) of their tag(s) by using URIs of Semantic Web resources. Certain concepts and relations from these ontologies are either used as-is or extended in the eParticipation ontology.

Reused concepts are sioc:Forum, sioc:Post, tag:RestrictedTagging, tag:Tag and moat:Meaning. As for the other classes, these are:

- **Deliberation:** The process described in Figure 1. The concept is defined as a subclass of the concept sioc:Space.
- **TopicSelectionPoll:** Poll which is conducted for determining the topics that will be discussed in a deliberation (extends sioc_t:Poll).
- **PotentialDeliberationTopic:** Topic which has been suggested for deliberation.
- **Document:** A document that contains information regarding a deliberation.
- **Document Library:** The set of documents that regard a specific deliberation. The concept is defined as a subclass of the concept Container of the SIOC ontology.

The relations that link the above concepts are shown in Figure 4.

---

[3] http://sioc-project.org/
[4] http://www.holygoat.co.uk/projects/tags/
[5] http://moat-project.org/

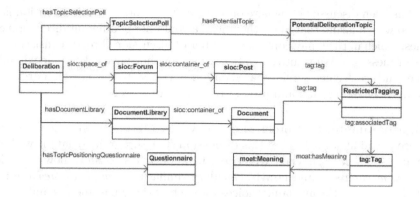

Fig. 4. Deliberation Ontology

4.2   Making Deliberation Content Available as Linked Data

Same as domain ontologies, the deliberation ontology serves a practical goal besides conceptually specifying the domain: it is used in order to make content generated on the platform available as Linked Data. We rely on existing work on the inbound/outbound Linked Data approach to make this possible [2].

As the eParticipation platform is implemented as a typical Web 2.0 n-tier application, all the entities and relations modelled in the eParticipation ontology live in a relational database. In order to make them available as Linked Data, we mapped the platform's database to the ontology using D2R as the tool to produce the mappings as well as publish the data via a SPARQL endpoint. Most of the mapping process was rather straightforward, as the vocabularies used are a natural match for our domain the eParticipation ontology is also modeled appropriately.

One point that deserves special attention is the use of the Tag and MOAT vocabularies to represent both taxonomical and user-provided tags. In both cases, Tags and Taggings are mapped in the same way, however the difference is that taxonomical tags have exactly 1 pre-specified meaning, which is the same for every tagging and corresponds to the concept of the ontology from which they originate while user-provided tags may have from 0 to N meanings, depending on their use and to whether the user has grounded them with some ontology concept or not. In our case, user-provided tags do not have meanings, for reasons we shall explain in Section 6.

4.3   Distributed Contextual Views Retrieval

Having the ontological infrastructure and the Linked Data mechanism in place, we utilize them in order to provide context for disussions taking place in deliberations. The idea is to enable people participating in the discussion to have an idea of what has been discussed elsewhere on the topic at hand. Each deliberation is associated with a forum that plays the role of a container of different discussion categories, which in turn may contain a number of discussion threads consisting of a series of messages. We want to locate discussions that have taken place on other sources and are deemed similar, based on some criteria, to the ones that are taking place in each deliberation and present them to forum users.

Design parameters. In order to do so, we need to define what it is we want to present and at what level of this discussion structure to associate it with and present it (*granularity*), where to retrieve from (*source selection*), how to retrieve it (*query mechanism*) and how to calculate similarity (*similarity measure*). We shall elaborate on the available choices for each of these parameters and how we define the positioning of our application on the selection space.

Regarding the choice of *query mechanism*, since we wanted to implement an application that does not rely on proprietary APIs in order to retrieve information from different sources, our choice was between using OpenSearch[6] and Linked Data. We decided to go with Linked Data, as it allows for more flexibility in specifying data structure, semantics and search criteria. OpenSearch only supports text-based queries and is also not transparent as to how the results returned are ranked, while we wanted to have control over the ranking. Additionally, Linked Data is gaining traction, so we expect to see an increasing number of discussion board providers supporting it in the near future.

The *source selection* dimension however highlights a contradiction with regard to the use of Linked Data as the foundation for building applications. On the one hand, basing our retrieval mechanism on Linked Data means that, if properly designed, it can be generic enough to be applicable to any Linked Data source. In practice however, our choice is rather limited since at this point the use of Linked Data to publish discussion board data in structured form is still very limited. For this reason, we chose to only interlink different instances of our platform, each one serving as a data provider and a consumer at the same time.

In terms of *granularity*, the two extremes would be to establish connections at the deliberation level and the message level. Single messages taken out of context do not provide enough information to create associations, while deliberations on the other hand are eParticipation-specific constructs, so establishing connections at this level would mean that the mechanism would not be applicable to any discussion board. So we chose to focus our interlinking algorithm on retrieving threads of discussion related to a certain category, which is generic enough to work for any discussion board, while also utilizing eParticipation-specific information in case it is present.

Finally, given these choices, we designed a first version of the contextual views retrieval mechanism that calculates *similarity* using a mixture of structural information and content similarity on the textual level, making no assumptions about the presence of annotations, but is also generic enough so that it can be extended to take such information into account, if present.

---

[6] http://www.opensearch.org

Implementation. Our distributed contextual views retrieval mechanism works as follows:

Source selection is currently controlled via a manually maintained list of SPARQL endpoints that provide discussion board data in a structured form, in compliance with the SIOC vocabulary. If the endpoints also provide deliberation data, then we assume that the endpoint is an instance of an eParticipation platform, so administrators are given the option to associate deliberations running locally with others residing on remote endpoints, using a special GUI to do so.

When presenting deliberation fora, users may choose to view relevant views for each discussion category by clicking the corresponding button. Then the name of the category is parsed (again using advanced language processing techniques) and the terms it contains are extracted and used to query endpoints, retrieve and rank relevant discussion threads and present links to them alongside the local threads.

There is a 'default' similarity measure used in case there is no annotation present, which is generic enough to be usable for any SIOC-enabled SPARQL endpoint: a SPARQL query is issued against the endpoint, searching for posts that contain at least one of the query terms in their content or title, or in their thread's title. This query returns information about Posts and their associated Threads that is processed locally to rank the results in terms of their syntactic relevance to the issued query terms, using information retrieval techniques similar to the ones used to rank local results.

Since this intermediate list of results contains discrete Posts and not Threads, we use it to produce a list of discrete Threads to be presented, based on: i) The sum of occurences of Posts belonging to each Thread in the intermediate list. The more Posts each Thread has, the higher it is ranked. ii) Possible association between the deliberation to which the local discussion category belongs and the deliberation to which the remote Thread belongs. If such an association exists, the Thread is promoted in the ranking. Further elaboration is beyond the scope of this paper and is identified as future work.

5   Evaluation

At the time of writing, the system had been in operation for a period of one month, running a total of 4 deliberations. Some early indicators on which we can judge the platform's impact and importance are the following:

- Number of citizens who have registered at the platform: 70.
- Number of citizens who participated in the first agenda setting e-poll: 25.
- Number of citizens who posted to the e-forum: 20 with 33 posts.
- Number of e-surveys submitted: 4 answered in total by 44 citizens.
- Monthly average statistics: 784 visits, 385 unique visitors, 6.469 page views.

Although the above numbers may seem small, when evaluating them we have to consider the limited amount of time the project has been running, the novel nature of the project and also the fact that in the Prefecture of Samos (with a population of 33.814 people), 42% of the population are internet users out of which 60% have broadband access[7]. Assuming that broadband users are the ones most likely to use such a sophisticated platform, then we can -very roughly- estimate that 1% of them became registered users and 10% participated in one way or another. We expect these figures to rise substantially in the coming months, as the recently launched publicity campaign for the project will reach its peak and word-of-mouth advertisement will also start taking effect.

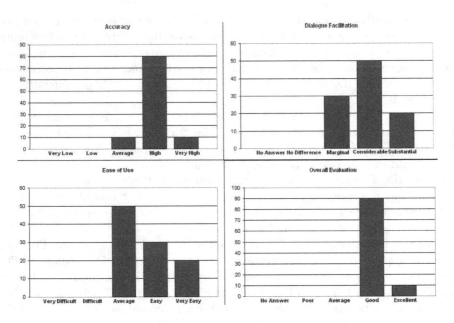

Fig. 5. Qualitative user evaluation

Besides quantitative indicators provided by usage statistics, a user survey has also been undertaken in order to evaluate the system qualitatively. A total of 12 users so far have provided feedback by means of filling in questionnaires to evaluate the accuracy of the retrieved results as well as overall satisfaction by the system. The results of the evaluation are depicted in Figure 5, showing that the system scores well on ease of use and extremely well in the other categories.

6   Conclusions and Future Work

In this paper we described how Semantic Web technologies were applied in our eParticipation platform, deployed in the Prefecture of Samos. We gave some

---

[7] Figures calculated and based on official data from the Observatory for the Information Society eEurope/i2010 July 08 report and the Census 2001 population data of the Greek National Statistics Office.

background on the domain and the platform and showed why the technology fits the domain, how it has been implemented using a Web 2.0 user-friendly approach as far as the user interface is concerned and what benefits it brings in terms of content annotation, browsing and search. We emphasized the sharing aspect of the platform, showed how it aligns with the Linked Data philosophy and infrastructure and described a distributed approach to contextual views retrieval that is based on it.

In terms of future work, we identify the following areas:

- **Improved support for annotation.** In order to assist users in the annotation process, we are looking to add a semi-automated annotation feature: the system will examine new content as well as the domain ontology in the context (deliberation) it has been generated and provide suggested taxonomical terms to use as annotations.

- **Incorporation of meanings for user-provided tags.** As part of an inbound/outbound Linked Data approach, we have been developing an application that grounds tag meanings with DBpedia concepts [2]. We shall include this application in the platform, as tag meanings can enhance search, disambiguate tag use and even be used for ontology alignment and evolution purposes, as soon as a Greek version of DBpedia is available.

- **Support for inference.** A known issue for the recipe we used to publish Linked Data is the lack of inference capabilities in the SPARQL endpoint provided by D2R [5], as 'a certain amount of inference (datatypes, basic RDFS, owl:sameAs) would be desirable and feasible'. Furthermore, by adding inference capabilities for each node to the eParticipation scenario we have, in which each community maintains control over its ontologies, it becomes an ideal match for a distributed reasoning scenario [3].

- **Refinement of similarity measure used in distributed contextual views assesment.** The similarity measure that we described in Section 4 is a first approach to assesing similarity between threaded discussions based on textual search. This has certain drawbacks, as on the one hand our D2R-based SPARQL endpoint does not currently support Semantic IR [13] features, therefore we have to rely on the limited matching capabilities offered by pure SPARQL, on the other hand we do not take into account the existence of annotation. While the former is beyond our control, for the latter we could utilize ontology alignment techniques and tools [8,7] in order to align ontologies used in different nodes and thus be able to assess similarity between resources annotated using these ontologies.

Concluding, we believe that the eParticipation domain is one that showcases very well the benefits of Semantic Web technology in action and we shall continue in pursuing this approach and further evolving it, in the hope that it can contribute to facilitating a dialogue ecosystem.

Acknowledgements

We would like to thank Mr. Vasilis Goulandris, for his contribution in the methodological part of the platform, the Prefecture of Samos Director, Mr. Manolis Karlas for his support in the implementation of the project, as well as the IT department of the Prefecture of Samos for their support during the platform's operation.

References

1. Alexopoulos, P., Wallace, M., Kafentzis, K.: A Fuzzy Ontology Framework for Customized Assessment of Semantic Similarity. In: 3rd International Workshop on Semantic Media and Adaptation (2008)
2. Anadiotis, G., Andriopoulos, P., Vekris, D., Zosakis, A.: Linked Data for the masses - using open source infrastructure and the inbound/outbound Linked Data approach to bring added value to end user applications. In: I-KNOW '09 and I-SEMANTICS '09 (to appear, 2009)
3. Anadiotis, G., Kotoulas, S., Siebes, R.: An Architecture for Peer-to-peer Reasoning. In: New Forms of Reasoning for the Semantic Web, CEUR Workshop Proceedings, vol. 291. CEUR-WS.org (2007)
4. Bhagdev, R., Chapman, S., Ciravegna, F., Lanfranchi, V., Petrelli, D.: Hybrid Search: Effectively Combining Keywords and Ontology-based Searches. In: Bechhofer, S., Hauswirth, M., Hoffmann, J., Koubarakis, M. (eds.) ESWC 2008. LNCS, vol. 5021, pp. 554–568. Springer, Heidelberg (2008)
5. Bizer, C., Cyganiak, R.: D2RQ - Lessons Learned. W3C Workshop on RDF Access to Relational Databases (October 2007)
6. Bizer, C., Heath, T., Idehen, K., Berners-Lee, T.: Linked data on the web. In: WWW '08: Proceedings of the 17th international conference on World Wide Web, pp. 1265–1266. ACM, New York (2008)
7. Bizer, C., Volz, J., Kobilarov, G., Gaedke, M.: Silk - A Link Discovery Framework for the Web of Data. In: 18th World Wide Web Conference (April 2009)
8. Euzenat, J., Shvaiko, P.: Ontology matching. Springer, Heidelberg (2007)
9. Kafentzis, K., Alexopoulos, P., Korakas, C., Goulandris, V., Baseas, I., Georgolios, P.: Enabling citizen participation in local governance using ict. In: 3rd National Conference of the Hellenic Society for Systemic Studies, Piraeus, Greece (2007)
10. Kotis, K.: On Supporting HCOME-3O Ontology Argumentation using Semantic Wiki Technology. In: Meersman, R., Tari, Z., Herrero, P. (eds.) OTM-WS 2008. LNCS, vol. 5333, pp. 193–199. Springer, Heidelberg (2008)
11. Kotis, K., Vouros, G.: Human-Centered Ontology Engineering: the HCOME Methodology. International Journal of Knowledge and Information Systems 10, 109–131 (2006)
12. Macintosh, A.: eParticipation in Policy-making: the Research and the Challenges. In: Exploiting the Knowledge Economy: Issues, Applications, Case Studies, IOS Press, Amsterdam (2006)
13. Minack, E., Siberski, W., Nejdl, W.: Benchmarking Fulltext Search Performance of RDF Stores. In: Aroyo, L., Traverso, P., Ciravegna, F., Cimiano, P., Heath, T., Hyvönen, E., Mizoguchi, R., Oren, E., Sabou, M., Simperl, E. (eds.) ESWC 2009. LNCS, vol. 5554, pp. 81–95. Springer, Heidelberg (2009)
14. Wimmer, M.: Ontology for an e-participation virtual resource centre. In: ICEGOV '07: Proceedings of the 1st international conference on Theory and practice of electronic governance, pp. 89–98. ACM, New York (2007)

Implementing Archaeological Time Periods Using CIDOC CRM and SKOS

Ceri Binding

University of Glamorgan, Pontypridd, UK
cbinding@glam.ac.uk

Abstract. Within the archaeology domain, datasets frequently refer to time periods using a variety of textual or numeric formats. Traditionally controlled vocabularies of time periods have used classification notation and the collocation of terms in the printed form to represent and convey tacit information about the relative order of concepts. The emergence of the semantic web entails encoding this knowledge into machine readable forms, and so the meaning of this informal ordering arrangement can be lost. Conversion of controlled vocabularies to Simple Knowledge Organisation System (SKOS) format provides a formal basis for semantic web indexing but does not facilitate chronological inference - as thesaurus relationship types are an inappropriate mechanism to fully describe temporal relationships. This becomes an issue in archaeological data where periods are often described in terms of (e.g.) named monarchs or emperors, without additional information concerning relative chronological context.

An exercise in supplementing existing controlled vocabularies of time period concepts with dates and temporal relationships was undertaken as part of the Semantic Technologies for Archaeological Resources (STAR) project. The general aim of the STAR project is to demonstrate the potential benefits in cross searching archaeological data conforming to a common overarching conceptual data structure schema - the CIDOC Conceptual Reference Model (CRM). This paper gives an overview of STAR applications and services and goes on to particularly focus on issues concerning the extraction and representation of time period information.

Keywords: CIDOC CRM, SKOS, semantic interoperability, time periods, archaeology.

1 Introduction

The work described here draws on work carried out for the AHRC funded Semantic Technologies for Archaeology Resources (STAR) project [1]. This is a 3 year project in collaboration with English Heritage, the broad aim of the research being to investigate the utility of mapping different archaeological datasets to a common overarching ontology, where the datasets are indexed using domain specific thesauri and glossaries. The goal is to demonstrate effective search across multiple different archaeological datasets and associated grey literature documents.

L. Aroyo et al. (Eds.): ESWC 2010, Part I, LNCS 6088, pp. 273–287, 2010.
© Springer-Verlag Berlin Heidelberg 2010

The current situation within archaeology is one of fragmented datasets and applications, with different terminology systems. The interpretation of a find (or free text report of an excavation) may not employ the same terms as the underlying dataset. Similarly searchers from different scientific perspectives may not use the same terminology. Separate datasets employ distinct schema for semantically equivalent information. Entities and relationships may have different names but be semantically equivalent. Even when datasets are made available on the Web, effective cross search is not possible due to these semantic interoperability issues [2].

STAR has aimed to address these concerns by exploiting the potential of a standard ontology for cultural heritage (extended for the archaeology excavation and analysis process) to link digital archive databases, vocabularies and the associated grey literature. This paper gives an overview of STAR applications and services and goes on to particularly focus on issues concerning the extraction and representation of time period information.

1.1 Extending CIDOC CRM for Use in Archaeology

Within the cultural heritage domain, the CIDOC Conceptual Reference Model (CRM) has emerged as a core ontological model [3]. The CRM is the outcome of more than a decade of work by the CIDOC Documentation Standards Working Group, and has more recently become an ISO Standard (ISO 21127:2006). The scope of the model encompasses the general cultural heritage domain and it is envisaged as 'semantic glue' useful for mediating between sometimes diverse information sources.

CIDOC CRM deals with concepts at a high level of generality. For working with archaeological datasets at a more detailed level, the English Heritage Centre for Archaeology developed an ontological model (CRM-EH) [4] as a CRM extension covering the archaeological excavation and analysis workflow. This model only existed in document form so in collaboration with staff at English Heritage an RDF implementation was first produced by Glamorgan [5], referencing and complementing the existing published (v4.2) RDFS implementation of the CRM [6]. Using this model, selections were extracted from multiple excavation datasets via SQL queries, and stored as RDF files. This work was significantly assisted by a semi-automatic mapping and data extraction tool. Further details of this process are discussed in [7].

1.2 STAR Architecture

The STAR system enables cross-search on multiple excavation datasets including Raunds Roman (RRAD), Raunds Prehistoric (RPRE), Museum of London (MoLAS), Silchester Roman (LEAP) and Stanwick sampling (STAN). The final system will extend this cross-search to data extracted from excavation reports originating from the OASIS index of grey literature, operated by the Archaeology Data Service (ADS).

The general architecture of the STAR system is shown in Fig. 1. A common RDF data store holds the CRM-EH ontology, thesauri and glossaries, and amalgamated data extracted from the previously separate databases. The data store will eventually also hold annotations extracted from the grey literature documents. Applications communicate to the server via web services (see section 1.3). Search result items offer

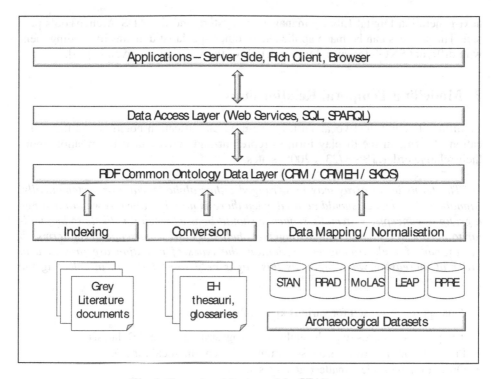

Fig. 1. General architecture of the STAR system

entry points into the structured data; allowing a user to browse to related data items via CRM relationship chains.

1.3 SKOS Based Terminology Services

STAR employs SKOS (Simple Knowledge Organization System) [8] as the representation format for domain specific thesauri and glossaries associated with the archaeological datasets. Seven English Heritage thesauri have been converted to SKOS RDF representation, along with various glossary term lists [9]. SKOS is a W3C Recommendation based on a formal data model intended as an RDF representation standard for the family of knowledge organization systems, with a lightweight semantics designed primarily for information retrieval purposes. This offers a cost effective approach for dealing with thesauri for STAR purposes. For other recent work employing SKOS see, for example, Isaac et al. [10] on aligning thesauri and Tuominen et al. [11] on various SKOS based semantic web services.

A set of terminology web services has been developed for the project [12] based on a subset of the SWAD Europe SKOS API [13] with extensions for concept expansion. The services provide term look up across the thesauri held in the system, allowing search systems to be augmented by SKOS-based vocabulary resources. Queries are often expressed at a different level of generalization from document content or meta-data, so concepts may be expanded by synonyms or by semantically related concepts [14]. In addition to STAR, the services have been used by the DelosDLMS prototype next-generation Digital Library management system and the ADS ArcheoTools project. The services can be made applicable to other specialist domains by loading them with different SKOS thesauri. Further details of the services are given in [15].

2   Modelling Temporal Relationships

Traditionally controlled vocabularies have used classification notation and the collocation of terms in the display form to represent and convey tacit information about their relative order. [BS 8723-2:2005] states:

"The terms in an array may be arranged either alphabetically or systematically. Alphabetical sequence should be used when there is no other obvious way to arrange a group of concepts. Systematic sequence should be used when it is likely to be familiar to most users, or when the arrangement helps to clarify the scope of the terms. In the example for electromagnetic radiation, the types of radiation are presented in order of increasing wavelength, as this might help some indexers in selecting the correct term(s). "

This approach is used for various kinds of sequence:

- Temporal sequences (e.g. chronological progression: earliest → latest).
- Property continua (e.g. visual spectrum, wavelength, vocal range).
- Order of magnitude (smallest → largest).
- Derivative sequences (e.g. an evolutionary or developmental order).

In archaeology datasets the relative temporal context of objects and events is useful and important both for indexing and display purposes. Alphabetical ordering can be illogical - a chronological arrangement often being more appropriate. A particular application for this would be displaying archaeological finds within their chronological context and establishing linear paths for navigation through the data.

The Getty Thesaurus of Geographic Names (TGN) [16] facilitates the presentation of multiple historical variants for place names. The online version lists these variants in reverse chronological order, to present the likely most sought after information at the top of the list, whilst also illustrating a historical progression. However thesaurus relationships are not the most comprehensive mechanism to fully describe temporal relationships.

2.1   Types of Temporal Relationship

Previous research effort has been devoted to the modelling of specialised operators to define relationships between periods and events. Knight & Ma [17] defined a set of relationships including *before, after, during, pre, post, circa*. Interval Temporal Logic (a.k.a. Allen Algebra) [18] described a method for reasoning about temporal intervals. The system defined 13 possible types of relationship between periods – the equality condition plus 6 reciprocal property pairs. OWL-Time [19] (formerly DAML-Time) includes a practical RDF encoding of these properties for the Semantic Web. The properties (*intervalEquals, intervalBefore, intervalAfter* etc.) occur between

ProperInterval OWL classes. CIDOC CRM similarly models an equivalent set of relationships (*P114F.is_equal_in_time_to*, *P120F.occurs_before*, *P120B.occurs_after* etc.) as occurring between *E2.TemporalEntity* conceptual entities, as listed in Table 1. These relationships give no indication of scale so without supplementary information we cannot know the degree of temporal affinity between resources - only their relative chronological context.

Table 1. Relationships between time periods, with their associated inverse property

CIDOC CRM Property	OWL-Time Property	Transitive?
P114F.is_equal_in_time_to	intervalEquals	✓
P115F.finishes P115B.is_finished_by	intervalFinishes intervalFinishedBy	✓
P116F.starts P116B.is_started_by	intervalStarts intervalStartedBy	✓
P117F.occurs_during P117B.includes	intervalDuring intervalContains	✓
P118F.overlaps_in_time_with P118B.is_overlapped_in_time_by	intervalOverlaps intervalOverlappedBy	✗
P119F.meets_in_time_with P119B.is_met_in_time_by	intervalMeets intervalMetBy	✗
P120F.occurs_before P120B.occurs_after	intervalBefore intervalAfter	✓

```
A is_equal_in_time_to B :- (A.start = B.start AND A.end = B.end)
A finishes B :- (A.start > B.start AND A.end = B.end)
A is_finished_by B :- (A.start < B.start AND A.end = B.end)
A starts B :- (A.start = B.start AND A.end < B.end)
A is_started_by B :- (A.start = B.start AND A.end > B.end)
A occurs_during B :- (A.start > B.start AND A.end < B.end)
A includes B :- (A.start < B.start AND A.end > B.end)
A overlaps_in_time_with B :-
(A.start < B.start AND A.end > B.start AND A.end < B.end)
A is_overlapped_in_time_by B :-
(A.start > B.start AND A.start < B.end AND A.end > B.end)
A meets_in_time_with B :- (A.end = B.start)
A is_met_in_time_by B :- (A.start = B.end)
A occurs_before B :- (A.end < B.start)
A occurs_after B :- (A.start > B.end)
```

Fig. 2. Pseudo-code logic for temporal relationships, assuming valid(X) :- (X.start <= X.end)

Note: *transitive*[1] in Table 1 refers to relationships that are logically transitive; transitivity is not formally stated for the interval relations in the RDF implementations of CIDOC CRM and OWL-Time (the latter does however include separate transitive versions of the *before* and *after* properties). Fig. 2 shows how each of these formal relationships between periods can be deduced based on start/end dates.

---

[1] If a *transitive* relationship applies between successive members of a sequence, then that same relationship must also apply between *any* two members of the sequence taken in order. I.e. if A *occurs_before* B, and B *occurs_before* C, then A *occurs_before* C.

2.2 Using Temporal Relationships to Extend Controlled Vocabularies

As previously discussed, an established technique for modelling sequences within thesauri has been the use of classification notation to define a specific order within contiguous sequences of sibling terms. However collocation of sequential homogeneous terms is not always guaranteed within mono-hierarchical thesaurus structure due to *subsumption*, as described by Doerr [20]. Some examples of temporal sequences defined by classification notation can be found within the Getty Art & Architecture Thesaurus (AAT) [16] within the *Styles and Periods* facet. Fig. 3 illustrates how it is possible for a logical chronological sequence to span boundaries imposed by the hierarchical structure.

The primary temporal sequences encountered in Fig. 3 are:

1. Tudor → Stuart → Georgian
2. Regency → Victorian → Edwardian

A cursory analysis of the date spans represented by these terms (obtained via the associated scope notes), coupled with some knowledge of British reigns indicates that sequence 2 overlaps (and continues) sequence 1. However the evidence of term proximity alone is not sufficient in this case and the classification notation cannot describe the continuation across the imposed hierarchical boundary. The inclusion of temporal relationships would clarify that an item indexed using the term *Queen Anne* has an *earlier* historical context to an item indexed using the term *Regency*, even though these terms occur at different hierarchical positions.

As the STAR project is using the CIDOC CRM as an overarching ontology we represent the required additional relationships in terms of CRM properties in Fig. 4.

This additional information now formally links the 2 previously separate hierarchies and clarifies the relative ordering of items within the hierarchies. It states that *Caroline* and *Restoration* are represented by overlapping time periods, and that there is an interval between the end of *Georgian* and the start of *Victorian* (this is because the reign of William IV is not represented in the data). We have implied by using CRM relationships that all the periods referenced can also be regarded as CRM *E2.TemporalEntity* elements. However *E2* is an abstract class having no direct instances so it would be appropriate to also include statements declaring the type to be a specific subclass of *E2*, e.g. *E4.Period*. Other pertinent relationships between these time periods (*occurs_before*, *occurs_after* etc.) can then be derived from this initial set of assertions.

These relationships were all created by examining the dates mentioned in the scope notes - so why not just use dates directly? This is certainly a viable approach in cases where dates are commonly known and agreed, however in archaeology often absolute dates may be unknown or disputed, while relative ordering may be better agreed and established through the process of grouping and phasing. Section 3 discusses in more detail how we approached the alignment of data records with controlled terminology.

```
Hierarchy                 Classification notation (truncated)  Date span

<British Renaissance-Baroque styles by reign>
. Tudor                   .ALO.ARI.BIQ.BIQ.AFU.ALO.AFU         [1485-1603]
. . Elizabethan           .ALO.ARI.BIQ.BIQ.AFU.ALO.AFU.AFU     [1551-1603]
. Stuart                  .ALO.ARI.BIQ.BIQ.AFU.ALO.ALO         [1603-1714]
. . Jacobean              .ALO.ARI.BIQ.BIQ.AFU.ALO.ALO.ALO     [1603-1625]
. . Caroline              .ALO.ARI.BIQ.BIQ.AFU.ALO.ALO.AFU     [1625-1685]
. . Restoration           .ALO.ARI.BIQ.BIQ.AFU.ALO.ALO.ARI     [1660-1688]
. . William and Mary      .ALO.ARI.BIQ.BIQ.AFU.ALO.ALO.AXC     [1688-1702]
. . Queen Anne            .ALO.ARI.BIQ.BIQ.AFU.ALO.ALO.BCW     [1702-1714]
. Georgian                .ALO.ARI.BIQ.BIQ.AFU.ALO.ARI         [1714-1830]
------------------------------------------------------------------------

Hierarchy                 Classification notation (truncated)  Date span

<modern British styles by reign>
. Regency                 .ALO.BCW.ALO.AXC.DIO.ALO.BCW.AFU     [1811-1830]
. Victorian               .ALO.BCW.ALO.AXC.DIO.ALO.BCW.ALO     [1837-1901]
. . Early Victorian       .ALO.BCW.ALO.AXC.DIO.ALO.BCW.ALO.AFU [1837-1850]
. . High Victorian        .ALO.BCW.ALO.AXC.DIO.ALO.BCW.ALO.ALO [1850-1870]
. . Late Victorian        .ALO.BCW.ALO.AXC.DIO.ALO.BCW.ALO.ARI [1870-1901]
. Edwardian               .ALO.BCW.ALO.AXC.DIO.ALO.BCW.ARI     [1901-1910]
```

Fig. 3. Temporal sequences spanning hierarchical boundary (dates obtained from scope notes)

```
@prefix crm: < http://cidoc.ics.forth.gr/rdfs/cidoc_v4.2.rdfs#>
@prefix : <http://tempuri/concept#>

<Elizabethan> crm:P115F.finishes <Tudor> .
<Tudor> crm:P119F.meets_in_time_with <Stuart> .
<Jacobean> crm:P116F.starts <Stuart> ;
          crm:P119F.meets_in_time_with <Caroline> .
<Caroline> crm:P118F.overlaps_in_time_with <Restoration> .
<Restoration> crm:P119F.meets_in_time_with <William_and_Mary> .
<William_and_Mary> crm:P119F.meets_in_time_with <Queen_Anne> .
<Queen_Anne> crm:P115F.finishes <Stuart> .
<Stuart> crm:P119F.meets_in_time_with <Georgian> .
<Regency> crm:P115F.finishes <Georgian> .
<Victorian> crm:P120B.occurs_after <Georgian> ;
          crm:P119F.meets_in_time_with <Edwardian> .
<Early_Victorian> crm:P116F.starts <Victorian> ;
          crm:P119F.meets_in_time_with <High_Victorian> .
<High_Victorian> crm:P117F.occurs_during <Victorian> ;
          crm:P119F.meets_in_time_with <Late_Victorian> .
<Late_Victorian> crm:P115F.finishes <Victorian> .
```

Fig. 4. TURTLE syntax triples describing relationships between time periods

The boundaries of *terminus ante quem* ("limit before which") and *terminus post quem* ("limit after which") commonly used in the archaeological dating process can be modelled in CRM, although in our case the data available did not always fully support this finer level of reasoning. Refer to [21] and [22] for related work discussing the potential for chronological reasoning supported by the CRM.

3   Establishing Known Time Periods

Five archaeological datasets had been previously identified as suitable for use within the main STAR project:

- Raunds Roman Analytical Database (RRAD)
- Stanwick sampling data (STAN)[2]
- Raunds Prehistoric Database (RPRE)
- Silchester Roman Database (LEAP)
- Museum of London (MoLAS)

Within these datasets archaeological entities were typically associated with a date range rather than an absolute date. Time spans were expressed in a variety of different textual forms e.g. centuries, AD/BC years, named Roman Emperors / British Monarchs, the Three Age System[3]:

- MLC2-C3
- AD341-6
- Iron Age
- First half 1st century?
- Antonine
- LC2/EC3
- MLA

Even within an individual database field the formats used could vary, and sometimes multiple fields of the same record contained conflicting dating information. Obviously dates were important within archaeological datasets but in order to use the dates represented in any meaningful way, we had to undertake a process of data cleansing to convert this data to a more regular form.

Firstly for reference a controlled list of known time periods was collated to ensure a consistent approach across all databases. The English Heritage *Timelines* thesaurus [23] developed by the English Heritage Data Standards Unit was adopted for this purpose. The *Timelines* thesaurus integrates historic, cultural, political and geological chronological terminology, and has the scope of "*the whole span of human occupation of the United Kingdom*". It is currently only made available on request in draft format, as it has not been formally published. The thesaurus data received was first converted to SKOS format and then manually supplemented with dates deduced from the scope notes and from certain online historical resources.

---

[2] The Stanwick sampling data represented the environmental sampling part of the Raunds Roman project, so the two databases were merged to enable easier subsequent data extraction.

[3] A chronological classification system originally attributed to Nicholas Mahudel (and later to Christian Jürgensen Thomsen) as a way to describe historical epochs based on the predominant tool making materials of the time.

3.1 Adding Century Subdivisions to Known Time Periods

Prior to supplementing the thesaurus with dates we first established a convention for century subdivision and boundaries with reference to advice received from English Heritage. Centuries start at year 1 and end at year 100. In some cases in the datasets centuries AD were also observed prefixed with subdivision terms such as *Early, Mid, Late*. For consistency we established the following split to apply to all centuries AD:

- Early = 01→32
- Mid = 33→66
- Late = 67→100

Possibly an overlapping split of 01→50, 25→75, 50→100 respectively would also not be unreasonable, given the inherent uncertainty in this style of dating. The use of quarter and half subdivisions of centuries AD was also occasional practice observed in the datasets:

- 1st Half = 01→50
- 2nd Half = 51→100
- 1st Quarter = 01→25
- 2nd Quarter = 26→50
- 3rd Quarter = 51→75
- 4th Quarter = 76→100

The various subdivisions described were not represented in the original *Timelines* thesaurus so terms were manually added for each century AD (i.e. *Early 1st Century, 1st quarter 1st century AD, 1st half 1st century AD* etc.).

3.2 Aligning Data Records with Known Time Periods

Records containing date information were first semi-automatically processed to give 2 numeric values representing the approximate lower and upper bounds of the time periods indicated by the data. This process involved some data cleansing and the identification of common textual patterns (e.g. "MLC2-C3", "AD341-6" etc.) in fields describing periods. The resultant records were next processed to assign known time period identifiers to each record. This allows clustering and searching for records, and also facilitates matching between periods mentioned in database records and within the grey literature documents. A semantic closeness calculation for time periods used in previous work at Glamorgan (described more fully in [24]) was incorporated into a custom application (STAR.TIMELINE) to batch process the cleansed data records, comparing the derived start/end dates against our collated list of known periods. Periods frequently overlapped or were contained within others, so the matching method accommodated these issues to suggest the most appropriate match. The matching calculation used is reproduced below:

$$\text{Match } (P1, P2) = W1 \, (MP \, / \, IU) + W2 \, (IU \, / \, (NM + IU)) + W3 \, (IU \, / \, (D + IU)).$$

- P1 & P2 are the periods being compared.
- D is the time elapsed between one period ending and another starting (expressed in years). Where the two periods overlap D will be 0.
- MP is the matching portion (overlap) between two periods – the number of years that the two periods have in common.
- NM is the non-matching portion between two periods – the number of years that the two periods *do not* have in common.
- IU is the duration in years of the period being used as the basis for the comparison.
- W1, W2 & W3 represent weightings for the appropriate factors. Following initial experimentation these weightings were set to 0.400, 0.200 and 0.400 respectively, resulting in a match value that is always within the range (0..1). Modification of these weights relative to each other could give higher precedence to e.g. overlapping terms.

Table 2. Calculation of the degree of match between periods P1 and P2

P1	P2	Relationship Type	D	MP	NM	IU	Match
0→150	200→300	P1 *occurs before* P2	50	0	250	150	0.375
0→150	150→250	P1 *meets* P2	0	0	250	150	0.475
0→150	100→200	P1 *overlaps* P2	0	50	200	150	0.619
0→150	50→150	P1 *includes* P2	0	100	50	150	0.817

The calculated match value is then used for ranking the results in decreasing order of match. An optional minimum match threshold can also be set to prevent results with a lower degree of match being returned.

As a practical example, comparing a period P1 [175→190] to the concepts from the Timelines thesaurus yields the (top 10) results as shown in Table 3.

The relationship types are calculated as previously described in Fig. 2, using the start and end dates of the periods being compared. All of the relationships listed in

Table 3. Calculation of top 10 closest matches for P1 [175→190]

P2	Relationship Type	D	MP	NM	IU	Match
LATE 2ND CENTURY [167→200]	P1 *occurs during* P2	0	15	18	15	0.891
4TH QUARTER 2ND CENTURY AD [176→200]	P1 *overlapped by* P2	0	14	11	15	0.889
2ND HALF 2ND CENTURY AD [151→200]	P1 *occurs during* P2	0	15	34	15	0.861
2ND CENTURY AD [101→200]	P1 *occurs during* P2	0	15	84	15	0.830
ROMAN [43→410]	P1 *occurs during* P2	0	15	352	15	0.808
COMMODUS [180→192]	P1 *overlapped by* P2	0	10	7	15	0.803
AURELIUS [161→180]	P1 *overlaps* P2	0	5	24	15	0.610
3RD QUARTER 2ND CENTURY AD [151→175]	P1 *met by* P2	0	0	39	15	0.456
PERTINAX [193→193]	P1 *occurs before* P2	3	0	16	15	0.430
DIDIUS JULIANUS [193→193]	P1 *occurs before* P2	3	0	16	15	0.430

Table 3 are factually correct, however to reduce the potential number of new assertions made; only the maximal match for each relationship type is retained. E.g. "P1 *occurs during* LATE 2nd CENTURY" would render the subsequent *occurs during* relationships superfluous.

The STAR.TIMELINE process was run against data records extracted from a number of tables in the archaeological datasets to output the closest known period matches. A small selection of processed results when aligned with the English Heritage *Timelines* thesaurus, listing only maximal matches for each relationship type and applying a minimum match threshold of 0.500, are shown in Table 4.

Table 4. Sample of data aligned with English Heritage Timelines Thesaurus

Data Record	Relationship Type	Period Matched	Match
"AD 69-79"	equals	VESPASIAN [69→79]	1.000
	occurs during	LATE 1st CENTURY [67→100]	0.861
	overlapped by	3rd QUARTER 1st CENTURY AD [51→75]	0.703
	met by	OTHO [69→69]	0.545
"AD 270-4"	equals	TETRICUS I [270→274]	1.000
	starts	AURELIAN [270→275]	0.960
	occurs during	3rd QUARTER 3rd CENTURY AD [251→275]	0.833
	met by	QUINTILLUS [270→270]	0.614
	finished by	TETRICUS II [274→274]	0.614
"AD 275-402"	includes	4TH CENTURY AD [301→400]	0.876
	occurs during	ROMAN [43→410]	0.869
	overlapped by	LATE 3rd CENTURY [267→300]	0.586
	started by	TACITUS [275→276]	0.504
"AD 268-70"	equals	CLAUDIUS II GOTHICUS [268→270]	1.000
	occurs during	3rd QUARTER 3rd CENTURY AD [251→275]	0.817
	met by	LUCIUS AELIANUS [268→268]	0.733
	includes	MARCUS AURELIUS MARIUS [269→269]	0.733
	finished by	VICTORINUS [269→270]	0.733
	overlapped by	POSTUMUS [260→269]	0.636
"AD 270-84"	occurs during	LATE 3RD CENTURY [267→300]	0.885
	overlaps	4th QUARTER 3rd CENTURY AD [276→300]	0.706
	includes	PROBUS [276→282]	0.699
	started by	AURELIAN [270→275]	0.665
	overlapped by	3rd QUARTER 3rd CENTURY AD [251→275]	0.610
	met by	QUINTILLUS [270→270]	0.532

As a result of this process we created a set of records originating from multiple datasets that could be effectively cross searched either directly by date or via thesaurus concept. It was noted that in certain cases the alignment process rediscovered links to specific Roman emperors that had previously only been implicit in the dates used (see e.g. *VESPASIAN*, *TETRICUS I* and *CLAUDIUS II GOTHICUS* in Table 4).

The matched thesaurus terms were limited specifically to the geographic and cultural scope of the associated thesaurus used; however the STAR.TIMELINE application may be loaded with alternative period lists to align the data with periods specific to other locations. The overall quantity of records processed for date alignment is shown in Table 5.

Table 5. Overall quantity of records processed for date alignment

Table.Column	Records processed
LEAP.FINDS	2,719
MOLAS.FND_DATE	1,834
MOLAS.FINDS_INVENTORIES	5,229
MOLAS.FND_PRPOT	1,674
MOLAS.FND_RF	1,814
RRAD.CONTEXT_PERIOD	5,291
RRAD.OBJECT_PERIOD	3,765
RRAD.CERAMICS_PERIOD	5,401
RRAD.SAMPLE_PERIOD	369
RPRE.OBJECTS	4,828
Total records processed	32,924

In the next stage of the work the processed data will be converted to RDF conforming to the CRM model for representing period information as shown in Fig. 5, for import to the main STAR data store.

This import will facilitate querying the aligned records using SPARQL in the context of other extracted STAR data, and manipulation using existing STAR interface controls, e.g. the experimental timeline component illustrated in Fig. 6.

```
@prefix crm: <http://cidoc.ics.forth.gr/rdfs/cidoc_v4.2.rdfs#>
@prefix thes: <http://tempuri/star/concept#>
@prefix : <http://tempuri/star/base#>

# Supplement existing SKOS Concept ('LATE 3rd CENTURY') with CRM
# properties describing a known period relative to other periods.
thes:135952 a crm:E4.Period;
   crm:P115F.finishes thes:900086;
   crm:P117F.occurs_during thes:134738;
   crm:P118F.overlaps_in_time_with thes:136180;
   crm:P4F.has_time-span [
      crm:P81F.ongoing_throughout '+267/+300'
   ] .

# Data record related to known periods using CRM relationships.
<dataX> a crm:E4.Period;
   crm:P117F.occurs_during thes:135952;
   crm:P118F.overlaps_in_time_with thes:900011;
   crm:P117B.includes thes:136172;
   crm:P116B.is_started_by thes:136162;
   crm:P118B.is_overlapped_in_time_by thes:900010;
   crm:P119B.is_met_in_time_by thes:136160;
   crm:P4F.has_time-span [
      crm:P82F.at_some_time_within '+270/+284'
   ] .
# [etc.]
```

Fig. 5. Processed data expressed as a series of CRM *E4.Period* entities

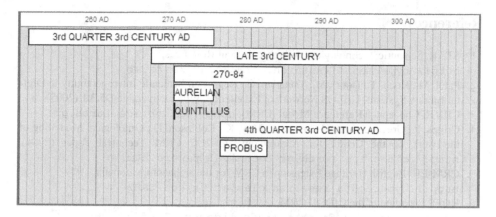

Fig. 6. Experimental STAR timeline interface component

4 Conclusions

This paper gave an overview of the STAR project and went on to discuss a particular aspect of the project in dealing with chronological information. We described suitable methods of modelling temporal relationships and demonstrated the use of CRM entities and properties to supplement existing controlled vocabularies, enabling temporal reasoning. We then described STAR.TIMELINE; a custom application that aligns archaeological records with a controlled set of known time periods, in the process rediscovering links to specific named periods that were only implicit in the original data. We acknowledge that archaeological dating can be uncertain while relative ordering may be better agreed and established. The processed records can be searched either by date range or by named period, and they facilitate temporal matching between database records and grey literature document content.

This work has potential uses beyond the immediate project, and we envisage reusing the implemented STAR.TIMELINE functionality to complement our existing suite of web services with a service for suggesting a ranked list of suitable named archaeological periods for any given dates, possibly making use of the distinction between period types e.g. century names, British Monarchs, Roman Emperors and extending to give further consideration to periods being specific to particular geographical locations.

Acknowledgements

The STAR project is funded by the UK Arts and Humanities Research Council (AHRC). Thanks are due to Phil Carlisle & Keith May (English Heritage), Douglas Tudhope and Andreas Vlachidis (University of Glamorgan), Renato Souza (Universidade Federal de Minas Gerais, Brazil).

References

1. STAR: Semantic Technologies for Archaeological Resources,
   http://hypermedia.research.glam.ac.uk/kos/star
2. Patel, M., Koch, T., Doerr, M., Tsinaraki, C.: Report on Semantic Interoperability in Digital Library Systems. DELOS Network of Excellence, WP5 Deliverable D5.3.1 (2005)
3. CIDOC Conceptual Reference Model (CRM), http://cidoc.ics.forth.gr
4. Cripps, P., Greenhalgh, A., Fellows, D., May, K., Robinson, D.: Ontological Modelling of the work of the Centre for Archaeology, CIDOC CRM Technical Paper (2004), http://cidoc.ics.forth.gr/technical_papers.html
5. CRM-EH: English Heritage Extension to CRM for the archaeology domain, http://hypermedia.research.glam.ac.uk/kos/CRM/
6. RDFS Encoding of the CIDOC CRM, http://cidoc.ics.forth.gr/rdfs/cidoc_v4.2.rdfs
7. Binding, C., Tudhope, D., May, K.: Semantic Interoperability in Archaeological Datasets: Data Mapping and Extraction via the CIDOC CRM. In: Christensen-Dalsgaard, B., Castelli, D., Ammitzbøll Jurik, B., Lippincott, J. (eds.) ECDL 2008. LNCS, vol. 5173, pp. 280–290. Springer, Heidelberg (2008)
8. SKOS: Simple Knowledge Organization Systems - W3C Semantic Web Deployment Working Group, http://www.w3.org/2004/02/skos
9. Tudhope, D., Binding, C., May, K.: Semantic interoperability issues from a case study in archaeology. In: Kollias, S., Cousins, J.(ed.) Semantic Interoperability in the European Digital Library, Proceedings of the First International Workshop (SIEDL) 2008, associated with 5th European Semantic Web Conference, Tenerife, pp. 88–99 (2008)
10. Isaac, A., Matthezing, H., van der Meij, L., Schlobach, S., Wang, S., Zinn, C.: Putting ontology alignment in context: Usage scenarios, deployment and evaluation in a library case. In: Bechhofer, S., Hauswirth, M., Hoffmann, J., Koubarakis, M. (eds.) ESWC 2008. LNCS, vol. 5021, pp. 402–417. Springer, Heidelberg (2008)
11. Tuominen, J., Frosterus, M., Kim Viljanen, K., Eero Hyvönen, E.: ONKI SKOS Server for Publishing and Utilizing SKOS Vocabularies and Ontologies as Services. In: Aroyo, L., Traverso, P., Ciravegna, F., Cimiano, P., Heath, T., Hyvönen, E., Mizoguchi, R., Oren, E., Sabou, M., Simperl, E. (eds.) ESWC 2009. LNCS, vol. 5554, pp. 768–780. Springer, Heidelberg (2009)
12. Terminology Services for the STAR Project, http://hypermedia.research.glam.ac.uk/resources/terminology/
13. SKOS API: SWAD EUROPE Thesaurus Project Output (2004), http://www.w3.org/2001/sw/Europe/reports/thes/skosapi.html
14. Binding, C., Tudhope, D.: KOS at your Service: Programmatic Access to Knowledge Organisation Systems. Journal of Digital Information 4(4) (2004), http://journals.tdl.org/jodi/article/view/110/109
15. Binding, C., Tudhope, D.: Terminology Services. Knowledge Organization, vol. 37. Ergon-Verlag (2010) (forthcoming) ISSN 0943-7444
16. Getty vocabulary databases, Paul Getty Trust, J.: http://www.getty.edu/research/tools/vocabulary/
17. Knight, B., Ma, J.: Time Representation: A Taxonomy of Temporal Models. Artificial Intelligence Review 7, 401–419 (1994)
18. Allen, J.F.: Maintaining knowledge about temporal intervals. Communications of the ACM 26 (1983)
19. OWL-Time, http://www.w3.org/TR/owl-time/

20. Doerr, M.: Semantic problems of thesaurus mapping. Journal of Digital Information 1(8) (2001), http://journals.tdl.org/jodi/article/view/31/32
21. Eide, O., Holmen, J., Ore, C.: Deducing event chronology in an archaeological documentation system. In: Proceedings Computer Applications and Quantitative Methods in Archaeology (CAA 2009), Williamsburg (2009)
22. Doerr, M., Plexousakis, D., Kopaka, K., Bekiari, C.: Supporting Chronological Reasoning in Archaeology. In: Proceedings Computer Applications and Quantitative Methods in Archaeology (CAA 2004), Prato (2004)
23. English Heritage Timelines Thesaurus, http://www.fish-forum.info/i_time.htm
24. Tudhope, D., Taylor, C.: Navigation via Similarity: automatic linking based on semantic closeness. Information Processing and Management 33(2), 233–242 (1997)

Facet Graphs: Complex Semantic Querying Made Easy

Philipp Heim[1], Thomas Ertl[1], and Jürgen Ziegler[2]

[1] Visualization and Interactive Systems Group (VIS), University of Stuttgart, Germany
{Philipp.Heim,Thomas.Ertl}@vis.uni-stuttgart.de
[2] Interactive Systems and Interaction Design, University of Duisburg-Essen, Germany
Juergen.Ziegler@uni-due.de

Abstract. While the Semantic Web is rapidly filling up, appropriate tools for searching it are still at infancy. In this paper we describe an approach that allows humans to access information contained in the Semantic Web according to its semantics and thus to leverage the specific characteristic of this Web. To avoid the ambiguity of natural language queries, users only select already defined attributes organized in facets to build their search queries. The facets are represented as nodes in a graph visualization and can be interactively added and removed by the users in order to produce individual search interfaces. This provides the possibility to generate interfaces in arbitrary complexities and access arbitrary domains. Even multiple and distantly connected facets can be integrated in the graph facilitating the access of information from different user-defined perspectives. Challenges include massive amounts of data, massive semantic relations within the data, highly complex search queries and users' unfamiliarity with the Semantic Web.

Keywords: Graph visualization, faceted search, query building, SPARQL, hierarchical facets, pivot operation.

1 Introduction

Ten years ago, Tim Berners-Lee planted the seed for the Semantic Web [1] which thereupon started to grow and expand over the years. At first, information was manually translated into semantic structures and added to the Semantic Web resulting in a rather moderate growth. The automation of the translation process at a later date allowed large amounts of existing information as available e.g., in encyclopedias, medical databases or in knowledge bases of other domains to be integrated in the Semantic Web causing a rapid acceleration of its growth rate. Today, the Semantic Web contains so much semantically annotated information that it seems ready for broader exploration. Alone appropriate tools are missing.

In this paper, such tools are defined as something, which allows humans to access information contained in the Semantic Web according to its semantic descriptions. Finding the right information, however, requires the semantic of what should be searched to be specified by the user. For this purpose it is not sufficient to enter words in an input field as it is usual for search engines in the common Web since natural language is ambiguous. A basic strategy to avoid the ambiguity of natural language

L. Aroyo et al. (Eds.): ESWC 2010, Part I, LNCS 6088, pp. 288–302, 2010.

are artificial query languages like *SPARQL[1]* that are uniquely defined. A growing amount of information in the Semantic Web (e.g. *DBpedia* [2] or the *LOD cloud* [3]) can be queried via SPARQL endpoints that are freely accessible over the Internet. However, building search queries in such an artificial language, as for example possible with *SNORQL[2]*, requires the language to be learned by the user and is thus rather a task for experts. The vast majority of users need intuitive interfaces to express search queries that are semantically unique but do not require any extra knowledge.

A popular approach for such interfaces is based on the concept of faceted search [4]. In faceted search, the search space gets partitioned using orthogonal conceptual dimensions whereas one acts as the result set and the others as facets. The facets can then be used to filter the result set by different attributes that can be selected independently from each other. Selecting an attribute in a facet adds it to the query and hence filters the result set accordingly. Whenever the result set gets changed, all the facets are updated to only those attributes that can be used for further filtering (Fig. 1). Therefore, users always see only attributes that can cause a reduction of the result set, but can never cause an empty set when selected. Moreover, since all attributes that can be used for filtering are extracted from the semantic structures of the Semantic Web, all search queries contain only uniquely defined objects, classes and properties and thus completely avoid ambiguity.

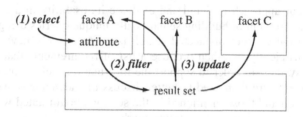

Fig. 1. In faceted search, selecting an attribute in a facet (1) filters the result set (2), which thereupon updates all facets (3)

In order to support a better understanding of our theoretical explanations throughout this paper, we use concrete examples and tasks from the field of football (soccer). In this domain, a faceted search would allow, for example, football players to be filtered by their clubs, their birthplaces, or their ages. Even so the concept of faceted search is successfully applied in popular applications such as *Apple's iTunes[3]*, using it to seek information in the Semantic Web entails several new problems that are not yet sufficiently solved. Most of the problems result from the vast number of objects, classes and properties that are contained in the Semantic Web. According to [5], the LOD cloud alone contained approximately two billion statements in 2008 already.

In this paper we introduce *Facet Graphs*, a new approach based on the concept of faceted search which allows the intuitive formulation of semantically unique search queries. Users can choose the result set as well as the facets to filter it and thereby

---

[1] http://www.w3.org/TR/rdf-sparql-query/
[2] http://dbpedia.org/snorql/
[3] http://www.apple.com/de/itunes/

produce a personalized interface to build search queries. Facets and result set are represented as nodes in a graph visualization and are connected by labeled edges that fosters users' understanding of the relationships between the facets and also allows for an easy extension by further nodes and edges. The graph provides a coherent representation of multiple, even distantly connected facets on one page that completely avoids any browsing activities and hence prevents users from getting 'Lost in Hyperspace'. Each node contains a list that provides sorting, paging and scrolling functionalities and thereby enables the easy handling of even large amounts of objects.

In Facet Graphs, users can build queries just by clicking certain objects in the nodes. All filtering effects caused by such selections are highlighted by different colors in the graph that can be used for both, a better understanding of the caused effects or a better traceability of reasons for filtering effects on a certain node. Since users may change their minds while searching, the result set can be changed at any time enabling a rather exploratory search when the domain, the way to achieve the goal, or the goal itself is not completely clear in advance. Altogether, the combination of graph visualization with faceted search allows for an easy formulation of even complex semantically unique search queries and thus to seek for information according to its semantic without expert knowledge.

The rest of this paper is organized as follows. First we review related work and use the identified weak points for the motivation of our approach of Facet Graphs. We then describe our approach in detail and evaluate its usability in a comparative user study. Since the problem of building semantically unique queries using intuitive interfaces based on the concept of faceted search is comparatively new and has not yet been solved sufficiently, we then propose a list of requirements that need to be fulfilled by such systems in order to support the information seeking process in general. These requirements are then used to better discuss the advantages and limitations of our own approach and those mentioned in the section about related work. Finally, we give a conclusion and an outlook on future work.

2   Related Work

A number of approaches to build semantically unique search queries using faceted search have been described in the literature. Most of the approaches display the facets as well as the result set as lists at different positions on the screen. Examples are tools like *mSpace* [6], *Flamenco* [4], *Longwell* [7] and *Haystack* [8]. Facets provided by these tools are limited to directly connected ones exclusively. So, football players could be filtered by facets containing the clubs they are playing for, the city they are living in or the number on their shirts. By selecting, for example, the football club 'FC Chelsea' in the facet with all existing clubs, the result set with all football players could be filtered to only those players that are playing for this club. Hierarchical filtering, however, that allows also indirectly connected facets to be used for query building (e.g. get only players playing for clubs in the Premier League) is not supported by these tools.

Tools like *Parallax* [9], *Humboldt* [10], *Tabulator* [11] and the *Nested Faceted Browser* [12], by comparison, allow for hierarchical filtering. Therefore, football players can be filtered by the cities where clubs they are playing for are located. Thus the possible options for building a query are not restricted to the direct periphery around a result set but can include dimensions that are distantly connected by other facets. Depending on the directness of their connections to the current result set, they can be integrated in a hierarchy and are therefore called *hierarchical facets*.

Fig. 2. Screenshots of Parallax (left) and Tabulator (right)

In Parallax (Fig. 2, left), Flamenco and Humboldt, the hierarchy of facets is never completely visible to the user but only parts of it. By providing ways to browse through the hierarchy, users are able to include attributes of also distantly connected facets in their search query. With the growth of the complexity of their queries, it is getting more difficult for users to keep an overview of all included attributes since the corresponding facets are often scattered over several different pages.

Tools like Tabulator (Fig. 2, right) and the Nested Faceted Browser, on the contrary, allow the whole hierarchy to be displayed on one page. By using a tree structure to display all available hierarchical facets, users can open and close even distantly connected facets in one coherent view and thus keep an overview of all attributes that are included in their queries. Since tree structures are used to depict all kinds of taxonomies in a wide range of well known applications, users need no extensive period of training to gain an understanding of how to use them.

In Tabulator and the Nested Faceted Browser, every attribute defines its own subtree that can be expanded by the user in order to see distantly connected facets and their attributes, which again can be expanded and so on (cp. Fig. 2, right). So for the football players, one of the clubs they are playing for (e.g. 'FC Chelsea'), could be expanded by the user to see, for example, the city of its location (here: 'London'). Selecting 'London' would cause the list of players to be filtered to only those that are playing for 'FC Chelsea' or any other club located in this city. A combined list of all the cities that could be selected in order to filter the clubs and also the players, however, is not provided by the tree structure. The cities are partitioned in different subtrees, each for every club, that all need to be expanded in order to see all available cities. Having many subtrees opened, however, places attributes that actually belong to one facet at many different positions in the tree, leading to an increased tree structure that can possibly not be displayed on one screen. If an attribute is shared by more than one object (e.g. many clubs are located in London), it also occurs repeatedly in different subtrees.

Altogether, a tree structure is a well known paradigm to visualize and interact with hierarchical data; however, when used for hierarchical facets, it tends to produce large and highly subdivided structures that cannot easily be overviewed by users. In this paper we therefore propose an alternative, graph-based approach to visualize and interact with hierarchical facets that aims at preventing large and confusing tree structures and hence facilitates an easy generation of semantically unique queries by the user.

3 Facet Graphs

In Facet Graphs, facets and result set are represented as nodes in a graph visualization. The semantic relations that exist between facets and result set as well as facets and other facets are represented by labeled directed edges between the nodes. Fig. 3 shows *gFacet*[4], a prototypical implementation of our approach of Facet Graphs.

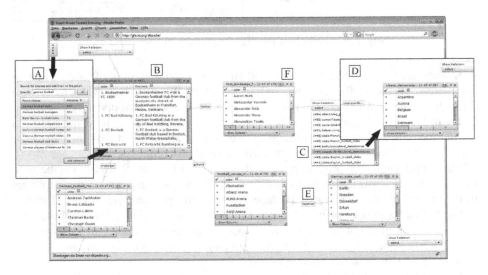

Fig. 3. In gFacet, the result set is defined by the user (A) and represented by the initial node in the graph (B). By selecting properties out of drop-down-lists (C), facets can be added as new nodes (D) that get connected by labeled edges (E).

In gFacet, the node representing the result set is marked by a darker background color (cp. Fig. 3, B) to better distinguish it from the nodes representing facets. The attributes of each facet are not located at different positions on the screen but are grouped within one single node (e.g. the cities where football venues are located in Fig. 3). Every node in the graph contains a list that can be scrolled, paged and sorted by the user allowing even large amounts of objects to be clearly arranged. If an attribute is shared by more than one object (e.g. several players are born in Poland) it still occurs only once in the list in comparison to the tree-based approaches described in related work.

---

[4] A description of an early version of this prototype with limited functionalities and access to dummy data only can be found in [13].

The graph can interactively be expanded by additional nodes with further facets that are not represented yet. For each node in the graph, facets that can be added are available via a drop-down list (e.g. facets for the 'First Bundesliga Footballers' in Fig. 3, C). The facets in the drop-down lists are ordered by the number of their attributes, with the largest numbers presented first. Selecting one of the facets in a list (e.g. the one containing the countries where footballers are born), adds this facet as a new node to the graph and connects it to the existing node by a labeled edge (cp. Fig. 3, D). Thus, the user can iteratively add and remove facets to the graph and hence produce a personalized interface to build search queries.

The nodes in the graph are positioned in an aesthetically pleasing way by performing a force-directed layout algorithm [14]. This can cause the nodes to often change their position, possibly making it hard to maintain visual focus and thus confusing the user. We therefore apply a pinning mechanism that forces nodes to hold their position. When a new node is added to the graph, the pinning of this node is executed after a short time period. This delay allows the force-directed algorithm to position new nodes in an appropriate way and at the same time prevents already existing information to change their location. Whether a node is pinned or not is indicated by the color of the needle symbol at the upper right corner of each node (cp. Fig. 3, F). This pinning can also be controlled by the user by clicking at the needle symbol. Thus, the user can decide whether a node should stay on a fixed position or should be rearranged by the force-directed algorithm in order to improve the overall appearance of the graph.

The general benefits of representing hierarchical facets as nodes in a graph are:

1. The attributes for each facet are grouped into one node.
2. All nodes are shown in a coherent presentation on one page.
3. Semantic relations between the nodes are represented by labeled edges (Fig. 3, E).
4. Facets can be added and removed by the user (Fig. 3, D).

3.1 Extracting Hierarchical Facets

In order to provide facets in drop-down lists to expand the graph, they first have to be extracted from the underlying data structure. In gFacet, we build SPARQL queries on the client side, send them to SPARQL endpoints using HTTP requests and extract the facets from the resulting XML data. The client-server communication as well as the graphical user interface are implemented in *Adobe Flex*[5] and thus compiled to a Flash movie, which runs in all Web browsers with Flash Player installed. An exemplary implementation of gFacet that uses DBpedia's SPARQL endpoint is accessible online[6]. Since gFacet does not need any modification on the server side, it can be used to access information from other SPARQL endpoints as well.

Our general strategy of how to extract facets from semantic structures by querying SPARQL endpoints is based on the links within these structures. The links are defined by properties like 'plays for' and connect objects like 'Franck Ribéry' with, for example, 'FC Bayern Munich'. So given a list with several objects including 'Franck

---

[5] http://www.adobe.com/products/flex
[6] http://gfacet.semanticweb.org

Ribéry', a possible facet to filter this list would be the football clubs at least one of the objects in the list are playing for. Other facets representing other properties of even other objects could also be used for filtering. With all the objects that exist in the underlying data structure (e.g. DBpedia) put together in one list, however, would result in so many possible facets to filter this list that they could not be read by the users. So, before selecting facets to filter the list, the users first have to restrict the list to only objects that are of a certain ontological class. This is always the first task when searching with gFacet and defines the result set for the current search.

By entering words in an input field, users can search for ontological classes that meet their interests (e.g. 'German football' in Fig. 3, A). The corresponding SPARQL query, which returns all the classes with labels containing the words entered by the users (here: "German Football"), is given in the following:

```
SELECT DISTINCT ?class ?label COUNT(?o) AS ?numOfObj
WHERE { ?class rdf:type skos:Concept .
?o skos:subject ?class .
?class rdfs:label ?label .
?label bif:contains "german and football" .
FILTER (lang(?label) = "en") }
ORDER BY DESC(?numOfObj) LIMIT 30
```

The found classes are shown in a list and are initially ordered according to the numbers of objects contained in each class, with the largest counts presented first. One of the suggested classes can then be selected by the user to become the first node in the graph and also the current result set (e.g. 'German football clubs'). The first node contains all the objects of the selected class and is the starting point for all further nodes in the graph (cp. Fig. 3, B).

Based on the properties of the objects in the result set, available facets to filter them are extracted automatically and are displayed in a drop-down list next to the result set. Each facet in the drop-down list consists of a property (e.g. 'ground') and one class of objects this property is leading to (e.g. 'Football venues in Germany'). So it is possible to have several facets with the same property but with different classes, or different properties but with the same class. The corresponding query looks like the following:

```
SELECT DISTINCT ?prop ?newClass
COUNT(DISTINCT ?objNewClass) AS ?numOfObj
WHERE {
?objCurrClass skos:subject <URIofGermanFootbalClubs> .
?objCurrClass ?prop ?objNewClass .
?objNewClass skos:subject ?newClass .
?newClass rdf:type skos:Concept .}
ORDER BY DESC(?objNewClass) ?prop ?newClass LIMIT 40
```

Similarly to adding first order facets to the result set, also facets of second or higher order can be added to the graph and thus used for filtering. The number of visible objects in higher order facets is restricted to only those that are connected to objects in other visible facets that are in turn directly or indirectly connected to objects in the result set. Fig. 4 shows a result set on the left, a first order facet in the middle and a

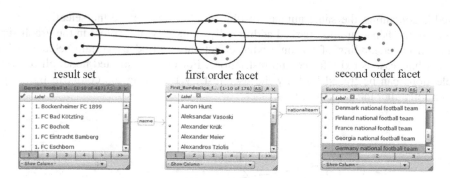

Fig. 4. Only objects that are connected to the result set are visible in the hierarchical facets: Here the national teams for which players of German clubs are playing

second order facet on the right together with a schematic representation of the visible and invisible objects. Black dots are visible objects and gray dots are invisible objects. The gray dots in the schematic representation of the second order facet represent objects that are of the same class but are not connected to an object in the result set and therefore not visible for the users. In this way, all the facets in the graph only contain objects that can be used for filtering but will never result in an empty result set.

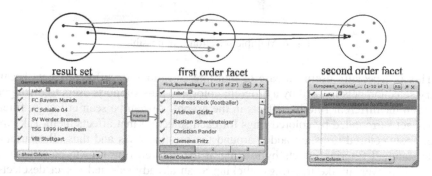

Fig. 5. Hierarchical facets can be used for filtering

3.2 Building Search Queries

Having chosen at least one facet to be represented as node in the graph, it can be used to build semantically unique search queries. By selecting one of the objects in a facet, the result set can be filtered to only objects that are directly or indirectly connected to the selected one. E.g. the selection of 'Germany national football team' in the second order facet in Fig. 4 filters the football clubs to only those with players playing for this national team (see the new result set in Fig. 5). If a selection actually filters the result set, all lists get updated within a few seconds.

To support the traceability of filtering effects we use color-coding. Every node has a certain color assigned to, which marks all filtering effects caused by selections in this node. If an object gets selected by the user, the selected object itself, all the filtered nodes and all the edges between them are marked with the same color (Fig. 5).

Nodes containing the same number of objects after and before the selection are not filtered and hence are not marked additionally. This way, the colors in the graph support an understanding of not only what effects are caused by certain selections but also what reasons exist for certain restrictions. For every restricted node, all relevant selections can be traced back by the user just by following the colors in the graph even long after the selections took place.

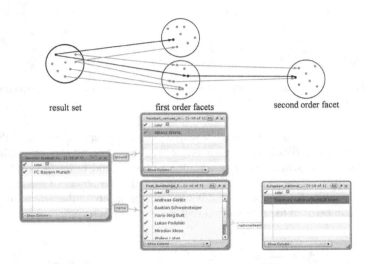

Fig. 6. Multiple selections are possible

This is especially useful in case of multiple selections in different facets because every selection gets marked by a different color and thus supports users to distinguish between the different filtering effects in the graph[7]. As can be seen in Fig. 6, filtered nodes get surrounded by colored rings for each selection that affects them. Like tree-rings, new colored rings are added around the existing ones and thus allow users to understand all filtering effects by looking at the colored ring growth patterns in the graph. However, unlike tree-rings, clicking at an already selected object deselects it and reverses the corresponding filtering effects with all their color-coding including also rings around nodes. In the current implementation, multiple selections are connected by a logical 'AND' and thus narrow down the result set to only objects that are connected to all selections. Thus by selecting a certain ground, the clubs in the result set in Fig. 6 are restricted to only those that have players playing in a certain national team and are tenants of a certain venue.

3.3 Pivot Operation

While choosing facets to add them to the graph or selecting objects to filter the result set, users may change their minds about what they want to search. When, for example, searching for 'German football clubs', users could realize that they rather want to

---

search for 'First Bundesliga footballers' and want to use the football clubs to filter the footballers instead of the other way around. This operation is called *pivot operation* since it allows leaving the used path and following another direction. The pivot operation is based on the operation in data drilling [15], where data can be represented according to different dimensions.

The Nested Faceted Browser [12] and Humboldt [10] are the only tools mentioned in the section about related work that allow users to perform a pivot operation and thus to change the focus of their search. In Humboldt, the user can replace the current result set, displayed in the centre of the screen, by one of its visible facets, arranged among each other on the right-hand side. The chosen facet becomes the new result set and vice versa, the replaced result set becomes a new facet. In Humboldt, only directly related facets are shown next to the result set and thus hierarchical facets can only be reached by operating pivots. Whenever a pivot is operated and a new result set is shown in the centre of the screen, the list of directly related facets is updated accordingly. This way, information is partitioned over multiple pages, placing substantial cognitive load on the users to keep track of former result sets and facets, which are not visible yet.

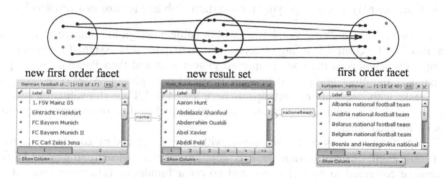

Fig. 7. Hierarchical facets can be used for filtering

Our graph-based approach, by contrast, allows a pivot operation to be performed without any changes of the displayed information structure and thus reduces the cognitive load to keep track of them. Clicking the 'RS'-Button (RS = result set) next to the pinning needle of any of the facets represented in the graph turns this facet into the new result set (e.g. 'First Bundesliga footballers' in the middle of Fig. 7) and vice versa the current result set into a new facet. Whereas other approaches have to rebuild their complete interface to keep the displayed facets up to date, in our approach even distantly related information can be shown on one page and hence can remain at their position while operating pivots. The only aspect that can change in gFacet when operating a pivot is the number of objects in both the result set and the visible facets.

In Fig.7, the current result set has moved from the node on the left to the node in the middle. Therefore, the number of objects in the new first order facet containing 'German football clubs' decreased from 467 (cp. Fig. 4) to 17 in Fig. 7. This is because the new result set contains only first Bundesliga footballers and thus the number of clubs is limited to only those of the first division (i.e. some of the dots are gray in the schematic representation of the left facet in Fig. 7). Because the data provided by

DBpedia is automatically extracted from Wikipedia and thus entails some minor errors, not all first Bundesliga footballers are connected to a German football club and therefore only 176 players were visible in Fig. 4 as it was a first order facet. Since this facet became the new result set, all German football players got visible without any restrictions and so the number of objects increased to 1165 (i.e. all dots are black in the schematic representation of the new result set in Fig. 7).

4   User study

In order to evaluate our approach and thus get a first opinion about its usability, we conducted a user study that compared gFacet with another tool that supports the building of semantically unique search queries based on the concept of faceted search. For both tools we measured to what extent participants were able to solve the following three task types of different levels of difficulty:

1. Find two players who are playing for a certain club.
2. Find two cities where players who are playing for a certain club are born.
3. Find one player who is playing for a certain club and is born in a certain city.

We applied a 2x3 (*tool type* x *task type*) within-subject design to compare gFacet with Parallax [9]. To control learning effects, each participant was assigned to one of two groups. Participants in the one group used gFacet first and then Parallax, while participants in the other group used Parallax first and then gFacet. After completing all three tasks with one tool, the participants were asked to fill out an evaluation sheet to rate this tool. In a final questionnaire, participants had to directly compare both tool types with each other.

Ten participants took part in the study, with an average age of 28.3 (ranging from 24 to 31). Eight of them were male; two were female with all ten participants having normal or corrected to normal vision and no color blindness. Education level of the participants was at least general qualification for university entrance and they were all familiar with computers. The functionalities of both, gFacet and Parallax were introduced by videos in which sample tasks were solved.

4.1   Results

Overall, gFacet performed very well for complex tasks. However, it performed less well for rather simple tasks that could also be accomplished just by following links.

The left bar chart in Fig. 8 shows the number of right solutions for each of the three different task types using the two different tool types. For task 1 and task 2, Parallax performed equally or even better than gFacet. This was mainly because in Parallax participants could accomplish both tasks just by following links and did not have to filter at all. In gFacet, by contrast, they had to filter despite the simplicity of the first two tasks and hence did not accomplish task 2 in four cases. The unfamiliar approach of graph-based facets seemed partly too complex to be properly used in average exploratory tasks. However, in order to find the right solution for more complex tasks, as for example for task 3, gFacet performed significantly better than Parallax. It was almost impossible so to find the right solution for task 3 just by following links in

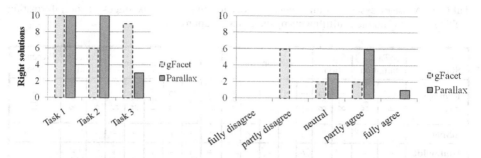

Fig. 8. Number of right solutions to the given tasks (left) and comments to the statements 'It was difficult to understand the relations between the information' (right)

Parallax. All the links had to be checked in a trial-and-error method to actually find the player that is born in the given city. Since this is quite time-consuming, participants were forced to apply filters in Parallax as well.

To find the right solution to task 3, participants had to filter the list of all football players to only players that are playing for a certain club and are born in a certain city. Even though Parallax generally supports applying multiple filters, participants felt uncertain about the solutions they found. A reason for this is the strict separation in Parallax between exploration, which can be realized by clicking links on the right side of the content, and filtering, which can be done by clicking links on the left side (cp. Fig. 2, left). If users explore a list of objects (e.g. cities where players are born) these objects cannot be used for filtering.

On the other hand, if users look at the filter options on the left side, they cannot further explore these options for hierarchical filters. To filter hierarchically, users first have to explore objects via links on the right side (e.g. cities where players are born) and then have to filter this list via links on the left side (e.g. to only cities located in Germany). Having to change from one side to the other can confuse users and thus can decrease their confidence in the found solutions. Moreover, clicking links to explore objects completely replaces the current content as well as the links at both sides. That way information gets partitioned over multiple pages and thus hampers users' understanding of the relations that exist between information (cp. right bar chart in Fig. 8). In gFacet, by contrast, all objects in all lists can be used for both filtering and the exploration of further facets and are all visible on one page.

5 Discussion

In order to better comprehend the advantages and limitations of our approach and also to better compare it to the existing approaches described in the section about related work, we go through the general information seeking process (ISP) as described in [16] and determine whether the different approaches are suitable to support it or not. The ISP from a human's perspective can be described in six stages: task initiation, selection, exploration, focus formulation, collection and presentation [16]. In a user study described in [16], different tasks were revealed that are considered most appropriate by

Table 1. A list of system requirements in order to support the six stages of the information seeking process and their fulfillments by the different approaches

ISP Stages	Task initiation		Selec -tion		Exploration					Focus formulation						Collec- tion		Presenta -tion
Require- ments	R1.1	R1.2	R2.1	R2.2	R3.1	R3.2	R3.3	R3.4	R3.5	R4.1	R4.2	R4.3	R4.4	R4.5	R4.6	R5.1	R5.2	R6.1
mSpace	-	-	-	-	+	+	-	-	-	+	+	+	-	-	-	-	-	-
Humboldt	-	-	-	-	/	-	-	-	-	+	+	+	+	-	+	-	-	-
Parallax	-	-	-	+	+	-	+	+	-	+	+	+	+	-	-	-	-	-
Tabulator	-	-	-	+	/	-	+	+	-	-	-	+	+	-	-	-	-	+
gFacet	-	-	-	+	+	+	+	+	-	+	+	+	+	+	+	-	-	-

users to move the process on to the subsequent stage of the ISP. In the following, we identify for each of these tasks requirements to support humans in accessing information in the Semantic Web and mark for each approach in Table 1 whether it is fulfilled or not.

The first stage of the ISP, the *task initiation*, begins with awareness of lack of knowledge and leads to a concrete definition of the problem and its relation to prior experience and knowledge. Requirements are: A continuous support of the whole ISP including the problem definition (R1.1) and, based on this definition, suggestions on how to address the information need considering previously operated ISPs (R1.2).

The next stage, the *selection*, includes tasks like the identification and selection of the general topic to be investigated. Requirements are: An overview of all available topics (R2.1), for instance in form of a map that can be zoomed in and out, together with automatic suggestions of topics (R2.2) based on the entered problem description, entered keywords or an auto complete functionality. Both requirements aim at lower-ing the barrier to start an ISP.

The selection is followed by the *exploration* stage. It includes the investigation of the general topic, locating information and relating it to what is already known. Re-quirements are: A graphical representation of information that can be understood by the user (R3.1), interaction possibilities that are self-explanatory and easy to use (R3.2), the accessibility of details on demand (R3.3), sorting and paging techniques to handle large datasets (R3.4) and zooming functionalities that are capable of showing information in different levels of detail (R3.5).

The *focus formulation* includes tasks like the identification and the selection of hy-potheses that result in the formulation of certain filters and thus allows a focused perspective of the topic. It is rather an iterative process than one that is strictly linear. Requirements are: The interactive and intuitive formulation and change of filters (R4.1), their immediate execution on the data (R4.2), the combination of different filters (R4.3), the possibility to build hierarchical filters (R4.4), the traceability of effects caused by each of them (R4.5) and a possibility to change the focus (R4.6).

After the focus formulation, the *collection* takes place. Tasks are to gather and se-lect information related to the focused topic. Requirements are: Easy mechanisms to select interesting findings (R5.1) and to export the selected information for further use in other systems (R5.2).

The last stage of the ISP, the *presentation*, consists of the task to present the found information. Requirements are: A broad range of opportunities to visualize the find-ings (R6.1).

Especially obvious in the pattern shown in Table 1 is the lack of all approaches to fulfill requirements regarding the first and the last stages of the ISP. Besides these pre- and post-processing stages, requirement R3.5 is also not fulfilled by any of them. Even so gFacet fulfills more requirements than every other approach listed in Table 1, not fulfilling requirement R3.5 is particularly problematic for our approach since its graph tends to get too large to fit on one screen and thus needs to be scrolled by the users. Therefore an appropriate zooming technique along with a better support for the pre- and post-processing would be highly preferable.

5.1 Conclusion and Future Work

In this paper we described Facet Graphs, a new approach for building semantically unique queries based on the concept of faceted search in combination with graph visualization. In addition to the general advantages of faceted search, the visualization of facets as nodes in a graph allows the direct representation of relationships between nodes by labeled edges and thus a connected presentation of the result set together with all relevant facets on one page. The user can add and remove facets to the graph to produce a personalized interface including even distantly connected and multiple facets that can be used to filter the result set from different user-defined perspectives. All caused filtering effects are color-coded in the graph making them better under-standable and traceable for users.

We introduced gFacet, a prototypical implementation of our approach that can query arbitrary SPARQL endpoints (e.g. DBpedia) to access information according to its semantics. We conducted a user study to compare gFacet with Parallax and found out that our tool is especially applicable in scenarios where multiple aspects from different domains need to be integrated in order to find certain information. Such scenarios seem to be particularly interesting for querying the Semantic Web because of its huge variety of domains with each containing large amounts of different classes, objects and properties. This opens up new and outstanding opportunities for users to access information; however, controlling such powerful opportunities remains a chal-lenging task.

Future work includes the integration of appropriate zooming functionalities in combination with a focus and context technique to foster users to retain an overview even when using massive amounts of facets in one graph. Another interesting idea is to provide an opportunity to save especially helpful combinations of facets and share such search interfaces with other users. This would further lower the barrier of accep-tance for using gFacet since users can load existing search interfaces that are built by more experienced users and thus do not need to start from scratch.

References

1. Berners-Lee, T., Fischetti, M.: Weaving the Web: The Original Design and Ultimate Destiny of the World Wide Web by its Inventor. Harper, USA (1999)
2. Auer, S., Bizer, C., Kobilarov, G., Lehmann, J., Cyganiak, R., Ives, Z.: DBpedia: A Nucleus for a Web of Open Data. In: Aberer, K., Choi, K.-S., Noy, N., Allemang, D., Lee, K.-I., Nixon, L.J.B., Golbeck, J., Mika, P., Maynard, D., Mizoguchi, R., Schreiber, G., Cudré-Mauroux, P. (eds.) ASWC 2007 and ISWC 2007. LNCS, vol. 4825, pp. 722–735. Springer, Heidelberg (2007)
3. Bizer, C., Heath, T., Kingsley, I., Berners-Lee, T.: Linked data on the Web. In: Proc. WWW 2008 Workshop: LDOW (2008)
4. Hearst, M., English, J., Sinha, R., Swearingen, K., Yee, P.: Finding the Flow in Web Site Search. Communications of the ACM 45(9), 42–49 (2002)
5. Hausenblas, M., Halb, W., Raimond, Y., Heath, T.: What is the size of the Semantic Web? In: Proc. I-SEMANTICS'08, JUCS, pp. 9–16 (2008)
6. Schraefel, m.c., Smith, D., Owens, A., Russell, A., Harris, C., Wilson, M.: The evolving mSpace platform: Leveraging the Semantic Web on the trail of the memex. In: Proc. Hypertext 2005, pp. 174–183. ACM Press, New York (2005)
7. Longwell RDF Browser, SIMILE (2005), http://simile.mit.edu/longwell/
8. Quan, D., Huynh, D., Karger, Haystack, D.: A Platform for Authoring End User Semantic Web Applications. In: Fensel, D., Sycara, K., Mylopoulos, J. (eds.) ISWC 2003. LNCS, vol. 2870, pp. 738–753. Springer, Heidelberg (2003)
9. Huynh, D., Karger, D.: Parallax and companion: Set-based browsing for the Data Web (2009)
10. Kobilarov, G., Dickinson, I.: Humboldt: Exploring Linked Data. In: Proc. WWW 2008 Workshop: LDOW (2008)
11. Berners-Lee, T., Hollenbach, J., Lu, K., Presbrey, J., Prud'ommeaux, E., Schraefel, m.c.: Tabulator Redux: Browsing and writing Linked Data. In: Proc. WWW 2008 Workshop: LDOW (2008)
12. Huynh, D.: Nested Faceted Browser (2009), http://people.csail.mit.edu/dfhuynh/projects/nfb/
13. Heim, P., Ziegler, J., Lohmann, S.: gFacet: A Browser for the Web of Data. In: Proc. SAMT 2008 Workshop: IMC-SSW, CEUR-WS, pp. 49–58 (2008)
14. Fruchterman, T., Reingold, E.: Graph drawing by force-directed placement. In: Softw. Pract. Exper. 1991, pp. 1129–1164. John Wiley & Sons, Chichester (1991)
15. Gray, J., Bosworth, A., Layman, A., Pirahesh, H.: Data cube: A relational aggregation operator generalizing group-by, cross-tab, and sub-totals. In: Proc. ICDE 1996, pp. 152–159. IEEE, Los Alamitos (1996)
16. Kuhlthau, C.C.: Developing a model of the library search process: cognitive and affective aspects. Reference Quarterly, 232–242 (1988)

Interactive Relationship Discovery via the Semantic Web

Philipp Heim[1], Steffen Lohmann[2], and Timo Stegemann[3]

[1] Visualization and Interactive Systems Group, University of Stuttgart, Germany
`philipp.heim@vis.uni-stuttgart.de`
[2] DEI Laboratory, Carlos III University of Madrid, Spain
`slohmann@inf.uc3m.es`
[3] Interactive Systems and Interaction Design, University of Duisburg-Essen, Germany
`timo.stegemann@uni-due.de`

Abstract. This paper presents an approach for the interactive discovery of relationships between selected elements via the Semantic Web. It emphasizes the human aspect of relationship discovery by offering sophisticated interaction support. Selected elements are first semi-automatically mapped to unique objects of Semantic Web datasets. These datasets are then crawled for relationships which are presented in detail and overview. Interactive features and visual clues allow for a sophisticated exploration of the found relationships. The general process is described and the RelFinder tool as a concrete implementation and proof-of-concept is presented and evaluated in a user study. The application potentials are illustrated by a scenario that uses the RelFinder and DBpedia to assist a business analyst in decision-making. Main contributions compared to previous and related work are data aggregations on several dimensions, a graph visualization that displays and connects relationships also between more than two given objects, and an advanced implementation that is highly configurable and applicable to arbitrary RDF datasets.

1 Introduction

Today's world is complex, and so are the relationships within most knowledge domains. Even experts in a field are often not aware of all relationships that exist between certain elements of interest. However, overlooking relevant relationships can have fatal consequences in many situations. To name just two examples of the financial and medical domains: Not considering crucial relationships when developing a portfolio of investments might be disastrous for a broker. Even more fatal could be the result if a physician overlooks negative effects caused by a combination of several drugs.

Typical reasons for overlooking and therefore not considering relevant relationships in decision-making and related activities are:

1. A large number of relationships that cannot all be cognitively grasped.
2. Relationships that do not follow logical human thinking.
3. Indirect relationships that are hard to derive by purely cognitive reasoning.

L. Aroyo et al. (Eds.): ESWC 2010, Part I, LNCS 6088, pp. 303–317, 2010.
© Springer-Verlag Berlin Heidelberg 2010

The Semantic Web offers suitable opportunities to assist humans in getting an overview on existing relationships. Since the information objects of the Semantic Web are interlinked via their properties, they altogether describe a "giant global graph" [3] that can be crawled for relationships[1] by appropriate algorithms [12]. That way, it is possible to find relationships that, in particular, deal with the above-mentioned challenges and therefore ideally supplement the relationships that are considered by human thinking.

However, since the information objects in the Semantic Web are ideally strongly interlinked, simply crawling for relationships and listing them is not sufficient in most cases. Instead, user-centered processes and interactive tools are needed that provide comprehensive assistance in the discovery of even very large numbers of relationships. Users must be able to efficiently get an overview on found relationships, to interactively explore them and to easily spot and separate relationships that are of relevance in a certain situation.

In this paper, we therefore define relationship discovery via the Semantic Web as a highly user-centered process. Even though the relationships are found automatically in the datasets, all steps of the process can be controlled and monitored by the user, allowing for a powerful combination of interactive and automatic mechanisms. The process is defined on an abstract level making it applicable in a wide range of domains. It consists of four steps: object mapping, relationship search, visualization, and interactive exploration.

With the RelFinder, we present a concrete implementation of this process. Each step is supported by sophisticated visualization and interaction techniques that aim to move the process on to the subsequent step. The mapping of selected elements to unique objects in the Semantic Web is supported by auto-completion and semi-automatic disambiguation features. Starting from these objects, an algorithm then automatically searches for relationships by following links in the dataset. After relationships are found, they get presented to the user by both a detailed view that shows a limited set of relationships in a graph visualization and an overview that shows the whole set of found relationships aggregated according to topological and semantic dimensions in lists. The aggregated representations can be used to determine what relationships should be shown in the graph visualization and to highlight nodes and edges according to their properties in the different dimensions. In addition, nodes in the graph visualization can be selected to get further information about them.

In the following sections we first define the process for interactive relationship discovery via the Semantic Web in general and present the RelFinder as a concrete implementation of it. With the RelFinder we aim to proof the applicability of our process definition and therewith also the potential of the general approach. We use a scenario to illustrate the benefits of using the RelFinder and evaluate it against existing approaches from the common Web. We conclude with a discussion and future work.

---

[1] Between two objects o_0 and o_n exists a relationship $o_0 \ l_1 \ o_1 \ l_2 \ o_2, \ ... \ l_{n-1} \ o_{n-1} \ l_n \ o_n \ (n > 0)$ if for each link and the two neighboring objects $o_{i-1} \ l_i \ o_i \ (0 < i \leq n)$ in the relationship, either $o_{i-1} \ l_i \ o_i$ or $o_i \ l_i \ o_{i-1}$ is a triple in the dataset (cp. [7]).

2   Process Definition

In this section we define the general process for our approach of interactive relationship discovery via the Semantic Web. We describe the process on an abstract level, independently from any concrete implementation or domain. We call it the ORVI process according to the initial letters of its four sequential steps (Object mapping, Relationship search, Visualization, and Interactive exploration). It can be used in any situation, in which relationships between certain elements are of interest. Knowing the labels of at least two elements is sufficient in order to trigger the process.[2] The selection of these elements is not part of the process as it can be realized in multiple ways. For instance, elements of interest can be manually chosen, the result of natural language processing or any other manual, automatic, or semi-automatic selection process.

In addition, it must be decided on which dataset the process is executed. This decision is also not part of the general process since it depends strongly on the domain in focus and the user goals. It might, for instance, be a large public dataset which covers general knowledge (such as DBpedia [4] or the LOD cloud[3]) or a domain-specific dataset that is privately hosted and maintained by a company.[4]

After the elements have been selected and the decision for a dataset has been made, the four steps of the ORVI process are sequentially executed. They are summarized in the following (cp. Fig. 1):

1. **Object Mapping:** As a common requirement of the Semantic Web, the selected elements must first be mapped to unique objects of the datasets. In order to minimize effort, manual disambiguation should only be required in cases where a unique automatic mapping is not feasible (e.g., in case of ambiguity). In addition, all manual disambiguation should be accompanied by appropriate user support (e.g., auto-completion).

2. **Relationship Search:** After all selected elements have been mapped to unique objects, the dataset is automatically crawled for relationships between these objects by appropriate algorithms. Since it is hard to generally determine which relationships are of relevance in a certain situation and which are not [1], filtering should at best only be used to clean the search results in this process step (e.g., suppressing cycles[5]). Thus, the general goal

---

[2] In contrast to related work, the process does explicitly not limit the elements between which relationships are to be found to only two but supports relationship discovery also between more than two elements.

[3] http://linkeddata.org/

[4] Since we defined the process with the average user in mind who has usually little or no expertise in Semantic Web topics, a dataset might be preselected in most cases that is appropriate for the user's tasks (i.e., contains interrelated objects that the user is interested in).

[5] "Suppressing cycles" means that the same object occurs at most once in the same relationship [9].

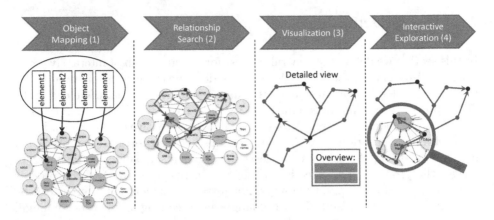

Fig. 1. The ORVI process: Selected elements are mapped to objects in the dataset (1) which are then used as starting objects to find relationships between them (2). The found relationships are visualized (3) and can be explored by the user (4).

in this step is to find as many relationships as possible since each single relationship could be valuable in a certain situation.[6]

3. **Visualization:** The found relationships are then presented to the user. The visualization must be capable to handle even large numbers of relationships. In many cases, only a small subset of the found relationships can be presented in a detailed view due to spatial limitations of the display area (usually, screen size is limited). Therefore, an overview is required that can aggregate the found relationships according to different dimensions (e.g., statistical, topological, or semantic ones) and thus facilitate users' understanding of the whole result set.

4. **Interactive Exploration:** The last step of the process is the interactive exploration of the found relationships. The main goal is the discovery of relationships that are of relevance in a certain situation. In order to reach this goal, interactive features (e.g., dynamic filtering) and visual clues (e.g., highlighting) are needed that enable a sophisticated exploration on the different views of the visualization.

3   RelFinder – An Implementation of the ORVI Process

We developed the RelFinder, a tool that demonstrates the applicability of the ORVI process and illustrates the support it can provide in real-world-contexts.[7] It is implemented in Adobe Flex[8] and gets compiled to a Flash movie which runs

---

[6] Though filtering should only be carefully applied in this process step, it might, however, in practice be necessary due to performance issues and/or resource limitations.

[7] A demo installation of the RelFinder can be tested online at: http://relfinder.semanticweb.org

[8] http://www.adobe.com/products/flex

in all Web browsers with installed Flash Player. SPARQL queries are generated
on the client side and can be sent to any SPARQL endpoint that is available either locally or via the Web. Thus, the RelFinder can be used to find relationships
in datasets of various domains without a need of modifying them.

In order to illustrate how the RelFinder implements the ORVI process and to
show its application potentials, we present a complete walkthrough and describe
the implemented features by means of a scenario. In this scenario, we simulate
the situation of a business analyst who uses the RelFinder to explore a large
number of relationships that were found between companies she is interested in.
We assume the analyst to hold shares from the following German automotive
companies: BMW, Porsche, Volkswagen, and MAN SE. Against the background
of recent developments in the German automotive sector[9], the analyst needs
a deeper understanding of the relationships between the four companies to establish an optimal trading strategy. She decides to use the RelFinder to get
supported in these tasks.

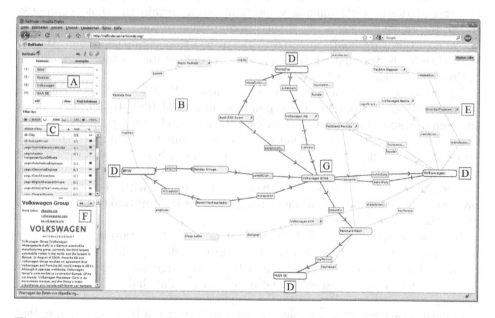

Fig. 2. Screenshot of the RelFinder with relationships between BMW, Porsche, Volkswagen and MAN SE found in the DBpedia dataset

3.1   Object Mapping

The labels of the elements are entered as strings in separate input fields in the
upper left corner of the user interface (Fig. 2, A). Initially, two input fields are
presented but additional ones can easily be added. The business analyst from

---

[9] VW to buy half of Porsche by 2010. BBC News. 2009-10-20. http://news.bbc.co.
uk/2/hi/business/8317010.stm. Retrieved 2009-12-13.

the scenario, for instance, adds two more input fields, since she is interested in relationships between four elements ("BMW", "Porsche", "Volkswagen" and "MAN SE"). As detailed in the following, the RelFinder assists the mapping of entered strings to objects in the dataset in various ways.

While the user is entering the element labels, possibly matching objects are displayed in a drop-down list below each input field. These suggestions are retrieved by SPARQL queries against selected properties of the dataset[10] and are ranked according to their popularity, if supported[11] (else according to string similarity using the Jaro-Winkler distance measure).

The user is not forced to use the auto-completion feature while she inputs her element labels.[12] Hence, all elements that have not been disambiguated via auto-completion need to get mapped to objects of the dataset before the relationship search can be performed. The RelFinder implements a semi-automatic mapping strategy that aims to maintain an optimal trade-off between user effort and false mappings (which should both be minimized). Automatic mapping is triggered in two cases: 1) if the user input matches exactly the property string of an object and the object's ranking value is above a certain threshold compared to the top-ranked object[13] , 2) if the ranking value of the top-ranked object is above a certain threshold compared to the object that is ranked second. Hence, both thresholds are relative; their values are configurable so that they can be optimized for each dataset separately.

Following this implementation, the user inputs "BMW" and "Porsche" can be automatically mapped to corresponding objects of the DBpedia dataset in the scenario, since they meet the first case (exact match and top-ranked object). "Volkswagen" is ranked second but can also be automatically mapped since it is an exact match and its ranking value is above the defined threshold compared to the top-ranked object ("Volkswagen Group").[14] The user input "MAN" cannot be automatically mapped as it has no exact match with one of the `label` properties of DBpedia and as the ranking value of the top-ranked object is not above the defined threshold.

If no automatic mapping is feasible, manual disambiguation is supported by an enhanced suggestion list displayed in a pop-up dialog. This dialog provides additional features such as links to the URIs of the suggested objects or a possibility to directly input and validate object URIs.[15] The dialog can also be used

---

[10] Configuration allows to freely define the queried dataset and the property types that are included in the search for suggestions (by default, the `label` property of the RDF Schema vocabulary is used).

[11] The RelFinder uses the `count` command for popularity ranking that is, however, not (yet) part of the SPARQL standard but was proposed as extension.

[12] Demanding a manual disambiguation for all elements would be against the ORVI principle of minimizing user effort.

[13] This case is only applicable for the popularity ranking based on the `count` value.

[14] The suggestions were ranked according to their `count` value (not string similarity) in the scenario. This results in 'Volkswagen Group' being ranked higher than 'Volkswagen'.

[15] If the URIs of the objects are known in advance, they can also be directly entered in the input fields.

to correct false disambiguations. Thus, the RelFinder provides twofold support for manual disambiguation with lightweight auto-completion during user input and more advanced functionalities in unclear cases (i.e., if no automatic mapping is possible or if entered strings match with more than one object). Ultimately, it ensures that each user input gets mapped to a unique object of the dataset with minimized effort for manual disambiguation. These objects serve as *starting objects* in the subsequent relationship search.

3.2   Relationship Search

Relationship search can be realized in various ways. The RelFinder uses an algorithm that was first introduced in [9] and further developed in [6]. It defines several parameters that can be configured to adapt relationship search and that are also used in related algorithms [1,7], such as *length*[16] and *directionality*[17].

As defined by the ORVI process, the general goal of this process step should be the extraction of as many relationships as possible since each single relationship can be valuable depending on the situation. Therefore, the parameters of the relationship search should generally be configured with this goal in mind. However, this idealized vision cannot be fully realized in many situations due to performance reasons or resource limitations. Thus, the RelFinder allows a configuration of the *length* and *directionality* parameters. In addition, it allows the definition of properties that should be ignored as they provide no benefits for relationship discovery (e.g., contain no valuable semantics).

The RelFinder installation of the scenario has been configured to search for all relationships that have a maximum length of two and contain no more than one change in the link directions. Furthermore, it has been defined to ignore the `wikilink` property of the DBpedia ontology [4] since it simply represents hyperlinks and provides therefore no valuable semantics for relationship discovery. In addition, all links of types `subject` from the SKOS vocabulary[18] and `type` from the RDF Schema vocabulary are ignored. Overall, this results in 64 relationships that were found between the four starting objects by the algorithm (26 of length 1 and 38 of length 2), with 16 object classes belonging to the YAGO ontology[19], four to OpenCyc[20] and three to DBpedia, and with 37 different link types.[21] The next challenge addressed by the RelFinder in accordance with the ORVI process is the visualization of these relationships in a user-centered way.

---

[16] We define the "length" of a relationship by the number of intermediate objects that are contained within this relationship. According to this definition, direct relationships (i.e., the starting objects are directly linked without intermediate objects) are of length 0 and indirect relationships that contain $x + 1$ links and x intermediate objects are of length x.

[17] The "directionality" expresses the number of changes in the directions of the links that a relationship consists of. See [7] for more information about this concept.

[18] http://www.w3.org/2004/02/skos/

[19] http://www.mpi-inf.mpg.de/yago-naga/yago/

[20] http://www.cyc.com/opencyc/

[21] These were the results at time of writing.

3.3 Visualization

The visualization of relationships in the RelFinder is organized in two separate parts, a detailed view of a limited number of relationships in the main area (Fig. 2, B) and an overview of the whole set in the sidebar on the left (Fig. 2, C).

Detailed View: The detailed view consists of a graph visualization that represents objects as nodes and links as directed labeled edges between them.[22] The nodes representing starting objects (all objects the selected elements got mapped to) are marked by a stronger border (Fig. 2, D) and are elliptically arranged in an oval on fixed positions on the screen. The found objects and links that are contained in the relationships between the starting objects span a graph between these fixed nodes and get automatically arranged by a force-directed layout [5].

Since the found energy level is not necessarily a global minimum, i.e. the graph layout is probably suboptimal, or the user might want to arrange nodes according to individual preferences, single nodes can be picked by the user and pinned at fixed positions on the screen decoupling them from the automatic layout.[23] Whether a node is pinned or not is indicated by a needle symbol (Fig. 2, E). By clicking the needle symbol of an already pinned node, this node releases its fixed position and gets again coupled to the automatic layout.

The graph building is animated incrementally by displaying the found relationships one after the other. This has three advantages: 1) An early impression of found relationships: Even though the search is still in progress, first results are already displayed; 2) Time for cognitive processing: Having a delay between each newly added relationship gives users time to adjust to the graph visualization (especially new users without any familiarity with graphs are often overstrained by their complexity); 3) An easy traceability of relationships: Since relationships are stepwise added to the graph, the layout needs to integrate only a few nodes and edges at a time and thus the nodes are changing their positions rather smoothly allowing the eyes to keep track of them.

Overview: In the overview, the found relationships get aggregated according to two topological and two semantic dimensions. The two topological dimensions are:

- *Relationship lengths* (see Section 3.2 and Footnote 19).
- *Connectivity levels* of found objects contained in the relationships.[24]

The two semantic dimensions are:

- *Link types* contained in the relationships.
- *Classes* of found objects contained in the relationships.

---

[22] Actually, edge labels are also handled as nodes in the graph layout for readability reasons.

[23] We call the manual adaption of the positions of single nodes in the graph *pick-and-pin* operation.

[24] We define the connectivity level of a found object by the number of distinct starting objects it connects in the graph. Each found object connects at least 2 and at most all starting objects.

For each of the four dimensions, all aggregated properties of the relationships are organized in lists that can be accessed via a tab menu in the sidebar (Fig. 2, C). Each row in the lists stands for a distinct property and contains its label, the numbers of aggregated relationships that are visible in the detailed view, the total number of aggregated relationships, and information whether the property is generally set visible or not (by an eye symbol).

If the number of found relationships exceeds a certain threshold, which defines the maximum number of relationships that can clearly be arranged in the graph visualization, not all of them get visualized in the detailed view initially. In order to decide which relationships should initially be visible in the graph visualization, we define a *measure of importance*. The questions are: In which relationships are the users most likely interested in? And even more important: What properties can be used to calculate the importance of relationships automatically?

Unfortunately, the definition of the importance of relationships seems to change profoundly with the current user task. Nevertheless, since we do not ask for the current user task in advance, at least in the current RelFinder implementation, we chose the relationship length as a general property to automatically measure the importance of relationships (cp. [1]). Thus, direct relationships or relationships with few intermediate objects are more likely to be shown in the initial graph visualization than relationships with more intermediate objects. If a property, as for example a certain relationship length, is set invisible, this is indicated in the corresponding row of the list in the overview by a closed eye symbol.

3.4 Interactive Exploration

The found relationships in the RelFinder can be explored by interacting with both the properties in the overview and the nodes and edges in the detailed view. The user can control what relationships are shown in the graph visualization, can highlight nodes, edges and relationships, and can get additional information about selected objects.

By interacting with the properties in the overview, relationships can be shown or hidden in the detailed view and nodes and edges can be highlighted. Clicking on the open eye symbol of a certain relationship length removes all relationships of this length from the graph visualization (e.g., all direct relationships). Clicking on the open eye symbol of a certain link type removes all relationships that contain links of this type and thus allows users to ignore links that are possibly irrelevant for the current analysis (e.g., "companyType"). Clicking on the open eye symbol of a certain connectivity level or ontology class removes all relationships that contain corresponding objects. This facilitates focusing on relationships via objects that belong to certain classes (Fig. 2, C) or that connect a certain number of starting objects (e.g., all starting objects). Selecting one of the properties in any of the four aggregation dimensions highlights all corresponding nodes and edges in the detailed view (e.g., selecting the class "HybridElectricVehicles" of the YAGO ontology highlights the "Porsche Cayenne" node in Fig. 2, E).

In the detailed view, nodes can be selected in order to highlight related information in both the detailed view and the overview. First, the properties of the selected object are highlighted in the aggregated lists to provide information about its class and connectivity level. Second, objects in the detailed view that share the same properties as the selected one are highlighted to provide some awareness of similar information in the graph. Third, all relationships that contain the selected object are highlighted as "red threads" in the detailed view helping the user to visually track relationships within the graph (e.g., all relationships that contain "Volkswagen Group" in Fig. 2, G). Furthermore, additional information about the selected node, such as an image and a short description, is shown in the sidebar (Fig. 2, F) to help users to interpret possibly unknown objects that were found between the starting objects and thus to better understand the found relationships in general.

The business analyst in the scenario interactively explores the found relationships mainly by using the semantic dimensions "class" and "link type". Since relationships based on spatial correlations (e.g., companies located in the same city) or on similar organizational structures (e.g., companies with a chief executive officer) are not of much interest to her, she sets all relationships that contain objects like "cities" or "countries" and links like "companyType" and "death-Place" invisible in the detailed view. Thus, the graph visualization shows only a limited but possibly valuable set of found relationships like those containing persons (e.g., "Bernd Pischetsrieder"), products (e.g., "Porsche Cayenne"), or organizations (e.g., "Volkswagen Group"). Such relationships can be indicators for personal, structural, or financial connections and dependencies between the four automotive companies and are thus of interest to the business analyst. A very prominent insight that can be gained by studying the graph visualization in Fig. 2 is the important role of the "Volkswagen Group" as a connector of all four starting objects. Dependencies based on this object should be considered very carefully when developing a trading strategy.

4 Evaluation

We performed a user study in which we compared relationship discovery via the Semantic Web according to the ORVI with relationship discovery as it can be commonly performed by Web users nowadays. We used the RelFinder as implementation of the ORVI process and decided for Google and Wikipedia as reference applications for relationship finding in the "common" Web.[25]

4.1 Study Design

The user study consisted of three tasks that had to be accomplished with all three applications (Google, Wikipedia, and RelFinder). One relationship had to

---

[25] We selected Google and Wikipedia for the following reasons: 1) These two applications were mentioned by most people in an informal poll when we asked for Web applications they would use for relationship discovery, 2) They are very popular representatives for the application classes search engine and Wiki, 3) We expected a high familiarity with these applications among the study participants lowering the need for explanations or trainings.

be found in the first task and three relationships in the second. The third task also asked for three relationships but additionally defined an object class that should be included in the found relationship (e.g., person, location, etc.). The relationships had always to be found between two given elements that varied across the applications.[26] Likewise, the class varied that was asked for in the third task.

The elements were selected from three thematic categories – persons, locations, and culture –, whereas each study participant received elements from each category. We run a pre-test to ensure that relationships between the given elements could be found in all three applications with relatively small effort.[27] For example, one text for the third task in the category *culture* was: "Name three movies that relate Quentin Tarantino and Samuel L. Jackson. Give also the kind of relationship" (with "Quentin Tarantino" and "Samuel L. Jackson" as given elements and "movie" as given class).

The time limit for each task was three minutes. If a study participant was not able to solve a task within this time, its execution was aborted and it was continued with the next task. The study participants were advised to disregard previous knowledge as much as possible. They were only allowed to name relationships they evidently found with the applications. Correspondingly, they were not permitted to use further terms for search that are based on their own knowledge. The DBpedia dataset was used for the RelFinder in the user study. We ensured that the study participants did not access Web pages from Wikipedia via Google. Further restrictions were not made so that participants could use their own preferred strategies to solve the tasks in each application.[28]

4.2   Procedure

Twelve participants, mainly students, took part in the study. Their familiarity with Google and Wikipedia was high[29] (Google: M=9, SD=1.2; Wikipedia: M=8.8, SD=1.0)[30].

The study began with a short introduction and explanation of the three tasks. Subsequently, the three applications (Google, Wikipedia, and RelFinder) were presented in systematically varying order. The tasks had to be accomplished

---

[26] We restricted relationship finding to only two elements in the user study since it is highly challenging to find relationships between more than two elements via Google and Wikipedia. Even more challenging is the selection of examples that work in all three applications if more than two given elements are considered.

[27] For instance, we ensured in the case of Google that relationships were preferable displayed on the first, at least on the second result page.

[28] The high diversity of the datasets accessed by the applications (DBpedia, Wikipedia, Google-indexed WWW) could not be avoided but was also not considered as a problem since the pre-tests ensured that all tasks could principally be solved with all applications and within the given time frame of three minutes.

[29] Familiarity was measured on a scale of 1 to 10 (with 1 = "unfamiliar" and 10 = "very familiar").

[30] M = mean; SD = standard deviation.

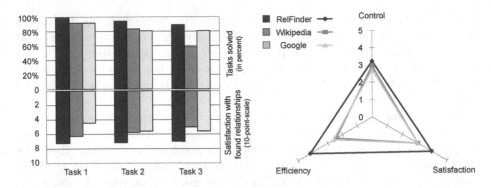

Fig. 3. Left: Average number of tasks solved (in percent) and average value of satisfaction with the task solutions (on scale of 1 to 10) for each application and task type; Right: User ratings for the three applications on the dimensions control, satisfaction, and efficiency (measured by 12 items on a five-point Likert-scale)

with all three applications.[31] For each task, the participants had to rate their satisfaction with the found relationships.[32] In addition, after the presentation of all three tasks, they had to rate how much the respective application helped in the discovery of relationships.[33]

4.3 Results

Fig. 3 shows the average number of tasks that were solved with each application (upper left diagram, separately listed for each task type). In this direct comparison, the RelFinder provides generally the best support. A similar result is shown by the satisfaction values that were measured after each task's solution (Fig. 3, lower left diagram). These results indicate that the ORVI process as implemented in the RelFinder is generally preferred to relationship discovery as it is currently possible in common Web applications such as Google and Wikipedia. This is also reflected by the answers on the statement: "If I would need to search for relationships between two elements, I would use the following tool". Eight participants decided for the RelFinder and only two for Google and two for Wikipedia.[34]

The diagram on the right of Fig. 3 shows the ratings of the participants on the dimensions *efficiency*, *satisfaction*, and *control* that we collected directly

---

[31] Since the given elements in the tasks were presented in the same order each time, they also varied systematically across the applications.

[32] Satisfaction was measured on a scale of 1 to 10 (with 1 = "not satisfied at all" and 10 = "totally satisfied").

[33] Support was measured according to twelve pre-defined items on a five-point Likert scale (with 1 = "not agree" and 5 = "fully agree"). The items were then mapped to aggregated measures on the dimensions *efficiency*, *satisfaction*, and *control*.

[34] The decision for Google and Wikipedia was mainly motivated with a higher familiarity with these applications.

after the presentation of each application via the twelve Likert-scaled items. The relationship discovery support as implemented in the RelFinder reached once again the highest satisfaction values on average. The ratings on the dimension *control* were nearly the same for all three applications. This result indicates a successful interaction design of the RelFinder since familiarity with Google and Wikipedia was much higher among the participants. The *satisfaction* values support this interpretation and the results given above. The largest differences shows the *efficiency* dimension: The RelFinder has foremost been considered as much more efficient than the other two applications.

5   Discussion

Overall, the RelFinder performed very well in the user study. This is not surprising since it has been developed exactly for the kind of tasks that were investigated in the study. Nevertheless, the results demonstrate the high applicability of this approach and the general potentials and benefits it offers for relationship discovery compared to common Web applications. Interestingly, the RelFinder was considered as very efficient, although the manual disambiguation and relationship search took longer time than entering and searching for terms in Google and Wikipedia. It seems as if this additional effort pays off and is ultimately appreciated by the users when they recognize its benefit. These results argue for the generally high suitability of the Semantic Web to support relationship discovery. They also argue for viewing relationship discovery as a highly user-oriented process that consists of several interactive steps, as proposed by our approach.

5.1   Related Work

This view on relationship discovery as an iterative and highly interactive process is a main difference to related work which mainly investigates querying strategies and algorithms for relationship search in the Semantic Web. Considerable research in this area has been conducted in the SemDis project[35]. A specific focus of this project was on the development of ranking measures for found relationships. The authors distinguish between semantic and statistical metrics and define a SemRank value that combines these metrics in different configurations [2]. In contrast to our topological and semantic classification dimensions, their ranking criteria do not include aggregations. However, our dimensions showed to provide very powerful assistance in the interactive exploration of the found relationships. This limitation holds also for the "DBpedia Relationship finder" [9] that has largely inspired our work and provided the basic algorithms for relationship search. The found relationships are simply listed as text strings in this tool but are neither aggregated nor extended by interactive functionalities.

Another related approach is SPARQLeR [7] that defines additional language constructs for SPARQL designed for relationship search. Unfortunately, SPARQLeR is not supported by common endpoints and could therefore not be used in

---

[35] http://lsdis.cs.uga.edu/projects/semdis/

the RelFinder. Further related work can be found in the research areas of ontology matching, learning, and enrichment. However, these approaches are rather interested in relationships on the conceptual level [11]. More distantly related research on the identification of semantic relationships in other data sources (e.g., text documents [10]) provides only few valuable input to the topic of interactive relationship discovery via the Semantic Web.[36] Though information seeking processes are generally a topic in related work [8], to the best of our knowledge it exists no approach for relationship discovery via the Semantic Web that covers the whole process, from object mapping to interactive exploration. Our approach aims to close this gap and, with the RelFinder, proposes an implementation that applies interactive relationship discovery via the Semantic Web to real-world-contexts.

5.2   Conclusion and Future Work

The most notable difference of our approach compared to related work is the emphasis on the *interactive* aspect of relationship discovery. In this understanding, "real" discovery is only possible with a human involved, since only the user can ultimately decide if a found relationship is relevant in a certain situation or not. However, this notion of "discovery" does explicitly not exclude any pre-selection and ranking of relationships as long as these are meant to support the interaction and do not restrict search results. An improved pre-selection of search results that are initially presented in the detailed view is therefore a main topic for future work. This will require some kind of context- or situation-awareness in order to adapt the pre-selection criteria to the users' information needs. Future work includes also the application of the RelFinder to use cases of different domains (e.g., health care, eLearning, etc.) and on datasets of different size (e.g., LODD[37], Semantic Wikis datasets, etc.) in order to get an improved understanding of the application potentials, benefits, and scalability of our approach.

Acknowledgments

We are grateful to Sebastian Hellmann and Jens Lehmann for the fruitful discussions and their contributions to the RelFinder implementation. We also thank Jürgen Ziegler for his valuable input and Lena Tetzlaff for assisting us with the user study. Last but not least, we thank Jörg Schüppel, Jens Lehmann, and Sören Auer for the development of the "DBpedia Relationship Finder" [9] which has largely inspired this work and provided basic algorithms for relationship search.

References

1. Aleman-Meza, B., Halaschek-Wiener, C., Budak Arpinar, I., Ramakrishnan, C., Sheth, A.P.: Ranking complex relationships on the semantic web. IEEE Internet Computing 9(3), 37–44 (2005)

---

[36] Refer to [12] for an overview on different types of semantic relationships in the Web.
[37] http://esw.w3.org/topic/HCLSIG/LODD

2. Anyanwu, K., Maduko, A., Sheth, A.P.: SemRank: ranking complex relationship search results on the semantic web. In: Proc. of the 14th International World Wide Web Conference (WWW '05), pp. 117–127 (2005)
3. Berners-Lee, T.: Giant Global Graph (2007), http://dig.csail.mit.edu/breadcrumbs/node/215 (last access, 2009/12/20)
4. Bizer, C., Lehmann, J., Kobilarov, G., Auer, S., Becker, C., Cyganiak, R., Hellmann, S.: DBpedia – a crystallization point for the web of data. Web Semantics: Science, Services and Agents on the World Wide Web 7(3), 154–165 (2009)
5. Fruchterman, T.M.J., Reingold, E.M.: Graph drawing by force-directed placement. Softw. Pract. Exper. 21(11), 1129–1164 (1991)
6. Heim, P., Hellmann, S., Lehmann, J., Lohmann, S., Stegemann, T.: Relfinder: Revealing relationships in RDF knowledge bases. In: SAMT 2009. LNCS, vol. 5887, pp. 182–187. Springer, Heidelberg (2009)
7. Kochut, K., Janik, M.: SPARQLeR: Extended SPARQL for semantic association discovery. In: Franconi, E., Kifer, M., May, W. (eds.) ESWC 2007. LNCS, vol. 4519, pp. 145–159. Springer, Heidelberg (2007)
8. Kuhlthau, C.C.: Seeking meaning: a process approach to library and information services. Libraries Unlimited (1993)
9. Lehmann, J., Schüppel, J., Auer, S.: Discovering unknown connections – the DBpedia relationship finder. In: Proc. of the 1st Conference on Social Semantic Web, CSSW'07 (2007)
10. Ramakrishnan, C., Kochut, K., Sheth, A.P.: A framework for schema-driven relationship discovery from unstructured text. In: Cruz, I., Decker, S., Allemang, D., Preist, C., Schwabe, D., Mika, P., Uschold, M., Aroyo, L.M. (eds.) ISWC 2006. LNCS, vol. 4273, pp. 583–596. Springer, Heidelberg (2006)
11. Sabou, M., d'Aquin, M., Motta, E.: Relation discovery from the semantic web. In: Proceedings of the Poster and Demonstration Session at the 7th International Semantic Web Conference (ISWC '08). CEUR, vol. 408, CEUR-WS.org (2008)
12. Sheth, A.P., Ramakrishnan, C.: Relationship web: Blazing semantic trails between web resources. IEEE Internet Computing 11(4), 77–81 (2007)

Put in Your Postcode, Out Comes the Data: A Case Study

Tope Omitola[1], Christos L. Koumenides[1], Igor O. Popov[1], Yang Yang[1],
Manuel Salvadores[1], Martin Szomszor[2], Tim Berners-Lee[1], Nicholas Gibbins[1],
Wendy Hall[1], mc schraefel[1], and Nigel Shadbolt[1]

[1] Intelligence, Agents, Multimedia (IAM) Group
School of Electronics and Computer Science
University of Southampton, UK
{t.omitola,clk1v07,ip2g09,yy1402,ms8,timbl,
nmg,wh,mc,nrs}@ecs.soton.ac.uk
[2] City eHealth Research Centre
City University London, UK
martin.szomszor.1@city.ac.uk

Abstract. A single datum or a set of a categorical data has little value
on its own. Combinations of disparate sets of data increase the value of
those data sets and helps to discover interesting patterns or relationships,
facilitating the construction of new applications and services. In this
paper, we describe an implementation of using open geographical data
as a core set of "join point"(s) to mesh different public datasets. We
describe the challenges faced during the implementation, which include,
sourcing the datasets, publishing them as linked data, and normalising
these linked data in terms of finding the appropriate "join points" from
the individual datasets, as well as developing the client application used
for data consumption. We describe the design decisions and our solutions
to these challenges. We conclude by drawing some general principles from
this work.

Keywords: Public Sector Information, Linked Data, Public Open Data,
Data Publication, Data Consumption, Semantic Web.

1 Introduction

In the private consumption of goods and services, there is a drive to put the
consumer at the centre of production, i.e. to co-produce the goods and services
consumers want. This drive has also come to the production and consumption
of public goods and services. Citizens want governments to improve the delivery
of public services. One way to improve the delivery is to put the citizen as the
co-producer of these goods and services. There are concrete cases of these, where
citizens are at the heart of service designs and accountability. A good example is
Patients Know Best[1], where the principle is the "empowerment of health workers

---

[1] http://www.patientsknowbest.com/

L. Aroyo et al. (Eds.): ESWC 2010, Part I, LNCS 6088, pp. 318–332, 2010.

and patients to be creative with information". An example of co-production here is the opening up of access and communications to:

- patients' records,
- their medical doctors and consultants, and
- other information, such as treatments, care, etc.

For this to be more seamless, citizens need to have access to public data, and there will need to be linkage of these data and records across organisational boundaries to help patients make informed decisions, and to enable the quality of care to be monitored. Therefore, the provision and opening up of government data contributes to the improvement of the delivery of public services.

With a view to this, governments around the world are opening up government data to enable, among other things, this process of citizens' co-production. Questions such as: "Where can I find a good school, hospital, investment advisor, employer?", and more complex questions, such as the integration of these domains and their potential relationships, can be more easily answered than they are at present, using open government data.

In the United States, the government has set up *data.gov*[2] for the publication of public data. The United Kingdom government has set up a public data store[3] where large quantities of public sector information have been freed up or published, ranging from geospatial, statistical, financial, and legal data. While most of these data are published in spreadsheet or comma-separated-values (csv) formats, publishing them in structured machine-processable formats will be highly useful for ease of linking to other data sources and for ease of re-use.

Although the Semantic Web offers solutions to publishing data in a structured machine-processable format, the requirement for agreed ontologies has often presented a hurdle in the deployment of these technologies [2]. The Linked Data[4] movement advocates a bottom-up approach to ontology agreement [6] by publishing data in a structured machine-processable formats, such as RDF, before agreeing on ontologies for specific applications. The benefits for making data available in a structured and machine-processable formats include:

1. End users know what to expect, and find content easier to read,
2. Online services can aggregate accurate, up to date, and comprehensive information, and
3. Data re-users will find it easier to create new combinations of data that are more relevant to end users.

There have been many efforts in publishing data as linked data. Some noteworthy examples include

---

[2] http://www.data.gov
[3] http://www.data.gov.uk
[4] The term "Linked Data" refers to a style of publishing and interlinking structured data on the Web [http://www.w3.org/DesignIssues/LinkedData.html].

1. The London Gazette[5], where linked data was used to maximise the re-use of the information within it, and as a vehicle for the government to serve semantically enabled official information, and
2. The New York Times[6], which, in 2009, published its news vocabularies as linked open data.

There are some examples of linking data sources from different domains. Such examples include:

1. BBC's Music Beta[7]. This links data across BBC[7] domains with data from MusicBrainz[8], and DBpedia[9]. The BBC maintains data of programmes, music, artists, etc, but most of these information are stored in data silos. For many years, it has been difficult for the BBC to have an "across domain" look at its data; Music Beta provides a solution to this.
2. Linked Movie Database[8]. This is an RDF data source of movies, which are the results of interlinking data from disparate data sources, such as RDF Book Mashup[10], MusicBrainz, Geonames[11], and DBpedia.

A noteworthy example in the public sector is the Postcode paper[12] which, by using London (United Kingdom) postcodes, provides an integrated view of local services, environmental information, and crime statistics of neighbourhoods. However, there are challenges with providing an integrated view of linked datasets. These include:

1. (the case of) sourcing, or discovering, the appropriate datasets,
2. their formats,
3. which "join point"(s) to use,
4. selecting the normal form to use and its representations, e.g. will it be RDF/XML or RDF/N3,
5. data interlinking issues (i.e. setting links between entities in different data sources), and
6. building the client applications to consume the data

This paper describes the results and analyses from experiments carried out from selecting and combining some United Kingdom public datasets that can be used to infer relationships amongst these data. Berners-Lee and Shadbolt [1] laid out the benefits of publishing non-personal public computer-readable data for reuse. We set out to implement some of the ideas set out in their paper, and to use administrative entities (geographic) data, from the UK's Ordnance Survey, as a "join point" to mesh data for crime, mortality rates, and hospital waiting times.

---

[5] http://www.london-gazette.co.uk/
[6] http://data.nytimes.com/
[7] http://www.bbc.co.uk
[8] http://musicbrainz.org/
[9] http://dbpedia.org/About
[10] http://www4.wiwiss.fu-berlin.de/bizer/bookmashup/
[11] http://www.geonames.org/
[12] http://blog.newspaperclub.co.uk/2009/10/16/data-gov-uk-newspaper/

By **meshing**, we mean the ability to naturally merge together a dynamic set of information sources, and a **join-point** is a point of reference shared by all datasets. As most of these data were not linked data and were published by different departments of government, we describe the processes we undertook to convert them into a linked data format, the challenges encountered, and the solutions we devised. Building clients to consume these data also posed its own challenges, which we describe.

2   Related Work

The provision and consumption of public data have been an ongoing effort for many years. These vary from the solutions used in the linked and the non-linked data space.

2.1   Non-linked Data Space

1. **Mashups.** used for many years as a mechanism to provide and consume public data. They fuse data from two or more Web applications to create a new service. The website, *GeoWorldBank*[13] is an example of a data mashup from Google[14] and the World Bank to display a country's statistics, such as its population and its income level. A mashup application is comprised of three different components that are disjoint, both logically and physically. These are: *the API/content providers, the mashup site*, and *the client's Web browser*. Mashups provide many benefits, such as the provision of access to massive amounts of content which no individual could gather on their own, and lowering the barriers to developing novel applications. They have some disadvantages, and these include:

   (a) Data pollution. Some of these data sources may contain erroneous or inconsistent data, compromising the value provided by the mashup.
   (b) If a mashup uses screen scraping as part of building it, one small change in the data markup of any of the source sites may compromise the quality of the mashup.
   (c) Mashups are implemented against a fixed number of data sources and can not take advantage of new data sources that appear on the Web.

2. **Other Third-party Datastores.** There are a few charity or non-profit based institutions who provide, through APIs and bulk file downloads, data of members of a country's governmental institutions. Some are: (a) *Gov-Track.us*[15], a website providing a set of tools used to research and track the activities in the U.S. Congress, using congressional district maps, or searching by name, or using the U.S. ZIP code. It provides two main access to its

---

[13] http://geo.worldbank.org/
[14] http://maps.google.co.uk/
[15] GovTrack.us.

data, via raw XML files and APIs, and (b) *TheyWorkForYou*[16] a website
that provides data on the Members' and the Houses of the United Kingdom
Parliament, through using a set of APIs and raw XML files.

2.2   Linked Data Space

There are many initiatives around the world making public data available. These
include:

- DBpedia: A community effort to extract structured information from
  Wikipedia, linking this information to other datasets, and making it available
  on the Web.
- GeoNames: GeoNames integrates geographical data, such as place names,
  population, etc, from various sources. It gives access to users to manually
  edit, correct, and add new names.
- Data.gov.uk[17]: This is U.K. government central place to publish public data
  as RDF.
- The Ordnance Survey[18]: Great Britain's national mapping agency, providing
  geographic data used by government, businesses, and individuals. It provides
  linked data format of the administrative and voting regions in Great Britain.
  This data includes the names, census code, and area of the regions of Great
  Britain.

In DBpedia and GeoNames, as they are user-community based initiatives, there
are risks of introducing data redundancy and/or data pollution. Data.gov.uk is
only open to registered members, and many of the data it points to are not yet
published in RDF format. The Ordnance Survey, however, is an authoritative
source of the data it produces.

3   Application Case Study

3.1   Introduction

We investigated the use of disparate sets of data in an effort to better understand the challenges of their integration using Semantic Web approaches. Part
of this investigation involved ascertaining the datasets that were available, their
formats, and converting them into (re)usable formats, asking our questions, and
also linking our data back into the linked data cloud[19]. The issue we started with
was how to deal with linked data that are centred around the democratic system
of political representation in the United Kingdom. We noticed that a lot of UK
governmental data are already referenced by geography. The Ordnance Survey
have produced a number of ontologies and an RDF data set that represents the

---

[16] http://www.theyworkforyou.com/
[17] http://data.hmg.gov.uk/about
[18] http://www.ordnancesurvey.co.uk/oswebsite/
[19] http://linkeddata.org

key administrative entities in the UK [3]. The questions we asked were what kinds of problems will be encountered from developing a service that uses an administrative entity, i.e. geography data, linked with other data, such as criminal statistics data, the Members of Parliament of these entities (their data), the mortality rates of these entities, and the National Health Service (NHS) hospital waiting times.

3.2 Design Decisions

1. Sourcing the datasets. Since many of the datasets of interest were not yet in linked data format, we could not take advantage of the automatic resource discovery process as enunciated in [10]. We sourced the data by going to the relevant department of government websites. Some datasets were in PDF and HTML formats, while some were in XLS formats. We decided against scraping, for reasons outlined in section 2.1. For reasons of data fidelity, ability to source from a wider range of public sector domains, and to have increased value that comes from many information linkages, we chose the ones in XLS formats. In future, we do expect many of these datasets to be sourced via the U.K. government's public datastore[20]. This should aid the discovery process of consuming (linked) data.

2. Selection of RDF as the normal form: We decided to use RDF as the normal form for the datasets. RDF offers many advantages, such as provision of an extensible schema, self-describing data, de-referenceable URIs, and, as RDF links are typed, safe merging (linking) of different datasets. We chose the RDF/Turtle representation of RDF triples for its compactness and clarity.

3. We chose a central 4store [4] system to store and manage our RDF triples. 4store provides a robust, scalable, and secure platform to manage RDF triples[21].

4. Modelling multidimensional data. The real world is complex, multidimensional (of space and time) and multivariate, and so are our chosen datasets. They contain dimensions such as time, geographical regions, employment organisations, etc. For example, one of the datasets, the datasets for recorded crime for England and Wales 2008/09, has dimensions such the "Police Force Areas of England and Wales" and the types of recorded crimes, e.g. burglary. To model this multi-dimensionality, we chose SCOVO[5]. SCOVO is an expressive modelling framework for representing complex statistics.

5. Many of the datasets we used have notions of geography or region. To join them together, we used geographical location data as the set of "join point"(s). We chose to use the Ordnance Survey's geographical datasets [3] as our set of join points. The Ordnance Survey datasets are relatively stable and fairly authoritative.

6. Although our datasets had concepts of geography, the names given to particular geographical regions differ. As many of these regions refer to the same

---

[20] http://data.hmg.gov.uk/about

[21] As of 2009-10-21 it's running with 15B triples in a production cluster to power the DataPatrol application(http://esw.w3.org/topic/LargeTripleStores)

geographical boundaries, we used `owl:sameAs` to assert equivalences between them.

7. Consumption of data. We used Exhibit[22] to develop the client application. Exhibit allows quick development of Web sites that support various data-centric interactions such as faceted browsing and various representation formats over data such as tables, timelines, thumbnail views, etc.

4   Public Sector DataSets - Publication and Consumption

4.1   Datasets

We used five major datasets. Table 1 lists the data sets used, their formats, and a brief description of the data. They include datasets of Members of Parliament (MPs), Lords, their corresponding constituencies and counties, relevant websites, MPs' expenses and votes, and statistical records about crime, hospital waiting time, and mortality rates.

Table 1. Targeted Government data sources, formats, and description of dataset

Data Source	Format	Dataset
Publicwhip.org.uk	HTML	MP Votes Records, Divisions, Policies
Theyworkforyou.com	XML Dump	Parliament, Parliament expenses
Homeoffice.gov.uk	Excel Spreadsheet	Recorded crime (English and Wales 2008/09)
Statistics.gov.uk	Excel Spreadsheet	Hospital Waiting List Statistics (English 2008/09)
Performance.doh.gov.uk	Excel Spreadsheet	Standardised mortality ratios by sex (English and Wales 2008)
Ordancesurvey.co.uk	Linked Data	National mapping agency, providing the most accurate and up-to-date geographic data

4.2   Modelling the Datasets

Most of our vocabularies come from Friend-of-a-Friend (FOAF)[23], Dublin Core (DC)[24], and SCOVO, thereby following the advice given in [9] to re-use terms from well-known vocabularies.

Modelling the datasets for Recorded Crimes. Each row, of the spreadsheet provided by the Home Office[25], consisted of data of each Police Force area in England and Wales, and for a particular row, its columns contained the recorded

---

[22] http://simile.mit.edu/wiki/Exhibit/API

[23] http://xmlns.com/foaf/spec/

[24] http://dublincore.org/documents/dcmes-xml/

[25] http://www.homeoffice.gov.uk/about-us/publications/non-personal-data/

crime values for the following offences, "Violence against the person", "Robbery", "Burglary", "Offences against vehicles", etc. The time period under discussion, i.e. 2008/09, the geographical areas and regions, and the different types of criminal offences are scovo:Dimension(s). A snippet of the RDF/Turtle schema representation is shown below:

```
:TimePeriod rdf:type owl:Class;
                          rdfs:subClassOf scovo:Dimension.
:TP2008_09 rdf:type :TimePeriod.
:GeographicalRegion rdfs:subClassOf scovo:Dimension;
    dc:title "Police force area, English region and Wales".
:CriminalOffenceType rdf:type owl:Class;
                          rdfs:subClassOf scovo:Dimension.
```

Modelling the Hospital Waiting List. Each row, of this dataset[26], consisted of data for each health care provider, or a National Health Service (NHS) Hospital Trust, in England and Wales. The columns consisted of various data that were of no interest to us. One of the columns, "Patients waiting for admission by weeks waiting", was made up of several columns which had data for patients waiting for hospital operations, and each of these columns was divided into weekly waiting times, from those waiting between 0 and 1 week, continuing to those waiting for more than thirty weeks. We modelled the data as follows. The time period, 2008/09, the NHS Hospital Trust (e.g. South Tyneside NHS Foundation Trust), and the waiting periods are scovo:Dimension(s). The value for patients that had been waiting for hospital operation from between zero to one week at South Tyneside NHS Foundation Trust is modelled as:

```
:A_RE9 rdf:type waitt:OrgName; dc:title "RE9";
    rdfs:label "South Tyneside NHS Foundation Trust";
    statistics:SHA "Q30"; statistics:org_code "RE9".
:ds1_1_2 rdf:type scovo:Item; rdf:value 185;
    scovo:dataset :ds1; scovo:dimension :w0to01week;
    scovo:dimension :A_RE9; scovo:dimension :TP2008_09.
```

Modelling the UK Parliament. The datasets of information for MPs, Lords, constituencies, counties, MPs' expenses and votes were downloaded from the Parliament Parser[27]. Most of these were raw XML files. The Parliament Parser provides structured versions of publicly available data from the UK parliament. Members of parliament and lords were modelled as foaf:person(s) with parliament identities corresponding to their roles in the Parliament at different time periods. Constituencies and counties were embodied as dc:jurisdiction(s) and linked to their corresponding MP and Lord identities via the dc:coverage property. Political parties and the Houses themselves were in turn modelled as foaf:group(s), while MPs expenses and votes were modelled using the SCOVO ontology.

---

[26] http://www.performance.doh.gov.uk/waitingtimes/index.htm
[27] http://ukparse.kforge.net/parlparse/

4.3   Converting Datasets to RDF

Most of our data were in spreadsheet or comma-separated-values (csv) formats. There are inherent problems with re-using data published in spreadsheet format. These include:

1. little or no explicit semantic description, or schema, of the data. An example of this can be seen from the Hospital Waiting List where there were codes given names such as "SHA Code", and "Org Code", without explanation of their relationships with the rest of the data in the spreadsheet.
2. more difficult to integrate, or link, data from disparate data sources. An example of this can be seen from the Home Office data where each area's value for a crime was given. It will be good to know how this data was arrived, and linking it with the data sources from whence they come would have been useful (e.g. for provenance and validation).

We developed a number of scripts to automatically convert the spreadsheets' data, and used the Jena Semantic Web Framework[28] to convert the Parliament data, into RDF triples. These triples were stored in our local 4store system.

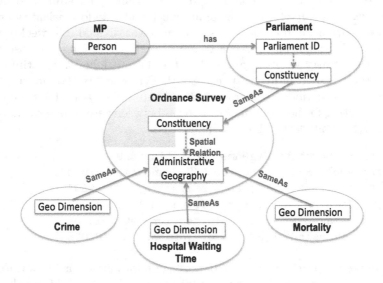

Fig. 1. Alignment of datasets using the Ordnance Survey Administrative Geography

4.4   Alignment of the Datasets

The process of aligning the datasets relied on the correct identification of owl: sameAs relations between the geographic concepts of the datasets and the corresponding relevant entities in the Ordnance Survey Administrative Geography (OS Admin Geo) (figure 1). The relevant entities here were constituencies data from the Ordnance Survey (OS).

---

[28] http://jena.sourceforge.net/

Aligning the datasets for Recorded Crimes We made use of our local 4store and also of the OS sparql endpoint at "http://api.talis.com/stores/ordnance-survey/services/sparql". Our goal was to set owl:sameAs equivalences between the geographical entities (geo names) in our dataset and respective (Westminster) constituencies as defined by the OS. The geographical entities in the OS are of several types, some are civil parishes, some are constituencies, and some are counties. A county usually contains a set of constituencies (and parishes). We queried the OS for the type of geo name in our dataset. If a constituency, we set the geo name to be the same as the OS identifier for that constituency. If the geo name is a county, we queried the OS for the list of constituencies it contained, and we set the geo name to be the same as the individual members' identifiers of that list. For example, the geo name Cumbria, represented in our 4store as http://enakting.ecs.soton.ac.uk/statistics/data/Cumbria, has many parishes, but only four constituencies. We set Cumbria to be the same as these four constituencies, shown below (to save space, only one is shown):

```
<http://enakting.ecs.soton.ac.uk/statistics/data/Cumbria>
    <http://www.w3.org/2002/07/owl#sameAs>
        <http://data.ordnancesurvey.co.uk/id/7000000000024876>.
```

However, we encountered a few special cases. A police force region in our dataset was known as "Yorkshire and the Humber Region", but the OS did not have this but had an entity called "Yorkshire & the Humber" which were the same. We manually had to query the OS for this and also to give us the constituencies under 'Yorkshire & the Humber", and set them to be the same as the "Yorkshire and the Humber Region" in our dataset.

Aligning the Hospital Waiting List. The geographical entity here was the full name of each NHS Trust in England and Wales, e.g. "South Tyneside NHS Foundation Trust". We employed the Google Maps API[29] to get the locations of these NHS Trusts. The Google Maps API returned for each geographical entity, with increasing precision, the Administrative Area, Sub Administrative Area, Locality, as well as their lat/long coordinates. We then manually queried the OS, using string matching, for the constituency names of this entity. In case the string matching operation failed, we queried TheyWorkForYou API, for the constituencies, giving it the lat/long values.

Aligning the UK Parliament Data. In the United Kingdom, boundaries of constituencies and constituency names change every few years. This affected the precise alignment of the data from the Parliament Parser and the OS Admin Geo. The Parliament Parser solves the problem of constituencies changes by assigning a new identifier to it[30]. The Ordnance Survey, however, only defines constituencies according to their latest classification by the UK Parliament. Therefore, only a partial alignment of these two datasets was possible.

---

[29] http://code.google.com/apis/maps/

[30] "Unique identifiers and alternative names for UK parliamentary constituencies. A constituency is given a new id whenever its boundaries change." [see http://ukparse.kforge.net/svn/parlparse/members/constituencies.xml].

4.5 Linked Data Consumption

The application scenario we envisaged is as follows: a user wants to find out some information about their geographical region - political, social etc. They have no knowledge, however, of the kind of data they might find nor are they knowledgeable in all the various geographical entities their place of residence is part of. Following on the methodology as described in the Postcode paper, the application acts as an aggregator of information based on the user's postal code, which they input at the start of the application. The application then tries to generate views of data from different topics along with widgets that allow the user to further explore the data retrieved.

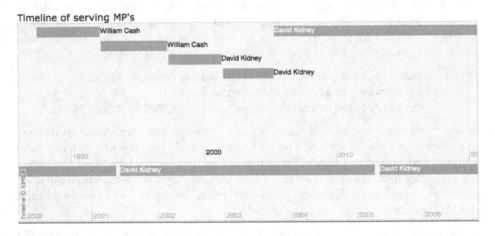

Fig. 2. Displaying data, as timeline, of some British Members of Parliament

In the application[31], the geographical region acts as the context for the displayed data, and is the central point from which the application follows links to find the data to display. For example, the application starts off showing political information, such as the political representatives for that area. Since in our data the constituency is the lowest geographic entity in the hierarchy, it starts by showing the political representation for that constituency. The interface shows the different MPs that have served or are in office for that constituency, plots a timeline view of their terms in office (Figure 2), and shows data about their voting records (Figure 3), and expenses (Figure 4). Additionally, the application generates facets for the user to quickly filter through the information. To keep the load of information low and present relevant information, we restrict the application to presenting data for MPs for the last two decades. We note that the application accounts for any temporal inconsistencies by matching the time periods between these aggregated data, as there are cases where a certain MP had served in two different constituencies and data on their expenses are available only for one of those terms. In such cases information is restricted only to

---

[31] The application is at http://psiusecase.enakting.org/

Voting record
Legislation supported

Member of Parliament	Voted in favor		
99 David Kidney	**107** Items		
10 William Cash			

Division	▼ MP	Time
Finance Bill	David Kidney and William Cash	2001-04-09 and 1997-07-28
Referendums (Scotland and Wales) Bill	William Cash	1997-05-22
Student Finance	William Cash	1997-11-04
European Communities (Amendment) Bill - Meaning of "the Treaties" and "the Community Treaties"	William Cash	1997-12-03
Education (Schools) Bill	William Cash	1997-06-05
Greater London Authority (Referendum) Bill	David Kidney and William Cash	1997-11-26 and 1997-11-10
Table - Tax credits	William Cash	1997-07-29
Table	William Cash	1997-07-29

Year
1 1997-05-22
1 1997-06-05
1 1997-06-17
1 1997-06-25
2 1997-07-07
2 1997-07-28

1 • 2 • 3 • 4 • 5 • 6 • 7 • 8 • 9 • 10 • 11 • 12 • 13 • 14   Next »

Fig. 3. Displaying voting record data for selected British Members of Parliament

MPs Expenses

Member of Parliament			
12 David Kidney	**12** exp		

Expense	▼ MP	Year	Amount
London Supplement	David Kidney	2002, 2003, 2001, 2006, 2007, 2004, and 2005	0
Centrally Purchased Stationery	David Kidney	2002, 2003, 2001, 2006, 2007, 2004, and 2005	1123, 1124, 1825, 2623, 1796, 2445, and 1774
Staffing Allowance	David Kidney	2002, 2003, 2001, 2006, 2007, 2004, and 2005	65043, 67940, 43929, 83791, 89082, 68705, and 69802
Member's Total Travel	David Kidney	2002, 2003, 2001, 2006, 2007, 2004, and 2005	4184, 4477, 3027, 5091, 5105, 4793, and 4901
Member's Staff Travel	David Kidney	2002, 2003, 2001, 2006, 2007, 2004, and 2005	444, 514, 713, 532, 940, 616, and 854
Incidental Expenses Provision	David Kidney	2002, 2003, 2001, 2006, 2007, 2004, and 2005	18214, 18618, 16783, 22684, 21442, 19322, and 25395
Centrally Provided Computer Equipment	David Kidney	2002, 2003, 2001, 2006, 2007, 2004, and 2005	1862, 1017, 1220, and 877

Year
9 2001
9 2002
10 2003
10 2004
10 2005
10 2006

Expense
1 Additional Costs Allowance
1 Centrally Provided Computer Equipment
1 Centrally

Fig. 4. Displaying expenses data for a selected British Member of Parliament

that which applied for the period they are in office for the constituency currently
under view. Going up the hierarchy, at each level the application tries to find
data about different topics. For example, it finds the county which contains the
constituency and tries to retrieve crime data for that county. If it finds data, it
displays them.

5   Conclusions and Future Work

In an effort to provide greater transparency amongst public sector departments and to target public services to areas of best need, governments are actively opening up public data. However much of these data are in non-linked formats. The data models are difficult to understand and re-use, and closed to web-scale integration. Publishing these data in linked data format would make it easier for them to be re-useable and interlinked.

In this work, we took data from disparate public data sources converting them into linked data format using geographical data, as the set of "join point"(s), to compose them together to form a linked integrated view. Several issues and challenges needed to be solved to build an integrated view of these disparate datasets.

5.1   Challenges in Data Publication

1. Although there is an increase in the amount of public data being made available, there is still a paucity of data in the right formats. Most data are still in HTML, PDF, and XLS formats, publishing and re-publishing these data in linked form will be very useful,
2. Many of these disparate datasets may not cover the same temporal intervals. This may make comparison over time complex. Most of the missing data are likely to be stored in hard-to-reach places in their respective government departments. As more of them are published, future temporal interval misalignments will be mitigated,
3. Data/Instance (Ontology) Alignment. Whenever there is more than one way to structure a body of data, there will be data and semantic heterogeneity when they are joined together. Because they are more flexible, semi-structured data exacerbates this problem, and as there will be more of them, the linked data cloud will add to this. Various mechanisms have addressed these problems. Semi-automatic mechanisms use an admixture of human and software, e.g. see [12], while fully automated methods, such as [13], aim to discover data and schema overlaps with no human intervention. We did not use any automatic methods in this exercise, and used mainly manual methods. Linking datasets required us to resort to string matching. This method is certainly unscalable to hundreds and thousands of linked datasets that are expected to come on stream in the next few years.

5.2   Challenges in Data Consumption

1. One of the biggest challenges we experienced was the low level of interoperability between the user interface (UI) and the underlying data. This meant that data consumption was not direct and needed to be converted and re-modelled in order to be shown in the UI. This conversion, however, was not straightforward as we had to frequently query the store and use a

proxy to construct an entirely new data model for the UI. This highlights two important issues pertaining to UI over heterogeneous data:

(a) The lack of UIs to quickly browse, search or visualise views on a wide range of differently modelled data, and
(b) Suitable tools which allow efficient aggregation and presentation of data to the UI from multiple datasets. The efficient and scalable retrieval of resources is particularly important for UIs which change views and require frequent querying of various datasets. Some approaches to tackling this problem were described in [11].

2. In the real world, the data publishers and consumers may be different entities, and this is what we enforced in our case study. Our data consumers had partial knowledge of the domain and found it difficult to understand the domain and the data being modelled. This is best illustrated in the case of the hierarchy of the administrative geography. Some constituencies can be mapped into the administrative region of counties, while some are parts of counties. Querying or browsing the data did not help in this instance. This points out the need for a mechanism, or a toolset, that helps developers give better description of the domain being modelled,

We have re-published the data we generated into the linked data cloud[32]. Resolving data and schema heterogeneity is a heuristic semi-automatic process. In future work, we aim to explore the application of data mining techniques to reduce the time it takes a human expert to align instances and/or schema. We have built a backlinking service[33] to the Linking Open Data cloud. We aim to further integrate the backlinking service to our datasets. In addition, we aim to provide an efficient scalable user interface able to visualise and search multiple datasets.

Acknowledgements

This work was supported by the EnAKTing project, funded by EPSRC project number EI/G008493/1.

References

1. Berners-Lee, T., Shadbolt, N.: Put in your postcode, out comes the data. In: The Times (November 18, 2009),
http://www.timesonline.co.uk/tol/comment/columnists/
guest_contributors/article6920761.ece
(last accessed December 13, 2009)

---

[32] mortality.psi.enakting.org, nhs.psi.enakting.org,
crime.psi.enakting.org
[33] backlinks.psi.enakting.org

2. Harith, A., David, D., John, S., Kieron, O., John, D., Nigel, S., Carol, T.: Unlocking the Potential of Public Sector Information with Semantic Web Technology. In: Aberer, K., Choi, K.-S., Noy, N., Allemang, D., Lee, K.-I., Nixon, L.J.B., Golbeck, J., Mika, P., Maynard, D., Mizoguchi, R., Schreiber, G., Cudré-Mauroux, P. (eds.) ASWC 2007 and ISWC 2007. LNCS, vol. 4825, pp. 708–721. Springer, Heidelberg (2007)
3. Ordnance Survey Data, http://data.ordnancesurvey.co.uk/
4. Harris, S., Lamb, N., Shadbolt, N.: 4store: The Design and Implementation of a Clustered RDF Store. In: The 5th International Workshop on Scalable Semantic Web Knowledge Base Systems SSWS 2009 (2009)
5. Hausenblas, M., Halb, W., Raimond, Y., Feigenbaum, L., Ayers, D.: SCOVO: Using Statistics on the Web of Data. In: Aroyo, L., Traverso, P., Ciravegna, F., Cimiano, P., Heath, T., Hyvönen, E., Mizoguchi, R., Oren, E., Sabou, M., Simperl, E. (eds.) ESWC 2009. LNCS, vol. 5554, pp. 708–722. Springer, Heidelberg (2009)
6. Tiropanis, T., Davis, H., Millard, D., Weal, M., White, S., Wills, G.: Semantic Technologies for Learning and Teaching in the Web 2.0 era - A survey. In: Web-Sci'09: Society On-Line (2009)
7. Kobilarov, G., Scott, T., Raimond, Y., Oliver, S., Sizemore, C., Smethurst, M., Bizer, C., Lee, R.: Media Meets Semantic Web - How the BBC Uses DBpedia and Linked Data to Make Connections. In: Aroyo, L., Traverso, P., Ciravegna, F., Cimiano, P., Heath, T., Hyvönen, E., Mizoguchi, R., Oren, E., Sabou, M., Simperl, E. (eds.) ESWC 2009. LNCS, vol. 5554, pp. 723–737. Springer, Heidelberg (2009)
8. Hassanzadeh, O., Consens, M.: Linked Movie Data Base. In: Linked Data on the Web, LDOW 2009 (2009)
9. Bizer, C., Cyganiak, R., Heath, T.: How to Publish Linked Data on the Web, http://www4.wiwiss.fu-berlin.de/bizer/pub/LinkedDataTutorial/
10. Hausenblas, M.: Linked Data Applications - The Genesis And The Challenges of Using Linked Data On The Web. Deri Technical Report 2009-07-26 (July 2009)
11. Smith, D., Schraefel, M.: Interactively using Semantic Web knowledge: Creating scalable abstractions with FacetOntology (unpublished), http://eprints.ecs.soton.ac.uk/17054/ (last accessed 2009-12-19)
12. Kalfoglou, Y., Schorlemmer, M.: Ontology mapping: the state of the art. The Knowledge Engineering Review Journal 18 (2003)
13. Salvadores, M., Correndo, G., Rodriguez-Castro, B., Gibbins, N., Darlington, J., Shadbolt, N.: LinksB2N: Automatic Data Integration for the Semantic Web. In: International Conference on Ontologies, DataBases and Applications of Semantics, ODBASE 2009 (2009)

Taking OWL to Athens
Semantic Web Technology Takes Ancient Greek History to Students

Jochen Reutelshoefer[1], Florian Lemmerich[1], Joachim Baumeister[1],
Jorit Wintjes[2], and Lorenz Haas[2]

[1] Institute of Computer Science, University of Würzburg, Germany
{lastname}@informatik.uni-wuerzburg.de
[2] Institute of Ancient History, University of Würzburg, Germany
{firstname.lastname}@uni-wuerzburg.de

Abstract. The HermesWiki project is a semantic wiki application on Ancient Greek History. As an e-learning platform, it aims at providing students effective access to concise and reliable domain knowledge, that is especially important for exam preparation. In this paper, we show how semantic technologies introduce new methods of learning by supporting teachers in the creation of contents and students in the personalized identification of required knowledge. Therefore, we give an overview of the project and characterize the semi-formalized content. Additionally, we present several use cases and describe the semantic web techniques that are used to support the application. Furthermore, we report on the user experiences regarding the usefulness and applicability of semantic technologies in this context.

1 Introduction

Students today are used to collect a large amount of required knowledge from the internet. While the number of available webpages is huge for almost any given topic, the quality of these pages is quite heterogeneous. Additionally, it is very difficult for students, especially undergraduate students, to extract the essential knowledge from extensive webpages. Therefore, students can significantly benefit from a reliable and concise knowledge base, that combines the advantages of traditional text books with the advantages of internet-based knowledge platforms, like accessibility, integration of multimedia resources, and the ability to update the contents easily. However, the creation of such a web application still is a tedious task, as texts and resources must be created, collected, and adapted to the context. Additionally, with the growing amount of content it again gets more difficult for students to find exactly the resources they require. In this paper, we describe how semantic technologies help to alleviate both problems in an e-learning project in the domain of Ancient Greek History, the HermesWiki.

The HermesWiki is a semantic wiki, developed to give students of history an introductory domain overview. As a full featured wiki system, HermesWiki allows for an effective collaborative composition of content. Furthermore, semantic

L. Aroyo et al. (Eds.): ESWC 2010, Part I, LNCS 6088, pp. 333–347, 2010.

technologies provide advanced functionality that generates additional value to the learning environment [1]: Formalized paragraphs and semantic annotations of the main text enable the contributors to easily generate additional content tailored to different tasks, such as tables of events, maps, or a quiz. Further, students have access to different forms of knowledge like narrative elements, ancient source texts, geo data, chronologic information and images. They can use semantic navigation to easily find the concepts they are looking for, filter the presented content by its relevancy on demand, and query the systems knowledge using an intuitive user interface.

The rest of the paper is organized as follows: In Section 2 we give an overview of the Hermes project and its context of use. Section 3 presents the underlying semantic model of the content that is created by the semantic wiki extension and discusses the Hermes ontology. Further, the use cases and the employed semantic technology are explained. Then, our experiences within the Hermes project are discussed. We present the technical basis of the implementation in Section 4 and conclude by presenting our ideas for future directions.

2   HermesWiki – An Overview

The HermesWiki is developed by the historians of the Department of Ancient History from the University of Würzburg, Germany, supported by the Department of Intelligent Systems of the Institute of Computer Science. The main purpose of the HermesWiki is to provide a concise and reliable overview of Ancient Greek History for teaching purposes of students. The project started in summer 2008 and its content is continuously growing since then. From the next semester on, the wiki is recommended as an alternative to traditional text books to all undergraduate students of the University of Würzburg, that take courses in Ancient History.

2.1   Project History

The development of the HermesWiki project was rather unusual compared to typical semantic application projects. The focused 'knowledge engineers' were historians with no experience in semantic technologies or knowledge management solutions. Initially, a web-based, easy to use content–management system, that supports collaborative development, was intended in order to structure e-learning content. Thus, at first a standard, non-semantic wiki was chosen as the favorable tool, since it was already known as a simple and flexible application. It soon became clear that this approach was a success as the wiki was quickly filled by a large knowledge base consisting mainly of textual content enriched with figures and an informal taxonomy for organizing the articles. Several intended use cases and the various possibilities of how to access and present the available content motivated the step-wise introduction of semantic technologies — possible due to the use of a semantic wiki [2].

2.2   The Content: Knowledge about Ancient Greek History

Currently, the HermesWiki contains about 700 pages which are written in German language. In general, we distinguish the following four categories:

1. A set of about 20 *essays* forms the core of the project. These essays of about 1,000 to 2,000 words each have been written especially for this project and provide a comprehensive overview of Ancient Greek History. Each essay covers one topic of the domain and is structured by a standardized template. Figure 1 shows the essay about *Tyrannis*. It includes a short list of the most important events generated from the ontology, an introductory section, that explains the context of this essay, a text description of the respective topic, an overview of ancient historical sources, and a formalized set of relevant events.

2. An extensive *glossary* of more than 500 articles provides students a short, but precise explanation of the used terminology. Described concepts include persons, geographic locations, and domain specific terms ("Autarky", "Polis", etc. . .) .

3. Around 60 translated excerpts of the referenced ancient *sources* are included in the wiki as separate wiki pages. Due to copyright reasons mostly own translations are used.

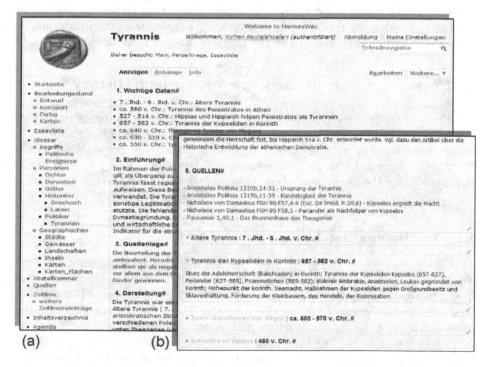

Fig. 1. The top (a) and bottom (b) of the wiki page containing the essay about *Tyrannis* taken from the HermesWiki. (Screenshots of the system, in German language).

4. The *organization and administration* is supported by several wiki pages. These include "todo-lists", authoring guidelines, technical tutorials, bug reports, and separate pages for specialized tools, e.g., for wiki-wide refactoring of concept names or (semantic) search.

2.3   The HermesWiki Community

The contents of HermesWiki are contributed by the group of Ancient History of the University of Würzburg. The team consists of about a dozen persons: One professor, an assistant professor, their research staff, and a few selected graduate students, which work in close cooperation. These users have basic knowledge about computers and wiki systems like wikipedia, but no special experience with semantic wikis or semantic technologies in general. While the relatively small size of the community obviously limits the amount of contributions in the wiki, the high educational level of the authors guarantees a consistently high quality of the content.

In practice, the professor and the assistant professor of the team approve the content of each wiki page before release. Thus, typically a new article is created as follows: The professor/assistant professor identifies the need of an additional article and assigns this task to a team member. He/she collects necessary information, writes the article, and tags the respective wiki page as "draft". Afterwards, the article is proof-read by the professor/assistant professor, who either returns the article to the original author with suggestions for improvements, improves it by himself, or approves the page by tagging it as "revised".

3   Social Semantic Technology for Ancient History

In this chapter, we first present some main aspects of the ontology developed in the HermesWiki. Next, the knowledge formalization process that helps us to obtain formalized knowledge from the content entered by the contributors is described. Afterwards, we give some examples, how the ontology is used in the HermesWiki for the augmented presentation of the content, semantic navigation and search, and interactive sessions.

3.1   The Hermes Ontology

As already mentioned the project was not intended to be a "semantically enriched" wiki application from the beginning. However, the authors by themselves began to create categories and hierarchies for the domain concepts like persons, locations, and events to organize the contents. Thus, for the creation of a domain ontology of the HermesWiki we had to consider several requirements. We needed to integrate the informal conceptualization already given implicitly by the content. Further, we had to enrich it to support the planned use cases of the e-learning application. To avoid risky barriers for the domain experts, it seemed reasonable to keep the ontology as simple and sparse as possible with respect to the intended use cases, as the historians are no trained ontology engineers.

The starting point of the HermesWiki domain ontology was inspired by the VICODI project [3], which also developed an ontology for the historical domain. Considering the requirements stated above we had to conduct several modifications. We followed the KISS principle (keep it simple, stupid) — which is in line with the wiki spirit — to obtain an ontology, that is easy to understand for the historians and at the same time suits our formalization requirements for the intended use cases. For example, the VICODI ontology heavily relies on the role pattern. Thus, a person fulfills a role, e.g., is a king for a fixed period of time. For our applications this precise approach appeared to be unnecessarily detailed, so it was omitted. Figure 2(a) shows an excerpt of the resulting Hermes ontology. The upper part shows some exemplary concepts from the system ontology (wiki object model) sketching how the Hermes domain ontology is embedded into the wiki system. That is, each *HermesConcept* 'isDefinedBy' a *TextOrigin* allowing to trace the location where the concept has been defined in the wiki text. This can be done, e.g., by a wiki page, a single paragraph or an annotation markup.

Below, the concept hierarchy for the historical data is shown. Unlabeled links define subclass relations between two concepts represented by the connected nodes. Main concepts of the VICODI ontology, such as *Individual, Location, Event, Social Stratum,* and *Ethnical Group* have been reused and integrated with concepts proposed by the domain experts. In the center of the figure, the concept *Event* is depicted, which plays a key role in the knowledge formalization of HermesWiki. To each event a *TimeStamp* is attached containing the (possibly vague or uncertain) date information of the event. Further, a title and an importance rating (regarding exam relevance) is specified. Events can be connected to other concepts by object properties like *involves* or *takesPlaceAt*.

These properties as well as the taxonomies can also be edited or created by users inside the wiki using dash-tree markup [4]. Any term being a dash-tree child, i.e., follows with an incremented number of dashes, is defined as a subclass of its parent. For instance, in Figure 2(b) *Dynasty* and *Social Stratum* are defined as subclasses of *Group of Persons*. Since ontology changes can have a deep impact on some wiki features, they are only performed by experienced contributors. Major changes in the ontology are discussed in the community in advance.

Generally, the ontology is not intended to cover as much of the domain knowledge or wiki content as possible but only contains knowledge that is necessary for advanced features. In the next sections, we discuss how this ontology is populated by the domain experts of HermesWiki by editing and annotating wiki pages.

3.2 Knowledge Formalization

The methods of knowledge formalization in HermesWiki were designed considering three aspects: First, the way the historians intuitively organized the domain knowledge in the wiki in a natural way. Second, what formalized relations are

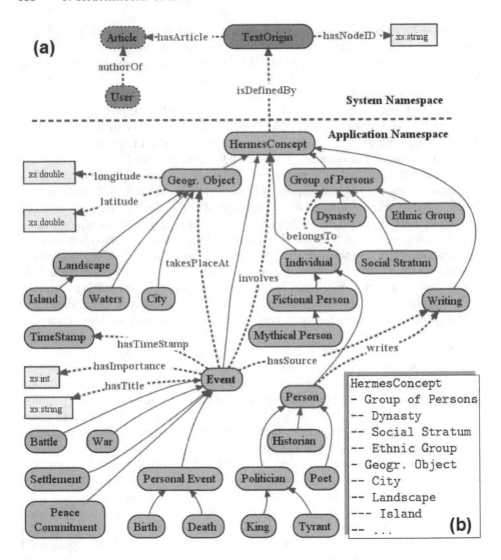

Fig. 2. (a) The Hermes Ontology (lower part) is connected to the system ontology (upper part). This figure is limited to the most important concepts of the project. (b) An example for dashtree markup for concept hierarchies.

required by use cases providing additional value to the e-learning application. Third, what are the additional costs, i.e., the workload, of this formalization. The content was continuously 'semantified', when an added value existed by enabling additional use cases.

The most common way to populate the ontology in semantic wikis is by annotating a page to represent an instance of some class. A large part of the knowledge in HermesWiki complies with this reasonable approach. However, often multiple relevant concepts are defined on one wiki page, when the 'one page – one instance' granularity is inappropriate, e.g., for events or geographical objects. As examples of knowledge formalization used in HermesWiki, we present a markup for the definition of geographical objects and time events. Further, we introduce the semi-automated workflow to connect the time events with other entities of the concept hierarchies like persons and geographic objects.

Definition of geographical objects. An important issue in the study of history is to set locations of historical events into context. As obtaining specialized maps can be a tedious (and costly) task, the HermesWiki offers easy to use possibilities to mark important places in maps. The longitude and latitude of geographic objects can be specified by a markup anywhere on any wiki page. For example the following (translated) markup specifies the geo-coordinates of the ontology instance "Marathon":

```
<<COORDINATES: Marathon, 38°9'N, 23°57'E>>
```

This markup can also be obtained by using a Google Maps based editor in the wiki, that allows for the creation of the markup by specifying the concept name and clicking the respective location in the displayed map. The editor also features automatic search using the provided API.

Specifying time events. Time events are the most important concepts in the HermesWiki knowledge base. Like sketched in Figure 2, time events can connect the individuals of the concept hierarchy. In the wiki, time events often are only described by a couple of sentences and are closely interrelated. Thus, it seemed not pragmatic to create a separate page for each of these events, but to allow the definition of multiple events in one page. To formalize these time events in a flexible way (at any place of some wiki page), a markup was designed in cooperation with the historians. The entire definition of one time event is enclosed by the brackets '<<' and '>>'. The following (translated) markup example describes the event *Lamian War*. As the first information the title of the event is given. It is followed by the importance rating defining its relevance for student exams. For instance, events with an importance rating of '1' are considered essential, while events with a rating of '3' are categorized as "additional knowledge". In the next line, the timestamp of the event is notated. The historians introduced a simple language for the definition of time intervals, which also includes annotations for different degrees of uncertainty (possibly resulting of inconsistent descriptions in different historical sources). The string "323b-322b" points out, that the event occurred from 323 BC until 322 BC. Next, the *body* of the markup follows consisting of a (free text) description of the actual event. The markup concludes with an (optional) list of historical sources where the event is mentioned, explicitly marked by the (translated) keyword "SOURCE:" as the first word of a new line (from *Diodor* and *Pausanias* in this example).

```
<<Lamian War (2)
323b-322b

After Alexanders death the Greeks revolted against
Macedonian rule under the lead of the Athenians.
[....]

SOURCE: Paus::1,25,3-6
SOURCE: Diod::18,8-18
>> ..
```

When the wiki page is saved, the time events are parsed and translated into the corresponding OWL concepts introduced in Figure 2. For each event an instance of type *Event* is created and the additional information is stored using the provided properties.

A semi-automated workflow for annotating time events. Events, locations, persons and other ontology instances, can be connected by adding appropriate relations into the ontology. This can be done by using a markup inside the wiki source text. However, to minimize the workload of the contributors, we additionally introduced a semi-automatic approach: Generally, the idea of semi-automated annotation in semantic wikis [2,5] is to use the background knowledge already given in the ontology, while processing the wiki text content and to propose probable relations to the user for confirmation. For the context of time event descriptions we assume, that any person or location important for this event is mentioned in its description. As those concepts are already present in the ontology they can be searched for (by name) in the description texts while parsing the time event markups. Although concept names in the event description strongly indicate a relation between the event and the respective concept, we use a semi-automated workflow to specify the kind of relation and to strictly avoid false positives, which is essential for the quality requirements of the project. Thus, whenever a concept is found, it is highlighted in the rendering of the event. Clicking on it will open up a popup window, which proposes some relations between the event and the mentioned concept, see Figure 3. The possible relations are suggested, in this case *takesPlaceAt* and *involves*, together with the default options *concept mismatch* and *do not ask again*. These proposals can either be confirmed or discarded by the domain experts. The relations are proposed by inspecting the domain and range definitions of the properties in the ontology. If, for example, the name of an instance of class *Person* is found in the text description of the event, all properties with *Event* as domain and *Person* as range are proposed. Thus, dynamic definition of new properties is supported by this approach. When a relation is confirmed by clicking an option in the popup, an annotation markup of the phrase is added to the wiki source text. The corresponding OWL relation is generated while processing the annotation markup within the wiki source update.

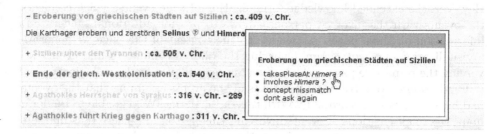

Fig. 3. Popups propose relations between the entities described in the text

The presented knowledge formalizations are extensively used in HermesWiki. For example, the ontology contains currently about 700 formally defined time events, 140 persons and 100 cities (with geo-coordinates), covering the knowledge in the intended scope of the project.

3.3   Use Cases

In this section we introduce use cases of semantic technologies. These are enabled by the advanced formalization features of HermesWiki and provide additional value for teachers and learners.

Inline queries for events. In HermesWiki the concept of inline queries, which is a common and beneficial feature of semantic wikis (e.g., [6]), has been adapted for filtering and displaying time events. Events are usually rendered at that place where they are defined but it might be didactically valuable to display specific selections of events in other contexts. For example, at the top of each essay a bullet list of the most important time events defined at the respective wiki page is displayed as depicted Figure 1(a). This can be done by using a flexible parameterized inline query mechanism. Inserting the respective tag into the wiki page sources allows to display events, that are related to some specific entity (e.g., Person, Geogr. Object), occurred in a defined period in time and/or have a minimum level of importance. For a seamless integration with full text descriptions, one can also specify the visualization of the events (e.g., as bullet lists or collapsible panels, with or without description).

Browsing through time – The Hermes Event Browser. While the inline queries allow to dynamically present selected time events in specific contexts to the students, the Hermes Event Browser enables the students themselves to search for time events by specifying a time interval. Additionally the search can be restricted to time events, that involve specific ontology instances, e.g, a Person or a Geogr. Object. The knowledge base is queried for time events fulfilling these constraints and the events are displayed, also providing links to related content.

Biographical timelines and maps. The wiki pages representing a person in most cases only contain a free text description with no further formalization.

However, the extended knowledge formalization of time events, which connects the events with the involved persons, allows to provide additional (generated) information on these pages. Appended to the content of the page we generate a visualization of a *curriculum*. Querying the ontology allows to find events involving the respective person. These events are displayed in chronological order.

Furthermore, we retrieve the locations of the events assuming that the events had been annotated accordingly. With this data, HermesWiki is able to render a map, where all locations of events involving this person are inserted as markers at the location of its occurrence. Hence, the generated map illustrates a complete overview of the lifeline and the travels of this character. The marker of an event gives more detailed information about the event and provides a link to the text passage in the wiki, where the event is defined and described. Figure 4 shows the wiki page of *Alexander the Great* containing a generated map displaying the locations of the most important events in the life of Alexander the Great.

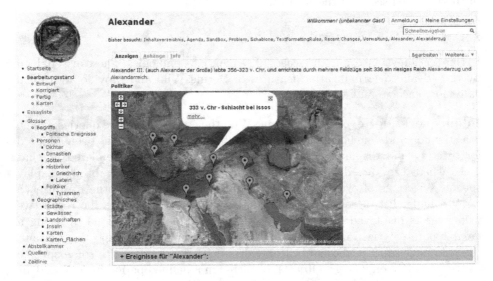

Fig. 4. The wiki page of Alexander the Great. It contains a map generated by the information in the ontology. It shows the most important events in the life of Alexander.

The HermesQuiz. The Hermes-Quiz is an interactive component, where students can answer (multiple-choice) questions to test their knowledge. The questions are generated by the system, based on the formal relations contained in the ontology. For example, the ontology contains the information, that the beginning of the Persian empire was about 552 BC. The system can generate two other dates (taken from some other randomly chosen time events) and pose the correct and the generated dates as a three-choice question. As depicted in Figure 5 the quiz panel shows a new question (lower box) and waits for the user to choose the correct date. In the upper box the solution of the last answered question is presented, also containing a link to the description of the corresponding time event. At the bottom, the score for the current quiz session is displayed, that is, the ratio of correctly answered questions.

The quiz could be extended in the future to ask for other types of relations contained in the ontology, however, generating good questions can be a non-trivial task in general (see for instance [7]).

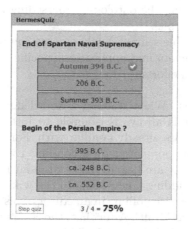

Fig. 5. The Hermes Quiz allows the user to test his knowledge with questions generated from the ontology

3.4 Experiences

Next, we describe some experiences on the usage of semantic technologies and the workflow in the HermesWiki community.

Experiences using semantic technology. In the context of this application we applied the approach of a *Decorated Semantic Wiki* [8]. This concept tackles the barrier for untrained users to contribute to semantic applications by hiding the semantic technology, considering formalization and use, behind 'interfaces' designed especially for the domain and user community. These interfaces are provided by formalization methods like special markups or popup questions and are tailored to the users comprehension of the domain and the data. They allow users with only little experience in ontology[1] engineering or its technical implementation, to contribute. Wikis aim to provide the lowest entry barrier possible and this extension of the wiki philosophy towards semantic data appears to be successful in our project, considering the high formalization level of the HermesWiki contents.

In this project, the use of semantic technologies such as OWL and SPARQL proved to be a very suitable basis for fulfilling the (extended) application requirements. The flexible knowledge repository in combination with the wiki allows for

---

[1] The term *ontology* exists in humanities considerably longer than in computer science, which can lead to misunderstandings in this domain.

incremental formalization of the content as well as for modifications/extensions in the ontological schema. Considering the pathway of the project, where the demand of advanced features developed step by step over time without pre-defined requirement specification, the use of semantic technology proved to be much more flexible at the implementation level when compared to conventional techniques. It appears that any (new) feature can be implemented fairly independently from the other using the ontology, superseding time-consuming changes in database or object schemas.

By utilizing an extensible semantic wiki as core component, the development could concentrate on domain and application specific issues, thus strongly limiting the implementation efforts.

Workflow experiences. When starting a knowledge engineering application with domain experts, it is always reasonable to integrate methods and tools that the domain experts are already familiar with. For example, in the VICODI project the ontology was populated by uploading Excel spreadsheets [3]. The contributors of our project are heavily using standard office software for other work. When the task of adding a new topic to the wiki is assigned to an author, the first version is often written offline in an editor of his choice. Then it is pasted into the wiki and tagged as 'draft'. After that, the community is invited to review, refine, extend and 'semantify' this article. This employed process model complies with the idea of *Seeding and Evolutionary Growth* in collaborative knowledge acquisition proposed by Fischer et al. [9]. Considering the total amount of content in the HermesWiki, this procedure yields a relatively small number of user-edits (about 6200 at the time of writing).

Most of the time, team members spend only a few hours a week working on HermesWiki. However, about twice per year the complete team meets for a half week workshop. In these workshops, major decisions of the project and new software features are discussed. The rest of the time is dedicated to the creation and improvement of wiki contents. This also showed to be beneficial for system developers, as it allowed to get insights of user behavior and thus identify helpful system improvements.

4   Implementation

The HermesWiki is a plugin for the semantic wiki KnowWE [10], which itself is a semantic extension of JSPWiki, an open source wiki engine implemented in Java[2]. For the management of RDF-data, KnowWE employs the Sesame framework[3] and (swift-) OWLIM[4], which also supports rule-based reasoning (e.g., of OWL-Horst rules [11]). The KnowWE system, bringing semantic wiki features for formalization and querying of knowledge out of the box, is primarily designed for extensibility [8]. The design concept aims to support customization

---

[2] http://www.jspwiki.org
[3] http://www.openrdf.org/
[4] http://www.ontotext.com/owlim/

towards specialized semantic wiki applications, that then can provide domain and user specific features. The Hermes extension uses the KnowWE API and the plugin mechanisms to introduce the custom features discussed in Section 3. The components contained in the Hermes extension can be classified into the two categories *formalization* and *presentation*:

- **Formalization:** Contains the parser components to create the parse-tree of the page and translation functions generating OWL data (e.g., markup for time events) for markup used beyond the standard KnowWE markup.
- **Presentation:** Contains the components for querying and visualization implementing the features presented in Section 3.3 (e.g., inline queries, biography visualization and the quiz). These components typically contain some SPARQL query expression containing some placeholder, which is replaced before execution according to the current context of use (e.g., page name and user input). With the results of the 'coined' SPARQL query retrieved from the RDF-store the result is rendered for the user by common HTML/CSS/DOM-scripting techniques, also utilizing the Google Maps API.

The Hermes plugin as well as KnowWE itself is available under LGPL license and can be downloaded at *https://isci.informatik.uni-wuerzburg.de.*

5   Related Work

Several general approaches using semantic technologies for e-learning have been proposed before, compare e.g., [1]. However, in humanities, especially history, semantic technologies have only received little attention with respect to e-learning applications so far. The *Perseus Project*[5] for example provides a freely available digital library, including source texts and multimedia content for Ancient Greek History. However, in contrary to HermesWiki it does not offer concise descriptions of historical events and is not using semantic technologies at all. On the contrary, within the VICODI project [3] a detailed ontology for the domain of history has been developed. However, this project was not focused on teaching or learning. While many concepts of the VICODI ontology could be reused for this project, major modifications were required for the deployment in our context of e-learning. In the related domain of cultural heritage documentation the *CIDOC CRM*[6] ontology with a slightly different scope has been developed.

Today for many domains, including history, general knowledge is collected by Wikipedia. In fact, it shows up that for most of the content of the HermesWiki there can be found some correspondence in the online encyclopedia. Much scientific work has been done reusing this vast accessible resource and processing the data for specific presentation, like for example done by Sipos et al. [12]. There are several reasons why this approach is not applicable for the HermesWiki application: Although the methods to extract formal relations from informal text

---

[5] www.perseus.tufts.edu

[6] http://cidoc.ics.forth.gr/

sources have made considerable progress during the last years (e.g., resulting in systems like DBpedia [13]), they still cannot guarantee the degree of correctness that is necessary in an e-learning scenario for exam relevant knowledge. Further, Wikipedia as a resource for scientific work is a heavily discussed topic. In the domain of history, often well established historic facts are mixed up with remarks lacking of historicity. Additionally, a main goal of the project is to provide a delimitation of the knowledge that needs to be learned for certain exams.

Schaffert et al. [14] propose the use of a semantic wiki in the e-learning context for combining the advantages of usability, knowledge formalization and full control of the contents. This approach complies with the spirit of our project.

6   Conclusions

In this paper we presented the benefits of semantic web technologies in the HermesWiki application, an e-learning project in the domain of Ancient Greek History. We provided an overview of the project itself and its community. Then, we explained how semantic technologies are employed to generate additional value for the application by describing the cycle of generation and use of formalized knowledge, and presented in-use experiences. Further, we briefly presented the implementation of the system and discussed related approaches. The HermesWiki project indicates that the additional employment of semantic technologies as an extension to well-established tools, and methods can generate considerable additional value at relatively low implementation costs. For future work, we plan to extend the quiz approach for asking general relations. To obtain even more formalized data we will evolve the semi-automated annotation approach.

As the domain overview on Ancient Greek History is approaching completion and HermesWiki shows to be successful, the community is also planning on extending the content of the wiki to Ancient Roman History. A table of contents and main time events have been already specified inside the wiki.

The HermesWiki is exclusively accessible for students of the University of Würzburg. Some exemplary pages will be released to the public under the URL *http://hermeswiki.informatik.uni-wuerzburg.de.*

References

1. Stojanovic, L., Staab, S., Studer, R.: eLearning based on the Semantic Web. In: WebNet 2001 - World Conference on the WWW and Internet, pp. 23–27 (2001)
2. Schaffert, S., Bry, F., Baumeister, J., Kiesel, M.: Semantic wikis. IEEE Software 25(4), 8–11 (2008)
3. Nagypál, G., Deswarte, R., Oosthoek, J.: Applying the Semantic Web – The VI-CODI Experience in Creating Visual Contextualization for History. Literary and Linguistic Computing 20(3), 327–349 (2005)
4. Baumeister, J., Reutelshoefer, J., Puppe, F.: Markups for Knowledge Wikis. In: SAAKM'07: Proceedings of the Semantic Authoring, Annotation and Knowledge Markup Workshop, Whistler, Canada, pp. 7–14 (2007)

5. Ruiz-Casado, M., Alfonseca, E., Castells, P.: From Wikipedia to Semantic Relationships: a Semi-automated Annotation Approach. In: SemWiki06: Proceedings of 1st Semantic Wiki workshop - From Wiki to Semantics (2006)
6. Völkel, M., Krötzsch, M., Vrandecic, D., Haller, H., Studer, R.: Semantic Wikipedia. In: WWW '06: Proceedings of the 15th international conference on World Wide Web, pp. 585–594. ACM, New York (2006)
7. Zitko, B., Stankov, S., Rosic, M., Grubisic, A.: Dynamic test generation over ontology-based knowledge representation in authoring shell. Expert Syst. Appl. 36(4), 8185–8196 (2009)
8. Reutelshoefer, J., Lemmerich, F., Haupt, F., Baumeister, J.: An Extensible Semantic Wiki Architecture. In: SemWiki'09: Fourth Workshop on Semantic Wikis – The Semantic Wiki Web (CEUR proceedings 464) (2009)
9. Fischer, G.: Seeding, Evolutionary Growth and Reseeding: Constructing, Capturing and Evolving Knowledge in Domain–Oriented Design Environments. Automated Software Engineering 5(4), 447–464 (1998)
10. Baumeister, J., Reutelshoefer, J., Puppe, F.: KnowWE: A Semantic Wiki for Knowledge Engineering. Applied Intelligence (2010)
11. ter Horst, H.J.: Combining RDF and Part of OWL with Rules: Semantics, Decidability, Complexity. In: Gil, Y., Motta, E., Benjamins, V.R., Musen, M.A. (eds.) ISWC 2005. LNCS, vol. 3729, pp. 668–684. Springer, Heidelberg (2005)
12. Sipos, R., Bhole, A., Fortuna, B., Grobelnik, M., Mladenic, D.: Demo: HistoryViz - Visualizing Events and Relations Extracted from Wikipedia. In: Aroyo, L., Traverso, P., Ciravegna, F., Cimiano, P., Heath, T., Hyvönen, E., Mizoguchi, R., Oren, E., Sabou, M., Simperl, E. (eds.) ESWC 2009. LNCS, vol. 5554, pp. 903–907. Springer, Heidelberg (2009)
13. Bizer, C., Lehmann, J., Kobilarov, G., Auer, S., Becker, C., Cyganiak, R., Hellmann, S.: DBpedia - A crystallization point for the Web of Data. Journal of Web Semantics: Science, Services and Agents on the World Wide Web 7(3), 154–165 (2009)
14. Schaffert, S., Bischof, D., Bürger, T., Gruber, A., Hilzensauer, W., Schaffert, S.: Learning with Semantic Wikis. In: SemWiki'06: Proceedings of 1st Semantic Wiki workshop - From Wiki to Semantics (2006)

Generating Innovation with Semantically Enabled TasLab Portal

Pavel Shvaiko[1], Alessandro Oltramari[2], Roberta Cuel[3],
Davide Pozza[4], and Giuseppe Angelini[5]

[1] TasLab, Informatica Trentina S.p.A., Trento, Italy
`pavel.shvaiko@infotn.it`
[2] ISTC-CNR, Trento, Italy
`oltramari@loa-cnr.it`
[3] DISA, University of Trento, Trento, Italy
`roberta.cuel@economia.unitn.it`
[4] OMNYS srl - Information Technology, Vicenza, Italy
`davide.pozza@omnys.it`
[5] WEBSS srl - Web Software Solutions, Trento, Italy
`gangelini@webss.it`

Abstract. In this paper we present a concrete case study in which semantic technology has been used to enable a territorial innovation. Firstly, we describe a scenario of the ICT regional demand in Trentino, Italy; where the main idea of territorial innovation is based on the so-called *innovation tripole*. Specifically, we believe that innovation arises as a result of the synergic coordination and technology transfer among three main innovation stakeholders: (*i*) final users, bringing domain knowledge, (*ii*) enterprises and SMEs, bringing knowledge of the market, and (*iii*) research centers, bringing the latest research results. The tripole is instantiated/generated for innovation projects, and, technically, can be viewed as a competence search (based on metadata) among the key innovation stakeholders for those projects. Secondly, we discuss the implementation of the tripole generation within the TasLab portal, including the use of domain ontologies and thesauri (e.g., Eurovoc), indexing and semantic search techniques we have employed. Finally, we provide a discussion on empirical and strategic evaluation of our solution, the results of which are encouraging.

1 Introduction

The technology transfer process can be described as the economic and/or organizational process, of technology, knowledge and products exchange among various stakeholders. It leads to the transfer of knowledge, usually from research centers to industries, in order to conduct firms to the development and commercialization of end user applications and products [11,13,17]. In the last decades we have assisted to a radical change in the forms of alliances, processes and governance models of technology transfer. Specifically, let us consider the shift from traditional joint ventures and in-house R&D laboratories to a more flexible forms and more open environments, such as science innovation parks, incubators, and Living Labs[1], see also [3,14]. This change introduced a new paradigm,

---

[1] `http://www.openlivinglabs.eu/`

L. Aroyo et al. (Eds.): ESWC 2010, Part I, LNCS 6088, pp. 348–363, 2010.

called *open innovation* [2], through which many actors use both internal and external assets to advance their technology of production and service providing. In fact, several companies nowadays operate as open innovation intermediaries and some others report on using multiple instruments to open up their innovation systems, e.g., by using venture capital funds, managing collaborations with universities [16].

Such an open environment is the motivation for our case study: *Trentino as a Lab* (TasLab), which is considered as a governance model for technology transfer supported by the Autonomous Province of Trento, Italy [9]. TasLab is meant to play a mediating role among business, research and public sector, thereby enhancing innovation. The activities of TasLab can be generally articulated as follows:

- *conception:* namely, creation of shared knowledge, economic/organizational conditions and opportunities to stimulate creativity and innovative products or services. This means creating and maintaining a network of companies, research departments, and final users (both citizens and public administrations), scouting the technology, disseminating results and opportunities, etc.
- *development:* once an innovative proposal has been identified, a project should be formalized and managed. This means providing services, e.g., project management, networking for new partnerships, support for intellectual property rights (IPR), etc.
- *production:* namely, refinement of a product or a service in order to transfer it to the actual exploitation by the final users.

In order to support these activities, among others, various technologies, such as knowledge portals have been adopted. Within such portals, various stakeholders should have a role and their special skills and knowledge should be managed and integrated to develop innovative ideas. Notice that Trentino is characterized by a myriad of small and medium enterprises (SMEs) which develop their own business assets, processes and knowledge that might enable innovation. Hence, a territorial innovation portal should provide knowledge management facilities in order to match these assets, interests, and competencies of all the various stakeholders. It should support flows of knowledge involving links and staff flows between firms, research centers, and public institutions. This means that this heterogeneity/diversity (e.g., in goals, languages, terminologies of the various innovation stakeholders) should be treated as a feature that eventually might generate innovation, and hence, should be respectively handled [8]. In turn, this requires an adequate semantic heterogeneity management that we believe can be implemented with the help of the semantic technology.

The contributions of the paper include: (i) description of the concrete problem, namely innovation generation, in a specific application domain, such as eGovernment, where the semantic technology is of help; (ii) an implementatinon of the solution devised within the TasLab portal; and (iii) a discussion of the empirical and economic evaluation of the solution employed.

The rest of the paper is organized as follows. Section 2 provides the problem statement. Section 3 overviews the solution proposed. Section 4 describes the use of the semantic technology within our solution as well as some of its implementation details. Section 5 discusses an empirical and strategic evaluation of the solution employed. Finally, Section 6 reports on the major findings of the paper and overviews future work.

2   The Problem: How to Generate Innovation

Our application domain is *eGovernment*. By eGovernment we mean here an area of application for information and communication technologies to modernize public administration by optimizing the work of various public institutions and by providing citizens and businesses with better (e.g., more efficient) services as well as with the new services (that did not exit before), see [20] for the latest developments in the area. More specifically, our goal is to introduce in a systematic manner (technological) innovation in the eGovernment projects being conducted in the Autonomous Province of Trento, Italy. We believe that semantic technology is among enabling (trasversal) technologies that can help achieving this goal.

2.1   Motivating Example

Let us briefly discuss a typical situation occurring at a public administration. A final user, such as a department of public administration (e.g., Urban Planning) which among others, has the goal of sharing of spatial information has to follow the INSPIRE[2] directive, see also [19]. In order to achieve this, one of the key components of the INSPIRE architecture is a discovery service, that ought to be implemented by means of the Catalogue Service for the Web (CSW)[3]. A usual request of a typical final user here would be to have a geo-catalog. An advanced, or the so-called *lead user* would ask for a semantic geo-catalog. Although, there have been provided several implementations for the CSW-based geo-catalog, at present there is no reference implementation for a semantic geo-catalog. Hence, semantic geo-catalog is an example of an innovative project (at the world level) the final user may want to run.

Now, the question is what are the competencies available to run such a project. There is a need for competencies on semantic layer of the system from a research center. For example, there could be already a prototype for a discover service implemented at a research center to be further adapted to a particular case at hand. There is a need for an industrial company to provide a robust implementation for the semantic geo-catalog system-to-be, see for details [18].

Moreover, there can be several variations of the scenario discussed above, including:

- a user may want to identify several research centers in order to contact them concerning the state of the art with geo-catalogs and actual feasibility of the eventual innovative requests;
- a public institution may need to perform a market verification before launching a public tender, by asking some industrial companies an estimate for the realization of certain functionalities of a geo-catalog;
- an industrial company may have a promising platform and may look for its further extensions, and hence, may want to identify the relevant research centers, or final users that may help with this extension, e.g., either by including some new functionalities (research centers) or by customizing some modules of that platform to particular user needs, what ultimately can be re-proposed in other projects;

---

[2] INSPIRE - INfrastructure for SPatial InfoRmation in Europe:
http://www.ec-gis.org/inspire/
[3] http://www.opengeospatial.org/standards/cat

– research centers or universities may have outstanding prototypes, and hence, may want to bring them down to production and final exploitation, or just find partners (e.g., industrial companies or final users) for a new project proposal.

From a technical viewpoint, the scenario mentioned above as well as its variations can be implemented as a search for competencies across the key innovation actors. Note that many research projects that employ ICT (e.g., semantic technology) correctly identify an application in which prototypes they develop can be eventually exploited. However, it is far rarely the case that *final users* are directly involved in the definition of requirements and use cases instantiating the applications under consideration within those projects. This is so because research projects are not usually concerned with bringing the original ideas developed within them down to the actual exploitation of these by the (expected) final users. Also enterprises that are often involved in larger research and development projects, for instance, of 4 years duration and with about 1K man-month effort, are primarily interested in acquiring know-how to be later exploited in their internal subsequent projects. Hence, in order to foster an early practical exploitation of the research prototypes, it is necessary to directly involve final users in the research and development cycles.

2.2   Problem Statement

Involving final users into the research and development cycles requires addressing a *social challenge* of integrating relevant actors and facilitating the cross-fertilization among research centers, technology providers and user institutions, see Figure 1; this is exactly what is pursued by TasLab.

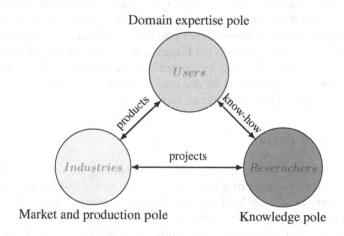

Fig. 1. The tripole model

As Figure 1 indicates, the *tripole* model for innovation includes three key poles, namely: (i) users (U) that possess an application domain expertise, (ii) research centers and universities (R) that possess knowledge of the state of the art technologies and innovative solutions, and (iii) industries (D) that possess market and production knowledge. The actors of these poles are put together through the innovation projects, thus being an enabling factor for amplifying potential gains by building on top of a larger volume of knowledge and experience compared with the other approaches, where final users usually have a limited role.

From a technical viewpoint, the problem of generating innovation is reduced to a competence search among the key innovation stakeholders and is as follows. Given:

- an innovation project theme (T), described as a phrase in a natural language, such as *semantic geo-catalog*;
- a finite set of user institutions $U = \{i \,|\, 1, \ldots, N_U\}$, e.g., urban planning, each of which annotated with respective metadata $M_U = \langle name, competencies, \ldots \rangle$, all together denoted as $\langle U, M_U \rangle$;
- a finite set of research centers and universities $R = \{j \,|\, 1, \ldots, N_R\}$, e.g., CNR (Italian National Research Council), each of which annotated with respective metadata $M_R = \langle name, recent\ projects, \ldots \rangle$, all together denoted as $\langle R, M_R \rangle$;
- a finite set of industrial companies $D = \{k \,|\, 1, \ldots, N_D\}$, e.g., WEBSS, OMNYS, each of which annotated with respective metadata $M_D = \langle name, market, \ldots \rangle$, all together denoted as $\langle D, M_D \rangle$;

discover (based on the available metadata) the best match between T and $\langle U, R, D \rangle$; or in other words generate a tripole for a given project theme.

N_U corresponds approximately to 350 entities, including various public administration departments and municipalities that are respectively structured, and which ultimately offer services to about 500.000 inhabitants of Trentino; $N_R = 13$, grouping about 750 researchers and $N_D = 684$ for the ICT sector (we started from), grouping about 3.400 professionals [1]. The system is not closed, and thus, can be extended, e.g., by adding the research centers and the industrial ICT companies outside Trentino. However, the system bootstrap is done only with the data of Trentino. Finally, notice that the metadata inserted into the system is not bounded by any vocabulary or predefined lists of terms, thus, allowing users to use their own terminology which they believe describes best their activities. This preserves the diversity, being the key feature, of the innovation stakeholders, and thus, facilitates innovation generation.

3   The TasLab Portal

We have implemented the tripole generation functionality within the TasLab portal[4], which is devoted to foster innovation by creating the conditions for a successful integration of the innovation stakeholders in the Trentino territory. The portal is available in English and Italian. It possesses various standard functionalities with public and private parts, including vision and mission of the initiative, related materials, news and events, services offered and so on. From now on, we concentrate only on a part of the back-end of the portal, which is related to the tripole generation.

Technically, the TasLab portal aims not only to model the pre-existing knowledge of the stakeholders but also to foster collaboration within public administration, companies

---

[4] http://www.taslab.eu/

and research centers, producing new structured knowledge. Specifically, it includes the following characteristics:

- federation of lightweight ontologies (for the ICT domain) based on the sharing of a common reference model, i.e., Descriptive Ontology for Linguistic and Cognitive Engineering - DOLCE [6];
- multilingual tools (computational ontologies and human-language technologies that converge in the task of providing the semantic description of contents);
- query answering system for semi-automatic construction of lightweight ontologies (as a guide for non-expert users in the task of ontology building and population; not covered here and retained as future work).

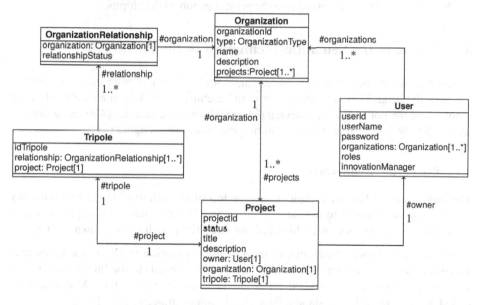

Fig. 2. Key business entities of the Taslab portal

The main business entities involved in the Taslab portal are shown in Figure 2 and are as follows:

Organization, which can be of the following types: *company, public company* (a final user in our case) and *research center.* An organization includes one or more users; it can own a project (if one of its users created it) or collaborate on a project created by another organization.

User, which identifies a person who accesses the reserved area of the portal and uses the available functions (e.g., tripole generation). A user can assume the following roles: *portal admin,* who manages all the portal areas; *organization owner,* who owns an organization which has been approved by the portal admin; *organization member,* who is a member of an organization, typically an employee; *simple user,* who simply created an account on the portal, without becoming a member or an owner of any organization.

Project, which can be created only by a user belonging at least to an organization which is directly associated to it. Once a project has been created it can assume one of the following statuses: draft, started, in process, closed, suspended. During the startup phase, the owner of the project is able to invite other organizations to participate in the innovative project proposal. This is enabled with the *tripole generation* functionality.

Tripole, which represents the group of organizations that have been involved in the project proposal through the following process: (i) the project owner has used the tripole generation functionality in order to semi-automatically identify the best matching organizations; (ii) the project owner has directly invited the identified organizations to participate in the project proposal; (iii) the invited organizations have accepted to be involved into the project proposal development.

4   The Use of the Semantic Technology in the Portal

In this section we describe how the semantic technology has been employed within the TasLab portal. First we present the portal architecture (§4.1), then we discuss the ontology of the portal (§4.2), indexing (§4.3) and semantic search (§4.4) techniques as well as finally the key interactions with the semantic search engine (§4.5).

4.1   The Portal Architecture

The TasLab portal has been implemented on top of the LifeRay[5] (v5.2.3 Community Edition) portal server. The tripole generation functionality has been implemented in Java. The system architecture, which follows three-tier paradigm, is shown in Figure 3.

Front-end tier. This is the front-end level of the application (also known as the presentation layer). It is responsible for serving the web contents to the Internet users. The software modules which provide the user interface and interact with the Middle tier are called *portlets* and follow a standardized development strategy - JSR 168/268 [6].

Middle end tier. This layer (also known as the business logic layer) is responsible for performing the required business processes and returning the required results.

Back-end tier. This tier consists of all the Data Access Objects (DAO). These objects are responsible for storing and retrieving data from the data providers involved in the scenario. This tier keeps data neutral and independent from the application servers or business logic.

Finally, the Solr search engine is hosted on a separate servlet engine instance in order to decouple it from the portal server and to make it more scalable independently from any other module. Its pipeline has been extended by adding the required plug-ins, which are responsible for automatically performing, e.g., all the required semantic enrichments to the indexed contents (coming from the portal) and so on.

---

[5] http://www.liferay.com/web/guest/home
[6] http://developers.sun.com/portalserver/reference/techart/jsr168/

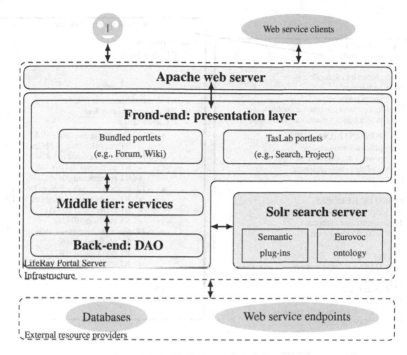

Fig. 3. The TasLab portal architecture

4.2   The Ontology of the Portal

The semantic layer of the portal is based on a hybrid model that integrates *Eurovoc* multilingual thesaurus[7] with a domain specific ontology. Eurovoc covers several domains and is available in 22 languages. It comprehends 21 fields, 127 micro-thesauri and 6645 descriptors (519 are the core terms). Moreover, there are 6669 occurrences of hierarchical links (broader term - BT/narrower term - NT) and 3636 associative relations (related term - RT), see Figure 4 for an example.

One of the main features of Eurovoc is the cross-lingual representation of terms and relations, allowing for coherent mappings between equivalent contents. Eurovoc has been preferred to alternative options, such as:

- a new thesaurus (or ontology) built from scratch: according to time and work constraints of the TasLab project, this direction has been considered too onerous.
- *eClass*[8]: a multilingual resource for product and service classification. Adapting this resource to the TasLab domain has not been considered as a feasible strategy, since the topic overlap between these is low.
- *EuroWordNet*[9]: This option has been discarded mainly for its genericity, where TasLab conversely needs coverage for specialized domains.

---

[7] http://europa.eu/eurovoc/
[8] http://www.eclass-online.com/
[9] http://www.illc.uva.nl/EuroWordNet/

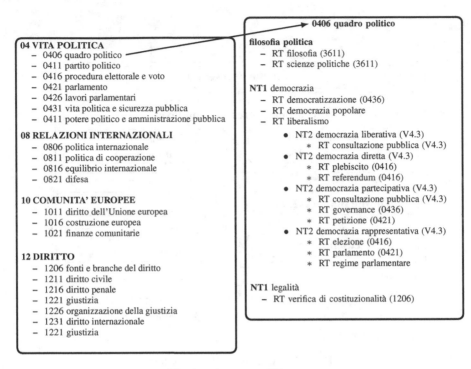

Fig. 4. A fragment of Eurovoc

The ontology underlying TasLab portal concerns two layers, namely top level and do-main level. In particular, at the top level, Eurovoc most general categories are aligned with DOLCE [6]. At the domain level, all the concepts used for describing TasLab entities (related to the institutional, research and administrative domains) are to be inte-grated into the Eurovoc structure (this is a future line work). In this sense, the ontology extends and enriches Eurovoc conceptual framework, both at top-down and bottom-up directions. The overall knowledge base has been implemented according to the SKOS W3C standard[10] (hence, converting Eurovoc from its native format to SKOS, etc.), which provides a unified method of knowledge representation, easier than the other languages, e.g., OWL, although exportable in that format.

4.3 Indexing

Every concept defined in the portal is assigned to a specific documental class and, after-wards, is converted into a Solr[11] document for indexing. In the initial stage, the specific fields of the documents are populated on the basis of their specific documental class. The following process, as shown in Figure 5, is applied to the relevant textual informa-tion/documents:

---

[10] http://www.w3.org/2004/02/skos/
[11] http://lucene.apache.org/solr/

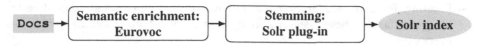

Fig. 5. Indexing

- Semantic enrichment, namely population of the TasLab domain specific ontology and its integration with Eurovoc.
- Stemming, namely reduction of the inflected (or sometimes derived) words to their stem, base or root form. For example, *progetto di sviluppo* being stemmed becomes *progett svilupp*. Since this process is language-dependent, there should ideally be as many stemming processes as the number of languages supported by the portal. In our case we have used it only for Italian and English, what improves the recall of the system, since queries are normalized and adapted to the linguistic knowledge units of the portal.
- Data entry, namely documents are indexed on Solr and immediately made available for querying.

4.4 Semantic Search

This functionality enables the tripole generation by executing semantic search for the required competencies. Search queries are processed as follows, see Figure 6:

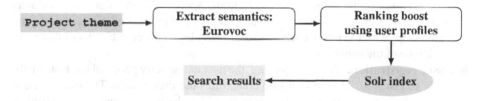

Fig. 6. Semantic search

- Semantic extraction, namely matching between every searched term (undergo stemming) and the following items of the system ontology: domains, micro-thesauri, descriptors, broader terms, non descriptors, related terms and the related query-expansion, e.g., for the query *office automation*, the results here include: *office automation* (in exact and stemmed way) or Eurovoc sector *education and communications* or Eurovoc micro-thesauri *information technology and data processing* or Eurovoc descriptor *office automation* or broader term *computer applications*.
- Matching on the index, the expanded search (like in the example above) for each language (English and Italian) is submitted to Solr; results are given on the basis of textual and Eurovoc code matching.
- Ranking boost, results are contextually organized according to user profiles, specifically on the one side, by considering the empirically established weight assigned to the Eurovoc hierarchy (sector, thesauri, descriptor) and, on the other side, by exploiting the *interests* metdata entries of the user profile.

– Faceting, for every search, Solr also provides clustering of results according to categories/facets. These categories are dynamic, as these are processed by Solr for every query.

The metadata used for navigation includes: domain, micro-thesaurus and Eurovoc descriptor, release date (organized per period); language; documental class; document format. Finally, it is possible to refine search results on the basis of facets - contextually visualized at the result page as well as by providing access to similar documents (through the TF/IDF measure - term frequency/inverse document frequency), exploiting existing links.

4.5 Interactions with the Semantic Search Engine

Let us discuss the key interactions between the specific functions supported by the portal and the semantic engine implemented as a Solr plug-in:

Semantic search over the contents of the portal. All the contents of the TasLab portal, suitably loaded through the LifeRay web content standard portlet, are retrieved using Eurovoc-based semantic search algorithms (see §4.4). Moreover, the Solr index is extended in order to manage the business entities discussed in Section 3.

Tripole generation. The metadata associated to the project is added to Solr and is exploited together with a list of keywords that the user can optionally indicate to guide the tripole generation according to the *best-each* modality for selecting the companies, research centers, public administrations. Specifically, the algorithm evaluates metadata of each organization entity and metadata of the related users, then it compares these with the project metadata and provides an ordered list (by ranking) for each type of the organization.

New user registration. When registering, the user can specify personal interests on the basis of Eurovoc. This information constitutes the user profile. The overall metadata and the URI's of the organization to which the user belongs are indexed by Solr. Notice that every change here forces the global re-indexing.

Adding new content. This process contextually requires necessary information for indexing, including: documental class, URI (automatically assigned by the system; this unique key is used for retrieving the document in the original format from the portal CMS repository), language (based on which the system determines the kind of stemming process to apply), title, release date (automatically assigned by the system). Every possible modification to metadata or contents forces the global re-indexing.

Adding new organization or project. The process of registration of a new organization foresees, after a first stage of moderation by the administrator, adding descriptive metadata to the Solr index, so that the new organization is made available for the semantic search and the tripole generation functionality. Every change here forces the global re-indexing. Similar argument applies when a new project is added.

5   Discussion

In this section we provide a discussion on some empirical (§5.1) and strategic (§5.2) evaluation of the solution employed together with a related work overview (§5.3).

5.1   Empirical Evaluation

We have run our tests on a PC with CPU Intel quadcore 3 Ghz, 8GB of RAM. TasLab semantic search module underlying the tripole generation functionality builds on top of the performance of "Solr as is" since for each indexing/search, it executes about 20.000 to 25.000 queries for each language (in our case for English and Italian). The overhead here depends on: number of the documents on index; size of the index; search parameters, such as query complexity, numbers of request fields, etc. In our tests we had 100.000 random documents on index, 1.2GB index size, queries of various length, such as uri, publishing date, title, facets on Eurovoc fields. Based on these tests the overhead was only about 100-200 ms, what suggests for the scalability of our solution.

The solution employed represents an improvement over the canonical (and commonly known) exact string matching search methods available in LifeRay. The user has the possibility of posing a query by using a natural language format and the semantic search algorithms used are able to return the most relevant documents related to the request. In fact, in all the examples we run so far our solution had demonstrated better characteristics (e.g., precision, recall) with respect to conventional approaches, such as a string-based search of LifeRay. For example, a user searching for *nuclear industry* obtains also results/documents on *plutonium* or *uranium* (the terms related to the nuclear industry argument) even if their contents never contain the searched string.

5.2   The SWOT Analysis

Usually an assessment of an application implies conducting an ex-post analysis, which takes into consideration the effectiveness of the technology based on the daily activity of users. At the moment of writing, the TasLab portal is still under testing, therefore a *prospective* assessment method has been adopted: the *strengths, weaknesses, opportunities, threats* (SWOT) analysis. Typically, the SWOT analysis is used to review the market position, foreseen directions of a business idea. We decided to use it here in order to assess what strategic actions should be adopted in order to make the TasLab portal a success. To this end, we start by enlisting the needs of the main innovation stakeholders, which are as follows:

- *Public administrations,* which aim at: catalyzing the innovation and demanding for innovative products and services for the local government, monitoring and funding innovation programs, increasing the internationalization of local SMEs by fostering new partnerships.
- *Research centers,* which aim at: developing a more structured channel of technology transfer among academia and industry, testing innovative ideas in real-life settings, obtaining funds for future research activities.

– *Industries,* which aim at: obtaining new funding opportunities for the development of innovative solutions, enforcing connections with academia, suggesting/selling to the public administration specific (innovative) solutions, participating to the transformation of innovation into business value.

Following the strengths/weaknesses of ICT itself and market opportunities/threats of the TasLab portal, below we discuss how the above mentioned aims might be met.

Internal strengths. By using the semantic technology the portal improves quality of stakeholders' content management and information access. For example, the semantic search engine improves the accuracy of tripole generation (over the conventional methods, see §5.1) and in general of information discovery on the portal. Moreover, TasLab is strongly related to the territoriality and the inner characteristics of the organizations of the innovation network, what, e.g., means that the project can count on the availability of (local) domain experts to tune the application.

Internal weaknesses. Companies, research centers, and final users might anyhow eventually desert the portal, perceiving it as too complex to understand, due to bureaucratic procedures or being conflicting with their interests. In fact, a combination of motivation/incentive mechanisms is still in a very early development stage here. In order to build, test and provide to the market an effective territorial innovation system, several more years are needed; e.g., effective IPR policies should be adopted. In our view, the weaknesses reside on the organizational side, rather than on the technological one.

External opportunities. Companies, research institutions and local governments spend billions of euros each year on data integration and portals in order to foster and sustain innovation. Thanks to the availability of public financing of research and innovation in Trentino and thanks to the presence of top notch researchers, local companies are becoming also more competitive on the global market. We expect an increasing demand here coming from the diffusion of the portal in the other areas of Italy and in Europe.

External threats. In general, the complexity of creating semantically enabled applications and the sometimes unclear business value of these in comparison with more traditional approaches to master data and metadata somewhat limited the semantic technology potential and appeal [7]. This should be overcame with concrete benefits coming from the actual portal usage.

Through an effective knowledge management within the portal, companies and research centers should become aware of new funding opportunities, develop new profitable partnerships, ultimately leading to the development of new products and services. In turn, public administrations can monitor the results of innovative projects, direct the innovation activities into specific priority areas, etc. The local public administration is interested in collaborative solutions and in TasLab as one of the important innovative initiatives in the region. A strategic action to be taken includes designing a set of incentives in order to guarantee sustainability and high usage of the portal.

5.3   Related Work

In the last years, semantic technology has played a key role in the ICT area. If semantics undoubtedly became a buzzword in the most advanced contexts of communication technologies (e.g., eGovernment, eHealth), only few systems are actually able to provide effective semantic functionalities. For example, looking at web-based communities in the area of knowledge management, it is not easy to find full-operational semantic portals, as also demonstrated in a recent survey in [12]. Here, the focus is on the general features of some of the most popular semantic portals: Esperonto[12], OntoWeb[13] (both developed for research tasks), Empolis K42[14], and Mondeca ITM[15] (commerce-oriented). These portals provide only static ontologies without any sufficient versioning mechanisms. In fact, none of these supply semantic web services, which conversely should be a core function of such systems. Within these four cases, only Ontoweb includes a hybrid semantic resource integrating an ontology with a suitable thesaurus, though making information access difficult. At this level, the navigation tools rely on conceptual models (the underlying ontologies) with no support for linguistic access. In general, the interface between ontologies and lexical resources has also an impact on semantic search, as recently stated in [10], since it represents a novel approach to user-centred information access based on computation of semantic relations between lexicalized concepts and not on syntactic parsing. In the variegate context of semantic search tools, such (a) user-based approaches to retrieve information and knowledge (e.g., SemSearch[16]) complement (b) user-centred search to retrieve ontologies (e.g., Swoogle[17] and Watson[18]) and (c) search based on structural query languages[19].

As from [12], the most relevant problem of the above mentioned semantic portals concerns the total lack of community-based features, corresponding to the absence of suitable dynamic functionalities for the evolution of portal contents according to users' practice and knowledge. In this sense, as we have illustrated in the previous sections, TasLab can be considered as a good candidate to overcome that limit, since it *delegates* to the tripole actors the construction of the information framework for the semantic portal[20]. This remark is in line with thesis of the work in [5] too: to globally take into account semantic technology into the eGovernment applications; i.e., it is not enough to focus on web services, but an ontological focus on people and organizations is also needed. For this reason, we think that - besides the critical considerations in [12] - what is important for the efficiency of semantic systems is to focus on the human dimension of information, reminding that the Web is not only an interlinked cluster of machines, but rather a network of humans negotiating linguistic meanings through machines. One

---

[12] http://www.esperonto.net/
[13] http://ontoweb-lt.dfki.de/
[14] http://www.empolis.com/
[15] http://www.mondeca.com/
[16] http://code.google.com/p/semsearch/
[17] http://swoogle.umbc.edu/
[18] http://watson.kmi.open.ac.uk/WatsonWUI/
[19] Such as SPARQL and ARQ (see, e.g., http://jena.sourceforge.net/ARQ/).
[20] Only providing a top-down resource (DOLCE-based domain ontologies + Eurovoc thesaurus) at the initial stage.

of the key issues in current R&D in semantic technology is to provide integrated solutions to address two core requirements of the Web: (i) natural language semantic facilities and (ii) flexible machine-encoding and processing of concepts. We can conclude that the above mentioned features of TasLab are going to satisfy these requirements.

6   Conclusions

In this paper we have discussed our solution to innovation generation in public administrations. Specifically, we reformulated the problem of innovation generation as competence search or the so-called tripole generation among the key innovation actors, namely: final users, industries and research centers. This is enabled with the semantic technology, in particular with the use of ontologies, indexing and semantic search. The evaluation results, though preliminary, demonstrate the strengths of our approach as from the technical viewpoint (e.g., scalability) as well as from the SWOT analysis.

Future work includes at least: (i) an in-depth evaluation of the techniques employed as well as including some other matching methods from [4] in order to fine-tune the solution; (ii) an enrichment of Eurovoc by customizing TMEO, a recently developed tutoring methodology for the enrichment of ontologies [15], to the TasLab requirements; and (iii) the development of an organizational structure which with an appropriate set of incentives should guarantee sustainability and high usage of the portal.

Acknowledgments. This work has been supported by the *TasLab network* project funded by the European Social Fund under the act n. 1637 (30.06.2008) of the Autonomous Province of Trento. We are thankful to the TasLab group members: Isabella Bressan, Ivan Pilati, Luca Mion, Valentina Ferrari, Marco Combetto and to Fausto Giunchiglia, Francesca Gleria, Italo Della Noce, Mauro Piffer, Andrea Simioni for many fruitful discussions on the various innovation aspects covered in this paper as well as to Gabriele Frati for some technical support.

References

1. Camussone, P.F., Dalmonego, I., Zaninotto, E.: Le tecnologie digitali nell'economia del Trentino. EGEA S.p.A., Italy (2007)
2. Chesbrough, H.W.: Open Innovation: The New Imperative for Creating and Profiting from Technology. Harvard Business School Press, Cambridge (2003)
3. Eriksson, M., Niitamo, V.-P., Kulkki, S., Hribernik, K.A.: Living labs as a multi-contextual R&D methodology. In: Proc. of ICE (2005)
4. Euzenat, J., Shvaiko, P.: Ontology matching. Springer, Heidelberg (2007)
5. Ferrario, R., Guarino, N.: A new ontological perspective for social services. In: Proc. of MeTTeG, pp. 41–51 (2008)
6. Gangemi, A., Guarino, N., Masolo, C., Oltramari, A.: Sweetening WordNet with DOLCE. AI Magazine 24(3), 13–24 (2003)
7. Gartner. Hype cycle for web and user interaction technologies (2009)
8. Giunchiglia, F.: Managing diversity in knowledge. Keynote talk at ECAI (2006)
9. Giunchiglia, F.: Il ruolo degli enti di ricerca per lo sviluppo dell'ict del trentino. Le tecnologie digitali nell'economia del Trentino (2007)

10. Giunchiglia, F., Kharkevich, U., Zaihrayeu, I.: Concept search. In: Aroyo, L., Traverso, P., Ciravegna, F., Cimiano, P., Heath, T., Hyvönen, E., Mizoguchi, R., Oren, E., Sabou, M., Simperl, E. (eds.) ESWC 2009. LNCS, vol. 5554, pp. 429–444. Springer, Heidelberg (2009)
11. Howells, J.: Intermediation and the role of intermediaries in innovation. Research Policy 35(5), 715–728 (2006)
12. Lausen, H., Ding, Y., Stollberg, M., Fensel, D., Lara Hernandez, R., Han, S.-K.: Semantic web portals: state-of-the-art survey. Journal of Knowledge Management 9(5), 40–49 (2005)
13. Levin, M.: Technology transfer as a learning and development process: an analysis of Norwegian programme on technology transfer. Technovation 13(8), 497–518 (1993)
14. Niitamo, V.-P., Kulkki, S., Eriksson, M., Hribernik, K.A.: State-of-the-art and good practice in the field of living labs. In: Proc. of ICE (2005)
15. Oltramari, A.: TMEO - tutoring methodology for the enrichment of ontologies. In: Proc. of LREC (to appear, 2010)
16. Rohrbeck, R., Hölzle, K., Gemünden, H.G.: Opening up for competitive advantage: How Deutsche Telekom creates an open innovation ecosystem. R&D Management 39(4), 420–430 (2009)
17. Shapira, P.: Modernizing small manufacturers in Japan: The role of local public technology centers. Journal of Technology Transfer 17(1), 40–57 (1992)
18. Shvaiko, P., Vaccari, L., Trecarichi, G.: Semantic geo-catalog: a scenario and requirements. In: Proc. of the workshop on Ontology Matching collocated with ISWC, pp. 240–241 (2009)
19. Vaccari, L., Shvaiko, P., Marchese, M.: A geo-service semantic integration in spatial data infrastructures. Journal of Spatial Data Infrastructures Research 4, 24–51 (2009)
20. Wimmer, M., Scholl, H.J., Janssen, M., Traunmüller, R. (eds.): Proc. of the 8th International Conference on Electronic Government, EGOV (2009)

Context-Driven Semantic Enrichment of Italian News Archive

Andrei Tamilin, Bernardo Magnini, Luciano Serafini, Christian Girardi,
Mathew Joseph, and Roberto Zanoli

FBK, Center for Information Technology - IRST
Via Sommarive 18, 38050 Povo di Trento, Italy

Abstract. *Semantic enrichment* of textual data is the operation of linking mentions[1] with the entities they refer to, and the subsequent enrichment of such entities with the background knowledge about them
available in one or more knowledge bases (or in the entire web). Information about the context in which a mention occurs, (e.g., information
about the time, the topic, and the space, which the text is relative to)
constitutes a critical resource for a correct semantic enrichment for two
reasons. First, without context, mentions are "too little text" to unambiguously refer to a single entity. Second, knowledge about entities
is also context dependent (e.g., speaking about political life of Illinois
during 1996, Obama is a Senator, while since 2009, Obama is the US
president). In this paper, we describe a concrete approach to *context-
driven semantic enrichment*, built upon four core sub-tasks: detection of
mentions in text (i.e., finding references to people, locations and organizations); determination of the context of discourses of the text, identification of the referred entities in the knowledge base, and enrichment
of the entity with the knowledge relevant to the context. In such approach, context-driven semantic enrichment needs also to have contextualized background knowledge. To cope with this aspect, we propose a
customization of Sesame, one of state-of-the-art knowledge repositories,
to support representation and reasoning with contextualized knowledge.
The approach has been fully implemented in a system, which has been
practically deployed and applied to the textual archive of the local Italian newspaper "L'Adige", covering the decade of years from 1999 to
2009.

1 Introduction

The exploitation of background knowledge for text understanding is nowadays
becoming a very appealing research area due to the wide availability of large
sources of structured background knowledge in form of semantic web data, as

---

[1] The terms "mentions" and "entities" have been introduced within the ACE Program
(Linguistic Data Consortium, 2004). "Mentions" are equivalent to "referring expressions", while "entities" are equivalent to "referents", as widely used in computational
linguistics.

L. Aroyo et al. (Eds.): ESWC 2010, Part I, LNCS 6088, pp. 364–378, 2010.

well as huge amount of unstructured textual data. Our intuition on how textual understanding using background knowledge should be implemented is by means of a two phase *loop* in which (i) knowledge is automatically extracted from text by exploiting some form of pre-existing background knowledge and (ii) the extracted knowledge is used to extend the background knowledge and in this way it will contribute to extract new knowledge from text. In this paper we focus on phase (i) and we show how the usage of the information about *context* can contribute to improve the quality of that phase.

Our approach is based on the observation that when humans read a piece of text, they exploit their capability of establishing a link between the mentions, which occur in the text, and knowledge they have previously acquired about corresponding entities mentions refer to (such as people, organization, locations, events, and etc.). The impossibility to create such a link prevents people from combining their previous knowledge with the information contained in the text. Why people can actually do this is by taking into account the context in which each mention occurs in. Information about the context (as for instance that the article is about a soccer match which took place in Milan) helps them to focus their attention, and to limit the scope of the knowledge they remember. For instance, if we are reading an article on the newspaper speaking about the certain soccer match between Milan and Juventus, which is part of the Italian League and was taken in Turin on the 20 of October 2000, reading the string "Boban", if we already know him, we will focus our attention on an ex-Yugoslavian soccer player Zvonimir Boban, who played with Milan from 1992 to 2001, considering the fact that he played the role of midfielder, and all the other knowledge about this person relevant given the context of the article. In this process, the context of discourse helps us to focus our attention on the soccer player and not Boban Marković, the Serbian trumpet player. Similarly, the context will limit the "activation of knowledge" to one necessary to understand the information contained in the article. So for instance, it will not be necessary to remember that before 1990 Boban played in Dinamo Zagabria team.

To implement the above schematic model into an automatic program, we should be able to realize the operation called *semantic enrichment* of textual data. This is the operation of automatically linking mentions with the entities they refer to and the subsequent enrichment of such entities with the background knowledge about them available in one or more knowledge bases (or in the entire web). Information about the context in which a mention occurs, (e.g., information about the time, the topic, and the space, which the text is relative to) constitutes a critical resource for a correct semantic enrichment for two reasons. First, without context, mentions are "too little text" to unambiguously refer to a single entity. Second, knowledge about entities is also context dependent (e.g., speaking about political life of Illinois during 1996, Obama is a Senator, while since 2009, Obama is the US president), and we need to know the context in order to identify the correct portion of knowledge the mention should be enriched with.

This paper defines and provides a concrete implementation of the *context-driven semantic enrichment* of text. Context-driven semantic enrichment is built upon four core sub-tasks:

- mention detection in the text (we will focus on people, locations and organizations);
- determination of the context of discourse of the text;
- identification of the referred entities in the knowledge base;
- enrichment of the entity with the knowledge relevant to the context.

Practically, this work describes the approach and implemented system for context-dependent semantic enrichment of Italian news archive. The approach integrates natural language processing tools for extraction of named entities with the background knowledge expressed in semantic web standards, such as RDF/OWL. In order to enable context-sensitive enrichment of the extracted named entities, we have extended the standard state of the art semantic repository Sesame for managing RDF with the capability of expressing contextually-qualified RDF/OWL knowledge bases, focusing on temporal, geographic and thematic contextual dimensions. Formally, for contextualization of background knowledge we adopted and extended the state of the art context as box representation framework [9], in which the contextual space is defined by a fixed number of partially-ordered contextual dimensions and the concrete context, containing RDF/OWL knowledge base, is defined by a vector of values the corresponding dimensions take. By virtue of dimension orders, in such a framework contexts automatically exhibit generalization/specialization ordering allowing further effectively localize contexts possibly containing knowledge relevant for enrichment of the given textual source.

The paper is further organized as follows. In Sect. 2 we describe the processing pipeline of the semantic enrichment process. Employed knowledge extraction techniques are described in Sect. 3. In Sect. 4 we present the approach to organize background knowledge in a context-sensitive way, shedding the light on the formal aspects of the approach. In-detail description of the context-dependent semantic enrichment process is depicted in Sect. 5. Practical issues related to application to real data set are described in Sect. 6. Relation with other similar approaches and systems is discussed in Sect. 7. Finally, Sect. 8 concludes and outlines the future work.

2   Enrichment Pipeline by Example

Semantic enrichment of a text aims at making available background knowledge that is supposed to be relevant while reading and interpreting that text. As an example of context-driven semantic enrichment, suppose we read the following piece of text about a soccer match:

```
Milan - Juventus (Friday, November 20, 2000)
```

"Milan was unlucky to hit the post with a Boban header in the
first half but came out of the dressing room determined to score
and win all three points."

In this case relevant background information about "Boban" would include
knowledge, among the other, about his team (i.e., Milan) at that time (i.e., 2000),
his role in the team (i.e., midfielder). We might also be interested in background
knowledge about the specific match (i.e., Milan-Juventus), or about the town in
which the match has been played (i.e., Milan).

Now, suppose we encounter "Boban" in the context of a different match, like
the one reported in the following text.

PARIS (Thursday, July 9, 1998)

"Croatia captain Zvonimir Boban won the ball at the top of the
box at Croatia's defensive end. Thuram, a right back who had
made a long run forward, didn't give up on the play, coming
behind the dawdling Boban and knocking the ball loose."

In this case, different background knowledge about the same person (i.e.,
Boban) should be selected. Specifically, the team, at that time (i.e., 1998), would
be Croatia, the match is France-Croatia, and the town of the match is Paris.

In order to provide appropriate background knowledge, the following steps
are necessary: (i) some understanding of the entities mentioned in the context,
including the fact that "Boban" is the name of a person and that "Milan" is
the name of an organization: this is referred in the literature as *named entitics
recognition*; (ii) understanding that "Boban" in the first context and "Zvonimir
Boban" in the second one, actually denote the same person: this is referred as
cross-document coreference; (iii) being able to recognize that the person mentioned in the two contexts is included in a repository of background knowledge:
this is referred as *entity disambiguation*, because there can be more than one
person with the same name; (iv) being able to select the correct portion of
knowledge available in the background repository with respect to the actual textual context, for instance the composition of the Milan team in the first example
and the composition of the Croatian team in the second: this is called *context selection*, and (v) being able to attach correct pieces of knowledge to corresponding
textual portions: this is referred as actual *enrichment*.

3 Automated Extraction of Named Entities

The ability to recognize and classify Named Entities (Named Entity Recognition), such as people and locations names, is an important task in various areas,
including topic detection and information retrieval. Cross-document coreference
extends the task into deciding whether or not different mentions refer to the

same entity, and the task becomes more complex when documents come from different sources, probably having different authors, conventions and style. Note that an entity (such as Valentino Rossi, the MotoGP World Champion) can be referred to by multiple surface forms (e.g., Valentino Rossi, Rossi and Valentino) and a surface form (e.g., Rossi) can refer to multiple entities (e.g., Vasco Rossi, the Italian rock star, and Paolo Rossi, the famous ex-football player); performing this task allows users to get information about a specific entity from multiple text sources at the same time.

3.1   Named Entity Recognition

Named Entity Recognition is a subtask of Information Extraction which aims to classify words in text into predefined categories. Examples of named entities are person names (PER), location (LOC) and organization names (ORG). Spurred on by the Message Understanding Conferences (MUC), a considerable amount of work has been done in last years on the Named Entity Recognition and a number of machine-learning approaches were proposed, such as: Hidden Markov Model (HMM), Support Vector Machines (SVMs), and Conditional Random Fields (CRFs). Drawing from our participation at Evalita 2007[2] and at ACE08[3], we built Typhoon [13], a system for Named Entity Recognition in which two different classifiers based on CRFs and HMM are combined in cascade to exploit global features such as *Data Redundancy* and *Patterns* extracted from a large text corpus of about one billion of words. *Data Redundancy* is attained when the same entity occurs in different places in documents, whereas *Patterns* are 2-grams, 3-grams, 4-grams and 5-grams preceding, and following recognized entities in the large corpus. The system can use additional features, such as that given by a Text Classifier able to recognize the category to which the story belongs (e.g. sport, economy). Typhoon consists of two classifiers in cascade, but it is possible to use a single classifier making the system faster (100 times faster, with a speed rate of about 20,000 tokens/sec); whereas the second classifier will be used in combination to the first one when more accuracy is needed. The system took part in Evalita 2009 Named Entity Recognition task [10] for Italian language performing as the best tagger (see Table 1).

Table 1. Evalita 2009 results

Entity type	Precision	Recall	F_1
PER	90.29	86.42	88.31
LOC	86.12	84.16	85.13
ORG	71.71	69.43	70.56

---

[2] http://evalita.fbk.eu/2007/
[3] http://www.itl.nist.gov/iad/mig/tests/ace/

3.2 Cross-Document Coreference

To corefer the Named Entities we used the system developed by Popescu and Magnini [12] in cascade to Typhoon. The system is based on agglomerative clustering technique able to exploit other Named Entities and professional categories co-occurring with the ambiguous entity in the same document; it was first tested in the SEMEVAL 2007 Web People Search task, performing the second best result among 16 systems with the following performance in terms of the harmonic mean of purity and inverse purity, which are standard clustering evaluation metrics: F_1=0.77 (Purity=0.75 and Inverse Purity=0.80).

4 Contextualized Background Knowledge Repository

The recognition of the fact that most of the knowledge available on the semantic web in form of RDF/OWL data is tailored to a specific context of use, has fostered recently the investigation on practical extensions of the semantic web languages to make explicit the representation of context associated to a knowledge resource. The use of explicit qualification of knowledge with contextual information has been investigated for such issues as provenance and trust of data [7,4], expressing propositional attitudes [11], dealing with temporally-stamped data [8], and access control [5]. In this work, we propose a lightweight *contextualized background knowledge repository* for managing and querying RDF/OWL data qualified with a set of contextual restrictions, practically limiting the scope to the temporal, geographic and thematic boundaries since those can be directly derived from a textual material.

4.1 Representation Framework

For representation of contextually qualified RDF/OWL knowledge we formally adopted and extended the state of the art *context as a box* framework [9]. According to this framework, a *context* is defined as a set of logical statements, or a knowledge base, inside the box, and an array of *contextual dimensions*, outside of the box. For example, if C is the context of the current Italian parliament, it can contain the information primeminister(berlusconi) and the parameters are for instance time(C) = 8may2008–now, location(C) = Italy, subject(C) = Politics.

In the present work, we pursue the additional requirement to the context as box framework demanding the values of each of contextual dimensions to be taken from structured domains with defined on them broad-narrow relations. For instance, the values for time(C) are time intervals, the values of location(C) are geographical regions, and the values of subject(C) are topics. For time and location dimensions the broad-narrow relation can be naturally defined as the interval and region containment respectively, while for subject dimension the topic-sub-topic relation can be considered.

As an example, Fig. 1 depicts a contextualized repository composed of three contexts describing governments in Italy. It can be easily observed that the context C_1 is broader than contexts C_2 and C_3.

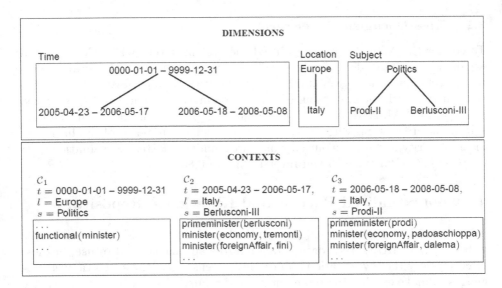

Fig. 1. Example of contextualized repository

4.2   Querying for Contextualized Knowledge

In answering queries, knowing the scope of the query is quite crucial. For instance, if one asks for the prime minister in the context of 2005 United States Politics or in the context 2005 Italian Politics he clearly obtains two different answers. From this elementary example one can see how relevant the context of the query for providing the right answer. That is why a query to a contextualized knowledge repository is in fact a contextualized query, composed from the query itself and also from the (set of) context(s) in which the query should be evaluated.

The choice of the most appropriate context for executing contextualized query is very crucial factor. Sending a query to the "wrong" context can produce an empty answer. On the other hand to precisely determine the correct context at which a query should be sent is in most of the cases a difficult task. To mitigate this problem, we introduce the notion of a *query shifting*, which is the operation of redirecting a query from one context to another relevant context, when query fails to find any fruitful information in the current context. The hierarchical structure of contexts, induced by partial orders of the context dimensions, provides the basic graph on which queries are shifted across contexts. More specifically, as a semantic metric of context closeness the relation "directly covers" and "is directly covered by" are exploited.

Let us see an example of such a shifting considering the contextualized knowledge repository shown in Fig. 1. Suppose we want to submit to the repository a query for knowing who was the minister of economy during the period 2005–2009 in Italy. This request can be encoded into the contextual query

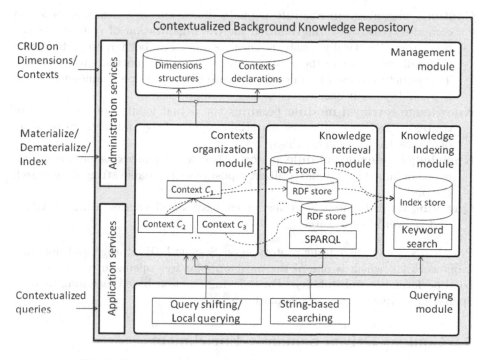

Fig. 2. System architecture of the contextualized repository

$(\text{minister}(\text{economy}, x), \langle 2005–2007, \text{Italy}, \text{Politics}\rangle)$. Since the context with dimensions $\langle 2005–2007, \text{Italy}, \text{Politics}\rangle$ does not exist in the repository, then a new context C_4 is created with empty content and its position in the context graph is computed (namely C_4 position is below C_1 and above C_2 and C_3). The query in C_4 will not produce any result. On the other hand if, we "zoom" into the contexts directly covered by C_4, namely C_2 and C_3, and submit the same query to both of them, we will obtain the following contextualized answers:

Context	Answer
2006-05-18 – 2008-05-08, Italy, Prodi-II	padoaschioppa
2005-04-23 – 2006-05-17, Italy, Berlusconi-III	tremonti

4.3   System Architecture

The implementation architecture of the contextualized knowledge repository is graphically depicted in Fig. 2. The repository is composed of four principal modules, whose functionalities are briefly described below.

The management module supports the functionalities for (a) defining and managing the dimensions structures and (b) defining and managing the set of contexts comprising the repository.

Contexts organization module exploits dimensions structures in order to
compute context covering relation for the organization of contexts of the
repository. Practically, context cover relation has been represented by a
Hasse diagram, one of the popular representations of partially ordered sets.
This structure is used in order to compute the context pairs among which it
is possible to shift queries.

Knowledge retrieval module performs the actual loading of knowledge of
contexts into the storage, i.e., materializing knowledge, for further execution
of knowledge retrieval queries.

Knowledge indexing module performs the textual indexing of the knowledge contained in the materialized repositories to enable string-base search
queries.

Querying module enables to answer contextualized queries using SPARQL
and keyword-based search.

Practically, we grounded our prototype on Sesame RDF storage and querying
framework [3], which is one of the most popular free open-source tool having
good performance and stability.[4] For indexing and text-based searching we used
open-source Apache Lucene Solr platform.[5]

5   Context-Driven Semantic Enrichment

Having on one side the textual material, annotated by automated entity ex-
tractor with textual mentions (referring to people, locations and organizations),
and the populated contextualized background knowledge repository, the task of
a context-driven semantic enrichment consists in mapping mentions to the entities in the repository and then retrieving the knowledge about these entities
relevant to the textual context mentions occur in. In the following we discuss
major steps in more details.

5.1   Entity Disambiguation

The first step to entity disambiguation consists in identification of the name
for the entity from the multiple possible ways it is referred to in the text. For
this task from the computed coreference clusters we select the longest and the
most frequent mention occurring in the text. This simple heuristic in practice
allows bringing from the text the most representative, complete name for the
frequently occurring entities, which is the combination of name and surname
for people, non abbreviated name for locations and organizations. Using the
complete name allows to establish the accurate match to the entities available
in the knowledge repository. Practically, the matching is performed by querying
the textual index constructed from ontologies of the repository using identifiers

---

[4] In the future we plan to investigate the use of OWLIM extension to Sesame for OWL
    data; more details on OWLIM can be found at http://www.ontotext.com/owlim
[5] http://lucene.apache.org/solr/

and available textual labels attached to ontological individuals. However, in the general setting, due to the name ambiguity problem, this procedure brings from the repository the set of entities having the same name but denoting different real-world entities. To eliminate further the entity ambiguity we employ the analysis of the text, the entity mentions occur in, in order to guess the imposed contextual constraints.

5.2 Context Selection

Topic and time are constraints we practically employed for identification of the entity context from text. Selection of topic is based on the use of automatically extracted from text keywords (using the algorithm presented in [1]) allowing to fall the textual source into the fixed list of categories, ranging from broad categories, such as for instance sport and politics, to the more detailed ones, such as soccer, soccer series and annual championships, government legislatures, and etc. For the identification of temporal constraint we at the moment adopted the simple strategy of using the publication year of the text. Currently we are working on automatic detection of temporal expressions from text for more accurate determination of the temporal constraint.

Identified contextual constraints are used for further filtering the list of matching entities and consequent retrieval of the relevant background knowledge from the corresponding contexts of the contextualized repository.

5.3 Enrichment

Using the detected entities and guessed contextual constraints, the concluding semantic enrichment phase extracts from the corresponding contexts of the repository the background knowledge on the entity. This later practically evaluates to execution of the SPARQL query asking for triples having in subject or object the given entity.

6 Practical Deployment

The presented context-driven semantic enrichment approach has been fully implemented in a system, which has been practically deployed and applied to the textual archive of the local Italian newspaper "L'Adige"[6]. The archive contains 620,641 articles in Italian from January 1st 1999 to October 15th 2009 ranging over the regional and national news in the domain of politics, sports, economics, culture, education, and etc. Practically, for the processed archive we have implemented the portal giving the possibility to search the news archive by entities addressed in the articles, see the relevant background knowledge attached to entities by semantic enrichment when reading the articles, as well as see the summary card assuming all background knowledge on interested entity. The screen shot of the implemented portal is shown in Fig. 3. In the following we give some figures describing the steps of the enrichment process.

---

[6] http://www.ladige.it

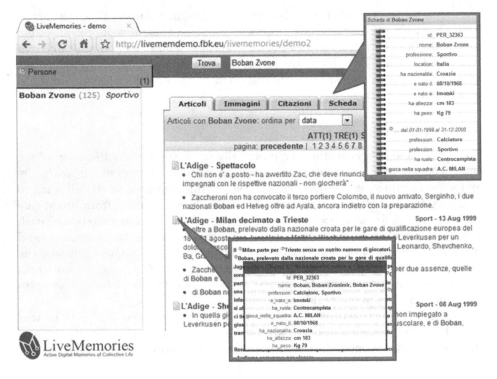

Fig. 3. Semantically enriched news portal for "L'Adige" archive

6.1   Extraction of Named Entities

For automated extraction of named entities from "L'Adige" dataset we practically used the Typhoon system described in Sect. 3. From total amount of 257,255,240 tokens constituting the dataset we have extracted 5,169,188 mentions referring to people; 2,977,960 - to organizations and 2,958,228 - to locations. We consider the reported in Sect. 3 evaluation obtained at Evalita a reasonable indicator of the accuracy of the extracted entities; considering also the fact that at Evalita systems were evaluated on a subset of documents extracted from "L'Adige" archive.

From the extracted Named Entities we further constructed 133,906 clusters corresponding to distinct persons, 34,270 clusters of organizations and 9,836 - of locations using the integrated in Typhoon coreference resolution algorithm by Popescu and Magnini [12]. The coreference system limited to deal with entities of type PER only has been extended by us to work also with ORG and LOC too. The system accuracy was computed on a gold standard constructed on a subset of "L'Adige" news stories from 1999 to 2006, containing 209 person names corresponding to 709 entities, for a total of 43,704 annotated documents [6]. On this corpus the system performed as F_1=0.80 (Purity=0.91 and Inverse Purity=0.75).

6.2   Feeding the Background Knowledge Repository

Looking for semantic resources on Italy and in Italian language we recognized the very limited availability of such models in RDF/OWL on the web. To bootstrap the construction of the background knowledge in Italian, we have developed a set of procedures for semi-automatic conversion of existing semi-structured resources. In particular, we used various public classifications of National Statistics Institute (ISTAT)[7], data tables of national and provincial Economical Registries (Camera di Commercio)[8], official web sites of Italian senate and chamber[9], National Olympic Committee (CONI)[10], and etc.) into the formal ontologies expressed in RDF/OWL. The ontologies has been constructed in Italian language and focused on the following domains of interest: sport (players, teams, regular championships and competitions in soccer, auto- and motosport, ice hockey, and others), education (Italian educational system and degrees, universities, and others), economy (economical activities and professions, industries and craftsmen, banks, and others), politics (Italian political system, national and regional legislatures, deputies, senators, political parties, and others), and geography (administrative division of Italy into regions, provinces, communes, detailed geographic composition of the Province of Trento in accordance with the Toponymy database[11]). All of the ontologies have been loaded into proper contexts of the repository presented in Sect. 4.

6.3   Semantic Enrichment of Named Entities

With relatively simple effort spent for creating the collection of knowledge for the contextualized repository, the execution of the semantic enrichment over the complete "L'Adige" dataset 45% of news articles has been enriched (272,253 article from total of 600,470 distinct news articles), counting if at least one recognized in article entity of type PER, LOC or ORG has been enriched. Clusters produced by coreference resolution algorithm have been mapped to the corresponding entities in the repository with the following numbers: 35% of people clusters, 42% of location clusters, and 2% of organization clusters. In order to perform the qualitative assessment of the performed enrichment we are planning to create in the near future the corresponding gold standard. Preliminary, using the gold standard for cross-document coreference evaluation of people [6], we have first manually attached to famous people clusters (i.e., those with ambiguous names, such as Paolo Rossi, Roberto Mancini, and etc.) their corresponding person entity available in the current version of the repository; and then we have performed the enrichment of the gold standard articles. As a result we got a fairly high precision of 91% when enriching these famous people due to the ability to recognize the specific detailed context (such as championship of the

---

[7] http://www.istat.it/dati/

[8] http://www.cameradicommercio.it/

[9] http://www.senato.it/, http://www.camera.it/

[10] http://www.coni.it/

[11] http://www.trentinocultura.net/territorio/toponomastica/

certain year in sport, or certain political legislature). Straightforwardly, when we disabled the consideration of context and performed the enrichment against the whole knowledge repository the precision fall down, because of the big number of wrong matches produced due to the name ambiguity problem.

7   Related Work

During the last decade the introduced semantic web vision has fostered the development and public sharing on the web of numerous structured resources containing the background knowledge on different domains of interest. Availability of high quality knowledge consequently drew attention to the development of systems for exploiting this knowledge. The task of semantic enrichment of text is one of such applications aiming at making computers comprehend and integrate the knowledge contained in text. From the number of integrated solutions for the semantic enrichment reported in the literature, we would like to mention several remarkable approaches which implement the complete semantic enrichment pipeline and are close to the one presented in this work, namely exploiting the notion of context.

In [2] the authors present the approach to using DBPedia for enriching and interconnecting the number of data sources within BBC.[12] The main idea of their system is to analyze the web pages on music offerings, TV channels and programs in order to provide contextual, semantic links for connecting and navigating the content described in different pages using the entities corresponding to artists, bands, musical albums, concerts, and etc. The interlinking approach with DBPedia exploits the notion of context' for disambiguation; the idea is to group entities co-occurring with one another in text and further to search for corresponding entities in the DBPedia such that they all fall into corresponding similarity cluster.

Enrycher, described in [14], is another similar example of the completely implemented pipeline for semantic enrichment of textual resources with the knowledge from DBPedia. In a similar vein, it exploits the notion of context in form of a group of co-occurring in text entities and further seeks to find a cluster of corresponding DBPedia entities matching those in context.

The main difference of the present study is that the background knowledge is "clustered" by construction of the repository into the contexts and the detection of context from a textual resource is based on its temporal and thematic analysis, rather than on co-occurrence of entities.

8   Conclusion and Future Extensions

In this work we presented the approach and implemented system for semantic enrichment of textual materials written in Italian with the background knowledge contextually relevant to a given text. A number of possible improvement steps

---

[12] http://bbc.co.uk

are planned for the future to increase the accuracy of the current version of the system and improve the overall utility and usability. On the one side, this means to improve the quality of extraction and enrichment, on the other side, this means to construct the practical services benefiting from the performed enrichment.

For entity disambiguation we currently considered only the mentions of type proper name available in text for finding matching entity in the knowledge repository. However, the state of the art named entity recognizers, as Typhoon we have used in the current implementation, are capable of extracting richer set of mentions, in particular, nominal expressions practically referring to the professions in case of people (such as "the mayor of Trento" for the entity "Alberto Pacher"), types of locations (such as city or lake), and types of organizations (such as gmbh or srl). We plan to elaborate that information in the future for establishing more accurate link to the repository.

The accuracy of the semantic enrichment crucially depends on the quality of the context detection from text: the topic, time and location. One of the simplifications in the proposed context detection scheme is the identification of relevant time by considering only the publication date of the text. We are working on attaching to the pipeline the recently developed Chronos system for automatic recognition in text of temporal expressions, and using them further to identify the temporal span of the article from these temporal expressions in a more sensitive, granular way.

As of the improvement of the background knowledge collection, we are currently exploiting the use of other publicly available structured resources of the background knowledge and the ability to import those into the presented contextualized knowledge repository. We are particularly interested in a high quality knowledge bases, such as for example Freebase[13] and DBPedia[14]. The crucial point for their applicability to the proposed semantic enrichment flow consists in the ability to partition these resources into the contexts, identified by temporal, spatial and thematic dimensions.

For the qualitative assessment of the enrichment procedure, in the near future we plan to work out the evaluation methodology and construct the gold standard for people/location/organization enrichment on top of the corresponding gold standard for evaluation of cross-document coreference.

Acknowledgements

This work has been supported by LiveMemories project (Active Digital Memories of Collective Life) funded for 2008-2011 by Autonomous Province of Trento under the call "Major Project". The authors express additional gratitude to Silvana Marianela Bernaola Biggio, Elena Cardillo, and to all members of the LiveMemories project contributing in different ways to the realization of the present work.

---

[13] http://www.freebase.com
[14] http://dbpedia.org

References

1. Ricca, F., Pianta, E., Tonella, P., Girardi, C.: Improving web site understanding with keyword-based clustering. Journal of Software Maintenance and Evolution: Research and Practice 20(1), 1–29 (2008)
2. Kobilarov, G., Scott, T., Raimond, Y., Oliver, S., Sizemore, C., Smethurst, M., Bizer, C., Lee, R.: Media meets semantic web – how the BBC uses dBpedia and linked data to make connections. In: Aroyo, L., Traverso, P., Ciravegna, F., Cimiano, P., Heath, T., Hyvönen, E., Mizoguchi, R., Oren, E., Sabou, M., Simperl, E. (eds.) ESWC 2009. LNCS, vol. 5554, pp. 723–737. Springer, Heidelberg (2009)
3. Broekstra, J., Kampman, A., van Harmelen, F.: Sesame: A Generic Architecture for Storing and Querying RDF and RDF Schema. In: Horrocks, I., Hendler, J. (eds.) ISWC 2002. LNCS, vol. 2342, pp. 54–68. Springer, Heidelberg (2002)
4. Carroll, J.J., Bizer, C., Hayes, P., Stickler, P.: Named graphs, provenance and trust. In: Proceedings of the 14th International Conference on World Wide Web (WWW-2005), pp. 613–622 (2005)
5. Ko, H.J., Kang, W.: Enhanced access control with semantic context hierarchy tree for ubiquitous computing. International Journal of Computer Science and Network Security 8(10), 114–120 (2008)
6. Bentivogli, L., Girardi, C., Pianta, E.: Creating a gold standard for person cross-document coreference resolution in italian news. In: Proceedings of the Workshop on Resource and Evaluation for Identity Matching, Entity Resolution and Entity Management (LREC-2008), Marrakech, Morocco, pp. 19–26 (2008)
7. Ding, L., Finin, T., Peng, Y., Pinheiro da Silva, P., McGuinness, D.L.: Tracking rdf graph provenance using rdf molecules (Poster paper). In: Gil, Y., Motta, E., Benjamins, V.R., Musen, M.A. (eds.) ISWC 2005. LNCS, vol. 3729, Springer, Heidelberg (2005) Poster paper
8. Liao, H.-C., Tu, C.-C.: A rdf and owl-based temporal context reasoning model for smart home. Information Technology Journal 6, 1130–1138 (2007)
9. Benerecetti, M., Bouquet, P., Ghidini, C.: On the dimensions of context dependence. In: Bouquet, P., Serafini, L., Thomason, R.H. (eds.) Perspectives on Contexts, ch. 1. CSLI Lecture Notes, pp. 1–18. Center for the Study of Language and Information/SRI (2007)
10. Speranza, M.: The named entity recognition task at evalita 2009. In: Proceedings of the Workshop Evalita 2009, Reggio Emilia, Italy (2009)
11. Nickles, M.: Social acquisition of ontologies from communication processes. Appl. Ontol. 2(3-4), 373–397 (2007)
12. Popescu, O., Magnini, B.: Web people search using name entities. In: Proceedings of the Workshop SemEval-2007, Prague, CZ (2009)
13. Zanoli, R., Pianta, E., Giuliano, C.: Named entity recognition through redundancy driven classifiers. In: Proceedings of the Workshop Evalita 2009, Reggio Emilia, Italy (2009)
14. Stajner, T., Rusu, D., Dali, L., Fortuna, B., Mladenic, D., Grobelnik, M.: Enrycher: service oriented text enrichment. In: Proceedings of the 11th International multiconference Information Society (IS-2009), Ljubljana, Slovenia (2009)

A Pragmatic Approach to Semantic Repositories Benchmarking

Dhavalkumar Thakker[1,2], Taha Osman[1], Shakti Gohil[1], and Phil Lakin[2]

[1] Nottingham Trent University, Clifton Lane, Nottingham NG11 8NS, UK
[2] Press Association, 16 Castle Boulevard, Pavilion House, Nottingham, UK
{Dhaval.Thakker,Phil.Lakin}@pressassociation.com,
{Taha.osman,N0239676}@ntu.ac.uk

Abstract. The aim of this paper is to benchmark various semantic repositories in order to evaluate their deployment in a commercial image retrieval and browsing application. We adopt a two-phase approach for evaluating the target semantic repositories: analytical parameters such as query language and reasoning support are used to select the pool of the target repositories, and practical parameters such as load and query response times are used to select the best match to application requirements. In addition to utilising a widely accepted benchmark for OWL repositories (UOBM), we also use a real-life dataset from the target application, which provides us with the opportunity of consolidating our findings. A distinctive advantage of this benchmarking study is that the essential requirements for the target system such as the semantic expressivity and data scalability are clearly defined, which allows us to claim contribution to the benchmarking methodology for this class of applications.

1 Introduction

Based on the concept of autonomous interpretation of machine-understandable meta-data, semantic web technologies can deliver intelligent management of user-transparent access to an increasingly complex mesh of interrelated information, which makes these technologies especially appealing to organizations with complex information taxonomy and rich data sets such as the BBC [1], Reuters [2] and Yahoo [3]. However, to promote the adoption of the semantic web technologies beyond organisations that are resourceful in technology-related innovation, clear benchmarks are required that indicate that the tools facilitating the deployment of the semantic technologies are capable of cost-effectively handling potentially enormous amounts of data and increasingly complex information structures. There are many aspects for the organisations to consider: the expertise required for semantically enabling the organization's information infrastructure, the costs involved in superimposing the extra layer of meta-data and the overheads related with processing it, the technical challenges in synchronising with existing data stores, etc. In this study, we focus on evaluating the computing engine of the semantic web technologies, semantic repositories (SR).

Kiryakov et al. define a semantic repository as "a tool, which combines the functionality of an RDF-based DBMS and an inference engine and can store data and

L. Aroyo et al. (Eds.): ESWC 2010, Part I, LNCS 6088, pp. 379–393, 2010.
© Springer-Verlag Berlin Heidelberg 2010

evaluate queries, regarding the semantics of ontologies and metadata schemata." [4]. As semantic technologies become more lucrative, an increasing number of commercial and freeware semantic repositories are being offered. These repositories vary significantly at a number of levels that might affect their deployment decision in the target systems, to mention few: supported query languages, semantic expressivity (reasoning capability), load and query response times, and scalability. It might also be necessary to analyze the combined effect of one or two parameters in the target systems, for instance the capacity of the semantic repositories in handling increasing dataset sizes has to be considered in tandem with the supported semantic expressivity and the retrieval throughput.

A distinctive feature of this study is that it is motivated by the practical deployment requirements for semantically-enabling an existing application for a digital images retailer's retrieval and browsing engine. This allows us to inform the benchmarking exercise about the precise essential and desirable requirements of the semantic repository, which we also claim presents a roadmap for benchmarking this rich class of applications.

We uniquely classify the benchmarking parameters into non-functional (analytical) and functional (practical). The analytical parameters, such as expected level of reasoning and query language support aid in narrowing down the pool of benchmarked semantic repositories, while the practical parameters such as the query response time helps to select the optimum repository for the target system.

In order to consolidate our results, we use a public benchmark that satisfies the requirements of our target system (the University Ontology benchmark - UOBM [5]), as well as devising a dataset from the applications knowledge base. This allows us to consolidate our results and vet them against published work on semantic repositories benchmarking.

The rest of the paper is structured as follows: section 2 surveys the current semantic repositories benchmarking approaches. Section 3 discusses the details the commercial deployment case study for benchmark. Section 4 studies the benchmarking methodology, while section 5 analyzes the experimental results. The paper's conclusion and plans for further work is detailed in section 6.

2   Benchmarking Semantic Web Technologies

Benchmarking semantic repositories is significantly more challenging than that of RDMS, primarily because of the complexity of evaluating the additional reasoning layer. For semantic repositories, unlike relational databases there exists no standard benchmark similar to TPC [6].

Benchmarking approaches can be classified into studies of the reasoning engines and studies of the semantic repositories (the RDF stores and the inferencing engine). The first approach [7] [8] mainly targets the description logic community or developers interested in optimising the reasoning engines and integrating them into their semantic datastores. This benchmarking exercise is motivated by the requirement of deploying semantic web technology in a commercial search and browsing engine, and hence is chiefly interested in benchmarking approaches evaluating ready-to-deploy semantic repositories. Below we discuss some of the published work on semantic repositories benchmarking.

The Lehigh University Benchmark LUBM [9] was the first standard platform to benchmark OWL systems, but it gradually fell behind with the increasing expressivity of OWL reasoning and could not support a modest reasoning logic such as OWL Lite [10]. The University Ontology Benchmark (UOBM) benchmark [5] was devised to improve the reasoning coverage of LUBM by adding TBox axioms that make use of all OWL Lite and OWL DL constructs. Both benchmarks predate the advent of the SPARQL RDF query language, and hence do not evaluate advanced query features such as OPTIONAL filters and UNION operations [11].

[12] introduces the Berlin SPARQL benchmark (BSBM) for comparing the performance of systems that expose SPARQL endpoints. The benchmark is built around an e-commerce use case, which extends its benefits to similar class of applications desiring to embrace semantic technologies. BSBM focuses provides comprehensive evaluation for SPARQL query features. However, the benchmark does not evaluate update operation on the RDF stores and has no information on precision/recall and primarily targets the throughput results with the assumption that the systems are precise and complete. The list of benchmarked systems by BSBM is not exhaustive.

All the works discussed above represent valuable contributions to the methodology of semantic technologies benchmarking and can also offer reusable datasets and query results at the practical level, which allow us to compare our results with other published benchmarking studies. However, we believe that for the decision to adopt a specific semantic repository for the deployment of our commercial application can only be based on a benchmarking study that mirrors the demands of our semantic retrieval and browsing engine within an enterprise setup. This entails using a similar dataset, evaluating the required level of expressivity, and considering the evaluation of all established semantic repositories including freeware systems such Jena TDB [13] and Sesame [14], as well as commercial offerings such as Allegrograph [15], Virtuoso [16] and BigOWLIM [17].

3 Commercial Deployment Case Study

This study has been conducted with a commercial deployment case study at the heart of its objectives. This section gives more details on the motivations of the exercise with the nature of the proposed application.

3.1 Motivation

Press Association (PA) is the UK's leading multimedia news and information provider and supplier of business-to-business media services. The photography arm of the PA, Press Association Images is looking into the utilization of semantic web technologies to improve the image browsing experience for their customers. Therefore this study focuses on the particular concerns of this implementation, such as the sheer volume of data and other fundamental performance measures such as load time, query response time and level of inference.

Along with gauging potential benefits of semantic technologies, our motivation to perform this benchmarking is to evaluate the scalability of current semantic technologies in handling potentially large datasets while maintaining reasoning and retrieval throughput. Our concern about the scalability stems from the fact that unplanned use of the OWL properties can result into impractical reasoning complexity. For the benefit of the reader, it is useful to highlight the complexity of the ontology we utilize in our implementation. The PA Images ontology in its current form has total 147 classes, 60 object properties and 30 data properties. The OWL species of the ontology is OWL-DL and the DL expressivity is ALCHOIN (D).

Apart from the standard classification hierarchy and object and data type properties, we utilize what we see as the "smart" properties of OWL. One example of these properties is the inverse property *"owl:inverseOf"*, which implicitly allows defining relationship in both directions [18]. For example, an application based on PA Images ontology has a relationship category where father-son, parent-child, husband-wife bi-directional relationship are heavily utilized. The other property which we find very useful is the value constraint in OWL-DL *"owl:hasValue"* that links a restriction class to a value. For example, "Actor is a person who has value for the property *profession* equal to *acting*". This is very useful property as it allows for the automatic classification of individuals into categories depending on the value of some of their properties. This is a desirable functionality as instead of relying on the annotator to remember category of an entity while entering data it could be automatically inferred based on the properties of entities.

These properties make reasoning challenging and require a level of language expressivity in the domains of OWL-LITE and OWL-DL. For example, when inverse properties are used in some of the reasoning engines, it prohibits the use of highly efficient optimization techniques [10]. The aim of this benchmarking study is to investigate how various repositories will handle such reasoning requirements while maintaining acceptable query response time.

As discussed, the PA Images ontology is light-weight DL ontology. For increasing the confidence of our benchmarking, we researched the availability of published benchmarks with datasets with characteristics similar to ours, i.e. datasets that support OWL-DL level of reasoning and contain few million triples. We selected UOBM for this purpose as the prime focus of the UOBM dataset has been inferencing and reasoning which meets our requirements. UOBM also supplies dataset of variable length ranging from 0.2 million triples in UOBM-1 to around 6.6 million triples in UOBM-30. We discarded using the BSBM [12] dataset as it is primarily designed to test Repositories in terms of RDF and SPARQL support instead of higher order of reasoning capabilities. The DBpedia [19] dataset was also not considered relevant to the task due to the lack of formal ontology structure in its datasets as it is governed by combination of external ontologies SKOS, UMBEL and WordNet in addition to its own custom ontology, making judgment on precision and recall challenging task.

3.2 PA Dataset

In this section, we provide useful information on the PA Dataset which contains three components: PA Images ontology, Knowledge base and image captions.

1. PA Images ontology
The first component of the dataset is layered owl-dl ontologies: one of these ontologies defines the entities in our domains primarily consisting of sports, news and entertainment images. This ontology contains entities such as footballers, sport teams, politicians, stadiums, tournaments, actors, award events. The set of ontologies contains another ontology – a media ontology defining image metadata attributes.

2. PA Knowledge base(KB)
PA KB is the data operating on the PA ontology. Manual generation of such data as part of a knowledge base is a colossal and quite cumbersome task. However, we alleviated the burden of manual compilation of creating such KB by leveraging the rich amount of structured knowledge publically available in DBpedia [19]. We see DBpedia being at the centre of the linked data cloud (LoD) efforts [20] mainly due to its knowledge coverage across multiple domains. LoD is a medium for domain experts to come together and share the knowledge about the domains they are expert in. We have successfully used SPARQL CONSTRUCT [11] queries to achieve ontology mapping between PA Images and DBpedia ontologies to extract the instances from DBpedia KB and generate a clean, contexualised PA KB.

3. Image captions
Image captions triples were generated randomly using an instance generator that links an image with list of entities from the KB. The images represent an adequate mixture of indices of People (player, actor, politician) at Events (Tournaments, Signing, Awards etc), or people seen with other people. Apart from the ontology, the dataset is expressed in N-Triples serialization fromat. Table 1 gives more information on the dynamics of PA dataset components.

Table 1. PA Dataset dynamics

Dataset	No of Triples	Entities/Images	Disk space
KB	6.6 Millions	1.2 Millions	1.23 GB
Image captions	8 Millions	5 Millions	1.57 GB
Schema			136 KB

4 Benchmarking Methodology

4.1 Semantic Repository Selection and Benchmarking Environment

We have selected the Semantic Repositories for this benchmarking based on the following selection criteria.

1. Minimum level of inference required is RDFS reasoning
2. Support for SPARQL or SPARQL-like RDF query language
3. As per the definition of the Semantic Repository, any tool that is combination of reasoner and storage backend. This criterion ruled out the selection of Pellet, Racer, and KAON2 as these tools need to be used in conjunction with the databases.

The repositories that satisfy the aforementioned criteria hence selected for bench-marking are: Virtuoso [16], Allegrograph [15], Sesame [14], Jena TDB [13], Oracle [23] and BigOWLIM [17].

Hardware Setup. The experiment was conducted on a DELL workstation (processor: Intel Core 2 Quad Q9400 2.66GHz; memory: 8GB DDR2 667; hard disks: 160GB (10,000 rpm) SATA2, 750GB (7,200 rpm) SATA2) running Windows XP profes-sional x64 edition, 2003, Service pack 2 as operating system using Java version 1.6.0_16.

4.2 Benchmarking Parameters

We uniquely classify the benchmarking parameters into non-functional (A=analytical) and functional (P=practical). This section gives more information on these parameters.

1. Identification of the Semantic Repositories storage technology in Native, Mem-ory-based or Database-based storage systems (A). Both native and database based techniques store data persistently while memory-based stores utilize main memory to store RDF graphs. The database technique uses RDBMS to store data while native store use a flat file structure. Understanding the behaviour of the semantic repositories in these classifications helps predicting the store's behaviour under various condi-tions, for example scalability of the memory based repositories will be limited to the amount of memory space available.
2. Identification of Semantic Repositories in forward, backward or hybrid chaining reasoning strategies (A). The forward-chaining repositories support materialisation where they compute and store the possible inferencing of facts at load time. The backward-chaining repositories perform the inferencing at the query time.
3. Load time (P) is a standard benchmarking parameter that measures the perform-ance of repositories in terms of the time it takes loading datasets. We believe that for the class of application similar to ours, update time is more relevant as the load time is generally one-off and could be performed offline. We cover update time in 6 below.
4. Using query response time (P), we measure the time for issuing a query and ob-taining the results. We have created a query-mix that exploits OWL-DL and OWL-Lite constructs from PA images ontology and we use the queries provided by the UOBM to exploits different construct of UOBM.
5. We use query results analysis (P) to measure completeness and correctness of the query results. The results of this analysis will allow us to judge a repository as sound, complete or both. With the query results analysis, where possible we also want to analyze the results to verify the OWL properties supported by a Semantic Repository under the dataset load in this experiment. The repositories advertise type of inferenc-ing supported by them however as observed by [7] [10], for larger datasets most of the tools seem to fail simplest of OWL reasoning queries.
6. Most triple-stores use SPARQL for querying RDF; however there is no stan-dardization for modification to RDF data. SPARQL/Update is an effort to standardize the update language for RDF graphs for updating graphs with modification opera-tions. The alternative is to use a programming language and custom APIs. With RDF store update tests (A&P) parameter, we test and analyze repositories by schemata and

data update queries and indentify the repositories that use either SPARQL/Update or custom APIs for doing so.

7. The identification of repository support for RDF serialization formats (A) allows us to study different serialisation (RDF/XML, N-Triples, N3, Turtle) offered by the repositories.

8. We also want to analyze the scalability (P) of the repositories, i.e. loading and querying time of semantic data is linear with the dataset sizes.

9. Reasoner Integration (A) is a parameter designed to identify the reasoners integration supported by a repository.

10. We will also identify query languages supported (A) by a repository.

11. Inferencing and reasoning is computationally challenging task and clustering support (A) is helpful for practical implementations. We want to identify semantic stores that supports clustering configuration in their standard setup.

12. From the application development perspective, we want to analyze the client API supported (A) in various programming languages.

13. Identification of different platform supported (A) by a semantic repository. This could be a crucial factor for many organisations.

14. The trend to move relational data to RDF graphs can be encouraged by repositories that have in-built support for converting relational data into RDF data (A). We will identify the stores that have in-built support for such functionality.

Table 2 Shows our observation for the selected repositories.

Table 2. Analytical Parameter observation

Parame ters	Jena TDB	Virtuoso	Allegrograph	BigOWLIM	Sesame	Oracle
Storage Type	Native	Native, RDBMS -based	Native	Memory, Native	Memory, Native, RDBMS	Native
Reasoni ng strategy	Backward chaining	Backward Chaining	Backward chaining	Forward chaining	Forward chaining	Forward chaining
Serializ ation format	rdf/xml, n3,ntriples	rdf/xml, n3	rdf/xml, n3, ntriples	rdf/xml, n3, triples	rdf/xml, n3, triples	rdf/xml, ntriples
Reason er Integrat ion	Built-in	Built-in, Jena, Sesame, Redland	Built-in, Jena, Racerpro, Sesame	Built-in, Sesame	Built-in	Built-in, Jena
RDFvie w support	No	Yes	Not conclusive	No	No	Not conclusive
RDF Update	sparql/ udpate	sparql/ update	api	api	api	api
Query Langua ge Support	tql, sparql	sparql, spasql	sparql, twinql, serql, prolog	sparql, serql	sparql, serql, rql	bespoke, sparql

Table 2. (*continued*)

Clusteri ng	No	Yes	Yes	Not conclusive	No	Not conclusive
Client side	Java	PL/SQL Java, C	Java, Python, Ruby, Lisp,	Java	Java	PL/SQL, Java
Platfor m support ed	Windows, Unix, Mac, Solaris	Windows Unix,Mac , Solaris	Mac, Windows, Unix, Solaris	Windows, Unix, Mac, Solaris	Windows, Unix, Mac, Solaris	Unix, Solaris, Windows, Mac
Licensi ng	Free	Free, Commerc ial	Free, Commercial	Free, Commercia l	Free	Commercia l

5 Benchmarking Results

5.1 UOBM Dataset Results and Analysis

UOBM Dataset Load timings. Although UOBM-30 is the super set of other datasets of UOBM, as an opportunity to gauge the load time scalability, we decided to load all the four datasets. The datasets were loaded in four different graphs as these datasets contain overlapping data and if loaded in the same graph it will generate redundancy and unexpected results when queried. The aim here was to evaluate the load time as the dataset size increases.

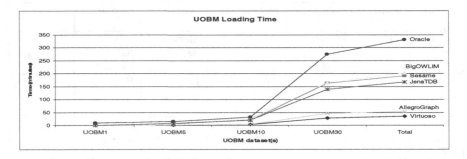

Fig. 1. UOBM Loading Time

From the graph in Figure 1, we can clearly identify that virtuoso performs best among these tools for loading A-Box by taking approx 27.5 minutes to load UOBM data-set with 30 university and allegro-graph is the closest competitor of virtuoso in loading data into a store. BigOWLIM performs second slowest among the tools as it performs the "forward-chaining" of facts and stores them explicitly. Oracle is the slowest in loading all four datasets as it take more time than BigOWLIM in forward chaining process. Another interesting observation can be made about the perform-ance of these repositories in terms of how well they scale for the increase in dataset sizes. Virtuoso and Allegrograph are quite consistent and scalable in terms of dataset sizes and takes almost same amount of time (linear) as the load increases.

Query Result and Execution Speed Analysis. UOBM supplied 15 queries with different levels of complexity where 12 queries fall under OWL-Lite and the remaining 3 queries are of OWL-DL expressivity. To our knowledge, the UOBM benchmark has not published a query result set. Therefore we had to generate the answer keys in order to enable checking the correctness and completeness of the returned results. We generated answer keys by modifying queries to remove complex inference and firing them against the benchmarked repositories. Our precision and recall analysis is based on this and for the scrutiny we publish the result sets [24].

Next, we analyze query response times taking into account the context of the precision and recall. In the Table 3, "N" against a query indicates empty result set when at least some results were expected. (P) next to a timing indicates that the repository took that much amount of time but returned partial results.

From Table 3, we can conclude that BigOWLIM answers 12 out of 15 queries completely while answering query no. 9 partially and performs the execution faster in most of the cases with the average time 0.038 seconds. Sesame answers 4 queries completely while answering 2 queries partially. Average time to answer these queries is 0.09 seconds. Allegrograph answers 7 queries completely, while answering 2 queries partially. However Allegrograph is the slowest and takes on average 219 seconds to answer queries. Virtuoso has the worst recall, as virtuoso answers 1 query partially and the other completely at the average speed of 3.388 seconds. We would also like to draw attention to virtuoso's different behaviour in answering a query from a SPARQL end-point and from the Jena Adapter API. From the API, Virtuoso repository is able

Table 3. UOBM Query execution speed and result analysis

No.	Execution Timings (seconds)					
	Virtuoso	Allegrograph	Oracle	Sesame	Jena TDB	BigOWLIM
Q1	6.766 (P)	21.921	0.141	0.203	0.031	0.047
Q2	N	8.906(P)	N	0.001(P)	0.001(P)	0.062
Q3	N	651.237	N	0.109	0.016	0.062
Q4	N	N(infinite)	N	0.14	120	0.063
Q5	N	1.281	N	N	N	0.047
Q6	N	1153.025	N	N	N	0.047
Q7	N	300.12	N	N	N	0.001
Q8	N	6.843(P)	N	N	N	0.031
Q9	N	N	N	N	N	0.031(P)
Q10	0	0.25	0.001(P)	0.001	0.001	0.016
Q11	N	N(infinite)	0.001(P)	0.094(P)	N(infinite)	0.062
Q12	N	476.507	N	N	N	0.016
Q13	N	N	N	N	N	N
Q14	N	N(infinite)	N	N	N	0.016
Q15	N	N	N	N	N	N

to answer only 2 query while from a SPARQL end-point it answer 3 queries. Moreover, for the UOBM query 1, virtuoso's SPARQL end-point returns 21 triple which is correct as well as complete but when we fire the same query from the API it returns 105 triples. 21 triples out of these 105 triples are correct. We believe that this can be attributed to a bug in the API implementation rather than problem with the soundness of the repository.

Jena TDB answers 4 queries completely while one partially. Average speed is 24 seconds which is skewed by the time it takes to answer Q4. Oracle answers 3 queries, among them one completely and two partially at the average speed of 0.048 seconds.

Closer examinations of queries show that queries Q5 and Q7 are not answered by all the repositories except Allegrograph and BigOWLIM. Queries Q5 and Q7 involves transitive (*owl:TransitiveProperty*) property based inference. As this is the case for both of the queries it is possible to conclude that this property is not supported by Virtuoso, Sesame, Jena TDB and Oracle. Q6 relies on semantic repositories to support (*owl:inverseOf*) and all except Allegrograph and BigOWLIM answers this query. However, to consolidate the conclusion that other tools do not yet support inverse property, we can rely on the PA Dataset results as the dataset includes some queries of the same complexity. Q10 requires symmetric property support and is correctly answered by all the SRs. Q13 requires support for OWL lite-level of cardinality and not answered by any of these tools. OWL Lite cardinality restrictions allow statements concerning cardinalities of value 0 or 1 i.e. min 1, max 1. Q15 requires support for dl-level of cardinality that is not answered by any of these tools.

At the time of compiling this paper, correspondence with the semantic technologies team at Oracle established that they introduced improved OWL reasoning capability in the new release of Oracle (11g Release 2). Unfortunately the release is currently not available for our benchmarking platform, Windows OS. Hence we decided to omit Oracle from experimentation with the PA Data set (below).

5.2 PA Dataset Experiment Analysis

Loading time for KB and Images. Allegrograph was able to load whole of the dataset in under 15 minutes. This result is inline with the UOBM results as it was comparatively

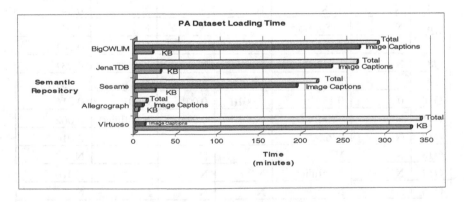

Fig. 2. PA Dataset Loading Timings

(second place to Virtuoso) faster. Similar to the UOBM benchmark results, BigOWLIM performs slower in loading PA datasets. This pattern repeats for Jena TDB and Sesame, which are again in the list of slower performers as is with UOBM results. However, the major difference in PA Dataset results from UOBM results is the performance of Virtuoso which took the least amount of time in loading all four of the UOBM datasets, for PA Dataset takes the maximum amount of the time among the repositories. There is an operational distinction between UOBM and PA Dataset, in which UOBM dataset is in RDF/XML serialization where PA Dataset is expressed in N-Triples. Virtuoso's Jena Adapter API lacks the functionality to load N-Triples and we had to load the PA Dataset using TTLP_MT function from the command line, which can explain the store's relatively lengthy loading time.

Query execution speed and results analysis. The list of PA Dataset queries is available here [24]. The results are outlined in Table 4Table 4. Carrying forward the observations from the UOBM query results, it is possible to conclude that inverse property of OWL expressivity as required to answer queries 6, 12, 15 is not supported by Virtuoso and Sesame.

In our tests, BigOWLIM was able to answer all the queries. Allegrograph answered all the queries except two. Sesame answered six queries completely while two queries partially. On a one-to-one comparison between Allegrograph and BigOWLIM , two repositories that answered maximum number of queries and between Sesame and BigOWLIM, two fastest repositories, it is clear to see that execution speed-wise BigOWLIM outperforms Allegrograph and sesame for almost all of the dataset queries.

Modifications Tests. Modifications to the data and ontology is an important task performed against a SR [12]. Although the complexity of modifications can change considerably across applications and usage patterns, the execution speed and correctness of modifications is vitally important for any commercial application. This area of

Table 4. PA Images Query Execution speed results

Query No.	Virtuoso	Allegrograph	Sesame	Jena TDB	BigOWLIM
Q1	2.234 (P)	26.422	0.469(P)	0.047	0.219
Q2	N	N	N	N	0.063
Q4	N	N	N	N	0.047
Q5	0.172	1.719	0.141	N	0.078
Q6	N	3.765	N	0.001	0.45
Q7	84.469	28.688	0.203	N	0.093
Q8	0.047	3.39	0.11	0.001	0.062
Q9	0.156	1.782	0.171	N	0.016
Q10	0.001	1.734	0.047	N	0
Q11	N	1.734	0.11	0.001	0.062
Q12	N	16.14	N	N	0.079
Q13	5.563(P)	1.812	0.016(P)	0.001	0.641
Q15	N	1.688	N	N	0.031

benchmarking has been ignored so far. As SPARQL specification in its current state provides no implementation of update or delete parameters these experiments also provide an insight to how each SR handles them in absence of standardization.

T-Box/ontology modifications. One of the main advantages of using a semantic ontology is the possibility of loose couplings of schemata from the data. In Virtuoso, the schema is loaded separately from the data and the repository requires any query to inform the SR which schema it shall use for the purpose of inferencing. This is done using *"define input:inference 'schema name'"* prefix as part of the query. We believe that this approach allows maximum loose coupling of data from schemata as the same dataset can be reasoned using different schemata. BigOWLIM protects and places restriction on deleting components of the base schema. In BigOWLIM, the schemata is stored as "imports" parameter of the repository configuration and are treated as "read-only", thus these schemata are protected from delete operations. Jena TDB, Oracle, Allegrograph expects an ontology to be present at its absolute or relative URL; hence modifications could be made to the schemata outside the scope of these repositories.

A-box Insertion operations. We believe that in most of the applications, loading of datasets of size of UOBM dataset is done once, while most of the loadings are insertion in small sizes. Here we test these tools on how they fare under small insertions and utilize the same methods we used for loading the whole of the dataset to perform insertions. The results in the Figure 3 illustrate this with small KB addition and small number of image additions to the PA Dataset. The results provide reassurance that all the repositories (virtuoso and Allegrograph when warmed up), can handle small amount of loading (insertions) relatively fast. It is also important to highlight here that all the repositories have approximately 12 million triples already stored when this loading call occurs.

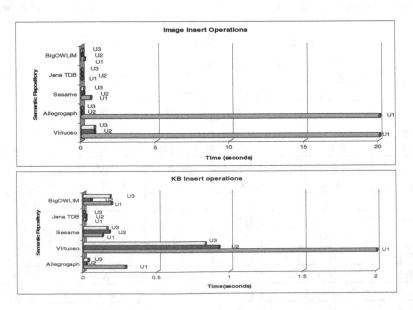

Fig. 3. Insertion operations

Table 5. Modification queries

U1= updating two actors relationship from "partner" to "spouse", U2= updating an image caption to identify previously incorrectly identified person, U3= updating ontology to make "Person" and "Group" classes to be disjoint classes., D1= Deleting relationship between two British Royalty., D2= Deleting a player's playing position, D3= Deleting a band's genre

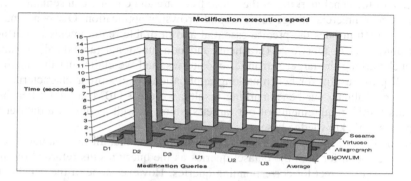

Fig. 4. Modification operation results

Update and deletion operations.

Again, similar to the small data insertions, it is important to test these SRs on their performance on small routine deletion or updates (Table 5) that happens in small amounts but in higher frequency. The aim here is to analyze the execution speed and also determine how they deal with modifications in the absence of a standardized SPARQL protocol. We treat the update and delete queries in the same frame and display and compare in the same graph (Figure 4). This is because for most of these tools the update operation is two step operation: a. delete a fact and b. insert a new fact instead of the deleted fact.

In BigOWLIM, deletion of the fact is performed from the API, as the repository does not implement a customized extension of SPARQL. There is also an area of concern for this class of repository that utilizes "forward chaining" as by nature the delete operation is slow, i.e. any fact deletion shall also delete any other facts that are inferred based on them. We found that the latest version of BigOWLIM (3.2.3) provided to us with a major improvement in delete operation, which means that upon delete, BigOWLIM invalidates only the inferred facts which are no longer inferable as opposed to dropping all inferred facts and inferring everything from scratch. However in these experiments, whenever this process (invalidating only the inferred facts) was involved such as in the query D2 the performance of system is slower than other simpler delete operations.

Allegrograph deals with the deletion of triples from the store using the base API and the execution speed is quite fast. Similar to Jena, Virtuoso provides an extension of SPARQL for the update and deletes queries. Using the SPARQL/UPDATE queries, Virtuoso runs very fast. We were not able to perform similar operations with Jena TDB as it runs out of the memory for each of these operations.

6 Conclusions and Future Work

Utilising semantic web technologies in commercial applications requires confidence by the decision makers that the underlying semantic repositories can deliver the required quality of service while managing the overhead of processing the metadata of potentially huge amount of information organized in complex taxonomies. This paper investigates the benchmarking of the major freeware and commercial semantic repositories for a commercial image retrieval and browsing application. Our benchmarking methodology translates the precise essential and desirable requirements of our application into a set of functional (practical) and non-functional (analytical) parameters for benchmarking the target semantic repositories, and we claim that this methodology will prove useful for benchmarking applications with similar characteristics. In order to consolidate our benchmarking results, we use UOBM, a public benchmark that satisfies the requirements of our target system, as well as devise a dataset from the application's knowledge base.

Our analysis of the benchmarking results established that all the evaluated repositories were sound for both the dataset queries as the query results returned by the repositories were correct for corresponding queries. However none of the benchmarked repositories were able to answer all the queries in the UOBM dataset, and hence we conclude that the evaluated repositories currently cannot handle the OWL reasoning level required to answer the UOBM queries.

In our tests, BigOWLIM provides the best average query response time and answers maximum number of queries for both the datasets. Sesame, Jena, Virtuoso and Oracle offered sub-second query response time for the majority of queries they answer. Allegrograph answers more queries than the former four repositories hence offers better coverage of OWL properties. However, we found that the average query response time for Allegrograph was the highest for both the dataset and believe that this repository requires further optimisation to handle complex OWL capabilities. The modifications operations testing confirmed that the forward chaining repositories offer slower response times compared to the backward chaining repositories. This is especially more noticeable for delete operation where sesame was consistently and BigOWLIM was variably slower in deleting triples.

Our plans for further work involve expanding this benchmark exercise to billion triples of extended PA Dataset and adding extra benchmarking parameters such as the performance impact of concurrent users and transaction-related operations. We would also like to test the new capabilities of the Oracle's semantic repository.

References

[1] Kobilarov, G., Scott, T., Raimond, Y., Oliver, S., Sizemore, C., Smethurst, M., Bizer, C., Lee, R.: Media meets semantic web – how the BBC uses dBpedia and linked data to make connections. In: Aroyo, L., Traverso, P., Ciravegna, F., Cimiano, P., Heath, T., Hyvönen, E., Mizoguchi, R., Oren, E., Sabou, M., Simperl, E. (eds.) ESWC 2009. LNCS, vol. 5554, pp. 723–737. Springer, Heidelberg (2009)

[2] http://www.opencalais.com/

[3] Mika, P.: Microsearch: An Interface for Semantic Search. In: Proceedings of the Workshop on Semantic Search (SemSearch 2008) at the 5th European Semantic Web Conference (ESWC 2008), Tenerife, Spain, June 2, vol. 334. CEUR-WS.org (2008)

[4] Kiryakov, A.: Measurable Targets for Scalable Reasoning, Ontotext Technology White Paper (November 2007)

[5] Ma, L., Yang, Y., Qiu, Z., Xie, G., Pan, Y., Liu, S.: Towards a Complete OWL Ontology Benchmark. In: Sure, Y., Domingue, J. (eds.) ESWC 2006. LNCS, vol. 4011, pp. 125–139. Springer, Heidelberg (2006)

[6] TPC Database Benchmark,
http://www.tpc.org/information/benchmarks.asp

[7] Bock, J., Haase, P., Ji, Q., Volz, R.: Benchmarking OWL Reasoners. In: Proc. of the ARea2008 Workshop, Tenerife, Spain (June 2008)

[8] Gardiner, T., Horrocks, I., Tsarkov, D.: Automatic benchmarking of description logic reasoners. In: Proceedings of the 2006 International Workshop on Description Logics (DL06), Windermere, UK (2006)

[9] Guo, Y., Pan, Z., Heflin, J.: An evaluation of knowledge base systems for large OWL datasets. In: McIlraith, S.A., Plexousakis, D., van Harmelen, F. (eds.) ISWC 2004. LNCS, vol. 3298, pp. 274–288. Springer, Heidelberg (2004)

[10] Weithöner, T., Liebig, T., Luther, M., Böhm, S.: What's Wrong with OWL Benchmarks? In: Proceedings of the Second International Workshop on Scalable Semantic Web Knowledge Base Systems (SSWS 2006), Athens, GA, USA (November 2006)

[11] http://www.w3.org/TR/rdf-sparql-query/

[12] Bizer, C., Schultz, A.: Benchmarking the Performance of Storage Systems that expose SPARQL Endpoints. In: Proceedings of the ISWC Workshop on Scalable Semantic Web Knowledge-base systems (SSWS), Karlsruhe, Germany (2008)

[13] http://openjena.org/TDB/

[14] Broekstra, J., Kampman, A., Harmelen, A.v.: Sesame: A generic architecture for storing and querying RDF and RDF schema. In: Horrocks, I., Hendler, J. (eds.) ISWC 2002. LNCS, vol. 2342, p. 54. Springer, Heidelberg (2002)

[15] http://www.franz.com/agraph/allegrograph/

[16] Erling, O., Mikhailov, I.: RDF Support in the Virtuoso DBMS. In: Proceedings of the 1st Conference on Social Semantic Web (CSSW), pp. 7–24. Springer, Heidelberg (2009)

[17] Kiryakov, A.: OWLIM: balancing between scalable repository and light-weight reasoner. In: Developer's Track, WWW 2006 (2006)

[18] http://www.w3.org/TR/owl-guide/

[19] Auer, S., Bizer, C., Cyganiak, R., Ives, Z.: DBpedia: A Nucleus for a Web of Open Data. In: 2nd Asian Semantic Web Conference, Springer, Heidelberg (2007)

[20] Hausenblas, M.: Exploiting Linked Data to Build Web Applications. IEEE Internet Computing 13(4), 68–73 (2009)

[21] Ding, Z., Peng, Y., Pan, R., Yu, Y.: A Bayesian Methodology towards Automatic Ontology Mapping. In: Proceedings of the AAAI-05 C&O Workshop on Contexts and Ontologies: Theory, Practice and Applications. AAAI Press, Menlo Park (2005)

[22] Mongiello, M., Totaro, R.: Automatic Ontology Mapping for Agent Communication in an e-Commerce Environment. In: Bauknecht, K., Pröll, B., Werthner, H. (eds.) EC-Web 2005. LNCS, vol. 3590, pp. 21–30. Springer, Heidelberg (2005)

[23] http://www.oracle.com/technology/tech/semantic_technologies/index.html

[24] http://realizingsemanticweb.blogspot.com/2010/03/benchmarking.html

A Web-Based Repository Service for Vocabularies and Alignments in the Cultural Heritage Domain

Lourens van der Meij[1,2], Antoine Isaac[1,2], and Claus Zinn[3]

[1] Vrije Universiteit Amsterdam
[2] Koninklijke Bibliotheek, Den Haag
{lourens,aisaac}@few.vu.nl
[3] Max Planck Institute for Psycholinguistics, Nijmegen
claus.zinn@mpi.nl

Abstract. Controlled vocabularies of various kinds (*e.g.*, thesauri, classification schemes) play an integral part in making Cultural Heritage collections accessible. The various institutions participating in the Dutch CATCH programme maintain and make use of a rich and diverse set of vocabularies. This makes it hard to provide a *uniform* point of access to all collections at once. Our SKOS-based vocabulary and alignment repository aims at providing technology for managing the various vocabularies, and for exploiting semantic alignments across any two of them. The repository system exposes web services that effectively support the construction of tools for searching and browsing across vocabularies and collections or for collection curation (indexing), as we demonstrate.

1   Introduction

Cultural Heritage (CH) collections are typically indexed with metadata derived from a range of different vocabularies or Knowledge Organization Systems (KOS, *e.g.*, thesauri, classification schemes, subject lists), such as the Art & Architecture Thesaurus (see http://www.getty.edu/research/conducting_research/vocabularies/aat/), Iconclass (http://www.iconclass.nl/), but also in-house standards. This makes it hard to facilitate uniform access to multiple collections in a semantically interoperable way. The aim to unify the main CH vocabularies into a standard, commonly-accepted vocabulary to use for all—and to migrate all metadata to such a new, overarching standard—is deemed unrealistic. Vocabularies evolved over many years, and will so in the future; also, there are good reasons for domain-, collection-, or institution-specific organisations of CH objects. A *vocabulary matching* approach acknowledges this, and aims at mapping together those concepts of any two given vocabularies that are semantically related to each other. Such vocabulary alignments can then be exploited to facilitate access to multiple collections via the vocabulary of a single one.

L. Aroyo et al. (Eds.): ESWC 2010, Part I, LNCS 6088, pp. 394–409, 2010.

The STITCH project (http://stitch.cs.vu.nl) of the Dutch CATCH programme (http://www.nwo.nl/CATCH) and the European TELplus project (www.theeuropeanlibrary.org/telplus/) investigated methods to support metadata interoperability by automatically identifying inter-vocabulary semantic mappings [1,2]. They showed that the automatic matching of vocabularies can be the basis of various real-world usage scenarios, including support for indexing and re-indexing collection items, inter-collection search and navigation, but also thesaurus management [3,4]. First tools for vocabulary services have been deployed at the National Library of the Netherlands, so that there is indeed an industrial uptake of Semantic Web technology in this context.

Our projects have dealt with a good number of industrial-strength, real-world vocabularies; they have used third party tools, but also developed in-house prototypes to align those vocabularies. A considerable effort was needed to convert the vocabularies' format to make them satisfy the input requirements of the various matching tools. Moreover, the output of some matching tools lacked precise definitions, so that higher-level tools (say, to support indexing) had to rely on interpretations of produced mappings, especially with respect to the *type* of mapping relation used. To support various applications that exploit (or contribute in creating) networks of vocabularies, we felt the need to adopt standardized middleware-level repository services, which we have subsequently developed and which is reported herein. Our middleware for managing vocabularies and their mappings is explicitly targeted at CH technologists, acknowledging the fact that the KOSs of CH institutions, and the application contexts where they are used, share many common features as well as a core of data management requirements.

Research on repository services for Semantic Web ontologies is very active. We focused on selecting and combining those elements from existing APIs and repositories that fit our application scenarios best. Rather than providing a framework for dealing with ontologies in general, we aim at technology to tackle the CH applications at hand. For this, we marry a simpler vocabulary modelling approach with results from the ontology alignment community, taking into account CH issues such as data distribution, scalability and maintenance. We have thus chosen to build our vocabulary and alignment repository services on the basis of a SKOS-based format for vocabularies to give unified, effective and fast access to vocabularies and vocabulary alignments, or their parts. Our semantic middleware is implemented as a distributed web-based architecture. Higher-level tools can now use the services, for instance, to look-up a concept within a vocabulary, to identify the vocabularies where a given concept occurs, to get all related concepts for a given concept within a vocabulary, or across vocabularies by exploiting concept mappings.

In the remainder of the paper, we discuss the repository services in greater detail. Sect. 2 discusses use cases, requirements, and other background, while Sect. 3 introduces data model and design, and lists the main services. Sect. 4 describes the current state of our middleware, and three demonstrator systems we have built with it; Sect. 5 concludes the paper with a discussion.

2   Use Cases, Requirements and Background

While the design of our repository services takes into account general needs of vocabulary experts, its current implementation responds to direct requirements of the STITCH project and its umbrella programme CATCH [4].

2.1   Use Cases and User Requirements

Indexing support. Support CH staff in finding a concept in a given vocabulary, for instance, through term search, including auto-completion, or vocabulary navigation (browsing concept hierarchies). Similarly, return other information attached to concepts such as preferred or alternative labels (possibly across languages), scope notes, or the semantic relationship of the concept in question to other concepts (following broader-than, narrower-than or related-to links). CH staff can then use the result of concept search to annotate literary works, for instance, with appropriate concept labels.

Semantic search and browsing. Support expert and novice users in performing semantic search across multiple collections, e.g., exploiting the object-concept links established by indexing staff. Where a search query returns insufficient hits, replace (some of) its search terms by others that are semantically broader than the given ones. Where CH items of interests are described by concepts of a different vocabulary, replace user-given search terms with equivalent or related terms of the other vocabulary (for the collections and their vocabularies at hand). Moreover, give users browsing access across any two collections using the vocabulary of one or the other, and an alignment between them.

Uniform vocabulary format and storage. Convert the vocabularies of a given CH institution into an electronic and uniform format, and store resulting data in a vocabulary repository; adapt existing CH software to access the new format (supporting the import/export of vocabulary from/to the repository).

Alignment management. Store an alignment between two given vocabularies in a uniform format, and allow users to browse alignment data, add new mappings, and to remove or modify existing mappings. Give access to individual mappings to support the attachment of evaluation marks. Provide support for the combination of existing alignments into a new one, or for selecting an alignment's subset given, say, some confidence threshold. Facilitate the testing of automatic alignment techniques by providing support to compare computed alignments with gold standard reference alignments.

Technical requirements. The vocabulary server should store all data in a commonly accepted format, preferably SKOS, the proposed W3C standard for porting Knowledge Organization Systems on the Semantic Web [5]. It ought therefore to support most of SKOS' constructs such as labels, semantic relations, and documentation aspects. API service functionality should meet the requirements stemming from the use cases and meet community best practices. Also, the vocabularies shall be restorable from their RDF sources. Moreover, the architecture shall provide authorization methods to facilitate the implementation of various access levels (*e.g.*, to support the updating or versioning of thesaurus data).

An architecture that builds upon a simple "standard" RDF repository is clearly not sufficient to satisfy all requirements at once. SPARQL, for instance, does neither support full text search in labels without appropriate extension nor the advanced sorting of results, which is often required for, *e.g.*, user interaction. It is also hard to constrain SPARQL queries to data subsets (restricted access), or guarantee fast response time when allowing arbitrary rather than optimized SPARQL queries. Consequently, our architecture cannot simply be a front-end to an RDF repository containing uncontrolled RDF triples. Neverthess, it makes use of RDF repositories, but all access is via a simple but standardized interface to (a part of) SKOS.

2.2   Background

There is an increased interest in services and technology around KOS resources. A recent JISC report reviews the state of the art in this area, in particular, with regard to vocabulary types, indicative use cases, best practise guidelines and current research [6]. Services and/or APIs such as [7,8,9,10,11,12,13,14] offer the functionality for accessing common vocabulary features, and are mostly compatible with KOS standards like SKOS, both for serving/exporting or ingesting data.

Following the spirit of the SKOS standard, KOS alignments are expressed in those tools by simple RDF triple statements. A more expressive representation is required, however, to meet realistic application requirements such as the ones we encountered in CATCH [4]. Here, mappings need to have properties of their own, for instance, "confidence measure", "producer", or "evaluated as". This issue is only acknowledged by [10,14]; and the approach of [8] is more motivated by the *provenance* problem rather than guided by the need to serving representations specifically adequate to alignment management.

The design of our middleware is inspired by the influential work of Euzenat [15] for the Ontology Alignment Evaluation Initiative (OAEI, see http://oaei. ontologymatching.org), who proposes a representation for alignments that is compatible with KOS (and SKOS) practices. To the best of our knowledge, our middleware is the only one that implements the frameworks introduced in both the KOS and the ontology matching community.

It is important to notice that the design of our middleware was purely driven by practical end-user and application requirements in the context of the STITCH project (and the larger CATCH umbrella). Our services thus cater for CH practitioners who expect computer-supported means for managing simple KOSs following well-established CH usages or workflows.

While ontology portals and services such as NeON [16] or BioPortal [17] also make use of the OAEI framework, they seem to have a more generic approach by supporting fully-fledged formal ontologies; in comparison, we are aiming at a different level of complexity, lowering the barrier for tool use in practise. This emphasis on simplicity also holds in comparison with other simple KOS-based services such as the aforementioned ones. Rather than providing users with advanced functionality such as calculating semantic proximity between two concepts based on the structure of KOSs [7], we deliberately focused on infrastructural work around core functionality, upon which one can later build more application-specific tools.

3   Service Description

In this section, we describe the data modelling approaches we followed, the overall design of the repository's architecture, and the various vocabulary and alignment services that our middleware provides.

3.1   Data Model

The data model builds upon SKOS and the alignment exchange format used in the Ontology Matching community [15].

SKOS. SKOS represents the elements of a KOS as *concepts*, provides them with various kinds of labels and documentation notes, and allows linking them together by three types of semantic relations, namely *broader*, *narrower* and *related*. SKOS represents entire KOSs as *concept scheme* objects, with explicit references to the concepts they contain. SKOS *collections* represent meaningful groupings of concepts within a KOS such as "persons by age." SKOS also provides a mechanism for the creation of RDF data. For instance, concepts are represented as resources with the `skos:Concept` class as type, and the property `skos:prefLabel` is used to indicate a concept's preferred lexicalization.

Our service supports the manipulation of the SKOS RDF constructs for data representation and exchange. The only exceptions are collection-related constructs, since such groupings of concepts were not observed in the thesauri at hand, and in many other KOSs.[1]

Unfortunately, SKOS lacks the ability to represent *concept subschemes* that belong semantically or functionally to a *concept scheme*. The GTT thesaurus used at the National Library of the Netherlands, for instance, is divided into 8 sub-vocabularies: "general subjects", "places", "genres" *etc.* We have therefore introduced the notion of *concept scheme groups* to represent the inclusion of KOSs into larger sets that can be used as concept schemes themselves.

OAEI format. OAEI represents individual mappings between concepts as *mapping cells* that indicate the type of relation that holds between these concepts, as well as a confidence measure. In addition, a cell may contain other metadata, for instance, users' assessment or evaluation of the mapping. OAEI also provides

---

[1] See the "vocabulary usage" section of the SKOS implementation report, http://www.w3.org/2006/07/SWD/SKOS/reference/20090315/implementation.html

explicit representations at the *alignment level*, allowing users to manipulate (*e.g.*, for composing alignments) or evaluate the result of matching efforts on a group basis by attaching metadata to the *alignment* resource itself.

When using the OAEI data model to represent mapping cells, we explicitly re-use the SKOS relations *exactMatch*, *closeMatch*, *broadMatch*, *narrowMatch* and *relatedMatch* as relation types. This illustrates the complementarity between the two models: SKOS does not support the annotations of mappings as we need it; on the other hand, OAEI does not make any commitment with regards to the semantic type of relations that mappings assert. SKOS mapping properties support the appropriate types to fill this gap.

3.2   Design

Fig. 1 depicts the interaction between the components of the vocabulary and alignment services. It considers an example case where alignment data comes from one (local) store, while vocabulary data is accessed from two data stores (one local store and one remote store).

Our vocabulary and alignment services, which have been implemented using Java, provide an abstract data access layer on top of existing RDF repositories. Implementations of the interface `VocabularyAndAlignmentAccess` support, for instance, the plug-in of SPARQL endpoints, and connections to different versions of local or remote RDF stores such as Sesame (see `http://openrdf.org`) via their API. The services can be accessed over SOAP (using the Apache Axis implementation, see `http://ws.apache.org/axis/`), or locally. Local access is being used by dedicated servlets that provide a simple HTTP REST-like access (see Sect. 4.2).

Crucially, a repository service instance can be connected to several vocabulary data sources at the same time, each of them providing its own set of vocabular-ies. Instances of our `SKOSAccess` interface for vocabularies may indeed connect to a single RDF source or to multiple other instances wrapped around differ-ent sources—as for the `SKOSMultiConnection` in Fig. 1. For this, instances of `SKOSAccess` make public the vocabularies or alignments they contain, which allows a repository service aggregating them to distribute data queries to the various sources available, and merge the obtained results. This allows our archi-tecture to easily scale up to dozens of vocabularies. It also makes it easier to maintain updates of vocabularies, or authorization mechanisms, as the owners of vocabularies can choose to implement and control their own components among the sources of a central repository.

We have chosen a similar distributed approach for vocabulary and alignment data. KOS and alignment providers (or consumers) may indeed come from dif-ferent institutions. Some actors may publish vocabularies without seeking to align them to external sources, while others would establish alignments between vocabularies they do not own. Whenever possible, we thus packaged the vocabu-lary and alignment functions into two distinct service specifications. This allows interested implementors to focus on just one dimension, while still fitting the wider picture.

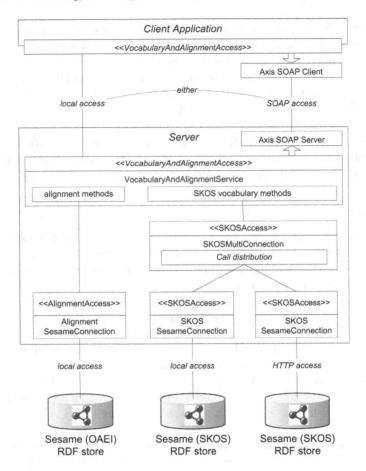

Fig. 1. Service architecture—angle brackets indicate the main interfaces implemented

3.3 Web Services Overview

Vocabularies. Entire KOSs can be imported to and exported from a repository. As required by CH institutions, the import function keeps track of the original information sources, so that the export function is capable of returning the exact copy of the original import (enabling lossless round-trips), leaving out potential later KOS enrichments (*e.g.*, when inference added new statements to a KOS' content).

The services give access to the *metadata* of the concept schemes and their groupings. There is functionality to search for schemes whose labels match a given string. Search can be restricted by specifying the type of label, or a label's language. Search results can be sorted or filtered given user-defined ranges, and are returned either as URI references, structured descriptions (*i.e.*, Java objects) or simple URI/label couples. Knowing a KOS' URI, there are methods to access either all of the KOS' concepts or only its "top" elements.

Access to KOS data (concepts, relations) is centered on concepts, which can be searched based on their (different types of) labels and notes, with similar options for sorting, filtering and output. There is also a method that returns all concepts which are semantically related to a given concept; here, standard SKOS relations are followed, but this can be easily extended to include other relation types of the KOS in question, if defined. Moreover, unlike traditional KOS approaches, in SKOS it is possible for a concept to belong to more than one concept scheme. Our implementation therefore allows users to specify the scheme to which the sought connected concepts shall belong, thus addressing a concept's potential multiple provenance.

The KOS services do not provide editing functionality. Here, we assume the existence and use of purpose-built tools that fit best each CH institute's existing workflow. Moreover, KOSs are more stable than alignments. Nonetheless, the versioning of KOS updates is an issue, which has not yet been dealt with satisfactorily within the SKOS community.

Alignments. Entire alignments can be imported and exported. All functionality for the creation and management of new alignments was inspired by Euzenat's Alignment API functions [15]. New alignments can result from subjecting existing alignments to e.g., filtering, intersection or union operations, the implementation of which is left to future extensions. A plug-in mechanism supports the integration of automatic alignment methods, in particular, with support for accessing existing KOSs of the vocabulary repository.

There are also methods for comparing alignments. Such comparisons form the basis for evaluation use cases where automatically generated alignments are set against existing reference alignments. The result of such a comparison, which is by default specified as a structured object, can be extended to reflect specific needs—precision, recall, various f-measures for evaluation; overlap and inclusion for more neutral comparison purposes *etc.*

The management of an alignment's metadata follows the standard OAEI format, but there are provisions for custom annotations to fit specific needs. All metadata is searchable to find all alignments that link together any given two vocabularies.

The individual *mapping cells* of an alignment can also be accessed. There is support to iterate through its (indexed) cells, but also to search for cells that match a given combination of concepts, mapping relation type and confidence measure. This facilitates access to cells that are not given a URI (blank nodes). The output can be sorted according to (extensible) presentation strategies.

Alignments are editable. Individual cells can be added to or removed from alignments, or modified. Cell metadata can be accessed and edited in a flexible way, *e.g.*, to reflect specific annotations resulting from a mapping's manual assessment.

4   Current Status

4.1   Repository Instances

At Vrije Universiteit (VU), we have deployed a repository instance hosting SKOS versions of five (groups of) vocabularies: *Iconclass*, a classification to describe images, *RAMEAU*, the subject headings of the French National Library, *Brinkman*, a thesaurus used at the National Library of the Netherlands, the noun subset of *Wordnet* and *RACM Glas*, an archeology KOS to describe glass material. Due to licensing issues, we have also deployed a richer, privately accessible, instance with nine additional KOSs used in the CATCH context. In total, we converted 10 out of the 13 KOSs to SKOS in the STITCH and TELPlus projects; the creation of two others was a joint effort with other research teams. The non-public instance now contains more than 1,700,000 concepts; its underlying (in-memory) RDF stores consume 6 GB of memory. Access to the service and further details, including statistics, are given at `http://stitch.cs.vu.nl/repository`, also see Appendix.

At the time of writing, the two service instances also host 15 alignments between various vocabularies to amount to almost a million mapping cells. In part, they were produced using lexical (using the concepts' labels) or instance-based (using objects annotated with the concepts) matching techniques as investigated in STITCH and TELplus [1,2]; in part they were created manually in the context of other projects.

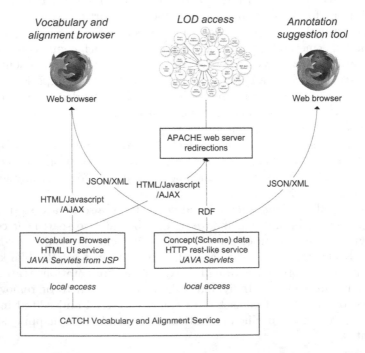

Fig. 2. Three deployments accessing the vocabulary and alignment services

4.2   Service Demonstrators

We have implemented three demonstrators, which are connected to our repository service instances as shown in Fig. 2.

Vocabulary and alignment browser. The *vocabulary and alignment browser*, shown in Fig. 3, consists of servlets that connect to a service instance to produce content (HTML, Javascript, AJAX) in response to browser-based user requests.

Fig. 3. Concept Information Service, HTML view

The demonstrator features an autocompletion function that helps users to search for concepts by partially typing concept labels. It supports the generation of RDF, JSON, and UI-oriented XML data for all elements viewed (see Fig. 4(b)). Also, RDFa markup [18] is included in all generated pages, see Fig. 4(a). Elementary data access functionality is implemented by a specific set of servlets, which then provide a HTTP REST-like access interface to services.

RAMEAU subject headings as linked data. In the TELplus project we converted the RAMEAU vocabulary of the French National Library to SKOS and ingested the result into our repository. We then implemented the recipes of [19] to have HTTP requests for RAMEAU concept URIs redirected so as to provide either HTML or RDF representation of these concepts, following the Linking Open Data (LOD) principles (see http://linkeddata.org/). This

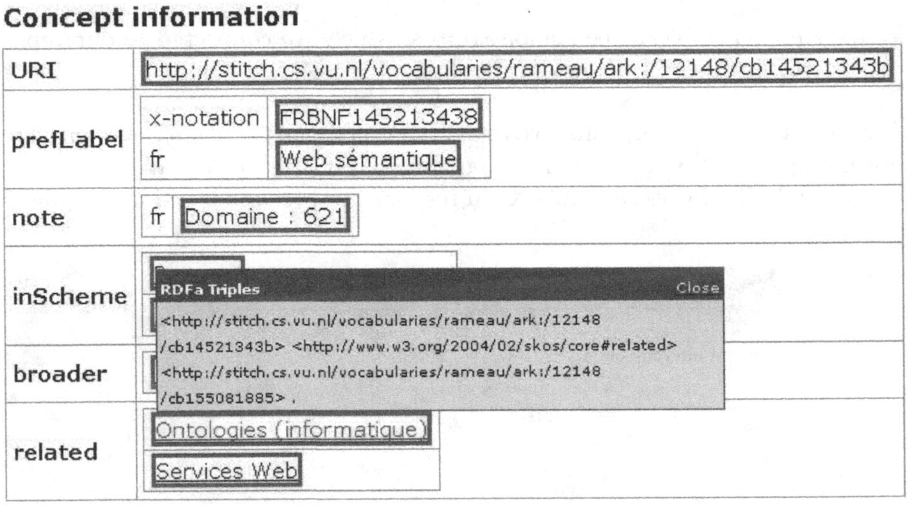

Concept information

URI	http://stitch.cs.vu.nl/vocabularies/rameau/ark:/12148/cb14521343b	
prefLabel	x-notation	FRBNF145213438
	fr	Web sémantique
note	fr	Domaine : 621
inScheme		
broader		
related	Ontologies (informatique)	
	Services Web	

RDFa Triples   Close

<http://stitch.cs.vu.nl/vocabularies/rameau/ark:/12148
/cb14521343b> <http://www.w3.org/2004/02/skos/core#related>
<http://stitch.cs.vu.nl/vocabularies/rameau/ark:/12148
/cb155081885> .

(a) RDFa markup—highlight with RDFa Bookmarklet

```
<rdf:RDF>
  <skos:Concept rdf:about="http://stitch.cs.vu.nl/vocabularies/rameau/ark:/12148/cb14521343b">
    <skos:prefLabel xml:lang="x-notation">FRBNF145213438</skos:prefLabel>
    <skos:prefLabel xml:lang="fr">Web sémantique</skos:prefLabel>
    <skos:note xml:lang="fr">Domaine : 621</skos:note>
    <skos:inScheme rdf:resource="http://stitch.cs.vu.nl/vocabularies/rameau/autorites_matieres"/>
    <skos:inScheme rdf:resource="http://stitch.cs.vu.nl/vocabularies/rameau/noms_communs"/>
    <skos:broader rdf:resource="http://stitch.cs.vu.nl/vocabularies/rameau/ark:/12148/cb13319953j"/>
    <skos:related rdf:resource="http://stitch.cs.vu.nl/vocabularies/rameau/ark:/12148/cb144109034"/>
    <skos:related rdf:resource="http://stitch.cs.vu.nl/vocabularies/rameau/ark:/12148/cb155081885"/>
    <skos:related rdf:resource="http://stitch.cs.vu.nl/vocabularies/rameau/ark:/12148/cb155081885"/>
    <skos:related rdf:resource="http://stitch.cs.vu.nl/vocabularies/rameau/ark:/12148/cb144109034"/>
  </skos:Concept>
  <rdf:Description rdf:about="http://stitch.cs.vu.nl/alignments/macs/manual_rameau_lcsh">
    <align:map>
      <align:Cell>
        <align:entity1 rdf:resource="http://stitch.cs.vu.nl/vocabularies/rameau/ark:/12148/cb14521343b"/>
        <align:entity2 rdf:resource="http://id.loc.gov/authorities/sh2002000569#concept"/>
        <align:measure rdf:datatype="http://www.w3.org/2001/XMLSchema#float">1.0</align:measure>
        <align:relation rdf:resource="http://www.w3.org/2004/02/skos/core#closeMatch"/>
      </align:Cell>
    </align:map>
  </rdf:Description>
</rdf:RDF>
```

(b) Concept Information Service, RDF response

Fig. 4. Serving RDF data

demonstrator, which is available at `http://stitch.cs.vu.nl/rameau`, also features an alignment between RAMEAU and LCSH (see `http://id.loc.gov`, [20]) as manually produced in the MACS project (see `http://macs.cenl.org`). The application of the Linked Data recipes allows users or RDF-consuming agents to seamlessly "follow their nose" from one KOS to the other.

Annotation suggestion tool. As part of the CATCH project, we have subjected a corpus of 250.000 *dually* indexed books of the National Library of the Netherlands (KB) to an instance-based method to derive an alignment between two KOSs, the *Brinkman* thesaurus and the *Biblion* one. We then implemented an alignment-based annotation suggestion tool to support KB employees indexing new, undescribed or singly indexed books. Library indexers get access to a list of subject suggestions, which they can accept or reject on a subject per subject basis [21]. For concepts they feel are missing, the tool gives browsing access to the vocabulary service. Feedback from KB staff is very positive as the annotation tool greatly supports the indexing task; the quality of automatically obtained rules reached a precision of 72.7% with a recall of 47.9%—and many mistakes are in fact near-matches. Further, the browser-based UI—dynamically generated HTML using XSLT—is perceived as more user-friendly than previously used software and paperwork for this task.

At the time of writing, the tool is only accessing the vocabulary service; we are working on adapting the alignment services to better fit the requirements of KB staff. In this respect, mappings between *combinations* of concepts from each KOS need to be exploited—for example, {'travel guides' + 'Spain' → 'Spain; travel guides'}. While the OAEI format supports many-to-many mappings, our current solution does not correspond yet to established practice in SKOS. This clearly points to further work determining representation and access means that fit existing (or anticipated) use cases and community best practices.

5 Discussion

RDF stores often result from conflating complex data models into huge sets of RDF triples. Making them accessible via SPARQL endpoints (or as Linked Data) leaves much freedom to application developers; on the other hand, the developers are on their own with constructing complex SPARQL queries to retrieve the data they require. A repository with well-defined services has many advantages for data consumers (implementors) but also for data providers and the community as a whole.

The implementation of the aforementioned three demonstrators, for instance, was greatly facilitated by the availability of our well-defined and fast repository services. The implementation of the autocompletion feature of the vocabulary and alignment browser, for instance, was helped by an appropriate service version of concept search via labels that only returns a lightweight representation of URI/label pairs. We hope that other application designers will profit from this and our other middleware services as well.

Data providers are in danger of running out of computing resources when making accessible a SPARQL endpoint with no restrictions. Here, consumers could easily formulate and submit queries that are far from optimized or tractable. Queries, for instance, that request the description of a vocabulary, including all the concepts that belong to this vocabulary (that is, following inbound `skos:inScheme` statements that have the concept scheme as object) are expensive, and it is more efficient to serve the same data via well-defined (and efficiently implemented) repository services.

Designing high-level repository services (and making them available to others) also pushes a community forward in terms of agreeing with common application requirements and best practises, but also in sharing expertise. Consider the example of Binding and Tudhope [22] on query expansion. Such mechanisms capitalize on a significant amount of existing research. Their implementation can be really tedious in any back-end engine, but it is hard, if not impossible, to reproduce it *via* SPARQL queries. It is not surprising thus that functionality of this kind is often provided at higher levels than SPARQL [23,17].

Sharing data at an appropriate level of abstraction is important for the CH institutions we work with. What makes our repository services unique with regard to others is that institutions can ingest and maintain their own KOS RDF data sources along with rich semantic alignments, a great help for institutions with little IT or expertise in this area.

Our future work will focus on scalability, improved speed and robustness. This includes the fine-tuning of services' description to reduce server/client communication. Also, we are currently investigating the provision of a local access API to complement the current network-based one. Having a local instance of the repository services would eliminate network bandwidth and yield significant better access times. Once there are locally-run repositories, the need may arise to synchronise their data with centrally-run repositories. The versioning problem, however, has not been tackled so far. Vocabularies (and alignments) evolve, and there is a strong requirement from CH practitioners to have our middleware handling this aspect. Unfortunately, we found that CH institutions employ rather *ad hoc* than systematic and easily implementable procedures for versioning vocabularies. Here, we would like to learn a lesson from more generic ontology repository systems and their versioning control.

Our web-based repository services for vocabularies and alignments are available at `http://stitch.cs.vu.nl/repository`. The webpage also gives access to the JavaDoc API. We would like to encourage interested parties to access and use it, and also to provide us with their feedback to improve the services.

Acknowledgements

This work was funded by the Dutch NWO CATCH programme (STITCH) and the eContentPlus programme of the European Union (TELplus). We are indepted to Stefan Schlobach, Shenghui Wang, Henk Matthezing, Frank van Harmelen and Hennie Brugman for valuable discussion time and advice.

References

1. Isaac, A., van der Meij, L., Schlobach, S., Wang, S.: An empirical study of instance-based ontology matching. In: Aberer, K., Choi, K.-S., Noy, N., Allemang, D., Lee, K.-I., Nixon, L.J.B., Golbeck, J., Mika, P., Maynard, D., Mizoguchi, R., Schreiber, G., Cudré-Mauroux, P. (eds.) ASWC 2007 and ISWC 2007. LNCS, vol. 4825, pp. 253–266. Springer, Heidelberg (2007)
2. Wang, S., Isaac, A., Schopman, B., Schlobach, S., van der Meij, L.: Matching multi-lingual subject vocabularies. In: Agosti, M., Borbinha, J., Kapidakis, S., Papatheodorou, C., Tsakonas, G. (eds.) ECDL. LNCS, vol. 5714, pp. 125–137. Springer, Heidelberg (2009)
3. Isaac, A., Schlobach, S., Matthezing, H., Zinn, C.: Integrated access to cultural heritage resources through representation and alignment of controlled vocabularies. Library Review 57(3), 187–199 (2008)
4. Isaac, A., Wang, S., Zinn, C., Matthezing, H., van der Meij, L., Schlobach, S.: Evaluating thesaurus alignments for semantic interoperability in the library domain. IEEE Intelligent Systems 24(2), 76–86 (2009)
5. Miles, A., Bechhofer, S.: SKOS Reference. W3C Recommendation (2009), http://www.w3.org/TR/skos-reference/
6. Tudhope, D., Koch, T., Heery, R.: Terminology Services and Technology – JISC state of the art review. Technical report, University of Glamorgan and UKOLN and University of Bath (September 2006)
7. Binding, C., Tudhope, D.: SKOS-based semantic web services: experiences from the STAR project. Presentation at the ISKO-UK KOnnecting KOmmunities Seminar: Sharing Vocabularies on the Web via SKOS (July 21, 2008)
8. Hillmann, D., Sutton, S.A., Phipps, J., Laundry, R.: A Metadata Registry from Vocabularies Up: The NSDL Registry Project. In: International Conference on Dublin Core and Metadata Applications (DC), Mexico (2006)
9. Jupp, S., Bechhofer, S., Stevens, R.: A Flexible API and Editor for SKOS. In: Aroyo, L., Traverso, P., Ciravegna, F., Cimiano, P., Heath, T., Hyvönen, E., Mizoguchi, R., Oren, E., Sabou, M., Simperl, E. (eds.) ESWC 2009. LNCS, vol. 5554, pp. 506–520. Springer, Heidelberg (2009)
10. Macgregor, G., McCulloch, E., Nicholson, D.: Terminology server for improved resource discovery: analysis of model and functions. In: International Conference on Metadata and Semantics Research, Corfu, Greece (2007)
11. Neubert, J.: Bringing the "thesaurus for economics" on to the web of linked data. In: WWW Worskhop on Linked Data on the Web (LDOW), Madrid, Spain (2009)
12. Sini, M., Lauser, B., Salokhe, G., Keizer, J., Katz, S.: The AGROVOC Concept Server: rationale, goals and usage. Library Review 57(3), 200–212 (2008)
13. Tuominen, J., Frosterus, M., Viljanen, K., Hyven, E.: ONKI SKOS Server for Publishing and Utilizing SKOS Vocabularies and Ontologies as Services. In: Aroyo, L., Traverso, P., Ciravegna, F., Cimiano, P., Heath, T., Hyvönen, E., Mizoguchi, R., Oren, E., Sabou, M., Simperl, E. (eds.) ESWC 2009. LNCS, vol. 5554. Springer, Heidelberg (2009)
14. Vizine-Goetz, D., Childress, E., Houghton, A.: Web services for genre vocabularies. In: International Conference on Dublin Core and Metadata Applications (DC), Madrid, Spain (2005)
15. Euzenat, J.: An API for Ontology Alignment. In: McIlraith, S.A., Plexousakis, D., van Harmelen, F. (eds.) ISWC 2004. LNCS, vol. 3298, pp. 698–712. Springer, Heidelberg (2004)

16. Duc, C.L., d'Aquin, M., Barrasa, J., David, J., Euzenat, J., Palma, R., Plaza, R., Sabou, M., Villazón-Terrazas, B.: Matching ontologies for context: The NeOn Alignment plug-in. Deliverable 3.3.2, NeOn project (2008)
17. Noy, N.F., Griffith, N., Musen, M.A.: Collecting community-based mappings in an ontology repository. In: Sheth, A.P., Staab, S., Dean, M., Paolucci, M., Maynard, D., Finin, T., Thirunarayan, K. (eds.) ISWC 2008. LNCS, vol. 5318, pp. 371–386. Springer, Heidelberg (2008)
18. Adida, B., Birbeck, M., McCarron, S., Pemberton, S.: RDFa in XHTML: Syntax and Processing. W3C Recommendation (2008),
    http://www.w3.org/TR/rdfa-syntax
19. Berrueta, D., Phipps, J.: Best Practice Recipes for Publishing RDF Vocabularies. W3C Working Group Note (2008), http://www.w3.org/TR/swbp-vocab-pub/
20. Summers, E., Isaac, A., Redding, C., Krech, D.: Lcsh, skos and linked data. In: International Conference on Dublin Core and Metadata Applications (DC), Berlin, Germany (2008)
21. Isaac, A., Kramer, D., van der Meij, L., Wang, S., Schlobach, S., Stapel, J.: Vocabulary matching for book indexing suggestion in linked libraries – a prototype implementation & evaluation. In: Bernstein, A., Karger, D.R., Heath, T., Feigenbaum, L., Maynard, D., Motta, E., Thirunarayan, K. (eds.) ISWC 2009. LNCS, vol. 5823, pp. 843–859. Springer, Heidelberg (2009)
22. Binding, C., Tudhope, D.: KOS at your Service: Programmatic Access to Knowledge Organisation Systems. J. Digital Information 4(4) (2004)
23. Daltio, J., Medeiros, C.B.: Aondê: An ontology web service for interoperability across biodiversity applications. Inf. Syst. 33(7-8), 724–753 (2008)

Appendix

Fig. 5 gives an overview of all vocabularies that are stored in the STITCH/CATCH/TELplus vocabulary repository ("source" column), and indicates their use of SKOS constructs (e.g., skos:ConceptScheme, skos:Concept, skos:note). For the complete table, and more details, please consult http://www.cs.vu.nl/STITCH/repository/stats.html.

Source name	ConceptScheme	hasTopConcept	Concept	prefLabel	altLabel	broader	related	note	scopeNote
Brinkman thesaurus	4	17169	12505	12505	1921	4704	2013	0	463
Mandragore voc.	1	13	16233	16390	2211	19097	0	2948	0
NBC (Dutch basic class.)	1	59	2143	6429	4286	2084	0	0	663
GOO thesaurus	9	78223	65297	104478	24418	26518	7559	0	5622
Glas voc.	11	141	337	337	0	240	0	0	0
Iconclass	2	14	24315	97209	1031867	26175	5462	0	0
GTAA thesaurus	6	0	160921	160921	1597	11658	42117	0	54566
Wordnet (nouns)	0	0	79689	79689	141691	81857	27243	0	0
SWD subject headings	9	0	805017	818364	1072714	292512	30042	230749	286816
Rameau subj. headings	7	0	154974	309979	196499	127161	59114	118467	27140
NBD/Biblion thesaurus	6	57968	49171	49171	5612	24820	2207	362	3067
Regiothesaurus KB	1	17	16410	20304	3174	16401	5560	0	9523
LCSH (lcsh.info)	13	0	340557	340557	310320	247112	21460	0	11118

Fig. 5. Statistics: vocabularies and usage of SKOS constructs (excerpt)

Ontology Management in an Event-Triggered Knowledge Network

Chen Zhou[1], Xuelian Xiao[2], Jeff DePree[2], Howard Beck[1], and Stanley Su[2]

[1] Department of Agricultural and Biological Engineering,
University of Florida, Gainesville, Florida 32611
1-352-392-3797
{czhou,hwb}@ufl.edu
[2] Database Systems RD Center 458 CSE Building,
University of Florida, Gainesville, Florida 32611
1-352-392-2693
{xxiao,jdepree,su}@cise.ufl.edu

Abstract. This paper presents an ontology management system and ontology processing techniques used to support a distributed event-triggered knowledge network (ETKnet), which has been developed for deployment in a national network for rapid detection and reporting of crop disease and pest outbreaks. The ontology management system, called Lyra, is improved to address issues of terminology mapping, rule discovery, and large ABox inference. A domain ontology that covers the concepts related to events, rules, roles and collaborating organizations for this application in ETKnet was developed. Terms used by different organizations can be located in the ontology by terminology searching. Services that implement knowledge rules and rule structures can be discovered through semantic matching using the concepts defined in the ontology. A tableau algorithm was extended to lazy-load only the needed instances and their relationships into main memory. With this extension, Lyra is capable of processing a large ontology database stored in secondary storage even when the ABox cannot be entirely loaded into memory.

1 Introduction

Government organizations worldwide are facing complex problems such as illegal immigration, terrorism, disease outbreaks, and natural disasters. Effective resource sharing, collaboration and coordination among government organizations are needed to solve these and other complex problems. They need to share not only data and application system functions, but also human and organizational knowledge useful for decision support, problem solving and activity coordination. The technology of sharing distributed, heterogeneous data has been extensively studied, but an effective way of sharing knowledge among collaborating organizations is still lacking.

The distributed event-triggered knowledge network (ETKnet) is an event and rule-based system, which was developed for deployment in a national network

L. Aroyo et al. (Eds.): ESWC 2010, Part I, LNCS 6088, pp. 410–424, 2010.

for rapid detection and reporting of plant disease and pest outbreaks. The National Plant Diagnostic Network (NPDN[1]) has been organized to strengthen the homeland security protection of the United State's agriculture by facilitating quick and accurate detection of disease and pest outbreaks in crops. NPDN has developed a general standard operating procedure (SOP [1]) to respond to a pest or disease outbreak. This SOP details the steps to be taken when such a bio-security event takes place. ETKnet uses events and different types of knowledge rules and rule structures to implement the SOP.

ETKnet is used to capture, manage, and apply the multifaceted knowledge embedded in organizational as well as inter-organizational policies, regulations, constraints, processes and operating procedures. A common means of representing knowledge is to use knowledge rules [2]. Three types of knowledge rules have been found to be useful in many applications [3,4]: integrity constraints [5], logic-based derivation rules [6], and condition-action rules [7,8]. One possible approach for the interoperability of these heterogeneous rules is to choose one rule type as a common format and convert the other rule types into this chosen representation [9]. This approach sounds attractive because it only needs a single rule engine to process all the converted rules. However, since different types of rules have significant semantic disparities, converting a rule from one representation to another may lead to loss of information. Another possible approach is to build wrappers around different types of rule engines [10], and provide a common interface to enable these rule engines to exchange the data generated by rules. This approach is not ideal either, because it will result in a very complex system that is difficult to operate and maintain. In our work, we extend the condition-action rule to allow the specification of a structure of operations that models a sharable process in the action clause to allow the process to be conditionally enacted. These operation structures can have the structural constructs selected from workflow process definition languages such as WPDL [11] and BPEL[12]. A single knowledge and process specification language is used for collaborating organizations to define different types of rules and rule structures that incorporate processes.

When organizations collaborate, it is usually to solve specific problems. Due to security and practical reasons, opening the database up in its entirety for access by other organizations is not a safe option. Thus it is important to devise a framework that allows organizations to share only those data and knowledge pertaining to specific problems. Our approach for achieving data and knowledge sharing is to augment an event subscription and notification system with knowledge sharing and processing capabilities. An event is anything of significance to collaborating organizations (e.g. an arrest, a terrorist incident, the detection of a disease, a special state of a database, a signal from a sensor, etc.) that occurs at a particular point in time. Data associated with an event occurrence (i.e., the event data) may trigger the processing of distributed rules and rule structures, which can produce new data or modify the event data. The new event data may trigger other rules and rule structures. Thus, multiple rounds of event data

---

[1] NPDN: National Plant Diagnostic Network, http://www.npdn.org

transmission, rule processing, and data aggregation may take place in order to produce all the data that are pertinent to the event occurrence.

There are a number of knowledge sharing challenges in such a distributed heterogeneous environment. The first issue is the heterogeneous terminology problem. Collaborating organizations may use their own terms to specify their events, event data, and rules, as well as the roles that their users play. The meanings of these terms need to be properly defined. Technologies for effective searching and processing of distributed, heterogeneous events, rules, roles and organizations are also needed. Our approach for meeting these needs is to develop a domain-specific ontology, which covers the concepts that are related to events, rules, roles, and organizations in the ETKnet system. Terms are mapped to ontology concepts that define the meaning of the terms to address the terminology discrepancy. The Lyra ontology management system is used to maintain the domain specific ontology and the terminology mapping. The second issue is the rule service's discovery. Collaborating organizations often want to find the applicable rules for certain event data. A rule or rule structure is applicable for an event if the input data it's expecting is a subset of the event data. Knowledge sharing is facilitated through a publish and subscription model. An ontology-enhanced registry is developed for the discovery of events, rules, roles and organizations. The third issue is the scalability problem. The ETKnet system may involve huge amounts of event data. Lyra needs to support large secondary storage management and a scalable inference engine. To meet this requirement, we have extended the tableau algorithm to lazy-load only the needed instances into main memory. Thus, a large ABox can be utilized even it cannot be fully loaded into memory.

In the following sections, we briefly describe the implemented ETKnet system and use a sample scenario taken from the implementation of SOP to explain ETKnet's distributed event and rule processing process so that the reader will know how the ontology support comes into play. We then present the domain-specific ontology defined for the implementation of the SOP, and present the ontology management system and its lazy-loading algorithm. Related work and a conclusion are given in the last two sections.

2   Background

2.1   ETKnet

ETKnet has a peer-to-peer server architecture as shown in Fig. 1. All collaborating organizations have identical subsystems installed at their sites. Each site creates and manages its own events, rules, rules structures and operations. Their specifications are registered at the host site of a collaborative federation. The host maintains a repository of these specifications. A user interface is used at each site to define sharable events, rules, rule structures, application system operations and operation structures.

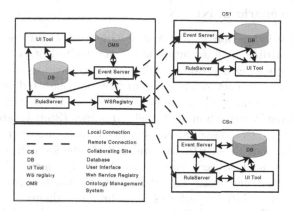

Fig. 1. System Architecture

Through a relatively simple progress, the defined rules and rule structures are translated into code and wrapped as web services for distributed knowledge and process sharing and interoperation. This approach avoids the use of multiple rule engines and workflow/process management systems, as well as the problem of rule-to-rule conversions.

The system supports three types of rules: logic-based derivation rule adopted from RuleML [13], constraint rule patterned after [14], and action-oriented rule [8]. A *rule structure* is a directed graph with different types of rules as nodes. These nodes are connected by link *split, and-join,* and *or-join* constructs, which specify sequential and parallel processing of rules and two alternative ways of rule synchronization. When a shared rule or a rule structure is defined, a relatively simple progress is used by the Rule Server at that site to convert it into program code, wraps the code as a Web service, stores the rule information in the local database and registers the generated Web service with the WSRegistry at the host site. This approach avoids the use of multiple rule engines and workflow/process management systems, as well as the problem of rule-to-rule conversions.

The Event Server is responsible for storing information about events defined at that particular site and information about event subscribers. Events defined at all sites are registered with the host site. Users of all organizations can browse or query the registry to subscribe to the event. They can also define triggers to link distributed events to distributed rules and rule structures. In both cases, they are "explicit subscribers". Triggers can also be generated automatically and dynamically by the system for those sites that contain "applicable" rules and rule structures. A rule or rule structure is applicable to an event if its input data requirement is a subset of the event data. The organization that defines the applicable rule or rule structure is an "implicit subscriber" to the event. The occurrence of an event will cause event data to be sent to explicit and implicit subscribers and be process by their rules and rule structures.

2.2   Sample Scenario in NPDN

The collaborative federation that serves as the application domain is NPDN. NPDN links plant diagnostic facilities across the United States and several US territories. The following is a sample submission scenario in the NDPN system (Figure 2). When a suspect sample of plant tissue suspected of having a new disease or insect is submitted to the NPDN disease diagnostics triage lab, an event, Presumptive-Positive-Sample-Observed occurs (Step 1, labeled E1 in the figure) E1 at the NPDN Triage Lab causes the event data containing the sample information to be sent to APHIS Lab and NPDN Regional Hub Lab (Step 2). This event data is sent to both sites as an XML document. These labs have applicable rules that can make use of the event data to provide some more relevant information. APHIS performs a preliminary diagnosis on the sample (Step 3). The NPDN Regional Hub Lab informs the appropriate personnel of the sample status (also Step 3). These procedures at the NPDN Triage Lab and the NPDN Regional Hub Lab are modeled using heterogeneous rules and rule structures. Details of these procedures are given later in this section.

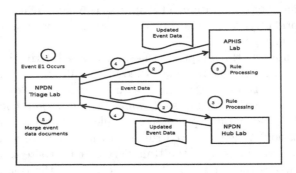

Fig. 2. Distributed Event and Rule Processing

The invocation of the applicable rules and rule structures in both the APHIS CDD Lab and the NPDN Regional Hub Lab may produce new data or modify the existing data. The new data and updates are then sent back to the NPDN Triage Lab as modifications to the original event data document (step 4) and are merged with the original event data (step 5). The new version of event data is sent (not shown in the figure) to the APHIS Lab and NPDN Regional Hub Lab to begin a second round of rule processing if there are applicable rules. Thus, multiple rounds of event data transmission, rule processing and data aggregation can take place as event data is dynamically changed by rules. The algorithms for aggregating event data to produce a new version of event data, and for avoiding cyclic processing of distributed rules can be found in [15].

Figure 3 describes the rule structure executed at the NPDN Triage Lab upon receiving a sample. The rule structure has both link and join relationships. The first rule, NTLR1, is concerned with acknowledging the receipt of the sample

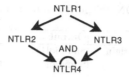

Fig. 3. Rule Structure upon Sample Received Event

by the sample submitting entity. It assigns a unique id to the sample, and asks the lab diagnostician to perform a preliminary diagnosis on the sample. Rule NTLR2 checks whether the sample has been reviewed by a diagnostician. If this is the case, it is classified as 'presumptive positive'. Meanwhile, NTLR3 instructs and guides the lab staff on how to contact the APHIS-CDD and NPDN hub, and how to store the sample securely. Then, an NPDN Sample event is posted in the NTLR4 to inform the system that a portion of the sample has been sent to the APHIS-CDD lab and NPDN Hub lab. For space reasons, we do not include the rules or rule structures at other NPDN labs.

3 Ontology for ETKnet System

3.1 Rules Definition and Matching

To support data interoperability and registry discovery, a domain ontology was defined to cover the concepts related to events, rules, roles and organizations in ETKnet. The ETKnet ontology defined in the NPDN domain contains the metadata definition for the rules, events, roles, and organizations in the context of the SOP. Each rule individual is an instance of CAARule, IntegrityRule, DerivativeRule, or their subclasses. In our system, each of these rules are converted to Java code, and wrapped as web services. The rule web service in the registry concerns only the input and outputs, and internally rules process actions. Hence the properties input, output, and action are defined in the rule ontology. For example, table 1 shows each rule's definition in Fig. 3. The NTLR1 rule becomes an individual in the ontology and is an instance of CAARule. Its input property has value StateOfOrigin, and its output property has values of SampleID and SampleExamined. Here are all NTLR rules definition according to the table 1:

$NTLR1 \in CAARule \sqcap \exists input.StateOfOrigin \sqcap \exists output.(SampleID \sqcup SampleExamined)$

$NTLR2 \in DerivationRule \sqcap \exists input.SampleExamined \sqcap \exists output.Classification$

$NTLR3 \in CAARule \sqcap \exists input.SampleExamed$

$NTLR4 \in CAARule \sqcap \exists output.(Sample \sqcup SampleId \sqcup State)$

These rule definitions are stored in the Lyra OMS, and the ontology reasoner can utilize these metadata definitions for rule discovery. For a given inquiry P, the reasoner returns the set of all the rule individuals which are compatible with P. The inquiry P and the rule individual r are compatible iff r is an instance of

Table 1. NPDN Triage Rules on Sample Received

Name	Type	Input	Output	Action
NTLR1	CAARule	StateOfOrigin	SampleID, SampleExamined	1. Acknowledge Receipt 2. Assign sample ID and examine sample
NTLR2	DerivationRule	SampleExamined	Classification	
NTLR3	CAARule	SampleExamined		Store sample securely
NTLR4	CAARule		Sample, SampleID, StateOfOrigin	1. Post NPDN_Sample_Event 2. Send sample to APHIS-CDD 3. Send sample to NPDN Hub

P, and r's input and output are compatible with P's input and output. A rule or rule structure is applicable for an event if its input data requirement is a subset of the event data. Algorithm 1 shows the algorithm for the rule web service's discovery. The user enters the rule's concept P, input concept I, and output concept O for the algorithm. Since all the result candidates must be an instance of P, the algorithm realizes the rule concept P and retrieves its instances as candidates. Among this candidate set, a comparison is made between each instance's input/output with the user's required input/output. The matching score is calculated after these comparisons are completed. An EXACT match implies that the required input R_I/output R_O and the candidate's input S_I/output S_O are equivalent concepts. It has the highest score, since this indicates that the inputs and the requirement are exactly the same. A SUBSUME matching denotes that the required input R_I is a subconcept of the candidate's input S_I, or that the candidate's output S_O is a subconcept of the required output R_O. It has a lower score, since the rule service requires fewer inputs than have been specified in the request. This guarantees that the rule will be executable with the provided inputs. In addition, the rule is expected to return more specific output data whose semantics are exactly the same or very close to what has been requested by the user. Other matches are treated as failures. According to this algorithm, the user's query is converted to the description logic (DL) concept realization problems, and answered by Lyra's inference engine. This algorithm is currently used for purpose of rule discovery. The result set does not have any specific order for rules with the same score. All the matched services are proposed for checking as candidate services.

Here is an example of the rule web service's reasoning. The user wants to find the CAA rule whose input includes the State class, and whose output contains SampleID and SampleExamined. The inquiry concept P can be expressed as:

$$P = CAARule \sqcap \exists input.State \sqcap \exists output.(SampleID \sqcup SampleExamined)$$

According to the example scenario, the candidate set by realization contains NTLR1. Meanwhile its input and output are compatible with the user's requirement, hence it is returned in the result set.

Algorithm 1. Rules Matching

1: candidate_set=realize(P)
2: result_set=empty
3: **for all** instance in candidate_set **do**
4:     input_score=match_score(instance.input, R_I)
5:     output_score=match_score(R_o, instance.output)
6:     **if** (input_score $\geq$ subsume and output_score $\geq$ subsume) **then**
7:         result_set.add(instance)
8:     **end if**
9: **end for**
10: **return** result_set

---

4 Lyra Ontology Management System and Lazy-Loading Algorithm

An ontology management system (OMS) is a database framework for creating, storing, modifying, and querying ontology information. Lyra, designed as an OMS, is used in a number of different application projects, such as the ETKnet project, digital library projects, and agricultural decision support systems [16]. In this section we will use the ETKnet NPDN project as an example and provide more detailed information about Lyra.

4.1 Terminology Mapping

Terminology mapping is integrated with Lyra's objects. Figure 4 shows the main data definition language for Lyra. The top portion of the figure creates a mapping from terminology to the ontology objects. It has a similar data definition as Wordnet [17]. Among them, a term is a single word or short phrase, which can have one or more specific meanings. Each of the specific meanings is represented by a word sense. Every SynSet represents a single concept and contains a set of terms that have the same meaning (synonyms). Different terms can point through word senses to the same SynSet.

SynSet's formal meaning is represented directly using an ontology object. That is, Each SynSet is mapped to exactly one object in the ontology. Lyra provides the lookup API to find the SynSet's ontology definition, and vice verse. This allows the reasoning engine to perform inferences according to the ontology's formal definition. For example, the relationships between SynSets can be checked by the reasoning engine. Two most typical relationships in SynSets are hyponym (subclass) and hypernym (superclass).

Lyra provides an API to search through the terminologies and get the SynSets. When an organization needs to define or search for some event data, Lyra's terminology information can be searched to get the candidate SynSets, or the hierarchy of the event data ontology can be browsed to identity an event.

For example, the NPDN ontology contains definitions of events, roles, and organizations specified in the SOP. In a collaborative environment, terms used

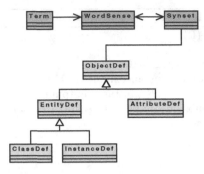

Fig. 4. Overview of Lyra Data Definition Language

by different organizations to describe the same thing can be quite different. To resolve this terminology level discrepancy, Lyra is used to maintain a mapping between the organizations' terminology and the ontology. Based on the mapping, Lyra can find the terminology's matched concepts for the user. The user does not need to know the exact concepts in the system, only terminology previously defined by his or other organizations. In the event that a concept needed by the user does not exist in the ontology, it must be added, along with associated terminology, under the supervision of an ontology administrator.

4.2   Lyra Data Definition Language and Reasoning Engine

Lyra's data definition language is designed according to description logic. It implements DL $\mathcal{SHIQ}$ and defines its own syntax for it. Table 2 shows the main language constructors in Lyra, as well as their interpretations. An interpretation $I = (\triangle^I, \cdot^I)$ consists of a mapping from every concept to a set $\triangle^I$ and from every role to a subset of $\triangle^I \times \triangle^I$ such that, for all concepts C, D, roles R, S, and non-negative integers n, the equations in table 2 are satisfied, where $\#M$ denotes the cardinality of a set M. Since OWL-DL's semantic model is based on description logic [18], most of the constructors in OWL-DL have a mapping to the constructors in Lyra. To facilitate knowledge sharing between different research groups, we have developed an OWL conversion tool to support the interoperability of OWL and Lyra.

The main objects in Lyra's data definition language are ClassDef, AttributeDef, and IndividualDef. They are presented at the bottom of Figure 4. They correspond to the concept, role, and individual definitions in the description logic respectively. Each of these objects contains an object identity and a display term. These are defined in ObjectDef, a parent class of ClassDef, AttributeDef, and IndividualDef, as shown in Figure 4. Object identity (OID) is used to uniquely identify the object in the Lyra object database. The display term represents the gloss of the object. All the objects that inherit ObjectDef in turn have these properties.

Lyra's object database supports two types of retrieval functions: SynSet retrieval and object retrieval. SynSet retrieval uses the term as the input, and

Table 2. Interpretation of Lyra Definition Language

Lyra	Interpret
Inverse	$(R^-)^I = \langle x, y \rangle \mid \langle y, x \rangle \in R^I$
Conjunction	$(C \sqcap D)^I = C^I \cap D^I$
Disjunction	$(C \sqcup D)^I = C^I \cup D^I$
Exists restriction	$(\exists R.C)^I = \{x \mid \exists y.\, \langle x, y \rangle \in R^I \text{ and } y \in C^I\}$
Value restriction	$(\forall R.C)^I = \{x \mid \forall y.\, \langle x, y \rangle \in R^I \text{ and } y \in C^I\}$
$\geq$ n number restriction	$(\geq nR.C)^I = \{x \mid \#\{y.\, \langle x, y \rangle \in R^I \text{ and } y \in C^I\} \geq n\}$
$\leq$ n number restriction	$(\leq nR.C)^I = \{x \mid \#\{y.\, \langle x, y \rangle \in R^I \text{ and } y \in C^I\} \leq n\}$

returns all related SynSets for this term. Users can identify whether the SynSet is the desired one by checking its definition in the ObjectDef. Object searching uses the OID as the input, and returns the ObjectDef definition for the user.

Lyra's reasoning engine provides consistency checking and realization services based on description logic semantics. The TBox contains the ontology's definition information. The ABox is a list of assertions about individuals and their memberships. The core of the reasoning engine is a tableau reasoner for description logic that can check the consistency of a concept. Many of our projects require the datatype inference in the realization tasks, hence we support number, string and many other XML schema datatype value inferences.

Integration has been carried out between the Lyra object database and the reasoning engine. The object database is treated as a persistent layer for storing and retrieving object definitions. The reasoner needs to retrieve the ClassDef, AttributeDef, and IndividualDef definitions from Lyra's persistent layer first, and then convert them into normalized format for the reasoner's processing. The concept's unique string object id (SOID), or the automatically assigned unique integer id (OID) can be used as the concept's unique representation in the DL reasoner. SOID representation is more human friendly for the result interpretation, while the OID representation provides better performance for inference.

4.3 Lazy-Loading Tableau Algorithm

When an ontology has a normal sized TBox and a large ABox, the ABox can be a bottleneck for the memory based tableau algorithm. We invent the lazy-loading algorithm to address this problem. The main idea in this algorithm is to avoid bringing individuals into main memory unless and until needed by the tableau algorithm. The $\forall$, $\leq$, or $\forall+$ rules are modified to lazy-load the individuals at runtime. In the lazy-loading algorithm, the idea is to identify when and where it is necessary to load the individuals' type definition and neighboring relationship information in the tableau algorithm's rules. Let's take the tableau algorithm for DL $\mathcal{SHIQ}$ as the example. Suppose that a and b are named individuals in A, x is an unnamed individual, C is a concept in A, and R is a role. A new relationship assertion $R(a, b)$ may influence the result of the tableau algorithm only if one of the following two conditions holds:

- The relationship assertion is used to trigger new applications of tableau rules that alter the ABox. For example, a role assertion can be used to add new membership assertions about the individuals by the application of the $\forall$ rule on a if a has the concept label $(\forall R.C)$, and b is an R-neighbor of a.
- The relationship assertion is involved in clash detection due to the violation of a maximum cardinality restriction. Here is an example: if a has label $\leq nR$ and b is one of $n+1$ mutually distinct R-neighbors of a, then $R(a,b)$ is needed to be loaded, and can cause the clash in tableau.

These conditions can only hold by either the application of the $\forall$, $\leq$, or $\forall+$ or the presence of a maximum cardinality constraint. In contrast, the $\exists$ and $\geq$ do not need to know the real role assertions $R(a,b)$, since they artificially create new role assertions and new unnamed individuals for satisfying the $\exists R.C$ and $\geq nR$ constraints. From these observation, we know that the role assertion $R(a,b)$ and the range instance can be delayed until the tableau algorithm requires such information. This helps to load only necessary information into memory.

Table 3. The Lazy Loading Tableau Rules

$\forall$-rule	if x is not loaded, lazy load x from secondary storage if 1. $\forall S.C \in \mathcal{L}_i(x)$, x is not indirectly blocked, and 2. there is an S-neighbour y of x with $C \not\in \mathcal{L}_i(y)$ then $\mathcal{L}_i(y) \to \mathcal{L}_i(y) \cup \{C\}$

$\forall_+$-rule:	if x is not loaded, lazy load x from secondary storage
	if 1. $\forall S.C \in \mathcal{L}_i(x)$, x is not indirectly blocked, and
	  2. there is some R with $\mathsf{Trans}(R)$ and $R \not\sqsubseteq S$,
	  3. there is an R-neighbour y of x with $\forall R.C \not\in \mathcal{L}_i(y)$
	then $\mathcal{L}_i(y) \to \mathcal{L}_i(y) \cup \{\forall R.C\}$

$\leq$-rule:	if x is not loaded, lazy load x from secondary storage
	if 1. $\leq nS.C \in \mathcal{L}_i(x)$, x is not indirectly blocked, and
	  2. $\sharp S_i^{\mathcal{F}}(x,C) > n$, there are S-neighbours y, z of x with not $y \neq z$,
	    y is neither a root node nor an ancestor of z, and $C \in \mathcal{L}_i(y) \cap \mathcal{L}_i(z)$,
	then 1. $\mathcal{L}_i(z) \to \mathcal{L}_i(z) \cup \mathcal{L}_i(y)$ and
	  2. if z is an ancestor of x
	    then $\mathcal{L}_i(\langle z,x \rangle) \to \mathcal{L}_i(\langle z,x \rangle) \cup \mathsf{Inv}(\mathcal{L}_i(\langle x,y \rangle))$
	    else $\mathcal{L}_i(\langle x,z \rangle) \to \mathcal{L}_i(\langle x,z \rangle) \cup \mathcal{L}_i(\langle x,y \rangle)$
	  3. $\mathcal{L}_i(\langle x,y \rangle) \to \emptyset$
	  4. Set $u \neq z$ for all u with $u \neq y$

$\leq_r$-rule:	if x is not loaded, lazy load x from secondary storage
	if 1. $\leq nS.C \in \mathcal{L}_i(x)$, and
	  2. $\sharp S_i^{\mathcal{F}}(x,C) > n$ and there are two S-neighbours y, z of x
	    which are both root nodes, $C \in \mathcal{L}_i(y) \cap \mathcal{L}_i(z)$, and not $y \neq z$
	then Merge (y, z)

Applying the lazy-loading algorithm to the Lyra reasoner, we assume that the ontology in the Lyra OMS is consistent, and we have loaded the classified TBox during preprocessing. When a query is issued to Lyra, the query concept is classified so that its equivalent concepts' and sub-concepts' instances are added into the result set. The query's direct super concepts' instances are added into the unknown set for further testing by the tableau algorithm. After adding the obvious individuals from the unknown set into the result set, the realization process starts on the remaining unknown set linearly or bulkily. Here we control the bulk size of this subset to fit in the memory. During the completion strategy in tableau algorithm, we modified the $\forall$, $\leq$, and $\forall+$ rules to lazy-load the individuals from Lyra secondary storage in the runtime only when necessary. This is shown in the Table 3. When any of these rules are triggered, it checks whether the named individual has already been loaded into memory. If not, the lazy-load process will load it in and process the initialization. After that, the rule continues and tableau algorithm will stop when either all the branches have conflicts or a satisfied branch is found.

4.4 Proof of Lazy-Loading Tableau Algorithm

In the following we show that the lazy-loading tableau algorithm for DL $\mathcal{SHIQ}$ generates the correct results. A lazy-loading ABox is an ABox A' corresponds to the original SHIQ ABox A, but the nodes in A' (except the root nodes) are loaded only at runtime when $\forall$, $\leq$, and $\forall+$ rules are triggered in the tableau algorithm. Here we want to prove: to the lazy-loading ABox A' obtained by applying the lazy-loading to A, A is consistent w.r.t. T and R, iff A' is consistent. This proof is straightforward. For any inference branches in the tableau algorithm, the processed subset of ABox A' is simply retrieved from the original ABox A. If there is any conflicts in A, it will also be found in A'. Hence if A' is consistent, the original A is also consistent. If there is no conflicts in A, they will not be found in A' either. Hence if A' is not consistent, the original A is also not consistent.

According to this proof, we can apply the tableau algorithm directly on the lazy ABox A' instead of original ABox A for the inference. The classification and realization are based on the tableau algorithm, so that we can apply them on A' directly as well. Our realization process requires that the whole TBox has been preprocessed and loaded in the memory. After the preprocessing, lazy-loading ABox A' has only the candidate individuals loaded while leaving all other individual information in the Lyra secondary storage. The tableau algorithm starts from this small candidate set in the A'. When $\forall$, $\leq$, and $\forall+$ rules are triggered in the tableau algorithm, the individual's definition and neighboring relationship will be lazy-loaded into A'. In the worst case, the tableau algorithm may load the whole ABox A into the memory, but normally only a small portion of the ABox A is needed during this process. Hence we can perform the inferencing on a lot of ABoxes that cannot fit into memory by the traditional tableau algorithm. In some cases (actually many cases in this application), there is only datatype reasoning involved in the query, and so the lazy-loading ABox needs only to load the individual's own data information.

A number of optimizations are adopted in the lazy-loading algorithm to improve the performance. Each individual in the unkown candidate set is pre-checked to find obvious conflicts to avoid invoking the tableau algorithm. The cached lazy-loading ABox is kept in different invocations of the tableau algorithm to get improved in-memory performance. When the memory usage reaches a threshold, the lazy-loading ABox is reinitialized to free unneeded memory usage. Our experiments on the LUBM(5, 0) [19] database, as well as other applications we have tested, confirm that lazy-loading produces the correct result. The lazy-loading tableau algorithm has runtime IO and instance insertion's overhead. The overhead depends on the query type and the loaded instance number. The time for various queries in the LUBM differs from one second to tens of seconds. The time for query in our publication database is within a few seconds, which is acceptable for normal end users.

5   Related Works

ETKnet system is a distributed rule system to support processing and sharing of knowledge. Web services are adopted in our system to improve the interoperability in the heterogeneous environment. In the last few years, a number of works have been reported for semantic web services. For example, OWL-S [20] presents specific ontology designed for web services and their process. Match-making algorithms, such as [21], help to discover the proper services according to their input, output, precondition, and effect (IOPE). Web Servcies Modeling Ontology (WSMO) [22] has some similarity with OWL-S, and provides additional mediator concept for service integration. Our system focuses more on the rules and their interoperability in the distributed environment. There is no specific global process defined in ETKnet. Event data will trigger the rules to process and share the knowledge.

Much research has been done on logic programming. SWSL [23] is a language for describing the concept of web services. The logic programing part of it, SWSL-Rules, is used to describe the services specification. SILK [24] is a recent work to study the proper enhancement on existing rule specification to achieve scalable and expressive semantic rules. These works provide the building blocks for annotation and inference of service descriptions. In contrast, our system studies how rules can be inferenced in a distrbuted way, and how the domain knowledge is used to sovle the interoperability problems.

The ontology management system plays a key role for data processing in a heterogeneous environment. One important issue in our system is scalable ABox reasoning. A number of previous works have dealt with this problem. Instance store [25] presents a role free ABox for instance retrieval. Its ABox allows only type assertions but not property assertions, while Lyra supports the normal DL constructors. DL-Lite [26] supports a subset of OWL-DL called DL-Lite. All the queries in DL-Lite can be translated into a set of SQL queries for processing. We supports the full OWL-DL, which is useful in some projects. SHER [27] stores instance data in the database, and creates a small summary ABox from the original ABox for query processing. It supports OWL-DL minus datatypes and nominals. This engine's ability is quite similar to the Lyra system. However, datatype inference is supported in our system to meet the projects' requirement.

By lazy loading the ABox instance during the tableaux procedure, Lyra helps to deal with large ABox that cannot be fit in the main memory.

6   Conclusion

This paper describes the approaches taken in ETKnet to achieve the sharing of distributed events and rules defined by collaborating organizations. Three types of commonly used rules and rule structures with imbedded application operations and operations structures are used to specify organizational and inter-organizational policies, constraints, regulations, processes and procedures. The distributed event and rule processing technique of ETKnet enables the activation of all the applicable rules and rule structures defined by collaborating organizations and ensures that these organizations receive all the data that are relevant to an event occurrence. The Lyra ontology management system manages the domain-specific ontology and enables terminology searching for events, roles and organizations and semantic searching for sharable rules. Rule web services' discovery assists the organizations to find shared rules in the ETKnet system. The lazy-loading algorithm helps to manage a large ABox even when it cannot fit main memory.

Acknowledgements

This project is supported by NSF under grant number IIS-0534065.

References

1. NPDN Scenario SubCommittee: The National Plant Diagnostic Network Standard Operating Procedure for APHIS-PPQ Pest of Concern Scenario - General SOP (2005)
2. Sowa, J.: Knowledge Representation: Logical, Philosophical and Computational Foundations. Brooks Cole Publishing Co., Pacific Grove (2000)
3. Group, B.R.: Defining Business Rules - What Are They Really? http://www.businessrulesgroup.org/first_paper/br01c0.htm
4. Grosof, B., Rouvellou, I., Degenaro, L., Chan, H.Y., Rasmus, K., Ehnebuske, D., McKee, B.: Combining different business rules technologies: a rationalization. In: OOPSLA Workshop on Best-practices in Business Rule Design and Implementation (2000)
5. Ullman, J.: Principles of Database Systems, 2nd edn. Computer Science Press, Rockville (1982)
6. Ullman, J.: Principles of Database and Knowledge-Base Systems. Computer Science Press, Rockville (1988)
7. Bry, F., Eckert, M., Ptrnjan, P., Romanenko, I.: Realizing business processes with ECA rules: benefits, challenges, limits. In: Int. Workshop on Principles and Practice of Semantic Web Reasoning, pp. 48–62 (2006)
8. Widom, J., Ceri, S.: Active Database Systems, Triggers and Rules for Advanced Database Processing. Morgan Kaufmann, San Francisco (1996)

9. Bassiliades, N., Vlahavas, I., Elmagarmid, A.K.: E-device: an extensible active knowledge base system with multiple rule type support. IEEE Transactions on Knowledge and Data Engineering 12, 824–844 (2000)
10. Rosenberg, F., Dustdar, S.: Towards a distributed service-oriented business rules system. In: IEEE Third European Conference on Web Services (November 2005)
11. Workow Management Coalition: Workow management coalition workow standard: Interface 1 process denition interchange process model (wfmc-tc-1016). Technical report, Lighthouse Point, Florida (1999)
12. IBM, BEA Systems, Microsoft, SAP AG, and Siebel Systems: Business Process Execution Language for Web Services version (BPEL4WS) 1.1. (2003), http://www-106.ibm.com/developerworks/library/ws-bpel/
13. RuleML committee: The rule markup initiative, http://www.ruleml.org
14. Object Management Group: Object constraint language specification (2001), http://www.omg.org
15. Degwekar, S., DePree, J., Beck, H., Thomas, C., Su, S.: Event-triggered data and knowledge sharing among collaborating government organizations. In: International Conference on Digital Government Research, Philadelphia, PA, pp. 102–111 (2007)
16. Beck, H.: Evolution of database designs for knowledge management in agriculture and natural resources. Journal of Information Technology in Agriculture 3(1) (2008)
17. Miller, G.A.: Wordnet, a lexical database for the english language, http://wordnet.princeton.edu/
18. W3C Committee: OWL Web Ontology Language Reference (February 2004), http://www.w3.org/TR/owl-ref/
19. Guo, Y., Pan, Z., Heflin, J.: LUBM: A Benchmark for OWL Knowledge Base Systems. Journal of Web Semantics 3(2), 158–182 (2005)
20. OWL-S Coalition: OWL-S: Semantic Markup for Web Services (2003), http://www.daml.org/services/owl-s/1.0/owl-s.html
21. Paolucci, M., Kawmura, T., Payne, T., Sycara, K.: Semantic matching of web services capabilities. In: First International Semantic Web Conference (2002)
22. Fensel, D., Lausen, H., de Bruijn, A.P.J., Stollberg, M., Domingue, D.R.J.: Enabling Semantic Web Services, 1st edn. Springer, Heidelberg (2007)
23. Semantic Web Services Committee: Semantic web services language (swsl) (2005), http://www.w3.org/Submission/SWSF-SWSL/
24. Grosof, B.N.: Silk: Higher level rules with defaults and semantic scalability. In: International Conference of Web Reasoning and Rule Systems, pp. 24–25 (2009)
25. Horrocks, I., Li, L., Turi, D., Bechhofer, S.: The instance store: Description logic reasoning with large numbers of individuals. In: IJCAR (2004)
26. Calvanese, D., Giacomo, G.D., Lembo, D., Lenzerini, M., Rosati, R.: Dl-lite: Tractable description logics for ontologies. In: AAAI (2005)
27. Dolby, J., Fokoue, A., Kalyanpur, A., Kershenbaum, A., Schonberg, E., Srinivas, K., Ma, L.: Scalable semantic retrieval through summarization and refinement. In: AAAI (2007)

Modeling and Querying Metadata in the Semantic Sensor Web: The Model stRDF and the Query Language stSPARQL*

Manolis Koubarakis and Kostis Kyzirakos

Dept. of Informatics and Telecommunications
National and Kapodistrian University of Athens Greece
{koubarak,kkyzir}@di.uoa.gr

Abstract. RDF will often be the metadata model of choice in the Semantic Sensor Web. However, RDF can only represent thematic metadata and needs to be extended if we want to model spatial and temporal information. For this purpose, we develop the data model stRDF and the query language stSPARQL. stRDF is a constraint data model that extends RDF with the ability to represent spatial and temporal data. stSPARQL extends SPARQL for querying stRDF data. In our extension to RDF, we follow the main ideas of constraint databases and represent spatial and temporal objects as quantifier-free formulas in a first-order logic of linear constraints. Thus an important contribution of stRDF is to bring to the RDF world the benefits of constraint databases and constraint-based reasoning so that spatial and temporal data can be represented in RDF using constraints.

1 Introduction

Sensors are rapidly becoming ubiquitous and may be found everywhere, ranging from consumer products to the medical, automotive and industrial markets. Collections of spatially distributed sensors with communication infrastructure form sensor networks. Semantically enriched sensor networks should allow the discovery and analysis of sensor data based on spatial, temporal and thematic information. In this paper we extend RDF, which will often be the metadata model of choice in the Semantic Sensor Web, with a uniform way to represent spatial and temporal characteristics of sensors and sensor networks such as the spatial location of a sensor, the trajectory of a moving sensor, the coverage of a sensor network, the valid time of sensor acquisitions etc.

Up to now, little attention has been paid to the problem of extending RDF to represent spatial and/or temporal information. The most important work that deal with representing temporal information in RDF is [1]. More recently, [2,3,4] proposed to represent spatial data in RDF(S) using spatial ontologies e.g., ontologies based on the GeoRSS GML specification [5]. [3] also compares

---

* This work was supported in part by the European Commission project Semsor-Grid4Env (http://www.semsorgrid4env.eu/)

L. Aroyo et al. (Eds.): ESWC 2010, Part I, LNCS 6088, pp. 425–439, 2010.

various ways to use SPARQL to query such spatial data, while [4] proposes a useful extension to SPARQL, called SPARQL-ST, to query data expressed in a spatial and temporal extension of RDF. The temporal extension of RDF in [4], uses the model of [1] to represent the valid time of triples.

The work presented in this paper has the same goal with the papers cited above: to enrich the Semantic Web with spatial and temporal data by extending RDF and SPARQL. To achieve this we diverge significantly from the papers cited above and follow the main ideas of *spatial and temporal constraint databases* [6,7,8,9]. We represent spatial geometries by *semi-linear* point sets in the n-dimensional space $\mathbb{Q}^n$ i.e., sets that can be defined by quantifier-free formulas in the first-order logic of linear equations and inequalities over $\mathbb{Q}^n$. Semi-linear sets can capture a great variety of spatial geometries, e.g., points, lines, line segments, polygons, k-dimensional unions of convex polygons possibly with holes, thus they give us a lot of expressive power [10]. Similarly, we represent the *valid times* of triples using *temporal constraints* (a very restricted class of linear constraints).

The main contributions of this paper are the following: Following the approach of Dédale [11] and CSQL [12], we develop a constraint-based extension of RDF, called stRDF, that can be used to represent thematic and spatial data that might change over time. The main contribution of stRDF is to bring to the RDF world the benefits of constraint databases and constraint-based reasoning so that spatial and temporal data can be represented in RDF using constraints. In this way, application areas with a rich spatial and temporal component such as the Semantic Sensor Web [13] and the Geospatial Semantic Web [14] can be tackled using Semantic Web technologies. The model stRDF and the query language stSPARQL are currently implemented (by extending the Sesame RDF store) in the context of the project SemsorGrid4Env where they serve as the data model and query language for the *semantic sensor registry*.

We also present an extension of SPARQL, called stSPARQL, to query spatial and temporal data expressed in stRDF, in a declarative way. We introduce stSPARQL by example and present a detailed semantics using the algebraic approach pioneered for SPARQL in [15]. Technically, stSPARQL follows closely the ideas in [12] and to a lesser extent the ideas in [11]; this allows us to have a useful language for expressing spatial and temporal queries while maintaining closure (i.e., staying within the realm of semi-linear point sets).

The organization of this paper is the following. In Section 2 we present the data model stRDF and in Section 3 we present the query language stSPARQL by means of examples. In Section 4 we give a formal definition of stSPARQL and define its semantics by following an algebraic approach. Comparison with related work is presented in Section 5 and in Section 6 we present our conclusions and discuss future work.

2   Data Model

To develop stRDF, we follow closely the ideas of constraint databases [6,8] and especially the work on CSQL [12]. First, we define the formulae that we allow as constraints. Then, we develop stRDF in two steps. The first step is to define the model sRDF which extends RDF with the ability to represent spatial data. Then, we extend sRDF to stRDF so that thematic and spatial data with a temporal dimension can be represented.

2.1   Linear Constraints

Constraints will be expressed in the first-order language $\mathcal{L} = \{\leq, +\} \cup \mathbb{Q}$ over the structure $\mathcal{Q} = \langle \mathbb{Q}, \leq, +, (q)_{q \in \mathbb{Q}} \rangle$ of the linearly ordered, dense and unbounded set of the rational numbers, denoted by $\mathbb{Q}$, with rational constants and addition. The atomic formulae of this language are *linear equations* and *inequalities* of the form: $\sum_{i=1}^{p} a_i x_i \Theta a_0$, where Θ is a predicate among =, or $\leq$, the x_i's denote variables and the a_i's are integer constants. Note that rational constants can always be avoided in linear equations and inequalities. The multiplication symbol is used as an abbreviation i.e., $a_i x_i$ stands for $x_i + \cdots + x_i$ (a_i times).

We now define semi-linear subsets of $\mathbb{Q}^k$, where k is a positive integer.

Definition 1. *Let S be a subset of $\mathbb{Q}^k$. S is called* semi-linear *if there is a quantifier-free formula $\phi(x_1, \ldots, x_k)$ of $\mathcal{L}$ where $x_1, \ldots, x_k$ are variables such that $(a_1, \ldots, a_k) \in S$ iff $\phi(a_1, \ldots, a_k)$ is true in the structure $\mathcal{Q}$.*

We will use $\varnothing$ to denote the empty subset of $\mathbb{Q}^k$ represented by any inconsistent formula of $\mathcal{L}$.

2.2   The sRDF Data Model

We now define sRDF. As in theoretical treatments of RDF [15], we assume the existence of pairwise-disjoint countably infinite sets I, B and L that contain IRIs, blank nodes and literals respectively. In sRDF, we also assume the existence of an infinite sequence of sets $C_1, C_2, \ldots$ that are pairwise-disjoint with I, B and L. The elements of each $C_k, k = 1, 2, \ldots$ are the quantifier-free formulae of the first-order language $\mathcal{L}$ with k free variables. We denote with C the infinite union $C_1 \cup C_2 \cup \cdots$.

Definition 2. *An sRDF triple is an element of the set $(I \cup B) \times I \times (I \cup B \cup L \cup C)$. If (s, p, o) is an sRDF triple, s will be called the subject, p the predicate and o the object of the triple. An sRDF graph is a set of sRDF triples.*

In the above definition, the standard RDF notion of a triple is extended, so that the object of a triple can be a quantifier-free formula with linear constraints. According to Definition 1 such a quantifier-free formula with k free variables is a finite representation of a (possibly infinite) semi-linear subset of $\mathbb{Q}^k$. Semi-linear subsets of $\mathbb{Q}^k$ can capture a great variety of spatial geometries, e.g., points, lines, line segments, polygons, k-dimensional unions of convex polygons possibly with holes, thus they give us a lot of expressive power. However, they cannot be used to represent other geometries that need higher-degree polynomials e.g., circles.

Example 1. The following are sRDF triples:

```
ex:s1 rdf:type, ex:Sensor .
ex:s1 ex:has_location "x=10 and y=20"^^strdf:SemiLinearPointSet
```

The above triples define a sensor and its location using a conjunction of linear constraints. The last triple is not a standard RDF triple since its object is an element of set C.

In terms of the W3C specification of RDF, sRDF can be realized as an extension of RDF with a new kind of *typed literals*: quantifier-free formulae with linear constraints. The datatype of these literals is e.g., `strdf:SemiLinearPointSet` (see Example 1 above) and can be defined using XML Schema. Alternatively, linear constraints can be expressed in RDF using MathML[1] and serialized as `rdf:XMLLiterals` as in [16]. [16] specifies a syntax and semantics for incorporating linear equations in OWL 2. We now move on to define stRDF.

2.3   The stRDF Data Model

We will now extend sRDF with time. Database researchers have differentiated among user-defined time, valid time and transaction time. RDF (and therefore sRDF) supports user-defined time since triples are allowed to have as objects literals of the following XML Schema datatypes: `textttxsd:dateTime, xsd:time, xsd:date, xsd:gYearMonth, xsd: gYear, xsd:gMonthDay, xsd:gDay, xsd:gMonth`.

stRDF extends sRDF with the ability to represent the *valid time* of a triple (i.e., the time that the triple was valid in reality) using the approach of Gutierrez et al. [1] where the a fourth component is added to each sRDF triple.

The *time structure* that we assume in stRDF is the set of rational numbers $\mathbb{Q}$ (i.e., time is assumed to be linear, dense and unbounded). Temporal constraints are expressed by quantifier-free formulas of the language $\mathcal{L}$ defined earlier, but their syntax is limited to elements of the set C_1. *Atomic* temporal constraints are formulas of $\mathcal{L}$ of the following form: $x \sim c$, where x is a variable, c is a rational number and $\sim$ is $<, \leq, \geq, >, =$ or $\neq$. *Temporal constraints* are Boolean combinations of atomic temporal constraints using a *single* variable.

The following definition extends the concepts of triple and graph of sRDF so that thematic and spatial data with a temporal dimension can be represented.

Definition 3. *An stRDF quad is an sRDF triple (a, b, c) with a fourth component τ which is a temporal constraint. For quads, we will use the notation (a, b, c, τ), where the temporal constraint τ defines the set of time points that the fact represented by the triple (a, b, c) is valid in the real world. An stRDF graph is a set of sRDF triples and stRDF quads.*

3   Query Language

We present the syntax of stSPARQL by means of examples involving sensor networks. The semantics of the language is presented in Section 4. More examples

---
[1] `http://www.w3.org/Math/`, last accessed February 20, 2010.

of stSPARQL from a GIS perspective are given in [17]. We will consider a dataset that describe static and moving sensors and use the CSIRO/SSN Ontology [18] to describe them . The main classes of interest in the SSN ontology is the class *Feature* that describes the observed domain, the class *Sensor* that describes the sensor, the class *SensorGrounding* that describes the physical characteristics and the location of the sensor and the class *Location* that is self explained. We extend the aforementioned ontology with the properties `strdf:hasGeometry` and `strdf:hasTrajectory` with range `strdf:SemiLinearPointSet`.

The stRDF description of a static sensor that measures temperature and has a certain location is the following (`ssn` is the namespace of the CSIRO/SSN ontology and `ex` an example ontology):

```
ex:sensor1 rdf:type ssn:Sensor.
ex:sensor1 ssn:measures ex:temperature.
ex:temperature ssn:type ssn:PhysicalQuality.
ex:sensor1 ssn:supports ex:grounding1.
ex:grounding1 rdf:type ssn:SensorGrounding.
ex:grounding1 ssn:hasLocation ex:location1.
ex:location1 rdf:type ssn:Location.
ex:location1 strdf:hasGeometry
            "x=10 and y=10"^^strdf:SemiLinearPointSet.
```

We choose to use the O&M-OWL ontology [19] to represent sensor observations. However, since we use stRDF to model space and time, we choose not to use the classes *Time*, *TimeInterval* and *TimeInstant* that come from OWL-Time and the classes *Geometry* and *Point* that come from GML. So our modeling is similar to the modeling in [19] but instead of relying on OWL-Time and GML we rely on the stRDF constructs. The stRDF representation of the sensor's observations is the following (`om` is the namespace of the O&M-OWL ontology):

```
ex:sensor1 rdf:type ex:TemperatureSensor.
ex:TemperatureSensor rdf:subClassOf om:Sensor.
ex:obs1 rdf:type om:Observation.
ex:obs1 om:procedure ex:sensor1.
ex:obs1 om:observedProperty ex:temperature.
ex:temperature rdf:type om:Property.
ex:obs1 om:observationLocation ex:obslocation1 .
ex:obslocation1 rdf:type om:Location.
ex:obslocation1 strdf:hasGeometry
                "x=10 and y=10"^^strdf:SemiLinearPointSet.
ex:obs1 om:result ex:obs1Result.
ex:obs1Result rdf:type om:ResultData.
ex:obs1Result om:uom ex:Celcius.
ex:obs1Result om:value "27"
                "(10 <= t <= 11)"^^strdf:SemiLinearPointSet.
```

Notice the last quad that capture the spatiotemporal information.

Let us now present an example of modeling *moving sensors* in stRDF. Note that trajectories of moving sensors are easily represented in stRDF.

```
ex:sensor2 rdf:type ssn:Sensor.
ex:sensor2 ssn:measures ex:temperature.
ex:sensor2 ssn:supports ex:grounding2.
ex:grounding2 rdf:type ssn:SensorGrounding.
ex:grounding2 ssn:hasLocation ex:location2.
ex:location2 rdf:type ssn:Location.
ex:location2 strdf:hasTrajectory
        "(x=10t and y=5t and 0<=t<=5) or
         (x=10t and y=25 and 5<=t<=10)"^^strdf:SemiLinearPointSet.
```

Finally, we assume that we have the stRDF descriptions of some rural area where the sensors are deployed. The stRDF description of such an area called Brovallen is the following:

```
ex:area1 rdf:type ex:RuralArea.
ex:area1 ex:hasName "Brovallen".
ex:area1 strdf:hasGeometry
        "(-10x+13y<=-50 and y<=79 and y>=13 and
          x<=133) or (y<=13 and x<=133 and
          x+2y>=129)"^^strdf:SemiLinearPointSet.
```

Example 2. Spatial selection. Find the URIs of the static sensors that are inside the rectangle R(0,0,100,100)?

```
select ?S
where {?S rdf:type ssn:Sensor. ?G rdf:type ssn:SensorGrounding.
       ?L rdf:type ssn:Location. ?S ssn:supports ?G.
       ?G ssn:haslocation ?L. ?L strdf:hasGeometry ?GEO.
       filter(?GEO inside "0<=x<=100 and 0<=y<=100")}
```

Let us now explain the new features of stSPARQL by referring to the above example. stSPARQL has a new kind of variables called . Spatial variables can be used in basic graph patterns to refer to spatial literals denoting semi-linear point sets. They can also be used in *spatial filters*, a new kind of filter expressions introduced by stSPARQL that is used to compare *spatial terms* using spatial predicates. Spatial terms include spatial constants (finite representations of semi-linear sets e.g., "0<=x<=10 and 0<=y<=10"), spatial variables and complex spatial terms (e.g., ?GEO INTER "x=10 and y=10" which denotes the intersection of the value of spatial variable ?GEO and the semi-linear set "x=10 and y=10"). There are several types of spatial predicates such as topological, distance, directional, etc. that one could introduce in a user-friendly spatial query language. In the current version of stSPARQL only the topological relations of [20] can be used as predicates in a spatial filter expression e.g., filter(?GEO1 inside ?GEO2).

Example 3. Temporal selection. Find the values of all observations that were valid at time 11 and the rural area they refer to.

```
select ?V ?RA
where {?OBS rdf:type om:Observation. ?LOC rdf:type om:Location.
       ?R rdf:type om:ResultData. ?RA rdf:type ex:RuralArea.
       ?OBS om:observationLocation ?LOC. ?OBS om:result ?R.
       ?R om:value ?V ?T. ?LOC strdf:hasGeometry ?OBSLOC.
       ?RA strdf:hasGeometry ?RAGEO.
       filter(?T contains (t = 11) && ?RAGEO contains ?OBSLOC)}
```

The above query demonstrates the features of stSPARQL that are used to query the valid times of triples. stSPARQL offers one more new kind of variables in addition to spatial ones: *temporal variables* . Temporal variables can be used as the last term in a new kind of basic graph pattern called *quad pattern* to refer to the valid time of a triple. Temporal variables can also appear in temporal filters, a new kind of filter that can be used in stSPARQL to constrain the valid time of triples.

The expressions that make up temporal filters are Boolean combinations of *interval predicates* that are used to compare temporal terms. A *temporal term* in stRDF is a temporal variable or a temporal constant (i.e., an element of the set C_1 e.g., `"(t>=0 and t<=2) or (t>=5 and t<=7)"`). We allow any of the thirteen interval relations identified by Allen in [21] to be used as the interval predicates e.g, `contains` in the above example .

Example 4. Intersection of an area with a trajectory. Which areas of Brovallen were sensed by a moving sensor and when?

```
select (?TR[1,2] INTER ?GEO) as ?SENSEDAREA  ?GEO[3] as ?T1
where {?SN rdf:type ssn:Sensor. ?RA rdf:type ex:RuralArea.
       ?X rdf:type ssn:SensorGrounding. ?Y rdf:type ssn:Location.
       ?SN ssn:supports ?X. ?X ssn:hasLocation ?Y.
       ?Y strdf:hasTrajectory ?TR. ?RA ex:hasName "Brovallen".
       ?RA strdf:hasGeometry ?GEO. filter(?TR[1,2] overlap ?GEO)}
```

The above query demonstrates the projection of spatial terms. Projections of spatial terms (e.g., `?TR[1,2]`) denote the projections of the corresponding point sets on the appropriate dimensions, and are written using the notation `Variable "[" Dimension1 "," ... "," DimensionN "]"`.

Example 5. Projection and spatial function application. Find the URIs of the sensors that are north of Brovallen.

```
select ?SN
where {?SN rdf:type ssn:Sensor. ?X rdf:type ssn:SensorGrounding.
       ?Y rdf:type ssn:Location. ?RA rdf:type ex:RuralArea.
       ?RA ex:hasName "Brovallen". ?RA strdf:hasGeometry ?GEO.
       ?SN ssn:supports ?X. ?X ssn:hasLocation ?Y.
       ?Y strdf:hasGeometry ?SN_LOC.
       filter(MAX(?GEO[2])<MIN(?SN_LOC[2]))}
```

The above query demonstrates the projection of spatial terms and the application of metric spatial functions to spatial terms. We allow expressions like MAX(?GEO[2]) that return the maximum value of the unary term ?GEO[2]. The metric functions allowed in stSPARQL will be defined in detail in Section 4.

4   Formalization and Semantics of stSPARQL

In this section, we give a formal definition of stSPARQL and define its semantics by following an algebraic approach like the one originally pioneered in [15]. We only cover the spatial features of stSPARQL in detail and their interactions with existing SPARQL concepts. The temporal features of stSPARQL (quad patterns and temporal filters) can be formalized similarly and are omitted.

Let us recall from Section 2.2 the definitions of sets $I, B, L, C_1, C_2, \ldots$ and C. We define $ILC = I \cup L \cup C$ and $T = I \cup B \cup L \cup C \cup \mathbb{R}$. We need to include the set of real numbers $\mathbb{R}$ in the set T since as we will see below (Definition 8) the application of certain metric functions such as $AREA$ etc. can result in real numbers as answers to stSPARQL queries.

We also assume the existence of the following disjoint sets of *variables*: (i) the set of non-spatial variables V_{ns}, (ii) an infinite sequence $V_s^1, V_s^2, \ldots$ of sets of variables that will be used to denote elements of the sets $C_1, C_2, \ldots$ and (iii) the set of real variables V_r. We use V_s to denote the infinite union $V_s^1 \cup V_s^2 \cup \ldots$ and V to denote the union $V_{ns} \cup V_s \cup V_r$. The set V is assumed to be disjoint from the set T.

Let us now define a concept of mapping appropriate for stSPARQL by modifying the definition of [15]. A *mapping* μ from V to T is a partial function $\mu : V \to T$ such that $\mu(x) \in I \cup B \cup L$ if $x \in V_{ns}$, $\mu(x) \in C_i$ if $x \in V_s^i$ for all $i = 1, 2, \ldots$ and $\mu(x) \in \mathbb{R}$ if $x \in V_r$.

Example 6. The following is a mapping:
$$\{?S \to s_1, \ ?O \to John, \ ?GEO \to \text{``}x \geq 1 \wedge y \geq 0 \wedge y \leq 5\text{''}\}$$

The notions of domain and compatibility of mappings is as in [15]. The *domain* of a mapping μ, denoted by $dom(\mu)$, is the subset of V where the mapping is defined. Two mappings μ_1 and μ_2 are *compatible* if for all $x \in dom(\mu_1) \cap dom(\mu_2)$ we have $\mu_1(x) = \mu_2(x)$. For two sets of mappings Ω_1 and Ω_2, the operations of join, union, difference and left outer-join are also defined exactly as in [15]:

$$\Omega_1 \bowtie \Omega_2 = \{\mu_1 \cup \mu_2 \mid \mu_1 \in \Omega_1, \mu_2 \in \Omega_2 \text{ are compatible mappings}\}$$
$$\Omega_1 \cup \Omega_2 = \{\mu \mid \mu \in \Omega_1 \text{ or } \mu \in \Omega_2\}$$
$$\Omega_1 \setminus \Omega_2 = \{\mu \in \Omega_1 \mid \text{ for all } \mu' \in \Omega_2, \mu \text{ and } \mu' \text{ are not compatible}\}$$
$$\Omega_1 \bowtie\!\!\!\!\!\!\!\!\!\!\bowtie \Omega_2 = (\Omega_1 \bowtie \Omega_2) \cup (\Omega_1 \setminus \Omega_2)$$

Using an algebraic syntax for stSPARQL graph patterns which extends the one introduced for SPARQL in [15], we now define the result of evaluating a graph pattern over an stRDF graph.

Definition 4. *Let G be an stRDF graph over T, p a triple pattern and P_1, P_2 graph patterns. Evaluating a graph pattern P over a graph G is denoted by $[[P]]_G$ and is defined as follows [15]:*

1. $[[p]]_G = \{\mu \mid dom(\mu) = var(p) \text{ and } \mu(p) \in G\}$, where $var(p)$ is the set of variables occurring in p.
2. $[[(P_1 \text{ AND } P_2)]]_G = [[P_1]]_G \bowtie [[P_2]]_G$
3. $[[(P_1 \text{ OPT } P_2)]]_G = [[P_1]]_G \bowtie [[P_2]]_G$
4. $[[(P_1 \text{ UNION } P_2)]]_G = [[P_1]]_G \cup [[P_2]]_G$

The semantics of $FILTER$ expressions in stSPARQL are defined as in [15] for filters that do not involve spatial predicates. To define the semantics of spatial filters formally, we first need the following definitions.

Definition 5. *A* k-*ary spatial term is an expression of the following form:*

(i) *a quantifier-free formula of* $\mathcal{L}$ *from the set* C_k *(in quotes).*
(ii) *a spatial variable from the set* V_s^k.
(iii) $t \cap t'$ *(intersection),* $t \cup t'$ *(union),* $t \setminus t'$ *(difference),* $BD(t)$ *(boundary),* $MBB(t)$ *(minimum bounding box),* $BF(t, a)$ *(buffer) where* t *and* t' *are* k-*ary spatial terms and* a *is a rational number.*
(iv) *the projection* $t[i_1, \ldots, i_{k'}]$ *of u* k-*ary spatial term* t *where* $i_1, \ldots, i_{k'}$ *are positive integers less than or equal to* k.

Example 7. The following are examples of binary spatial terms:
$$\text{“}(x \geq 1 \wedge x = y) \vee y = 7\text{”}$$
$$?GEO \cap \text{“}(x \geq 1 \wedge x = y) \vee y = 7\text{”}$$
$$BD(?GEO \cap \text{“}(x \geq 1 \wedge x = y) \vee y = 7\text{”})$$
$$\text{“}(x \geq 1 \wedge x \leq 10 \wedge y \geq 0 \wedge x = y)\text{”}[1,2] \cap \text{“}(z \geq 0 \wedge z \leq 10)\text{”}$$

Definition 6. *A metric spatial term is an expression of the form* $f(t)$ *where* f *is one of the metric functions* VOL *(volume),* $AREA$ *(area or surface),* LEN *(length),* MAX *(maximal value) or* MIN *(minimal value) and* t *is a* k-*ary spatial term. In the case of* $AREA$ *we require* $k \geq 2$. *In the case of* LEN, MAX *and* MIN, *we require* $k = 1$.

Example 8. The following are examples of metric spatial terms:
$$AREA(\text{“}(x \geq 1 \wedge x \leq 10 \wedge y \geq 0 \wedge x = y)\text{”})$$
$$MIN(\text{“}(x \geq 1 \wedge x \leq 10 \wedge y \geq 0 \wedge x = y)\text{”}[1])$$

Note that Definition 6 is not recursive like Definition 5 i.e., f can only be applied once to a k-ary spatial term. The result of the application of f is a real number and the definition of mapping has already catered for this possibility.

Definition 7. *A spatial term is a* k-*ary spatial term or a metric spatial term.*

We will be interested in the value of a k-ary spatial term t for a given mapping μ such that the variables of t are all among the spatial variables of μ. This is captured by the following definition.

Definition 8. *Let* t *be a spatial term. Let* μ *be a mapping such that all the spatial variables of* t *are elements of* $dom(\mu)$. *The value of* t *for* μ *is denoted by* $\mu(t)$ *and is defined as follows:*

(i) *If t is an element of C_k then $\mu(t) = t$.*

(ii) *If t is a spatial variable x then $\mu(t) = \mu(x)$.*

(iii) *If t is a projection expression of the form $t'[i_1, \ldots, i_{k'}]$ then $\mu(t)$ is a quantifier-free formula ϕ of $\mathcal{L}$ which is obtained after eliminating from $\mu(t')$ the variables corresponding to all the other dimensions except $i_1, \ldots, i_{k'}$.*

(iv) *If t is the intersection $t' \cap t''$ of two k-ary spatial terms then $\mu(t) = \mu(t' \cap t'') = \mu(t') \wedge \mu(t'')$.[2]*

(v) *If t is the union $t' \cup t''$ of two k-ary spatial terms then $\mu(t) = \mu(t' \cup t'') = \mu(t') \vee \mu(t'')$.*

(vi) *If t is the difference $t' \setminus t''$ of two k-ary spatial terms then $\mu(t) = \mu(t' \setminus t'') = \mu(t') \wedge \neg\mu(t'')$.*

(vii) *If t is $MBB(t')$ where t' is a k-ary spatial term, then $\mu(t)$ is a quantifier-free formula of the language $\mathcal{L}$ that represents the minimum bounding box of $\mu(t')$.*

(viii) *If t is $BD(t')$ where t' is a k-ary spatial term, then $\mu(t)$ is a quantifier-free formula of the language $\mathcal{L}$ that represents the boundary of $\mu(t')$.*

(ix) *If t is $BF(t', a)$ where t' is a k-ary spatial term and a is a rational number, then $\mu(t)$ is a quantifier-free formula of the language $\mathcal{L}$ that represents the buffer of $\mu(t')$ within distance a. The buffer of t contains t and a zone of width a around t.*

(x) *If t is $VOL(t')$, $AREA(t')$ or $LEN(t')$ where t' is a k-ary spatial term, then $\mu(t)$ is a real number that represents the volume, surface (or area) or length of $\mu(t')$.*

(xi) *If t is $MIN(t')$, $MAX(t')$ where t' is a unary spatial term, then $\mu(t)$ is a real number that represents the minimum or the maximum value of $\mu(t')$.*

To guarantee closure of stSPARQL, it is important to point out that the value $\mu(t)$ in the above definition is a well-defined formula of $\mathcal{L}$ in the cases *(i)-(ix)* and a real number in the cases of *(x)* and *(xi)*. This is easy to see for cases *(i)-(vi)*. For the case $t = MBB(t')$, $\mu(t)$ is $\bigwedge_{i=1}^{k} (l_i \leq x_i \wedge x_i \leq u_i)$ where l_i, u_i are the minimum and maximum values of x_i for which the formula $\mu(t')$ holds in the structure $\mathcal{Q}$. For the case $t = BD(t')$, the formula $\mu(t)$ can be constructed by performing quantifier elimination in the quantified formula defining the boundary given in Proposition 3.1 of [10]. For the case $t = BF(t', a)$ and the standard definition of buffer that uses the Euclidean distance , the formula $\mu(t)$ is not general an element of $\mathcal{L}$ (e.g., BF("x=0 and y=0",1) is the unit circle with center $(0,0)$). There are two alternative non-standard definitions of BF that allow us to stay in the realm of linear constraints. In the first case, BF can be defined using the *Manhattan distance* which measures the distance between two points along axes at right angles. For example, in the case of two dimensions, the formula $\mu(t)$ would now be the formula that remains if we eliminate variables x', y' from the formula:

---

[2] In this and subsequent definitions, we assume that standardization of variables takes place before forming the conjunction, disjunction of formulas etc.

$$(\phi(x', y') \wedge 0 \le x - x' \le a \wedge 0 \le y - y' \le a) \vee$$
$$(\phi(x', y') \wedge 0 \le x - x' \le a \wedge 0 \le y' - y \le a) \vee$$
$$(\phi(x', y') \wedge 0 \le x' - x \le a \wedge 0 \le y - y' \le a) \vee$$
$$(\phi(x', y') \wedge 0 \le x' - x \le a \wedge 0 \le y' - y \le a)$$

where $\phi(x', y')$ is the formula $\mu(t')$. If using Manhattan distance seems like a crude alternative to the standard definition then more detailed alternatives are possible. For example, if t defines a polygon then $BF(t, a)$ is a new polygon that contains t and the zone of width a around the polygon (however, "circular" curves are approximated by polylines). Note that the same approach is followed by vector data models e.g. the computational geometry library CGAL[3]. The cases *(x)* and *(xi)* are easy to see as well.

Definition 9. *An* atomic *spatial condition* *is an expression in any of the following forms:*

(i) t_1 *R* t_2 *where* t_1 *and* t_2 *are k-ary spatial terms and R is one of the topological relationships DISJOINT, TOUCH, EQUALS, INSIDE, COV-EREDBY, CONTAINS, COVERS, OVERLAPBDDISJOINT (overlap with disjoint boundaries) or OVERLAPBDINTER (overlap with intersecting boundaries).*

(ii) *a linear equation or inequality of* $\mathcal{L}$ *with metric spatial terms in the place of variables.*

Note that the form (ii) does not destroy closure of our language since these equations/inequalities allows linear equations or inequalities with terms that evaluate to real numbers and they will only be checked for satisfaction (see Definition 11), not used as constraints i.e., as elements of sets C_k.

Example 9. The following are atomic spatial selection conditions:
$$?GEO1 \ INSIDE \ "x \ge 1 \wedge x \le 5 \wedge y \ge 0 \wedge y \le 5"$$
$$AREA(?GEO1) \ge 2 \cdot AREA(?GEO2)$$

Definition 10. *A* spatial condition *is a Boolean combination of atomic spatial conditions.*

Definition 11. *A mapping* μ *satisfies a spatial condition R (denoted* $\mu \models R$*) if*

1. *R is atomic and the spatial condition that results from substituting every spatial variable x of R with* $\mu(x)$ *holds for semi-linear sets in* $\mathbb{Q}^n$.
2. *R is* $(\neg R_1)$*,* R_1 *is a spatial condition, and it is not the case that* $\mu \models R_1$.
3. *R is* $(R_1 \vee R_2)$*,* R_1 *and* R_2 *are spatial conditions, and* $\mu \models R_1$ *or* $\mu \models R_2$.
4. *R is* $(R_1 \wedge R_2)$*,* R_1 *and* R_2 *are spatial conditions, and* $\mu \models R_1$ *and* $\mu \models R_2$.

The semantics of spatial filters can now be defined as follows.

Definition 12. *Given an stRDF graph G over T, a graph pattern P and a spatial condition R, we have:* $[[P \ FILTER \ R]]_G = \{\mu \in [[P]]_G \mid \mu \models R\}$.

---

[3] CGAL, http://www.cgal.org/, last accessed February 20, 2010.

Now we can define the semantics of the SELECT clause of an stSPARQL expression where variables (spatial or non-spatial) are selected and new spatial terms are computed. To capture the peculiarities of the SELECT clause of stSPARQL, we first need the following definitions.

Definition 13. *Let t be a spatial (resp. metric spatial) term and z a spatial (resp. real) variable that does not appear in t. Then, t AS z is called an* extended spatial term *with* target variable z.

Example 10. $(BD(?GEO) \cap$ "$x = 1$") AS $?L$ is an extended spatial term.

Definition 14. *A* projection specification *is a set consisting of non-spatial variables, spatial variables and extended spatial terms such that all the target variables of the extended spatial terms are different from each other and different from each spatial variable.*

Definition 15. *Let μ be a mapping and W a projection specification with spatial and non-spatial variables $x_1, \ldots, x_l$ and extended spatial terms t_1 AS $z_1, \ldots, t_m$ AS z_m. Then, $\pi_W(\mu)$ is a new mapping such that*

   (i) $dom(\pi_W(\mu)) = \{x_1, \ldots, x_l, z_1, \ldots, z_m\}$.
   (ii) $\pi_W(\mu)(x_i) = \mu(x_i)$ *for* $1 \leq i \leq l$ *and* $\pi_W(\mu)(z_j) = \mu(t_j)$ *for* $1 \leq j \leq m$.

Example 11. Let μ be the mapping $\{?S \to s_1, ?O \to John, ?GEO \to$ "$x \geq 1 \wedge x \leq 5 \wedge y \geq 0 \wedge y \leq 5$"$\}$ and W the projection specification $\{?O, (BD(?GEO) \cap$ "$x = 1$") AS $?L\}$ then $\pi_W(\mu)$ is the following mapping:
$$\{?O \to John, ?L \to \text{"}x = 1 \wedge y \geq 0 \wedge y \leq 5\text{"}\}.$$

The next definition gives the semantics of an arbitrary stSPARQL query.

Definition 16. *An stSPARQL query is a pair (W, P) where W is a projection specification and P is a graph pattern. The* answer *to an stSPARQL query (W, P) over a graph G is the set of mappings $\{\pi_W(\mu) \mid \mu \in [[P]]\}$.*

Example 12. Let G be the following stRDF graph:
$\{(s_1, geom,$ "$x \geq 1 \wedge x \leq 5 \wedge y \geq 0 \wedge y \leq 5$"$), (s_1, owner, John)\}$
and consider the query with $W = \{?O, BD(?GEO) \cap$ "$x = 1$" AS $?L\}$ and $P = (?S, owner, ?O)$ AND $(?S, geom, ?GEO)$. Then, the answer to (W, P) over G is the set which consists of the mapping: $\{?O \to John, ?L \to$ "$x = 1 \wedge y \leq 5 \wedge y \geq 0$"$\}$.

5   Related Work

Let us now compare stRDF and stSPARQL with relevant proposals in the literature. The closest language to stSPARQL is SPARQL-ST presented in Perry's Ph.D. thesis [4]. SPARQL-ST adopts the model of temporal RDF graphs of [1] to represent the valid time of a triple. Similarly, stSPARQL offers support for valid time of a triple but uses a temporal constraint language to define a valid time. As a result, the notion of valid time in stSPARQL is more expressive (thus it requires a more sophisticated implementation). The spatial part of stSPARQL and SPARQL-ST are significantly different. SPARQL-ST assumes a particular upper ontology expressed in RDFS for modeling theme, space and time [4]. The spatial part of this upper ontology uses the class geo:SpatialRegion and its subclasses (e.g., geo:Polygon) defined in GeoRSS in order to model spatial geometries (e.g., polygons). Thematic data (e.g., a city) can then be connected to their spatial geometry (e.g., a polygon) using the property stt:located_at. Spatial geometries in SPARQL-ST are specified by sets of RDF triples that give various details of the geometry depending on its type (e.g., for a 2-dimensional polygonal area, they give the coordinates of its boundary and the relevant coordinate reference system). SPARQL-ST provides a set of built-in spatial conditions that can be used in SPATIAL FILTER clauses to constrain the geometries that are returned as answers to queries. Although a semantics for SPARQL-ST is presented in [4], the treatment of spatial conditions in these semantics is unsatisfactory in our opinion. The notion of "when a spatial condition evaluates to true" that is used to give semantics to built-in spatial conditions (page 99 of [4]) is not defined formally but is left to the intuition of the reader. When this definition is given explicitly, it will have to rely on the different types of geometries (e.g., geo:Polygon) allowed by the spatial ontology of [4], properties of these geometries (e.g., geo:lrPosList) and relevant co-ordinate systems (e.g., geo:CRS_NAD83). Currently, these semantics are hardwired in the implementation of SPARQL-ST presented in [4]. This means that if someone wants to use a different spatial ontology (e.g., an ontology based on the Open GIS SQL geometry types), this cannot be done unless the semantics of SPARQL-ST and its implementation are modified appropriately. Since geometries in stRDF and stSPARQL are based on the mathematical concept of semi-linear subsets of $\mathbb{Q}^k$, stSPARQL (as opposed to SPARQL-ST) can be given an elegant semantics based on well-understood mathematical machinery from constraint databases as we showed in Section 4 of this paper.

In addition, the new literal datatype strdf:SemiLinearPointSet of stRDF alluded to in Section 2.2 can be used together with spatial ontologies expressed in RDFS to give the same kind of class-based modeling capabilities offered by SPARQL-ST. Thus, stRDF and stSPARQL impose very minimal requirements to Semantic Web developers that want to use our approach: all they have to do is utilize a new literal datatype such as strdf:SemiLinearPointSet.

Two other papers related to our work on stSPARQL are [2,3] by Kolas and colleagues. Compared with our work on stRDF and stSPARQL, the system SPAUK presented in [2] has problems similar to the ones we pointed out for SPARQL-ST. First, no semantics for query evaluation are given. Secondly, even if these semantics are given in great detail, they will rely on the spatial ontologies assumed by SPAUK. Thus, any query processor that implements these semantics will need to be extended if users of the system decide to use different spatial ontologies (this is said explicitly in [2]).

To summarize, the constraint extension to RDF and SPARQL that we have advocated in this paper gives us the following benefits. First, our extension is general and its only primitive (semi-linear point set) does not depend on the application at hand. This is in contrast to approaches based on spatial/temporal ontologies which need to choose an ontology with classes (e.g., Point, Interval, Polygon etc.) appropriate for the application at hand. This is reminiscent of spatial DBMSs based on data types (e.g., PostGIS and Oracle) that offer their own, often incompatible, spatial data type systems. Second, the elaboration of a query in a constraint-based query language such as stSPARQL does not depend on the spatial data type (or class) of the objects queried or the results that will be returned. Thus, the programmer does not need to think about composition of operators, closure etc. In approaches based on classes or data types, the programmer needs constantly to be thinking about the classes/data types of the objects queried (this point has been also made in [3]). Third, our extensions can be given a natural and intuitive semantics by extending the standard algebraic semantics of SPARQL [15]. Finally, as we showed in Section 3, our extensions to RDF and SPARQL can easily be integrated with current work on sensor network ontologies to realize the vision of the Semantic Sensor Web.

6   Conclusions and Future Work

In this paper we studied the problem of designing a data model and a query language that can be used in the Semantic Sensor Web for representing and querying spatial and temporal data. We proposed the data model stRDF and the query language stSPARQL. We gave a formal definition of stRDF, introduced stSPARQL by examples and presented a detailed semantics of stSPARQL using the algebraic approach pioneered for SPARQL in [15]. Finally, we compared our approach with related work. Our future work concentrates on studying the complexity of stSPARQL query processing theoretically, and carrying out an implementation of the language for the cases of 2 and 3 dimensions that are the most interesting ones in practice. In these cases, we would like to apply the lessons learned from the implementation of relational constraint databases [11] and demonstrate that our proposal can be implemented efficiently in comparison with competitive approaches.

Acknowledgements

We thank Jianwen Su and Gabi Kuper who were always available to answer questions regarding CSQL. We also thank Peter Revesz for interesting discussions on constraint databases.

References

1. Gutierrez, C., Hurtado, C., Vaisman, A.: Introducing Time into RDF. IEEE TKDE (2007)
2. Kolas, D., Self, T.: Spatially Augmented Knowledgebase. In: ISWC/ASWC 2007 (2007)

3. Kolas, D.: Supporting Spatial Semantics with SPARQL. In: Terra Cognita Workshop (2008)
4. Perry, M.: A Framework to Support Spatial, Temporal and Thematic Analytics over Semantic Web Data. PhD thesis, Wright State University (2008)
5. Singh, R., Turner, A., Maron, M., Doyle, A.: GeoRSS: Geographically Encoded Objects for RSS Feeds (2008), http://georss.org/gml (last accessed February 20, 2010)
6. Kanellakis, P., Kuper, G., Revesz, P.: Constraint Query Languages. In: PODS (1990)
7. Rigaux, P., Scholl, M., Voisard, A.: Introduction to Spatial Databases: Applications to GIS. Morgan Kaufmann, San Francisco (2000)
8. Revesz, P.Z.: Introduction to Constraint Databases. Springer, Heidelberg (2002)
9. Koubarakis, M.: Database Models for Infinite and Indefinite Temporal Information. Information Systems 19, 141–173 (1994)
10. Vandeurzen, L., Gyssens, M., Gucht, D.V.: On the expressiveness of linear-constraint query languages for spatial databases. Theoretical Computer Science (2001)
11. Rigaux, P., Scholl, M., Segoufin, L., Grumbach, S.: Building a constraint-based spatial database system: model, languages, and implementation. Information Systems 28(6), 563–595 (2003)
12. Kuper, G., Ramaswamy, S., Shim, K., Su, J.: A Constraint-based Spatial Extension to SQL. In: Proceedings of the 6th International Symposium on Advances in Geographic Information Systems (1998)
13. Sheth, A., Henson, C., Sahoo, S.S.: Semantic Sensor Web. Internet Computing, IEEE 12(4), 78–83 (2008)
14. Egenhofer, M.J.: Toward the Semantic Geospatial Web. In: ACM-GIS, New York, NY, USA (2002)
15. Pérez, J., Arenas, M., Gutierrez, C.: Semantics and complexity of SPARQL. In: Cruz, I., Decker, S., Allemang, D., Preist, C., Schwabe, D., Mika, P., Uschold, M., Aroyo, L.M. (eds.) ISWC 2006. LNCS, vol. 4273, pp. 30–43. Springer, Heidelberg (2006)
16. Parsia, B., Sattler, U.: OWL 2 Web Ontology Language, Data Range Extension: Linear Equations. W3C Working Group Note (October 2009), http://www.w3.org/TR/2009/NOTE-owl2-dr-linear-20091027/ (last accessed February 20, 2010)
17. Kyzirakos, K., Koubarakis, M., Kaoudi, Z.: Data models and languages for registries in SemsorGrid4Env. Deliverable D3.1, SemSorGrid4Env (2009)
18. Neuhaus, H., Compton, M.: The Semantic Sensor Network Ontology: A Generic Language to Describe Sensor Assets. In: AGILE 2009 Pre-Conference Workshop Challenges in Geospatial Data Harmonisation (2009)
19. Henson, C., Pschorr, J., Sheth, A., Thirunarayan, K.: SemSOS: Semantic Sensor Observation Service. In: CTS (2009)
20. Cui, Z., Cohn, A.G., Randell, D.A.: Qualitative and Topological Relationships in Spatial Databases. In: Advances in Spatial Databases (1993)
21. Allen, J.: Maintaining Knowledge about Temporal Intervals. CACM 26(11) (1983)

Author Index